CALIFORNIA
Real Estate Principles

Charles O. Stapleton III and Martha R. Williams, JD

W9-CSC-108

Dearborn™
Real Estate Education

President: Dr. Andrew Temte
Executive Director, Real Estate Education: Melissa Kleeman-Moy
Development Editor: Jody Manderfeld

CALIFORNIA REAL ESTATE PRINCIPLES TENTH EDITION
©2017 Kaplan, Inc.
Published by DF Institute, Inc., d/b/a Dearborn Real Estate Education
332 Front St. S., Suite 501
La Crosse, WI 54601

Printed in the United States of America
First revision, April 2018
ISBN: 978-1-4754-4699-9

CONTENTS

INTRODUCTION

California Real Estate Principles is an introduction to the many interesting aspects of the real estate business. This book has been written primarily for the prospective real estate broker or salesperson, but it will also be of interest to the consumer or investor.

Throughout this book you will find website addresses. We encourage you to explore the internet resources mentioned in this book to expand on what you read here. To make it easy to find site references, they are highlighted in the margins of the text. There is also a complete list of all site references in Appendix B at the back of the book. As with any resource, you are cautioned to use good judgment when considering the validity of the information you find on the internet. Some of the best sources are the.gov (government) or.edu (education) sites.

This new edition of California Real Estate Principles has been revised to reflect current market conditions as well as the numerous legislative and regulatory changes that resulted from the mortgage foreclosure crisis and the market recovery that has already begun to take place. Additional information is available at www.dearborn.com. Click on the link that takes you to the Instructor Resources page.

HOW TO USE THIS BOOK

Each unit of this book begins with a list of Key Terms that are highlighted in bold type when they first appear in the discussion that follows. Knowing the definitions of the Key Terms is especially important for students who plan to take a real estate licensing examination. Learning objectives are provided next to alert you to the important concepts that will be covered.

Each unit then is divided into sections. Usually, each section has one or more examples of how the material covered may be applied to real-life situations.

Throughout each unit are exercises that will require you to use what you have learned to solve problems involving practical applications of the topics covered. After you complete an exercise, you can check your answers by turning to the Answer Key at the back of the book.

The text of each unit concludes with a summary of the material covered, with most Key Terms highlighted once again in bold type. If you are familiar with the Key Terms listed at the beginning of a unit, you should have no problem successfully completing the review questions at the end of the unit.

Monitoring Your Progress

You should not be discouraged if at first you do poorly on the unit review questions despite your best efforts. Part of learning how to succeed at a review is learning how to take a test. This skill may require some practice, particularly if you have been out of school for some time. If you are using this book to prepare for a licensing exam, you should restudy any material you are unsure of and answer the unit review questions until you can answer most of the questions correctly. Your instructor can provide you with more review questions.

Don't forget that the Answer Key at the back of the book provides an answer for every exercise and unit review question. Check your work as often as necessary to make sure you understand what you have read. By doing so, you will be more likely to retain what you have learned as well.

ACKNOWLEDGMENTS

The authors wish to thank the real estate educators and professionals who contributed their very helpful criticism of one or more of the earlier editions of this book, or who assisted by providing forms and other materials. They included:

- Professor Olivia Vasquez Anderson, East Los Angeles College
- Thurza B. Andrew, GRI, Butte Community College
- Leonel A. Bello, MBA, real estate broker, City College of San Francisco
- Ray Benningson, College of Marin
- Yin Bihr, GRI, Century 21® Masters, San Marino
- Stephanie Booker, Vice President, Commonwealth Title Insurance Company
- Mark R. Chamberlin, Chamberlin Real Estate School, Inc.
- Victoria Chen, GRI, SRES, e-PRO, Masters Realty, San Marino
- Jacqueline Cheou, Certified Escrow Officer, Champion Escrow, Inc., Temple City
- Llewellyn Chin, Senior Counsel, California Association of REALTORS®
- Larry Copeland, Coastline Community College
- Jim Cunningham, Professor of Real Estate, Long Beach City College
- Frank Diaz, Mission College, Santa Clara
- Jennifer Dodge, California Association of REALTORS®, Director, Professional and Promotional Products
- Thomas E. Duffy Jr., Los Angeles City College
- Faz Elahi, Los Angeles Community Colleges
- Dean Abraham Farkas, Academic Affairs, West Los Angeles College
- Russell H. Gatlin, Television Education, Inc.

- Richard Gaylord, GRI, CRS, CRB, CIPS, 2000 President of CAR and 2008 President of the National Association of REALTORS®
- Ignacio Gonzalez, Mendocino Community College
- Richard Gonzalez, College of Marin
- Professor Donna Grogan, MBA, GRI, CPM, CRS, El Camino College
- James R. Gromley, Prudential California Realty School of Real Estate
- Dr. Joan M. Harrison, Harrison Seminars, Laguna Beach
- Ernie Hubert, 2000 School of Real Estate
- Lois Kadosh, REALTOR®
- Don Kalal, GRI, California Brokers Institute
- Dr. Alan R. Klofkorn, Irvine Valley College
- Keiko Lam, Certified Escrow Officer, City Escrow, Temple City
- Melody Langager, Diablo Valley College
- George Lawrence, Broker-Owner, Commercial Real Estate Lending and Consulting, Palmdale
- Regina Lawrence, Marketing Representative, Fidelity National Financial, Lancaster
- Minnie Lush, GRI, Lush Enterprises
- Judith Meadows
- George H. Miller, West Valley College
- Kathleen Monaco, Mesa College
- Don Names, Mt. San Antonio College
- Arthur L. Olderich, Chaffey College
- James R. Overton, Yuba Community College
- Gordon Peterson, Account Executive, First American Title Company, Los Angeles
- C. Anthony Phillips, CPA, BS, MBA, MBT, Downstream Exchange, Pasadena
- Millet Pineda, Alhambra Adult School
- William H. Pivar, College of the Desert
- Dennie L. Rowland, President, First American Title Company, Los Angeles
- J. D. Ryan, Irvine Valley College
- Larry Scheer, Anthony Schools of San Diego
- Sherry Shindler, Fullerton College
- Bobra G. Tahan, Senior Instructor, Kaplan Professional Schools
- Juliana Tu, Certified Escrow Officer, Arch Escrow, San Marino
- Fred Weber, Saddleback College

- Jason K. Wolins, Anthony Schools
- Bud Zeller, broker, GRI, CRS, RECS, SRES, CREA, RIM, IREI, Sierra-Properties.com

In addition, North American Title provided material for earlier editions of this book.

The California Bureau of Real Estate, California Association of REALTORS®, First American Title Company, Los Angeles, and others noted throughout the text generously allowed material from their publications to be reprinted. Special thanks go to Joy Alafia, Director of Business Products for Real Estate Business Services, Inc., a subsidiary of the California Association of REALTORS®, for her assistance in providing copies of the many CAR forms that appear here.

Charles O. Stapleton III

Martha R. Williams, JD

ABOUT THE AUTHORS

Charles "Buck" Stapleton, MA, holds the GRI, SRES, and e-PRO designations and has practiced commercial, residential, and international real estate. He is the broker/owner of a real estate office in Pasadena and has managed offices ranging in size from 10 to 150 sales associates. A national speaker, he has written numerous California courses and coordinates the California Association of REALTORS® GRI program. He has chaired numerous committees for his local REALTORS® association.

Martha R. Williams, JD, has practiced law in Texas and California and taught at the University of San Francisco and City College of San Francisco. She is coauthor of California Mortgage Loan Brokerage, Fundamentals of Real Estate Appraisal, The Art of Real Estate Appraisal, and other publications and courses. A past president of the California Real Estate Education Association (CREEA), she was named 2000 California Real Estate Educator of the Year.

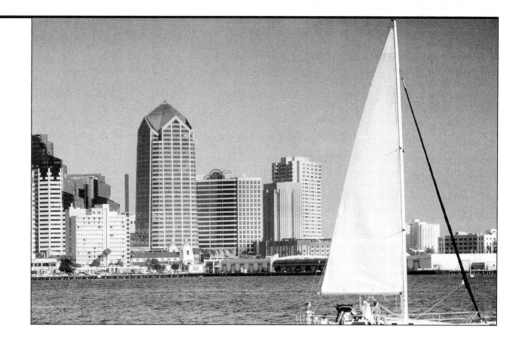

THE BUSINESS OF REAL ESTATE

LEARNING OBJECTIVES

When you have completed this unit, you will be able to

- **describe** the role of the Real Estate Commissioner;
- **identify** the ways in which a real estate brokerage may be owned;
- **list** the allowed activities of a real estate broker and salesperson;
- **describe** what may be included in a business opportunity transaction;
- **list** the requirements for a prepaid rental listing service;
- **list** the requirements to become a real estate broker or real estate salesperson;
- **describe** how the Real Estate Law is enforced by the Real Estate Commissioner;
- **identify** the types of prohibited conduct that can result in disciplinary action; and
- **explain** the purpose and funding of the Real Estate Education and Research Fund.

KEY TERMS

associate licensee	fictitious business name	Real Estate Education
blind advertising	statement	and Research Fund
broker-officer	franchise	Real Estate Law
bulk transfer of goods	manufactured home	real estate salesperson
Business and	mobilehome dealer	Recovery Account
Professions Code	mortgage loan	Regulations of the Real
business opportunity	brokerage	Estate Commissioner
California Bureau	mortgage loan	restricted license
of Real Estate	originator (MLO)	sales associate
(CalBRE)	Prepaid Rental Listing	Uniform Commercial
caveat emptor	Service (PRLS)	Code
certificate of status	real estate broker	
codes	real estate brokerage	

THE REAL ESTATE LAW

Only a century ago, buyers had few protections from unscrupulous sellers and real estate agents. Instead, the common-law doctrine of **caveat emptor** (a Latin phrase meaning "let the buyer beware") prevailed.

In 1917, California became the first state to legislate licensing requirements for real estate brokers and salespersons. Although that initial legislation was declared unconstitutional, it was quickly amended, and the California Supreme Court upheld the *Real Estate Act of 1919*. Now, all 50 states and the District of Columbia license real estate agents. This means that to conduct business as a real estate agent in any state, you must be licensed by that state. In California, there are over 400,000 real estate licensees, more than in any other state.

> The state's police power allows it to license real estate agents.

The state's licensing ability is an exercise of its *police power* to enact laws within constitutional limits to promote the public health, safety, and general welfare.

Major Provisions of the Law

California legislation has been compiled into a series of books called **codes**. What is commonly referred to as the **Real Estate Law** is Division 4 of the **Business and Professions Code**. The Real Estate Law has two parts:

1. Part 1 covers licensing.
2. Part 2 covers transactions and includes the *Subdivided Lands Law*.

> http://leginfo.legislature.ca.gov

The complete text of all 29 volumes of the California codes, as well as information on bills pending before the California legislature, can be found at http://leginfo.legislature.ca.gov.

Real estate licensees are also subject to the **Regulations of the Real Estate Commissioner**, which serve to clarify and interpret the Real Estate Law. They have the force and effect of law.

The primary purpose of both the Real Estate Law and the Regulations of the Real Estate Commissioner is to protect the members of the public with whom real estate licensees come into contact in their business activities.

California Bureau of Real Estate (CalBRE)

The **California Bureau of Real Estate** (CalBRE), formerly the Department of Real Estate, headed by the **Real Estate Commissioner**, administers the Real Estate Law in California. Every state has a similar department or agency responsible for enforcing laws concerning real estate licensees.

www.bre.ca.gov

Information about the California Bureau of Real Estate, including the current status of all real estate licensees, can be found at www.bre.ca.gov.

California Bureau of Real Estate Office Locations

Sacramento (Main Office)
1651 Exposition Blvd.
Sacramento, CA 95815
1-877-373-4542

San Diego
1350 Front Street, Suite 1063
San Diego, CA 92101-3687
1-877-373-4542

Los Angeles
320 W. 4th St., Suite 350
Los Angeles, CA 90013-1105
1-877-373-4542

Fresno
2550 Mariposa Mall, Room 3070
Fresno, CA 93721-2273
1-877-373-4542

Oakland
1515 Clay St., Suite 702
Oakland, CA 94612-1462
1-877-373-4542

All offices are open 8:00 am–5:00 pm weekdays.

Real Estate Commissioner

The Real Estate Commissioner is appointed by the governor and serves at the governor's discretion. The person selected as commissioner must have been a practicing real estate broker in California for five years or engaged in some form of real estate activity for five of the past 10 years.

The Real Estate Commissioner determines administrative policy and enforces that policy in the best interests of those dealing with real estate licensees. The responsibilities of the Real Estate Commissioner are highlighted in the following box.

> **The Real Estate Commissioner**
>
> Assisted by California Bureau of Real Estate staff members, the Real Estate Commissioner
>
> - screens candidates for licensing;
> - prepares subdivision public reports;
> - conducts licensee disciplinary action;
> - investigates nonlicensees performing activities for which a license is required; and
> - regulates nonexempt franchises and real property securities.

REAL ESTATE BROKERAGE

To represent someone else in a real estate transaction in California, you must be licensed by CalBRE as a **real estate broker** or **real estate salesperson**, with some exceptions. A real estate salesperson (often referred to as a **sales associate** or **associate licensee**) can act only under the control and supervision of a *responsible broker*; that is, the real estate broker by whom the salesperson is employed.

A **real estate brokerage** is a business in which real estate license–related activities are performed under the supervision of a real estate broker. A real estate brokerage may consist of only one broker of record and no employees. However, a brokerage may be large enough to have specialized departments with many salespeople, a support staff that includes administrative and clerical workers, and a number of branch offices.

No matter how large a real estate office is or how its ownership is structured, there must always be at least one broker under whose license the real estate activities of the firm are carried out.

Sole proprietorship   A real estate brokerage that is a sole proprietorship may be owned by a licensed real estate broker, a salesperson, or a nonlicensee. Real estate activities can only be carried out by or under the authority of a licensed real estate broker, however. No separate formalities are required to start a business as a sole proprietor. For business liability and tax purposes, however, most brokerages choose to incorporate.

Corporation   A brokerage may be set up as a corporation, provided that at least one officer of the corporation is a licensed broker and is designated the responsible **broker-officer**. The corporation must submit the following to CalBRE:

- The corporation license application and fee
- A **certificate of status** issued by the secretary of state within 30 days before submission of the application; *or* the Articles of Incorporation filed with the secretary of state if a California stock corporation originally filed the articles within six months of the application
- A statement of officers as filed with the secretary of state

Partnership   A brokerage can be a partnership if at least one of the partners is a licensed real estate broker. Every partner who performs activities that require a real estate license must be licensed as a real estate broker but there can be only one broker partner of record. At least one broker partner must obtain an additional license for each branch office location. The partnership itself needs no separate license.

Use of a Fictitious Business Name

A fictitious name is any name other than that of a real estate licensee.

A brokerage, whether a sole proprietorship, corporation, or partnership, can do business under a fictitious name as long as the real estate license is in that name. First, a **fictitious business name statement** must be filed with the county clerk in the county of the broker's principal business address. The statement is effective for five years from December 31 of the year filed and is commonly referred to as a *DBA* (doing business as). Then, an original or legible copy of the DBA, showing the "Filed" and "Certified" stamps from the county clerk's office, must be sent to the Real Estate Commissioner. The business cards of a real estate licensee should use exactly the same name that appears on the license. *Note:* The filing requirements for fictitious business names also apply to internet domains used to identify a real estate brokerage or licensee.

Often, two or more real estate licensees work together to provide licensed real estate services as part of a team, group, or association. A team name is not considered a fictitious business name and does not require the filing of a fictitious business name statement, as long as the team name includes the surname of at least one of its licensee members and the team name does not include a term or terms, such as "real estate broker," "real estate brokerage," "broker," or "brokerage," which would imply or suggest the existence of a real estate entity independent of a responsible broker. Advertising and solicitation materials must include the name and license number of at least one of the licensed members of the team and the responsible broker's identity must be displayed as prominently as the team name.

License Inspection

The broker's license must be available for inspection by the commissioner (or the commissioner's representative) at the broker's principal place of business. If a broker maintains more than one place of business, each branch office must be separately licensed and the license must be available for inspection there. The license of any salesperson(s) working for the broker must also be available for inspection at the broker's main office.

The Broker-Salesperson Relationship

For purposes of the Real Estate Law, a salesperson is always considered the *employee* of the broker. This means that the broker is held accountable for the salesperson's conduct in performing business activities. For compensation, tax, and other purposes, a salesperson can be treated as either an employee or an independent contractor (as discussed in Unit 6).

A salesperson's license is activated only after the name of the employing broker is provided to CalBRE. The broker and salesperson are required by the Real Estate Law to have a *written agreement*. Regulation 2726 of the Real Estate Commissioner states: "The agreement shall be dated and signed by the parties and shall cover material aspects of the relationship between the parties, including supervision of licensed activities, duties and compensation."

www.bre.ca.gov

When a Salesperson Changes Brokers

The following steps must be taken when a salesperson changes employment from one broker to another. Detailed information and printable forms are available at the CalBRE website, www.bre.ca.gov.

1. The former employing broker must notify the California Bureau of Real Estate's Sacramento headquarters immediately, in writing.

2. The former employer must return the salesperson's license certificate within three days of termination of employment and sign the Salesperson Change Application, R/E Form 214.

3. R/E Form 214 must be completed by the salesperson and new employer within five days and sent to:

   California Bureau of Real Estate
   PO Box 137003
   Sacramento, CA 95813-7003

When a Salesperson Is Discharged

If an employing broker discharges a salesperson for a violation of the Real Estate Law, the broker must immediately file a certified, written statement of the facts with the Real Estate Commissioner.

A sample broker-salesperson contract, with the salesperson treated as independent contractor is shown in Figure 1.1. The form provides for mediation of any dispute between broker and associate licensee; there is also a form that provides for binding arbitration of disputes.

This is the first of many forms that appear in this book. You should be alert to the differences in the types of forms that you will see:

■ The content of some forms is *proprietary*, which means that the form is unique to the entity that created it. You will see a copyright notice on such forms, which indicates that you are not allowed to copy the form without permission of the copyright holder.

■ Other forms consist of wording that is dictated by state law—what we refer to as *statutory language*. Even though the wording of the form is mandated (and even the style and size of the type used may be dictated by state law), the overall design of the form may still be copyrighted.

■ Lastly, some forms combine state requirements and those of an association or company. Most of these customized forms also are copyrighted.

With the rapid changes in both California and federal law, form updates are an ongoing process. By the time you see them, the forms in this book may have already been revised. To keep up with the pace of change, the two largest forms publishers in the state have websites where form updates can be ordered and even downloaded for immediate use. The California Association of REALTORS® is headquartered in Los Angeles and found at www.car.org. The forms of Professional Publishing, Inc., can be found at www.trueforms.com.

www.car.org
www.trueforms.com

Exercise 1-1

May a broker-salesperson agreement transfer responsibility for all brokerage activities to the salesperson?

ACTIVITIES OF A REAL ESTATE BROKER

The Real Estate Law sets out the activities that require a real estate broker's license. Those activities also may be performed by a licensed real estate salesperson. The law defines a real estate salesperson as someone who is employed for compensation (salary or commissions) by a licensed real estate broker to perform acts that require a real estate license. The salesperson can only conduct business as the employee of the broker. All of the salesperson's contracts with clients and customers will be executed in the broker's name.

FIGURE 1.1:   Independent Contractor Agreement ICA Revised 04/15

CALIFORNIA
ASSOCIATION
OF REALTORS®

**INDEPENDENT CONTRACTOR AGREEMENT
WITHOUT ARBITRATION
(Between Broker and Associate-Licensee)**
(C.A.R. Form ICA-NA, 4/15)

This Agreement, dated _____ , is made between _____
_____ ("Broker")
and_____ ("Associate-Licensee").
In consideration of the covenants and representations contained in this Agreement, Broker and Associate-Licensee agree as follows:

1. **BROKER:** Broker represents that Broker is duly licensed as a real estate broker by the State of California, ☐ doing business as _____ (firm name), ☐ a sole proprietorship, ☐ a partnership, or ☐ a corporation. Broker is a member of the _____ Association(s) of REALTORS®, and a participant to the_____ Multiple Listing Service(s). Broker shall keep Broker's license current during the term of this Agreement.

2. **ASSOCIATE-LICENSEE:** Associate-Licensee represents that: **(i)** he/she is duly licensed by the State of California as a ☐ real estate broker, ☐ real estate salesperson, and **(ii)** he/she has not used any other names within the past five years, except _____. Associate-Licensee shall keep his/her license current during the term of this Agreement, including satisfying all applicable continuing education and provisional license requirements.

3. **INDEPENDENT CONTRACTOR RELATIONSHIP:**
   A. Broker and Associate-Licensee intend that, to the maximum extent permissible by law: **(i)** This Agreement does not constitute an employment agreement by either party; **(ii)** Broker and Associate-Licensee are independent contracting parties with respect to all services rendered under this Agreement; and **(iii)** This Agreement shall not be construed as a partnership.
   B. Broker shall not: **(i)** restrict Associate-Licensee's activities to particular geographical areas, or **(ii)** dictate Associate-Licensee's activities with regard to hours, leads, open houses, opportunity or floor time, production, prospects, sales meetings, schedule, inventory, time off, vacation, or similar activities, except to the extent required by law.
   C. Associate-Licensee shall not be required to accept an assignment by Broker to service any particular current or prospective listing or parties.
   D. Except as required by law: **(i)** Associate-Licensee retains sole and absolute discretion and judgment in the methods, techniques, and procedures to be used in soliciting and obtaining listings, sales, exchanges, leases, rentals, or other transactions, and in carrying out Associate-Licensee's selling and soliciting activities; **(ii)** Associate-Licensee is under the control of Broker as to the results of Associate-Licensee's work only, and not as to the means by which those results are accomplished; **(iii)** Associate-Licensee has no authority to bind Broker by any promise or representation; and **(iv)** Broker shall not be liable for any obligation or liability incurred by Associate-Licensee.
   E. Associate-Licensee's only remuneration shall be the compensation specified in paragraph 8.
   F. Associate-Licensee who only performs as a real estate sales agent, shall not be treated as an employee for state and federal tax purposes. However, an Associate-Licensee who performs loan activity shall be treated as an employee for state and federal tax purposes unless the activity satisfies the legal requirements to establish an independent contractor relationship.
   G. The fact the Broker may carry workers' compensation insurance for Broker's own benefit and for the mutual benefit of Broker and licensees associated with Broker, including Associate-Licensee, shall not create an inference of employment. (Workers' Compensation Advisory: Even though a Real Estate salesperson may be treated as independent contractors for tax and other purposes, the California Labor and Workforce Development Agency considers them to be employees for workers' compensation purposes. According to that Agency: **(i)** Broker must obtain workers' compensation insurance for a real estate salesperson and **(ii)** Broker, not a Real Estate sales person, must bear the cost of workers' compensation insurance. Penalties for failure to carry workers' compensation include, among others, the issuance of stop-work orders and fines of up to $1,000 per agent, not to exceed $100,000 per company.)

4. **LICENSED ACTIVITY:**
   A. All listings of property, and all agreements, acts or actions for performance of licensed acts, which are taken or performed in connection with this Agreement, shall be taken and performed in the name of Broker. Associate-Licensee agrees to and does hereby contribute all right and title to such listings to Broker for the benefit and use of Broker, Associate-Licensee, and other licensees associated with Broker.
   B. Broker shall make available to Associate-Licensee, equally with other licensees associated with Broker, all current listings in Broker's office, except any listing which Broker may choose to place in the exclusive servicing of Associate-Licensee or one or more other specific licensees associated with Broker.

Broker's Initials (_____)   Associate-Licensee's Initials (_____)

© 2015, California Association of REALTORS®, Inc.

ICA-NA 4/15 (PAGE 1 OF 4)

FIGURE 1.1:   Independent Contractor Agreement ICA Revised 04/15 (continued)

C. Associate-Licensee shall provide and pay for all professional licenses, supplies, services, and other items required in connection with Associate-Licensee's activities under this Agreement, or any listing or transaction, without reimbursement from Broker except as required by law.

D. Associate-Licensee shall work diligently and with his/her best efforts to: **(i)** sell, exchange, lease, or rent properties listed with Broker or other cooperating Brokers; **(ii)** solicit additional listings, clients, and customers; and **(iii)** otherwise promote the business of serving the public in real estate transactions to the end that Broker and Associate-Licensee may derive the greatest benefit possible, in accordance with law.

E. Associate-Licensee shall not commit any unlawful act under federal, state or local law or regulation while conducting licensed activity. Associate-Licensee shall at all times be familiar, and comply, with all applicable federal, state and local laws, including, but not limited to, anti-discrimination laws and restrictions against the giving or accepting a fee, or other thing of value, for the referral of business to title companies, escrow companies, home inspection companies, pest control companies and other settlement service providers pursuant to the California Business and Professions Code and the Real Estate Settlement Procedures Acts (RESPA).

F. Broker shall make available for Associate-Licensee's use, along with other licensees associated with Broker, the facilities of the real estate office operated by Broker at _____ and the facilities of any other office locations made available by Broker pursuant to this Agreement.

G. PROHIBITED ACTIVITIES: Associate-Licensee agrees not to engage in any of the following Real Estate licensed activities without the express written consent of Broker:
☐ Property Management; ☐ Loan Brokerage ☐ Business Brokerage; ☐ _____
☐ _____
However, if Associate-Licensee has a Real Estate Broker's License, Associate-Licensee may nonetheless engage in the following prohibited activity(ies) only: _____
provided that (1) such prohibited activities are not done under the Broker's License, (2) no facilities of Broker (including but not limited to phones, fax, computers, and office space) are used for any such prohibited activities, (3) Associate-Licensee shall not use any marketing, solicitation or contact information that include Broker's name (including business cards) for such prohibited activities, (4) Associate-Licensee informs any actual or intended Principal for whom Associate-Licensee performs or intends to perform such prohibited activities the name of the broker under whose license the prohibited activities are performed, and (5) if Associate-Licensee is performing other permitted licensed activity for that Principal under Broker's license, then Associate-Licensee shall inform any actual or intended Principal for whom the prohibited activities are performed that the prohibited activities are not performed under Broker's license.

5. PROPRIETARY INFORMATION AND FILES:
A. All files and documents pertaining to listings, leads and transactions are the property of Broker and shall be delivered to Broker by Associate-Licensee immediately upon request or termination of this Agreement.
B. Associate-Licensee acknowledges that Broker's method of conducting business is a protected trade secret.
C. Associate-Licensee shall not use to his/her own advantage, or the advantage of any other person, business, or entity, except as specifically agreed in writing, either during Associate-Licensee's association with Broker, or thereafter, any information gained for or from the business, or files of Broker.

6. SUPERVISION: Associate-Licensee, within 24 hours (or ☐ _____) after preparing,signing, or receiving same, shall submit to Broker, or Broker's designated licensee: **(i)** all documents which may have a material effect upon the rights and duties of principals in a transaction; **(ii)** any documents or other items connected with a transaction pursuant to this Agreement in the possession of or available to Associate Licensee; and **(iii)** all documents associated with any real estate transaction in which Associate-Licensee is a principal.

7. TRUST FUNDS: All trust funds shall be handled through the Broker's trust account and in compliance with the Business and Professions Code, and other applicable laws.

8. COMPENSATION:
A. TO BROKER: Compensation shall be charged to parties who enter into listing or other agreements for services requiring a real estate license:
☐ as shown in "Exhibit A" attached, which is incorporated as a part of this Agreement by reference, or
☐ as follows:_____
_____
Any deviation which is not approved in writing in advance by Broker, shall be: (1) deducted from Associate-Licensee's compensation, if lower than the amount or rate approved above; and, (2) subject to Broker approval, if higher than the amount approved above. Any permanent change in commission schedule shall be disseminated by Broker to Associate-Licensee.
B. TO ASSOCIATE-LICENSEE: Associate-Licensee shall receive a share of compensation actually collected by Broker, on listings or other agreements for services requiring a real estate license, which are solicited and obtained by Associate-Licensee, and on transactions of which Associate-Licensee's activities are the procuring cause, as follows:
☐ as shown in "Exhibit B" attached, which is incorporated as a part of this Agreement by reference, or
☐ other: _____
_____
_____

Broker's Initials (_____)   Associate-Licensee's Initials (_____)

INDEPENDENT CONTRACTOR AGREEMENT (ICA-NA PAGE 2 OF 4)

FIGURE 1.1:   Independent Contractor Agreement ICA Revised 04/15 (continued)

C. PARTNERS, TEAMS, AND AGREEMENTS WITH OTHER ASSOCIATE-LICENSEES IN OFFICE: If Associate-Licensee and one or more other Associate-Licensees affiliated with Broker participate on the same side (either listing or selling) of a transaction, the commission allocated to their combined activities shall be divided by Broker and paid to them according to their written agreement. Broker shall have the right to withhold total compensation if there is a dispute between associate-licensees, or if there is no written agreement, or if no written agreement has been provided to Broker.

D. EXPENSES AND OFFSETS: If Broker elects to advance funds to pay expenses or liabilities of Associate-Licensee, or for an advance payment of, or draw upon, future compensation, Broker may deduct the full amount advanced from compensation payable to Associate-Licensee on any transaction without notice. If Associate-Licensee's compensation is subject to a lien, garnishment or other restriction on payment, Broker shall charge Associate-Licensee a fee for complying with such restriction.

E. PAYMENT: (i) All compensation collected by Broker and due to Associate-Licensee shall be paid to Associate-Licensee, after deduction of expenses and offsets, immediately or as soon thereafter as practicable, except as otherwise provided in this Agreement, or a separate written agreement between Broker and Associate-Licensee. **(ii)** Compensation shall not be paid to Associate-Licensee until both the transaction and file are complete. **(iii)** Broker is under no obligation to pursue collection of compensation from any person or entity responsible for payment. Associate-Licensee does not have the independent right to pursue collection of compensation for activities which require a real estate license which were done in the name of Broker. **(iv)** Expenses which are incurred in the attempt to collect compensation shall be paid by Broker and Associate-Licensee in the same proportion as set forth for the division of compensation (paragraph 8(B)). **(v)** If there is a known or pending claim against Broker or Associate-Licensee on transactions for which Associate-Licensee has not yet been paid, Broker may withhold from compensation due Associate-Licensee on that transaction amounts for which Associate-Licensee could be responsible under paragraph 14, until such claim is resolved. **(vi)** Associate-Licensee shall not be entitled to any advance payment from Broker upon future compensation.

F. UPON OR AFTER TERMINATION: If this Agreement is terminated while Associate-Licensee has listings or pending transactions that require further work normally rendered by Associate-Licensee, Broker shall make arrangements with another associate-licensee to perform the required work, or Broker shall perform the work him/herself. The licensee performing the work shall be reasonably compensated for completing work on those listings or transactions, and such reasonable compensation shall be deducted from Associate-Licensee's share of compensation. Except for such offset, Associate-Licensee shall receive the compensation due as specified above.

9. **TERMINATION OF RELATIONSHIP:** Broker or Associate-Licensee may terminate their relationship under this Agreement at any time, with or without cause. After termination, Associate-Licensee shall not solicit: **(i)** prospective or existing clients or customers based upon company-generated leads obtained during the time Associate-Licensee was affiliated with Broker; **(ii)** any principal with existing contractual obligations to Broker; or **(iii)** any principal with a contractual transactional obligation for which Broker is entitled to be compensated. Even after termination, this Agreement, inclusive of Paragraph 12, shall govern all disputes and claims between Broker and Associate-Licensee connected with their relationship under this Agreement, including obligations and liabilities arising from existing and completed listings, transactions, and services.

10. **AUTOMOBILE:** Associate-Licensee shall maintain automobile insurance coverage for liability and property damage in the following amounts $_____/$_____. Broker shall be named as an additional insured party on Associate-Licensee's policies. A copy of the endorsement showing Broker as an additional insured shall be provided to Broker.

11. **PERSONAL ASSISTANTS:** Associate-Licensee may make use of a personal assistant, provided the following requirements are satisfied. Associate-Licensee shall have a written agreement with the personal assistant which establishes the terms and responsibilities of the parties to the employment agreement, including, but not limited to, compensation, supervision and compliance with applicable law. The agreement shall be subject to Broker's review and approval. Unless otherwise agreed, if the personal assistant has a real estate license, that license must be provided to the Broker. Both Associate-Licensee and personal assistant must sign any agreement that Broker has established for such purposes.

12. **AGREEMENT TO MEDIATE DISPUTES:**
    (1) Broker and Associate-Licensee agree to timely notify the other person and mediate all disputes and claims between them arising from or connected in any way with this Agreement before resorting to arbitration or court action. **(2)** If any dispute or claim is not resolved through mediation, or otherwise, Broker and Associate-Licensee may mutually agree to submit disputes involving commissions for property transactions to binding arbitration by the procedures and rules set forth in the California Code of Ethics and Arbitration Manual, a copy of which is available at the following link: www.car.org/legal/calarbrules/.

Broker's Initials (_____)   Associate-Licensee's Initials (_____)

INDEPENDENT CONTRACTOR AGREEMENT (ICA-NA PAGE 3 OF 4)

FIGURE 1.1:   Independent Contractor Agreement ICA Revised 04/15 (continued)

13. **OFFICE POLICY MANUAL:** If Broker's office policy manual, now or as modified in the future, conflicts with or differs from the terms of this Agreement, the terms of the office policy manual shall govern the relationship between Broker and Associate-Licensee.

14. **INDEMNITY AND HOLD HARMLESS; NOTICE OF CLAIMS:**
    A. Regarding any action taken or omitted by Associate-Licensee, or others working through, or on behalf of Associate-Licensee in connection with services rendered or to be rendered pursuant to this Agreement or real estate licensed activity prohibited by this agreement: **(i)** Associate-Licensee agrees to indemnify, defend and hold Broker harmless from all claims, disputes, litigation, judgments, awards, costs and attorney fees, arising therefrom and **(ii)** Associate-Licensee shall immediately notify Broker if Associate-Licensee is served with or becomes aware of a lawsuit or claim regarding any such action.
    B. Any such claims or costs payable pursuant to this Agreement, are due as follows:
       ☐ Paid in full by Associate-Licensee, who hereby agrees to indemnify and hold harmless Broker for all such sums, or
       ☐ In the same ratio as the compensation split as it existed at the time the compensation was earned by Associate-Licensee ☐ Other: _____
       Payment from Associate-Licensee is due at the time Broker makes such payment and can be offset from any compensation due Associate-Licensee as above. Broker retains the authority to settle claims or disputes, whether or not Associate-Licensee consents to such settlement.

15. **ADDITIONAL PROVISIONS:** _____
    _____

16. **DEFINITIONS:** As used in this Agreement, the following terms have the meanings indicated:
    A. "Listing" means an agreement with a property owner or other party to locate a buyer, exchange party, lessee, or other party to a transaction involving real property, a mobile home, or other property or transaction which may be brokered by a real estate licensee, or an agreement with a party to locate or negotiate for any such property or transaction.
    B. "Compensation" means compensation for acts requiring a real estate license, regardless of whether calculated as a percentage of transaction price, flat fee, hourly rate, or in any other manner.
    C. "Transaction" means a sale, exchange, lease, or rental of real property, a business opportunity, or a manufactured home, which may lawfully be brokered by a real estate licensee.

17. **ATTORNEY FEES:** In any action, proceeding, or arbitration between Broker and Associate-Licensee arising from or related to this Agreement, the prevailing Broker or Associate-Licensee shall be entitled to reasonable attorney fees and costs.

18. **ENTIRE AGREEMENT:** All prior agreements between the parties concerning their relationship as Broker and Associate-Licensee are incorporated in this Agreement, which constitutes the entire contract. Its terms are intended by the parties as a final and complete expression of their agreement with respect to its subject matter, and may not be contradicted by evidence of any prior agreement or contemporaneous oral agreement. This Agreement may not be amended, modified, altered, or changed except by a further agreement in writing executed by Broker and Associate-Licensee.

Broker: _____

(Brokerage firm name)

By _____
Its Broker/Office manager (circle one)

_____
(Print name)

_____
(Address)

_____
(City, State, Zip)

_____
(Telephone)   (Fax)

Broker's Initials (_____)

Associate-Licensee: _____

(Signature)

_____
(Print name)

_____
(Address)

_____
(City, State, Zip)

_____
(Telephone)   (Fax)

Associate-Licensee's Initials (_____)

Published and Distributed by:
REAL ESTATE BUSINESS SERVICES, INC.
a subsidiary of the California Association of REALTORS®
525 South Virgil Avenue, Los Angeles, California 90020

Reviewed by _____ Date _____

ICA-NA 4/15 (PAGE 4 OF 4)

INDEPENDENT CONTRACTOR AGREEMENT (ICA-NA PAGE 4 OF 4)

Real Property Transactions

The Real Estate Law permits a real estate licensee (broker or salesperson) to represent someone else in any of the following transactions involving real property or a business opportunity:

- Selling or offering to sell, including soliciting prospective sellers
- Purchasing or offering to purchase, including soliciting prospective purchasers
- Exchanging
- Soliciting or obtaining property listings for sale or exchange
- Leasing, renting, or offering to lease or rent
- Selling, purchasing, or exchanging leases
- Filing an application for purchase or lease involving land owned by the state or federal governments

The Real Estate Law does *not* require licensing for the resident manager of an apartment building or complex; the manager (or employees of the manager) of a hotel, motel, or auto or trailer park; an employee of a property management company who merely opens vacant units to prospective tenants; and a real estate assistant who does not perform acts that require a real estate license.

Manufactured/Mobilehomes

The Real Estate Law permits a real estate agent to handle transactions involving a *mobilehome* (termed a *manufactured home* in federal regulations discussed in Unit 14). The home must be registered in compliance with the Health and Safety Code. If it is, the agent can perform the following activities:

- Sell
- Purchase
- Exchange

If the real estate agent displays or offers for sale two or more registered mobilehomes at the agent's place of business, the agent must also be licensed as a **mobilehome dealer**. The requirements for that license, which is obtained from the Department of Housing and Community Development (HCD), are in the Health and Safety Code. Information also can be found at the HCD website, www.hcd.ca.gov.

www.hcd.ca.gov

Mortgage Loan Transactions

In California, a real estate brokerage can also act as a **mortgage loan brokerage**. A real estate agent can represent someone else in any of the following acts involving loans secured by real property or a business opportunity:

- Soliciting borrowers or lenders for loans
- Negotiating loans
- Servicing loans (collecting payments or performing other services for borrowers or lenders)

In addition, a real estate agent can act as a principal (party to the transaction) in a transaction involving a sales contract or promissory note secured by real estate in the following cases:

- Purchase, sale, or exchange of such an obligation with a member of the public (consumer)
- Servicing of such an obligation by agreement with a member of the public

www.nmls.org

As of January 1, 2011, a licensee who acts as a residential **mortgage loan originator** (MLO) must register annually on the Nationwide Mortgage Licensing System & Registry (NMLS), found at www.nmls.org, and meet other requirements.

The federal and state registration requirements for mortgage loan brokers, lenders, branches, and originators are detailed in Unit 8, Financing Real Estate. All Cal-BRE licensees who conduct MLO activities for residential property of one to four units must obtain an MLO license endorsement that is attached to the real estate license and renewed annually.

Mineral, Oil, and Gas Transactions

A real estate brokerage is permitted to handle the following activities involving mineral, oil, and gas property for others:

- Sell or offer for sale
- Purchase or offer for purchase
- Solicit prospective sellers or purchasers
- Solicit or obtain listings
- Lease or offer to lease
- Collect rent or royalties from such property or its improvements
- Exchange
- Assist or offer to assist in filing an application for the purchase or lease of such property owned by the state or federal government (An exception is made for an officer or employee of the state or federal government.)

A real estate agent can also act as the principal in a transaction involving one of the following:

- Buying or leasing or taking an option on mineral, oil, or gas property for the purpose of sale, exchange, lease, sublease, or assignment of a lease of all or part of the property
- Offering mining claims for sale or assignment

There is no longer a separate *mineral, oil, and gas (MOG) broker license*. Anyone (individual or corporation) who still has an MOG license is entitled to continue to perform the listed activities, but no new MOG licenses are being issued. Existing MOG licenses must be renewed and renewal fees paid, but there is no continuing education requirement for MOG licensees.

BUSINESS OPPORTUNITY BROKERAGE

As noted earlier, the Real Estate Law allows a licensed real estate broker to represent others in the purchase or sale of a business. A transaction involving a **business opportunity** includes business assets that are personal property, such as inventory, trade fixtures, and the business's *goodwill* (the benefit derived from the business's favorable relationship with its customers). A business opportunity may also include or take the form of a **franchise** agreement. When real property is sold at the same time, the sales usually are treated as separate, concurrent transactions.

A business opportunity transaction may involve transfer of stock. Ordinarily, a stock transfer requires a securities license, as set out in the Corporations Code. But a stock transfer that is part of a transaction involving a business opportunity can be handled by a licensed real estate brokerage.

www.sba.gov

Business brokerage is a growing area of real estate practice. In many areas, retail stores, restaurants, manufacturing, and other businesses make up a significant number of transactions every year. The Small Business Administration (SBA), a federal agency found at www.sba.gov, defines a small business as one with no more than $1 million in annual sales or, if a manufacturer, with no more than 250 employees. In fact, 95% of U.S. businesses qualify as small businesses, and most of them change ownership every five to eight years. Some brokers specialize in business transactions, even limiting their activities to a particular type or size of business, such as retail stores of a certain square footage or annual gross income, gas stations, or warehouse storage facilities.

Franchises

A **franchise** is defined in California's Franchise Investment Law as a contract or agreement, either expressed or implied, whether oral or written, between two or more persons by which

- a franchisee is granted the right to engage in the business of offering, selling, or distributing goods or services under a marketing plan or system prescribed in substantial part by a franchisor;

- the operation of the franchisee's business pursuant to such plan or system is substantially associated with the franchisor's trademark, service mark, trade name, logotype, advertising, or other commercial symbol designating the franchisor or its affiliate; and

- the franchisee is required to pay, directly or indirectly, a franchise fee.

Taking and Handling the Business Opportunity Listing

The agent should evaluate carefully the business's location and operation, as well as the seller's records and financial statements.

Ideally, the business owner should provide profit and loss statements, or at least business tax reports, for the past three years, for review by the buyer's accountant. These documents also are important because the business's income stream and assets will determine the selling price. The agent should be aware of all factors that might influence the soundness of the business as an investment.

Uniform Commercial Code Requirements

California has adopted the **Uniform Commercial Code**. The Uniform Commercial Code governs the sale or transfer of goods ordinarily held for sale in the course of business. Goods held for sale by a business probably were obtained on credit from a supplier or manufacturer.

A **bulk transfer of goods** is any transfer of a substantial part of the materials, supplies, merchandise, equipment, or other inventory that is not in the ordinary course of the transferor's business. The Uniform Commercial Code protects creditors of the seller in such a transfer by requiring that notice of the transfer be given to the transferor's creditors. The notice is made once, at least 12 business days before the transfer is to take place. Notice is given by recordation with the county recorder, publication in a newspaper, and registered or certified mail to the County Tax Collector. Other requirements also may apply.

The prospective buyer may be an experienced businessperson, but often the business buyer will be young or inexperienced. The agent should be able to alert the buyer to federal, state, and local government requirements that must be met to obtain the necessary business permits, licenses, and clearances. In addition to federal withholding taxes, the buyer may be liable for sales tax, state payroll tax withholding, and workers' compensation insurance. The box above highlights concerns that arise under the Uniform Commercial Code. In an effort to streamline the permitting process, the California Environmental Protection Agency has created Permit Assistance Centers that can be contacted by calling 1-800-GOV-1-STOP or by visiting www.calgold.ca.gov, which lists permit requirements by city.

www.calgold.ca.gov

In short, a business opportunity listing should not be taken unless the agent is fully informed of the business's assets and liabilities and is able to convey that information to purchasers. Because of the complexities involved in the sale of a business opportunity, some brokers will not allow an associate to handle this type of transaction.

PREPAID RENTAL LISTING SERVICE LICENSE

A **Prepaid Rental Listing Service** (PRLS) is a business that supplies prospective tenants with listings of residential real property on payment of a fee collected at the same time or in advance of when the listings are supplied. Anyone licensed as a real estate broker may conduct a PRLS business without obtaining a separate PRLS license. The real estate broker must use a contract with the tenant/client that is approved in advance by CalBRE. Either the broker or a salesperson employed by the broker must be designated to supervise the PRLS activities.

An individual or a corporation may obtain a separate two-year license to conduct PRLS activities. Applicants must submit

- an application form;
- a properly completed fingerprint card;

- security in the form of a $10,000 surety bond or cash deposit for each location; and
- the appropriate license fees.

The security requirement does not apply to a PRLS operated by a tax-exempt entity; an agency of the federal, state, or local government; or a real estate broker conducting a PRLS under a real estate license.

Application requirements must be met for every location to be operated by the PRLS licensee. Before issuance of the PRLS license, the applicant must submit a copy of the contract to be entered into with prospective tenants/clients to Cal-BRE for approval. No examination is required.

Further information on the PRLS license may be obtained by mail from the California Bureau of Real Estate, PRLS Desk, PO Box 137000, Sacramento, CA 95813-7000, or by phoning 1-877-373-4542 toll free.

EXEMPTIONS FROM REAL ESTATE LICENSING REQUIREMENTS

A real estate license is *not* needed by the following people:

- A person who deals only with her own property
- A corporation that performs any of the specified activities through one of its regular officers, who receives no special compensation for doing so
- A licensed securities broker or dealer involved in the sale, lease, or exchange of a business opportunity in that capacity
- Anyone holding a duly executed power of attorney from the owner of property
- An attorney-at-law rendering services in the performance of his duties as attorney
- A receiver, trustee in bankruptcy, or person acting under order of any court
- A trustee selling under a deed of trust
- Employees of lending institutions, pension trusts, credit unions, or insurance companies, in connection with loans secured by liens on real property or a business opportunity
- Escrow agents collecting funds in connection with loans secured by liens on real property, when the funds are deposited in the escrow agent's trust account

Other examples include cemetery authorities and persons making 10 or fewer collections (in amounts of $40,000 or less in a calendar year) on notes secured by liens on real property.

To provide more time for client and customer contact, many real estate licensees are hiring one or more assistants to help with administrative and other tasks that do not require a real estate license. Activities that can be performed by an unlicensed real estate assistant include the following:

- Record filing, such as rent receipts, loan payments, or escrow sheets
- Meeting nonprincipals, such as the appraiser, home inspector, pest control, or fire inspector
- Computer data entry or retrieval, such as maintaining a client database or gathering title company records for the licensee's client record files
- Word processing, such as downloading digital photos and graphics for flyer composition or distribution

It is important to note that unlicensed assistants cannot perform any of the activities that require a real estate license. Those activities are listed in the Business and Professions Code starting in Section 10130. The employing broker has ultimate responsibility for complying with the law, making adequate supervision of the activities of unlicensed assistants imperative. The office policy manual should cover the use of unlicensed assistants.

REAL ESTATE LICENSING REQUIREMENTS

www.bre.ca.gov
www.bre.ca.gov/files/pdf/re4
.pdf

An application for a real estate licensing examination can be obtained from any CalBRE office. Forms, instructions, and licensing information are also available at CalBRE's website, www.bre.ca.gov. The licensing handbook is at www.bre.ca.gov /files/pdf/re4.pdf. Instructions are included with the application. A license application is sent to an examinee who has successfully completed the licensing exam.

A completed license application, together with the required fingerprints and processing fee, may be taken to a department office or mailed to the California Bureau of Real Estate, PO Box 137001, Sacramento, CA 95813-7001.

An applicant for a real estate license must be honest and truthful. Conviction of a crime that is either a felony or involves moral turpitude may result in the denial of a license. Failure to reveal a criminal conviction or disciplinary action that occurred at any time in the applicant's history on an original license application may also result in denial of a license.

Any fraud, misrepresentation, deceit, or material misstatement of fact in a licensing application can result in a suspension of the license without hearing within 90 days of issuance.

A license or renewal applicant must provide a *Social Security number* to CalBRE. This requirement does not apply to corporations with federal tax identification numbers.

CalBRE cannot issue or renew a license if the applicant is on a list of persons who are delinquent in making court-ordered child support payments. The list is compiled by the Department of Child Support Services from information provided by the local child support agencies in California:

- CalBRE will issue a 150-day license to a listed license applicant, if the applicant fulfills all other requirements. A regular license will not be issued unless a release is obtained from the appropriate district attorney's office within the 150 days.

- A currently licensed individual who is placed on the list will be notified by CalBRE that, if the obligation is not cleared within 150 days, the license will be suspended.

Real Estate Broker's License

An applicant for a real estate broker's license must be at least 18 years old at the time the license is issued. The applicant must pass a qualifying examination and meet the following requirements for experience and education:

- The applicant must have been actively engaged as a real estate salesperson for at least two of the five years preceding the application or provide satisfactory proof to the commissioner of other experience equivalent to two years of full-time experience as a real estate salesperson. An applicant with a four-year degree from an accredited college with a major or minor emphasis in real estate may be exempt from the experience requirement.

Proof of Legal Presence in the United States

As of January 1, 2016, proof of legal presence is no longer required for

- applicants for a license,
- license renewal applicants, and
- applicants for payment from the Real Estate Recovery Fund.

This means that, except as specified, any entity within the department may not deny licensure to an applicant based on citizenship status or immigration status.

- The applicant must have successfully completed eight three-semester-unit (or equivalent) college-level courses taken at an accredited institution of higher learning or a private vocational school approved by the commissioner. The courses include the following:
  — Real Estate Practice
  — Legal Aspects of Real Estate
  — Real Estate Finance
  — Real Estate Appraisal
  — Real Estate Economics (or General Accounting)
- The applicant also must have taken any three of the following:
  — Real Estate Principles
  — Business Law

— Property Management

— Real Estate Office Administration

— Escrows

— Mortgage Loan Brokering and Lending

— Advanced Legal Aspects of Real Estate

— Advanced Real Estate Finance

— Advanced Real Estate Appraisal

— Computer Applications in Real Estate

— Common Interest Developments

If both Real Estate Economics and General Accounting are taken, only two courses from the second group are required. Attorneys who are members of the bar of any state in the United States generally are exempt from both education and experience requirements, but must still pass the licensing exam.

Real Estate Salesperson's License

An applicant for a real estate salesperson's license must be at least 18 years old at the time the license is issued. The applicant must pass a qualifying exam and meet educational requirements. Before taking the licensing examination, the applicant must successfully complete three college-level courses in Real Estate Principles, Real Estate Practice, and one of the following courses:

■ Real Estate Appraisal

■ Property Management

■ Real Estate Finance

■ Real Estate Economics

■ Legal Aspects of Real Estate

■ Real Estate Office Administration

■ Mortgage Loan Brokering and Lending

■ General Accounting

■ Business Law

■ Escrows

■ Computer Applications in Real Estate

■ Common Interest Developments

License Examinations

The licensing examinations consist of multiple-choice questions that are similar in format to the achievement examinations in this book, but much more complex, including lengthy fact situations, with the same concept covered from different perspectives in different questions. The topics covered on the examinations are distributed as shown in Figure 1.2.

The salesperson's exam contains 150 questions, and at least 70% (105 questions) must be answered correctly to pass. Salesperson applicants have one 3¼-hour session to complete the exam.

The broker's exam contains 200 questions, and at least 75% (150) must be answered correctly to pass. Broker applicants have a 2½-hour morning and 2½-hour afternoon session to complete the exam.

The written license examination is intended to show whether the applicant has sufficient knowledge of the required topics. It also indicates whether the applicant has the ability to read and comprehend the English language. In addition, the applicant may be required to perform arithmetic computations common to real estate.

Interactive Voice Response System

CalBRE has an Interactive Voice Response (IVR) system, available 24 hours a day and seven days a week. Call 1-877-373-4321 toll free to

- confirm a licensing examination date, time, and location;
- confirm examination results;
- verify that an original salesperson or broker license number has been issued; and
- learn how to file a complaint against a licensee.

These verifications are also available at www.bre.ca.gov.

License Term and Renewal

The full term for a broker's or salesperson's license is four years. To renew the license for an additional four years, the licensee must successfully complete 45 hours of continuing education (CE). All courses must be approved by CalBRE. For all license renewals, the renewal applicant must complete 45 clock hours of education, including at least 18 hours related to consumer protection in addition to separate three-hour courses in the following:

- Ethics, Professional Conduct, and Legal Aspects of Real Estate
- Agency Relationships and Duties in a Real Estate Brokerage Practice
- Trust Fund Accounting and Handling
- Fair Housing
- Risk Management

Brokers renewing for the first time also must take a three-hour course in the management of real estate offices and supervision of real estate activities (Management and Supervision). For subsequent renewals, salesperson and broker licensees must complete an eight-hour continuing education survey course that includes topics in ethics, agency, trust fund handling, fair housing, risk management, and management and supervision.

The eLicensing online system offered by CalBRE at www.bre.ca.gov can be used to expedite processing of salesperson and broker license renewals at any time and day of the week.

There is a continuing education exemption for a licensee who is 70 years of age or older and has been a licensee in good standing for 30 continuous years in California. Details on filing for this status are found in the licensing handbook. A first-time application for a continuing education exemption must be filed by mail or in person.

FIGURE 1.2:   **Approximate Breakdown of Examination Topics in Broker's and Salesperson's Examinations**

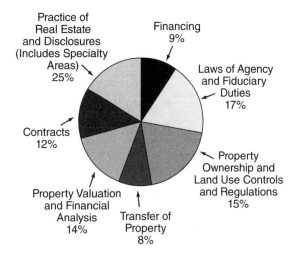

There is a separate renewal process for an MLO license endorsement, which must be renewed annually and requires completion of eight hours of continuing education.

Expiration and Late Renewal

If a license is not renewed before it expires, the licensee's real estate activities must cease immediately. If the license of an employing broker expires, the consequences can be profound. Expiration of the employing broker's license will place all licensees (whether salespersons or brokers) who work for the employing broker on nonworking status.

A license that is not renewed before it expires may be renewed at any time up to two years from the expiration date. A late renewal fee will be required. After the two-year period, the licensee must qualify for and successfully pass the appropriate real estate examination.

The Real Estate License Number

CalBRE requires that the real estate licensee's identification number appear on materials used to solicit consumers, including the following:

- Business cards
- Stationery
- Websites owned, controlled, and/or maintained by the soliciting real estate licensee
- Promotional and advertising flyers, brochures, email and regular mail, leaflets, and other marketing or promotional materials designed to solicit the creation of a professional relationship between the licensee and a consumer, or intended to induce a consumer to contact the licensee about any licensed services

The following are not considered solicitation materials under the license number requirement:

- Advertisements in electronic media, including radio, cinema, and television ads, and the opening section of streaming video and audio
- Print advertising in any newspaper or periodical
- For Sale signs placed on or around a property intended to alert the public the property is available for purchase or lease

The license number must be in a type size no smaller than the smallest type size used in the solicitation material. If the name of more than one licensee appears in the solicitation, each person's license number must be disclosed. The license number of employing brokers or corporate brokers whose names, logos, or trademarks appear on solicitation materials along with the names and license numbers of licensed employees or broker-associates, need not appear on those materials.

In addition to the CalBRE license number, a mortgage loan originator must include in an advertisement for a loan that is disseminated primarily in California the unique identifier assigned to that licensee by the Nationwide Mortgage Licensing System and Registry under which the loan would be made or arranged. The CalBRE licensing information telephone number is not required on advertisements for loan activities, but it is required on the Lender/Purchaser Disclosure Statement and the Mortgage Loan Disclosure Statement, which are discussed in Unit 8, Financing Real Estate.

ENFORCEMENT OF THE REAL ESTATE LAW

The Real Estate Commissioner investigates complaints regarding the activities of real estate licensees. A complaint may come from a member of the public or from a private group, such as a local association of REALTORS®. The commissioner is allowed to initiate an investigation and must do so if a verified complaint is made in writing by someone who believes he was wronged by a licensee acting in that capacity.

The CalBRE investigation may include a statement by the licensee and examination of the licensee's records, bank records, title company records, and public records. An informal conference including the parties may be held to determine the necessity for a formal hearing. If a formal hearing is held, it will be presided over by an administrative law judge. At that point, the commissioner becomes the complainant, and the licensee is the respondent. The licensee may appear with or without an attorney. The person who initiated the complaint is a witness. Other evidence also may be presented. Testimony is taken under oath.

The most common violations of the Real Estate Law involve trust fund record keeping and shortages, failure to supervise, unlicensed activity, misrepresentations, disclosure issues, and criminal convictions.

Outcome of the Hearing

Charges not proven by the evidence are dismissed. If the charges are proven, the licensee is subject to license *suspension* or *revocation*, depending on the seriousness of the charges. If the license is revoked, an application for reinstatement cannot be made for one year. When a violation involves an unlicensed individual, a *desist and refrain order* will be issued.

Restricted license   In certain circumstances, such as a violation of the Real Estate Law, the Real Estate Commissioner may decide to issue a **restricted license**. The restriction imposed could

- limit the length of the license term;
- require (for a salesperson) employment by a particular real estate broker; or
- contain some other condition, such as the filing of surety bonds for the protection of persons with whom the licensee does business.

The holder of a restricted license cannot renew the license unless and until the restriction is lifted. The commissioner has the right to suspend a restricted license without a hearing, pending a final determination after a formal hearing.

Other penalties   The Real Estate Commissioner also has the discretion to order one or more of the following penalties for violation of the Real Estate Law:

- Education—requiring the offender to successfully complete one or more courses, such as a course in ethics
- Payment of a fine
- Return of documents or other materials
- Reimbursement to the Real Estate Recovery Account of any amounts paid to victims of the violation on the offender's behalf, as explained later in this unit

Types of Violations

The Real Estate Law specifies many activities that can result in a suspension or revocation of a real estate license. Most of the prohibited activities listed below, which are found in Business and Professions Code Section 10176, are discussed in Units 6 and 7:

- *Misrepresentation.* This is a statement or act of deception on a matter of significance to the transaction, such as the condition of the property. Failure to disclose a property defect is probably the most common form of misrepresentation.

- *False promise.* This includes making any false promises of a character to influence, persuade, or induce. An offer of a rebate or gift to a prospective client is acceptable, as long as the terms of the offer are expressed and fulfilled.

- *Continued misrepresentation.* This is a continued and flagrant course of misrepresentation or making of false promises through real estate agents or salespersons.

- *Undisclosed dual agency.* This is acting for more than one party in a transaction without the knowledge and consent of all parties.

- *Commingling.* This includes placing the licensee's own money in the same account with the money of others. (The licensee can place up to $200 in an account to cover account fees.)

- *Not specifying listing termination date.* Any exclusive listing or other agreement authorized by the Real Estate Law must specify a definite ending date.

- *Making a secret profit.* No compensation of any form may be received by the licensee without the knowledge of the licensee's client. This can happen when the licensee purchases property through a "dummy" buyer, then resells it at a higher price.

- *Combining listing with option without informed consent of seller.* No option to purchase combined with a listing agreement is allowed unless the licensee's profit is stated when the option is exercised and agreed to by the seller in writing.

- *Dishonest dealing.* This is any other conduct that constitutes fraud or dishonest dealing.

- *Obtaining signature of prospective purchaser of a business opportunity without owner's authority.* No agreement to represent someone or receive compensation for the purchase, lease, rent, or exchange of a business opportunity can be obtained without prior authorization of the business owner.

- *Willfully or repeatedly violating any provision of the Civil Code regarding real property transfer disclosures.*

A real estate license may be suspended or revoked or issuance of a license may be denied if the licensee or applicant (or person owning or controlling more than 10% of a corporate applicant's stock) has engaged in any of the following activities, which appear in Business and Professions Code Section 10177:

- *Obtaining license by fraud.* This includes obtaining a real estate license or license renewal by fraud, misrepresentation, or deceit, or making any material misstatement of fact in an application for a real estate license, license renewal, or reinstatement.

■ *Criminal activities resulting in conviction.* This includes suffering a conviction of a felony or a crime involving moral turpitude that is related to the qualifications or duties of a real estate licensee.

■ *False advertising.* This is knowingly authorizing, directing, conniving at, or aiding in the publication, advertisement, distribution, or circulation of any material false statement or representation concerning any business, business opportunity, or land or subdivision offered for sale. When advertising a property, a licensee must disclose that the property is offered through a licensed real estate agent. Failure to disclose this fact and provide the name of the licensee is called **blind advertising** and is illegal.

■ *Violations of other sections.* This includes disregarding or violating any of the provisions of the Real Estate Law or the rules and regulations of the commissioner regarding administration and enforcement of the Real Estate Law.

■ *Misuse of trade name.* This includes using the term *REALTOR* or any trade name or insignia of membership (such as the term *Realtist*) in any real estate organization of which the licensee is not a member.

■ *Conduct warranting denial.* This is acting in a manner that would have resulted in denial of a real estate license, such as conviction for a felony or a crime involving moral turpitude.

■ *Negligence or incompetence.* This is demonstrating such carelessness or incompetence as a licensee that the interests of clients or customers are endangered.

■ *Negligent supervision of salespersons.* This is failing, as a broker-licensee or broker-officer of a corporation, to exercise reasonable supervision over the licensed activities of salespersons or the corporation.

■ *Violating government trust.* This includes using one's employment by a governmental agency to violate the confidential nature of government records.

■ *Other dishonest conduct.* This includes engaging in any other conduct constituting fraud or dishonest dealing.

■ *Restricted license violation.* This includes violating any of the terms of a restricted license.

■ *Inducement of panic selling.* This includes soliciting or inducing the sale, lease, or listing for sale or lease of residential property on the grounds, wholly or in part, of loss of value or of increase in crime or decline of the quality of the schools, due to the present or prospective entry into the neighborhood of a person or persons of another race, color, religion, ancestry, or national origin.

Manufactured/Mobilehomes

Real estate licensees handling manufactured homes (mobilehomes) are subject to the general requirements and prohibitions applicable to all real estate transactions. In addition, the Real Estate Law imposes the following restrictions on mobilehome sales:

- A mobilehome may not be advertised or offered for sale unless it is in place in a mobilehome park or located in a location where it can legally remain for at least one year.

- An advertisement of a mobilehome for sale must be withdrawn within 48 hours after receipt of notice that the mobilehome is no longer available for sale, lease, or exchange.

- License or transfer of title fees may not be prorated unless buyer and seller agree or the licensee was required to pay the fees to avoid penalties that would have been imposed for late payment.

- Only a mobilehome that meets Vehicle Code requirements can be represented as transportable on a California highway. All material facts pertaining to equipment requirements must be revealed. A permit from the Department of Transportation or local agency must be obtained to authorize the moving of a mobilehome.

- It may not be advertised or represented that no down payment is required if in fact the buyer will be advised to secure an additional loan for that purpose.

- The licensee is responsible for making sure that the certificate of ownership or certificate of title of the mobilehome is endorsed, dated, and delivered to the purchaser.

- No later than 10 days after the sale of a mobilehome, a real estate broker must give written notice of the transfer to the headquarters office of the Department of Housing and Community Development.

The following are grounds for revocation or suspension of a real estate license:

- Using a false or fictitious name, knowingly making a false statement, knowingly concealing a material fact, or otherwise committing a fraud in any application for registration of a mobilehome

- Failing to provide for delivery of a properly endorsed certificate of title or ownership from seller to buyer

- Knowingly participating in the purchase or sale of a stolen mobilehome

- Violating any requirement of the Health and Safety Code, Revenue and Taxation Code, or Civil Code regarding mobilehome registration, transfer, or taxation

- Submitting a check, draft, or money order to the Department of Housing and Community Development for any fee or other payment due the state for which payment is refused

LICENSEE CONDUCT

www.dre.ca.gov/publication
/referencebook.html

Every licensee should have a copy of the *Reference Book—A Real Estate Guide* published by CalBRE and available at www.dre.ca.gov/publications/referencebook .html. The latest edition (2010) lists examples of unlawful conduct by real estate licensees. These are shown in Figure 1.3.

In previous editions of the *Reference Book*, the Real Estate Commissioner has issued suggestions for professional conduct—desirable actions for those engaged in licensed activities. They appear in Figure 1.4. While these are now considered beyond the scope of the commissioner's authority, they are worth reading as good advice for real estate practitioners. It is also worth noting the reference to the Code of Ethics of the National Association of REALTORS®, which has more than one million members.

Trade groups often set the standard of practice for those in the profession. Membership requirements and ethical concerns can be the most direct evidence of the manner in which all professionals should carry out their responsibilities. Unfortunately, there is not enough space in this book to reproduce the directives of all of the trade groups active in California. We encourage you to obtain the most recent versions of that information from the associations listed later in this unit.

FIGURE 1.3: Unlawful Conduct

EXAMPLES OF UNLAWFUL CONDUCT IN SALE, LEASE, OR EXCHANGE TRANSACTIONS

1. Knowingly making a substantial misrepresentation of the likely value of real property to:

   ■ Its owner either for the purpose of securing a listing or for the purpose of acquiring an interest in the property for the licensee's own account.

   ■ A prospective buyer for the purpose of inducing the buyer to make an offer to purchase the real property.

2. Representing to an owner of real property when seeking a listing that the licensee has obtained a bona fide written offer to purchase the property, unless at the time of the representation the licensee has possession of a bona fide written offer to purchase.

3. Stating or implying to an owner of real property during listing negotiations that the licensee is precluded by law, by regulation, or by the rules of any organization, other than the broker firm seeking the listing, from charging less than the commission or fee quoted to the owner by the licensee.

4. Knowingly making substantial misrepresentations regarding the licensee's relationship with an individual broker, corporate broker, or franchised brokerage company or that entity's/person's responsibility for the licensee's activities.

5. Knowingly underestimating the probable closing costs in a communication to the prospective buyer or seller of real property in order to induce that person to make or to accept an offer to purchase the property.

6. Knowingly making a false or misleading representation to the seller of real property as to the form, amount, and/or treatment of a deposit toward the purchase of the property made by an offeror.

7. Knowingly making a false or misleading representation to a seller of real property, who has agreed to finance all or part of a purchase price by carrying back a loan, about a buyer's ability to repay the loan in accordance with its terms and conditions.

8. Making an addition to or modification of the terms of an instrument previously signed or initialed by a party to a transaction without the knowledge and consent of the party.

9. A representation made as a principal or agent to a prospective purchaser of a promissory note secured by real property about the market value of the securing property without a reasonable basis for believing the truth and accuracy of the representation.

10. Knowingly making a false or misleading representation or representing, without a reasonable basis for believing its truth, the nature and/or condition of the interior or exterior features of a property when soliciting an offer.

11. Knowingly making a false or misleading representation or representing, without a reasonable basis for believing its truth, the size of a parcel, square footage of improvements, or the location of the boundary lines of real property being offered for sale, lease, or exchange.

12. Knowingly making a false or misleading representation or representing to a prospective buyer or lessee of real property, without a reasonable basis to believe its truth, that the property can be used for certain purposes with the intent of inducing the prospective buyer or lessee to acquire an interest in the real property.

FIGURE 1.3:   Unlawful Conduct (continued)

13. When acting in the capacity of an agent in a transaction for the sale, lease, or exchange of real property, failing to disclose to a prospective purchaser or lessee facts known to the licensee materially affecting the value or desirability of the property, when the licensee has reason to believe that such facts are not known to or readily observable by a prospective purchaser or lessee.

14. Willfully failing, when acting as a listing agent, to present or cause to be presented to the owner of the property any written offer to purchase received prior to the closing of a sale, unless expressly instructed by the owner not to present such an offer, or unless the offer is patently frivolous.

15. When acting as the listing agent, presenting competing written offers to purchase real property to the owner in such a manner as to induce the owner to accept the offer that will provide the greatest compensation to the listing broker without regard to the benefits, advantages and/or disadvantages to the owner.

16. Failing to explain to the parties or prospective parties to a real estate transaction for whom the licensee is acting as an agent the meaning and probable significance of a contingency in an offer or contract that the licensee knows or reasonably believes may affect the closing date of the transaction, or the timing of the vacating of the property by the seller or its occupancy by the buyer.

17. Failing to disclose to the seller of real property in a transaction in which the licensee is an agent for the seller the nature and extent of any direct or indirect interest that the licensee expects to acquire as a result of the sale. (The licensee should disclose to the seller: prospective purchase of the property by a person related to the licensee by blood or marriage; purchase by an entity in which the licensee has an ownership interest; or purchase by any other person with whom the licensee occupies a special relationship where there is a reasonable probability that the licensee could be indirectly acquiring an interest in the property.)

18. Failing to disclose to the buyer of real property in a transaction in which the licensee is an agent for the buyer the nature and extent of a licensee's direct or indirect ownership interest in such real property: e.g., the direct or indirect ownership interest in the property by a person related to the licensee by blood or marriage; by an entity in which the licensee has an ownership interest; or by any other person with whom the licensee occupies a special relationship.

19. Failing to disclose to a principal for whom the licensee is acting as an agent any significant interest the licensee has in a particular entity when the licensee recommends the use of the services or products of such entity.

Exercise 1-2

Broker Bob opened his first real estate brokerage office and immediately hired salesperson Sally. Sally printed and circulated a newsletter throughout the neighborhood. She gave a few mortgage loan statistics in her newsletter and stressed the record high property values in the area. She concluded with the statement, "I've never handled a listing I couldn't sell." In fact, Sally had never handled any listing. Has she violated the Code of Ethics? Has broker Bob?

OTHER ACTIVITIES OF THE CALIFORNIA BUREAU OF REAL ESTATE

CalBRE performs many functions in addition to regulating the business activities of brokers and salespersons.

Through the **Real Estate Education and Research Fund,** research in land use and real estate development is made possible at both public and private universities and research entities throughout the state. The fund is financed by a fixed percentage of license fees.

The **Recovery Account** is another fund financed by license fees. It is available to aid victims of licensee fraud, misrepresentation, deceit, or conversion (theft) of trust fund, who are awarded money damages by a court or as the result of a CalBRE administrative proceeding that are noncollectible. A maximum of $50,000 per transaction or $250,000 per licensee can be paid from the Recovery Account. Reimbursement to the fund by the offender will be required as part of the disciplinary process.

FIGURE 1.4:   Desirable Conduct

RECOMMENDED CONDUCT
IN SALE, LEASE, OR EXCHANGE TRANSACTIONS

Real estate licensees are encouraged to adhere to the following suggestions in conducting their business activities:

1. Aspire to give a high level of competent, ethical, and quality service to buyers and sellers in real estate transactions.

2. Stay in close communication with clients or customers to ensure that questions are promptly answered and all significant events or problems in a transaction are conveyed in a timely manner.

3. Cooperate with the California Department of Real Estate's enforcement of, and report to that department evident violations of, the Real Estate Law.

4. Use care in the preparation of any advertisement to present an accurate picture or message to the reader, viewer, or listener.

5. Submit all written offers in a prompt and timely manner.

6. Keep oneself informed and current on factors affecting the real estate market in which the licensee operates as an agent.

7. Make a full, open, and sincere effort to cooperate with other licensees, unless the principal has instructed the licensee to the contrary.

8. Attempt to settle disputes with other licensees through mediation or arbitration.

9. Advertise or claim to be an expert in an area of specialization in real estate brokerage activity, e.g., appraisal, property management, industrial siting, mortgage loan, etc., only if the licensee has had special training, preparation, or experience in such area.

10. Strive to provide equal opportunity for quality housing and a high level of service to all persons regardless of race, color, sex, religion, ancestry, physical handicap, marital status, or national origin.

11. Base opinions of value, whether for the purpose of advertising or promoting real estate brokerage business, upon documented objective data.

12. Make every attempt to comply with these Guidelines for Professional Conduct and the Code of Ethics of any organized real estate industry group of which the licensee is a member.

PROFESSIONAL ASSOCIATIONS

One of the best ways for the real estate licensee to become involved in and remain enthusiastic about the profession is to become a member of a professional association. Trade associations provide sources of information, training, and contact with other professionals. Associations also help shape the law and the industry by establishing and enforcing standards of practice and also by providing an effective voice for their members.

REALTORS®

There have been voluntary associations of real estate professionals in California since 1887, when the San Diego Realty Board was formed. As more cities formed such groups, the California Real Estate Association was organized in 1905. On January 1, 1975, the name of that organization was changed to the California Association of REALTORS® (CAR), demonstrating its affiliation with the national organization. CAR (headquartered in Los Angeles) can be found on the web at www.car.org.

www.car.org
www.realtor.com

The term *REALTOR* is a registered trademark of the National Association of REALTORS® (NAR) and may be used only by REALTOR® members of NAR. NAR has offices in Chicago, Illinois, and Washington, D.C., and its web address is www.realtor.org. NAR's consumer website that includes property listings is www .realtor.com. With more than one million members across the country, NAR is a powerful force in lobbying on behalf of its members. Real estate licensees who fulfill NAR membership requirements may use the REALTOR® or REALTOR-Associate® trademark. Use of either of these registered trademarks by anyone not authorized to do so may result in a license suspension or revocation, in addition to damages in a legal action brought by NAR. NAR also has an affiliate membership classification open to lenders, escrow companies, and others engaged in real estate-related activities.

Realtists

www.nareb.com

Realtist is the member designation of the National Association of Real Estate Brokers, Inc., or NAREB. NAREB's website is www.nareb.com. This group was formed in 1947 in Tampa, Florida, of predominantly African American members, and it now has local boards nationwide. In California, local boards include Associated Real Property Brokers, Oakland; North Bay Board of Realtists, Richmond; and the Consolidated Realty Board, Los Angeles. Members of NAREB must belong to the local group as well as to the national organization, which is headquartered in Washington, D.C. Unauthorized use of the term *Realtist* is unlawful (misrepresentation) and unethical.

Local Associations

Most local real estate associations are affiliated with CAR and NAR or NAREB. Local organizations bring members together to assist in community outreach as well as charitable programs. They frequently offer continuing education and other informational seminars. In addition, the local real estate association typically conducts what may be the real estate broker and salesperson's most valuable marketing tool—the multiple listing service (MLS). All licensees benefit by sharing information on available properties. The number and variety of properties included in the larger MLSs would be impossible for any one company to duplicate. Local and regional property listings now are part of statewide and national databases accessible by both agents and consumers on the internet.

www.bre.ca.gov

Major Real Estate Trade Associations

The CalBRE website (www.bre.ca.gov) lists state and federal resources, as well as the major real estate-related trade associations in California. The following are some of the trade and related groups that maintain websites:

Asian Real Estate Association of America: www.areaa.org

California Association of Business Brokers: www.californiabusinessbrokers.biz

California Association of Community Managers: www.cacm.org

California Association of Mortgage Professionals: www.ca-amp.org

California Association of Real Estate Brokers: www.careb.org

California Association of REALTORS®: www.car.org

California Building Industry Association: www.cbia.org

California Mortgage Association: www.californiamortgageassociation.com

California Mortgage Bankers Association: www.cmba.com

Executive Council of Homeowners: www.echo-ca.org

National Association of Hispanic Real Estate Professionals: www.nahrep.org

SUMMARY

The business of real estate entails many responsibilities for the licensee. The responsibilities begin with completing qualifying courses and passing a licensing examination. They also include the obligation to make sure that the licensee obeys both the **Real Estate Law** and the **Regulations of the Real Estate Commissioner**.

The foundation of all of the activities and requirements of the **California Bureau of Real Estate** is the element of fair dealing. We have come far from the days when the concept of **caveat emptor** served as a shield for the unscrupulous. Now the police power of the government has brought about the Real Estate Law found in the **Business and Professions Code**. The **Real Estate Commissioner** and California Bureau of Real Estate are charged with the task of supervising the education, licensing, and conduct of those who call themselves real estate professionals.

The **real estate brokerage** office always has one responsible **broker** who may have one or more **salespersons** (or **brokers**) working out of the office. A **broker-officer** enables a brokerage to be incorporated. A corporate brokerage also must file a **certificate of status**. A partnership of real estate licensees also is possible. A fictitious name for a brokerage requires the filing of a **fictitious business name statement** (DBA).

Real estate licensees may deal in business opportunities, which may involve many requirements, including those of the **Uniform Commercial Code**.

The Real Estate Law contains many mandates and prohibitions for the licensee. Through the **Real Estate Education and Research Fund**, the California Bureau of Real Estate makes use of part of the license fees collected to finance real estate research. It also compensates victims of licensee wrongdoing from the **Recovery Account**.

By joining a local professional organization, the licensee benefits in many ways, from use of a **multiple listing service** to attending educational programs and contributing to various charitable events.

OPEN FOR DISCUSSION

It has been suggested that all real estate licensees be required to have at least a two-year Associate of Arts degree from a community college.

1. Make at least two arguments in favor of the idea.
2. Make at least two arguments against it.

REVIEW QUESTIONS

1. The Real Estate Law is found in
   a. the Licensing Code.
   b. the Business and Professions Code.
   c. the Health and Safety Code.
   d. the Corporations Code.

2. The Real Estate Commissioner reports to
   a. the California Bureau of Real Estate.
   b. the governor.
   c. the Department of Housing and Urban Development.
   d. the legislature.

3. A salesperson owns 25% of the outstanding shares of Rollo Realty, Inc., and the broker owns the remaining shares. This division of ownership is
   a. acceptable.
   b. mandated.
   c. discouraged.
   d. prohibited.

4. A salesperson is part owner of Rollo Realty, Inc. In the broker's absence, the salesperson frequently reviews the work of sales associates. This is
   a. acceptable.
   b. mandated.
   c. discouraged.
   d. prohibited.

5. A real estate business that is a partnership can have more than one office location, provided
   a. a broker partner obtains an additional license for each location.
   b. all partners are real estate licensees.
   c. there is a designated broker-officer.
   d. there is at least one partner at each location.

6. The sale or transfer of goods ordinarily held for sale in the course of business is governed in California by
   a. the Business Opportunity Code.
   b. the Commercial Transfer Law.
   c. the Uniform Commercial Code.
   d. the Real Estate Law.

7. An officer of Ajax Corporation, who is not a real estate licensee, successfully negotiated the purchase of the Smith Widget Plant on behalf of Ajax. The officer received a commission on the sale in addition to his normal salary. The officer of Ajax Corporation
   a. did not need a real estate license for the deal.
   b. should have had a real estate license.
   c. is exempt from licensing requirements.
   d. None of these

8. If a real estate license is NOT renewed before it expires, the licensee
   a. is allowed to complete transactions in progress.
   b. is allowed to finish transactions that are substantially complete.
   c. must cease all real estate activities.
   d. may act under authority of another agent's license for a period not to exceed 60 days.

9. A real estate licensee can offer a mobilehome for sale that is
   a. in a manufacturing plant, ready for delivery.
   b. transportable under an exemption from the Vehicle Code.
   c. presold.
   d. in a location where it can legally remain for one year.

10. A couple desperately wants to move to Pine Bend, and they like the seller's house, which is listed with a broker. The couple tells the broker they will "make it worth his while" if he can persuade the sellers to accept their offer, and they send an expensive food basket to the broker as a sign of their good faith. The broker neglects to mention this to the sellers. This practice is
    a. acceptable.
    b. mandated.
    c. discouraged.
    d. prohibited.

11. A broker routinely places earnest money deposits in his personal account for overnight safekeeping. This practice is
    a. acceptable.
    b. mandated.
    c. discouraged.
    d. prohibited.

12. A broker has an exclusive listing agreement with a property owner. The listing will terminate "when the parties agree." This practice is
    a. acceptable.
    b. mandated.
    c. discouraged.
    d. prohibited.

13. When a broker exercised his option to buy Whiteacre, he presented to the owner of Whiteacre a written statement of his expected profit in the transaction. The seller agreed in writing to proceed with the sale. This conduct is
    a. acceptable.
    b. mandated.
    c. discouraged.
    d. prohibited.

14. The broker-officer of XYZ Realty, Inc., does not like the overly aggressive sales tactics of XYZ's salespeople but has not reprimanded them because business is so good. The broker's conduct is
    a. acceptable.
    b. mandated.
    c. discouraged.
    d. prohibited.

15. A broker wants to help out his neighbor's son, who recently acquired a B.A. in history from Back East University. The broker hires the graduate to show property to prospective buyers. Because the new employee has no real estate license, the broker handles all of the negotiating. This practice is
    a. acceptable.
    b. mandated.
    c. discouraged.
    d. prohibited.

16. A salesperson is selling the Greenacre Estate. An offer has been accepted, and the closing will take place in two weeks. While the owners are out of town, the buyer asks if the closing can be put off for one day. The salesperson agrees on behalf of the owners, for she is sure they will not object. The salesperson's conduct is
    a. acceptable.
    b. mandated.
    c. discouraged.
    d. prohibited.

17. A house is for sale following a murder in the house six months earlier. A salesperson, showing an out-of-town prospect through the house, decides to keep information about the murder to himself. The salesperson's conduct is
    a. acceptable.
    b. mandated.
    c. discouraged.
    d. prohibited.

18. A broker is so busy that he never has the time to return the phone calls of his principals. He prefers to spend his time in the field making sales and acquiring new listings. This practice is
    a. acceptable.
    b. mandated.
    c. discouraged.
    d. prohibited.

19. After attending a get-rich-quick real estate seminar, an attendee wants to buy a house "cheap." She tells a broker that she will offer $50,000, with seller financing and no down payment, on the Monroe Street house, which has an asking price of $125,000. The broker presents the offer with one of his own for $85,000, telling the owners that unexpected market conditions make their asking price unrealistic. His conduct is
    a. acceptable.
    b. mandated.
    c. discouraged.
    d. prohibited.

20. A new broker opens a brokerage office and immediately places an ad in the local newspaper: *List Your House with Me and I Will Pay You $500 at Closing.* This practice is
    a. acceptable.
    b. mandated.
    c. discouraged.
    d. prohibited.

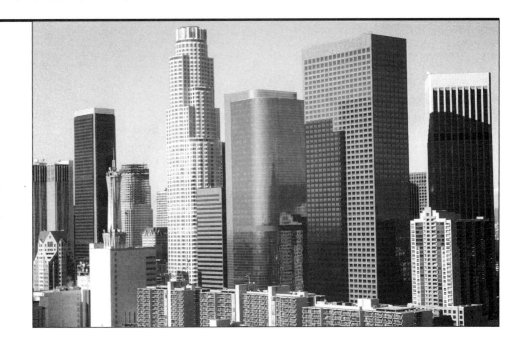

THE NATURE OF REAL PROPERTY

LEARNING OBJECTIVES

When you have completed this unit, you will be able to

- **identify** the origins of the California legal system;
- **define** the elements of real property;
- **describe** the forms of water rights found in California;
- **list** the tests for a fixture;
- **identify** and **explain** the methods of legal description of land; and
- **compute** the size of a parcel of land described using the rectangular survey system.

KEY TERMS

air rights
appurtenance
base line
bill of sale
bundle of rights
civil law
common law
community property
correction line
correlative use
emblements
fixture
fructus industriales
fructus naturales
guide meridian
land

legal description
littoral rights
lot and block system
markers
meridians
metes and bounds
mineral rights
monuments
personal property
plat map
point of beginning
ranges
real estate
real property
rectangular survey
    system

right of appropriation
riparian rights
section
section and township
    system
subdivision map
subdivision system
tiers
township
underground water
    rights
U.S. government
    survey system
water rights

HISTORICAL PERSPECTIVE

Many forces have shaped the landscape of California. Nature provides an abundance of both benefits and hazards, but cultural, political, and economic forces often have brought about more changes than even the most severe earthquake or fire. The earliest settlers of the region suffered greatly at the hands of those who followed, but the state is now home to one of the most diverse populations in the world.

This unit surveys the history of California very briefly to give you some idea of the dramatic origin of our system of land ownership. Then, real property is defined and distinguished from personal property. Finally, the most common ways of describing real property are discussed.

Spanish Conquest and Settlement

In 1513, Vasco Nuñez de Balboa, at the head of an advancing army of conquistadores, claimed all lands washed by the Pacific Ocean for the King of Spain. California became—in principle, at least—part of the Spanish Empire. But the distance from Spain to that far-flung outpost meant that it would be hundreds of years before it was fully explored.

For the most part, the Native Americans who emigrated from Asia and the great tribes of the nation's heartland had ignored the land we now call California. Still, as many as 300,000 people were living in California at the time of European exploration.

During the 20th century, California's Native American population grew to 100,000, in part because of immigration to California from other states.

Missions and presidios   The major impetus to Spanish settlement of California was the establishment of the *missions*. Franciscan missionaries converted some of the Native Americans to Christianity and resettled them in mission communities, where they were taught agriculture and crafts. Of course, living in such communities made the converts easy prey to epidemic disease. By 1900, only 15,000 Native Americans were estimated to be living in California.

The missions also provided a convenient source of supplies for the *presidios*, the military posts. The first mission and the first presidio were founded at San Diego in 1769. Twenty more missions were to follow by 1823, with the northernmost in Sonoma. Additional presidios were located in Santa Barbara, Monterey, and San Francisco. U.S. Highway 101 follows the route of *El Camino Real*, the main thoroughfare of Spanish California.

Pueblos   During Spanish rule, ownership of all the land was held by the crown—the King of Spain—with *rancho grants* made only for limited uses, such as grazing or farming. Cities, called *pueblos*, received four square leagues of land without need for a formal grant. Because a league was 4,440 acres, city officials carried much authority. The mayor and council of the pueblo could grant house lots and farm lots to inhabitants.

FIGURE 2.1:   **Mission**

From San Diego northward, the missions established a Spanish presence in the territory that became California.

Treaty of Guadalupe Hidalgo

Mexico, a territorial possession of Spain, established its independence in 1822. California became a possession of Mexico. But the tide of settlement brought Americans to the Pacific Coast, eventually leading to war with Mexico. The war ended with the signing of the *Treaty of Guadalupe Hidalgo* in 1848.

Following the Treaty of Guadalupe Hidalgo, California became a possession of the United States. Existing property rights of Mexicans in California were to be "inviolably respected." In the 26 years of Mexican rule from 1822 to 1848, mission lands had been confiscated, private land ownership encouraged, and large tracts given out. After the Treaty of Guadalupe Hidalgo, American squatters claimed some of that land, creating much conflict.

There would have been confusion in any event, because the transfer from Spanish/Mexican rule to the status of an American colony meant a change in the entire legal system. The Spanish **civil law**, consisting of detailed legal codes, was replaced by the English **common law**, an inheritance of the United States from the period before the American Revolution. This meant that Californians were to follow the laws established by the legislature, as well as the common-law customs and usages established by judicial decisions. Significantly, property could be held in absolute ownership by individuals.

A holdover from Spanish law is the concept of **community property**, which is property acquired by spouses during marriage. Community property is discussed in Unit 3.

Statehood

In the midst of the postwar land problems, gold was discovered at Sutter's Mill in 1848. This discovery, coming within weeks of the end of the war, gave new importance to America's westernmost frontier. In 1850, California became a state.

The federal government retained certain rights in the area known as California. The new state became owner of all lands lying under navigable streams and lakes and above the ordinary high-tide line. Tidelands are held in trust for public navigation, fishing, and recreation. Certain rights to public lands can be transferred, however, which allows the collection of income from oil and gas production.

The *Board of Land Commissioners* was formed by Congress in 1851 to settle claims to private land in California. Appeal from the commissioners was to the U.S. district court, and from there to the U.S. Supreme Court. Most of the Mexican land grants were upheld, to the dismay of numerous squatters. Of the more than 100 million acres of California's total area, the federal government still owns about 45%. Basically, these federal lands include everything that was not conveyed by Spanish or Mexican grant or granted to the state for education and recreation uses. Other large federal land grants were made to railroad companies to encourage the development of transportation

www.ca.gov

www.sos.ca.gov/archives
/collections/ussg/

You will find more information about California's history and culture at the State of California website, www.ca.gov. Information about the California State Archives, which contain official state copies of land grants from the Spanish and Mexican periods, can be found at www.sos.ca.gov/archives/collections/ussg/.

California Today

City dwellers may receive the impression that California is fully developed and generally urbanized. However, there still are vast tracts of land in the state that contradict its urban, progressive reputation.

Land ownership California land is owned approximately in the proportions shown below. About 29% of the total land area is devoted to agriculture.

	Number of Acres	Percent of Total
Federal	44,904,000	45
State	2,332,000	2
Local	2,050,000	2
Private	50,785,000	51
Total Acres	100,071,000	100

The 2012 United States Department of Agriculture Census of Agriculture, compiled every five years, indicates that, of all the states, California produces the greatest value of agricultural products sold, though the state has neither the greatest number of farms nor the largest number of acres of farmland. The complete report and subsequent studies can be found at www.agcensus.usda.gov /Publications/2012/.

www.agcensus.usda.gov /Publications/2012/
www.census.gov

Population The United States Census Bureau, found at www.census.gov, makes frequent demographic, income, and home value reports. For 2015, the Census Bureau estimated the population of California at over 39.1 million, which means that about one out of every eight Americans lives in California.

In many ways, the diversity of California's population and economy makes the state unique. Census Bureau population surveys for 2015 placed the white (not Hispanic or Latino) population of California, the largest segment, at 34% of the state's total but 60% of the nation's total. More than one-third of the California population (38.8%) was identified as Hispanic or Latino, while the nation as a whole had Hispanic or Latino population of only 18%. California also had a higher proportion of those identifying themselves as Asian alone (14.6%) than the 6% in the nation as a whole. California had a lower proportion of African Americans (6.4%), however, than the nation as a whole (13%). In 2013, 26.9% of Californians were identified as foreign born, in contrast to 12.9% for the nation as a whole.

California's population is not only more diverse than that of the nation as a whole, it is also younger. In 2015, the median age of California's residents was 35 years, while the median age for the nation as a whole was 37.8 years. Home value statistics continue to show great disparity between the state and the nation. The median existing home value for the nation in 2014 was $208,900, while the median existing home value in California that year was $447,010. Both numbers continue to rise, though the disparity does not correlate with household income. Median household income for California residents in 2015 was reported as $64,500, while nationwide, median household income was reported as $55,775—not a very great difference, considering that home values are so much higher in California. California is simply a very desirable place to live, and demand for housing reflects that fact.

California's economy is the sixth largest in the world. www.bea.gov

Economy With a 2015 gross domestic product (GDP) of $2.46 trillion, California's economy is about one-seventh of the total for the nation, according to the Bureau of Economic Analysis (BEA) of the United States Department of Commerce, found at www.bea.gov. By itself, California qualifies as the sixth largest economy in the world, following the United States, China, Japan, Germany, and the United Kingdom. Urban development generally has been concentrated in coastal and central valley areas. Eventually, Los Angeles and San Diego will form one continuous urban area, or megalopolis. The cities surrounding San Francisco Bay now have few recognizable boundaries. Attractive housing and commercial development costs have benefited Sacramento and other central valley cities.

www.dof.ca.gov

For updates on California's employment and income statistics, including breakdowns by county and city, visit the California Department of Finance website at www.dof.ca.gov.

REAL PROPERTY AND PERSONAL PROPERTY

Real property is often described as a **bundle of rights** that includes the legal rights of ownership shown in Figure 2.2.

The five major rights, which can be remembered by the acronym PUEDE, are known as the following:

1. Right of *possession*
2. Right to control the property's *use*
3. Right of *enjoyment* of the property
4. Right to *dispose* of the property
5. Right to *exclude* others from the property

From these rights flow other privileges of ownership. A property owner usually has the power to mortgage, cultivate, explore, lease, give away, share, trade, or exchange the property owned. The Spanish rancho grants, for instance, conveyed the right to use the land for such purposes as grazing or cultivation.

FIGURE 2.2:   **Bundle of Rights**

California law recognizes that property may be possessed by one or more persons to the exclusion of all others. All California property can be categorized as either *real property* or *personal property*.

Real Property

In California, the term **real property** is synonymous with the term **real estate**. The California Civil Code definition of *real property* includes all of the following elements:

- Land

- Fixtures (attachments) to land

- Anything incidental or appurtenant to land

- Anything immovable by law

Land   **Land** is the soil, the material that makes up what is called *earth*. Land includes the substances beneath the surface that extend to the center of the earth. These include oil, gas, and water, and they may be many times more valuable than the surface itself. Land also includes the airspace above the earth's surface for an indefinite distance upward.

In practice, use of airspace (as well as the surface and subsurface) is subject to many limitations imposed by law. These limitations will be discussed throughout this book, particularly in Unit 15. Figure 2.3 illustrates the general concept of land rights.

Mineral rights refer to the right to remove substances from the land, usually from beneath the surface. The term includes solid minerals, such as gold, coal, iron, and gravel from the soil as well as riverbeds.

FIGURE 2.3:   Rights in Land

Land
Earth's surface to the center of
the earth and the airspace above the
land, including the trees and water

Real Estate
Land plus permanent
human-made additions

Real Property
Real estate plus
"bundle of legal rights"

Mineral rights also include minerals that have a fugitive or fluid nature, such as oil and gas. All or some of the minerals may be transferred apart from the rest of the land.

FOR EXAMPLE   Mel Muller owns 100 acres of undeveloped land in San Bernardino County. Hearing that oil might be found in the area, Mel drills a well under his property. He finds nothing, but he thinks he will be successful if he drills a well slanted to reach under his neighbor's ranch. Can Mel do so?

No, because Mel can take from the earth only what is directly under his own land. Mel can capture a fluid substance, such as oil, only when it is found within the boundaries of his property.

In California—as in other states—**water rights** are becoming increasingly important. Growing demand for commercial and residential uses must be balanced against agricultural use of both surface and underground water resources, and all of these must consider both present and future needs. California's recent drought conditions have resulted in water conservation measures that are discussed in Unit 15.

Air rights have been modified from the historic concept of infinite airspace having no limitation. Federal law (the Air Commerce Act of 1926 and the Civil Aeronautics Act of 1938) allows use of airspace by aircraft. Local laws impose building height restrictions. In central city locations, air rights may be a profitable commodity. They may be transferable from one property owner to another to allow construction of skyscrapers on limited and expensive ground area.

The rules can be found at www.faa.gov/uas/.

Aerial photography is now a feature of many property listings, but has raised concerns. The Department of Transportation's Federal Aviation Administration (FAA) has issued rules for the use of small unmanned aircraft systems (UAS), commonly referred to as *drones*. The new rules, which took effect August 29, 2016, provide safety regulations for drones weighing less than 55 pounds that are conducting non-hobbyist operations, to minimize risks to other aircraft as well as people and property on the ground. The drone operator must be at least 16 years old and have a remote pilot certificate.

Fixtures   A **fixture** is anything, including improvements, that is attached, or affixed, to land. A fixture can be attached by its roots (trees or shrubs) or imbedded in the land (walls). A fixture might also be something permanently resting on the land, such as a building. A building would include all things customarily considered permanently attached to it, such as siding, plaster, nails, doors, and windows.

Water Rights

Riparian rights belong to owners of land bordering a river or other flowing stream. Owners of riparian rights do not own the water but have the right to make reasonable use of it on their own property. If the stream is navigable, the state owns the land under the stream and the riparian landowner's property line is the mean high water line of the stream; otherwise, the landowner's property line is the center of the stream.

Littoral rights belong to owners of land bordering a still body of water, such as a lake. Owners of littoral rights have the right to make reasonable use of the water on their own property.

Underground water rights belong to landowners, who have a right of **correlative use** of the water under their land. They may withdraw only water for which they have a beneficial use on their own property. Underground water that is not confined to a defined stream is *percolating water.* The *water table* (*groundwater level*) is the upper limit of percolating water below the earth's surface, at a depth of a few feet or hundreds of feet. A *mutual water company* may be formed when a subdivision is created and is owned by individual lot owners, who are its shareholders. An adequate potable water supply and distribution system for domestic use and fire protection must exist, and other requirements of the Corporations Code, starting at Section 14310, must be met if the mutual water company was created on or after January 1, 1998.

Appropriative water rights are subject to priority of claims filed before December 19, 1914; the claims remain valid as long as the water is put to a beneficial use. Since that time, permits have been issued for use of water in an area adjoining or distant from a body of water. The state may exercise its **right of appropriation** if there is reason to divert water for public use. The California Water Project and the Central Valley Project are just two examples of the massive developments that have moved water throughout the state. Water litigation disputes may be referred by a court of law to the California State Water Resources Control Board for hearing, then returned to the court for final adjudication. More information can be found at www.waterboards.ca.gov/waterrights/index.shtml.

www.waterboards.ca.gov
/waterrights/index.shtml

FOR EXAMPLE   Speedy Service Station has two hydraulic lifts in place in the repair bays. If Speedy's owner decides to sell the station, will the hydraulic lifts be included?

Yes, the hydraulic lifts will be included in a sale of the property (in the absence of an agreement to the contrary). Such fixtures are ordinarily permanent installations.

Appurtenances   An **appurtenance** to land is anything used with the land for the benefit of its owners, such as a roadway or waterway. Examples of appurtenances are some easements, rights-of-way, and condominium parking spaces. An appurtenance is said to "run with the land" because it is transferred when the land is transferred. An appurtenance could even be a passage for light, air, or heat from or across someone else's land. Stock in a mutual water company may be appurtenant to land. If it is, it can only be transferred with the land.

FOR EXAMPLE A homeowner lives at the end of a private road owned by the Bashir family. The homeowner owns an easement over the Bashirs' land; that is, the homeowner has the right to use the Bashirs' roadway to enter or leave his property. If the homeowner sells his land, the new owner will have the right to use the easement.

Easements are discussed in Unit 5.

Emblements Cultivated crops are called **emblements**. They are considered part of the land until they are harvested. Then, they become personal property. If grown by a tenant on leased land, however, they are considered personal property both while growing and after harvest. The sale of growing crops is governed by the provisions of the Uniform Commercial Code.

Crops produced by human labor (lettuce, cotton, grapes, and so on) are also referred to by the legal term, **fructus industriales**. They are distinguished from naturally occurring plant growth (such as grasses), which are termed **fructus naturales**.

Personal Property

Personal property is every kind of property that is not real property. In general, real property (*realty*) is considered immovable, while personal property (*personalty*) is considered movable. It is possible for property to change its character as realty or personalty, depending on how it is used.

FOR EXAMPLE Trees are real property while they are growing in the ground. When the trees are cut down, they become personal property. Tree logs may be cut into boards and used in the construction of a building that is considered part of the land. Thus, the wood from the tree that began as real property may again become real property.

Tests for a Fixture

The listing agreement between seller and agent should identify the items the seller wants to remove.

A *fixture* is anything attached to land. This simple definition is not always simple to apply. There are times when the status of a thing as a fixture to real estate, rather than personal property, is not clear-cut.

Fixtures are personal property before being attached to the land, but what kind of attachment will convert personal property to real property? California courts use five general tests in determining whether a specific thing is a fixture—that is, considered a permanent attachment to land. The five tests for a fixture can be remembered by the acronym MARIA, as explained in the box below.

FOR EXAMPLE   A homeowner, Mary, has remodeled her family room and installed a wood-burning stove. The heavy cast-iron stove sits on a brick base, and the chimney vents through a special opening in the roof. Unexpectedly, Mary is transferred by her company and decides to sell her house. The buyers and seller sign a contract of sale that does not specifically mention the stove but does include "all fixtures" in the sale. Can the seller take the stove with her?

Tests for a Fixture

Method by which the thing is affixed. The greater the degree of permanence in the attachment, the more likely it is a fixture. A wood gazebo on a concrete foundation is attached permanently; a screened enclosure fastened to the ground with tent stakes is not.

Adaptability of the thing for the land's ordinary use. The better adapted, the more likely it will be considered a fixture. A custom-fitted item, such as a swimming pool cover, would fall into this category.

Relationship of the parties. If a residential tenant attaches something to the premises, there will be a presumption that it is personal property and removable by the tenant. The court favors tenant over landlord and buyer over seller.

Intent in placing the item on the land. This is the most important consideration. The intent may be for reasons of health and safety rather than to improve the property, such as installation of a fire extinguisher.

Agreement of the parties. If the parties are knowledgeable, they can avoid ambiguities by specifying *in writing* whether various items are fixtures or personal property and how those items will be affected by the transaction.

No. The installation, permanence, and use of the stove all indicate it is a fixture that should stay with the house. If Mary (or her broker) had thought of it beforehand, she could have stipulated in the contract of sale that the stove would not be included and that Mary would repair any damage caused by its removal. The expense of doing that would probably be greater than the cost of a new stove, however.

Fixtures on leased premises   Parties to a lease of real property are free to make any agreement as to fixtures. In the absence of an agreement, several laws can be applied.

If a tenant has attached personal property to the premises, the property may be removed before the end of the lease term if

- it was installed for purposes of trade, manufacture, ornament, or domestic use; and

- it can be removed without substantial damage to the premises.

A tenant may remove a fixture installed for some other purpose only if the tenant believed in good faith that the fixture could be installed and subsequently removed. To summarize, an item attached for use in a trade or business (a *trade fixture*) or for residential use may be removed. The tenant must repair or pay for any property damage resulting from the removal.

Real Property vs. Personal Property

Why bother with labeling something as either real property or personal property? There are a number of reasons:

- The distinction between real and personal property is particularly important when property is sold or leased. When real estate is sold, fixtures are usually considered part of the land and go to the buyer.

A court of another state can't decide an issue involving California real estate.

- Ownership and transfer of title to real property are subject to the laws of the state within which the land is located. The only exceptions are for federally owned lands and land that is part of a federal proceeding, such as bankruptcy. Ownership and transfer of personal property are subject to the laws of the state where the property owner resides, even if the personal property is located elsewhere.

- The distinction between real property and personal property also is important in the formation of a contract of sale. Most contracts involving real property must be in writing. For personal property, a written document generally is required only when the value of the property exceeds $5,000 (California Civil Code Section 1624.5). A written instrument also may be required for transactions involving personal property that fall within the rules of the Uniform Commercial Code, such as bulk sales of goods, sales of securities, and formation of security agreements.

- Ownership of real property is usually transferred by an instrument called a *deed*. Ownership of personal property usually is transferred by a **bill of sale**.

- As you will learn in Unit 4, transfers of real property can be recorded with the county recorder to give notice of the transfer to other parties. Instruments conveying personal property generally cannot be recorded, and recording may not be considered notice of the conveyance.

- Real property and personal property are subject to separate tax laws.

Exercise 2-1

Identify each of the following as either a fixture or personal property and explain your choice.

house	patio furniture
room air conditioner	wall-to-wall carpeting
motor home	wood deck
space heater	room-size rug
brick patio	hot tub
fireplace	chandelier

LAND DESCRIPTION

It would be impossible to own or lease land if we had no adequate way to describe or define it. Street names and numbers can be used to identify buildings. What is described by such an address is a particular parcel of real estate. Usually, all the improvements within the perimeter of an identified parcel of land are included. Using only a street address to identify real estate presents several problems. First, some property, such as rural, undeveloped land, cannot be identified by street address. Second, a street name may change, a driveway may be moved, or the land may be developed in a way that was not anticipated. The best practice is to use the

- legal description;
- APN—the tax assessor's parcel number; and
- street address, when available.

Most deeds show the legal description followed by a.k.a. (also known as) and the street address.

In the United States, most parcels of land are defined by one of three methods of **legal description**. More than one method may be used in the same property description. Following are the three types of legal description of land (from earliest to most recent):

1. Metes and bounds
2. Rectangular survey system
3. Lot and block

Metes and Bounds

In a **metes and bounds** description, a surveyor uses boundary markers and measures the distance from marker to marker to determine a property's perimeter. The term *metes* refers to distances, which may be measured in inches, feet, yards, or rods. *Bounds* are natural or artificial boundaries, such as rivers and roads. Single **monuments**, or **markers**, such as rocks, fences, iron pipes, or other natural or artificial objects also may be used. If an *angle of measurement* is given, it will be based on the degree of deviation from either north or south, as shown in Figure 2.4.

Method of description   A metes and bounds description starts at a designated point, called the **point of beginning**. It then follows each boundary for a given distance, in a clockwise direction, and at a precise angle from the last point. The simplest type of description using metes and bounds would be to follow the dimensions of a tract, as in the example that follows.

F O R E X A M P L E   Using metes and bounds, describe lot 3 below.

Plat Map
Lots 1 to 8, Block 12, Tract 1045

Beginning at a point on the southerly line of Apple Street, 100 feet westerly of the SW corner of the intersection of Apple and Edith Streets; running thence due south 150 feet; thence westerly 100 feet; thence northerly and parallel to the first course, 150 feet, to the southerly line of Apple Street; thence easterly along the southerly line of Apple Street, 100 feet, to the point of beginning.

Unfortunately, rivers change their courses, and trees can burn or be cut down. Over time, bounds and markers may be impossible to locate or may simply have disappeared. Where the distance between monuments differs from that in the description, the actual distance takes precedence.

Because of the unpredictability of markers and boundaries, the metes and bounds method of land survey is not very accurate. In addition, only a professional surveyor may be able to follow a complex metes and bounds description, which severely limits its usefulness. This system of land description is not often used in California, although it can be found in older documents. It is used in many other states, including Hawaii.

FIGURE 2.4:   **Angles of Measurement**

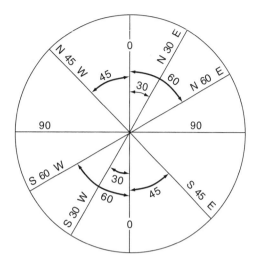

Source: California Department of Real Estate *Reference Book*, 1989-1990, p. 71.

The following is an early example of a metes and bounds description of the land illustrated in Figure 2.5. As you read this description, consider how the boundaries specified may have changed over the past 200 years.

A tract of land located in the Village of Red Skull, described as follows: Beginning at the intersection of the East line of Jones Road and the South line of Skull Drive; thence East along the South line of Skull Drive 200 feet; thence South 15° East 216.5 feet, more or less, to the center thread of Red Skull Creek; thence Northwesterly along the center line of said Creek to its intersection with the East line of Jones Road; thence North 105 feet, more or less, along the East line of Jones Road to the place of beginning.

FIGURE 2.5:   **Metes and Bounds/Tract**

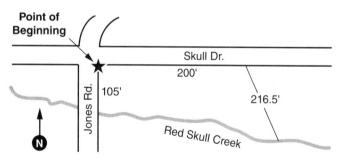

Rectangular Survey System

The **rectangular survey system** also is called the **section and township system** or **U.S. government survey system**.

This is the method used by the U.S. Surveyor General to survey public lands. This system bases descriptions of land on its distance from a **base line** that runs east-west and a **meridian** that runs north-south from a reference point.

The map in Figure 2.6 shows the three principal baselines and meridians used in California land descriptions. The Humboldt Baseline and Meridian were established on Mt. Pierre in Humboldt County in 1853; the Mt. Diablo Baseline and Meridian were established on Mt. Diablo in Contra Costa County in 1851; and the San Bernardino Baseline and Meridian were established on San Bernardino Mountain in San Bernardino County in 1852. A parcel may be described using different reference points. For example, property in the City of Fresno, as shown in Figure 2.6, may be described as ____ miles South and ____ miles East of the Mt. Diablo Baseline and Meridian, or as ____ miles North and ____ miles West of the San Bernardino Baseline and Meridian.

FIGURE 2.6: **California Township and Range Survey System**

Land division Land area, is divided into **townships** that are measured and numbered in each direction from the point of intersection of the base line and the meridian. A township does not refer to a town or community; instead, it is an area of six miles square (36 square miles).

Because of the curvature of the earth, the lines that set off each township are not perfectly parallel, and there must be some way to compensate for this. Every four townships north and south of the base line, a **correction line** is measured at the full interval (six miles) for that side of each township it borders. Every four townships east and west of the principal meridian, a **guide meridian** establishes the full interval of six miles for that side of each township it borders. This is illustrated in Figure 2.7.

Townships run north-south in groups called tiers (think of the **tiers** of a wedding cake) and east-west in groups called **ranges** (think of a vertical slice of cake layers). The township identified as T2N, R3E is the township in the second tier north of the baseline and the third range east of the meridian. It is highlighted in Figure 2.7.

A township is composed of 36 *sections*. One standard **section** is one square mile, which contains 640 acres. A section may be further divided as shown in Figure 2.8.

The sections composing a township are numbered in a particular order, starting with section number 1 in the northeast corner of the township. The numbering system is shown in Figure 2.8.

FIGURE 2.7:   Townships

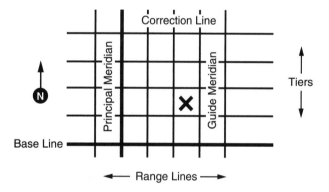

FIGURE 2.8:   Divisions of a Section and Section in a Township

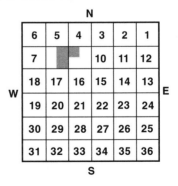

Method of description   The important dimensions of any rectangular survey description are the compass points: north, south, east, and west. The smallest area described is given first and the largest area last, so to find a parcel, you should work backward from the largest area described.

In Figure 2.8, the parcel labeled "A" is the northeast quarter of the southwest quarter of Section 30. For greater accuracy, legal descriptions will spell out directions and fractional parts, and then abbreviate them in parentheses (or vice versa).

F O R   E X A M P L E   Describe the parcel of land indicated by the shaded area of the township below. The shaded area is the east half (E½) of Section 8, and the northwest quarter (NW¼) of Section 9.

Computing land area   Land area is based on the following units of measurement. While the length of a rod, furlong, or league is interesting to know, the measurements for foot, yard, acre, and mile have more practical applications for the real estate licensee and should be memorized.

Units of Measurement

1 foot	12 inches.
1 yard	3 feet or 36 inches
1 acre	43,560 square feet
1 rod	5½ yards or 16½ feet
1 furlong	40 rods
6.06 rods	100 feet
1 mile	5,280 feet, or 8 furlongs, or 320 rods, or 1,760 yards
1 league	3 miles

The area of a parcel also can be computed using the rectangular survey system. Multiply the number of acres in a section by the fractional parts of a section described.

FOR EXAMPLE   A developer wants to buy the parcel described in the last example but doesn't want to pay more than $5,000 per acre. What is her maximum purchase price?

We know that a section has 640 acres, so we can multiply 640 acres by the fractional parts of the section that are involved.

For Section 8:

$$640 \times \tfrac{1}{2} = 320 \text{ acres}$$

For Section 9:

$$640 \times \tfrac{1}{4} = 160 \text{ acres}$$

The total acreage is 320 plus 160, or 480 acres. At $5,000 per acre, the maximum price the developer will pay is $2,400,000.

MATH CONCEPTS

There are several different ways to compute the size of a parcel of land.

Let's say you want to find the total area of a parcel described as the "south ½ of the East ½ of the Northeast ¼ of the Northwest ¼ of Section 1. This could appear on a deed as the "S½ of E½ of NE¼ of NW¼ of Section 1."

Method #1

Multiply the last fraction by the number of acres in a section. Then, working backward, multiply your answer by each of the remaining fractions.

$$640 \times \tfrac{1}{4} = 160 \text{ acres}$$
$$160 \times \tfrac{1}{4} = 40 \text{ acres}$$
$$40 \times \tfrac{1}{2} = 20 \text{ acres}$$
$$20 \times \tfrac{1}{2} = 10 \text{ acres}$$

The described parcel has 10 acres.

Method #2

This is a faster method, if you know how to multiply fractions. Multiply the fractions, then multiply that number by the number of acres in a section.

$$(\tfrac{1}{2} \times \tfrac{1}{2} \times \tfrac{1}{4} \times \tfrac{1}{4}) \times 640 \text{ acres} = \text{size of parcel}$$
$$\tfrac{1}{64} \times 640 \text{ acres} = \text{size of parcel}$$
$$\tfrac{640}{64} \text{ acres} = 10 \text{ acres}$$

To multiply fractions, multiply their numerators (the top part of the fraction) and multiply their denominators (the bottom part of the fraction).

$\frac{1}{2} \times \frac{1}{3} = \frac{1}{6}$

$\frac{2}{3} \times \frac{1}{4} = \frac{2}{12} = \frac{1}{6}$

Sometimes, you will find the size of a parcel of land by adding fractional parts of one or more sections.

Example.   Let's say you want to find the total area of a parcel described as the North ½ and the Southeast ¼ of Section 17.

Method #1

640 × ½ = 320 acres

640 × ¼ = 160 acres

320 + 160 = 480 acres

The described parcel has 480 acres.

Method #2

In the problem above, you would go through the following steps:

(½ + ¼) × 640 acres = (²⁄₄ + ¼) × 640 acres = ¾ × 640 acres = 480 acres

Method #3

If all else fails, you can draw the equivalent section(s), mark the parcels to be added, determine the number of acres in each parcel, and total the number of acres indicated.

Lot and Block

The **lot and block system** is also called the *lot, block, and tract system* or **subdivision system**. A **subdivision map** shows the boundaries of all of the parcels in the subdivision. The subdivision map is filed in the county recorder's office, usually by the developer. Each parcel in the subdivision is identified by tract, lot, and block numbers. The tract is the largest land area. The tract is divided into blocks, which are divided into lots.

FIGURE 2.9:   **Plat Map**

Plat Map
Lots 1 to 8, Block 12, Tract 1045

The deed to each parcel of land in the subdivision refers to the tract, block, and lot numbers shown on the subdivision map. The subdivision map may also be referred to as a **plat map**. Figure 2.9 shows part of a plat map, with a block that has been divided into eight residential building lots.

In a lot and block legal description, it is usually sufficient to give the city name, county name, tract name and number, and block and lot numbers. It is a better practice to give the book and page number in the county recorder's office where the map appears, as well as the date the map was recorded.

FOR EXAMPLE   A developer sold a house located at 491 Rose Avenue, which is lot 28 of block 15 of the Tice Elms Subdivision, Walnut Creek, Contra Costa County, California. The subdivision map was recorded August 16, 1968, and can be found in book 38, on page 106. How would the property be described by the developer and in the deed to the buyer?

The developer would describe the property as 491 Rose Avenue, Tice Elms Subdivision, Walnut Creek, Lot 28, Block 15, Contra Costa County, California, as shown in Book 38, Page 106, recorded 08-16-1968. The deed the buyer receives would describe the property as Lot 28, Block 15, Tice Elms Subdivision (as recorded August 16, 1968, Book 38, Page 106 of maps), City of Walnut Creek, County of Contra Costa, State of California.

SUMMARY

The State of California has a unique history of settlement, conquest, growth, and prosperity. The rancho grants and the vast lands surrounding the pueblos formed the basis for private land ownership after the Treaty of Guadalupe Hidalgo in 1848. The Board of Land Commissioners solved problems of conflicting claims of property ownership. With adoption of the English **common law**, admission to the Union as a state, and the discovery of gold, California quickly assumed the importance it deserved. Even today, however, the state retains elements of its Spanish heritage, such as **community property**.

Real property is land, both at and below the surface and above the surface. Real property includes **mineral rights, water rights**, and **air rights**. A **fixture** is something attached or placed permanently on the land. An **appurtenance** is used with land and benefits the landowner.

Personal property is all property that is not real property. Something may be personal property but become real property when it is affixed to land. Five tests can be used to determine whether something is a fixture and thus part of the real estate. *Trade fixtures* remain the personal property of a business.

A **legal description** identifies a specific parcel of land to the exclusion of all others. The **metes and bounds system** uses natural or manufactured **monuments, angles of measurement**, and distances to describe a property.

The **rectangular survey system** uses a grid-like division of land area into **townships** set in **tiers** and **ranges** along geographical dimensions called **meridians** and **base lines**. Townships are divided into **sections**, which are further divided into fractional parts.

The **lot and block system** uses the **subdivision map**, which shows streets and lot dimensions.

OPEN FOR DISCUSSION

California's population growth depends on the availability of water for both residential and nonresidential use.

1. Should growth be limited to conserve water resources?
2. Should water resources be limited to control growth?

REVIEW QUESTIONS

1. During the days of Spanish rule, all land was owned by
   a. the missions.
   b. the government.
   c. the crown.
   d. the conquistadores.

2. The Treaty of Guadalupe Hidalgo ended
   a. the gold rush.
   b. Spanish rule.
   c. the war with Mexico.
   d. the missions.

3. Real Estate Law, which relies on court decisions as well as legislation, is based on
   a. Spanish civil law.
   b. French civil law.
   c. the right of appropriation.
   d. English common law.

4. Land disputes over the Spanish and Mexican land grants were settled by
   a. the Board of Land Commissioners.
   b. the State of California.
   c. the Spanish legal code.
   d. taking all land for public use.

5. In California, the term *real estate* is synonymous with
   a. land.
   b. fixtures.
   c. real property.
   d. personal property.

6. Real property is *NOT*
   a. land.
   b. real estate.
   c. appurtenances to land.
   d. movable.

7. The sale of real property generally is governed by the laws of
   a. the state where the real property is located.
   b. the state where the owner of the real property resides.
   c. any of the states.
   d. the federal government.

8. The sale of personal property generally is governed by the laws of
   a. the state where the personal property is located.
   b. the state where the owner of the property resides.
   c. any of the states.
   d. the federal government.

9. In California, the Uniform Commercial Code governs sales transactions involving
   a. real estate.
   b. bulk sales of goods.
   c. fixtures to real estate.
   d. riparian rights.

10. For real estate to be conveyed, there must be an accurate
    a. fence line.
    b. description.
    c. soil chemical analysis.
    d. water test.

11. A subdivision map is
    a. rarely accurate.
    b. good only to describe the entire subdivision.
    c. never required.
    d. a good reference for a legal description.

12. The MOST useful method of describing a subdivision parcel is probably
    a. the lot and block system.
    b. the rectangular survey system.
    c. the metes and bounds system.
    d. the U.S. government survey system.

13. The rectangular survey system is also called
    a. the U.S. government survey system.
    b. the province and township system.
    c. the subdivision system.
    d. the California system.

14. California has how many principal baselines?
    a. One
    b. Two
    c. Three
    d. Four

15. A township consists of how many sections?
    a. 12
    b. 18
    c. 4
    d. 36

16. A section is
    a. 640 acres.
    b. six square miles.
    c. 5,000 feet by 5,000 feet.
    d. three leagues.

17. Section 6 lies in what direction from Section 1 of a township?
    a. North
    b. South
    c. East
    d. West

18. Section 22 lies in what direction from Section 17 of a township?
    a. Northeast
    b. Northwest
    c. Southeast
    d. Southwest

19. Land described as the South ½ of the North ½ of Section 18 contains how many acres?
    a. 80
    b. 120
    c. 160
    d. 320

20. The point of beginning is used in
    a. the rectangular survey system.
    b. the metes and bounds system.
    c. the lot and block system.
    d. all legal descriptions.

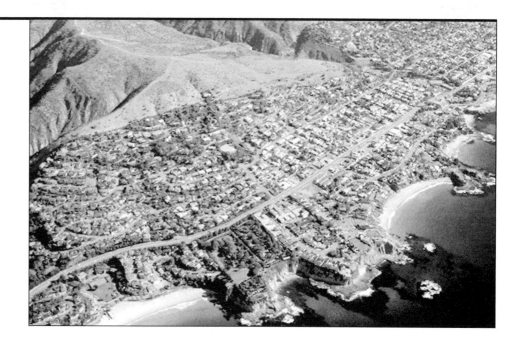

OWNERSHIP OF REAL PROPERTY

LEARNING OBJECTIVES

When you have completed this unit, you will be able to

- **identify** the various estates in land, including freehold estates of ownership and leasehold estates of tenancy;

- **describe** the difference between a reversion and a remainder;

- **list** the ways in which title to real estate may be taken by an individual;

- **distinguish** the forms of concurrent ownership;

- **describe** the attributes and ways of acquiring community property;

- **list** the forms of business ownership of real estate; and

- **define** a trust and **describe** how a trust can own real estate.

KEY TERMS

beneficiary	life estate	registered domestic
commingling	life tenant	partner
community property	limited liability	remainder
community property	company (LLC)	reversion
with right of	limited partnership	right of survivorship
survivorship	living trust	S corporation
concurrent ownership	measuring life	separate property
condition subsequent	ownership in severalty	sole proprietorship
corporation	partition action	successor trustee
estate	partners	tenancy in common
estates of tenancy	partnership	tenancy in partnership
fee simple absolute	power of termination	testamentary trust
fee simple estate	quasi-community	trust
freehold estate	property	trustee
general partnership	Real Estate Investment	trustor
inter vivos trust	Trust (REIT)	unity of possession
joint tenancy	real estate syndicate	vesting of title
leaseholds		

ESTATES IN LAND

In the previous unit, you learned that in California the term *real property* means the same thing as *real estate*. The terms are used interchangeably to refer to

- land;

- fixtures to land;

- anything incidental or appurtenant to land; and

- anything immovable by law.

The ownership of property consists of a "bundle of rights" or interests in it. Rights of ownership include the power to possess, use, exclude others, and dispose of the property.

An **estate** is an interest in property. All property that is not real property is personal property.

The rights of land ownership that are covered in this unit are shown in Figure 3.1.

Freehold Estates

In medieval England, the **freehold estate** was the highest form of land ownership. The owner of a freehold estate in land could use the property in any way, without being subject to the demands of the overlord. Today's owner of real estate also enjoys a freehold estate. But there usually are some restraints on how the land may be used.

A freehold estate can be held for an unlimited time, or the period of ownership may be limited in some way.

FIGURE 3.1:   Estates in Land

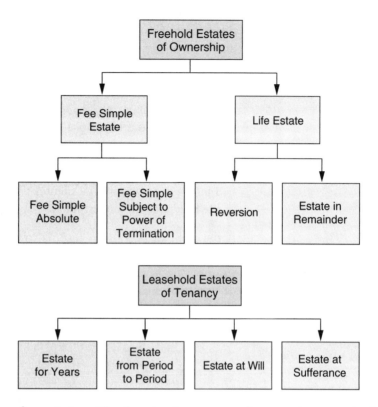

Fee simple estate   The **fee simple estate** is what may be termed a "present, possessory interest." It carries the maximum bundle of rights. The owner of a fee simple estate has the right to use the property right now and for an indefinite period in the future.

The highest (most complete) form of ownership is a **fee simple absolute**. If the right of possession is restricted in some way, it is a fee simple subject to a **power of termination**, or *fee simple defeasible*. A fee simple estate may be granted subject to a *limitation* on the use of the property or a *condition* that the property holder must (or must not) perform. The power of termination expires 30 years after the recording of the document creating it, unless it is extended for an additional 30 years by recording notice of the extension before termination of the prior 30-year term. A power of termination will not expire during the lifetime of the grantor, if the grantor is a natural person and the grant was made without consideration to a governmental entity or a tax-exempt organization.

With a fee simple estate subject to a **condition subsequent**, there is some action or activity that the fee simple owner must *not* perform. If the condition is broken, the former owner can retake possession of the property. Enforcement of a fee simple subject to a power of termination or condition subsequent is by filing a notice of that intention or bringing a civil action. The notice must be given, or action brought, within five years of the breach of the restriction or the power of termination will expire.

FOR EXAMPLE   A rancher gives a 1,000-acre parcel of rural land to the church youth fellowship "on the condition that" there is no sale or manufacture of alcoholic beverages on the property. Years later, the rancher visits the property and is surprised to find a reception in progress and a "no host" bar at which drinks are being purchased. What can the rancher do?

The fellowship has broken the condition subsequent to its fee simple right of ownership. The rancher can file a notice of his intent to reenter the property and claim possession or he can bring a legal action against the group.

Life estate   The owner of a **life estate** has the right to possession and use of property, but the estate lasts only as long as the life of a person (or persons) identified in the deed or will that creates the estate. Usually, the **measuring life** is that of the holder of the life estate.

If the right of possession returns to the original property owner when the life estate ends, the original owner has a **reversion**. If the right of possession goes to a third person when the life estate ends, that person has a **remainder**. The *remainderman* holds an *estate in remainder* during the existence of the life estate and a fee simple estate on termination of the life estate.

Fee Simple   Life Estate   OR   Remainder →   Fee Simple

— — — — — Reversion — — — — —

Mortgage interest is considered the responsibility of the life tenant.

The holder of a life estate (the **life tenant**) must keep up the property and pay taxes. If the life tenant pays a debt, such as mortgage principal, which also benefits the reversioner or remainderman, the life tenant is entitled to reimbursement.

The use of the life estate can be transferred by gift, lease, or sale, but the right to use and possession ends with the measuring life. Because there can be no guarantee that anyone will live to a certain age, the value of a life estate will be based on the life expectancy of the individual(s) against whose life the estate is measured.

A special situation arises when the measuring life is that of someone other than the holder of the life estate. The life tenant may die before the person against whose life the estate is measured dies. In that case, the life tenant's interest passes to that person's heirs and will last until the end of the measuring life. The reversioner or remainderman can give, sell, or lease that interest, but no right of possession will take effect until the termination of the life estate.

FOR EXAMPLE   A widower died, leaving a life estate in his home to his sister and the remainder to his only son. The sister had been living in an apartment and was very pleased to have the use of the house. The son, upset when he found out what his father had done, insisted on being allowed to live in the house, for it was "really" his. Does the son have that right?

No. The deceased's sister, the life tenant, has the sole right of use and possession of the property while she lives.

Leasehold Estates

Tenants are those who rent or lease property from **landlords**.

Tenants own nonfreehold (less than freehold) estates called **leaseholds** or **estates of tenancy**. Instead of an ownership interest, the tenant has the right to use the property for the stated period. The length of the lease term determines the type of tenancy. Estates of tenancy are discussed in more detail in Unit 12.

Exercise 3-1

Identify each of the following types of ownership interest in land:

1. Dennis has sole possession of Blackacre for as long as he lives.

2. The Middle Falls School has sole possession of Whiteacre on the condition that it is used for educational purposes.

3. The town of Merry Meadows has a beautiful library building. The building is a former mansion that was donated to the town with the stipulation that it be used only as a library. What kind of estate does the town have?

4. A renter has lived at 316 Iowa Street for 15 years on a month-to-month lease term. Although his rent has been increased every few years, the landlord has never drawn up a lease agreement. What kind of estate does the renter have in the residence on Iowa Street?

5. In her will, Chau left her residence in Palm Springs to her nephew, Simon, for the life of Simon's sister, Annette. On Annette's death, the home is to go to Annette's daughter, Yvonne. What estate does Simon have? What estate does Yvonne have? What happens if Simon dies before Annette does?

TAKING TITLE TO REAL ESTATE

A conveyance of real estate is called a *grant*. The person conveying the property (the owner) is the *grantor*; the person receiving the property is the *grantee*. There will be many possible roles for the owner of real estate discussed throughout this book; a good rule of thumb to remember is a word that ends in "or" stands for the property **owner**.

Title to real estate (its ownership) can be taken by one person or by more than one person. When a conveyance of real estate is done correctly, title **vests** in (is transferred to) the grantee. Advising someone on how to take title is a legal question that may have tax and other consequences. Such advice should come from an attorney or CPA (certified public accountant). A real estate licensee is prohibited from giving legal advice. Individuals taking title to property should indicate their status as

- single (never married);
- married;
- registered domestic partners;
- unmarried (divorced);
- widow (if the husband has died); or
- widower (if the wife has died).

For example, title may be conveyed to "Sarah Smith, a single woman" or "John Jones and Robert Lopez, registered domestic partners."

Ownership in Severalty

Ownership in severalty, also called *separate ownership* or *sole ownership*, is ownership by one person. The property owner (who can be an individual or a legal entity, such as a corporation or trust) is the only person to receive the benefits of ownership. The separate owner also is the only person responsible for the burdens of ownership, such as the payment of taxes.

Concurrent Ownership

Concurrent ownership is ownership by more than one person at the same time. There are four types of concurrent ownership, as shown in Figure 3.2.

Tenancy in common is the default form of ownership for two or more unmarried people.

Tenancy in common   A tenancy in common is created when it is specified by name. It also is created when more than one person takes title, they are not married to each other, and no other method of taking title is specified.

Tenants in common may take title at different times and may own equal or unequal shares. If no distribution is specified, tenants in common are presumed to own equal shares.

Tenants in common have what is called **unity of possession**, which means that each tenant has the right to possession of the property and cannot be excluded by the cotenants. Even if they own unequal shares in the property, each has the right to use all of it. If the property is rented, tenants in common share the rent according to their individual shares. Expenses of the property, such as taxes, also are shared.

FIGURE 3.2:   Concurrent Ownership

	Tenancy in Common	Joint Tenancy	Community Property	Tenancy in Partnership
Parties	Any number	Any number	Spouses or registered domestic partners	Any number
Time	Any time	Same time	Same time	Any time
Title	Separate titles to each interest	Only one title	Only one title	Only one title
Interest	Separate, undivided interests	Equal, undivided interests	Equal, undivided interests	Equal, undivided interests
Possession and Control of Property	Equal right for each owner	Equal right for each owner	Equal right for each owner	Equal right except for personal property
Conveyance	Yes, of each share separately	Yes, but creates tenancy in common as to that share	Only if both spouses join in the conveyance	Only if all partners join in the conveyance
Deceased's Share on Death	Passes by will or intestacy	Passes to surviving joint tenant(s)	Half to surviving spouse; half by will or intestacy	Can pass to surviving partners; heirs have right to deceased's share of profits
New Owner of Partial Interest	Tenant in common	Tenant in common	Tenant in common; no community interest	Tenant in common
Creditor Sale	Sale of individual tenant's interest	Sale of individual tenant's interest	Entire property available to satisfy debt	Entire property available to satisfy partnership debt

A tenant in common can give away, sell, or devise (will) her share of the property to someone else. The recipient receives the share of the tenant in common and full right of possession.

A tenant in common may want to dissolve the shared ownership. This can be accomplished by agreement of all cotenants or, if there is a dispute, by a lawsuit known as a **partition action**. If it is possible to divide the property among the owners in equitable shares, the court will do so. Otherwise, the property will be sold. If a sale is ordered by the court, the proceeds of the sale will be distributed to the cotenants in the same shares as their ownership interests, less a proportionate part of any expenses owed.

FOR EXAMPLE   Al, Sara, and Joe are all owners of Paradise Acres, a mountain retreat. They own a fee simple estate as tenants in common. Each has a one-third share of Paradise Acres. Gibbon Properties manages Paradise Acres. Who pays the management fee? Who gets the profits, if any?

Each of the tenants in common is responsible for one-third of the management fee. Each will take one-third of the profits, if any, after the management fee and expenses are paid.

A joint tenancy requires unity of time, title, interest, and possession.

Joint tenancy   A **joint tenancy** is a special form of co-ownership. It requires that all co-owners take title to the property at the same time, by the same document. In addition, each must have an equal share of the property. These four unities of a joint tenancy, which can be remembered by the acronym TTIP, are as follows:

1. **T**—unity of *time* (each takes title at the same time)
2. **T**—unity of *title* (each receives title through the same deed)
3. **I**—unity of *interest* (each owns an equal share)
4. **P**—unity of *possession* (each has the right to use all of the property)

If the joint tenancy is created properly, the joint tenants benefit from the **right of survivorship**. This means that when a cotenant dies, the survivors receive the deceased's share. If there are only two joint tenants, when one dies the other becomes sole owner of the property. One of the most important features of a joint tenancy is that, when ownership transfers by right of survivorship, whether to a sole surviving joint tenant or more than one surviving joint tenants, the property does not go through probate. As a result, however, a joint tenant cannot *will* (name an heir to) his share of the property. As long as the joint tenancy exists, the right of survivorship in the other joint tenant(s) takes precedence.

FOR EXAMPLE   Jessica and Sophie are cousins. Ten years ago they bought a house as joint tenants. Their deed did not include the words "with right of survivorship." Sophie married Trevor and moved out of the house she shared with Jessica. Before Jessica and Sophie could sell the house, as they had agreed, Sophie died unexpectedly. Who owns the house?

Jessica is sole owner of the house. Jessica and Sophie had taken title as joint tenants. Because one of the characteristics of a joint tenancy in California is the right of survivorship, those words do not need to be written into the deed transferring title to the joint tenants. Even if Sophie had made a will leaving all of her property to Trevor, the will would be ineffective as to her share of property held in joint tenancy.

A joint tenant can terminate a joint tenancy, but the advice of an attorney should be sought to avoid problems. It is also possible for a joint tenant's share to be transferred to someone else while the joint tenant is still alive. Again, legal requirements must be followed. Such a transfer will sever the joint tenancy only as to that tenant, however. The new owner becomes a tenant in common. If there is only one other cotenant, the joint tenancy has been completely destroyed. If there is more than one cotenant, the joint tenancy remains in existence as to the other tenants. They still have the right of survivorship with respect to their interests.

Any two people can be joint tenants, including a married couple and registered domestic partners (discussed in the next section). Because spouses and registered domestic partners also can hold title to real estate as community property, they will want to consider the benefits of each form of ownership, preferably with the advice of an attorney. As pointed out earlier, a licensed real estate agent may not give advice on how to hold title.

Community property   Community property is real or personal property acquired by a spouse during marriage or by a **registered domestic partner** as defined in Family Code Section 297. Each also may own *separate* (noncommunity) real or personal property, however, and acquire *separate property*. The rules described below for spouses apply also to registered domestic partners.

Property that was a married person's separate property before marriage remains separate property after marriage. Property acquired during marriage may be either the separate property of one spouse or community property belonging to both spouses, depending on its source, the actions of the parties, and legal presumptions.

Separate property is property acquired

- by gift or inheritance to one spouse,
- with the proceeds of other separate property, or
- as income from separate property.

Most other property acquired during marriage is community property. Spouses are allowed to change community property to separate property by written agreement. The handling of money can change its character as separate property. If there is **commingling** of separate funds (placed in the same account) with community funds, they lose their status as separate property.

If the ownership status of property is unclear, the courts will follow the legal presumption that *real property* in California acquired during marriage and *personal property*, wherever it is located, that is acquired during marriage are community property. Community property cannot be sold, mortgaged, or leased for one year or longer without the agreement of both spouses. Both must sign all documents.

> Spouses can agree to change community property to separate property.

A spouse can convey her interest in community property by will. The inheritor and the surviving spouse would then be tenants in common. If a spouse dies without a will, the surviving spouse is entitled to half of the community property as her own interest and also receives the deceased spouse's half.

Community Property With Right of Survivorship

As of July 1, 2001, spouses can take title to property as **community property with right of survivorship**. The document of transfer would have to stipulate that form of title, and both spouses would accept title in that form by writing on the face of the document a statement signed or initialed by both. With the right of survivorship, title passes to the surviving spouse without probate, just as if it were held in joint tenancy. Prior to the death of either spouse, the right of survivorship may be terminated in the same way that a joint tenancy may be severed. (Civil Code 682.1)

FOR EXAMPLE   Ignacio, a married man, signs a contract to sell the mountain cabin he owns as community property with his spouse, Manuela. Manuela is away on a business trip at the time the contract is drawn up and isn't interested in selling the cabin anyway. Can the buyer enforce the contract?

No, because the cabin is community property. Both spouses must sign any instrument of sale.

The concept of community property is a holdover from Spanish and Mexican rule. Only California and seven other states still treat marital property in this way, and there are important differences in each state's law. In any move from state to state, the applicable laws should be determined to avoid conflict regarding property status.

Quasi-Community Property

New California residents should be aware of the concept of **quasi-community property**. Quasi-community property is

■ any California real estate acquired by an out-of-state married person that would have been considered community property if it had been acquired by a resident of California; and

■ any California real estate acquired in exchange for real or personal property located anywhere, when the California real estate would have been considered community property if it had been acquired by a California resident.

Tenancy in partnership   The members of a partnership can own property for partnership purposes.

A **general partnership** is established when two or more persons carry on a business for profit as co-owners. Property owned by the partnership is owned by the individual **partners** as a **tenancy in partnership**. All partners have the right to possession of partnership property for partnership purposes. Partnership property can be attached only by partnership creditors.

When rights to partnership property are assigned, the rights of all partners must be assigned. The death of a partner will dissolve the partnership, unless there was a prior written agreement to continue the business. If a business is dissolved, its assets are sold, creditors are paid, and the remainder is distributed to the partners. If a partner dies and the business continues, that partner's right to possession of partnership property (the business) goes to the surviving partner(s). The heirs of the deceased partner have no right to the property, although they are entitled to the deceased's share of the profits. The partners may agree in writing to a different distribution.

A partner's right in property owned by the partnership cannot be community property. For some purposes, however, a partner's interest in the partnership itself is treated as community property.

| All partners are liable for debts of the partnership. |

For tax purposes, all partnership income is distributed to the partners, who report that income individually. An important feature of a partnership is that each partner is liable for partnership debts. For that reason alone, the decision to form a partnership requires careful consideration.

FOR EXAMPLE   George is a partner in Realty Agents, Inc. The partnership leases office space in four buildings. George needs storage space for some furniture he is giving his son. May he store the furniture in the partnership's office?

No. As a partner, George may not use partnership property for personal purposes.

Exercise 3-2

What form of ownership does each of the following people have in the property described?

1. Jane and her brother own a farm and have a right of survivorship.

2. Fred and Alita own their home as spouses. No form of ownership was specified in their deed, as Fred and Alita have not yet consulted an attorney.

3. Cal and Lou, both single men, bought a three-story Victorian home in Sacramento. No form of ownership was specified.

4. Helen is a partner in Real Estate Consultants, which owns a shopping center.

5. Fred, a married man, inherited a cattle ranch from his uncle. Fred is the uncle's sole heir.

BUSINESS OWNERSHIP OF REAL ESTATE

Other types of business also can acquire, use, and sell real estate. This section discusses the following:

- Sole proprietorship
- Corporation
- General partnership
- Limited partnership
- Limited liability company
- Trust

Sole Proprietorship

The **sole proprietorship** is the simplest form of business ownership, because it has only one owner. The sole proprietor

- conducts business in his own name or under a trade name,
- reports business income on his individual income tax return, and
- is responsible for the business's debts.

The sole proprietor may or may not have employees, such as personal assistants.

Corporation

Every state has specific laws regulating the formation, operation, and dissolution of **corporations**. The owners of a corporation are called *shareholders*.

The Corporation

- is a separate, legally recognized entity, apart from owners (shareholders);
- must be chartered by a state;
- acts through its board of directors and officers;
- may own, lease, and convey real property; and
- limits liability of officers, directors, and shareholders.

A corporation could be formed for a nonprofit motive. A nonprofit corporation is owned by *members* rather than shareholders. It can own, lease, and convey real estate.

Corporations are called *domestic corporations* by the state in which they are chartered (created). Corporations created in any other location are called *foreign corporations*. In California, for instance, corporations chartered by any other state are considered foreign corporations in their dealings in California.

Liability   A major benefit of doing business as a corporation is that individual officers, directors, and shareholders are usually not held personally accountable for corporate decisions and corporate debts. Increasingly, legislation such as the federal Sarbanes-Oxley Act of 2002, also known as the Public Company Accounting Reform and Investor Protection Act of 2002, has imposed a greater level of accountability on officers and directors of public companies.

S corporation   One disadvantage of a corporation is that profits are taxed twice. The corporation pays taxes on income, and income is taxed again when it is distributed to shareholders in the form of dividends. Federal tax law provides an alternative method of taxation to corporations with 100 or fewer shareholders. If the corporation is formed under the requirements of *Subchapter S of the Internal Revenue Code*, income is allowed to flow directly to shareholders, avoiding double taxation. In an **S corporation**, all shareholders must be individuals rather than other corporations.

To be treated as an S corporation, shareholders must file Form 2553 with the IRS; if they do nothing, they will be taxed as a C corporation (under Subchapter C) and be subject to the double taxation mentioned above. To qualify as an S corporation, the corporation must be a domestic (U.S.) corporation with only one class of stock and no more than 100 shareholders, all of whom consent in writing to filing as an S corporation. The shareholders of an S corporation can be individuals, estates, exempt organizations, or certain trusts, but cannot be nonresident aliens. For complete information about filing as an S corporation, consult your tax advisor and the instructions for Form 2553 that can be found at the website of the Internal Revenue Service, www.irs.gov.

www.irs.gov

Partnership

A **partnership** is an association of two or more persons to carry on a business as co-owners for profit. In a general partnership, each of the partners by definition has authority to act on behalf of the partnership, and each is liable for the debts of the partnership.

Limited Partnership

To avoid the unlimited liability of being a general partner, an investor can take part in a **limited partnership**. A limited partnership can be created only in compliance with state law. In California, this includes filing certain information with the secretary of state.

The *California limited partnership* must have one or more general partners who run the business and have unlimited liability for partnership obligations. Other investors can join as limited partners, and their liability will be no more than the amount they have invested in the partnership. By law, limited partners can take no part in the management of the partnership. If they do so, they will be considered general partners and will lose their limited liability.

Real estate syndicate   A **real estate syndicate** can take the form of a REIT, corporation, general partnership, or other entity but is usually formed as a limited partnership. In California, real estate syndicates are popular methods of investment for both corporations and individuals. A syndicate of 100 or more participants must be approved by the Department of Business Oversight before syndicate interests may be offered for sale. Strict rules and regulations must be followed.

Limited Liability Company

Almost all states permit property ownership by a **limited liability company** (LLC). Although each state's law is unique, an LLC typically provides the single-level tax benefit of a partnership with a flexible organizational structure.

In California, an LLC is created by filing a one-page form with the secretary of state. LLC members are not required to have a written operating agreement setting out their rights and responsibilities, although one is advisable. LLC members may adopt corporate formalities, such as resolutions and annual meetings, but are not required to do so.

Taxes and fees are higher for an LLC than for a partnership.

Unlike an S corporation, an LLC places no restriction on the number of shareholders who take part and who they are. The LLC provides something closer to the limited liability for corporate shareholders than the greater protection afforded to limited partners. Unlike limited partners, however, members of an LLC can take part in the running of the organization without incurring personal liability for business obligations. This freedom from liability does have a cost. In California, an LLC incurs higher taxes and fees than either a general or limited partnership.

Information Available on the Web

The Secretary of State Business Service Center website at www.sos.ca.gov/business/ provides information on corporations, limited liability companies, limited liability partnerships, general partnerships, and other entities, including lists of officers and directors.

Trust

Using a trust to hold title is a way to keep the true owner's identity hidden.

A **trust** can be a form of property ownership. Title to property is conveyed by the **trustor** (the property owner) to the **trustee**. Title is held by the trustee on behalf of a **beneficiary**.

Who controls the property held in trust? The trustee's powers generally are defined by the document establishing the trust. If the trustor fails to define the trustee's powers, the law of the state in which the trust is created is followed. A trust can last for a short or relatively long time, depending on the trustor's intent. Trusts often are created by the terms of a will (a **testamentary trust**) to care for the decedent's children until they reach adulthood.

Real Estate Investment Trust   The **Real Estate Investment Trust** (REIT) holds various forms of real estate or mortgages for the benefit of investors who own shares of the trust. REIT shares may be publicly traded. More information about REITs can be found in the following box.

REITs

In California, a Real Estate Investment Trust (REIT)

- is regulated by the Commissioner of Corporations;
- must comply with federal and state tax law;
- must be owned by at least 100 different investors;
- cannot have any five investors own more than 50% of the trust;
- must receive at least 95% of its income from investments; and
- must receive at least 75% of its investment income from real estate.

www.nareit.com

The *National Association of Real Estate Investment Trusts (NAREIT)* serves REIT owners, managers, and related companies. Information on various forms of REITs can be found at the association's website, www.nareit.com.

Living trust   The **living trust** (or **inter vivos trust**) is an increasingly popular form of property ownership. A living trust can be used to hold title to property during the lifetime of the trustor, who is also named as the trustee of the trust. When the trustor dies or becomes incapacitated, control of the property held in trust passes to a **successor trustee** named in the trust document. In this way, property can be transferred without going through an expensive probate process. A living trust also can be created by a married couple, with the property held in trust going to the successor trustee on the death of the second spouse.

Properly drafted, a living trust can be an effective estate-planning tool that provides the easiest and quickest way to transfer property at death.

Exercise 3-3

What form of ownership does each example below illustrate?

1. The Spice Company owns a processing plant and leases dock space for its shipments. The company is doing very well, and it paid an excellent dividend to shareholders last year.

2. Joseph Marine owns World Wide Real Estate. Joseph, a licensed real estate broker, is the only owner of World Wide and reports company income on his personal tax return.

3. Mountain Properties is a real estate syndicate of 127 investors. Only five members of the syndicate are allowed to participate in investment decisions.

4. When Grandpa Peter died he left his farm to his grandson, but his grandson will not receive title to the farm until he is 25. In the meantime, Cattlemen's Bank will manage and hold title to the property.

SUMMARY

In California, the terms *real estate* and *real property* are synonymous. The highest form of ownership in real property is the estate in **fee simple absolute**. It is also possible to own a **life estate** to enjoy property for a time measured by one's own or another's life. A **reversion** or **remainder** is the right to possess the property after the death of the holder of the life estate. A fee simple subject to a **power of termination** or **condition subsequent** may be lost on breach of a limitation or restriction.

A conveyance of real estate takes place by a *grant* from the *grantor* (owner) to the *grantee*. Property owned by only one individual is **separate property**. Both real property and personal property can be separate property. Property acquired during marriage or by a **registered domestic partner** by gift, inheritance, or with the income or proceeds of separate property is separate property unless *commingled*. Most other property acquired by a spouse or registered domestic partner is **community property**.

Two or more persons may have **concurrent ownership** of real estate as **tenants in common**, **joint tenants with the right of survivorship**, or **tenants in partnership**. Tenants in common share **unity of possession**, which means that each tenant has the right to use the entire property. Joint tenants share the four unities of *time*, *title*, *interest*, and *possession*. A **partition action** can be brought by a cotenant who wants to have the entire property divided or sold.

A **general partnership** can own property as a **tenancy in partnership**. All general partners have the right to use partnership property for partnership purposes. All general partners are liable for partnership debts, and all share partnership income.

In a **sole proprietorship**, the sole proprietor may take property in her own name or under the business's trade name. A **corporation**, whether chartered in or out of California, may own property even if the corporation is nonprofit.

A **trust** enables a **trustee** to hold property conveyed by a **trustor** (property owner) for the **beneficiary** of the trust. A **testamentary trust** is established by will. A **living trust (inter vivos trust)** can be used to convey property on death without the difficulty and expense of probate.

A **real estate syndicate** comprises a group of investors, generally organized as a **limited partnership**. The *limited partners* can benefit from the greater bargaining power of the syndicate while avoiding the liabilities of general partners. A limited partnership must comply with state law to protect the limited partners. A **limited liability company** offers the tax benefit of a partnership with the opportunity to take an active role in running the company.

OPEN FOR DISCUSSION

After gradually increasing over many years, home ownership in the United States has decreased slightly in the last decade.

1. Should home ownership be encouraged as a matter of government policy? Why or why not?

REVIEW QUESTIONS

1. A fee simple estate and a life estate are
   a. freehold estates.
   b. fee simple estates.
   c. leasehold estates.
   d. estates of tenancy.

2. The highest form of ownership is
   a. the life estate.
   b. the real estate syndicate.
   c. the fee simple absolute.
   d. the estate at will.

3. Victor and Karen are not married but together own community property because they are
   a. brother and sister.
   b. joint tenants.
   c. registered domestic partners.
   d. holders of a life estate.

4. A fee simple estate that may be lost when some act is performed is
   a. a life estate.
   b. a fee simple absolute.
   c. a remainder.
   d. a fee simple on condition subsequent.

5. A fee simple estate that has no conditions is
   a. a life estate.
   b. a remainder.
   c. a fee simple on condition subsequent.
   d. a fee simple absolute.

6. If Greenacre is deeded by Lou to Mary for Mary's life, Mary has
   a. a life estate.
   b. an estate in remainder.
   c. an estate in reversion.
   d. no interest.

7. If Greenacre is deeded by Lou to Mary for Mary's life, Lou has
   a. a life estate.
   b. an estate in remainder.
   c. an estate in reversion.
   d. no interest.

8. When Aunt Winifred died, she left a life estate in Whiteacre to her nephew George. When George dies, Whiteacre will go to George's daughter Elizabeth. Elizabeth is
   a. a reversioner.
   b. a remainderman.
   c. a holder of a life estate.
   d. a joint tenant with right of survivorship.

9. If Greenacre is deeded by Lou to Mary for the life of Nancy, Nancy has
   a. a life estate.
   b. an estate in remainder.
   c. an estate in reversion.
   d. no interest.

10. The owner of a life estate can
    a. sell only the life estate.
    b. never will the life estate.
    c. sell the fee simple estate.
    d. sell both the life estate and the fee simple estate.

11. Joint tenants have unity of
    a. interest but not possession.
    b. title but not interest.
    c. possession and title only.
    d. time, title, interest, and possession.

12. Jessica and John own Blackacre as joint tenants. Jessica's will specifies that on her death her interest in Blackacre is to go to her sister Mona. When Jessica dies
    a. Mona will be a tenant in common of Blackacre with John.
    b. Mona will be a joint tenant of Blackacre with John.
    c. John will be sole owner of Blackacre.
    d. the probate court will have to sell Blackacre and distribute the proceeds to John and Mona.

13. Three joint tenants share interest in a property. If one joint tenant's share is sold using the proper legal formalities, the new owner will then be
    a. a joint tenant with the other joint tenants.
    b. a tenant in common with the other joint tenants.
    c. a tenant at sufferance.
    d. a remainderman.

14. Community property is
    a. all property acquired by a spouse or registered domestic partner.
    b. all property acquired by the spouse during marriage.
    c. the only form of ownership during marriage.
    d. all property acquired by a spouse or registered domestic partner that is not separate property.

15. One of the forms of concurrent ownership is
    a. ownership in severalty.
    b. tenancy in partnership.
    c. sole proprietorship.
    d. separate ownership.

16. A partner has
    a. an absolute right to use partnership property.
    b. the right to assign partnership property.
    c. the right to convey partnership property by will.
    d. the right to possession of partnership property for partnership purposes.

17. Absolute control, as well as absolute liability, belongs to
    a. a sole proprietor.
    b. a corporate shareholder.
    c. a limited partner.
    d. a trustee.

18. When doing business in California, a corporation chartered in California is
    a. a domestic corporation.
    b. a foreign corporation.
    c. a Real Estate Investment Trust.
    d. a general partnership.

19. Title to a spouse's marital property can be transferred upon death by use of
    a. an oral will.
    b. a tenancy in common.
    c. a living trust.
    d. a letter of intent.

20. A limited partner is
    a. responsible for partnership activities.
    b. a general partner in some instances.
    c. not liable for partnership debts beyond the amount invested.
    d. required to take part in partnership business.

TRANSFERRING REAL ESTATE

LEARNING OBJECTIVES

When you have completed this unit, you will be able to

- **describe** what happens when someone dies and leaves a will;

- **describe** how the California Law of Intestate Succession affects the disposition of community property and separate property;

- **list** the steps involved in a probate sale of real estate;

- **identify** the ways in which property can be increased or acquired that do not involve a purchase;

- **define** the ways in which title to property can be transferred;

- **explain** the requirements for a valid deed; and

- **list** the types of deed used in California.

KEY TERMS

abandonment	easement	probate
accession	easement by	Probate Code
accretion	prescription	quitclaim deed
acknowledgment	eminent domain	Real Estate Fraud
action for declaratory	equitable estoppel	Prosecution Trust
relief	erosion	Fund
action to quiet title	escheat	reconveyance deed
administrator	executor	recording
adverse possession	forfeiture	reliction
after-acquired title	gift deed	request for
alienation	grant	reconveyance
alluvion	grant deed	revocable transfer on
avulsion	grantee	death (TOD) deed
bequest	granting clause	sheriff's deed
certificate of sale	grantor	statutory dedication
chain of title	holographic will	tack
codicil	intestate	tax deed
color of title	intestate succession	testate
common-law	inverse condemnation	testator
dedication	judgment	trust deed
condemnation	judicial foreclosure	trustee in bankruptcy
decedent	action	trustee's deed
deed	legacy	warranty deed
devise	legatee	will
devisee	partition action	writ of execution
devisor	power of sale	

HOW REAL ESTATE MAY BE ACQUIRED

When California was still under Spanish and Mexican rule, no written document was needed to transfer title to California land. A buyer could take title by taking possession at the time of sale. The seller would hand over to the buyer some part of the land (perhaps a twig or clump of dirt) to show transfer of ownership. California courts eventually decided that a written document was necessary to transfer title to land. An exception was made for a contract of sale, in which case the transfer of possession in the old ceremonial way was permissible. After California became a state, the legislature authorized the placing of a written document of transfer in the public records to provide evidence of a land transaction. A deed that is recorded in the county recorder's office is the modern equivalent of the ceremonial transfer of possession.

Real estate can be acquired in any of the following ways, which are discussed in this section:

■ The estate of someone who dies

■ Improvements to land

- Natural forces
- Possession of someone else's property
- Transfer from a private or public owner
- Alienation by operation of law or court action

Will or Succession?

Perhaps the least complicated way to acquire title to real estate is to receive it as part of the estate of someone who has died. The deceased can name the property's new owners in a document called a *will*. If the **decedent**—the person who died— leaves no will, the law determines the property's new owners.

Succession A person who dies without having made a will is said to have died **intestate**. All states make provision by law for distribution of the property of intestate persons. This legal determination of property ownership is called **intestate succession**. Figure 4.1 shows how property ownership is determined under California law. The law applies to both real and personal property. Community, quasi-community, and separate property were defined in Unit 3.

FOR EXAMPLE   A married couple own Sunny Acres as community property. The couple have no children. Who will have title to Sunny Acres if one of the spouses dies without a will? If the couple have eight children and one spouse dies without a will, who will receive title to Sunny Acres?

If a spouse dies without a will specifying otherwise, that spouse's half of the community property, including Sunny Acres, will go to the surviving spouse—regardless of the number of children. The surviving spouse already owns the other half of Sunny Acres, because it is community property. When the first spouse dies, the surviving spouse will own all of Sunny Acres.

Will   A **will** is a document made by an owner of property who is legally competent to do so, to pass title to the property to another after death. The person making a will is called the **testator** (property owner) and is said to die **testate**.

The transfer of title to real estate by a will is called a **devise**. The deceased owner is the **devisor** (property **owner**). The person receiving property by will is a **devisee**. The transfer of property by will, particularly personal property, is also referred to as the **bequest** of a **legacy**; the recipient is a **legatee**.

> A codicil is the easiest way to change the terms of a will.

A transfer of title by will takes effect on the death of the testator. During life, the testator has the right to make a new will or to change a will by adding new or amended provisions through a document called a **codicil**. For this reason, until the testator's death, a devisee has no present interest in the property interest specified in a will.

FIGURE 4.1: **Intestate Succession**

CALIFORNIA LAW OF INTESTATE SUCCESSION

Community Property

If there is a surviving spouse:

■ ½ already belongs to surviving spouse

■ Remaining ½ goes to surviving spouse after decedent's liabilities have been paid

Community Property with Right of Survivorship

If there is a surviving spouse, surviving spouse takes entire property

Separate Property

If there is a surviving spouse and no child:

■ Surviving spouse takes ½

■ Surviving parent; brother or sister; or child of deceased brother or sister; or

■ (if none of these) spouse takes ½

If there is a surviving spouse and one child:

■ Surviving spouse takes ½

■ Child takes ½

If there is a surviving spouse and more than one child:

■ Surviving spouse takes ⅓

■ Children divide ⅔ equally

If there is no surviving spouse or child:

■ Property is distributed to next of kin in order prescribed by California law; if no heirs can be located, the property will escheat to the state

There are two types of wills currently recognized in California: the formal *witnessed will* and the *holographic* (handwritten) *will*. Oral wills are no longer considered legally valid in California.

California Statutory Will

To encourage people to make a will, the California Bar Association has prepared two printed will forms that are available to the public:

■ The California Statutory Will form provides for disposition of the testator's property to the named devisees, typically the testator's spouse and/or children. Space for witnesses' signatures is included.

■ The California Statutory Will with Trust form provides for the establishment of a trust that will hold property for children of the testator until the youngest child is 21 years old. The property held in trust could be used by the named trustee (manager of the trust) for the support and education of the children before the youngest is 21.

The statutory will forms can be obtained from the State Bar of California, 555 Franklin Street, San Francisco, or 1149 South Hill Street, Los Angeles. Addresses of bar association offices can be found at www.calbar.ca.gov. Stationery supply stores also may carry statutory will forms.

www.calbar.ca.gov

Witnessed will   The formal *witnessed will* is a written document. It is normally prepared by an attorney and signed by the testator. The will lists all of the testator's property, specifying the desired disposition of that property on the testator's death. After the testator declares the will to be his, the testator signs it in the presence of at least two witnesses, who then sign the will at the testator's request and in the testator's presence.

> A holographic will is valid if the signature and material provisions are in the handwriting of the testator.

Holographic will   A **holographic will** is one written by hand, dated, and signed by the testator. A holographic will does not need to be witnessed, but it must be entirely handwritten. There can be *no* printed or typewritten parts of a holographic will.

Probate   When properly drawn, a will names an **executor** to act as the decedent's representative in ensuring that the terms of the will are carried out. **Probate** is the name of the court process that determines the decedent's heirs and creditors, pays debts owed by the estate, and transfers title to any remaining property from the decedent to the decedent's heirs.

If there is a will, the decedent's representative presents the will to the probate court and receives permission to carry out its provisions. Sometimes, the deceased leaves no will or fails to name a representative, or the named representative refuses to serve in that capacity. In any of those cases, the court may appoint an **administrator** to handle the estate.

Duties of the estate representative include the following:

- Publishing a *notice to creditors* of the decedent's death
- Conducting an *inventory* and obtaining an *appraisal* of the property in the decedent's estate
- Making a *report* to the probate court of the estate assets and liabilities
- Distributing the *proceeds* of the estate as the court directs

With the court's approval, estate representatives and attorneys may be paid a fee. Expenses incurred in administering the estate, federal and state estate taxes, and claims of creditors are provided for as the probate court approves. Any estate property remaining is distributed to the heirs and devisees.

Probate Sales of Real Estate

The **Probate Code** governs the sale of real property that is part of a probate proceeding. The executor or administrator may sell real property if it is in the best interests of the estate to do so (such as to pay debts or make specific bequests). For probate sales, the following apply:

- The real property may be offered for sale by the estate representative directly *or* through one or more brokers.
- With court permission, the estate representative may grant an exclusive right to sell the property for up to 90 days.
- The estate representative can accept an offer that is then subject to *court confirmation.*
- Broker commissions are subject to statute and court approval.

Accession Accession refers to an increase in the property owned. Manmade or natural additions to property may extend the owner's title to include those additions. These can occur by the construction of *improvements* or by the process of *accretion* or *reliction*.

> Improving land is one way to enhance its value.

Improvements If a landowner puts up a building on the land, that manmade improvement becomes part of the owner's title to the land. If a fixture, such as a new heating system, is added to an existing building, the fixture then becomes part of the real property.

The Unintended Improvement

Sometimes, an improvement is added to land by mistake. There may be a mistake in the address given to the builder, or the lot may have an incorrect address posted on it. Sometimes, the legal description in a deed is recorded incorrectly.

California law provides for what is known as a mistaken improvement. If a fixture is added to property by a person who acted innocently but on mistaken belief as to the property's owner, the fixture may be removed. The owner must be compensated for any damage to the property. The law thus protects an individual acting in good faith but under a mistake of fact (such as property location) or a mistake of law (identity of the rightful owner).

Accretion Land area can be increased by forces of nature. **Accretion** is the process by which land adjacent to a flowing body of water accumulates new soil. The buildup of new soil, called **alluvion** or alluvium, may be so gradual that it is not noticed. Buildup also can be quite dramatic and obvious, as when land is flooded.

FOR EXAMPLE A family owns a vacation cottage on the Russian River. Over the years, the river has deposited soil at the water line. The property's shoreline now extends one foot farther than the last recorded distance to the nearest landmark, a marker in the roadway. Has there been any increase in the square footage owned by the family?

Yes. A survey would show that the total property has increased due to accretion.

But land also may be lost. The natural force of a moving body of water acting gradually or suddenly may wash away or tear land in a process called **avulsion**. You should note that avulsion is distinct from **erosion**, the process by which precipitation (rainfall) wears away the surface of the soil.

Reliction Waters of any moving body of water may permanently recede, uncovering new land that was once under the water. This process, called **reliction**, increases the adjacent owner's property.

Occupancy

Sometimes, you can acquire an ownership right to property by occupying (using) it. Your use must be without the present owner's permission, and the land cannot be publicly owned. The following are three ways in which property, or the right to use property, can be acquired by occupancy:

1. Adverse possession

2. Prescription

3. Abandonment

Adverse possession The concept of taking over someone else's property and occupying it long enough to acquire ownership of it can be appealing, but the reality is much more complex and rarely accomplished. You can acquire title to real estate by **adverse possession** if you follow these five steps:

1. You must occupy the property *openly* and *notoriously*—that is, without hiding the fact from anyone.

2. Your occupancy must be *hostile to the true owner's interests*—in other words, without permission.

3. You must *claim title* to the real estate, whether your claim of right is initiated by the fact of occupancy or by *color of title*. **Color of title** is the possession of a document erroneously appearing to convey title to the occupant. Land boundaries must be fenced or otherwise documented. If the person in possession has color of title, that document will provide a legal description of the land.

4. There must be *continuous possession* for a period of *five years*. You cannot abandon the property during that time, no matter how briefly.

5. You must *pay all real property taxes* during the five years of possession.

An easy way to remember the requirements for adverse possession is by using the acronym *ONCHA*. The possessor's occupancy must be

- **o**pen,

- **n**otorious,

- **c**ontinuous,

- **h**ostile, and

- **a**dverse to the interests of the real owner for five years.

Although the occupancy must be continuous for five years, successive adverse holders may add together, or **tack**, their periods of occupancy. Successive occupiers must take possession under color of title, which means that the new occupier receives a deed from the previous occupier. Even though the deed would not survive a challenge by the property's owner, it must appear on its face to be valid.

Title acquired by adverse possession cannot be insured and generally cannot be conveyed until it has been verified by court decree. The court decree can then be recorded in the county recorder's office.

FOR EXAMPLE Floyd would like to own the acreage next to Mustang Canyon. The Hendersons own the land but rarely visit it. Floyd moves onto the property, builds a shack, fences in 50 acres, and places a sign, "Floyd's Ranch," over the locked entrance gate. Whenever anyone asks about his use of the property, he tells them, "It's mine." Floyd pays the property taxes and lives only on the property.

After two years, Floyd sells "all my right, title, and interest of whatever kind" in the ranch to Jud, giving Jud a deed. Floyd moves off the ranch and Jud promptly moves in, bringing his spouse and six children with him. Jud pays the property taxes and proclaims to everyone that he now owns Floyd's Ranch. After about three years, Jud sells Floyd's Ranch to Aria, who in good faith records the deed Jud gives her and moves onto the land. A few months later, Harry Henderson shows up and is quite upset over what he finds. It has been more than five years since Floyd first moved onto the land. Who owns the land?

Aria owns the land. The adverse possession begun by Floyd and continued by Jud and Aria under color of title ripened into good title at the end of five years. Aria will have to bring a legal action to quiet title (discussed later in this unit) to get the court decree she needs to give notice to the world of the validity of her title.

An individual can claim an easement by prescription.

Prescription   The right to use or to travel over someone else's land is called an **easement**. If an easement is used without permission and the user fulfills all the other requirements for adverse possession—except for paying property taxes—an **easement by prescription** will be created. The use must be exclusive. This means that the person claiming the easement is doing so as the assertion of a private, rather than a public, use. The easement right will be recognized as a result of legal action or by agreement of the parties.

FOR EXAMPLE Marcy owns a small house in La Jolla, California. Although Marcy's house is on a quiet, meandering residential street, she would prefer to have a more direct way to reach the commercial street that lies on the opposite side of the property behind hers. One day, Marcy discovers that there is just enough room along the side of her neighbor's lot for her to drive her car across her neighbor's property to the commercial street. She proceeds to do just that and does so at least once a day for the next six years. Marcy and her neighbor never discuss her use of what has taken on the appearance of a driveway. One day, when she drives home after work, she discovers that her neighbor has erected a chain link fence across the front of his property, blocking the entrance to the driveway she has been using. Does Marcy have the right to object?

Yes, Marcy can object to the fence her neighbor has built. By her continuing use of the driveway for more than five years, Marcy has acquired an easement by prescription to that portion of her neighbor's property. The neighbor may build a fence, but there will have to be a gate so that Marcy can have access.

In the previous example, what would happen if Marcy decided to stop using the driveway across her neighbor's lot? Just as an easement by prescription can be acquired by use, it can be lost by nonuse. If the holder of an easement by prescription fails to use the easement for five years, the easement right is extinguished.

Abandonment   If leased property is abandoned by the lessee (tenant), the lessor (landlord) has the right to reacquire its possession and use. **Abandonment** is more than simple nonuse. A lessee abandons the leasehold interest by leaving the premises and acting in a way that is inconsistent with continuing possession, such as by failing to make rent payments when due, removing one's property from the premises, and filing a change of address with the post office.

Transfer

The ways in which title to real estate can be transferred from the present owner to someone else are highlighted in Figure 4.2 and explained next.

FIGURE 4.2:   Ways to Transfer Real Estate

- Private grant
- Public grant
- Public dedication
- Alienation by operation of law or court action
- Execution sale
- Forfeiture
- Bankruptcy
- Marriage
- Escheat
- Eminent domain
- Equitable estoppel

Private grant   A private grant, also called a **grant deed**, is a written instrument giving the names of both parties and a legal description of the property. The transfer of ownership may be a gift, which requires no consideration (payment) for the deed. The requirements for a deed are explained later in this unit.

Public grant   Title to real estate that was not passed by land grant and affirmed after the war with Mexico became *public land* and part of the territory of the United States. Some public land became the property of the State of California after statehood was granted. It is still possible for the federal or state government to deed public lands by public grant to private parties, as is done when old military installations are sold to developers.

F O R   E X A M P L E   Fort Megan is an Air Force base that has not been used for 25 years because its runways are too short for modern aircraft. The base buildings are in disrepair, and the old landing strips have been devastated by earth movement and neglect. Nevertheless, Fort Megan is located in a densely populated urban area and could be sold for a high price per acre for any purpose allowed by local ordinances.

Public dedication   *Private land* can be transferred for public use or ownership by common-law dedication, statutory dedication, or deed.

A **common-law dedication** occurs when a landowner devotes land to a public use, as when a roadway is opened to public use or described as such in the deeds to adjoining parcels. Under the requirements of the Subdivision Map Act (described in Unit 15), certain areas will be set aside for public use, such as parks, school grounds, and streets. This **statutory dedication** generally transfers an easement for the intended public use, although transfer of fee simple ownership by **deed** is becoming the preferred method of public acquisition. Fee simple title preserves the public character of the land despite the failure of the subdivision itself.

Alienation by operation of law or court action   It is possible to bring a legal action in court for the purpose of clearing or establishing title to real estate, despite the opposition of the owner of record. **Alienation** (transfer) of title may be involuntary, that is, without the original owner's consent.

An **action to quiet title** is brought to force others who have claims to the property to prove those claims or have the claims ruled invalid by the court. This is the usual method of establishing title by adverse possession and of clearing tax titles or title acquired on a forfeited contract of sale.

A **partition action** is brought by a co-owner of property to force a severance of the co-owners' respective interests. As explained in Unit 3, the co-owner can be a tenant in common or a joint tenant. The property is divided, if possible, or sold. After a sale, the court divides the proceeds according to the owners' shares.

FOR EXAMPLE   Linda and Sheila, twin sisters, own a house as tenants in common. Linda wants to sell her share but can't find a buyer, and Sheila doesn't want to sell. What can Linda do?

Linda can bring a partition action in court. The court will sell the house unless the property can be divided into two equal parcels, and it will distribute the proceeds to the two sisters.

A **power of sale** gives the trustee under a trust deed the ability to sell the property to satisfy the unpaid debt if the debtor defaults. A mortgage or another lien document also may provide a power of sale for the mortgagee or lienholder. Trust deeds and mortgages are discussed in Unit 8.

In a **judicial foreclosure action**, the holder of a trust deed, a mortgage, or other lien on property requests a court-supervised sale of the property to cover the unpaid balance on the delinquent debt.

In an **action for declaratory relief**, the parties petition the court for a determination of their respective rights before a controversy arises. When a deed is ambiguous, an action for declaratory relief may be brought to avoid later problems.

Execution sale   The party who wins a legal action may receive a **judgment** from the court that includes the award of money damages against the losing party. The holder of the judgment can file the judgment in any county in the state in which the debtor owns property and then seek a writ of execution.

> If you buy real estate at an execution sale, you will receive a sheriff's deed.

A **writ of execution** is a court order directing the county sheriff or another officer to satisfy a judgment out of the debtor's property. The property available to satisfy the judgment includes any nonexempt real property owned by the debtor. The property is sold at public auction, and the proceeds are used to pay the judgment.

When *personal property* is sold at auction, the buyer receives a **certificate of sale**. When real property is sold at auction, the buyer receives a **sheriff's deed**. The officer who conducts the sale must record a duplicate of the sheriff's deed in the office of the county recorder.

Forfeiture **Forfeiture** occurs if a condition subsequent in a deed is breached. The grantor (or the grantor's successor) then has the right to reacquire title.

Bankruptcy The U.S. Congress has sole authority to enact bankruptcy laws, and it enforces those laws through the *federal bankruptcy courts*. In a liquidation bankruptcy, a debtor's property is sold to cover debts. The **trustee in bankruptcy** carries out the sale, and the buyer receives a *trustee's deed*.

Marriage Property acquired during marriage or by registered domestic partners that is not separate property is *community property* by operation of law, as explained in Unit 3. One spouse acting alone cannot defeat the other spouse's interest in that property.

Escheat California law presumes that every person who dies has an heir who could take title to the decedent's property. Sometimes, however, it is impossible to locate an heir. The attorney general acts on behalf of the state to bring a claim against the estate and, if no claimant comes forward within five years, title to the property vests in the state. This process is called **escheat**.

Eminent domain The federal and state governments have the right to acquire title to property by **eminent domain**. If property is for a public purpose such as highway construction, it is first subject to **condemnation**, a process that gives notice to the property owner that the property is being taken. The property owner receives compensation based on an *appraisal*, which usually is the property's fair market value. *Fair market value*, the price a property should bring on the open market, will be explained more fully in Unit 13.

Sometimes, property that has not been condemned is damaged or its use is affected by a nearby public activity. When that happens, the affected property owners may seek money damages in a legal action claiming **inverse condemnation**. For instance, if a new highway blocks off the access road to adjoining properties, those properties will lose value. The property owners will expect to be compensated for the loss in value.

The U.S. Supreme Court, in *Kelo v. New London*, 545 U.S. 469 (2005), held that private property can be condemned by a public entity for transfer to a new private owner to further economic development. There was a strong response to this decision at all levels of government. President George W. Bush issued an executive order in 2006 limiting the federal government's use of eminent domain to purposes that benefit the general public and not merely for the purpose of the economic interest of private parties. Various states, including Arizona, have passed legislation prohibiting use of eminent domain for other than public purposes. Proposition 99, passed by California voters in 2008, amends the state constitution to affirm existing California law by prohibiting state and local governments from acquiring an owner-occupied residence by eminent domain for conveyance to a private person or business entity, with a few exceptions.

Equitable estoppel   A person may convey or appear to convey a property interest she does not yet own but may acquire at some future time. Such **after-acquired title** must be transferred to the new owner. The doctrine of **equitable estoppel** (a common-law theory meant to prevent unjust enrichment) prohibits a refusal to make the transfer. Equitable estoppel also prevents fraud or misrepresentation by the present owner of property. If a property owner misrepresents her ownership (whether by act or omission) to a person who then buys the property from another person who is the apparent owner, the true owner must convey the property to the innocent party.

FOR EXAMPLE   Max owns Blackacre but does not want Jose to know. One day, when Max, Jose, and Carlo are together, Jose asks Max and Carlo if one of them owns Blackacre. Carlo says he owns Blackacre, and Max doesn't object. Jose then pays Carlo for Blackacre. Who owns Blackacre?

Jose owns Blackacre. Max is equitably estopped from denying Jose's ownership. By his conduct, Max allowed Jose to believe he was buying Blackacre from Carlo. Max will be left with an action for damages against Carlo, who has pocketed the money Jose paid for Blackacre.

Exercise 4-1

1. George married Helen in January 2008. In March 2010, Helen's father died, leaving Helen his condominium in Palm Springs. Who owns the condominium and in what form of ownership?

2. George and Helen, who married in 2008, purchased a house in 2012. Who will the law presume to own the house and in what form of ownership?

3. In 2016, George and Helen are notified by the city that their property is being considered as the site of a new sports arena. They protest the city's plans at a public hearing but are unsuccessful in halting the construction. Can the city take their house?

4. George and Helen paid $746,000 for their house in 2012. In 2016, the city offers them $746,000 for the property. Do they have to accept?

5. George decides to leave his half of the community property he owns with Helen to his sister Davida and has a will drawn up to that effect. When George dies, Helen is surprised when Davida claims to own half of "her" home. Can George do that?

6. Angel knows that "squatters" have moved onto the "back 40" of his ranch and have even put up a fence, but Angel is too busy to do anything about it. Even after he hears that the squatters are building a house, Angel doesn't object. He feels smug that somebody is stupid enough to build a house on his land—and pay taxes, to boot. Six years later, Angel tries to sell his ranch, but the buyer says that he can't get a loan because Angel doesn't have clear title to all of the land. Angel brings an action to quiet title in court. Will he win?

7. Tim Brown holds a mortgage on the house of Sara Nelson, who is having financial difficulties and has missed all of her mortgage payments for the past six months. What can Tim do?

8. Uncle Henry died without a will. Did he die testate? What is the name of the legal process by which his property will be distributed to his heirs?

9. Lydia and Miguel own a small resort on the Colorado River with about 200 feet of lawn on a small bluff overlooking the river. Following torrential rains and flooding, Lydia and Miguel find they have only 130 feet of lawn area. What happened to the 70 feet of ground? What is this process called?

DEEDS

A deed is the document that transfers title to real property. There are many types of deeds that can be used to convey title to real estate. This section describes the requirements for a valid conveyance by deed and examines the different forms of deeds and their legal distinctions.

Elements of a Valid Deed

A **deed** is a written instrument that, when properly executed, delivered, and accepted, conveys title to real property. Title is conveyed by **grant** (transfer) from one person (the **grantor**, who is the property owner) to another (the **grantee**). The words of conveyance appear in the **granting clause**. Transfer of title by deed may be the voluntary or involuntary act of the parties, as in the case of a foreclosure sale when title is transferred by operation of law.

The specific legal requirements for a valid deed are listed in Figure 4.3. If all of the requirements for a valid deed are not met, the deed may be questioned even years after the property has been conveyed.

FIGURE 4.3:   Requirements for a Valid Deed

1. The deed must be in writing.

2. There must be a description of the parties. The full name and marital status of each should be given.

3. The grantor must be legally capable of executing a written conveyance. Generally, this means the grantor must be an adult of sound mind. The requirements are the same as those to create a valid contract (discussed in Unit 7). The grantee of a gift can be an incompetent or a minor but cannot be a fictitious person.

4. There must be an adequate description of the property being conveyed, preferably using one or more of the methods discussed in Unit 2.

5. There must be a granting clause in which the necessary language of conveyance is used, such as the words *grant* or *convey*. The words "to have and to hold" (the *habendum clause*) are not necessary.

6. The deed must be signed by the grantor(s).

7. The deed must be delivered to the grantee and accepted by the grantee. The grantor must have the present intention of conveying and the ability to convey the property.

FOR EXAMPLE   Ted gives a deed to Nicole, telling her it will take effect on his death. Is the deed valid?

The deed is not a valid conveyance, even at Ted's death. Delivery means exactly that—the grantor holds nothing back. There can be no conditions.

It is possible to deliver a deed to a third party to be released to the grantee on the fulfillment of a *condition precedent*. In that case, however, the acceptance is conditioned, not the delivery. A *condition subsequent* might be placed in the deed itself that would invalidate it if the grantee failed to fulfill the condition.

Note that although there is no legal requirement that a deed be dated, in practice, dating a deed is preferred because delivery and acceptance will be presumed to have occurred on that date.

> "Love and affection" are the only considerations needed for a valid deed.

You should remember that a deed is not a contract. A deed has different elements and is subject to different rules regarding validity. The elements of a contract are discussed in Unit 7. A deed, unlike a contract, does not need to be supported by consideration; that is, the grantee does not need to pay anything in return for the conveyance. If fraud is suspected, however, as when property is deeded without consideration or with nominal consideration—say, $10—shortly before the grantor declares bankruptcy, the deed may be set aside by a court.

There is no legal requirement that a deed be witnessed, that the grantor's signature be verified by any third person, or that the deed be recorded in the county recorder's office. Nevertheless, these steps are practical necessities to prevent future problems. Acknowledgment and recording of deeds are discussed following the exercise.

Exercise 4-2

Assuming all other requirements have been met, has a valid deed been created in each of the following cases?

1. Gerald Stone is selling Greenacre, the family estate. Gerald is out of the country at the time the sale is to be closed but phones the broker handling the transaction to tell her to go ahead with the sale and deliver possession to the buyer. Gerald intends to sign the deed when he returns.

2. Aunt Nellie is incapable of caring for herself. To help her out, her niece Roberta takes Aunt Nellie into her home. In return, Roberta asks Aunt Nellie to deed her condominium to her. Aunt Nellie does not realize what is happening, and Roberta guides her hand as she signs a deed. Who owns the condo?

3. Jed is a high-powered real estate investor. Over the phone he persuades Sol to sell him a 20-unit apartment building in San Diego. Jed is anxious to get the property and tells Sol to convey the property to him over the phone while his secretary takes notes. Jed tells Sol, "Your word is as good as gold."

4. Angela Dell agrees to sell her farm to her friend Diego. The deed from Angela describes the property as "the old Dell place, including 100 acres, more or less." Does Diego have a problem?

5. Uncle Anthony decides to make a present of his Hillsborough estate to his nephew Richard. He prepares a deed, reciting "love and affection" as the consideration, and places the deed in an envelope marked, "To be opened upon my death." He then places the envelope in his safe-deposit box. Will Richard own the estate when his uncle dies?

Acknowledgment and Recording

California law requires that most written instruments affecting title to real property be acknowledged before they can be recorded in the county recorder's office. Besides deeds, those instruments include the following:

- Loan documents
- Agreements for sale
- Option agreements
- Deposit receipts
- Commission receipts
- Any affidavits concerning one of these documents

A document does not have to be recorded to be valid. The process of recording is important, however, because it is the primary way to give notice to the world of an interest that affects title to real estate.

Acknowledgment A document is *executed* when it is signed. A person who has executed a document can make a declaration, called an **acknowledgment**, that the execution is the person's own act. An acknowledgment may be made anywhere within California before an authorized official—typically, a notary public—who cannot be a party to the transaction or related to a party to the transaction. An acknowledgment may be made outside California if local laws are followed and that fact is certified by the person taking the acknowledgment.

> A notary public will verify your signature and take your thumbprint.

Persons authorized to take an acknowledgment in California include judges, court clerks, and notary publics. A notary public, in addition to signing the document, must stamp it with the seal required by the state. When notarizing a deed (including a quitclaim deed or deed of trust, discussed later in this unit), the thumbprint of the grantor must be placed in the notary's official journal.

An acknowledgment alone, without recording the document, serves as notice of the conveyance to the parties and to persons knowing of it. Possession of the property involved also gives notice of ownership. The legal protection of an acknowledged but unrecorded document is not very great. The ordinary transaction does not involve many people, and only those who already know of the transaction are considered aware of it.

Recording The safest way of ensuring that one's title to property is unquestioned is by **recording** the deed that conveys the property. The deed is brought to the office of the county recorder in the county where the property is located. As a general rule, "first in time is first in right." This means that, if more than one person claims title from the same grantor, the first to record a deed will be the successful claimant.

To be recorded, a deed must give an address of the grantee to which tax bills can be sent. A county may add up to $2 to its recording fees for a **Real Estate Fraud Prosecution Trust Fund** to help district attorneys and law enforcement agencies deter, investigate, and prosecute real property fraud crimes.

Building the Chain of Title

The recorder's office files instruments under the parties' names, so the full name of both grantor and grantee must be given. If the grantor's name is not given exactly as it appears in the conveyance to the grantor, it may not be possible to complete that "link" in the **chain of title**.

Most title searches are conducted by tracking the grantor's interest backward in time, then tracking the first recorded grantee's interest forward. To discover all the links in the chain of title, the grantor of the present conveyance should be found as the grantee of a preceding conveyance, the grantor of that conveyance should be the grantee of an earlier conveyance, and so on.

Although variance in the use of a middle name is not necessarily fatal to the validity of a deed, the better practice is to use the full name rather than an initial in place of the middle name.

A fictitious name, or *alias*, may be used to receive title to property, provided the same name is used in any subsequent conveyance. Title cannot be conveyed to a fictitious person, however. Title can be conveyed to a corporation, because a corporation is a recognized legal entity.

The system of making documents a part of the public record works to the advantage of the property owner as well as a prospective buyer or lessee. The property owner is able to give constructive notice to the world of the fact of his ownership. In theory, by inspecting the public record the prospective buyer or lessee can have the confidence of knowing that he is dealing with the recorded owner of the property. (The buyer or lessee still needs to verify that someone else isn't in possession of the property, of course.)

Financing instruments are also recorded to give constructive notice of the lien rights of the lender and are discussed in Unit 8.

Types of Deeds

Grant deed A typical form of **grant deed** appears in Figure 4.4. Notice that the form contains the word *grant(s)*. The deed form is simple and provides for the deed to be acknowledged and recorded.

The grantor makes *implied warranties* in executing a grant deed. These are items the grantee must assume to be true, or the deed would be meaningless. Implied warranties are legally enforceable even though they are not mentioned in the deed. The grantor warrants that

- the grantor's interest in the property has not already been conveyed, and

- there are no undisclosed encumbrances on the property, such as tax liens, brought about by the grantor or any person who might claim title from the grantor.

FIGURE 4.4: **Individual Grant Deed**

RECORDING REQUESTED BY

WHEN RECORDED MAIL TO
AND MAIL TAX STATEMENTS TO

NAME

ADDRESS

CITY
STATE & ZIP

GRANT DEED

TITLE ORDER NO.   ESCROW NO.   APN NO.

THE UNDERSIGNED GRANTOR(s) DECLARE(s)
DOCUMENTARY TRANSFER TAX is $_____ CITY TAX $_____
☐ computed on full value of property conveyed, or ☐ computed on full value less value of liens or encumbrances remaining at time of sale,
☐ Unincorporated area: ☐ City of _____, and

FOR A VALUABLE CONSIDERATION, receipt of which is hereby acknowledged,

hereby GRANT(s) to

the following described real property in the County of   State of California:

Dated_____   _____

                                                     _____

State of California
County of _____
On _____before me, (here insert name and title of the officer), personally appeared _____,
who proved to me on the basis of satisfactory evidence to be the person(s) whose name(s) is/are subscribed to the within
instrument and acknowledged to me that he/she/they executed the same in his/her/their authorized capacity(ies), and that by
his/her/their signature(s) on the instrument the person(s), or the entity upon behalf of which the person(s) acted, executed the
instrument.
**I certify under PENALTY OF PERJURY under the laws of the State of California that the foregoing paragraph is true
and correct.**
WITNESS my hand and official seal.
Signature _____ (Seal)

DOCUMENT PROVIDED BY STEWART TITLE OF CALIFORNIA, INC.   GRNTDEED.DOC

Source: Reprinted by permission of Stewart Title of California, Inc.

Note that the grantor does not warrant that she has a present interest in the property to convey. If the grantor attempts to convey property the grantor will acquire after the execution of the grant deed, the deed will become effective at the time such after-acquired title is received by the grantor. The grant deed is the only form of deed that conveys after-acquired title.

Gift deed Although the grant deed form leaves space for the consideration paid by the grantee, it may be used to convey property as a **gift deed** by supplying the words "love and affection" as the consideration received. As noted earlier, such a conveyance may not be made to defraud creditors of the grantor.

Quitclaim deed A **quitclaim deed** conveys any interest the grantor may have in the property at the time the deed is executed. No implied warranties are made by a quitclaim deed, and there is no express or implied warranty that the grantor owns any interest at all in the property. A quitclaim deed should never be used when a grant deed can be used.

A quitclaim deed does ensure that whatever interest the grantor may have in the property is conveyed to the grantee. The quitclaim deed is a commonly used way of clearing a *cloud on the title* and eliminating any future claim by the grantor of the quitclaim deed. There can be no after-acquired title with a quitclaim, however.

The grantor of a quitclaim deed remains liable for any loans made using the property as security.

FOR EXAMPLE Harvey Anderson bought Whiteacre after he married Anna, but Harvey used money from the sale of his separate property to do so. When Harvey sold Whiteacre, he signed the deed as Harvey Anderson, a married man. His spouse did not sign the deed. The grantee of Whiteacre questioned the validity of that conveyance when years later a would-be purchaser was unable to acquire title insurance.

The *cloud on the title* of the present owner of Whiteacre was cleared by having Anna Anderson sign a quitclaim deed, relinquishing whatever claim she might have in the property.

Warranty deed A **warranty deed** expressly warrants that the grantor has good title. The grantor's warranty makes the grantor liable for a flaw in the title affecting the buyer's interest that may be discovered later, even if the grantor had no previous knowledge of it. This form of guarantee, while attractive to a property buyer, could be devastating to a property seller. It is one reason why title insurance is required (particularly by lenders) in most transactions in California. By shifting the liability to the insurer, the seller can be assured that there will be no future liability caused by an undiscovered defect in the seller's title. In turn, the buyer can rely on the resources of the title insurer if any problem covered by the title insurance should arise.

Trust deed The **trust deed**, also called *deed of trust* (shown in Figure 8.3) is used when property serves as security for a debt. The debt typically is the loan used to purchase the property, but it can be any loan using the property as collateral to guarantee payment of the amount borrowed. The requirements for creation of a security interest in real estate are in Unit 8.

When the purchaser of property borrows money to finance the purchase, the borrower (new *owner*) is the *trustor* (the *grantor*) of the trust deed. The *trustee* (the *grantee*) is the party who holds title until the debt is paid. The *beneficiary*, the party on whose behalf the title is held, is the *lender*. If the underlying debt is not paid, the trustee has the power to sell the property at a foreclosure sale and pay the beneficiary the amount of the remaining indebtedness from the proceeds. Any money left over would go to the trustor. The purchaser would receive a **trustee's deed** from the trustee.

Reconveyance deed   A **reconveyance deed** executed by the trustee is the means by which the trustee returns title to the trustor when the debt is paid off. The beneficiary notifies the trustee that the debt has been cleared by sending the trustee a document called a **request for reconveyance**.

Sheriff's deed   A sheriff's deed is given to the purchaser at a court-ordered sale to satisfy a judgment. A sheriff's deed carries no warranties.

Tax deed   A **tax deed** is issued by the county tax collector if property is sold because of nonpayment of taxes. Tax collection procedures are discussed in Unit 11.

Transfer on Death Deed   A new form of nonprobate transfer of real property was created in 2015 by statute, though the statute will be in effect only until January 1, 2021. A **revocable transfer on death (TOD) deed** transfers real property on the death of its owner without a probate proceeding, provided it is lawfully created. The grantor must have the capacity to contract to make or revoke the deed, the deed must be in the required form, and it must be signed, dated, acknowledged, and recorded. During the owner's life, the deed does not affect ownership rights and is part of the owner's estate for the purpose of Medi-Cal eligibility and reimbursement. The TOD deed is only available for use on a residence of one to four units, a condominium, or a parcel of agricultural land of 40 acres or less that contains a residence.

If, at the time of the owner's death, the property is titled in joint tenancy or as community property with right of survivorship, the deed is void. The law establishes priorities for creditor claims against the property owner and the beneficiary of the deed in connection with the property, as well as limits on the liability of the beneficiary. There is also a procedure for contesting the transfer of real property by a revocable TOD deed.

The California Law Revision commission will study the success of the TOD deed and make recommendations regarding its findings to the legislature by January 1, 2020.

Exercise 4-3

What type of deed would most likely be used in each of the following situations?

1. All-cash sale of a single-family residence

2. Deed from possible former co-owner of property

3. Loan secured by deed

4. Conveyance from grandfather to grandson in consideration of grandson's "love and affection"

5. Deed to someone who has just paid off a home loan

6. Deed received after purchase of property at a court-ordered sale

SUMMARY

A person who dies **testate** leaves a **will**. The **testator (decedent)** can devise her property to a **devisee**. By **bequest**, a **legacy** of personal property can be transferred to a **legatee**. A formal witnessed will is a written document complying with legal formalities. A **holographic will** is written entirely in the handwriting of the testator. The law of **intestate succession** provides for distribution of the property of a person who dies without leaving a valid will.

Land situated along a moving body of water may be increased by **accretion** as **alluvion** (alluvium) is deposited on the shoreline. If water recedes, there may be **reliction** of land. The movement of water may diminish the land area at shoreline by **avulsion**.

By occupying land for five years, paying taxes, and claiming possession, one can acquire title by **adverse possession**. Successive owners under **color of title** can **tack** their periods of ownership. An **easement by prescription** to travel over land may be acquired in a similar fashion, but without paying taxes.

The holder of a *leasehold* interest may abandon that interest, and the landlord again may have the right of present use or possession.

Title to real estate may be transferred by **deed**, whether private or public. Land may be *dedicated* to public use, as when a developer builds streets through a subdivision.

Alienation is an involuntary transfer of title. An **action to quiet title**, a **partition action**, a **foreclosure action**, and an **action for declaratory relief** are some of the ways the courts can be called on to settle property disputes.

A **writ of execution** by the court orders the sheriff to sell a debtor's property. The buyer receives a **certificate of sale** or a **sheriff's deed**. Title could change by **forfeiture** if a **condition subsequent** were breached. A **trustee in bankruptcy** may sell real property to acquire funds for creditors. The buyer receives a **trustee's**

deed. Property acquired during marriage that is not separate property is *community property*.

The right of **eminent domain** enables a governing body to *condemn*, or take, land for a public purpose. The actions of a property owner or prospective property owner may later **equitably estop**, or prevent, him from denying the property rights of another.

Transfer of ownership of property by **deed** must name a **grantor** and **grantee** and describe the property to be conveyed. The correct words of grant must be used, depending on the type of deed. The deed is effective once it has been delivered to the grantee and accepted. If the grantor's action is acknowledged, the deed can be **recorded** and will enter the property's **chain of title**.

Implied warranties are given in a **grant deed** by the **grantor**, who also may convey **after-acquired title**. A **quitclaim deed** gives no such warranties and cannot convey after-acquired title, but it may clear a *cloud on the title*. A **warranty deed** gives *express* (stated) *warranties*. A **trust deed** enables a *trustee* to hold title until a debt is paid to the *beneficiary* by the *trustor*. If the debt is paid, a **reconveyance deed** will put title back in the trustor. A **sheriff's deed** is given following a forced sale of real estate. A **revocable transfer on death (TOD) deed**, when properly created, will transfer title without going through a probate proceeding.

OPEN FOR DISCUSSION

A claim of title by adverse possession often is used as a fallback position when title is challenged by legal action.

1. When could such a claim be made?

REVIEW QUESTIONS

1. A person who dies without a will dies
   a. testate.
   b. intestate.
   c. with an executor.
   d. in eminent domain.

2. The testator names
   a. an executor or executrix.
   b. a testator.
   c. a devisor.
   d. an administrator or administratrix.

3. Someone who receives real property by will is called
   a. a devise.
   b. a devisee.
   c. a testator.
   d. a codicil.

4. A typewritten will must be
   a. made by a competent person.
   b. signed by the testator.
   c. witnessed.
   d. all of these.

5. A statutory will is
   a. signed and witnessed.
   b. telegraphic.
   c. oral.
   d. invalid.

6. A holographic will is
   a. oral.
   b. telegraphic.
   c. handwritten.
   d. witnessed.

7. The probate court appoints
   a. an executor or executrix.
   b. a testator.
   c. a devisee.
   d. an administrator or administratrix.

8. When soil is deposited on a riverbank, gradually building out the land, this process is called
   a. accretion.
   b. alluvion.
   c. avulsion.
   d. subsidence.

9. When flood conditions cause land to be washed away, this is known as
   a. accretion.
   b. alluvion.
   c. avulsion.
   d. accession.

10. When water recedes, creating a new shoreline, the process is called
   a. accretion.
   b. alluvion.
   c. avulsion.
   d. reliction.

11. Elena moves onto Mike's land, builds a home, pays the property taxes, and claims she owns the property. When will she have good title, even against Mike?
   a. After 1 year
   b. After 3 years
   c. After 5 years
   d. After 10 years

12. Elena's friend Carl, who used to own the property in question 11, gave her a phony deed to Mike's land. Elena, who does not know the deed is phony, has
   a. a worthless document.
   b. color of title.
   c. a good title.
   d. to share the title with Mike.

13. The right to travel over the property of someone else is
   a. an easement.
   b. equitable estoppel.
   c. a fixture.
   d. statutory dedication by deed.

14. A cotenant who wants property that is co-owned to be sold would bring
    a. a foreclosure action.
    b. an action for declaratory relief.
    c. an action to quiet title.
    d. a partition action.

15. In event of default, real property may be sold without court action if the mortgage or other lien instrument contains
    a. a trust deed.
    b. a power of sale.
    c. a tax deed.
    d. a right of entry.

16. The court order following a judgment for money is
    a. a certificate of sale.
    b. a special limitation.
    c. a writ of execution.
    d. a trustee in bankruptcy.

17. The power of the state to take private property for public use is called
    a. eminent domain.
    b. equitable estoppel.
    c. a public grant.
    d. abandonment.

18. To be effective, a deed must be
    a. made on a printed form.
    b. signed by the grantor.
    c. delivered to the grantee by the grantor personally.
    d. all of these.

19. The transfer of title from grantor to grantee, and from that grantee to a subsequent grantee, and so on, is called
    a. a cloud on the title.
    b. the chain of title.
    c. delivery and acceptance.
    d. an acknowledgment.

20. Legal title conveyed by a deed of trust may be regained by
    a. a warranty deed.
    b. a trust deed.
    c. a reconveyance deed.
    d. a sheriff's deed.

UNIT FIVE

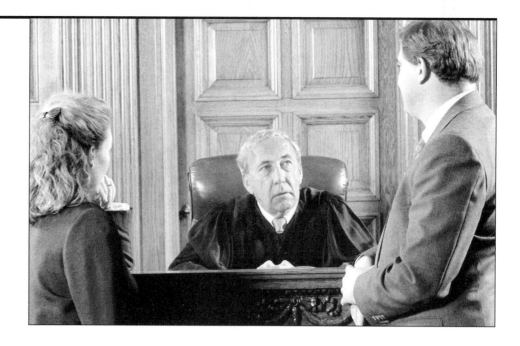

ENCUMBRANCES

LEARNING OBJECTIVES

When you have completed this unit, you will be able to

- **distinguish** a voluntary and involuntary lien;

- **identify** the persons entitled to a mechanic's lien;

- **describe** the notice requirements applicable to a mechanic's lien;

- **define** an attachment, judgment, and writ of execution;

- **describe** the bankruptcy proceeding;

- **list** the types of easements and licenses and **describe** how they can be created;

- **list** the most common forms of property restriction; and

- **identify** the persons entitled to a homestead exemption and the amount of the exemption in each case.

KEY TERMS

abstract of judgment	encumbrance	payment bond
attachment	equity	plaintiff
bankruptcy	express grant	power of eminent
CC&Rs	express reservation	domain
cloud on the title	general lien	preliminary notice
condition	homestead	priority of claims
covenant	homestead exemption	restraint on alienation
deed restriction	injunction	restriction
defendant	involuntary lien	satisfaction
dominant tenement	judgment	servient tenement
easement	license	six-month rule
easement appurtenant	lien	specific lien
easement by	lien release	starting time
condemnation	lien release bond	tax lien
easement by	marketable title	trustee in bankruptcy
implication of law	mechanic's lien	trustee's deed
easement by necessity	notice of cessation	voluntary lien
easement by	notice of completion	writ of execution
prescription	notice of	zoning
easement in gross	nonresponsibility	
encroachment		

ENCUMBRANCES TO REAL ESTATE

An **encumbrance** is anything that has an effect on an owner's

- fee simple title to real estate or
- use of the property.

Some limitations on property use benefit property owners. Property use is often regulated by deed restrictions and other devices of control. Deeds to property in most housing subdivisions require that owners maintain property improvements for the benefit of all property owners in the subdivision. Government controls, such as zoning ordinances, also serve to regulate property use for the public good.

Because it can limit the transferability or use of property, an encumbrance may affect the property's value. A **marketable title** to real estate is one that a prudent buyer would accept. Certain encumbrances will not affect the property's marketability, but others will, meaning that the property will not be worth as much as long as it is burdened by the encumbrance.

There may be a **cloud on the title**. This means that there is some reason why the owner's interest is less than perfect. With a cloud on the title, the property may not be marketable or it may be marketable only at a reduced price because of the questionable title. A careful buyer may demand that the cloud be removed before title to the property is conveyed. The quitclaim deed (mentioned in Unit 4) is one way in which a cloud on the title can be cleared.

This unit examines many possible encumbrances, including liens, judgments, easements, deed restrictions, and encroachments. One of the most important impediments to good title to real estate is the *lien*.

LIENS

A **lien** is an encumbrance that makes property security for the payment of a debt or discharge of an obligation. A **general lien** applies to all property of the debtor and a **specific lien** applies only to identified property, such as a parcel of real estate. Examples of liens include the following:

- The judgment of a court (general)

- A financing instrument, such as a trust deed (specific)

- The mechanic's lien given to someone who helps improve property (specific)

It would be much more difficult to finance land purchases and building construction if a lien on the real estate were not possible. A lien also may be used to refinance a loan, borrow additional money, or initiate a line of credit. The fact that land and improvements to land can be used as security gives lenders and builders some guarantee of payment.

A **voluntary lien** is one agreed to by the property owner. A mortgage or deed of trust that an owner of real estate gives to obtain financing is an example of a voluntary lien. Voluntary liens are covered in Unit 8.

An **involuntary lien** is one that is imposed without the agreement of the property owner. Involuntary liens are made possible by laws that prescribe ways in which unpaid debts can be used by creditors or government agencies to create the burden of a lien on the property. A **tax lien**, for example, is an involuntary lien that arises from a taxpayer's obligation to pay

- real property taxes,

- state income and estate taxes, or

- federal income, gift, and estate taxes.

Tax liens will be covered in Unit 11. Some other forms of involuntary liens are mechanics' liens, judgments, and attachments, discussed in this unit.

Mechanics' Liens

The **mechanic's lien** is used to help secure payment for any labor, service, equipment, or materials used in the construction of improvements to real estate. The mechanic's lien is an important protection rooted in the California Constitution. It is considered so important, any contract provision that purports to waive the right to a mechanic's lien has been held to be against public policy, void, and unenforceable.

A mechanic is anyone who performs such work or furnishes the material used in the work. Persons entitled to a mechanic's lien include all those who work or supply materials at the request of the property owner, or any contractor, subcontractor, sub-subcontractor, architect, builder, or other person placed in charge of all or part of a project. A mechanic's lien is available to the following:

- Material suppliers
- Contractors
- Subcontractors
- Equipment lessors
- Architects
- Registered engineers
- Licensed land surveyors
- Machinists
- Truckers
- Laborers

A mechanic's lien thus can be claimed by a subcontractor, such as a plumber, electrician, or roofer, even though the property's owner never dealt directly with the person claiming the lien. One way to guard against possible claims is to require that the contractor obtain a **payment bond**. The bonding company compensates the owner if the contractor defaults in the performance of contract obligations, such as the payment of workers and suppliers.

Important notice and filing requirements are specified by law for making a mechanic's lien claim. The summary shown here should not be used as the sole guide as to when to initiate a lien. As with any form of legal action, the advice of an attorney experienced in such matters should be sought first.

Enforcement and termination   A mechanic's lien may be terminated by the claimant's voluntary release of the lien. A **lien release** should be filed with the county recorder to prevent a cloud on the owner's title.

A mechanic's lien must be enforced within 90 days after the filing of the lien claim. If credit is extended, notice of the extension must be filed within 90 days after filing the lien, and the extension cannot be for more than one year after completion of the work.

Enforcement of a mechanic's lien is by *foreclosure*, which will bring about a judicial sale of the property. The lienholder is paid out of the proceeds of the sale. The owner receives only what remains after all claimants have been paid.

The Mechanic's Lien

Preliminary Notice

Notice of the right to file a mechanic's lien should be made within 20 days of the time the work begins or the materials are furnished. A direct contract with the property owner serves this purpose. Otherwise, a **preliminary notice** is hand-delivered or sent by first-class registered or certified mail to the

- property owner,
- general contractor (if any), and
- construction lender (if any).

Preliminary notice need not be given by someone who is under direct contract with the owner, performs actual labor for wages, or is entitled to a lien or payment bond.

Starting Time

The **starting time** is the date the construction project begins. The starting time determines when the preliminary notice (if required) must be given.

Completion Time

The project is completed when

- work stops and the owner (or owner's agent) uses the improvement;
- the owner (or owner's agent) accepts the work;
- work has been stopped for 60 continuous days; or
- the owner has filed a **notice of cessation** after work has been stopped for 30 continuous days.

The **notice of completion** may be filed by the owner with the county recorder within 10 days after the work is completed.

Filing Time

A mechanic's lien for unpaid work or materials is filed with the county recorder.

If notice of completion (or cessation) was not filed by the owner, all claimants have **90 days** after completion of the work of improvement to file the mechanic's lien.

If notice of completion (or cessation) was filed, a contractor of all or part of the job must file the mechanic's lien within **60 days** from the filing date of the notice. Everyone else has **30 days** from the filing date of the notice in which to file a mechanic's lien.

Notice of nonresponsibility   What protection does the owner of real estate have if unauthorized work is begun on the property? The owner can *post* a **notice of nonresponsibility** in a conspicuous place on the land and *record* a copy of the notice with the county recorder. The same procedure may be followed by anyone else having an interest in the land, such as the holder of a lease, who notices unauthorized work being done.

If you didn't authorize work on your property, you must post and record within 10 days.

The notice of nonresponsibility must be posted and recorded within 10 days of learning of the construction, repair, or other work. The notice of nonresponsibility must include the following:

- A property description

■ The name, address, and property interest of the person giving notice

■ A brief statement that the person giving notice is not responsible for any claims arising from the work

FOR EXAMPLE   Landlord Inosencia Rivera saw a contractor's truck outside her small apartment building on Sacramento Street. When she inquired, Inosencia was told by a man in a painter's jumpsuit, "The building is being remodeled." Inosencia never agreed to remodel the building, and she manages the building herself. What can she do?

As soon as possible, but at least within 10 days, Inosencia should post a notice of nonresponsibility at the entrance to the building and file a copy of the notice in the county recorder's office.

How to Stop a Lien Foreclosure

A property owner who disputes the correctness or validity of a mechanic's lien can stop the foreclosure on the property.

The owner must file a **lien release bond** in the county recorder's office where the lien was recorded. The bond must be issued by an authorized California surety. The amount of the bond must equal 150% of either the entire claim or the portion of the claim allocated to the parcel(s) sought to be released. The amount of the bond will be available to cover the lien claimant's possible recovery, including costs of bringing legal action.

A lien release bond also can be filed by anyone having an interest in the property, such as the lender, or by any original contractor or subcontractor affected by the claimed lien.

Exercise 5-1

C. L. Drake is general contractor on the Bigelow Building remodeling job. C. L. signed a written agreement for the work with Busby Bigelow, the property's owner. Busby, a wealthy but eccentric individual, decided halfway through the project that the design was "all wrong." It has been two months since Busby stopped the project. He has not filed either a notice of completion or a notice of cessation. C. L. is owed a considerable amount for materials he furnished and wages he paid. What can he do?

Attachments and Judgments

Attachment   The **plaintiff** is the person who files a lawsuit against a **defendant**. Sometimes, the plaintiff has reason to believe that the defendant will try to sell or conceal assets that might be awarded by the court to the plaintiff if the case is decided in the plaintiff's favor. At the plaintiff's request, even before the outcome of the case is decided, the court may order that title to real or personal property of the defendant be "seized" and held by the court as security for satisfaction of the potential award to the plaintiff. This process, called **attachment**, is restricted primarily to cases involving a business, trade, or profession.

Judgment   The **judgment** of a court is its determination of the rights of the parties to a legal action. The losing party has the right to appeal the decision to a higher court. After the time for appeal has passed (or an appellate review has taken place and the lower court's judgment is affirmed), the judgment becomes final. The judgment could take effect as it was originally made or as it was reversed or amended by the higher court. The higher court could also order a retrial and vacate the original judgment. A judgment granting money damages may come from a California or federal court.

> The court of another state cannot render a judgment affecting California real estate.

A final judgment will become a *lien* on property of the judgment debtor when it is recorded by the party to whom it was awarded. An **abstract of judgment** can be recorded in any or all of the state's 58 counties.

After it has been created by recording, a judgment lien is effective against all non-exempt real property of the debtor located in the county of filing. This includes any real property acquired within the term of the lien, which normally is 10 years. Homestead property, which is covered later in this unit, is an example of exempt real property.

Writ of execution   Any nonexempt property (or exempt property, as the court decides) may be sold to pay a judgment debt. The lienholder requests a **writ of execution** from the court, which directs the sheriff or other officer to sell the property.

Discharge of debt   A judgment lien may be discharged before the end of its term by payment of the total damages owed. This results in **satisfaction** of the debt.

Notice of satisfaction of a debt should be filed with the clerk of the court. Partial payment of money owed could result in a *release* as to some (but not all) of the property of the debtor.

FOR EXAMPLE   Gladys Street sued Len Flimflam in a California court, claiming that Len had defrauded her of $100,000 in a real estate scam. Gladys won her lawsuit, and the judge awarded her damages of $100,000 plus interest. Len did not appeal the decision but has not volunteered any money to Gladys. Now what?

Gladys can file her judgment in any county in which Len has sufficient property to cover what she is owed. If Len persists in ignoring the judgment, Gladys can ask for a writ of execution to sell enough of his nonexempt property to cover her award.

BANKRUPTCY

Bankruptcy is a federal court proceeding. There are various forms of bankruptcy, identified by their chapter in the federal Bankruptcy Code. In a Chapter 11 reorganization, the court approves a plan to repay creditors. In a Chapter 7 liquidation, the court takes possession of the assets of the debtor and sells the assets to pay off creditors on a pro rata basis. Under Chapter 13, the debts of an individual who earns a regular income are reduced. A debtor may voluntarily petition for bankruptcy, or an involuntary petition may be filed by the debtor's creditors to force a liquidation and distribution of the debtor's assets.

In a liquidation, a **trustee in bankruptcy** holds title to the debtor's assets. The trustee is responsible for the sale of the assets, as necessary, and issues a **trustee's deed** to the buyer of real property. Some property is exempt from sale, and all property is subject first to the claims of lienholders.

EASEMENTS

The encumbrances already discussed in this unit affect the transfer of title to real estate. Other encumbrances affect the condition or use of property. An **easement** is the right to use the land of another for a particular purpose.

Easement Appurtenant

An easement usually is the right of the owner of one parcel of land to travel over an adjoining parcel. The land over which the easement runs is called the **servient tenement**. The land benefited by the easement is the **dominant tenement**.

Unless the deed creating it specifies otherwise, an **easement appurtenant** belongs to, or "runs with," the land. If the dominant tenement is sold, the new owner has the same right to use the easement that the previous owner had. If the servient tenement is sold, the new owner takes title subject to the easement. The fact that there is an easement will be recorded as part of the seller's deed or will be obvious from an inspection of the property.

F O R   E X A M P L E   Al owns property that he divides into two lots, lot A and lot B. Al sells lot B to Betty. Betty builds a house on lot B.

The deed to Betty conveys an easement over Al's driveway so that Betty can get to and from her land. The illustration below shows the location of lot B in relation to lot A.

If Betty sells lot B, the new owner also will be entitled to use Al's driveway to go to and from the road. If Al sells lot A, the new owner must allow the owner of lot B to use the driveway.

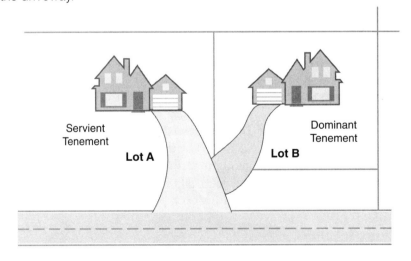

Easement in Gross

Even though an easement is a real property interest, its use may be purely personal. An **easement in gross** is a personal right to use land. The right belongs to an individual (a person or business corporation) and is not appurtenant to any ownership interest in land. The instrument creating the easement in gross can be made binding on future owners of the land, in which case it will "run with the land." Sometimes, a railroad's right-of-way is an easement in gross. The railroad does not own any adjacent land but has the right to travel over the land on which the easement lies. Pipeline and power line easements are other examples.

Because an easement in gross is a personal interest, it usually is not assignable by its owner and terminates on the owner's death.

Creation of Easements

The owner of land may execute a contract that provides an easement right over the land. The recipient of the easement right may or may not be the owner of adjoining land, depending on the type of easement created. Other ways in which easements can arise are discussed next.

Easement created by express grant or express reservation   An easement may be created by **express grant** or **express reservation** in a grant deed. The wording of the deed will depend on whether the grantor is to be the holder of the dominant or the servient tenement.

The owner of the land that will be the dominant tenement will *reserve* an easement right in the deed to the new owner of the land that will be the servient tenement.

F O R   E X A M P L E   In the previous example, if Al had sold lot A to Betty and kept lot B for himself, he would have *reserved* an easement over Betty's driveway to get to and from lot B.

> ## How to Create an Easement
>
> An easement may be created by
> - contract;
> - express grant from the owner of the easement property;
> - reserving an easement over land that is sold;
> - implication of law;
> - long use; or
> - condemnation for a public purpose.

The owner of the land that will be the servient tenement will *grant* an easement right to the new owner of the land that will be the dominant tenement.

FOR EXAMPLE In the previous example, Al *granted* Betty an easement when he sold lot B to her.

Only the fee owner of the servient tenement can grant an easement (whether the easement is appurtenant or in gross). Once an easement appurtenant is granted, however, the owner of the dominant tenement can convey the easement along with the land it benefits.

Easement by implication of law In some cases, the law will imply an easement to travel over someone else's land. If a subdivision plat map shows streets, an easement to use those streets is an **easement by implication of law**.

Suppose landowner A sells a parcel of land that can be reached only by traveling over another parcel of land also owned by A. It is evident from examining both parcels that landowner A has used the easement for many years. Even if landowner A doesn't specifically grant the right to use the easement, the right may be implied by law. Factors taken into account include the nature of the easement, the length of time it has been used, and whether it could be considered permanent.

> Every parcel of land will be allowed some form of access.

Another form of easement by implication of law is the **easement by necessity**. A tract of land may be landlocked—that is, there may not be a road adjacent to any part of it. The owner of such a tract has an easement by necessity implied by law over any land of the seller that is adjacent and provides access to a roadway. If the seller owns no land adjacent to the landlocked parcel, there will be an implied easement over the land that provides the most efficient road access, even though that land now belongs to a "stranger" to the transaction, provided both parcels were once owned by the same person.

FOR EXAMPLE As shown in the illustration that follows, *A* sells *B* a landlocked tract. Even if *A* never expressly mentions an easement in the grant deed to *B*, *B* has an implied easement over the land of *A* to the nearest roadway.

Suppose that *A, B, C, D, E, F,* and *G* all bought their land from *H*. Suppose also that no easement was expressly reserved for *B*'s land and that no easement ever has been used to get to *B*'s land for any extended period. *B* then would petition the court for an implied easement over the property that would give him the shortest reasonable access to a street. In our illustration, the easement granted would most likely be over the land of *F*.

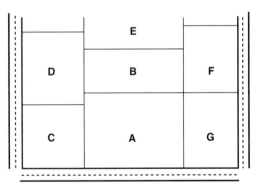

Easement by prescription An **easement by prescription** is acquired in much the same way that ownership of land is acquired by adverse possession. The major difference is that to acquire an easement, property taxes need not be paid. An easement use will become a legal right if it is

- open and notorious (not hidden in any way);

- continuous for five years;

- hostile to the interests of the owner (without permission); and

- under some claim of right or color of title.

Easement by condemnation Fee ownership of land may be acquired for a public purpose by the government's **power of eminent domain**, which will be discussed in Unit 15. Rights to use land also can be acquired by eminent domain.

The creation of an **easement by condemnation** begins with the condemnation of the right of use on behalf of the holder of the new easement.

Some easements benefit property owners.

The easement use acquired (such as an easement for utility line installation and maintenance) may benefit the land over which the easement runs. In such a case, compensation of the landowner may not be required. Other uses, such as a railroad right-of-way or construction of major power transmission lines, are likely to require payment to the owner for the loss in value to the property caused by the easement.

Termination of an Easement

There are many ways to *terminate* an easement. They include the following eight actions:

1. **Express agreement of the parties.** This may be accomplished by quitclaim deed from the owner of the dominant tenement to the owner of the servient tenement, or from the owner of an easement in gross to the owner of the land over which the easement runs.

2. **Lawsuit.** An action to quiet title can be brought against anyone claiming an easement.

3. **Abandonment of a prescriptive easement.** Although a prescriptive easement is acquired after five years of continuous use, it also can be lost if the easement is unused for five years. This is not true of an easement obtained by grant, unless the additional conditions described next are met.

4. **Estoppel.** Regardless of how it was acquired, an easement may terminate if

    - it is not used, *and*

- the owner of the dominant tenement reasonably indicates that no further use is intended, *and*

- the owner of the servient tenement makes use of the land in reasonable reliance on the representations of the owner of the dominant tenement.

If all of these conditions are met, the owner of the dominant tenement will be prevented (estopped) from complaining of the new use.

5. **Merger of the dominant and servient tenements.** When the owner of either dominant or servient tenements becomes the owner of both properties, the easement is extinguished. The easement can be revived by a subsequent sale of the dominant tenement.

6. **Destruction of the servient tenement.** Two buildings may share a common wall, called a *party wall*. The owner of each building has an easement over the other's property to the extent that the wall intrudes on that property. If the buildings are demolished and the wall destroyed, the easement terminates.

7. **Adverse possession.** If the owner of the servient tenement performs the conditions for adverse possession as to the land over which the easement lies, the easement right of the owner of the dominant tenement will terminate.

8. **Excessive use.** An easement can be terminated if the easement's use is improper or much greater than originally intended. The owner of the servient tenement could object, for instance, if land sold for residential purposes was used as a gravel pit and noisy, dusty trucks began to use the easement.

You can remember the ways to terminate an easement by the following acronym *ADAM E LEE*:

- **A**bandonment
- **D**estruction
- **A**dverse possession
- **M**erger
- **E**xpress agreement
- **L**awsuit
- **E**stoppel
- **E**xcessive use

License to Use Land

As you learned in Unit 3, the right to *use* land may not be an ownership right. Instead of being a *freehold* interest, it may be a *leasehold* interest. It also may be an easement, as you have learned in this unit.

One more way to transfer a right to use land is by a **license**, the permission given to another to come onto one's land. A license is a nonexclusive right, which means that the person to whom it is given has no right to exclude others from the owner's land. A license is *personal property* rather than real property and *temporary* rather than permanent. A license may be terminated at any time without prior notice.

An example of a license would be the permission given by an owner to neighbors to store their lawn mower in the owner's garage. The neighbors are not charged for this privilege, nor does the owner give them exclusive use of the garage but retains the right to tell them to remove their lawn mower at any time. Under this arrangement, the neighbors have a license to enter the property to retrieve and return their lawn mower. They have no easement, lease, or other interest in the real estate.

Exercise 5-2

Harvey returned home to California after a six-year absence. Harvey went directly to his empty house, a palatial building on 20 acres of land.

While touring his property the next morning, Harvey was surprised to find a new power line running across the back of his land, a conspicuous and unwelcome addition. Harvey also noticed a dirt road cutting across a corner of his land to the highway from a little house just off his property.

Can the power company put up such a line? By what authority?

The little house in this exercise is located on a roadway. Can its owner create a new road across Harvey's property? How?

RESTRICTIONS

Any form of **restriction** is a limitation on the use of land. The most common private restrictions are the "covenants, conditions, and restrictions" found in a deed. The most common public (government) restriction is the zoning ordinance.

Covenants, Conditions, and Restrictions (CC&Rs)

CC&Rs all serve to control land use. They are commonly found in the Declaration of Restrictions filed by a developer when a subdivision plan is recorded. The deed to each buyer of a subdivision lot will include the CC&Rs by reference to the book and page number in which they are recorded.

A house in a subdivision probably has CC&Rs.

CC&Rs are commonly referred to simply as *restrictions*. Because they benefit the other property in the subdivision, they usually "run with the land." This means that when the property is sold, the new owner receives both the burden and benefits of the CC&Rs. Creation of a formal organization of property owners, such as a homeowners association, usually is the most efficient and cost-effective method to enforce the CC&Rs. Even though the CC&Rs are recorded, they are useless unless they are known to property owners and have a practical method of enforcement.

CC&Rs generally can be removed only by agreement of all those who have the right to enforce them (that is, the other property owners in the subdivision). The provisions of CC&Rs also may be written so that they apply only to the original grantee and not to subsequent owners.

Covenants   A **covenant** is a promise

- to do something or
- to refrain from doing something.

FOR EXAMPLE   Property owners in the Willow Creek subdivision covenant that they will keep buildings in good repair. They also agree to follow specific architectural guidelines for additions and design changes to buildings in the subdivision.

If a covenant is breached, the other property owners may seek an **injunction** from a court prohibiting or ordering the removal of the cause of the breach, or they may seek money damages.

A covenant also may be found in a lease. For instance, a tenant might promise to use the property only for a specified purpose.

Conditions   A **condition** generally is enforceable by the person imposing the condition. In a sale transaction, that would be the seller. A **condition subsequent**, if performed, will enable the seller to regain title to the land. Because a condition limits the estate granted, it should appear on the face of the deed.

The remedy for breach of a condition is forfeiture of the land, a much harsher result than the money damages or injunction that can follow the breach of a covenant. Because a condition can have such a severe consequence, courts will construe any ambiguous language in a deed as a covenant, rather than a condition.

FOR EXAMPLE   Terry deeded Greenacre to his church, to be used for church purposes. When the church used the land as a public parking lot, Terry objected, claiming the right to retake possession of the land.

The court, called on to determine the rights of the parties, found that the church *covenanted* to use the property for church purposes. Assuming that a use was not for a church purpose, Terry's remedy, the court said, would be an action for money damages or an injunction to prohibit the use.

A condition cannot require the performance of an unlawful act or an act that would be impossible to perform. There could not, for instance, be a condition that would require a crime to be committed or that would prohibit the sale of the property to a person of a certain race.

A condition also cannot impose a *restraint on alienation*. A **restraint on alienation** is any condition that prohibits a property owner from transferring title to the property. An example of a restraint on alienation would be a condition that the grantor's consent be obtained before the grantee could sell the property. Such a restraint is void—totally ineffective—and the grantee holds the property free of the restraint.

Deed restrictions   A **deed restriction** is a prohibition against a property use that is imposed in the grantee's deed. Homeowners associations frequently make use of deed restrictions to ensure that the uniform appearance of the homes in a subdivision is maintained. Some typical property maintenance standards are shown in Figure 5.1.

F O R   E X A M P L E   Ann and Anthony Rush purchased a house in Montrose Manor, which is governed by the Montrose Homeowners Association. Ann and Anthony are aware that there are CC&Rs on their property. They have seen the latest property maintenance standards, which are the ones that appear in Figure 5.1. Ann and Anthony have decided to re-landscape their property, so they are "letting it go" until next spring. They now have more weeds than plantings. Do they have a problem?

Yes, the Rushes do have a problem. The property standards specify that all properties must be landscaped, "trimmed, cultivated, weeded, and maintained continuously." The Rushes can expect to hear from the homeowners association soon.

Covenants sometimes sound like deed restrictions, and vice versa. As with a covenant, the remedy available when a deed restriction must be enforced will be an injunction or money damages. A deed restriction also may be illegal from its inception, making enforcement impossible.

FIGURE 5.1:   Property Maintenance Standards

Montrose Homeowners Association, Inc.
Property Maintenance Standards

1. **Dwellings**

   a. Building exteriors will be maintained and painted as needed. Prior to altering an existing paint color, a written request and color samples must be reviewed and approved by the Architectural Committee.

   b. Appurtenances, including but not limited to decks, overhangs, lights, attic ventilators, gutters, downspouts, and solar-heating equipment, must be properly maintained and promptly repaired.

   c. Broken windows, screens, garage and entry doors, and fences must be repaired or replaced within 30 days of breakage.

2. **Property**

   a. All lots must be landscaped. Landscaping of every kind and character, including lawn, shrubs, trees, and plantings, must be trimmed, cultivated, weeded, and maintained continuously to provide a safe, clean, and groomed appearance.

   b. Trees and shrubs that overhang on public sidewalks and streets must be trimmed to provide a minimum clearance of seven feet from grade. Open strips of land between fences and sidewalks are the responsibility of the property owners and should be kept neat and weeded.

   c. Accumulations of rubbish, wood, or any other household or garden debris visible from other properties or the street will not be allowed for more than seven days or the next scheduled trash pickup.

   d. Prolonged repair of automobiles on the street or driveway is prohibited.

3. **Miscellaneous**

   a. Any other condition not covered above that contributes to the general appearance or disrepair of a property will be addressed by the association on an individual basis.

> ### Expunging an Illegal Covenant
>
> A person who holds a recorded ownership interest in property that she believes is subject to an unlawful discriminatory restrictive covenant can submit a Restrictive Covenant Modification form, along with a copy of the original document (with the illegal language crossed out), to the county recorder. After a determination by the county counsel that the crossed-out language is illegal, the county recorder records the Restrictive Covenant Modification and may choose to waive the recording fee.

Termination   Restrictions (CC&Rs) may be terminated by

- expiration of the terms of the restriction;

- voluntary cancellation;

- merger of ownership, if one individual owns both the encumbered and the benefited properties;

- government act, such as a legal prohibition against restrictions based on race or religion; or

- a change in condition that prompts a court action to remove the restriction.

Subdivision restrictions often include a provision that allows their modification on approval of the homeowners association. That is accomplished by vote of all or a specified number of the homeowners.

FOR EXAMPLE   Clare's family has owned their home for 20 years. When it was first deeded to them by the developer, it carried a restriction that only wood shingles be used for roofing. Because of the fire hazard of a wood roof, Clare and other homeowners in her development ask the homeowners association that the restriction be terminated.

The restriction is modified by the homeowners association to require fireproof shingles on new or replacement roofs.

In some cases, an overriding public interest in allowing or disallowing certain property uses will take precedence over a deed restriction, or even a property use limitation found in a lease. For example, Sections 1940.20 and 1950.10 of the Civil Code provide that a landlord, or a governing body such as a homeowners association, cannot prohibit a tenant's or owner's use of an outside clothesline or drying rack that meets reasonable location and privacy standards. Another example is Civil Code Section 4735, which has been amended to declare as void and unenforceable any provision of a governing document that prohibits a homeowner's use of low water-using plants or artificial turf.

Zoning

Zoning is an act of city or county government. Zoning laws or ordinances specify the possible uses of property in a defined area. Zoning is a 20th-century invention intended to promote the public health or general public welfare. It has been the subject of many legal battles involving the extent to which public interests can take priority over private ones. We will consider zoning and other governmental controls of land use in more detail in Unit 15.

Exercise 5-3

1. Aria is very concerned that her neighborhood retain its quiet, well-maintained atmosphere. Herb, her neighbor, has his house up for sale. He promises Aria that he will require anyone who buys the house to care for it properly. Can he do that?

2. Aria has decided to move to Alaska and give her home in California to her nephew. Aria is very concerned that the neighborhood's appearance be kept up for the benefit of her old neighbors. Her deed to her nephew stipulates that she must approve any future transfer of the property. Can she do that?

ENCROACHMENTS

An encroachment can occur on land, in airspace, or underground (a footing for a fence or building).

An **encroachment** occurs when part of an improvement extends over the boundary line between properties without permission. Fences and buildings are typical forms of encroachment. Even the roof eave of a building can be an encroachment if it extends into the airspace of a neighboring lot.

An encroaching party who fulfills the conditions for an easement by prescription or ownership by adverse possession may earn the legal right to use the land occupied by the encroachment. If not, the owner of the occupied land can bring a legal action. The decision of the court will depend on

- the extent of the encroachment,
- the relative difficulty of removing it, and
- whether the encroaching party acted by mistake.

FOR EXAMPLE   Lester is an excellent surveyor, but he has a careless office assistant. Lester neglected to note that his assistant transposed some measurements on the plans for the Skyway Office Tower. As a result, the foundation for the tower was poured 11 inches inside an adjacent vacant lot's boundary line, along the entire 200-foot width of the building. The building was completed within two years. One year after that, the owner of the vacant lot went forward with her development plans and discovered the unfortunate mistake. Can she force the owner of Skyway to demolish the 50-floor office building (or at least the 11 inches that extend onto her property)?

No. To do so would be prohibitively expensive, and courts will not require such an uneconomic outcome, particularly when the cause was inadvertent.

The Skyway owner probably will have to pay damages for the encroachment, however. The amount of damages owed could be substantial, particularly if the vacant lot owner's plans must be extensively revised.

HOMESTEADS

California and other states provide homeowners with special protection from creditors. Some or all of the value of the owner's equity in the **homestead** is exempt from the claims of unsecured creditors.

The homestead exemption is separate from other benefits for homeowners, such as the homeowner's exemption from property tax that is discussed in Unit 11. Also, do not confuse the *homestead exemption* with the federal *homesteading* laws. Homesteading was discontinued after 1976, except in Alaska. Individuals may no longer homestead on public land in California as a way to acquire title.

The homeowner's **equity** is the market value of the home less any liens and encumbrances. If the homeowner's equity is greater than the amount of the exemption, the home could be sold at the court's direction to satisfy any unpaid creditors. A sale will not be ordered if the homeowner's equity is no more than

- the remaining amount owed on the mortgage loan, *plus*
- the amount of the **homestead exemption**.

If the homeowner chooses to sell the property, the amount of the exemption will be safe from creditors if the homeowner has filed a *Declaration of Homestead* and the sale proceeds are reinvested in a new homestead within *six months*. This could help a financially beleaguered homeowner. The **six-month rule** could allow the homeowner to move into a less costly home, for instance, and perhaps provide some equity from the sale of the former home to pay off creditors. The generous tax exclusion rules for homeowners (discussed in Unit 11) could allow the homeowner to avoid paying any tax on profit realized on the sale of the more expensive home.

Defining the Homestead

The homestead exemption applies only to an owner-occupied dwelling. The dwelling can be any of the following (among other forms of dwelling):

- House and land
- Mobilehome and land
- Boat
- Condominium
- Planned development
- Stock cooperative
- Community apartment project

The homestead can be community or separate property of spouses or registered domestic partners, or the separate property of an unmarried individual. If two unmarried persons share ownership, each can claim a separate homestead exemption on the dwelling they occupy.

Amount of the Homestead Exemption

The amount of the homestead exemption depends on the homeowner's status, as found in Section 704.730 of the Code of Civil Procedure and shown in Figure 5.2.

FIGURE 5.2:   **Homestead Exemption**

Amount of the Homestead Exemption as of January 1, 2010

Homeowner	$75,000
Homeowner who is a member of a family unit	$100,000
Homeowner, or spouse who resides with homeowner, is 65 years of age or older	$175,000
Homeowner, or spouse who resides with homeowner, is physically or mentally disabled and unable to engage in substantial gainful employment	$175,000
Homeowner is 55 years of age or older with a gross annual income of not more than $25,000 or, if the homeowner is married, with a combined gross annual income with the spouse of not more than $35,000, and the homestead is subject to an involuntary sale	$175,000

The Family Unit

A homeowner is entitled to an exemption of at least $75,000, but being a member of a family unit of two or more persons qualifies a homeowner for a $100,000 exemption. At least one member of the family unit must own no interest in the property or the interest must be a community property interest with the person claiming the exemption. The various forms of family unit are listed in the box that follows.

The Family Unit

The following qualify as family units for purposes of the homestead exemption:

1. Homeowner and spouse, if they reside together

2. Homeowner and, if cared for and maintained in the homestead, the minor child or minor grandchild of the homeowner, spouse, or deceased or former spouse

3. Homeowner and, if cared for and maintained in the homestead, the minor brother or sister of the homeowner or homeowner's spouse or the minor child of a deceased brother or sister of either spouse

4. Homeowner and, if cared for and maintained in the homestead, the father, mother, grandfather, or grandmother of the homeowner, spouse, or deceased spouse

5. Homeowner and, if cared for and maintained in the homestead, an unmarried adult relative who is unable to care for or support himself or herself

6. Homeowner's spouse and one of the other relatives mentioned in categories 2, 3, 4, or 5 above, if that person is unable to care for or support himself

Priority of Claims

The **priority of claims** is the order in which creditors are paid. The priority of claims against a declared homestead has been established by law. The proceeds of a forced sale go to

1. holders of liens and encumbrances on the homestead (with any tax lien paid off first); *then*
2. the homeowner in the amount of the homestead exemption only; *then*
3. the levying officer for reimbursement of costs for which an advance has not been made; *then*
4. judgment creditors; and *finally*, if anything remains,
5. the homeowner.

If a Declaration of Homestead has not been filed, or until it is, the homeowner's automatic homestead exemption will be subject to any judgments recorded up to that time.

Exercise 5-4

1. Harold and Cynthia Potter, spouses, own a houseboat docked at Lake Shasta as community property. Do they qualify for a homestead exemption?

2. Harold and Cynthia have a $95,000 mortgage on their houseboat, which has a market value of $130,000. If creditors try to force the sale of the houseboat, are they likely to succeed?

SUMMARY

A property owner has **marketable title** if the property is readily salable to a prudent purchaser. An **encumbrance** may create a **cloud on the title** and impede the property's marketability.

A **lien** is **voluntary** if the owner places it on the property or **involuntary** if someone else does. A **mechanic's lien** is available to anyone providing work or material for a property improvement. A *contractor's payment bond* helps minimize the risk of numerous mechanics' liens.

If a mechanic's lien is to be filed, **preliminary notice** may be required to be given to the owner, the construction manager (if any), and the construction lender (if any). It is important to establish the starting time and completion time of the work or materials supply. After work has been completed, the property owner may file a *notice of completion*. An owner also can stop work and file a *notice of cessation*.

A mechanic's lien is enforced by *foreclosure*. If unsolicited work is performed, a **notice of nonresponsibility** can be filed and posted on the land.

The **plaintiff** in a legal action can ask to have the court retain title to the **defendant's** property by **attachment** even before a **judgment** is rendered. A court will make a judgment after hearing the claims that a plaintiff has against a defendant. The court may grant *money damages*, and that judgment can become a lien on property of the debtor if it is filed in the county where the property is located. A **writ of execution** orders the sheriff to sell the property to pay the judgment. The owner can satisfy the debt by paying it off or can pay part of the debt and have some of the property *released*.

A *debtor's* property may be taken over by a *bankruptcy court*. The *trustee in bankruptcy* holds title.

Easements allow use of another's land for a particular purpose. The owner of a **dominant tenement** has the right to use the land of the owner of a **servient tenement**. Generally, an easement is conveyed with the land. An **easement in gross** is a personal right and may not be transferable.

Easements may be created by **deed, by implication of law**, or **by necessity** (if a parcel is landlocked), **by prescription** (similar to *adverse possession*), and **by condemnation** (through the **power of eminent domain**). An easement may be *terminated* by agreement, lawsuit, nonuse of a prescriptive easement, abandonment, merger of the easement and servient tenement, destruction of the servient tenement, adverse possession, or excessive use.

The **covenants, conditions, and restrictions** in a deed are private forms of limitation on land use and may bind the grantee. A court may issue an **injunction** ordering a property to refrain from activity prohibited by the **CC&Rs**. CC&Rs cannot act as a **restraint on alienation** of the property, require the performance of a crime or an impossible act, or have an illegal purpose.

Zoning is a public form of limitation on land use. An **encroachment** occurs when an improvement is placed on the wrong property.

A **homestead exemption** protects from $75,000 to $175,000 of the homeowner's equity in the dwelling from creditors. Filing a Declaration of Homestead offers the homeowner the greatest benefit from the exemption.

OPEN FOR DISCUSSION

Deed restrictions are the most popular method of maintaining uniformity of architectural style, appearance, and upkeep of subdivision properties.

1. Do you think that deed restrictions serve a useful purpose?
2. Do you think that deed restrictions should be allowed to continue indefinitely, or should they automatically terminate after a certain period? If so, what should that time be?

REVIEW QUESTIONS

1. A cloud on the title is
   a. not important.
   b. easily remedied.
   c. no impediment to a property sale.
   d. a possible impediment to a property sale.

2. A mechanic's lien can be filed by
   a. a laborer.
   b. a tenant.
   c. an advertiser.
   d. a customer.

3. Which is *NOT* a mechanic?
   a. An engineer
   b. An architect
   c. An apartment lessor
   d. An equipment lessor

4. When required, preliminary notice of right to file a mechanic's lien should be given
   a. 90 days after notice of completion.
   b. 60 days after notice of completion.
   c. within 10 days of the starting time.
   d. within 20 days of the starting time.

5. A notice of cessation is appropriate
   a. when the work has been stopped for 30 days.
   b. when an improvement is complete.
   c. at any time after the work is substantially finished.
   d. after work has stopped for a number of days.

6. A notice of completion should be *filed* within
   a. 20 days after completion of the work of improvement.
   b. 10 days after completion of the work of improvement.
   c. 20 days after work stops.
   d. 10 days after supplies have been received.

7. Generally, the action to enforce a mechanic's lien claim must be filed within how many days after the lien is recorded?
   a. 30 days
   b. 60 days
   c. 90 days
   d. 120 days

8. If unauthorized work is being done, a property owner can
   a. file a preliminary notice.
   b. file a notice of cessation.
   c. allow the job to be completed and then refuse to pay.
   d. file a notice of nonresponsibility.

9. Liens and judgments are
   a. encumbrances.
   b. encroachments.
   c. easements.
   d. void on homestead property.

10. The sheriff is directed to sell property by
    a. a writ of attachment.
    b. a writ of execution.
    c. a satisfaction.
    d. a release.

11. The right to use adjacent land to go to and from a roadway is
    a. an encroachment.
    b. an easement.
    c. a restriction.
    d. a condition.

12. Betty's property includes an easement over Al's land. Al's property is
    a. the dominant tenement.
    b. the servient tenement.
    c. the easement.
    d. the encroachment.

13. Betty's property includes an easement over Al's land. Betty's property is
    a. the dominant tenement.
    b. the servient tenement.
    c. the easement.
    d. the encroachment.

14. George does not own any land but has an easement over Al's and Betty's property to go down to the river. George has
    a. an easement by necessity.
    b. an easement by implication of law.
    c. an easement in gross.
    d. an encroachment.

15. Marilyn's 40-acre tract, purchased from Alan, is landlocked, which means that she
    a. has to enter it by helicopter.
    b. has an easement in gross over any land she chooses.
    c. has an easement by implication of law over any land she chooses.
    d. can get an easement by necessity over Alan's adjoining parcel.

16. Al sold Blackacre to Betty, giving her an easement over Whiteacre. Years later, Al bought Blackacre back from Betty. What effect did his purchase have on the easement?
    a. The easement stayed with Betty.
    b. The easement is owned by Al.
    c. The purchase terminated the easement.
    d. The purchase had no effect on the easement.

17. The maximum homestead exemption may be claimed by a homeowner who is
    a. a member of a family unit.
    b. older than 65 years of age.
    c. married.
    d. single.

18. A family unit is
    a. defined by law.
    b. limited in size.
    c. limited to the relatives of one's spouse.
    d. at least three people.

19. The homestead exemption for a single person is at *LEAST*
    a. $175,000.
    b. $100,000.
    c. $75,000.
    d. $50,000.

20. The homestead exemption for a homeowner who is a member of a family unit is at *LEAST*
    a. $175,000.
    b. $150,000.
    c. $125,000.
    d. $100,000.

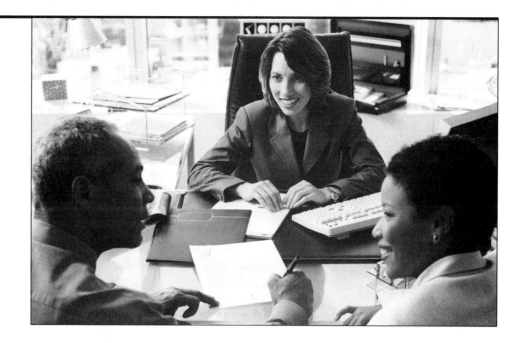

THE LAW OF AGENCY

LEARNING OBJECTIVES

When you have completed this unit, you will be able to

- **define** the agency relationship and the parties to an agency;

- **distinguish** the employee from the independent contractor;

- **describe** a single agency and dual agency;

- **identify** the ways in which an agency relationship can be created;

- **list** the types of listing agreements and **describe** them;

- **describe** the contents of a typical residential listing agreement and buyer broker agreement;

- **list** the rights and duties of principal and agent;

- **explain** the contents of the Real Estate Transfer Disclosure Statement and the agent's inspection disclosure; and

- **recognize** the ways in which an agency relationship may be terminated.

KEY TERMS

accounting	equal dignities rule	obedience
actual authority	estoppel	open listing
agency	exclusive agency listing	option listing
agency confirmation form	exclusive authorization and right-to-sell listing	ostensible agency
agency disclosure form		pocket listing
agent	express agreement	power of attorney
apparent authority	fiduciary	principal
associate licensee	full disclosure of material facts	procuring cause
attorney-in-fact		prospective economic advantage
bilateral contract	general agent	ratification
commingling	general power of attorney	Recovery Account
compensation		safety clause
confidentiality	good faith and honesty	secret profit
conflict of interest	implied agency	single agency
cooperating brokers	independent contractor	special agent
cooperating split	inherent authority	special power of attorney
dual agency	loyalty	
due diligence	multiple listing clause	subagent
duty of care	multiple listing service (MLS)	unilateral contract
employee		
employer	net listing	

THE CONCEPT OF AGENCY

Whom does the real estate agent represent? In the traditional view of agency law, the agent most often represented the seller. This was true even when it was the buyer who first contacted the real estate agent. The buyer could be shown dozens of homes and helped through a complicated real estate purchase contract. The agent could even assist the buyer through the escrow process. Despite all that, the real estate agent was first and foremost the agent of the seller. Most buyers never realized that "their" agent was the seller's agent. It probably never occurred to the agent that the buyer should know.

The traditional view of agency law in California has changed. Recent studies, public opinion, court decisions, legislation, and the redefinition of the market-place thanks to the internet have brought the role of the real estate agent into sharper focus. As the agency relationship is more clearly defined, it becomes easier for all agents to recognize and meet the challenges of that relationship. The real estate agent can better serve both buyers and sellers when all parties concerned know exactly whom the agent represents.

www.leginfo.ca.gov

The California Civil Code provides most of the laws dealing with the formation of an agency relationship. The definitions that follow and most of the information in this unit can be found there. To read a specific section of the law, go to www.leginfo.ca.gov. As you read through this unit, remember that the law—no matter how well established by statute or precedent—is always subject to change.

What an Agency Is

An **agent** represents a **principal** in dealing with a *third person*. The act of representing someone else is called an **agency**.

California Civil Code Section 2079.13(a) defines the agent in a real estate transaction as the broker "under whose license a listing is executed or an offer to purchase is obtained." It is important to remember that all of a real estate brokerage's associate licensees (real estate salespersons or brokers who work under the supervision of the company's designated broker), including those who work in branch offices, are considered one "agent" for the purpose of agency duties and liabilities.

In the practice of real estate, there are many possible *agency relationships*. The listing broker acts as the agent of the seller, but the salesperson is the agent of the broker. There may be a different broker representing the buyer and that broker may have a salesperson as his agent.

Who May Take Part in an Agency Relationship

In every agency relationship, there is always a *principal*, an *agent*, and a *third person* with whom the agent conducts business on behalf of the principal.

The principal can be anyone who has the ability to enter into a contract. For example, a person who is mentally incompetent cannot enter into a valid agency relationship.

In California, as in all states, a real estate agent must obtain the appropriate license. All California real estate licensees must be at least 18 years old and have fulfilled the education and other requirements discussed in Unit 1. A minor (someone under the age of 18) cannot obtain a real estate license.

Special Agent vs. General Agent

A **special agent** is one appointed to carry out a single act or transaction. Any other agent is called a **general agent**. The difference between a special agent and a general agent lies in the scope of authority the agent possesses. Typically, a general agent can enter into an agreement that will bind the principal to its terms, while the authority of a special agent will be subject to the approval of the principal.

FOR EXAMPLE   Broker Bob is engaged by Ramon and Rosa Garcia to sell their home. Bob is a special agent for that purpose. When he sells the Garcia home, his agency relationship with the Garcias will terminate.

The Garcias, performers who are planning a move from Los Angeles to Las Vegas, employ a manager and give that person full authority to carry out their business affairs. What kind of agent is that person?

That person is a general agent because of the broad authority given to the agent by the Garcias.

Delegating Authority

Some of an agent's authority may be delegated to someone else. The agent may do so without express authority of the principal when the responsibility being delegated involves a clerical or administrative act. Other activities will require the principal's agreement before they can be delegated.

FOR EXAMPLE   Broker Maya employs an administrative assistant, who performs secretarial duties, including typing sales brochures. Maya's assistant performs none of the tasks that require a real estate license, such as soliciting property sellers and buyers. Maya does not need the approval of her clients to employ her assistant.

A complete discussion of real estate listing agreements appears later in this unit. The typical listing contract allows the listing broker to make use of the efforts of the listing broker's staff as well as the services of *cooperating brokers*.

Cooperating brokers are agents who try to sell a property that is currently listed for sale by a broker but who work for someone other than the listing broker. Historically, it was taken for granted that the agency relationship was between the listing broker and the seller. Any agent who wrote an offer on behalf of a buyer was considered a **subagent** of the seller's broker, and, with the seller's consent, the listing broker agreed to share the commission with the subagent. Unless subagency was rejected, the cooperating broker was automatically the subagent of the seller and owed all of the duties of a fiduciary to the seller.

Under the practice of subagency, the buyer was not *represented* by the cooperating broker but instead was *assisted* by the cooperating broker. The problem? Almost 70% of buyers believed the agent working *with* them was working *for* them. In reality, the buyer was the third party in an agency relationship, and all of the agents were loyal to the seller. California legislation has changed this relationship. The cooperating broker is no longer automatically the subagent of the seller, even though the cooperating broker may be entitled to a share of the commission that the listing agent receives from the seller. (The cooperating broker's share of the commission is called the **cooperating split**, or *commission to the selling office*.) Now, a cooperating broker may be

- the agent of the listing broker,
- the subagent of the seller (with the seller's authorization, typically through use of the multiple listing service), or
- the agent of the buyer.

It is important to remember that the seller's authorization does not necessarily require a written agreement. As you will learn later in this unit, in the section entitled "How an Agency Relationship Is Created," the conduct of the seller (the principal) also can authorize an agency relationship.

Multiple listing service   A **multiple listing service** (MLS) is an organization of real estate agents that receives information from individual members on their property listings and makes that information available to participating members.

MLS members agree to abide by the rules of the MLS. The MLS benefits sellers by making more agents aware of the availability of their property. Buyers benefit from a wide choice of properties from which an agent can present those that meet the buyers' needs.

When a real estate broker enters into a listing agreement with a property owner, the owner may authorize the agent to place the listing in the MLS. Information placed in the MLS informs other agents of the asking price, provides a property description, indicates how the property may be shown, and tells the agent representing a buyer—the cooperating broker—what the commission to the selling agent will be. The cooperating broker is entitled to the compensation offered in the MLS, regardless of agency relationships. The MLS listing will also inform other agents if subagency is optional or mandatory. A **pocket listing** is one that the listing agent markets privately before entering it in the MLS. Unless specifically authorized by the seller, this practice usually is a violation of MLS rules as well as the employing broker's policies.

FOR EXAMPLE   Broker Bob is the exclusive agent for the O'Connors, who are selling a four-unit apartment building. The MLS has not been authorized and is not being used, although the property is being advertised for sale. If a cooperating broker brings in a buyer, what is the relationship of that broker to the O'Connors and broker Bob?

In this case, a cooperating broker would be the subagent of broker Bob and have no direct relationship with the O'Connors.

Employment Relationship of Principal and Agent

An agency agreement is a form of employment contract. It can be structured in several ways. The principal is the **employer**, but the agent may act as either an **employee** or an **independent contractor**. The main difference is in the type of control the principal exercises over the agent. Another difference is the form of compensation paid to the agent.

> Real estate sales associates don't have a typical "9-to-5" job with evenings and weekends off.

An employee typically is under very close control as to the place where work is performed, the hours spent on the work, and the manner in which the work is carried out. An employee receives wages from which payroll taxes are deducted and may receive other employee benefits. Employee status also subjects the employer to certain liability for acts performed in the course of employment, which will be discussed later. An independent contractor, on the other hand, usually has great flexibility in accomplishing the task undertaken and will receive a commission based on completed transactions, instead of a salary, with no payroll deductions.

Real estate agents generally act as independent contractors in their dealings with clients as well as in their dealings with each other.

> ### Don't Forget
>
> A real estate salesperson can conduct business only as the agent of a broker and they must have a written employment agreement.
>
> The Real Estate License Law always considers a salesperson to be an **employee** acting under the direct supervision and control of the broker.
>
> This is true even when the salesperson is treated by the broker as an **independent contractor** for compensation, work assignment, and tax purposes.

FOR EXAMPLE CPU Home Loans has a staff of 12 salespeople, all of whom are assigned office time and all of whom are paid a salary plus a commission on sales. CPU deducts income taxes and Social Security from the salaries of all salespeople and also makes payments for unemployment insurance and workers' compensation. For purposes of work assignments and compensation, are the salespeople of CPU Home Loans employees or independent contractors?

The salespeople of CPU Home Loans clearly are employees.

Throughout the rest of this unit, we will refer to the role of the real estate broker rather than that of the real estate salesperson. (Keep in mind that a salesperson acts *always* as the agent of the employing broker and that someone with a broker's license may choose to be employed by another broker.) A real estate licensee employed by the broker will be referred to as an **associate licensee**.

All of the associate licensees in a real estate brokerage, including all branch offices, are considered one "agent" for the purpose of agency duties and liabilities. The designated broker is responsible for all acts of the associate licensee with regard to duties owed to the principal, third party, and other brokers. In most cases, all of the listings in a real estate company belong to the broker and not the associate licensee. If an associate licensee changes employing brokers, the listings stay with the broker under whose name they were taken, unless the broker allows the associate licensee to retain them.

Single vs. Dual Agency

In a **single agency**, an agent represents only one principal. Each principal in a transaction is represented by a different broker, as shown in Figure 6.1.

In a **dual agency**, the same agent represents two principals in the same transaction. A listing broker may find a buyer for the property. A dual agency can also occur when two associate licensees in the same brokerage work on behalf of the employing broker to represent both buyer and seller.

FIGURE 6.1:   Agency Relationships

Solid lines indicate agency relationships. Dotted lines indicate nonagency relationships.

A dual agency places the agent in the precarious position of carrying out agency responsibilities to two principals whose interests are in opposition. Any agent who acts on behalf of both parties to a transaction is required by law to inform both parties and obtain their written consent to the dual representation.

The law is very specific with regard to the activities of real estate agents. A real estate broker in a dual agency relationship must make sure that both clients know of and consent to the dual representation. Otherwise, the agent faces temporary suspension or even permanent revocation of the real estate license, in addition to having to return any commission received on the transaction. The penalty may seem severe, but the chance or even the appearance of taking advantage of the special knowledge an agent possesses makes a dual agency a difficult enterprise. Not only does the broker have a real estate license to consider, a party acting without knowledge of the dual agency also could ask the court to rescind any contract that results.

Agency disclosure form   As of January 1, 1988, the details of the agency relationship must be disclosed in any transaction involving property of one to four residential units. A written document that explains the various relationships of those involved in a residential property sale, and exactly whom the agent is representing, must be presented to both buyer and seller "as soon as practicable." The written disclosure must be made by

- the listing agent to the seller before the seller signs the listing agreement;

- the selling agent (who may also be the listing agent) to the buyer before the buyer makes an offer to purchase; and

- the selling agent (if different from the listing agent) to the seller before an offer to purchase is accepted.

An example of an **agency disclosure form** is shown in Figure 6.2. The wording of the form must follow the wording required by Civil Code Section 2375. In addition, the rest of the code sections dealing with the disclosure requirements must be printed on the back of the form.

The *selling* agent's relationship must be confirmed in writing in

- the purchase contract or

- a separate writing executed or acknowledged by the seller, the buyer, and the selling agent before or at the same time the purchase contract is executed by buyer and seller.

The *listing* agent's relationship must be confirmed in writing in

- the purchase contract or

- a separate writing executed or acknowledged by the seller and the listing agent before or at the same time the purchase contract is executed by the seller.

The agency disclosure form shown here makes clear that, in addition to listing and sales transactions, agency disclosure obligations apply to a lease of a dwelling when the lease term will exceed one year. An example of an **agency confirmation form** is shown in Figure 6.3. The most recent revision of this form allows for its use by licensees representing landlord and/or tenant as well as seller and/or buyer.

Power of Attorney

An *attorney-at-law* is someone licensed by the state to practice law.

An **attorney-in-fact** is an agent who has been granted a *power of attorney* by a principal. A **power of attorney** authorizes an agent to act in the capacity of the principal.

FIGURE 6.2:   Disclosure Regarding Real Estate Agency Relationship

CALIFORNIA
ASSOCIATION
OF REALTORS ®

**DISCLOSURE REGARDING
REAL ESTATE AGENCY RELATIONSHIP**
(As required by the Civil Code)
(C.A.R. Form AD, Revised 12/14)

❏ (If checked) This form is being provided in connection with a transaction for a leasehold interest exceeding one year as per Civil Code section 2079.13(k), (l), and (m).

When you enter into a discussion with a real estate agent regarding a real estate transaction, you should from the outset understand what type of agency relationship or representation you wish to have with the agent in the transaction.

SELLER'S AGENT
A Seller's agent under a listing agreement with the Seller acts as the agent for the Seller only. A Seller's agent or a subagent of that agent has the following affirmative obligations:
To the Seller: A Fiduciary duty of utmost care, integrity, honesty and loyalty in dealings with the Seller.
To the Buyer and the Seller:
    (a) Diligent exercise of reasonable skill and care in performance of the agent's duties.
    (b) A duty of honest and fair dealing and good faith.
    (c) A duty to disclose all facts known to the agent materially affecting the value or desirability of the property that are not known to, or within the diligent attention and observation of, the parties. An agent is not obligated to reveal to either party any confidential information obtained from the other party that does not involve the affirmative duties set forth above.

BUYER'S AGENT
A selling agent can, with a Buyer's consent, agree to act as agent for the Buyer only. In these situations, the agent is not the Seller's agent, even if by agreement the agent may receive compensation for services rendered, either in full or in part from the Seller. An agent acting only for a Buyer has the following affirmative obligations:
To the Buyer: A fiduciary duty of utmost care, integrity, honesty and loyalty in dealings with the Buyer.
To the Buyer and the Seller:
    (a) Diligent exercise of reasonable skill and care in performance of the agent's duties.
    (b) A duty of honest and fair dealing and good faith.
    (c) A duty to disclose all facts known to the agent materially affecting the value or desirability of the property that are not known to, or within the diligent attention and observation of, the parties.
An agent is not obligated to reveal to either party any confidential information obtained from the other party that does not involve the affirmative duties set forth above.

AGENT REPRESENTING BOTH SELLER AND BUYER
A real estate agent, either acting directly or through one or more associate licensees, can legally be the agent of both the Seller and the Buyer in a transaction, but only with the knowledge and consent of both the Seller and the Buyer.
In a dual agency situation, the agent has the following affirmative obligations to both the Seller and the Buyer:
    (a) A fiduciary duty of utmost care, integrity, honesty and loyalty in the dealings with either the Seller or the Buyer.
    (b) Other duties to the Seller and the Buyer as stated above in their respective sections.
In representing both Seller and Buyer, the agent may not, without the express permission of the respective party, disclose to the other party that the
Seller will accept a price less than the listing price or that the Buyer will pay a price greater than the price offered.
The above duties of the agent in a real estate transaction do not relieve a Seller or Buyer from the responsibility to protect his or her own interests. You should carefully read all agreements to assure that they adequately express your understanding of the transaction. A real estate agent is a person qualified to advise about real estate. If legal or tax advice is desired, consult a competent professional.
Throughout your real property transaction you may receive more than one disclosure form, depending upon the number of agents assisting in the transaction. The law requires each agent with whom you have more than a casual relationship to present you with this disclosure form. You should read its contents each time it is presented to you, considering the relationship between you and the real estate agent in your specific transaction. **This disclosure form includes the provisions of Sections 2079.13 to 2079.24, inclusive, of the Civil Code set forth on page 2. Read it carefully. I/WE ACKNOWLEDGE RECEIPT OF A COPY OF THIS DISCLOSURE AND THE PORTIONS OF THE CIVIL CODE PRINTED ON THE BACK (OR A SEPARATE PAGE).**

Buyer/Seller/Landlord/Tenant _____ Date _____

Buyer/Seller/Landlord/Tenant _____ Date _____

Agent _____ BRE Lic. # _____
                   Real Estate Broker (Firm)
By _____ BRE Lic. # _____ Date _____
              (Salesperson or Broker-Associate)

Agency Disclosure Compliance (Civil Code §2079.14):
• When the listing brokerage company also represents Buyer/Tenant: The Listing Agent shall have one AD form signed by Seller/Landlord and a different AD form signed by Buyer/Tenant.
• When Seller/Landlord and Buyer/Tenant are represented by different brokerage companies: (i) the Listing Agent shall have one AD form signed by Seller/Landlord and (ii) the Buyer's/Tenant's Agent shall have one AD form signed by Buyer/Tenant and either that same or a different AD form presented to Seller/Landlord for signature prior to presentation of the offer. If the same form is used, Seller may sign here:

_____   _____
Seller/Landlord   Date   Seller/Landlord   Date

EQUAL HOUSING
OPPORTUNITY

Reviewed by _____ Date _____

AD REVISED 12/14 (PAGE 1 OF 2)   Print Date

DISCLOSURE REGARDING REAL ESTATE AGENCY RELATIONSHIP (AD PAGE 1 OF 2)

Source: Reprinted with permission, California Association of REALTORS®. Endorsement not implied.

FIGURE 6.2:   Disclosure Regarding Real Estate Agency Relationship (continued)

CIVIL CODE SECTIONS 2079.24 (2079.16 APPEARS ON THE FRONT)

2079.13 As used in Sections 2079.14 to 2079.24, inclusive, the following terms have the following meanings: **(a)** "Agent" means a person acting under provisions of Title 9 (commencing with Section 2295) in a real property transaction, and includes a person who is licensed as a real estate broker under Chapter 3 (commencing with Section 10130) of Part 1 of Division 4 of the Business and Professions Code, and under whose license a listing is executed or an offer to purchase is obtained. **(b)** "Associate licensee" means a person who is licensed as a real estate broker or salesperson under Chapter 3 (commencing with Section 10130) of Part 1 of Division 4 of the Business and Professions Code and who is either licensed under a broker or has entered into a written contract with a broker to act as the broker's agent in connection with acts requiring a real estate license and to function under the broker's supervision in the capacity of an associate licensee. The agent in the real property transaction bears responsibility for his or her associate licensees who perform as agents of the agent. When an associate licensee owes a duty to any principal, or to any buyer or seller who is not a principal, in a real property transaction, that duty is equivalent to the duty owed to that party by the broker for whom the associate licensee functions. **(c)** "Buyer" means a transferee in a real property transaction, and includes a person who executes an offer to purchase real property from a seller through an agent, or who seeks the services of an agent in more than a casual, transitory, or preliminary manner, with the object of entering into a real property transaction. "Buyer" includes vendee or lessee. **(d)** "Commercial real property" means all real property in the state, except single-family residential real property, dwelling units made subject to Chapter 2 (commencing with Section 1940) of Title 5, mobilehomes, as defined in Section 798.3, or recreational vehicles, as defined in Section 799.29. **(e)** "Dual agent" means an agent acting, either directly or through an associate licensee, as agent for both the seller and the buyer in a real property transaction. **(f)** "Listing agreement" means a contract between an owner of real property and an agent, by which the agent has been authorized to sell the real property or to find or obtain a buyer. **(g)** "Listing agent" means a person who has obtained a listing of real property to act as an agent for compensation. **(h)** "Listing price" is the amount expressed in dollars specified in the listing for which the seller is willing to sell the real property through the listing agent. **(i)** "Offering price" is the amount expressed in dollars specified in an offer to purchase for which the buyer is willing to buy the real property. **(j)** "Offer to purchase" means a written contract executed by a buyer acting through a selling agent that becomes the contract for the sale of the real property upon acceptance by the seller. **(k)** "Real property" means any estate specified by subdivision (1) or (2) of Section 761 in property that constitutes or is improved with one to four dwelling units, any commercial real property, any leasehold in these types of property exceeding one year's duration, and mobilehomes, when offered for sale or sold through an agent pursuant to the authority contained in Section 10131.6 of the Business and Professions Code. **(l)** "Real property transaction" means a transaction for the sale of real property in which an agent is employed by one or more of the principals to act in that transaction, and includes a listing or an offer to purchase. **(m)** "Sell," "sale," or "sold" refers to a transaction for the transfer of real property from the seller to the buyer, and includes exchanges of real property between the seller and buyer, transactions for the creation of a real property sales contract within the meaning of Section 2985, and transactions for the creation of a leasehold exceeding one year's duration. **(n)** "Seller" means the transferor in a real property transaction, and includes an owner who lists real property with an agent, whether or not a transfer results, or who receives an offer to purchase real property of which he or she is the owner from an agent on behalf of another. "Seller" includes both a vendor and a lessor. **(o)** "Selling agent" means a listing agent who acts alone, or an agent who acts in cooperation with a listing agent, and who sells or finds and obtains a buyer for the real property, or an agent who locates property for a buyer or who finds a buyer for a property for which no listing exists and presents an offer to purchase to the seller. **(p)** "Subagent" means a person to whom an agent delegates agency powers as provided in Article 5 (commencing with Section 2349) of Chapter 1 of Title 9. However, "subagent" does not include an associate licensee who is acting under the supervision of an agent in a real property transaction.

2079.14 Listing agents and selling agents shall provide the seller and buyer in a real property transaction with a copy of the disclosure form specified in Section 2079.16, and, except as provided in subdivision (c), shall obtain a signed acknowledgement of receipt from that seller or buyer, except as provided in this section or Section 2079.15, as follows: **(a)** The listing agent, if any, shall provide the disclosure form to the seller prior to entering into the listing agreement. **(b)** The selling agent shall provide the disclosure form to the seller as soon as practicable prior to presenting the seller with an offer to purchase, unless the selling agent previously provided the seller with a copy of the disclosure form pursuant to subdivision (a). **(c)** Where the selling agent does not deal on a face-to-face basis with the seller, the disclosure form prepared by the selling agent may be furnished to the seller (and acknowledgement of receipt obtained for the selling agent from the seller) by the listing agent, or the selling agent may deliver the disclosure form by certified mail addressed to the seller at his or her last known address, in which case no signed acknowledgement of receipt is required. **(d)** The selling agent shall provide the disclosure form to the buyer as soon as practicable prior to execution of the buyer's offer to purchase, except that if the offer to purchase is not prepared by the selling agent, the selling agent shall present the disclosure form to the buyer not later than the next business day after the selling agent receives the offer to purchase from the buyer.

2079.15 In any circumstance in which the seller or buyer refuses to sign an acknowledgement of receipt pursuant to Section 2079.14, the agent, or an associate licensee acting for an agent, shall set forth, sign, and date a written declaration of the facts of the refusal.

2079.16 Reproduced on Page 1 of this AD form.

2079.17(a) As soon as practicable, the selling agent shall disclose to the seller and buyer whether the selling agent is acting in the real property transaction exclusively as the buyer's agent, exclusively as the seller's agent, or as a dual agent representing both the buyer and the seller. This relationship shall be confirmed in the contract to purchase and sell real property or in a separate writing executed or acknowledged by the seller, the buyer, and the selling agent prior to or coincident with execution of that contract by the buyer and the seller, respectively. **(b)** As soon as practicable, the listing agent shall disclose to the seller whether the listing agent is acting in the real property transaction exclusively as the seller's agent, or as a dual agent representing both the buyer and seller. This relationship shall be confirmed in the contract to purchase and sell real property or in a separate writing executed or acknowledged by the seller and the listing agent prior to or coincident with the execution of that contract by the seller.

(c) The confirmation required by subdivisions (a) and (b) shall be in the following form.

_____(DO NOT COMPLETE. SAMPLE ONLY)_____ is the agent of (check one): ❏ the seller exclusively; or ❏ both the buyer and seller.
(Name of Listing Agent)

_____(DO NOT COMPLETE. SAMPLE ONLY)_____ is the agent of (check one): ❏ the buyer exclusively; or ❏ the seller exclusively; or
(Name of Selling Agent if not the same as the Listing Agent)   ❏ both the buyer and seller.

(d) The disclosures and confirmation required by this section shall be in addition to the disclosure required by Section 2079.14.

2079.18 No selling agent in a real property transaction may act as an agent for the buyer only, when the selling agent is also acting as the listing agent in the transaction.

2079.19 The payment of compensation or the obligation to pay compensation to an agent by the seller or buyer is not necessarily determinative of a particular agency relationship between an agent and the seller or buyer. A listing agent and a selling agent may agree to share any compensation or commission paid, or any right to any compensation or commission for which an obligation arises as the result of a real estate transaction, and the terms of any such agreement shall not necessarily be determinative of a particular relationship.

2079.20 Nothing in this article prevents an agent from selecting, as a condition of the agent's employment, a specific form of agency relationship not specifically prohibited by this article if the requirements of Section 2079.14 and Section 2079.17 are complied with.

2079.21 A dual agent shall not disclose to the buyer that the seller is willing to sell the property at a price less than the listing price, without the express written consent of the seller. A dual agent shall not disclose to the seller that the buyer is willing to pay a price greater than the offering price, without the express written consent of the buyer. This section does not alter in any way the duty or responsibility of a dual agent to any principal with respect to confidential information other than price.

2079.22 Nothing in this article precludes a listing agent from also being a selling agent, and the combination of these functions in one agent does not, of itself, make that agent a dual agent.

2079.23 A contract between the principal and agent may be modified or altered to change the agency relationship at any time before the performance of the act which is the object of the agency with the written consent of the parties to the agency relationship.

2079.24 Nothing in this article shall be construed to either diminish the duty of disclosure owed buyers and sellers by agents and their associate licensees, subagents, and employees or to relieve agents and their associate licensees, subagents, and employees from liability for their conduct in connection with acts governed by this article or for any breach of a fiduciary duty or a duty of disclosure.

Reviewed by _____ Date _____

EQUAL HOUSING OPPORTUNITY

AD REVISED 12/14 (PAGE 2 OF 2)

DISCLOSURE REGARDING REAL ESTATE AGENCY RELATIONSHIP (AD PAGE 2 OF 2)

| An attorney takes someone else's place. | A **special power of attorney** gives an agent authority to carry out a specific act or acts. A **general power of attorney** authorizes an agent to carry out all of the business dealings of the principal. |

Exercise 6-1

The following case problems illustrate some of the concepts you have just learned. Identify those concepts and answer the questions asked about them.

1. Glenda Golden has been declared mentally incompetent and resides in a nursing home. Her parents, who have moved to Retirement City, transferred title to their ranch to a trust established for Glenda, their only heir. Glenda learns of this and contacts Helen Silver, leading salesperson for XYZ Realty, about selling the ranch. Helen knows the property will sell quickly. Should Helen take the listing?

2. All of the salespeople at ABC Real Estate work strictly on commission. No deductions are made from their commissions, which they share with ABC. They have no office duties and are billed for any use of secretarial staff, phones, conference rooms, and so on. They do receive referrals from ABC, which they can accept or reject. Describe the relationship between ABC Real Estate and its salespeople.

3. Salesperson Sam is a good friend of the Patels, who ask Sam to help them find a small office building for their mail-order business. The Patels tell Sam they will pay him $1,000 as a fee if within 30 days he can find a suitable building available for occupancy. The Patels and Sam sign a written agency agreement to that effect. The next day, Sam is approached by Jim Nelson, who wishes to sell an office building that meets the Patels' specifications exactly. Can Sam sign an agency agreement on behalf of his broker with Jim Nelson? In other words, can he list the Nelson property for sale? If Sam lists the Nelson property, can he then show that property to the Patels? Should he?

HOW AN AGENCY RELATIONSHIP IS CREATED

The agreement between principal and agent that forms the basis of the agency may come about in one of several ways. This section discusses the creation of an agency relationship by

- express agreement;
- ratification; and
- estoppel.

FIGURE 6.3: **Agency Confirmation Form**

CALIFORNIA ASSOCIATION OF REALTORS ®

CONFIRMATION OF REAL ESTATE AGENCY RELATIONSHIPS
(As required by the Civil Code)
(C.A.R. Form AC, Revised 04/08)

Subject Property Address _____

The following agency relationship(s) is/are hereby confirmed for this transaction:

LISTING AGENT: _____
(Print Firm Name)

is the agent of (check one):

❏ the Seller/ Landlord exclusively; or

❏ both the Buyer/Tenant and Seller/Landlord

SELLING AGENT: _____
(Print Firm Name)
(if not the same as Listing Agent)

is the agent of (check one):

❏ the Buyer/Tenant exclusively; or

❏ the Seller/Landlord exclusively; or

❏ both the Buyer/Tenant and Seller/Landlord

I/WE ACKNOWLEDGE RECEIPT OF A COPY OF THIS CONFIRMATION.

Seller/Landlord _____ Date _____

Seller/Landlord _____ Date _____

Buyer/Tenant _____ Date _____

Buyer/Tenant _____ Date _____

Real Estate Broker (Selling Firm) _____

By _____ Date _____

Real Estate Broker (Listing Firm) _____

By _____ Date _____

A REAL ESTATE BROKER IS QUALIFIED TO ADVISE ON REAL ESTATE. IF YOU DESIRE LEGAL ADVICE, CONSULT YOUR ATTORNEY.

Published and Distributed by:
REAL ESTATE BUSINESS SERVICES, INC.
a subsidiary of the California Association of REALTORS
525 South Virgil Avenue, Los Angeles, California 90020

Reviewed by _____ Date _____

EQUAL HOUSING OPPORTUNITY

CONFIRMATION REAL ESTATE AGENCY RELATIONSHIPS (AC PAGE 1 OF 1)

Source: Reprinted with permission, California Association of REALTORS®. Endorsement not implied.

Express Agreement

An **express agreement** is established by an act of the parties that both parties acknowledge. The agreement does not have to be in writing, unless

- the law requires a writing, or

- the agent is to perform an act on behalf of the principal that requires a writing.

This is known as the **equal dignities rule**. An agency permitting an agent to establish such a contract for the principal must itself be in writing. The *statute of frauds* stipulates the kinds of contracts that must be written to be enforceable. Three rules applicable to real estate are summarized as follows:

1. The California Real Estate Law requires that the employment agreement between a real estate broker and salesperson be in writing.

2. The statute of frauds dictates that a contract for the sale of real estate or the lease of real estate for longer than one year must be in writing. This means that any agency agreement authorizing those actions must be written.

3. The statute of frauds also requires that a contract that authorizes an agent to find a purchaser or lessee (for more than one year) of real estate—a listing agreement—be written.

Ratification

An agency could also be established by a subsequent **ratification** (authorization) by either the principal or the agent of an activity of the other that held out an agency relationship.

FOR EXAMPLE   Broker Al Teller knows that his neighbor Woody is trying to sell a small lot in the downtown area that is zoned for commercial use. Because of its size, the lot is worth about $5,000. Al offers to find a buyer if he is given a 10% commission. Woody does not make a commitment but says he will think it over. The next day at a Chamber of Commerce luncheon, Joe Everett mentions to Al that he is looking for a small lot downtown to open a sandwich shop. Al tells Joe about his neighbor's property, and Joe is enthusiastic. Later that day, Al brings Joe to see the lot, and Joe states that he is willing to offer $4,500 for it. Al brings Joe's offer to Woody. If Woody accepts Joe's offer, will he have to pay Al a commission?

If Woody accepts the offer, he will ratify an agency agreement with Al on the terms discussed earlier.

Caution: If an agency agreement for the sale of real estate is formed by ratification, the ratification must be in writing and comply with all of the other formalities that would ordinarily be required for a valid real estate contract.

Estoppel

Another way to form an agency by operation of law is by **estoppel**. Someone may represent that another person is her agent, and a third person may rely on that representation and deal with the "agent" accordingly. If so, the "principal" will not be able to evade the agency relationship. An agency created by estoppel is also called an **ostensible agency** or **implied agency**.

FOR EXAMPLE Smith tells Jones that broker Bob is selling the Smith home. Jones brings an offer to Bob, who prepares a written offer to purchase, listing himself as the broker and stipulating a commission rate. Smith can accept the offer by signing it. If he does so, will an agency be created?

Yes, if Smith accepts the offer, which lists broker Bob as the selling agent entitled to the sales commission. Smith's acceptance by signing the agreement would satisfy the requirement for a writing.

Exercise 6-2

1. Richard and Roberta Simpson have decided to sell their condominium in Long Beach. They talk to broker Bonita, who does a market analysis for them and recommends a selling price in the $380,000–$400,000 range. Richard and Roberta tell Bonita they will think it over, but if they decide to sell, they will want to ask for $410,000, so that they will have at least $380,000 left after paying the sales commission and closing costs.

   Is broker Bonita the Simpsons' agent?

2. The next day, Bonita calls the Simpsons and tells them that an out-of-town buyer, anxious to close a deal on a condominium, is in her office and would like to see their home. The Simpsons allow Bonita to bring the prospective buyer through their condominium.

   Is broker Bonita the Simpsons' agent?

3. The out-of-town buyer makes an offer, through Bonita, of $395,000. The real estate purchase contract, signed by the buyer and broker Bonita, lists Bonita as selling broker, to receive a 6% commission on the sale. After talking it over, the Simpsons decide the offer is a good one, and they accept it by signing the contract.

   Is broker Bonita the Simpsons' agent?

AGENCY AGREEMENTS

An agreement creating an agency is a form of contract. Unit 1 included an example of an independent contractor agreement between broker and associate licensee. This section begins with a discussion of general contract requirements. Then, the types of listing agreement are explained. Finally, examples of a listing agreement and a buyer brokerage agreement are discussed.

Requirements for a Valid Contract

A real estate agency agreement must comply with the following legal requirements to create a valid contract (discussed in detail in Unit 7):

- The agency agreement must be made by parties who have the capacity to contract.

- Both parties must consent to the terms of the contract.

- The contract must have a lawful objective.

- There must be consideration—that is, an obligation on both parties.

A real estate listing agreement generally requires the broker (the agent) to find a buyer. If a buyer is found, the seller (the principal) will be required to pay the agent a commission based on the sales price agreed on by the seller and buyer.

If all of the above requirements are met, a **bilateral contract** has been formed. Each party to the contract has a separate obligation to perform, as provided in the contract. When only one party has an obligation under the contract, a **unilateral contract** is formed. A seller of real estate, for example, must pay a commission if the broker finds a ready, willing, and able buyer. But if a listing agreement is a unilateral contract, the broker is not obligated to exert any effort to find such a buyer.

Due diligence implies a good-faith effort to fulfill contract obligations.

For obvious reasons, unilateral contracts to sell real estate are not common in California. Listing agreements as well as other agency agreements (such as the broker-salesperson contract discussed in this unit) require the agent to use **due diligence** in carrying out the purpose of the contract.

FOR EXAMPLE   Salesperson Sam signs a broker-salesperson contract with broker Bob. Sam is to use due diligence in handling the listings of Bob's company. In return, Sam will receive a percentage of the commission on every sale he makes. What is Bob's obligation under the contract? What is Bob's obligation if Sam fails to sell, lease, or rent any listings?

Broker Bob will pay salesperson Sam a share of the commission received on a completed transaction. Bob has no obligation to pay Sam unless Sam brings about a sale or other transaction.

The Real Estate Agent's Commission

- In California, real estate commissions are negotiable.

- There is no predetermined commission rate.

- Seller and broker are free to set whatever rate they agree on.

Authority of an Agent

The **actual authority** of an agent is what is specified in the agency agreement. An agent can be given authority to do any lawful thing short of a personal act that only the principal can perform. A real estate agent, for example, can be authorized to conduct an open house but will not be able to order repair work done on the property. An agent's authority may be broadened in an emergency, if immediate action is required and the principal is unavailable.

> The role of the agent is defined in the agency agreement.

A typical real estate listing agreement specifies the obligation of the broker in soliciting offers. Under a broker-salesperson contract, a salesperson is employed by a broker, for compensation or in expectation of compensation, to perform an act the broker could perform.

An agent also has **inherent authority**, depending on the nature of the agent's obligations. There always are activities the agent needs to perform that are not mentioned in the contract, no matter how detailed. In conducting an open house, for instance, a real estate licensee may advertise, distribute flyers in the neighborhood, and post signs at nearby intersections, none of which is likely to be specified in the listing agreement.

An agent may appear to have authority he does not have. This **apparent authority** places no obligation on the party the agent claims to represent, but it will make the agent liable for his representations.

FOR EXAMPLE Broker Murphy meets Paula Phillips, who is looking for a house in Murphy's area. Paula describes what she wants, and Murphy realizes that his neighbor's house meets Paula's specifications exactly. Broker Murphy describes the house to Paula, who makes a special trip to town to see it. He did not tell Paula that the house he has described is not for sale. He is unable to persuade his neighbor that she should put her house up for sale, and he cannot reach Paula in time to call off her trip. Does Murphy have any liability to Paula?

At the least, Murphy will be dealing with a disappointed customer, and he may have to pay her expenses in traveling to his area. At the worst, Paula will complain to the Real Estate Commissioner, who may discipline Murphy for his misrepresentation.

Handling deposits One of a real estate licensee's most important obligations, as expressed in standard listing agreement forms, is to receive a deposit from a prospective buyer. The form of the deposit must be clearly disclosed to the seller and may influence the seller's decision to accept or reject the offer. For example, the offer may be accompanied by a demand note ("pay to buyer" note) or post-dated check, either of which will be less desirable than an immediately negotiable check.

Within three business days following receipt of deposit funds by the broker or broker's salesperson, if the funds have not been returned to their owner, they must be placed in a neutral escrow depository or in a trust fund account set up for the specific purpose of handling client and customer monies. A deposit check may be held uncashed by the broker until acceptance of the offer if

- the check is not negotiable by the broker, or the offeror has given written instructions that the check may not be deposited or cashed until acceptance of the offer, *and*
- the offeree is informed that the check is being held uncashed.

In most cases, the deposit is placed in an escrow account if the contract offer is accepted by the seller. If the offer is not accepted, the deposit is returned to the buyer. In either situation, the agent should make a record of the check's disposition.

Unless specifically authorized by the seller in a listing or other agreement, a real estate broker or salesperson taking possession of a buyer's deposit is acting as the buyer's agent. A buyer's representative who agrees to transmit the buyer's deposit to a seller should make sure the deposit is made out correctly and held in a safe place until it is delivered.

Above all, the real estate agent must avoid **commingling** funds. This occurs if the agent places client or customer funds in the agent's personal account. The Real Estate Commissioner can bring disciplinary action for any violation of this rule. The easiest way to avoid problems is to have the deposit check made out to the escrow (closing) agent.

Exercise 6-3

1. Frank Rice, a licensed real estate broker, lists the Marlow house for sale. If Frank becomes ill and is unable to carry out the terms of his agreement, can he delegate that responsibility to another broker?

2. Broker Rice has received an offer on the Marlow house along with a deposit check for $1,000, which his agency agreement authorizes him to receive. It is early evening when Rice receives the check, which he will present the offer to the seller the next morning. What should Rice do with the check in the meantime?

3. Broker Rice has been given a deposit check for $2,000 by a buyer. He neglected to tell the buyer to whom to make out the check, and the buyer made the check out to him. The buyer's offer is accepted. Broker Rice deposits the check in his personal account and immediately writes out his own check to the title company that will handle the sale. Has broker Rice acted correctly?

Listing Agreements

An agreement establishing an agency relationship between a real estate property owner and a real estate broker, for the purpose of selling or buying real estate, must be in writing. A written agreement should be signed by both parties as soon as possible after the client has indicated a willingness to list property.

The following box summarizes all forms of written real estate listing agreements. Note that all refer only to the real estate broker, because a salesperson (associate licensee) can act only on behalf of a broker. An associate licensee who acts with that authority can perform as the broker would in any of these situations.

Listing Agreements

Open Listing

Nonexclusive
Commission earned only if listing broker is procuring cause of sale

Exclusive Agency Listing

No other broker authorized
Owner may sell without owing commission

Exclusive Authorization and Right-to-Sell Listing

No other broker authorized
Cooperating broker may be brought in
Commission owed no matter who sells the property

Net Listing

No other broker authorized
Seller receives predetermined amount and broker receives excess

Option Listing

No other broker authorized
Broker has right to purchase the property
Requires full disclosure to seller of broker's profit if option exercised

Note also that there must be a *definite termination date* in any agreement that makes the listing broker the exclusive agent of the seller. The Business and Professions Code provides for suspension or revocation of a real estate license if the licensee claims, demands, or receives any compensation under any exclusive agreement, if the agreement "does not contain a definite, specified date of final and complete termination."

Open listing   An **open listing**, also called a *nonexclusive listing*, provides for a commission to the broker if the broker is the procuring cause of a sale. It provides no compensation if another broker fulfills that task or if the owner does. To be the procuring cause of a sale, the agent must be the one who brings the parties together or at least must initiate the contact that leads to a sale. Because there is no assurance that the listing broker will be the one to sell the listed property, this form of listing generally is avoided in residential transactions. It is often used in industrial and commercial property transactions, however.

Exclusive agency listing   With an **exclusive agency listing**, the property owner cannot list the property with another broker at the same time. The listing broker thus has the protection of getting at least a share of the commission if another broker finds a buyer. The protection is not complete, however, because the owner still may find a buyer without the broker's assistance and thus avoid paying any commission. In effect, the listing may become a "sale by owner."

Exclusive authorization and right-to-sell listing   The most commonly used form of agreement, and the only one that will be accepted by most employing brokers, is the **exclusive authorization and right-to-sell** listing. With this type of listing, the broker is entitled to a commission no matter who sells the property, even if the owner appears to find a buyer without the broker's assistance. The buyer may have found the property address on the internet, for example, or may have seen a sign on the property and contacted the owner directly. The listing broker is the owner's agent but has the option of being a dual agent. The commission typically is shared with any cooperating broker or subagent who procures a buyer. This type of listing agreement usually contains a **safety clause** that will cover a buyer the broker is working with even after the listing expires, as long as the broker has registered that buyer with the owner. The contract will specify the length of time after the listing expires during which the broker may still be compensated, whether or not the owner signs a new listing agreement with a different broker.

The **multiple listing clause** that is a part of the exclusive authorization and right-to-sell listing allows the property to be made available to other brokers participating in the MLS. The requirements of the broker's MLS determine whether the broker must place every listing into the MLS and how members of the MLS will be treated.

FOR EXAMPLE   Lydia lists her residence for sale. Broker Reina has an MLS clause in her exclusive authorization and right-to-sell listing agreement with Lydia. If broker Bob, a member of the MLS, finds a buyer, does broker Reina deserve a commission?

Yes. Broker Reina is entitled to the listing broker's share of the commission.

Net listing   In a **net listing**, the broker's compensation is whatever amount the property sells for over a previously agreed (net) amount. If the selling price is equal to or less than the agreed-on net listing amount, the broker receives no compensation.

Before it is accepted by the seller, this kind of agreement requires full disclosure of

- the selling price and
- the amount of compensation the broker will receive.

Without these disclosures, the broker and associate licensee may face license revocation or suspension. Because such an arrangement is both inherently risky (the broker may earn little or no compensation) and inherently suspect (a high commission may hint at a too-low net listing price), it should be avoided.

FOR EXAMPLE   A property's owners are selling a buildable lot in Palm Springs, and want to receive $143,000 after the commission and all costs are paid. Broker Bob signs a net listing agreement with the owners, specifying that they are to receive $143,000 for their property. What is Broker Bob's commission if the property is sold for $158,000? For $147,000?

$158,000	Selling price
− 143,000	Net listing price
$15,000	
− 2,000	Costs of sale
$13,000	Broker's commission

$147,000	Selling price
− 143,000	Net listing price
$4,000	
− 2,000	Costs of sale
$2,000	Broker's commission

Option listing   An **option listing** gives the broker the right to purchase the property. The broker thus can possibly be both a principal and agent in the same transaction. The broker must be scrupulous in fulfilling all obligations to the principal, particularly in informing the principal of all offers. If the broker exercises the option, the principal must be informed of the broker's profit in the transaction and agree to it in writing.

Terms of the Listing

Figure 6.4 is a typical exclusive authorization and right-to-sell listing contract. This form was prepared by the California Association of REALTORS®. The features of the contract are explained in the following list. The numbered paragraphs refer to the numbered sections of the contract:

1. Space is provided for the seller's name, the broker's name, the dates the listing will begin and end, the city and county in which the property is located, the assessor's parcel number, and a detailed enough description to exclude all other property.

2. Listing price is indicated in words and numbers. The seller's preferred purchase terms also can be indicated.

3. The commission rate on the sale of a single-family residence is negotiable. This fact is required by law to appear in the listing agreement for property of one to four residential units. Section 3A2 is the broker's "safety clause." The parties agree to a reasonable time after the expiration of the listing agreement during which the seller will be obliged to pay a commission if anyone brought to the seller by the broker (or a cooperating broker) during the listing term buys the property. The broker should give the names of such prospective buyers to the seller within three calendar days of termination of the contract.

Other clauses provide for the broker's compensation in the event of a property exchange, the seller's default, or the default of anyone other than the seller. In Section 3D, the broker is authorized to cooperate with other brokers through the MLS or otherwise. In Section 3E, the seller agrees to pay the broker's compensation through escrow. Section 3F provides for compensation to a broker with whom the seller has previously listed the property, if the name of the buyer is identified in this section.

4A. The contract should stipulate any fixtures the owner is excluding or personal property (such as furniture) the owner is including in the sale.

4B. Indicate any items on the property that are leased, such as a water softener, solar system, or alarm system.

5. The broker is authorized to use the MLS unless the seller gives written authorization to exclude the listing from the MLS in a separate form. The seller can exclude the property from display on internet sites or electronic displays of MLS participants and subscribers, but that exclusion may not limit access to property information made available by other internet sites that are not under the control of the MLS.

6. Seller knows of no loan delinquency, bankruptcy, or other legal action that would affect the property or its transfer.

7. The broker promises to use reasonable effort and act with due diligence to find a buyer for the listed property. The broker is authorized to advertise and market the property. The seller promises to consider all offers presented by the broker and to act in good faith. The seller agrees to indemnify the broker (including paying the broker's legal fees) in the event of a dispute stemming from any incorrect information supplied by the seller.

8. The broker is authorized to accept a buyer's deposit for the seller.

9. The seller will receive an agency disclosure form. The broker will act as agent of the seller. Any other agency relationship requires agreement of seller and broker. Seller agrees that broker can act as a dual agent in procuring a buyer.

10. It is the seller's responsibility to insure and protect household belongings while the property is listed for sale.

11. The seller may or may not give the broker permission to use electronic images of the property, but the seller acknowledges that the broker cannot control the taking of property photographs by prospective buyers or other persons.

12. The seller may or may not allow the use of a lockbox attached outside the house (with the house key inside, accessible to brokers).

13. The seller may or may not allow a For Sale or Sold sign on the property.

14. An antidiscrimination clause is evidence of the parties' intent to obey all applicable laws.

15. Both broker and seller are made aware that if a legal action ensues, reasonable attorney's fees and other costs will be awarded to the successful party.

16. The listing agreement may be subject to lender requirements if the property is lender-owned (REO) or is being sold for less than the remaining loan balance (short sale). Any other items not already covered can be mentioned here, such as repairs to be made by the seller. This is also the place to mention any potential buyers the seller has already contacted with whom the seller wishes to deal without paying the broker a commission.

17. If an associate licensee signs the contract on behalf of the broker, the broker or the broker's manager has a five-day right of cancellation.

18. The contract can be assigned.

19. The broker and seller agree to submit any differences of opinion to mediation before going through a formal arbitration process or beginning legal action in court subject to the exceptions noted in this clause. The broker and seller may agree to submit their differences, if any, to binding arbitration, except as the clause specifies. *Note:* In 2005, the California Supreme Court held in *Grafton Partners v. Superior Court* that any pre-dispute contractual waiver of the right to a jury trial is constitutionally invalid.

20. The agreement incorporates any prior understanding of the broker and seller, whether written or oral.

21. The seller must indicate that she owns the property and any other ownership interest, if applicable.

FIGURE 6.4:   Exclusive Authorization and Right-to-Sell Listing

---

CALIFORNIA
ASSOCIATION
OF REALTORS®

RESIDENTIAL LISTING AGREEMENT
(Exclusive Authorization and Right to Sell)
(C.A.R. Form RLA, Revised 12/15)

Date Prepared: _____

1. **EXCLUSIVE RIGHT TO SELL:** _____ ("Seller")
    hereby employs and grants _____ ("Broker")
    beginning (date) _____ and ending at 11:59 P.M. on (date) _____ ("Listing Period")
    the exclusive and irrevocable right to sell or exchange the real property described as_____
    _____, situated in _____ (City),
    _____ (County), California, _____ (Zip Code), Assessor's Parcel No. _____ ("Property").
    ☐ This Property is a manufactured (mobile) home. See addendum for additional terms.
    ☐ This Property is being sold as part of a probate, conservatorship or guardianship. See addendum for additional terms.
2. **LISTING PRICE AND TERMS:**
    A. The listing price shall be: _____
    _____ Dollars ($ _____).
    B. Listing Terms: _____
    _____.
3. **COMPENSATION TO BROKER:**
    Notice: The amount or rate of real estate commissions is not fixed by law. They are set by each Broker individually and may be negotiable between Seller and Broker (real estate commissions include all compensation and fees to Broker).
    A. Seller agrees to pay to Broker as compensation for services irrespective of agency relationship(s), either ☐ _____ percent of the listing price (or if a purchase agreement is entered into, of the purchase price), or ☐ $ _____.
    AND _____, as follows:
    (1) If during the Listing Period, or any extension, Broker, cooperating broker, Seller or any other person procures a ready, willing, and able buyer(s) whose offer to purchase the Property on any price and terms is accepted by Seller, provided the Buyer completes the transaction or is prevented from doing so by Seller. (Broker is entitled to compensation whether any escrow resulting from such offer closes during or after the expiration of the Listing Period, or any extension.)
    OR (2) If within _____ calendar days (a) after the end of the Listing Period or any extension; or (b) after any cancellation of this Agreement, unless otherwise agreed, Seller enters into a contract to sell, convey, lease or otherwise transfer the Property to anyone ("Prospective Buyer") or that person's related entity: (i) who physically entered and was shown the Property during the Listing Period or any extension by Broker or a cooperating broker; or (ii) for whom Broker or any cooperating broker submitted to Seller a signed, written offer to acquire, lease, exchange or obtain an option on the Property. Seller, however, shall have no obligation to Broker under paragraph 3A(2) unless, not later than the end of the Listing Period or any extension or cancellation, Broker has given Seller a written notice of the names of such Prospective Buyers.
    OR (3) If, without Broker's prior written consent, the Property is withdrawn from sale, conveyed, leased, rented, otherwise transferred, or made unmarketable by a voluntary act of Seller during the Listing Period, or any extension.
    B. If completion of the sale is prevented by a party to the transaction other than Seller, then compensation which otherwise would have been earned under paragraph 3A shall be payable only if and when Seller collects damages by suit, arbitration, settlement or otherwise, and then in an amount equal to the lesser of one-half of the damages recovered or the above compensation, after first deducting title and escrow expenses and the expenses of collection, if any.
    C. In addition, Seller agrees to pay Broker: _____
    D. Seller has been advised of Broker's policy regarding cooperation with, and the amount of compensation offered to, other brokers.
    (1) Broker is authorized to cooperate with and compensate brokers participating through the multiple listing service(s) ("MLS") by offering to MLS brokers out of Broker's compensation specified in 3A, either ☐ _____ percent of the purchase price, or ☐ $ _____.
    (2) Broker is authorized to cooperate with and compensate brokers operating outside the MLS as per Broker's policy.
    E. Seller hereby irrevocably assigns to Broker the above compensation from Seller's funds and proceeds in escrow. Broker may submit this Agreement, as instructions to compensate Broker pursuant to paragraph 3A, to any escrow regarding the Property involving Seller and a buyer, Prospective Buyer or other transferee.
    F. **(1)** Seller represents that Seller has not previously entered into a listing agreement with another broker regarding the Property, unless specified as follows: _____
    (2) Seller warrants that Seller has no obligation to pay compensation to any other broker regarding the Property unless the Property is transferred to any of the following individuals or entities: _____
    (3) If the Property is sold to anyone listed above during the time Seller is obligated to compensate another broker: (i) Broker is not entitled to compensation under this Agreement; and (ii) Broker is not obligated to represent Seller in such transaction.
4. **A.** **ITEMS EXCLUDED AND INCLUDED:** Unless otherwise specified in a real estate purchase agreement, all fixtures and fittings that are attached to the Property are included, and personal property items are excluded, from the purchase price.
    ADDITIONAL ITEMS EXCLUDED: _____
    ADDITIONAL ITEMS INCLUDED: _____

Seller's Initials (_____)(_____)

© 2015, California Association of REALTORS®, Inc.
RLA REVISED 12/15 (PAGE 1 OF 5)   Print Date

EQUAL HOUSING
OPPORTUNITY

RESIDENTIAL LISTING AGREEMENT - EXCLUSIVE (RLA PAGE 1 OF 5)

FIGURE 6.4: Exclusive Authorization and Right-to-Sell Listing (continued)

Property Address:_____ Date:_____

Seller intends that the above items be excluded or included in offering the Property for sale, but understands that: (i) the purchase agreement supersedes any intention expressed above and will ultimately determine which items are excluded and included in the sale; and (ii) Broker is not responsible for and does not guarantee that the above exclusions and/or inclusions will be in the purchase agreement.

B. (1) Leased Items: The following items are leased:

☐ Solar power system ☐ Alarm system ☐ Propane tank ☐ Water Softener
☐ Other _____

(2) Liened Items: The following items have been financed and a lien has been placed on the Property to secure payment:

☐ Solar power system ☐ Windows or doors ☐ Heating/Ventilation/Air conditioning system
☐ Other _____

Seller will provide to Buyer, as part of the sales agreement, copies of lease documents, or other documents obligating Seller to pay for any such leased or liened item.

5. MULTIPLE LISTING SERVICE:

A. Broker is a participant/subscriber to _____ Multiple Listing Service (MLS) and possibly others. Unless otherwise instructed in writing the Property will be listed with the MLS(s) specified above. That MLS is (or if checked ☐ is not) the primary MLS for the geographic area of the Property. All terms of the transaction, including sales price and financing, if applicable, (i) will be provided to the MLS in which the property is listed for publication, dissemination and use by persons and entities on terms approved by the MLS and (ii) may be provided to the MLS even if the Property was not listed with the MLS.

BENEFITS OF USING THE MLS; IMPACT OF OPTING OUT OF THE MLS; PRESENTING ALL OFFERS

WHAT IS AN MLS? The MLS is a database of properties for sale that is available and disseminated to and accessible by all other real estate agents who are participants or subscribers to the MLS. Property information submitted to the MLS describes the price, terms and conditions under which the Seller's property is offered for sale (including but not limited to the listing broker's offer of compensation to other brokers). It is likely that a significant number of real estate practitioners in any given area are participants or subscribers to the MLS. The MLS may also be part of a reciprocal agreement to which other multiple listing services belong. Real estate agents belonging to other multiple listing services that have reciprocal agreements with the MLS also have access to the information submitted to the MLS. The MLS may further transmit listing information to Internet sites that post property listings online.

EXPOSURE TO BUYERS THROUGH MLS: Listing property with an MLS exposes a seller's property to all real estate agents and brokers (and their potential buyer clients) who are participants or subscribers to the MLS or a reciprocating MLS.

CLOSED/PRIVATE LISTING CLUBS OR GROUPS: Closed or private listing clubs or groups are not the same as the MLS. The MLS referred to above is accessible to all eligible real estate licensees and provides broad exposure for a listed property. Private or closed listing clubs or groups of licensees may have been formed outside the MLS. Private or closed listing clubs or groups are accessible to a more limited number of licensees and generally offer less exposure for listed property. Whether listing property through a closed, private network - and excluding it from the MLS - is advantageous or disadvantageous to a seller, and why, should be discussed with the agent taking the Seller's listing.

NOT LISTING PROPERTY IN A LOCAL MLS: If the Property is listed in an MLS which does not cover the geographic area where the Property is located then real estate agents and brokers working that territory, and Buyers they represent looking for property in the neighborhood, may not be aware the Property is for sale.

OPTING OUT OF MLS: If Seller elects to exclude the Property from the MLS, Seller understands and acknowledges that: (a) real estate agents and brokers from other real estate offices, and their buyer clients, who have access to that MLS may not be aware that Seller's Property is offered for sale; (b) Information about Seller's Property will not be transmitted from the MLS to various real estate Internet sites that are used by the public to search for property listings; (c) real estate agents, brokers and members of the public may be unaware of the terms and conditions under which Seller is marketing the Property.

REDUCTION IN EXPOSURE: Any reduction in exposure of the Property may lower the number of offers and negatively impact the sales price.

PRESENTING ALL OFFERS: Seller understands that Broker must present all offers received for Seller's Property unless Seller gives Broker written instructions to the contrary.

Seller's Initials (____)(____)   Broker's/agent's Initials (____)(____)

B. MLS rules generally provide that residential real property and vacant lot listings be submitted to the MLS within 2 days or some other period of time after all necessary signatures have been obtained on the listing agreement. Broker will not have to submit this listing to the MLS if, within that time, Broker submits to the MLS an appropriate form signed by Seller. ☐ Seller elects to exclude the Property from the MLS as provided by C.A.R. Form SELM or the local equivalent form.

Seller's Initials (_____)(_____)

RESIDENTIAL LISTING AGREEMENT - EXCLUSIVE (RLA PAGE 2 OF 5)

FIGURE 6.4:   Exclusive Authorization and Right-to-Sell Listing (continued)

Property Address:_____ Date:_____

C. MLS rules allow MLS data to be made available by the MLS to additional Internet sites unless Broker gives the MLS instructions to the contrary. Seller acknowledges that for any of the below opt-out instructions to be effective, Seller must make them on a separate instruction to Broker signed by Seller. Specific information that can be excluded from the Internet as permitted by (or in accordance with) the MLS is as follows:

(1) Property Availability: Seller can instruct Broker to have the MLS not display the Property on the Internet.

(2) Property Address: Seller can instruct Broker to have the MLS not display the Property address on the Internet. Seller understands that the above opt-outs would mean consumers searching for listings on the Internet may not see the Property or Property's address in response to their search.

(3) Feature Opt-Outs: Seller can instruct Broker to advise the MLS that Seller does not want visitors to MLS Participant or Subscriber Websites or Electronic Displays that display the Property listing to have the features below. Seller understands (i) that these opt-outs apply only to Websites or Electronic Displays of MLS Participants and Subscribers who are real estate broker and agent members of the MLS; (ii) that other Internet sites may or may not have the features set forth herein; and (iii) that neither Broker nor the MLS may have the ability to control or block such features on other Internet sites.

(a) Comments And Reviews: The ability to write comments or reviews about the Property on those sites; or the ability to link to another site containing such comments or reviews if the link is in immediate conjunction with the Property display.

(b) Automated Estimate Of Value: The ability to create an automated estimate of value or to link to another site containing such an estimate of value if the link is in immediate conjunction with the Property display. ☐ Seller elects to opt out of certain Internet features as provided by C.A.R. Form SELI or the local equivalent form.

6.   SELLER REPRESENTATIONS: Seller represents that, unless otherwise specified in writing, Seller is unaware of: (i) any Notice of Default recorded against the Property; (ii) any delinquent amounts due under any loan secured by, or other obligation affecting, the Property; (iii) any bankruptcy, insolvency or similar proceeding affecting the Property; (iv) any litigation, arbitration, administrative action, government investigation or other pending or threatened action that affects or may affect the Property or Seller's ability to transfer it; and (v) any current, pending or proposed special assessments affecting the Property. Seller shall promptly notify Broker in writing if Seller becomes aware of any of these items during the Listing Period or any extension thereof.

7.   BROKER'S AND SELLER'S DUTIES:

A. Broker agrees to exercise reasonable effort and due diligence to achieve the purposes of this Agreement. Unless Seller gives Broker written instructions to the contrary, Broker is authorized, but not required, to (i) order reports and disclosures including those specified in 7C as necessary, (ii) advertise and market the Property by any method and in any medium selected by Broker, including MLS and the Internet, and, to the extent permitted by these media, control the dissemination of the information submitted to any medium; and (iii) disclose to any real estate licensee making an inquiry the receipt of any offers on the Property and the offering price of such offers.

B. Seller agrees to consider offers presented by Broker, and to act in good faith to accomplish the sale of the Property by, among other things, making the Property available for showing at reasonable times and, subject to paragraph 4F, referring to Broker all inquiries of any party interested in the Property. Seller is responsible for determining at what price to list and sell the Property.

C. Investigations and Reports: Seller agrees, within 5 (or___) Days of the beginning date of this Agreement, to pay for the following pre-sale reports: ☐ Structural Pest Control ☐ General Property Inspection ☐ Homeowners Association Documents ☐ Other _____.

D. Seller further agrees to indemnify, defend and hold Broker harmless from all claims, disputes, litigation, judgments attorney fees and costs arising from any incorrect or incomplete information supplied by Seller, or from any material facts that Seller knows but fails to disclose.

8.   DEPOSIT: Broker is authorized to accept and hold on Seller's behalf any deposits to be applied toward the purchase price.

9.   AGENCY RELATIONSHIPS:

A. Disclosure: The Seller acknowledges receipt of a ☑"Disclosure Regarding Real Estate Agency Relationships" (C.A.R. Form AD).

B. Seller Representation: Broker shall represent Seller in any resulting transaction, except as specified in paragraph 3F.

C. Possible Dual Agency With Buyer: Depending upon the circumstances, it may be necessary or appropriate for Broker to act as an agent for both Seller and buyer, exchange party, or one or more additional parties ("Buyer"). Broker shall, as soon as practicable, disclose to Seller any election to act as a dual agent representing both Seller and Buyer. If a Buyer is procured directly by Broker or an associate-licensee in Broker's firm, Seller hereby consents to Broker acting as a dual agent for Seller and Buyer. In the event of an exchange, Seller hereby consents to Broker collecting compensation from additional parties for services rendered, provided there is disclosure to all parties of such agency and compensation. Seller understands and agrees that: (i) Broker, without the prior written consent of Seller, will not disclose to Buyer that Seller is willing to sell the Property at a price less than the listing price; (ii) Broker, without the prior written consent of Buyer, will not disclose to Seller that Buyer is willing to pay a price greater than the offered price; and (iii) except for (i) and (ii) above, a dual agent is obligated to disclose known facts materially affecting the value or desirability of the Property to both parties.

D. Confirmation: If the Property includes residential property with one-to-four dwelling units, Broker shall confirm the agency relationship described above, or as modified, in writing, prior to or concurrent with Seller's execution of a purchase agreement.

E. Potentially Competing Sellers and Buyers: Seller understands that Broker may have or obtain listings on other properties, and that potential buyers may consider, make offers on, or purchase through Broker, property the same as or similar to Seller's Property. Seller consents to Broker's representation of sellers and buyers of other properties before, during and after the end of this Agreement. Seller acknowledges receipt of a ☑"Possible Representation of More than One Buyer or Seller - Disclosure and Consent" (C.A.R. Form PRBS).

RLA REVISED 12/15 (PAGE 3 OF 5)   Seller's Initials (_____)(_____)

RESIDENTIAL LISTING AGREEMENT - EXCLUSIVE (RLA PAGE 3 OF 5)

FIGURE 6.4: **Exclusive Authorization and Right-to-Sell Listing (continued)**

Property Address: _____ Date:_____

10. **SECURITY AND INSURANCE:** Broker is not responsible for loss of or damage to personal or real property, or person, whether attributable to use of a keysafe/lockbox, a showing of the Property, or otherwise. Third parties, including, but not limited to, appraisers, inspectors, brokers and prospective buyers, may have access to, and take videos and photographs of, the interior of the Property. Seller agrees: (i) to take reasonable precautions to safeguard and protect valuables that might be accessible during showings of the Property; and (ii) to obtain insurance to protect against these risks. Broker does not maintain insurance to protect Seller.

11. **PHOTOGRAPHS AND INTERNET ADVERTISING:**
    A. In order to effectively market the Property for sale it is often necessary to provide photographs, virtual tours and other media to buyers. Seller agrees (or ☐ if checked, does not agree) that Broker may photograph or otherwise electronically capture images of the exterior and interior of the Property ("Images") for static and/or virtual tours of the Property by buyers and others for use on Broker's website, the MLS, and other marketing materials and sites. Seller acknowledges that once Images are placed on the Internet neither Broker nor Seller has control over who can view such Images and what use viewers may make of the Images, or how long such Images may remain available on the Internet. Seller further assigns any rights in all Images to the Broker and agrees that such Images are the property of Broker and that Broker may use such Images for advertising, including post sale and for Broker's business in the future.
    B. Seller acknowledges that prospective buyers and/or other persons coming onto the property may take photographs, videos or other images of the property. Seller understands that Broker does not have the ability to control or block the taking and use of Images by any such persons. (If checked) ☐ Seller instructs Broker to publish in the MLS that taking of Images is limited to those persons preparing Appraisal or Inspection reports. Seller acknowledges that unauthorized persons may take images who do not have access to or have not read any limiting instruction in the MLS or who take images regardless of any limiting instruction in the MLS. Once Images are taken and/or put into electronic display on the Internet or otherwise, neither Broker nor Seller has control over who views such Images nor what use viewers may make of the Images.

12. **KEYSAFE/LOCKBOX:** A keysafe/lockbox is designed to hold a key to the Property to permit access to the Property by Broker, cooperating brokers, MLS participants, their authorized licensees and representatives, authorized inspectors, and accompanied prospective buyers. Broker, cooperating brokers, MLS and Associations/Boards of REALTORS® are not insurers against injury, theft, loss, vandalism or damage attributed to the use of a keysafe/lockbox. Seller does (or if checked ☐ does not) authorize Broker to install a keysafe/lockbox. If Seller does not occupy the Property, Seller shall be responsible for obtaining occupant(s)' written permission for use of a keysafe/lockbox (C.A.R. Form KLA).

13. **SIGN:** Seller does (or if checked ☐ does not) authorize Broker to install a FOR SALE/SOLD sign on the Property.

14. **EQUAL HOUSING OPPORTUNITY:** The Property is offered in compliance with federal, state and local anti-discrimination laws.

15. **ATTORNEY FEES:** In any action, proceeding or arbitration between Seller and Broker regarding the obligation to pay compensation under this Agreement, the prevailing Seller or Broker shall be entitled to reasonable attorney fees and costs from the non-prevailing Seller or Broker, except as provided in paragraph 19A.

16. **ADDITIONAL TERMS:** ☐ REO Advisory Listing (C.A.R. Form REOL) ☐ Short Sale Information and Advisory (C.A.R. Form SSIA)

    ☐ Trust Advisory (C.A.R. Form TAL) _____
    _____
    _____
    _____
    _____

17. **MANAGEMENT APPROVAL:** If an associate-licensee in Broker's office (salesperson or broker-associate) enters into this Agreement on Broker's behalf, and Broker or Manager does not approve of its terms, Broker or Manager has the right to cancel this Agreement, in writing, within **5 Days** After its execution.

18. **SUCCESSORS AND ASSIGNS:** This Agreement shall be binding upon Seller and Seller's successors and assigns.

19. **DISPUTE RESOLUTION:**
    A. **MEDIATION:** Seller and Broker agree to mediate any dispute or claim arising between them regarding the obligation to pay compensation under this Agreement, before resorting to arbitration or court action. Mediation fees, if any, shall be divided equally among the parties involved. If, for any dispute or claim to which this paragraph applies, any party (i) commences an action without first attempting to resolve the matter through mediation, or (ii) before commencement of an action, refuses to mediate after a request has been made, then that party shall not be entitled to recover attorney fees, even if they would otherwise be available to that party in any such action. THIS MEDIATION PROVISION APPLIES WHETHER OR NOT THE ARBITRATION PROVISION IS INITIALED. **Exclusions from this mediation agreement are specified in paragraph 19C.**
    B. **ARBITRATION OF DISPUTES:**
    Seller and Broker agree that any dispute or claim in Law or equity arising between them regarding the obligation to pay compensation under this Agreement, which is not settled through mediation, shall be decided by neutral, binding arbitration. The arbitrator shall be a retired judge or justice, or an attorney with at least 5 years of residential real estate Law experience, unless the parties mutually agree to a different arbitrator. The parties shall have the right to discovery in accordance with Code of Civil Procedure §1283.05. In all other respects, the arbitration shall be conducted in accordance with Title 9 of Part 3 of the Code of Civil Procedure. Judgment upon the award of the arbitrator(s) may be entered into any court having jurisdiction. Enforcement of this agreement to arbitrate shall be governed by the Federal Arbitration Act. Exclusions from this arbitration agreement are specified in paragraph 19C.

RLA REVISED 12/15 (PAGE 4 OF 5)

Seller's Initials (_____)(_____)

RESIDENTIAL LISTING AGREEMENT - EXCLUSIVE (RLA PAGE 4 OF 5)

FIGURE 6.4:   Exclusive Authorization and Right-to-Sell Listing (continued)

Property Address:_____ Date:_____

"NOTICE: BY INITIALING IN THE SPACE BELOW YOU ARE AGREEING TO HAVE ANY DISPUTE ARISING OUT OF THE MATTERS INCLUDED IN THE 'ARBITRATION OF DISPUTES' PROVISION DECIDED BY NEUTRAL ARBITRATION AS PROVIDED BY CALIFORNIA LAW AND YOU ARE GIVING UP ANY RIGHTS YOU MIGHT POSSESS TO HAVE THE DISPUTE LITIGATED IN A COURT OR JURY TRIAL. BY INITIALING IN THE SPACE BELOW YOU ARE GIVING UP YOUR JUDICIAL RIGHTS TO DISCOVERY AND APPEAL, UNLESS THOSE RIGHTS ARE SPECIFICALLY INCLUDED IN THE 'ARBITRATION OF DISPUTES' PROVISION. IF YOU REFUSE TO SUBMIT TO ARBITRATION AFTER AGREEING TO THIS PROVISION, YOU MAY BE COMPELLED TO ARBITRATE UNDER THE AUTHORITY OF THE CALIFORNIA CODE OF CIVIL PROCEDURE. YOUR AGREEMENT TO THIS ARBITRATION PROVISION IS VOLUNTARY."

"WE HAVE READ AND UNDERSTAND THE FOREGOING AND AGREE TO SUBMIT DISPUTES ARISING OUT OF THE MATTERS INCLUDED IN THE 'ARBITRATION OF DISPUTES' PROVISION TO NEUTRAL ARBITRATION."

| Seller's Initials _____ / _____ | Broker's/agent's Initials _____ / _____ |

C. **ADDITIONAL MEDIATION AND ARBITRATION TERMS:** The following matters shall be excluded from mediation and arbitration: (i) a judicial or non-judicial foreclosure or other action or proceeding to enforce a deed of trust, mortgage or installment land sale contract as defined in Civil Code §2985; (ii) an unlawful detainer action; (iii) the filing or enforcement of a mechanic's lien; and (iv) any matter that is within the jurisdiction of a probate, small claims or bankruptcy court. The filing of a court action to enable the recording of a notice of pending action, for order of attachment, receivership, injunction, or other provisional remedies, shall not constitute a waiver or violation of the mediation and arbitration provisions.

20. **ENTIRE AGREEMENT:** All prior discussions, negotiations and agreements between the parties concerning the subject matter of this Agreement are superseded by this Agreement, which constitutes the entire contract and a complete and exclusive expression of their agreement, and may not be contradicted by evidence of any prior agreement or contemporaneous oral agreement. If any provision of this Agreement is held to be ineffective or invalid, the remaining provisions will nevertheless be given full force and effect. This Agreement and any supplement, addendum or modification, including any photocopy or facsimile, may be executed in counterparts.

21. **OWNERSHIP, TITLE AND AUTHORITY:** Seller warrants that: (i) Seller is the owner of the Property; (ii) no other persons or entities have title to the Property; and (iii) Seller has the authority to both execute this Agreement and sell the Property. Exceptions to ownership, title and authority are as follows: _____
_____.

☐ **REPRESENTATIVE CAPACITY:** This Listing Agreement is being signed for Seller by an individual acting in a Representative Capacity as specified in the attached Representative Capacity Signature Disclosure (C.A.R. Form RCSD-S). Wherever the signature or initials of the representative identified in the RCSD appear on this Agreement or any related documents, it shall be deemed to be in a representative capacity for the entity described and not in an individual capacity, unless otherwise indicated. Seller (i) represents that the entity for which the individual is signing already exists and (ii) shall Deliver to Broker, within 3 Days After Execution of this Agreement, evidence of authority to act (such as but not limited to: applicable trust document, or portion thereof, letters testamentary, court order, power of attorney, resolution, or formation documents of the business entity).

By signing below, Seller acknowledges that Seller has read, understands, received a copy of and agrees to the terms of this Agreement.

Seller_____ Date _____

Address _____ City _____ State _____ Zip _____

Telephone _____ Fax _____ E-mail _____

Seller _____ Date _____

Address _____ City _____ State _____ Zip _____

Telephone _____ Fax _____ E-mail _____

Real Estate Broker (Firm) _____ Cal BRE Lic.# _____

Address _____ City _____ State ___ Zip _____

By_____ Tel._____ E-mail_____ CalBRE Lic.#_____ Date _____

By_____ Tel._____ E-mail_____ CalBRE Lic.#_____ Date _____

☐ Two Brokers with different companies are co-listing the property. Co-listing Broker information is on the attached Additional Broker Acknowledgement (C.A.R. Form ABA).

Published and Distributed by:
REAL ESTATE BUSINESS SERVICES, INC.
a subsidiary of the California Association of REALTORS®
525 South Virgil Avenue, Los Angeles, California 90020

| Reviewed by _____ Date _____ |

RLA REVISED 12/15 (PAGE 5 OF 5)

RESIDENTIAL LISTING AGREEMENT - EXCLUSIVE (RLA PAGE 5 OF 5)

Source: Reprinted with permission, California Association of REALTORS®. Endorsement not implied.

The date of signing is given, and the seller signs. If an owner is married—even if the real estate is the seller's separate property—the other spouse's signature should also be obtained, either directly or through a power of attorney. The correct address of the seller(s) and other contact information are also important.

The broker signs and dates the contract. If an associate licensee initiates the contract, the associate signs her name next to the name of the broker or firm. The firm's mailing address and other contact information is provided.

In completing a listing agreement, the real estate agent will be guiding the property owner through a legally binding contract. Yet the agent is not permitted to give legal advice. If the owner is confused about the meaning or ramifications of any of the contract terms, the agent should recommend in writing that the owner consult an attorney before signing.

Buyer Broker Agreements

The real estate broker does not always represent the property seller. Increasingly, property buyers are recognizing the important advantages that can be obtained by having their own broker represent them in a transaction. As with other real estate contracts, the terms under which the buyer's broker will function must be specified in writing. Figure 6.5 is a typical form of buyer broker agreement. Note the following contract clauses:

- Clause 1A specifies the type of property the buyer is seeking.

- Clause 2C(1) states the limitations on the broker in a possible dual agency representation.

- Clause 2D provides for the buyer's acceptance of the broker's representation of other buyers seeking the same or similar properties.

- Clause 3 stipulates the type of compensation to be paid to the broker. This could be a fee to be paid to the broker, based on a stated amount or percentage of the purchase price of the property. Provision is made for compensating the broker in the event that the buyer enters into an agreement to purchase property that the broker introduced to the buyer, so long as the agreement is entered into within the specified number of days of the expiration of the representation period. The terms under which compensation is to be paid are stated, as is the fact that any compensation that the buyer's broker collects from anyone other than the buyer is to be credited against the fee due from the buyer.

- Clause 4 explains that the broker has no control over comments or postings on the internet regarding properties that have been shown to the buyer.

FIGURE 6.5:   **Exclusive Right to Represent Buyer**

CALIFORNIA
ASSOCIATION
OF REALTORS®

BUYER REPRESENTATION AGREEMENT - EXCLUSIVE

(C.A.R. Form BRE, Revised 4/13)

1. **EXCLUSIVE RIGHT TO REPRESENT:** _____ ("Buyer")
   grants _____ ("Broker")
   beginning on (date) _____ and ending at: **(i)** 11:59 P.M. on (date) _____, or **(ii)** completion of
   a resulting transaction, whichever occurs first ("Representation Period"), the exclusive and irrevocable right, on the terms specified
   in this Agreement, to represent Buyer in acquiring real property or a manufactured home as follows:
   A.   **PROPERTY TO BE ACQUIRED:**
        (1) Any purchase, lease or other acquisition of any real property or manufactured home described as
        Location:_____
        Other:_____
        Price range: $_____ to $_____
   OR ☐ **(2)** The following specified properties only:_____
   OR ☐ **(3)** Only the properties identified on the attached list.
   B.   Broker agrees to exercise due diligence and reasonable efforts to fulfill the following authorizations and obligations.
   C.   Broker will perform its obligations under this Agreement through the individual signing for Broker below or another real estate
        licensee assigned by Broker, who is either Broker individually or an associate-licensee (an individual licensed as a real estate
        salesperson or Broker who works under Broker's real estate license). Buyer agrees that Broker's duties are limited by the terms of
        this Agreement, including those limitations set forth in paragraphs 5 and 6.
2. **AGENCY RELATIONSHIPS:**
   A.   **DISCLOSURE:** If the property described in paragraph 4 includes residential property with one to four dwelling units, Buyer
        acknowledges receipt of the "Disclosure Regarding Real Estate Agency Relationships" (C.A.R. Form AD) prior to entering into
        this Agreement.
   B.   **BUYER REPRESENTATION:** Broker will represent, as described in this Agreement, Buyer in any resulting transaction.
   C.   **(1) POSSIBLE DUAL AGENCY WITH SELLER:** (C(1) APPLIES UNLESS C(2)(i) or (ii) is checked below.)
        Depending on the circumstances, it may be necessary or appropriate for Broker to act as an agent for both Buyer and a seller,
        exchange party, or one or more additional parties ("Seller"). Broker shall, as soon as practicable, disclose to Buyer any election
        to act as a dual agent representing both Buyer and Seller. If Buyer is shown property listed with Broker, Buyer consents to
        Broker becoming a dual agent representing both Buyer and Seller with respect to those properties. In event of dual agency,
        Buyer agrees that: **(a)** Broker, without the prior written consent of Buyer, will not disclose to Seller that the Buyer is willing to pay
        a price greater than the price offered; **(b)** Broker, without the prior written consent of Seller, will not disclose to Buyer that Seller
        is willing to sell Property at a price less than the listing price; and **(c)** other than as set forth in (a) and (b) above, a dual agent
        is obligated to disclose known facts materially affecting the value or desirability of the property to both parties.
   OR **(2) SINGLE AGENCY ONLY:** (APPLIES ONLY IF (i) or (ii) is checked below.)
        ☐ **(i) Broker's firm lists properties for sale:** Buyer understands that this election will prevent Broker from showing Buyer
        those properties that are listed with Broker's firm or from representing Buyer in connection with those properties. Buyer's
        acquisition of a property listed with Broker's firm shall not affect Broker's right to be compensated under paragraph 3. In any
        resulting transaction in which Seller's property is not listed with Broker's firm, Broker will be the exclusive agent of Buyer and not
        a dual agent also representing Seller.
   OR ☐ **(ii) Broker's firm DOES NOT list property:** Entire brokerage firm only represents buyers and does not list property. In any
        resulting transaction, Broker will be the exclusive agent of Buyer and not a dual agent also representing Seller.
   D.   **OTHER POTENTIAL BUYERS:** Buyer understands that other potential buyers may, through Broker, consider, make offers on
        or acquire the same or similar properties as those Buyer is seeking to acquire. Buyer consents to Broker's representation of such
        other potential buyers before, during and after the Representation Period, or any extension thereof.
   E.   **NON CONFIDENTIALITY OF OFFERS:** Buyer is advised that Seller or Listing Agent may disclose the existence, terms, or
        conditions of Buyer's offer unless all parties and their agent have signed a written confidentiality agreement. Whether any such
        information is actually disclosed depends on many factors, such as current market conditions, the prevailing practice in the real
        estate community, the Listing Agent's marketing strategy and the instructions of the Seller.
   F.   **CONFIRMATION:** If the Property (as defined below) includes residential property with one to four dwelling units, Broker shall
        confirm the agency relationship described above, or as modified, in writing, prior to or coincident with Buyer's execution of a
        Property Contract (as defined below).
3. **COMPENSATION TO BROKER:**
   **NOTICE: The amount or rate of real estate commissions is not fixed by law. They are set by each Broker
   individually and may be negotiable between Buyer and Broker (real estate commissions include all
   compensation and fees to Broker).**
   Buyer agrees to pay to Broker, irrespective of agency relationship(s), as follows:
   A.   **AMOUNT OF COMPENSATION: (Check (1), (2) or (3). Check only one.)**
        ☐ **(1)** _____ percent of the acquisition price AND (if checked ☐) $_____,
   OR ☐ **(2)** $_____,
   OR ☐ **(3)** Pursuant to the compensation schedule attached as an addendum _____.

   Buyer's Initials (_____)(_____)

BRE REVISED 4/13 (PAGE 1 OF 4) Print Date

Reviewed by _____ Date _____

EQUAL HOUSING
OPPORTUNITY

BUYER REPRESENTATION AGREEMENT – EXCLUSIVE (BRE PAGE 1 OF 4)

FIGURE 6.5:   Exclusive Right to Represent Buyer (continued)

Buyer: _____ Date: _____

B. COMPENSATION PAYMENTS AND CREDITS: Buyer is responsible for payment of compensation provided for in this Agreement. **However, if anyone other than Buyer compensates Broker for services covered by this Agreement, that amount shall be credited toward Buyer's obligation to pay compensation.** If the amount of compensation Broker receives from anyone other than Buyer exceeds Buyer's obligation, the excess amount shall be disclosed to Buyer and if allowed by law paid to Broker, or (if checked) ☐ credited to Buyer, or ☐ other _____ .

C. BROKER RIGHT TO COMPENSATION: Broker shall be entitled to the compensation provided for in paragraph 3A:

(1) If during the Representation Period, or any extension thereof, Buyer enters into an agreement to acquire property described in paragraph **1A**, on terms acceptable to Buyer provided Seller completes the transaction or is prevented from doing so by Buyer. (Broker shall be entitled to compensation whether any escrow resulting from such agreement closes during or after the expiration of the Representation Period.)

(2) If, within ____ **calendar days** after expiration of the Representation Period or any extension thereof, Buyer enters into an agreement to acquire property described in paragraph 1, which property Broker introduced to Buyer, or for which Broker acted on Buyer's behalf. The obligation to pay compensation pursuant to this paragraph shall arise only if, prior to or within **3 (or** ☐ _____ **) calendar days** after expiration of this Agreement or any extension thereof, Broker gives Buyer a written notice of those properties which Broker introduced to Buyer, or for which Broker acted on Buyer's behalf.

D. TIMING OF COMPENSATION: Compensation is payable:

(1) Upon completion of any resulting transaction, and if an escrow is used, through escrow.

(2) If acquisition is prevented by default of Buyer, upon Buyer's default.

(3) If acquisition is prevented by a party to the transaction other than Buyer, when Buyer collects damages by suit, settlement or otherwise. Compensation shall equal one-half of the damages recovered, not to exceed the compensation provided for in paragraph 3A, after first deducting the unreimbursed payments, credits and expenses of collection, if any.

E. Buyer hereby irrevocably assigns to Broker the compensation provided for in paragraph 3A from Buyer's funds and proceeds in escrow. Buyer agrees to submit to escrow any funds needed to compensate Broker under this Agreement. Broker may submit this Agreement, as instructions to compensate Broker, to any escrow regarding property involving Buyer and a seller or other transferor.

F. **"BUYER"** includes any person or entity, other than Broker, related to Buyer or who in any manner acts on Buyer's behalf to acquire property described in paragraph **1A**

G. (1) Buyer has not previously entered into a representation agreement with another broker regarding property described in paragraph **1A**, unless specified as follows (name other broker here): _____
_____

(2) Buyer warrants that Buyer has no obligation to pay compensation to any other broker regarding property described in paragraph **1A**, unless Buyer acquires the following property(ies): _____

(3) If Buyer acquires a property specified in G(2) above during the time Buyer is obligated to compensate another broker, Broker is neither: **(i)** entitled to compensation under this Agreement, nor **(ii)** obligated to represent Buyer in such transaction.

4. INTERNET ADVERTISING; INTERNET BLOGS; SOCIAL MEDIA: Buyer acknowledges and agrees that: (i) properties presented to them may have been marketed through a "virtual tour" on the Internet, permitting potential buyers to view properties over the Internet, or that the properties may have been the subject of comments or opinions of value by others on Internet blogs or other social media sites; (ii) neither the service provider(s) nor Broker has control over who will obtain access to such services or what action such persons might take; and (iii) Broker has no control over how long the information concerning the properties will be available on the Internet or social media sites.

5. BROKER AUTHORIZATIONS AND OBLIGATIONS:

A. Buyer authorizes Broker to: **(i)** locate and present selected properties to Buyer, present offers authorized by Buyer, and assist Buyer in negotiating for acceptance of such offers; **(ii)** assist Buyer with the financing process, including obtaining loan pre-qualification; **(iii)** upon request, provide Buyer with a list of professionals or vendors who perform the services described in the attached Buyer's Inspection Advisory; **(iv)** order reports, and schedule and attend meetings and appointments with professionals chosen by Buyer; **(v)** provide guidance to help Buyer with the acquisition of property; and **(vi)** obtain a credit report on Buyer.

B. For property transactions of which Broker is aware and not precluded from participating in by Buyer, Broker shall provide and review forms to create a property contract ("Property Contract") for the acquisition of a specific property ("Property"). With respect to such Property, Broker shall: **(i)** if the Property contains residential property with one to four dwelling units, conduct a reasonably competent and diligent on-site visual inspection of the accessible areas of the Property (excluding any common areas), and disclose to Buyer all facts materially affecting the value or desirability of such Property that are revealed by this inspection; **(ii)** deliver or communicate to Buyer any disclosures, materials or information received by, in the personal possession of or personally known to the individual signing for Broker below during the Representation Period; and **(iii)** facilitate the escrow process, including assisting Buyer in negotiating with Seller. Unless otherwise specified in writing, any information provided through Broker in the course of representing Buyer has not been and will not be verified by Broker. Broker's services are

Buyer's Initials (_____)(_____)

Reviewed by _____ Date _____

EQUAL HOUSING OPPORTUNITY

BRE REVISED 4/13 (PAGE 2 OF 4)

BUYER REPRESENTATION AGREEMENT – EXCLUSIVE (BRE PAGE 2 OF 4)

FIGURE 6.5:   **Exclusive Right to Represent Buyer (continued)**

Buyer: _____   Date: _____

performed in compliance with federal, state and local anti-discrimination laws.

6. **SCOPE OF BROKER DUTY:**

   A. While Broker will perform the duties described in paragraph 6B, Broker recommends that Buyer select other professionals, as described in the attached Buyer's Inspection Advisory, to investigate the Property through inspections, investigations, tests, surveys, reports, studies and other available information ("Inspections") during the transaction. Buyer agrees that these Inspections, to the extent they exceed the obligations described in paragraph 6B, are not within the scope of Broker's agency duties. Broker informs Buyer that it is in Buyer's best interest to obtain such Inspections.

   B. Buyer acknowledges and agrees that Broker: **(i)** does not decide what price Buyer should pay or Seller should accept; **(ii)** does not guarantee the condition of the Property; **(iii)** does not guarantee the performance, adequacy or completeness of inspections, services, products or repairs provided or made by Seller or others; **(iv)** does not have an obligation to conduct an inspection of common areas or offsite areas of the Property; **(v)** shall not be responsible for identifying defects on the Property, in common areas or offsite unless such defects are visually observable by an inspection of reasonably accessible areas of the Property or are known to Broker; **(vi)** shall not be responsible for inspecting public records or permits concerning the title or use of the Property; **(vii)** shall not be responsible for identifying the location of boundary lines or other items affecting title; **(viii)** shall not be responsible for verifying square footage, representations of others or information contained in Investigation reports, Multiple Listing Service, advertisements, flyers or other promotional material; **(ix)** shall not be responsible for providing legal or tax advice regarding any aspect of a transaction entered into by Buyer or Seller; and **(x)** shall not be responsible for providing other advice or information that exceeds the knowledge, education and experience required to perform real estate licensed activity. Buyer agrees to seek legal, tax, insurance, title and other desired assistance from appropriate professionals.

   C. Broker owes no duty to inspect for common environmental hazards, earthquake weaknesses, or geologic and seismic hazards. If Buyer receives the booklets titled "Environmental Hazards: A Guide for Homeowners, Buyers, Landlords and Tenants," "The Homeowner's Guide to Earthquake Safety," or "The Commercial Property Owner's Guide to Earthquake Safety," the booklets are deemed adequate to inform Buyer regarding the information contained in the booklets and, other than as specified in 6B above, Broker is not required to provide Buyer with additional information about the matters described in the booklets.

7. **BUYER OBLIGATIONS:**

   A. Buyer agrees to timely view and consider properties selected by Broker and to negotiate in good faith to acquire a property. Buyer further agrees to act in good faith toward the completion of any Property Contract entered into in furtherance of this Agreement. Within **5 (or ☐ _____) calendar days** from the execution of this Agreement, Buyer shall provide relevant personal and financial information to Broker to assure Buyer's ability to acquire property described in paragraph 4. If Buyer fails to provide such information, or if Buyer does not qualify financially to acquire property described in paragraph 4, then Broker may cancel this Agreement in writing. Buyer has an affirmative duty to take steps to protect him/herself, including discovery of the legal, practical and technical implications of discovered or disclosed facts, and investigation of information and facts which are known to Buyer or are within the diligent attention and observation of Buyer. Buyer is obligated, and agrees, to read all documents provided to Buyer. Buyer agrees to seek desired assistance from appropriate professionals, selected by Buyer, such as those referenced in the attached Buyer's Inspection Advisory.

   B. Buyer shall notify Broker in writing (C.A.R. Form BMI) of any material issue to Buyer, such as, but not limited to, Buyer requests for information on, or concerns regarding, any particular area of interest or importance to Buyer ("Material Issues").

   C. **Buyer agrees to: (i) indemnify, defend and hold Broker harmless from all claims, disputes, litigation, judgments, costs and attorney fees arising from any incorrect information supplied by Buyer, or from any Material Issues that Buyer fails to disclose in writing to Broker; and (ii) pay for reports, Inspections and meetings arranged by Broker on Buyer's behalf.**

   D. Buyer is advised to read the attached Buyer's Inspection Advisory for a list of items and other concerns that typically warrant Inspections or investigation by Buyer or other professionals.

8. **OTHER TERMS AND CONDITIONS:** The following disclosures or addenda are attached:

   A. ☑ Buyer's Inspection Advisory (C.A.R. Form BIA-B) _____

   B. ☐ Statewide Buyer and Seller Advisory (C.A.R. Form SBSA) _____

   C. ☐ _____

   D. ☐ _____

9. **ATTORNEY FEES:** In any action, proceeding or arbitration between Buyer and Broker regarding the obligation to pay compensation under this Agreement, the prevailing Buyer or Broker shall be entitled to reasonable attorney fees and costs, except as provided in paragraph 11A.

10. **ENTIRE AGREEMENT:** All understandings between the parties are incorporated in this Agreement. Its terms are intended by the parties as a final, complete and exclusive expression of their agreement with respect to its subject matter, and may not be contradicted by evidence of any prior agreement or contemporaneous oral agreement. This Agreement may not be extended, amended, modified, altered or changed, except in writing signed by Buyer and Broker. In the event that any provision of this Agreement is held to be ineffective or invalid, the remaining provisions will nevertheless be given full force and effect. This Agreement and any supplement, addendum or modification, including any copy, whether by copier, facsimile, NCR or electronic, may

Buyer's Initials (_____)(_____)

BRE REVISED 4/13 (PAGE 3 OF 4)

Reviewed by _____ Date _____

EQUAL HOUSING
OPPORTUNITY

BUYER REPRESENTATION AGREEMENT – EXCLUSIVE (BRE PAGE 3 OF 4)

FIGURE 6.5: **Exclusive Right to Represent Buyer (continued)**

Buyer: _____ Date: _____

be signed in two or more counterparts, all of which shall constitute one and the same writing.

11. DISPUTE RESOLUTION:

A. **MEDIATION:** Buyer and Broker agree to mediate any dispute or claim arising between them out of this Agreement, or any resulting transaction, before resorting to arbitration or court action, subject to paragraph 11B(2) below. Paragraph 11B(2) below applies whether or not the arbitration provision is initialed. Mediation fees, if any, shall be divided equally among the parties involved. If, for any dispute or claim to which this paragraph applies, any party commences an action without first attempting to resolve the matter through mediation, or refuses to mediate after a request has been made, then that party shall not be entitled to recover attorney's fees, even if they would otherwise be available to that party in any such action. THIS MEDIATION PROVISION APPLIES WHETHER OR NOT THE ARBITRATION PROVISION IS INITIALED.

B. **ARBITRATION OF DISPUTES: (1) Buyer and Broker agree that any dispute or claim in Law or equity arising between them regarding the obligation to pay compensation under this Agreement, which is not settled through mediation, shall be decided by neutral, binding arbitration, including and subject to paragraph 11B(2) below. The arbitrator shall be a retired judge or justice, or an attorney with at least five years of residential real estate law experience, unless the parties mutually agree to a different arbitrator, who shall render an award in accordance with substantive California law. The parties shall have the right to discovery in accordance with California Code of Civil Procedure §1283.05. In all other respects, the arbitration shall be conducted in accordance with Title 9 of Part III, of the California Code of Civil Procedure. Judgment upon the award of the arbitrator(s) may be entered in any court having jurisdiction. Interpretation of this Agreement to arbitrate shall be governed by the Federal Arbitration Act.**

(2) EXCLUSIONS FROM MEDIATION AND ARBITRATION: The following matters are excluded from mediation and arbitration: (i) a judicial or non-judicial foreclosure or other action or proceeding to enforce a deed of trust, mortgage or installment land sale contract as defined in California Civil Code §2985; (ii) an unlawful detainer action; (iii) the filing or enforcement of a mechanic's lien; and (iv) any matter that is within the jurisdiction of a probate, small claims or bankruptcy court. The filing of a court action to enable the recording of a notice of pending action, for order of attachment, receivership, injunction, or other provisional remedies, shall not constitute a waiver of the mediation and arbitration provisions.

"NOTICE: BY INITIALING IN THE SPACE BELOW YOU ARE AGREEING TO HAVE ANY DISPUTE ARISING OUT OF THE MATTERS INCLUDED IN THE 'ARBITRATION OF DISPUTES' PROVISION DECIDED BY NEUTRAL ARBITRATION AS PROVIDED BY CALIFORNIA LAW. YOU ARE GIVING UP ANY RIGHTS YOU MIGHT POSSESS TO HAVE THE DISPUTE LITIGATED IN A COURT OR JURY TRIAL. BY INITIALING IN THE SPACE BELOW YOU ARE GIVING UP YOUR JUDICIAL RIGHTS TO DISCOVERY AND APPEAL, UNLESS THOSE RIGHTS ARE SPECIFICALLY INCLUDED IN THE 'ARBITRATION OF DISPUTES' PROVISION. IF YOU REFUSE TO SUBMIT TO ARBITRATION AFTER AGREEING TO THIS PROVISION, YOU MAY BE COMPELLED TO ARBITRATE UNDER THE AUTHORITY OF THE CALIFORNIA CODE OF CIVIL PROCEDURE. YOUR AGREEMENT TO THIS ARBITRATION PROVISION IS VOLUNTARY."

"WE HAVE READ AND UNDERSTAND THE FOREGOING AND AGREE TO SUBMIT DISPUTES ARISING OUT OF THE MATTERS INCLUDED IN THE 'ARBITRATION OF DISPUTES' PROVISION TO NEUTRAL ARBITRATION."

Buyer's Initials _____ / _____	**Broker's Initials** _____ / _____

Buyer acknowledges that Buyer has read, understands, received a copy of and agrees to the terms of this Agreement.

Buyer _____ Date _____

Address _____ City _____ State _____ Zip _____

Telephone _____ Fax_____ E-mail _____

Buyer _____ Date _____

Address _____ City _____ State _____ Zip _____

Telephone _____ Fax_____ E-mail _____

Real Estate Broker (Firm) _____ DRE License # _____

By (Agent) _____ DRE License # _____ Date _____

Address _____ City _____ State _____ Zip _____

Telephone _____ Fax_____ E-mail _____

Published and Distributed by:
REAL ESTATE BUSINESS SERVICES, INC.
a subsidiary of the California Association of REALTORS®
525 South Virgil Avenue, Los Angeles, California 90020

BRE REVISED 4/13 (PAGE 4 OF 4)

Reviewed by _____ Date _____

BUYER REPRESENTATION AGREEMENT – EXCLUSIVE (BRE PAGE 4 OF 4)

Source: Reprinted with permission, California Association of REALTORS®. Endorsement not implied.

RIGHTS AND DUTIES OF PRINCIPAL AND AGENT

Both parties to an agency agreement have obligations. An obligation owed by one party is a corresponding right of the other party. The agent has the obligation to use **due diligence** in fulfilling the purpose of the agency agreement. This obligation also may be expressed as the right of the principal to have the agent use such diligence. This section examines the duties each owes the other and the consequences of any failure by either to perform those duties.

Duties of Agent to Principal

The real estate agent owes the principal the following duties of a fiduciary and OLD CAR:

- Obedience
- Loyalty
- Disclosure
- Confidentiality
- Accounting
- Reasonable care and skill

One of the most important duties the agent owes the principal is the duty of **loyalty**. The agent in a real estate transaction acts as a **fiduciary**, a person to whom property or the power to act is entrusted on behalf of someone else. The agent's role in the transaction is to consider the interests of the principal first and foremost.

The agent's fulfillment of the duties of **good faith and honesty** will allow the agent to fairly represent the principal's interests. The agent must respect the **confidentiality** of personal information made known to the agent by the principal. This duty extends to computerized data compiled or obtained in the course of business. Civil Code Section 1798.29 requires notification to any resident of California in the event of a breach of such data. The "Notice of Data Breach" must follow the prescribed statutory format.

To the extent required by their agreement, the agent owes the principal the duty of **obedience** in relevant matters. The principal cannot obstruct the agent's activities but can direct the agent generally. For example, a real estate agent cannot insist on showing a seller's property to prospective buyers at any time but must respect the seller's wishes. The seller, on the other hand, should comply with reasonable requests to show the property.

The agent must make **full disclosure** of all material facts concerning the transaction to the principal. The agent makes an **accounting** to the principal of the details of the transaction. This is a sensitive area for a real estate broker representing the seller in a transaction. A listing agent who brings a buyer to a seller should have qualified the buyer financially and discussed the buyer's purpose in buying real estate. Even if the listing agent legally represents only the seller, the agent inevitably is made aware of information that is useful to the seller.

For example, the agent may have learned that the buyer is an out-of-state transferee with only a limited time in which to find a house. In such a case, the seller may have a stronger bargaining position. By law, the agent must disclose such information to the client, the seller. Most real estate licensees walk a fine line in balancing their obligations to their principal against their desire to gain the confidence of the person they want to bring to a successful transaction.

The agent also must disclose to the principal any possible **conflict of interest**, such as dual representation. The agent must disclose to the principal any relationship the agent has to another party to the transaction, even if the agent or other party will derive no benefit from the relationship. At times, even the appearance of impropriety is sufficient to require the agent to act. Of course, the agent can make no **secret profit** in a transaction.

FOR EXAMPLE   XYZ Realty has listed the Rey house for sale. Mabel Perkins, an aunt of the broker who owns XYZ Realty, wants to make an offer on the Rey house. Can XYZ take the offer to the Reys?

Yes, but the relationship of Mabel Perkins to the broker must be disclosed to the sellers first, *regardless of the terms of the offer.*

The agent owes the principal the duty of **reasonable care and skill** in carrying out the tasks dictated by the agency agreement. This is true even if the relationship is gratuitous (one in which the agent receives no compensation). After the agent has performed services on behalf of the principal, whether or not for compensation, the agent owes the principal the duties of a fiduciary.

> The agent's job is to find a ready, willing, and able buyer.

The agent's primary goal in a real estate listing agreement is to find a **ready, willing, and able buyer** for the property being offered for sale. When the agent has secured an offer that is at the seller's original price and terms, and if the buyer has the cash necessary to complete the purchase or the buyer can qualify for financing by a closing date within the seller's time frame, the agent's part of the agreement has been completed. If the prospective buyer's offer, suggested terms, or both are different from the owner's original stipulation, the owner can accept the different terms or make a counteroffer. When an agreement is reached, the licensee's contractual obligations have been met.

FOR EXAMPLE   Sally and Tom Benson have listed their house at Lake Shastina for sale with broker Luis. The asking price is $165,000, and the listing is for three months. Within two months Luis procures an offer from Mary Ivers for $163,750. All other terms are as stipulated by the Bensons, and Luis has determined that Ivers should qualify for the necessary loan. The Bensons accept the offer, and the sale is carried out. Has Luis earned his commission?

Yes. Broker Luis has produced a ready, willing, and able buyer who made an offer that was acceptable to his clients.

Duties of Subagent to Principal and Agent

A **subagent** owes to the principal the *same* duties as the agent and also owes those duties to the agent. The agent bears the responsibility of taking reasonable steps to ensure that the subagent acts with the required loyalty and care. Otherwise, the agent may be liable for any improper act, or failure to act, of the subagent. If the subagency was authorized by the principal, the principal shares that liability.

Duties of Principal to Agent

If the agent's contract obligations have been fulfilled, the agent is entitled to the agreed-on **compensation**. The agent must be the **procuring cause** of the sale, lease, rental, or other transaction. In other words, the agent must be the person who initiated the contact that brought the third party to the principal.

In a listing for sale, the seller usually agrees to pay the broker a commission that is a percentage of the actual sales price. In a lease or rental agreement, the agent's compensation may be a percentage of the lease or rental value, or a flat fee.

When Is a Commission Earned?

In a real estate listing agreement, the commission is earned when the real estate broker finds a buyer who is ready, willing, and able to purchase the subject property on the seller's original terms, or when the seller accepts a purchase offer at an agreed-on price, terms, or both.

The principal can revoke the agency agreement but is liable for the expenses the agent has incurred and may be liable for the full amount of the agent's commission. In an open listing, if the seller accepts an offer that was not secured by the listing broker, the seller need not compensate the listing broker. If more than one acceptable buyer is brought to the seller, the listing broker will receive a commission only if his buyer is the first in time.

FOR EXAMPLE   XYZ Realty has an open listing agreement with the Carters. XYZ brings to the Carters a buyer who will pay their asking price and is otherwise qualified financially. While the Carters are considering the offer, a good friend offers to buy their property for $3,000 less than the asking price. Because they will come out ahead if they do not have to pay a sales commission, the Carters accept the offer. Do the Carters owe the XYZ broker a commission?

Yes, because the first acceptable offer came through XYZ Realty. If the offer through XYZ was not at the sellers' original terms, they would be free to accept their friend's offer without obligation to pay a sales commission.

With the protection offered by an exclusive authorization and right-to-sell listing agreement, the listing broker will receive a commission regardless of who produces the buyer. A rare exception to this general rule may occur if the seller identifies a prospective buyer in the listing agreement as someone to whom the property may be sold without payment of compensation to the broker, and that person buys the property.

If a different broker sells the property, the listing broker and selling broker usually share the commission according to the terms of the purchase agreement. The commission usually is paid through escrow, an efficient and usually the safest way to distribute the commission proceeds.

A principal owes an agent a **duty of care** in that the principal may not interfere with the agent's **prospective economic advantage**. This legal term means that the principal may not sabotage the agent's business. If a seller rejects a buyer brought by a broker, the seller may not turn around and make her own deal with that buyer, even if the broker and seller have an open listing agreement. If the broker is the procuring cause of a transaction, the broker has earned the agreed-on compensation.

Duties to Third Persons

A real estate agent owes to a third person a duty of **full disclosure of material facts** that the agent knows or should have known regarding the property that is the subject matter of their dealings. The agent bears this responsibility independent of any instruction received from the property owner. If the property owner tells the agent not to reveal certain defects, such as termite damage, the agent must inform the principal that the agent cannot hide such information. To do otherwise would make the agent liable for money damages and place the agent's license in jeopardy.

Material Facts

A material fact can be anything that would affect the value or desirability of the subject property. Because this is such a broad definition, the legislature and courts have created their own interpretations of just what the prospective purchaser needs to know. Conspicuous physical defects must be revealed, certainly. But other factors may not be as easy to understand. It is not necessary, for instance, to reveal a death on the premises that occurred more than three years before an offer to purchase or lease is made. Nevertheless, the agent handling such a property may not make a misrepresentation if asked a direct question by the buyer. But the agent need not reveal that an occupant of the property was afflicted with, or died from, Acquired Immunodeficiency Syndrome (AIDS). This provision appears in Civil Code Section 1710.2.

Easton v. Strassburger   The decision in the California case of *Easton v. Strassburger* (1984) expanded the broker's duty of disclosure to third persons. The court held that a real estate broker has an affirmative duty to conduct a reasonably competent and diligent inspection of residential property and to disclose to prospective purchasers all facts revealed by the investigation that materially affect the value or desirability of the property. This duty was subsequently recognized by the California legislature and made a part of the Civil Code, starting at Section 2079. It applies to residential property of one to four units.

The *Easton* case involved a house built on landfill. That fact, and the fact that one of the broker's agents noticed an "uneven floor," should have acted as red flags warranting further investigation and disclosure to the buyer. If there is a substantial property defect the agent could have discovered by a thorough inspection of the property, even if the agent failed to notice the defect, the agent may be liable to a buyer for any resulting damages.

Easton renewed interest not only in the broker's duties to prospective purchasers of residential property but also in the seller's duties to prospective purchasers. The *seller* must disclose *any material fact* known to the seller that affects the value or desirability of the property, including defects that could not be discovered from casual observation of the property. In addition, every seller of a residential property of one to four dwelling units must disclose to a potential buyer whether, during the course of the seller's ownership (or through previous knowledge), any structural additions or alterations were made to the property, and whether they were made with or without benefit of an appropriate permit.

The seller of residential property of one to four units must provide the buyer with a written **Real Estate Transfer Disclosure Statement** that details the mechanical and structural conditions of the property in a form specified by law. The disclosure requirements are subject to change. Use of a form such as that prepared by the California Association of REALTORS® (shown in Figure 6.6) is the best way for the seller and broker to be sure that the buyer is fully informed of the property's condition and that all legal requirements are met. The Agent Visual Inspection Disclosure form that is shown in Figure 14.7 in Unit 14 was prepared by the California Association of REALTORS® to help the agent clarify the limitations on the inspection that the agent performs.

Seller disclosure is also required in a sale of a used manufactured home or mobilehome if the home is classified as personal property. Wording of the disclosure form is provided in Civil Code 1102.6d.

Environmental disclosures, such as the possible presence of lead-based paint, are discussed in Unit 14.

Other duties   As in dealing with the principal, a real estate agent may not make a **secret profit** in dealing with a third party to a transaction. To do so would make the agent liable to the third party buyer or lessee.

Exaggerating the attributes or benefits of property may subject a real estate licensee to liability if persons with whom the licensee deals accept the statements as accurate. Current concern for truth in advertising has made unacceptable what once may have been considered acceptable distortions of the literal truth. The "best school district in the state" should be exactly that by some objective standard, such as student test scores, or that representation should not be made. An agent is allowed to express an opinion, of course, but the opinion should neither be presented as fact nor misrepresent the facts.

An **agent** is liable to third persons for any tort (physical injury or property damage) or other act, such as a fraudulent misrepresentation, that the agent performs. The agent also is liable for torts or other acts committed by the principal in which the agent acquiesces, whether the agent does so by act or by omission.

The **principal** is liable for

- his own acts,
- acts of an agent or a subagent that were performed on the principal's behalf, and
- torts committed by an agent who is an employee (not an independent contractor) acting in the scope of the employment.

FOR EXAMPLE   Real estate broker Luis hires Sally and agrees to pay her a salary as well as a commission on sales she makes. When showing a house, Sally carelessly neglects to lock the back door. Before the owner returns, someone enters the house and steals a video game player. Is broker Luis liable for the owner's loss?

Yes, because Sally was acting within the scope of her employment while showing the house.

FIGURE 6.6: **Real Estate Transfer Disclosure Statement**

CALIFORNIA
ASSOCIATION
OF REALTORS®

REAL ESTATE TRANSFER DISCLOSURE STATEMENT
(CALIFORNIA CIVIL CODE §1102, ET SEQ.)
(C.A.R. Form TDS, Revised 4/14)

THIS DISCLOSURE STATEMENT CONCERNS THE REAL PROPERTY SITUATED IN THE CITY OF _____
_____, COUNTY OF _____, STATE OF CALIFORNIA,
DESCRIBED AS _____.

THIS STATEMENT IS A DISCLOSURE OF THE CONDITION OF THE ABOVE DESCRIBED PROPERTY IN COMPLIANCE
WITH SECTION 1102 OF THE CIVIL CODE AS OF (date) _____. IT IS NOT A WARRANTY OF ANY
KIND BY THE SELLER(S) OR ANY AGENT(S) REPRESENTING ANY PRINCIPAL(S) IN THIS TRANSACTION, AND IS
NOT A SUBSTITUTE FOR ANY INSPECTIONS OR WARRANTIES THE PRINCIPAL(S) MAY WISH TO OBTAIN.

I. COORDINATION WITH OTHER DISCLOSURE FORMS

This Real Estate Transfer Disclosure Statement is made pursuant to Section 1102 of the Civil Code. Other statutes require disclosures,
depending upon the details of the particular real estate transaction (for example: special study zone and purchase-money liens on
residential property).

Substituted Disclosures: The following disclosures and other disclosures required by law, including the Natural Hazard Disclosure
Report/Statement that may include airport annoyances, earthquake, fire, flood, or special assessment information, have or will be made
in connection with this real estate transfer, and are intended to satisfy the disclosure obligations on this form, where the subject matter is
the same:

☐ Inspection reports completed pursuant to the contract of sale or receipt for deposit.
☐ Additional inspection reports or disclosures: _____
_____

II. SELLER'S INFORMATION

The Seller discloses the following information with the knowledge that even though this is not a warranty, prospective
Buyers may rely on this information in deciding whether and on what terms to purchase the subject property. Seller hereby
authorizes any agent(s) representing any principal(s) in this transaction to provide a copy of this statement to any person or
entity in connection with any actual or anticipated sale of the property.

THE FOLLOWING ARE REPRESENTATIONS MADE BY THE SELLER(S) AND ARE NOT THE
REPRESENTATIONS OF THE AGENT(S), IF ANY. THIS INFORMATION IS A DISCLOSURE AND IS NOT
INTENDED TO BE PART OF ANY CONTRACT BETWEEN THE BUYER AND SELLER.

Seller ☐ is ☐ is not occupying the property.

A. The subject property has the items checked below:*

☐ Range
☐ Oven
☐ Microwave
☐ Dishwasher
☐ Trash Compactor
☐ Garbage Disposal
☐ Washer/Dryer Hookups
☐ Rain Gutters
☐ Burglar Alarms
☐ Carbon Monoxide Device(s)
☐ Smoke Detector(s)
☐ Fire Alarm
☐ TV Antenna
☐ Satellite Dish
☐ Intercom
☐ Central Heating
☐ Central Air Conditioning
☐ Evaporator Cooler(s)

☐ Wall/Window Air Conditioning
☐ Sprinklers
☐ Public Sewer System
☐ Septic Tank
☐ Sump Pump
☐ Water Softener
☐ Patio/Decking
☐ Built-in Barbecue
☐ Gazebo
☐ Security Gate(s)
☐ Garage:
  ☐ Attached ☐ Not Attached
  ☐ Carport
  ☐ Automatic Garage Door Opener(s)
    ☐ Number Remote Controls ____
☐ Sauna
☐ Hot Tub/Spa:
  ☐ Locking Safety Cover

☐ Pool:
  ☐ Child Resistant Barrier
☐ Pool/Spa Heater:
  ☐ Gas ☐ Solar ☐ Electric
☐ Water Heater:
  ☐ Gas ☐ Solar ☐ Electric
☐ Water Supply:
  ☐ City ☐ Well
  ☐ Private Utility or
    Other_____
☐ Gas Supply:
  ☐ Utility ☐ Bottled (Tank)
☐ Window Screens
☐ Window Security Bars
  ☐ Quick Release Mechanism on
    Bedroom Windows
☐ Water-Conserving Plumbing Fixtures

Exhaust Fan(s) in _____ 220 Volt Wiring in _____ Fireplace(s) in _____
☐ Gas Starter _____ ☐ Roof(s): Type: _____ Age: _____ (approx.)
☐ Other: _____
Are there, to the best of your (Seller's) knowledge, any of the above that are not in operating condition? ☐ Yes ☐ No. If yes, then
describe. (Attach additional sheets if necessary):_____
_____

(*see note on page 2)

Buyer's Initials (_____)(_____)   Seller's Initials (_____)(_____)

© 2014, California Association of REALTORS®, Inc. .

TDS REVISED 4/14 (PAGE 1 OF 3) Print Date

| Reviewed by _____ Date _____ |

EQUAL HOUSING
OPPORTUNITY

REAL ESTATE TRANSFER DISCLOSURE STATEMENT (TDS PAGE 1 OF 3)

FIGURE 6.6:   Real Estate Transfer Disclosure Statement (continued)

Property Address: _____ Date:_____

B. Are you (Seller) aware of any significant defects/malfunctions in any of the following? ☐ Yes ☐ No. If yes, check appropriate space(s) below.

☐ Interior Walls ☐ Ceilings ☐ Floors ☐ Exterior Walls ☐ Insulation ☐ Roof(s) ☐ Windows ☐ Doors ☐ Foundation ☐ Slab(s)
☐ Driveways ☐ Sidewalks ☐ Walls/Fences ☐ Electrical Systems ☐ Plumbing/Sewers/Septics ☐ Other Structural Components
(Describe: _____
_____)

If any of the above is checked, explain. (Attach additional sheets if necessary.): _____
_____

*Installation of a listed appliance, device, or amenity is not a precondition of sale or transfer of the dwelling. The carbon monoxide device, garage door opener, or child-resistant pool barrier may not be in compliance with the safety standards relating to, respectively, carbon monoxide device standards of Chapter 8 (commencing with Section 13260) of Part 2 of Division 12 of, automatic reversing device standards of Chapter 12.5 (commencing with Section 19890) of Part 3 of Division 13 of, or the pool safety standards of Article 2.5 (commencing with Section 115920) of Chapter 5 of Part 10 of Division 104 of, the Health and Safety Code. Window security bars may not have quick-release mechanisms in compliance with the 1995 edition of the California Building Standards Code. Section 1101.4 of the Civil Code requires all single-family residences built on or before January 1, 1994, to be equipped with water-conserving plumbing fixtures after January 1, 2017. Additionally, on and after January 1, 2014, a single-family residence built on or before January 1, 1994, that is altered or improved is required to be equipped with water-conserving plumbing fixtures as a condition of final approval. Fixtures in this dwelling may not comply with section 1101.4 of the Civil Code.

C. Are you (Seller) aware of any of the following:

1. Substances, materials, or products which may be an environmental hazard such as, but not limited to, asbestos, formaldehyde, radon gas, lead-based paint, mold, fuel or chemical storage tanks, and contaminated soil or water on the subject property .... ☐ Yes ☐ No
2. Features of the property shared in common with adjoining landowners, such as walls, fences, and driveways, whose use or responsibility for maintenance may have an effect on the subject property .... ☐ Yes ☐ No
3. Any encroachments, easements or similar matters that may affect your interest in the subject property .... ☐ Yes ☐ No
4. Room additions, structural modifications, or other alterations or repairs made without necessary permits................ ☐ Yes ☐ No
5. Room additions, structural modifications, or other alterations or repairs not in compliance with building codes......... ☐ Yes ☐ No
6. Fill (compacted or otherwise) on the property or any portion thereof.. ☐ Yes ☐ No
7. Any settling from any cause, or slippage, sliding, or other soil problems.. ☐ Yes ☐ No
8. Flooding, drainage or grading problems .... ☐ Yes ☐ No
9. Major damage to the property or any of the structures from fire, earthquake, floods, or landslides .... ☐ Yes ☐ No
10. Any zoning violations, nonconforming uses, violations of "setback" requirements .... ☐ Yes ☐ No
11. Neighborhood noise problems or other nuisances .... ☐ Yes ☐ No
12. CC&R's or other deed restrictions or obligations .... ☐ Yes ☐ No
13. Homeowners' Association which has any authority over the subject property.. ☐ Yes ☐ No
14. Any "common area" (facilities such as pools, tennis courts, walkways, or other areas co-owned in undivided interest with others)... ☐ Yes ☐ No
15. Any notices of abatement or citations against the property .... ☐ Yes ☐ No
16. Any lawsuits by or against the Seller threatening to or affecting this real property, claims for damages by the Seller pursuant to Section 910 or 914 threatening to or affecting this real property, claims for breach of warranty pursuant to Section 900 threatening to or affecting this real property, or claims for breach of an enhanced protection agreement pursuant to Section 903 threatening to or affecting this real property, including any lawsuits or claims for damages pursuant to Section 910 or 914 alleging a defect or deficiency in this real property or "common areas" (facilities such as pools, tennis courts, walkways, or other areas co-owned in undivided interest with others) .... ☐ Yes ☐ No

If the answer to any of these is yes, explain. (Attach additional sheets if necessary.): _____
_____
_____
_____

D. 1. The Seller certifies that the property, as of the close of escrow, will be in compliance with Section 13113.8 of the Health and Safety Code by having operable smoke detector(s) which are approved, listed, and installed in accordance with the State Fire Marshal's regulations and applicable local standards.
2. The Seller certifies that the property, as of the close of escrow, will be in compliance with Section 19211 of the Health and Safety Code by having the water heater tank(s) braced, anchored, or strapped in place in accordance with applicable law.

Buyer's Initials (_____)(_____)   Seller's Initials (_____)(_____)

TDS REVISED 4/14 (PAGE 2 OF 3)   Reviewed by _____ Date _____

REAL ESTATE TRANSFER DISCLOSURE STATEMENT (TDS PAGE 2 OF 3)

FIGURE 6.6:   Real Estate Transfer Disclosure Statement (continued)

Property Address: _____ Date:_____

Seller certifies that the information herein is true and correct to the best of the Seller's knowledge as of the date signed by the Seller.

Seller_____ Date _____

Seller_____ Date _____

III. AGENT'S INSPECTION DISCLOSURE
(To be completed only if the Seller is represented by an agent in this transaction.)

THE UNDERSIGNED, BASED ON THE ABOVE INQUIRY OF THE SELLER(S) AS TO THE CONDITION OF THE PROPERTY AND BASED ON A REASONABLY COMPETENT AND DILIGENT VISUAL INSPECTION OF THE ACCESSIBLE AREAS OF THE PROPERTY IN CONJUNCTION WITH THAT INQUIRY, STATES THE FOLLOWING:

☐ See attached Agent Visual Inspection Disclosure (AVID Form)

☐ Agent notes no items for disclosure.

☐ Agent notes the following items: _____
_____
_____
_____

Agent (Broker Representing Seller) _____ By _____ Date_____
                                       (Please Print)   (Associate Licensee or Broker Signature)

IV. AGENT'S INSPECTION DISCLOSURE
(To be completed only if the agent who has obtained the offer is other than the agent above.)

THE UNDERSIGNED, BASED ON A REASONABLY COMPETENT AND DILIGENT VISUAL INSPECTION OF THE ACCESSIBLE AREAS OF THE PROPERTY, STATES THE FOLLOWING:

☐ See attached Agent Visual Inspection Disclosure (AVID Form)

☐ Agent notes no items for disclosure.

☐ Agent notes the following items: _____
_____
_____
_____

Agent (Broker Obtaining the Offer) _____ By _____ Date_____
                                      (Please Print)   (Associate Licensee or Broker Signature)

V. BUYER(S) AND SELLER(S) MAY WISH TO OBTAIN PROFESSIONAL ADVICE AND/OR INSPECTIONS OF THE PROPERTY AND TO PROVIDE FOR APPROPRIATE PROVISIONS IN A CONTRACT BETWEEN BUYER AND SELLER(S) WITH RESPECT TO ANY ADVICE/INSPECTIONS/DEFECTS.

I/WE ACKNOWLEDGE RECEIPT OF A COPY OF THIS STATEMENT.

Seller _____ Date _____ Buyer _____ Date_____

Seller _____ Date _____ Buyer _____ Date_____

Agent (Broker Representing Seller) _____ By _____ Date_____
                                  (Please Print)   (Associate Licensee or Broker Signature)

Agent (Broker Obtaining the Offer) _____ By _____ Date_____
                                  (Please Print)   (Associate Licensee or Broker Signature)

SECTION 1102.3 OF THE CIVIL CODE PROVIDES A BUYER WITH THE RIGHT TO RESCIND A PURCHASE CONTRACT FOR AT LEAST THREE DAYS AFTER THE DELIVERY OF THIS DISCLOSURE IF DELIVERY OCCURS AFTER THE SIGNING OF AN OFFER TO PURCHASE. IF YOU WISH TO RESCIND THE CONTRACT, YOU MUST ACT WITHIN THE PRESCRIBED PERIOD.

A REAL ESTATE BROKER IS QUALIFIED TO ADVISE ON REAL ESTATE. IF YOU DESIRE LEGAL ADVICE, CONSULT YOUR ATTORNEY.

© 2014, California Association of REALTORS®, Inc. THIS FORM HAS BEEN APPROVED BY THE CALIFORNIA ASSOCIATION OF REALTORS® (C.A.R.). NO REPRESENTATION IS MADE AS TO THE LEGAL VALIDITY OR ACCURACY OF ANY PROVISION IN ANY SPECIFIC TRANSACTION. A REAL ESTATE BROKER IS THE PERSON QUALIFIED TO ADVISE ON REAL ESTATE TRANSACTIONS. IF YOU DESIRE LEGAL OR TAX ADVICE, CONSULT AN APPROPRIATE PROFESSIONAL.

Published and Distributed by:
REAL ESTATE BUSINESS SERVICES, INC.
a subsidiary of the California Association of REALTORS®
525 South Virgil Avenue, Los Angeles, California 90020

TDS REVISED 4/14 (PAGE 3 OF 3)

| Reviewed by _____ Date _____ |

REAL ESTATE TRANSFER DISCLOSURE STATEMENT (TDS PAGE 3 OF 3)

Recovery Account

The responsibilities of real estate licensees to their clients and customers are taken seriously by the California legislature. A **Recovery Account** has been established to help compensate victims of fraud, misrepresentation, deceit, or conversion (the legal term for theft) of trust funds when they cannot collect a court-ordered judgment against a real estate licensee. The Recovery Account is funded by 5% of all real estate license fees collected. The amount paid out is limited to $50,000 per transaction and $250,000 per licensee, regardless of the number of victims.

If a recovery is allowed against a licensee, the real estate license of that person is automatically suspended. Reinstatement cannot be considered until the licensee has fully reimbursed the fund for the amount paid out plus interest.

Exercise 6-4

Broker Cindy Carroll of ABC Realty would like to list the Meyer estate. She offers to handle the sale at a commission of 5% of the selling price. Meyer, a widow, signs a listing agreement with Carroll. Carroll discusses the Meyer estate with an investor she knows. She agrees to bring the investor's offer to Meyer and, if the offer is accepted, to represent the investor when he resells the property, which will take place immediately after the first sale. The investor offers somewhat less than the asking price, but Carroll persuades Meyer to accept the offer. A few weeks after the sale, Carroll sells the property for the investor, who makes a 20% profit on the transaction. She earns two commissions.

Comment on broker Carroll's activities.

TERMINATION OF AN AGENCY

The California Civil Code lists the ways in which an agency relationship may be terminated. They are summarized in the box below.

> ### Ways to Terminate an Agency
>
> ■ Fulfillment of the agency agreement
>
> ■ Expiration of the term of the agreement
>
> ■ Destruction of the property
>
> ■ Death of either the principal or agent
>
> ■ Incapacity of the agent to act as an agent, or incapacity of the principal to enter into a contract
>
> ■ Agreement of the principal and agent
>
> ■ By operation of law, as in a bankruptcy

The principal or agent always has the power to terminate the agency unilaterally (without the other person's consent) in writing. But the person who terminates the agency may be liable for damages to the other party. An early cancellation of a listing agreement by a seller is an example of a situation in which the seller may be liable to the listing broker for expenses or a commission.

Notice of termination must be given to third parties with whom the principal and agent are dealing.

FOR EXAMPLE   Sara and Sam Schuster decided to move from Laguna Beach to Boise and listed their home for sale with broker Bonita Fish. After an extended vacation in Boise, the Schusters decided to stay in Laguna Beach and notified Fish that they were taking their house off the market. Can they cancel the listing agreement?

Yes, the Schusters can unilaterally cancel the listing agreement. Broker Fish must decide whether she wants to charge the Schusters for any expenses she incurred in marketing their property. If Fish had already found a ready, willing, and able buyer for the Schuster house, she could also insist on payment of her commission on the transaction.

SUMMARY

The *agency relationship* establishes the authority of the **agent** as a **special agent** or **general agent** to act on behalf of a **principal** in dealing with third parties.

A *real estate listing agreement* authorizes a broker to receive a deposit on behalf of the seller, market the property, and authorize payment to **cooperating brokers**. The **multiple listing service** (MLS) is an association of real estate agents who place properties listed for sale in a network that may be accessed by other MLS members. A seller may make an offer of **subagency** through the MLS.

An agent may be an **employee** or an **independent contractor**. The California Real Estate Law will always treat a salesperson or another associate licensee as an employee of a broker in considering the associate's rights and responsibilities to buyers, sellers, and other parties to a real estate transaction.

A **dual agent** serves both buyer and seller in the same transaction. All transactions of residential properties of up to four units require *written disclosure* of the agent's representation. A **power of attorney** granted to an **attorney-in-fact** will enable that person to act in the capacity of the principal.

An agency may be established by **express agreement**. A principal may *ratify* conduct that establishes an agency, or an **ostensible (implied) agency** could be formed by **estoppel**.

A contract between broker and salesperson must have the same formalities as any contract, including consideration by both parties.

An agent's **authority** may be **actual**, **inherent**, or **apparent**. If a real estate licensee receives funds on behalf of a client or customer, those funds must not be **commingled** with the licensee's own funds.

Listing agreements, which must be written, establish the agency relationship of real estate broker and client. The parties may agree to an **open (nonexclusive) listing**, an **exclusive agency listing**, an **exclusive authorization and right-to-sell listing** (which may have a **multiple listing clause**), a **net listing**, or an **option listing**.

Buyer broker agreements, which must also be written, provide important benefits and protections for property buyers through representation by their own real estate broker.

The real estate agent owes the duties of a **fiduciary** to the principal, whether a buyer or seller. The agent must reveal any possible **conflict of interest** and may not make a **secret profit**.

The real estate agent's main task in listing property for sale is to find a **ready, willing, and able buyer**. The principal must pay the agreed-on compensation if the agent fulfills the agreement. In a real estate transaction, that means that the agent is the **procuring cause** of a sale, a lease, a rental, or another agreement.

Both principal and agent owe certain duties to third persons. Both must make **full disclosure of all material facts** and defects affecting the desirability of the property. Both must *inspect* the property and reveal its *condition* to a potential buyer. The agent must not make a **secret profit** at the expense of a third person.

The **Recovery Account** has been formed to help compensate victims of misconduct by real estate licensees.

OPEN FOR DISCUSSION

In some large real estate offices, the broker of record manages the work of many associate licensees.

1. Do you think there should be a limit on the number of licensees that are supervised by one broker?
2. If so, what should that limit be?

REVIEW QUESTIONS

1. Generally an agent works for
   a. the principal.
   b. the third person.
   c. the subagent.
   d. the California Bureau of Real Estate.

2. A minor
   a. may be a licensed real estate agent.
   b. is anyone younger than 21 years of age.
   c. may be a licensed real estate salesperson.
   d. is anyone younger than 18 years of age.

3. Someone appointed to carry out a particular transaction is
   a. a general agent.
   b. a special agent.
   c. a secret agent.
   d. a subagent.

4. An independent contractor is distinguished by
   a. responsibility for Social Security and other payments.
   b. no flexibility in setting work hours.
   c. little control over work methods.
   d. no legal obligation to employer.

5. The California Real Estate Law treats a real estate salesperson as
   a. an independent contractor of the broker.
   b. an employee of the broker.
   c. a sole proprietor.
   d. a partner of the broker.

6. A salesperson is a broker's
   a. principal.
   b. agent.
   c. subagent.
   d. third person.

7. An agency agreement to perform an act that requires a writing
   a. must itself be in writing.
   b. may be oral or written.
   c. cannot be an express agreement.
   d. violates the statute of frauds.

8. To be enforceable, all real estate sales contracts
   a. may be oral or written.
   b. must be in writing.
   c. must comply with the equal equities rule.
   d. must be completed within 90 days of origination.

9. As a contract, a real estate agency agreement
   a. can have any objective.
   b. needs only to be made by parties with the capacity to contract.
   c. does not need to be supported by consideration.
   d. must meet the requirements for a valid contract.

10. Real estate commission rates
    a. are established by the California Bureau of Real Estate.
    b. should be no lower than 2%.
    c. should be no higher than 10%.
    d. are not fixed by law.

11. All real estate agency agreements must
    a. expire in 90 days.
    b. be in writing.
    c. be signed before a buyer is solicited.
    d. be approved by the California Bureau of Real Estate.

12. The MOST commonly used form of real estate listing agreement is
    a. the open listing.
    b. the exclusive agency listing.
    c. the exclusive authorization and right-to-sell listing.
    d. the net listing.

13. A real estate agent owes duties to
    a. the principal.
    b. the third person.
    c. the subagent.
    d. all of these.

14. The agent owes the principal the duty of
    a. loyalty.
    b. compensation.
    c. extraordinary care and skill.
    d. dual representation.

15. A real estate agent must make full disclosure of
    a. all material facts known by the agent.
    b. all material facts revealed by the owner of the property.
    c. material facts that are known by the agent or that would be revealed by a reasonable inspection of the property.
    d. all actual or potential property defects, of whatever kind.

16. The principal owes the agent
    a. only the duty of compensation.
    b. the duty of obedience.
    c. the duty of care.
    d. the duties of a fiduciary.

17. A real estate seller must disclose
    a. only visible property defects.
    b. structural additions or repairs only if made by the seller.
    c. material facts concerning the property's value or desirability.
    d. only defects that would be revealed by a property inspection.

18. Exaggerating a property's value or desirability
    a. is permissible.
    b. is expected in the average transaction.
    c. is justifiable as harmless "puffing."
    d. is never permitted.

19. The Recovery Account is available to
    a. brokers.
    b. salespeople.
    c. people victimized by a real estate licensee.
    d. real estate licensees victimized by their clients.

20. An agency relationship may NOT be terminated by
    a. completion of the agreement.
    b. expiration of the terms of the agreement.
    c. agreement of the parties.
    d. someone outside the agency relationship.

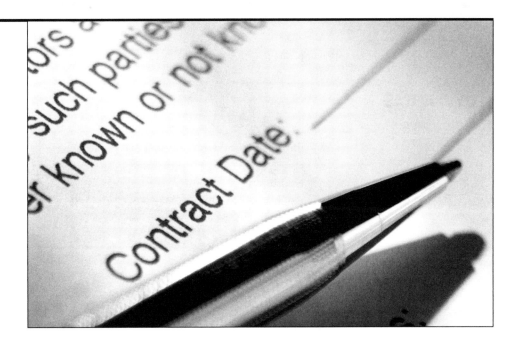

CONTRACTS

LEARNING OBJECTIVES

When you have completed this unit, you will be able to

- **define** executory, executed, express, implied, bilateral, and unilateral contracts;
- **explain** the elements of a valid contract and how a contract becomes void, voidable, or unenforceable;
- **describe** the effect of a counteroffer or rejection of an offer;
- **explain** how an offer can be revoked;
- **identify** the provisions of the statute of frauds and the statute of limitations;
- **list** the ways in which a contract can be discharged; and
- **define** an option and exchange.

KEY TERMS

actual fraud	fraudulent	offeror
affirmative fraud	misrepresentation	option
assignee	implied contract	oral contract
assignment	impossibility of	performance
assignor	performance	real estate purchase
bilateral contract	impracticability of	contract
breach of contract	performance	reformation
commercial frustration	lawful object	rejection
consideration	legal capacity	release
constructive fraud	liquidated damages	rescission
contract	minor	revocation
contractual obligation	mutual consent	specific performance
counteroffer	mutuality of contract	statute of frauds
default	Natural Hazard	statute of limitations
discharged contract	Disclosure Statement	tender
emancipated minor	negative fraud	undue influence
exchange	negligent	unenforceable contract
executed contract	misrepresentation	unilateral contract
executory contract	novation	valid contract
express contract	offer and acceptance	void contract
	offeree	voidable contract

WHAT IS A CONTRACT?

A **contract** is a promise made by one person to another to do something *or* to refrain from doing something. A person who takes part in a contract is referred to as a *party* to the contract. The contract promise may be made by only one of the parties, or a separate promise may be made by each of the parties. The promise each party makes is called that party's **contractual obligation**. An offer to perform a contractual obligation is called a **tender**.

A contract must meet certain requirements to be legally valid. If the contract is valid, each party has the *duty to perform* their specified contractual obligations. A party who does not fulfill the promise made—who **defaults** in completing the contract terms—will be liable to the other party for **breach of contract**.

A *real estate listing agreement* and a *real estate purchase contract* are examples of the most common types of contracts used by real estate agents. Listing agreements were covered in Unit 6. This unit will examine a typical form of real estate purchase contract. We begin with definitions of some of the terms we will use throughout this unit. They include the following:

- Executory and executed contracts
- Express and implied contracts
- Bilateral and unilateral contracts
- Valid, void, voidable, and unenforceable contracts

Executory and Executed Contracts

A contract is said to be an **executory contract** when some future contract obligation is yet to be performed. A listing agreement is executory, because the real estate broker must find a buyer for the listed property to earn the compensation promised by the seller. Until the sale is closed, a real estate purchase contract also is executory. The buyer must find financing for the purchase, and other conditions must be met before title is transferred.

When all of the contract obligations have been performed, the transaction is completed and the contract becomes an **executed contract**.

Note: Don't be confused by use of the word *execute* to mean contract performance as well as the signing of a document. For example, after the terms of a property listing agreement have been decided on and prepared in written form, both seller and broker *execute* the agreement by signing it. Then, the parties *execute* the agreement by performing all of its obligations.

Express and Implied Contracts

An **express contract** is a contract of words established by an oral or a written agreement in which the parties declare their intention to make a contract. An **implied contract** is established by the conduct of the parties, without a specific oral or written agreement.

F O R   E X A M P L E   Wanda and William South moved to Imperial City but never notified the local waste disposal company to start service at their address. The Souths leave their trash out at the usual pickup time, and it is removed by the disposal company. Can the waste company bill them for the service?

Yes. By making use of the waste disposal company's service, the Souths made an implied contract to pay for the service.

Bilateral and Unilateral Contracts

In a **bilateral contract**, both parties make a promise to do something or to refrain from doing something and both are obligated to perform. In a **unilateral contract**, only one party promises, and only that party is obligated to perform. The promise is accepted by the performance of the other party.

F O R   E X A M P L E   Hearth Homes is offering an extra incentive to agents to attract more buyers to the newest Hearth Homes subdivision. For every sale that is closed before Labor Day, the selling agent will earn an extra $1,000 commission. This offer is advertised in a flyer sent to each brokerage office. Broker Luis brings a client to the Hearth Homes subdivision, and the client purchases a home. The sale is finalized on August 31. Is Luis entitled to the $1,000 bonus?

Yes. Because broker Luis met the terms of the unilateral offer, he is entitled to the extra compensation.

The typical real estate purchase contract is *bilateral*. One party promises to transfer the right of ownership or use of real estate, and the other party promises to pay some form of compensation for that right.

Valid, Void, Voidable, and Unenforceable Contracts

A **valid contract** can be created easily, if all of the required elements are present:

1. The parties must have the *legal capacity* to enter into a contract.
2. There must be an *offer* by one party and *acceptance* of that offer by the other party.
3. There must be a *lawful object* to the contract.
4. There must be some form of *consideration*, or payment, supporting the contract.
5. The contract may have to be *written*.

Each of these elements is discussed in the next section, "Elements of a Contract."

A **void contract** is one that has no legal effect from its inception. An agreement to do something that is illegal is void.

A **voidable contract** is one that may be disavowed by one or both parties, depending on the circumstances. An example of a voidable contract is one that someone signs while intoxicated.

An **unenforceable contract** is valid on its face, but its enforcement would violate some law. An example is an **oral contract** on a matter that the law requires to be *in writing*. An oral contract to purchase real estate is unenforceable, no matter what its terms, because it is oral and not written. The kinds of contracts that require a written agreement will be covered later in this unit.

Another example of an unenforceable contract is one signed under duress, such as the threat of physical or economic harm. Deceit can also lead to an unenforceable contract. *Fraud in the inducement* is a defense to contract enforcement by a party who was deceived into entering the agreement.

ELEMENTS OF A CONTRACT

1. Legal Capacity to Contract

All parties must have the **legal capacity** to contract. This means that they must have the legal ability to make a contract. If they do not, either the contract will be voidable by the person who lacks the capacity to contract or the contract will be void from its inception.

A **minor** (in California, anyone younger than 18) generally cannot make a contract concerning real estate. Any such contract is *void*. Some contracts by a minor are *voidable*, which means they can be disaffirmed by the minor before the minor reaches adulthood, although contracts for "necessaries"—items needed for the support of the minor or the minor's family when the minor is not under the care of a parent or guardian—cannot be disaffirmed (canceled).

A minor can contract as an adult for all purposes as an **emancipated minor**. A minor becomes emancipated by marrying, joining the armed forces, or petitioning the court, which may approve the petition.

Contracts in Languages Other Than English

Many California real estate transactions involve parties for whom a language other than English is their first language—in some cases, the only language. As a result, contracts are frequently negotiated in a language other than English. Civil Code Section 1632 imposes special requirements on any person engaged in a trade or business (such as a real estate licensee) who negotiates orally or in writing primarily in Spanish, Chinese, Tagalog, Vietnamese, or Korean in the course of entering into any of a variety of agreements or required disclosures, including the following:

■ Lease, sublease, or rental agreement, for a period of longer than one month, of a dwelling, apartment, mobilehome, or other dwelling unit normally occupied as a residence

■ Loan negotiated by a real estate broker and secured by a lien on a dwelling of one to four units—the law applies to the loan disclosure statement made by the broker

■ Reverse mortgage

Before the English-language version of the contract is signed, the party to the contract must be given an unexecuted translation of the contract. A translation in the applicable language also is required for disclosures made by financial organizations under the Financial Code or the federal Truth in Lending Act.

The law does not apply if the party to the contract uses his own interpreter.

The interpreter

■ cannot be a minor,

■ must be able to speak fluently and read with full understanding both the English language and the specified language in which the contract or agreement was negotiated, and

■ cannot be employed by, or made available through, the trade or business.

Any minor may receive property as a gift or an inheritance, usually taking title without the appointment of an adult guardian. A guardian must be appointed, however, to handle any property conveyance, lease, encumbrance, or other transaction on behalf of an unemancipated minor.

If someone makes a contract while drugged or intoxicated, the contract is *voidable* by that person. He can let the contract stand or can disaffirm it.

FOR EXAMPLE   Harvey Lock, feeling no pain after six margaritas, gripes at a party that he is so fed up with his job he will sell his house to the first person who offers him a motor home in trade for it so he can fulfill his lifelong dream of visiting all 50 states. Sue Wilson offers Harvey her well-used "Minnie-Winnie" in exchange for his Beverly Hills home. Harvey, amid much laughter, accepts the offer and tells Sue to get the paperwork ready to sign the next day. Sue shows up at Harvey's the next day with her attorney. Now what?

Harvey, who only vaguely remembers the "deal" of the night before, can do one of two things. He can disaffirm the contract because he was intoxicated at the time and lacked the capacity to enter an agreement. Or he can thank Sue for the terrific motor home as he signs the deed that her attorney has prepared.

A *mentally incompetent person* cannot form a valid contract. Any such contract would be *void*. A person may be determined by a court to be mentally incompetent. Even without a judicial determination, however, evidence may show that a person is without understanding and thus unable to form a contract.

The property of a *deceased person* is handled by the personal representative of the estate. This can be either an executor named in the deceased's will or an administrator appointed by the court if no executor was named by the deceased or if the named representative declined to serve. The actions of the estate representative must always have the approval of the probate court.

Contracts by Businesses

A business entity can make a contract concerning real estate.

A *sole proprietor* acts in her own name, or with a spouse.

A *partnership* may hold real property in the name of the partnership, the name of one of the partners, or the name of a trustee. Any authorized partner (and spouse) may contract to transfer the real estate.

A *corporation* acts through its officers, as authorized by the board of directors. The directors may be personally liable for actions taken on behalf of the corporation.

When dealing with a business entity, it is important that the authority of the person acting on behalf of the business be verified and documented.

2. Offer and Acceptance

A *contract* is not created until the parties show that they have given their **mutual consent** to its terms. There must be some form of a "meeting of the minds" to create a valid and enforceable contract. This normally takes place in a process called **offer and acceptance.** An *offer* by one party is *accepted* by the other party and the acceptance is communicated to the person making the offer.

An *offer* exists only when the **offeror** (the person making the offer) has communicated its terms to the **offeree** (the person receiving the offer). The fact that an offer is being made should be clear. Because a standard, well-detailed form is used in most real estate transactions, establishing the intent of the offeror usually is not a problem.

Rejection The offeree can refuse to accept the offer. **Rejection** of an offer can be accomplished by simply taking no action that would indicate acceptance and allowing the offer to expire. An offer is also rejected if the offeree makes a change in its terms as a condition of acceptance, resulting in a counteroffer to the offeror.

Then, their roles are reversed. The person making the counteroffer becomes the *offeror* and the person to whom the counteroffer is made becomes the *offeree*.

Counteroffer   A **counteroffer** is created by any change in the terms of an offer as originally made. There may be considerable negotiation required to finalize a contract. At each step, an offer by one side may be met by a counteroffer from the other side. Any counteroffer has the effect of rejecting the offer that it counters. The previous offer, on the terms proposed, is terminated. It can no longer be accepted by the party to whom it was made. This means that, if a counteroffer is rejected, there is no longer an offer that can be accepted by either party because both the original offer and counteroffer have terminated.

FOR EXAMPLE   The asking price for the Barino residence is $495,000. John and Jane Murray offer $488,600 for the house. George Barino makes a counteroffer of $492,000. John and Jane reject the counteroffer. George decides $488,600 is not such a bad offer after all and signs the original purchase contract, returning it to the Murrays. Can he do that?

No. Once George made a counteroffer, he effectively turned down the Murrays' original offer. Of course, the Murrays can treat George's "acceptance" as an invitation to remake their original offer and proceed with the transaction on those terms.

Revocation of an offer   In general, an offer may be revoked before it is accepted if the offeror communicates the **revocation** directly to the offeree. It also is revoked if the offeree learns of the revocation from a reliable source (such as the real estate agent) and observes the offeror do something that is not consistent with the offer still being considered.

FOR EXAMPLE   Maria Burns wants to rent an apartment. She fills out a rental application at Ocean Villas and is told that she can expect to hear back in two days. The next day, Maria learns that her company is moving its office to Modesto. News of the move appears in the newspaper the same morning and the manager at Ocean Villas sees the article. He phones Maria's place of business and learns that all employees, including Maria, will be relocating to Modesto. Before Maria can get back to Ocean Villas to withdraw her rental application, the manager signs it and faxes a copy of the rental agreement to her. Does the manager have a new tenant?

No. Once he learned of Maria's change of circumstance from a reliable source and verified it with a phone call to her place of business, the manager had sufficient notice of Maria's intended revocation of the application.

The Exception to the Revocation Rule

An offer is revocable before acceptance *unless* it is supported by some form of consideration (payment). An example is an option agreement entered into by a prospective purchaser and seller. The prospective purchaser gives the seller some consideration for the option—usually money. In return, the purchaser receives the right to purchase the property during the option period. During that time, the seller is not allowed to revoke the buyer's right to exercise the option and is not allowed to sell the property to anyone else.

Offer made freely and voluntarily For a valid acceptance, the offeree must *not* be acting under

- threat of harm,

- undue influence,

- mistake, or

- as a result of a fraudulent misrepresentation by the offeror.

A contract is *voidable* if it is entered into under threat of harm to a person or thing.

No undue influence or fraud **Undue influence** may not be used to gain an acceptance. Most often, this happens when the parties are related or known to each other, and one of them takes advantage of that position of confidence.

FOR EXAMPLE   Jim is the neighbor, good friend, and accountant of Clara, who is 82 years old and legally blind. Jim wants to buy Clara's condominium. He tells her that property values are going down, and she should sell her unit while she has the chance. Jim then offers Clara $200,000 for her condo, about $150,000 less than it is worth, based on what similar properties have sold for recently. Because Clara paid $43,000 for her condo in 1977, she is very impressed with the offer and accepts. Shortly after the offer is accepted but before the sale is closed, Clara is visited by her niece. Clara's niece informs her of what a poor deal she has made. Can Clara do anything about it?

Yes. Clara should contact an attorney immediately to disaffirm the contract with Jim. She should have no problem doing so, because the offer Jim persuaded her to take is so obviously inadequate. Clara's attorney should also advise her that it may be in her best interest to seek another accountant.

A fraudulent act is either affirmative or negative:

- Fraud is **affirmative fraud** when it is a deliberate statement of a material fact that the speaker knows to be false and on which the speaker intends another person to rely, to that person's detriment.

- Fraud is **negative fraud** when it is a deliberate concealment of something that should be revealed.

Actual fraud can be any of the following actions, as long as it is performed with the intent to deceive:

- The suggestion as a fact of that which is not true by one who knows it is not true

- The positive assertion, in a manner not warranted by the information of the person making it, of that which is not true, though the person believes it to be true (that is, the belief is not justified)

- The suppression of that which is true by one who knows of or believes the fact

- A promise made without any intention of performing it

- Any other act of deception

Constructive fraud is a misrepresentation made without fraudulent intent, that is, deliberate intent to deceive. An agent can reasonably rely on some information, such as the owner's report of the results of a termite inspection, though it would be better practice to ask for a copy of all pertinent reports. Other information, however, such as the construction of a new school, should be verified. The agent could be guilty of constructive fraud if the information turns out to be false.

FOR EXAMPLE   Jim and Janet Day want to buy a house in Woodville. They contact broker Charles Charton, who shows them several houses, including one near a major thoroughfare. The Days talk to the owner, who tells them that the traffic noise will be reduced considerably after the city puts up a cement block wall along the property closest to the roadway. Broker Charton, who is present, knows that such a wall has been proposed to the city council but has not yet been approved. He does not contradict the owner, however. The Days make an offer, which is accepted. Before the close of the sale, they check with the city authorities to find out when the soundproofing wall will be erected. The Days discover the truth. Can the Days back out of their deal with the seller?

Probably, for the seller misrepresented the condition of the property—that the noise problem would be alleviated. Broker Charton knowingly went along with that misrepresentation, for he was present when it was made but did not object. Broker Charton's conduct could be reported to the Real Estate Commissioner.

Penalties for Fraud

A contract induced by fraud is *voidable* by the injured party. Action must be taken within a reasonable time after the fraud is discovered, as specified by the statute of limitations.

The injured party may also seek *money damages*, including punitive damages.

A *criminal prosecution* may be brought against the person who committed the fraud, resulting in a fine, imprisonment, or both.

A *real estate agent* who takes part in fraud may suffer loss or suspension of the real estate license, in addition to the penalties mentioned above.

Note that a **fraudulent misrepresentation** is different from a **negligent misrepresentation**. A negligent misrepresentation is not made with criminal intent to deceive. It is the result of carelessness. Although negligent misrepresentation carries no criminal penalties, it can result in a voidable contract, civil damages, and disciplinary action against the licensee.

Definite terms   The subject matter of the contract must be clearly expressed in *definite terms:*

■ If the subject matter is real estate, there must be an adequate *description* of the property.

■ *All parties* must be identified unambiguously; the full name and address of each are preferred.

- The *price* must be specified in a real estate contract, unlike contracts for other types of property in which a reasonable (market) price may be inferred. It would be sufficient in a real estate contract to state the manner in which the price is to be determined, such as the opinion of market value of an identified licensed appraiser as of a specified date.

- The terms that specify the *nature* of the transaction and any *conditions* to its performance must be clear.

- The *time of performance* is important. Particularly in real estate purchase contracts, deadlines for certain activities, such as qualifying for and obtaining a loan, should be given.

FOR EXAMPLE The Murrays offer to purchase the Barino residence. The offer describes the property as the George Barino residence on Gray Street, Meadowville, Yolo County. Is this description adequate? Is it advisable?

The description could be adequate if George Barino owns only one house on Gray Street. It is not advisable, however. Not only could George Belton own more than one house on Gray Street—there is no description of the land involved.

3. Lawful Object

One cannot make a valid contract to perform an *illegal activity*. An example is an agreement to use real estate for an unlawful purpose, such as the manufacture of illegal drugs. If the contract has a lawful as well as an unlawful objective, it will be valid only to the extent that the **lawful object** alone can be carried out.

4. Consideration

A contract must be supported by **consideration**—an obligation or a payment on the part of each party—to be enforceable. The fact that each party supplies consideration is referred to as **mutuality of contract**. The consideration can be a promise to do something (or refrain from doing something) in the future.

As noted earlier, if consideration has been given to create a valid **option**, the option agreement cannot be revoked by the person giving the option before the end of the option period.

FOR EXAMPLE Harvey gives Cecilia a one-year lease and an option to buy his house, in exchange for $5,000 and monthly lease payments of $3,000. Before the year is up, Harvey decides to give the house to his son Hal. Harvey notifies Cecilia by certified mail, enclosing a money order for $5,000. Does Cecilia still have an option to buy the house? What can Cecilia do?

Cecilia still has a valid option contract but will have to return the $5,000 to Harvey. If she delays, she may be understood as approving his revocation of the agreement. If Cecilia had already decided—or decides when she gets the $5,000—that she will not exercise the option, she is $5,000 richer than she would have been had Harvey not returned her money. Either way, Cecilia should talk to her attorney.

5. Writing

Certain agreements are *enforceable* only if they are *in writing*. A "handshake deal" may work perfectly well as long as the parties have no problems. But if something goes wrong and one party backs out, the other party won't be able to enforce the agreement.

A summary of the types of agreements involving real estate that *must* be in writing to be enforceable appears in the box that follows.

FOR EXAMPLE   Jim and Janet Day make an offer, through broker Luis, to purchase the Castle estate. The Days love the furniture in the family room and want to purchase that as well. Their offer is countered by the Castles, and after considerable negotiation a purchase price of $347,000 is agreed on. Somewhere along the line, the request for the family room furnishings is omitted, and the signed purchase offer does not include them. What can the Days do?

If the omission was inadvertent (a mistake), the Days may be able to reform the contract to conform to the understanding of the parties. A separate agreement and bill of sale for personal property, stating at least a nominal consideration (such as $10), is preferable.

The Statute of Frauds

The **statute of frauds** is a part of the California Civil Code that originated in the English common law. The statute of frauds lists the types of contract that must be *in writing*. They include the following:

1. An agreement that will not be completed within a year

2. An agreement for the sale of real property or an interest in real property, or the lease of real property for more than one year (and an agent making such an agreement on behalf of a principal must be authorized to do so by a written agreement)

3. An agreement that employs an agent, a broker, or any other person to

   ■ purchase or sell real property,

   ■ lease real property for a period longer than one year, or

   ■ find a purchaser or seller of real property or a lessee or lessor of real property where the lease period is for longer than one year.

4. An agreement by a purchaser of real property to pay a debt secured by a mortgage or deed of trust on the property purchased, unless the purchaser is to assume the debt

Exercise 7-1

1. Homeowner Clive Lentil is trying to sell his house without the assistance of a real estate agent. After four months in which he receives no offers on the house, Clive places an ad in the newspaper that states, "Three percent commission paid to buyer's agent at closing." Salesperson Sally phones Clive, identifies herself as a real estate agent, and makes an appointment to show Clive's house to one of her clients. Do Sally and Clive have an agreement? If Clive accepts the offer made by Sally's client, and the offer does not mention any commission for Sally, do Sally and Clive have an agreement? At closing, is Clive obliged to pay Sally the 3% commission? If the purchase offer that Clive accepted stipulates that Sally will receive a 3% commission on the transaction, will Clive and Sally have had an agreement at that point?

2. Jerry Kramer decides to make an all-cash offer on the Hardecker house. He fills out a standard offer to purchase, giving the street address of the property, and notes that the selling price is to be "agreed to by the parties." If Hardecker signs the contract, can Kramer enforce it?

3. When Jerry Kramer is shown the Hardecker house in Pasadena, the listing broker tells him the house was designed by Frank Lloyd Wright. Kramer immediately decides to buy the house. He questions Hardecker on the house's designer, and Hardecker also tells him the designer was Frank Lloyd Wright. Kramer makes an offer that is accepted by Hardecker. Before the sale closes, Kramer checks the city records and learns that Floyd White designed the house. Does Jerry have to go ahead with the sale?

4. On Monday, January 6, Sally Berman agreed to a one-year lease on an apartment at Shady Acres. The lease term began on Monday, January 13. Is the oral lease contract valid? Can the management of Shady Acres enforce the oral contract if Sally moves out before the end of the lease term?

DISCHARGING A CONTRACT

A **discharged contract** is one that is terminated. As discussed next, there are many ways to terminate a contract or change one or more of its terms, including the following:

- Performance
- Rescission
- Release

- Novation
- Reformation
- Assignment
- Breach

Performance

Performance of its terms discharges a contract.

A contract may be discharged if some intervening cause creates an **impossibility of performance**, such as when the property that is the subject matter of the contract is destroyed. If a buyer of real estate suffers an unexpected disability and job loss, making it impossible to go through with the purchase, the buyer's performance will be excused.

Performance may be excused in the event of **impracticability of performance**, also called **commercial frustration**. If changed circumstances make a purchase uneconomic, there may be an excuse for nonperformance. This might be the case if a buyer's financial condition were to take a downturn (say, a sudden, extreme drop in market value of the buyer's company's stock), so that the purchase, although not impossible, would impose an extreme financial hardship. There also could be other reasons that were not known at the time the contract was formed.

Rescission

If both parties agree, they may take back (rescind) the contract in the process called **rescission**.

Release

A party to whom an obligation is owed may sign a written **release**, possibly for further consideration. The contract is then discharged, and the other party no longer has an obligation to perform.

Novation

By a **novation** the parties may substitute a new agreement for the original one, discharging the original agreement. If the new agreement falls within the statute of frauds, it must be written.

FOR EXAMPLE   Jim and Janet Day make an offer to purchase the Castle estate. The offer is accepted, and the closing of the sale is to take place in two months. Before the closing date, Jim and Janet decide to dissolve their marriage and live apart. Alone, neither can qualify for a loan to purchase the Castle estate. What can Jim and Janet do to get out of their offer of purchase?

The Days should immediately inform the Castles, who may agree to rescind the contract. If not, the Days could refuse to perform on the grounds of impracticability but should consult an attorney first.

Reformation

At some point during the life of the contract, one of the parties may determine that a mistake has been made in the contract terms or that certain information should be made a part of the contract. There may be an inaccurate description of the subject property, the financing terms may need to be clarified, or new information may be discovered about the true condition of the property, particularly following an appraisal or property inspection. In any of those instances, it may be possible to bring about a **reformation** of the contract.

If all parties agree to the reformation, it is simply a matter of redrafting the contract or amending the escrow instructions. If one party objects, it is possible to bring a legal action to reform a contract, although the time and expense of a legal action usually make this alternative undesirable.

Assignment

Unless the contract requires a personal service or specifically prohibits an **assignment**, it probably can be assigned. In an assignment, the **assignee** is the new party who takes on the duties of the **assignor**, the party who makes the assignment. In return, the assignee receives the compensation that would have gone to the assignor.

Breach

A contract also may be discharged by a **breach of contract**. A breach occurs when one of the parties fails to perform all or part of the obligations required by the contract. The nonbreaching party who is injured by the breach is entitled to legal relief.

An injury due to breach of contract entitles the injured party to ask for *money damages*. With some forms of contracts, **specific performance** of the contract also may be sought. If a court grants specific performance, the breaching party must fulfill the terms of the contract. Specific performance will be ordered only if the subject of the contract is considered unique and not readily replaceable. By definition, no parcel of real estate is exactly like any other parcel of real estate.

No two parcels of real estate are exactly alike.

A court will not order specific performance unless the contract is supported by adequate consideration. This requires an offer (tender) of the entire purchase price by the offeror. Specific performance also will not be granted if the contract involves a personal service of the breaching party or if the agreement involves securing the consent or conduct of a third party.

Specific performance can only be obtained by bringing a lawsuit, which is expensive and time-consuming. As a result, this remedy is not sought very often. Most buyers of residential real estate have neither the ability nor the inclination to litigate a claim to a particular parcel of real estate.

The injured party in the breach of a real estate contract can ask for either money damages or specific performance. In some cases both may be sought. Damages may include the return of any consideration already given to the breaching party (if specific performance is not being sought) and payment of any expenses incurred because of the breach.

FOR EXAMPLE   A week before closing, Jim and Janet Day, who have reconciled their differences, decide against buying the Castle estate. What recourse do the Castles have when informed of the Days' decision?

The Castles can agree to rescind their contract and either keep or return the Days' earnest money deposit. If the Castles keep the deposit, the Days could sue for its return. The Castles could agree to release the Days from their contractual obligation but retain the security deposit as consideration for the release. Or the Castles could sue the Days for specific performance. Most likely, the Castles will sell the property as soon as possible to someone else and sue the Days for any loss in value that might result.

The injured party also could decide to *waive* the matter breached and enforce the contract on its remaining terms. Another use of a waiver is to remove a condition that a party has the right to enforce.

FOR EXAMPLE   The Yees offer to buy the King residence is conditioned on the Yees selling their home within the next 30 days. The Kings receive another offer that has no contingencies. The Kings ask the Yees to remove the home sale contingency from their offer to purchase within 48 hours, as is permitted by the contract. The Yees decide to go forward with the purchase, even though they have not yet sold their old home. To do so, the Yees sign a waiver of the home sale contingency in their contract with the Kings.

Often, the facts of a case may support more than one remedy. In any situation potentially involving a lawsuit, the advice of a real estate attorney should be sought as early as possible to ensure that no legal rights are lost.

Statute of Limitations

A legal action (lawsuit) must be brought within a specific period after the act that gives rise to it. The **statute of limitations** prescribes time limits for various lawsuits. You can remember the deadlines below by remembering the numbers 5-4-3-2-10.

■ A lawsuit to recover *title* to real property must be brought within *five years.*

■ An action based on a *written instrument* (such as a real estate sales contract) must be brought within *four years.*

■ An action based on *fraud* must be brought within *three years* of the discovery of the fraud.

■ An action based on an *oral agreement* (such as a lease for only a few months) must be brought within *two years.*

■ An action based on a *judgment* must be brought within *10 years* of the awarding of the judgment.

Exercise 7-2

1. Brad and Richa Turner want to buy a house. They make an offer to purchase the Markham house for $365,000. Ted Markham, who is single, accepts. Before the sale is closed, Brad Turner is seriously injured on the job. The Turners can no longer expect to comfortably make the house payments. What can they do?

2. The Wilsons are in the process of buying the Mulholland farm. Their offer was accepted, and they have received a loan commitment from a lender. Before the closing, however, the Mulhollands inform the Wilsons that they no longer wish to sell their property "for sentimental reasons." What recourse do the Wilsons have?

3. The Harleys purchased a home from the Davidsons, closing the transaction on March 15, 2007, and moving into the home a week later. In a period of unusually heavy rainfall in November 2009, the Harleys experienced water damage to the living room ceiling. When part of the ceiling was removed, extensive prior water damage and earlier repairs were revealed. The Harleys homeowners' insurance policy does not cover water damage. Do the Harleys have any recourse against the Davidsons?

REAL ESTATE CONTRACTS

This section examines one of the forms of real estate purchase contract and receipt for deposit currently used in California.

Real Estate Purchase Contracts

When someone is ready to make a purchase offer, the next step is the preparation of a *purchase contract*. The offer to purchase usually includes a *deposit* on the purchase price, so the purchase contract will also serve to acknowledge *receipt of the deposit*, if the offer is accepted.

As with any contract, a **real estate purchase contract** must be made by parties who have the *legal capacity* to do so. There must be an *offer* made on *definite terms* and with a *lawful objective*. There must be *acceptance* of those terms by all parties, and the contract must be supported by some form of payment, or *consideration*.

Use of a printed form Figure 7.1 is a typical form of a purchase contract that also serves as escrow instructions. Figure 7.2 is a two-page Buyer's Inspection Advisory form. This form adds information that the buyer should know.

FIGURE 7.1:   **Residential Purchase Agreement**

CALIFORNIA
ASSOCIATION
OF REALTORS®

**CALIFORNIA
RESIDENTIAL PURCHASE AGREEMENT
AND JOINT ESCROW INSTRUCTIONS**
(C.A.R. Form RPA-CA, Revised 12/15)

Date Prepared: _____

1. **OFFER:**
    A. **THIS IS AN OFFER FROM** _____ ("Buyer").
    B. **THE REAL PROPERTY** to be acquired is _____, situated in
        _____ (City), _____ (County), California, _____ (Zip Code), Assessor's Parcel No. _____ ("Property").
    C. **THE PURCHASE PRICE** offered is _____
        _____ Dollars $ _____.
    D. **CLOSE OF ESCROW** shall occur on _____ (date)(or _____ **Days** After Acceptance).
    E. Buyer and Seller are referred to herein as the "Parties." Brokers are not Parties to this Agreement.
2. **AGENCY:**
    A. **DISCLOSURE:** The Parties each acknowledge receipt of a ☑"Disclosure Regarding Real Estate Agency Relationships" (C.A.R. Form AD).
    B. **CONFIRMATION:** The following agency relationships are hereby confirmed for this transaction:
        Listing Agent _____ (Print Firm Name) is the agent of (check one):
        ☐ the Seller exclusively; or ☐ both the Buyer and Seller.
        Selling Agent _____ (Print Firm Name) (if not the same as the
        Listing Agent) is the agent of (check one): ☐ the Buyer exclusively; or ☐ the Seller exclusively; or ☐ both the Buyer and Seller.
    C. **POTENTIALLY COMPETING BUYERS AND SELLERS:** The Parties each acknowledge receipt of a ☑"Possible Representation
        of More than One Buyer or Seller - Disclosure and Consent" (C.A.R. Form PRBS).
3. **FINANCE TERMS:** Buyer represents that funds will be good when deposited with Escrow Holder.
    A. **INITIAL DEPOSIT**: Deposit shall be in the amount of ....$ _____
        (1) Buyer Direct Deposit: Buyer shall deliver deposit directly to Escrow Holder by electronic funds
        transfer, ☐ cashier's check, ☐ personal check, ☐ other _____ within 3 business days
        after Acceptance (or _____);
        OR (2) ☐ Buyer Deposit with Agent: Buyer has given the deposit by personal check (or _____
        to the agent submitting the offer (or to _____), made payable to
        _____. The deposit shall be held uncashed until Acceptance and then deposited
        with Escrow Holder within **3** business days after Acceptance (or _____).
        Deposit checks given to agent shall be an original signed check and not a copy.
        (Note: Initial and increased deposits checks received by agent shall be recorded in Broker's trust fund log.)
    B. **INCREASED DEPOSIT:** Buyer shall deposit with Escrow Holder an increased deposit in the amount of ....$ _____
        within ____ **Days** After Acceptance (or _____).
        If the Parties agree to liquidated damages in this Agreement, they also agree to incorporate the increased
        deposit into the liquidated damages amount in a separate liquidated damages clause (C.A.R. Form RID)
        at the time the increased deposit is delivered to Escrow Holder.
    C. ☐ **ALL CASH OFFER:** No loan is needed to purchase the Property. This offer is NOT contingent on Buyer
        obtaining a loan. Written verification of sufficient funds to close this transaction IS ATTACHED to this offer
        or ☐ Buyer shall, within **3 (or _____) Days** After Acceptance, Deliver to Seller such verification.
    D. **LOAN(S):**
        (1) FIRST LOAN: in the amount of ....$ _____
        This loan will be conventional financing or ☐ FHA, ☐ VA, ☐ Seller financing (C.A.R. Form SFA),
        ☐ assumed financing (C.A.R. Form AFA), ☐ Other _____. This loan shall be at a fixed
        rate not to exceed _____% or, ☐ an adjustable rate loan with initial rate not to exceed _____%.
        Regardless of the type of loan, Buyer shall pay points not to exceed _____% of the loan amount.
        (2) ☐ **SECOND LOAN** in the amount of ....$ _____
        This loan will be conventional financing or ☐ Seller financing (C.A.R. Form SFA), ☐ assumed
        financing (C.A.R. Form AFA), ☐ Other _____. This loan shall be at a fixed rate not to
        exceed _____% or, ☐ an adjustable rate loan with initial rate not to exceed _____%. Regardless of
        the type of loan, Buyer shall pay points not to exceed _____% of the loan amount.
        (3) FHA/VA: For any FHA or VA loan specified in 3D(1), Buyer has **17 (or ___) Days** After Acceptance
        to Deliver to Seller written notice (C.A.R. Form FVA) of any lender-required repairs or costs that
        Buyer requests Seller to pay for or otherwise correct. Seller has no obligation to pay or satisfy lender
        requirements unless agreed in writing. A FHA/VA amendatory clause (C.A.R. Form FVAC) shall be a
        part of this Agreement.
    E. **ADDITIONAL FINANCING TERMS:** _____
        _____
    F. **BALANCE OF DOWN PAYMENT OR PURCHASE PRICE** in the amount of..................................$ _____
        to be deposited with Escrow Holder pursuant to Escrow Holder instructions.
    G. **PURCHASE PRICE (TOTAL):** ....$ _____

Buyer's Initials (_____)(_____)

Seller's Initials (_____)(_____)

© 1991-2015, California Association of REALTORS®, Inc.
RPA-CA REVISED 12/15 (PAGE 1 OF 10) Print Date

EQUAL HOUSING
OPPORTUNITY

CALIFORNIA RESIDENTIAL PURCHASE AGREEMENT (RPA-CA PAGE 1 OF 10)

FIGURE 7.1:   **Residential Purchase Agreement (continued)**

Property Address: _____   Date: _____

H.   **VERIFICATION OF DOWN PAYMENT AND CLOSING COSTS:** Buyer (or Buyer's lender or loan broker pursuant to paragraph 3J(1)) shall, within **3 (or ___) Days** After Acceptance, Deliver to Seller written verification of Buyer's down payment and closing costs. (☐ Verification attached.)

I.   **APPRAISAL CONTINGENCY AND REMOVAL:** This Agreement is (**or** ☐ **is NOT**) contingent upon a written appraisal of the Property by a licensed or certified appraiser at no less than the purchase price. Buyer shall, as specified in paragraph 14B(3), in writing, remove the appraisal contingency or cancel this Agreement within **17 (or ___) Days** After Acceptance.

J.   **LOAN TERMS:**
   (1) LOAN APPLICATIONS: Within **3 (or ___) Days** After Acceptance, Buyer shall Deliver to Seller a letter from Buyer's lender or loan broker stating that, based on a review of Buyer's written application and credit report, Buyer is prequalified or preapproved for any NEW loan specified in paragraph 3D. If any loan specified in paragraph 3D is an adjustable rate loan, the prequalification or preapproval letter shall be based on the qualifying rate, not the initial loan rate. (☐ Letter attached.)
   (2) LOAN CONTINGENCY: Buyer shall act diligently and in good faith to obtain the designated loan(s). Buyer's qualification for the loan(s) specified above **is a contingency** of this Agreement unless otherwise agreed in writing. If there is no appraisal contingency or the appraisal contingency has been waived or removed, then failure of the Property to appraise at the purchase price does not entitle Buyer to exercise the cancellation right pursuant to the loan contingency if Buyer is otherwise qualified for the specified loan. Buyer's contractual obligations regarding deposit, balance of down payment and closing costs **are not contingencies** of this Agreement.
   (3) LOAN CONTINGENCY REMOVAL:
   Within **21 (or ___) Days** After Acceptance, Buyer shall, as specified in paragraph 14, in writing, remove the loan contingency or cancel this Agreement. If there is an appraisal contingency, removal of the loan contingency shall not be deemed removal of the appraisal contingency.
   (4) ☐ NO LOAN CONTINGENCY: Obtaining any loan specified above is NOT a contingency of this Agreement. If Buyer does not obtain the loan and as a result does not purchase the Property, Seller may be entitled to Buyer's deposit or other legal remedies.
   (5) LENDER LIMITS ON BUYER CREDITS: Any credit to Buyer, from any source, for closing or other costs that is agreed to by the Parties ("Contractual Credit") shall be disclosed to Buyer's lender. If the total credit allowed by Buyer's lender ("Lender Allowable Credit") is less than the Contractual Credit, then (i) the Contractual Credit shall be reduced to the Lender Allowable Credit, and (ii) in the absence of a separate written agreement between the Parties, there shall be no automatic adjustment to the purchase price to make up for the difference between the Contractual Credit and the Lender Allowable Credit.

K.   **BUYER STATED FINANCING:** Seller is relying on Buyer's representation of the type of financing specified (including but not limited to, as applicable, all cash, amount of down payment, or contingent or non-contingent loan). Seller has agreed to a specific closing date, purchase price and to sell to Buyer in reliance on Buyer's covenant concerning financing. Buyer shall pursue the financing specified in this Agreement. Seller has no obligation to cooperate with Buyer's efforts to obtain any financing other than that specified in the Agreement and the availability of any such alternate financing does not excuse Buyer from the obligation to purchase the Property and close escrow as specified in this Agreement.

4.   **SALE OF BUYER'S PROPERTY:**
   A. This Agreement and Buyer's ability to obtain financing are NOT contingent upon the sale of any property owned by Buyer.
   OR   B. ☐ This Agreement and Buyer's ability to obtain financing are contingent upon the sale of property owned by Buyer as specified in the attached addendum (C.A.R. Form COP).

5.   **ADDENDA AND ADVISORIES:**
   A.   ADDENDA: ☐ Addendum # _____ (C.A.R. Form ADM) _____
      ☐ Back Up Offer Addendum (C.A.R. Form BUO)   ☐ Court Confirmation Addendum (C.A.R. Form CCA) ___
      ☐ Septic, Well and Property Monument Addendum (C.A.R. Form SWPI) _____
      ☐ Short Sale Addendum (C.A.R. Form SSA)   ☐ Other _____

   B.   BUYER AND SELLER ADVISORIES: ☑ Buyer's Inspection Advisory (C.A.R. Form BIA)
      ☐ Probate Advisory (C.A.R. Form PA)   ☐ Statewide Buyer and Seller Advisory (C.A.R. Form SBSA)
      ☐ Trust Advisory (C.A.R. Form TA)   ☐ REO Advisory (C.A.R. Form REO)
      ☐ Short Sale Information and Advisory (C.A.R. Form SSIA)   ☐ Other _____

6.   **OTHER TERMS:** _____
   _____
   _____
   _____

7.   **ALLOCATION OF COSTS**
   A.   **INSPECTIONS, REPORTS AND CERTIFICATES:** Unless otherwise agreed in writing, this paragraph only determines who is to pay for the inspection, test, certificate or service ("Report") mentioned; it **does not determine who is to pay for any work recommended or identified in the Report.**
      (1) ☐ Buyer ☐ Seller shall pay for a natural hazard zone disclosure report, including tax ☐ environmental ☐ Other: _____
         _____ prepared by _____.
      (2) ☐ Buyer ☐ Seller shall pay for the following Report _____
         prepared by _____.
      (3) ☐ Buyer ☐ Seller shall pay for the following Report _____
         prepared by _____.
   B.   **GOVERNMENT REQUIREMENTS AND RETROFIT:**
      (1) ☐ Buyer ☐ Seller shall pay for smoke alarm and carbon monoxide device installation and water heater bracing, if required by Law. Prior to Close Of Escrow ("COE"), Seller shall provide Buyer written statement(s) of compliance in accordance with state and local Law, unless Seller is exempt.

Buyer's Initials (_____)(_____)   Seller's Initials (_____)(_____)

RPA-CA REVISED 12/15 (PAGE 2 OF 10) Print Date   EQUAL HOUSING OPPORTUNITY

CALIFORNIA RESIDENTIAL PURCHASE AGREEMENT   (RPA-CA PAGE 2 OF 10)

Source: Reprinted with permission, California Association of REALTORS®. Endorsement not implied.

FIGURE 7.1:   Residential Purchase Agreement (continued)

Property Address: _____   Date: _____

(2) (i) ☐ Buyer ☐ Seller shall pay the cost of compliance with any other minimum mandatory government inspections and reports if required as a condition of closing escrow under any Law.
(ii) ☐ Buyer ☐ Seller shall pay the cost of compliance with any other minimum mandatory government retrofit standards required as a condition of closing escrow under any Law, whether the work is required to be completed before or after COE.
(iii) Buyer shall be provided, within the time specified in paragraph 14A, a copy of any required government conducted or point-of-sale inspection report prepared pursuant to this Agreement or in anticipation of this sale of the Property.

C. **ESCROW AND TITLE:**
(1) (a) ☐ Buyer ☐ Seller shall pay escrow fee _____
(b) Escrow Holder shall be _____
(c) The Parties shall, within **5 (or ___) Days** After receipt, sign and return Escrow Holder's general provisions.
(2) (a) ☐ Buyer ☐ Seller shall pay for **owner's** title insurance policy specified in paragraph 13E _____
(b) Owner's title policy to be issued by _____
(Buyer shall pay for any title insurance policy insuring Buyer's **lender**, unless otherwise agreed in writing.)

D. **OTHER COSTS:**
(1) ☐ Buyer ☐ Seller shall pay County transfer tax or fee _____
(2) ☐ Buyer ☐ Seller shall pay City transfer tax or fee _____
(3) ☐ Buyer ☐ Seller shall pay Homeowners' Association ("HOA") transfer fee _____
(4) Seller shall pay HOA fees for preparing documents required to be delivered by Civil Code §4525.
(5) ☐ Buyer ☐ Seller shall pay HOA fees for preparing all documents other than those required by Civil Code §4525.
(6) Buyer to pay for any HOA certification fee.
(7) ☐ Buyer ☐ Seller shall pay for any private transfer fee _____
(8) ☐ Buyer ☐ Seller shall pay for _____
(9) ☐ Buyer ☐ Seller shall pay for _____
(10) ☐ Buyer ☐ Seller shall pay for the cost, not to exceed $ _____, of a standard (or ☐ upgraded) one-year home warranty plan, issued by _____, with the following optional coverages: ☐ Air Conditioner ☐ Pool/Spa ☐ Other: _____
Buyer is informed that home warranty plans have many optional coverages in addition to those listed above. Buyer is advised to investigate these coverages to determine those that may be suitable for Buyer.
OR ☐ Buyer waives the purchase of a home warranty plan. Nothing in this paragraph precludes Buyer's purchasing a home warranty plan during the term of this Agreement.

8. **ITEMS INCLUDED IN AND EXCLUDED FROM SALE:**
A. **NOTE TO BUYER AND SELLER:** Items listed as included or excluded in the MLS, flyers or marketing materials are **not** included in the purchase price or excluded from the sale unless specified in paragraph 8 B or C.
B. **ITEMS INCLUDED IN SALE:** Except as otherwise specified or disclosed,
(1) All EXISTING fixtures and fittings that are attached to the Property;
(2) EXISTING electrical, mechanical, lighting, plumbing and heating fixtures, ceiling fans, fireplace inserts, gas logs and grates, solar power systems, built-in appliances, window and door screens, awnings, shutters, window coverings, attached floor coverings, television antennas, satellite dishes, air coolers/conditioners, pool/spa equipment, garage door openers/remote controls, mailbox, in-ground landscaping, trees/shrubs, water features and fountains, water softeners, water purifiers, security systems/alarms and the following if checked: ☐ all stove(s), except _____; ☐ all refrigerator(s) except _____; ☐ all washer(s) and dryer(s), except _____.
(3) The following additional items: _____
(4) Existing integrated phone and home automation systems, including necessary components such as intranet and Internet-connected hardware or devices, control units (other than non-dedicated mobile devices, electronics and computers) and applicable software, permissions, passwords, codes and access information, are (☐ are NOT) included in the sale.
(5) **LEASED OR LIENED ITEMS AND SYSTEMS:** Seller shall, within the time specified in paragraph 14A, (i) disclose to Buyer if any item or system specified in paragraph 8B or otherwise included in the sale is leased, or not owned by Seller, or specifically subject to a lien or other encumbrance, and (ii) Deliver to Buyer all written materials (such as lease, warranty, etc.) concerning any such item. Buyer's ability to assume any such lease, or willingness to accept the Property subject to any such lien or encumbrance, is a contingency in favor of Buyer and Seller as specified in paragraph 14B and C.
(6) Seller represents that all items included in the purchase price, unless otherwise specified, (i) are owned by Seller and shall be transferred free and clear of liens and encumbrances, except the items and systems identified pursuant to 8B(5) and _____, and (ii) are transferred without Seller warranty regardless of value.
C. **ITEMS EXCLUDED FROM SALE:** Unless otherwise specified, the following items are excluded from sale: (i) audio and video components (such as flat screen TVs, speakers and other items) if any such item is not itself attached to the Property, even if a bracket or other mechanism attached to the component or item is attached to the Property; (ii) furniture and other items secured to the Property for earthquake purposes; and (iii) _____
_____. **Brackets attached to walls, floors or ceilings for any such component, furniture or item shall remain with the Property (or ☐ will be removed and holes or other damage shall be repaired, but not painted).**

9. **CLOSING AND POSSESSION:**
A. Buyer intends (or ☐ does not intend) to occupy the Property as Buyer's primary residence.
B. **Seller-occupied or vacant property:** Possession shall be delivered to Buyer: (i) at 6 PM or (____ ☐ AM/☐ PM) on the date of Close Of Escrow; (ii) ☐ no later than ____ calendar days after Close Of Escrow; or (iii) ☐ at ____ ☐ AM/☐ PM on _____.

Buyer's Initials (_____)(_____)   Seller's Initials (_____)(_____)

RPA-CA REVISED 12/15 (PAGE 3 OF 10) Print Date

CALIFORNIA RESIDENTIAL PURCHASE AGREEMENT (RPA-CA PAGE 3 OF 10)

FIGURE 7.1: **Residential Purchase Agreement (continued)**

Property Address: _____ Date: _____

C. **Seller remaining in possession After Close Of Escrow:** If Seller has the right to remain in possession after Close Of Escrow, (i) the Parties are advised to sign a separate occupancy agreement such as ☐ C.A.R. Form SIP, for Seller continued occupancy of less than 30 days, ☐ C.A.R. Form RLAS for Seller continued occupancy of 30 days or more; and (ii) the Parties are advised to consult with their insurance and legal advisors for information about liability and damage or injury to persons and personal and real property; and (iii) Buyer is advised to consult with Buyer's lender about the impact of Seller's occupancy on Buyer's loan.

D. **Tenant-occupied property: Property shall be vacant** at least **5 (or ___) Days** Prior to Close Of Escrow, unless otherwise agreed in writing. **Note to Seller: If you are unable to deliver Property vacant in accordance with rent control and other applicable Law, you may be in breach of this Agreement.**

OR ☐ **Tenant to remain in possession** (C.A.R. Form TIP).

E. At Close Of Escrow, Seller assigns to Buyer any assignable warranty rights for items included in the sale; and Seller shall Deliver to Buyer available Copies of any such warranties. Brokers cannot and will not determine the assignability of any warranties.

F. At Close Of Escrow, unless otherwise agreed in writing, Seller shall provide keys, passwords, codes and/or means to operate all locks, mailboxes, security systems, alarms, home automation systems and intranet and Internet-connected devices included in the purchase price, and garage door openers. If the Property is a condominium or located in a common interest subdivision, Buyer may be required to pay a deposit to the Homeowners' Association ("HOA") to obtain keys to accessible HOA facilities.

10. **STATUTORY AND OTHER DISCLOSURES (INCLUDING LEAD-BASED PAINT HAZARD DISCLOSURES) AND CANCELLATION RIGHTS:**

A. **(1)** Seller shall, within the time specified in paragraph 14A, Deliver to Buyer: (i) if required by Law, a fully completed: Federal Lead-Based Paint Disclosures (C.A.R. Form FLD) and pamphlet ("Lead Disclosures"); and **(ii)** unless exempt, fully completed disclosures or notices required by sections 1102 et. seq. and 1103 et. seq. of the Civil Code ("Statutory Disclosures"). Statutory Disclosures include, but are not limited to, a Real Estate Transfer Disclosure Statement ("TDS"), Natural Hazard Disclosure Statement ("NHD"), notice or actual knowledge of release of illegal controlled substance, notice of special tax and/or assessments (or, if allowed, substantially equivalent notice regarding the Mello-Roos Community Facilities Act of 1982 and Improvement Bond Act of 1915) and, if Seller has actual knowledge, of industrial use and military ordnance location (C.A.R. Form SPQ or ESD).

(2) Any Statutory Disclosure required by this paragraph is considered fully completed if Seller has answered all questions and completed and signed the Seller section(s) and the Listing Agent, if any, has completed and signed the Listing Broker section(s), or, if applicable, an Agent Visual Inspection Disclosure (C.A.R. Form AVID). Nothing stated herein relieves a Buyer's Broker, if any, from the obligation to (i) conduct a reasonably competent and diligent visual inspection of the accessible areas of the Property and disclose, on Section IV of the TDS, or an AVID, material facts affecting the value or desirability of the Property that were or should have been revealed by such an inspection or (ii) complete any sections on all disclosures required to be completed by Buyer's Broker.

(3) Note to Buyer and Seller: Waiver of Statutory and Lead Disclosures is prohibited by Law.

(4) Within the time specified in paragraph 14A, (i) Seller, unless exempt from the obligation to provide a TDS, shall, complete and provide Buyer with a Seller Property Questionnaire (C.A.R. Form SPQ); (ii) if Seller is not required to provide a TDS, Seller shall complete and provide Buyer with an Exempt Seller Disclosure (C.A.R. Form ESD).

(5) Buyer shall, within the time specified in paragraph 14B(1), return Signed Copies of the Statutory, Lead and other disclosures to Seller.

(6) In the event Seller or Listing Broker, prior to Close Of Escrow, becomes aware of adverse conditions materially affecting the Property, or any material inaccuracy in disclosures, information or representations previously provided to Buyer, Seller shall promptly provide a subsequent or amended disclosure or notice, in writing, covering those items. **However, a subsequent or amended disclosure shall not be required for conditions and material inaccuracies** of which Buyer is otherwise aware, or which are **disclosed in reports provided to or obtained by Buyer or ordered and paid for by Buyer.**

(7) If any disclosure or notice specified in paragraph 10A(1), or subsequent or amended disclosure or notice is Delivered to Buyer after the offer is Signed, Buyer shall have the right to cancel this Agreement within **3 Days** After Delivery in person, or **5 Days** After Delivery by deposit in the mail, by giving written notice of cancellation to Seller or Seller's agent.

B. **NATURAL AND ENVIRONMENTAL HAZARD DISCLOSURES AND OTHER BOOKLETS:** Within the time specified in paragraph 14A, Seller shall, if required by Law: **(i)** Deliver to Buyer earthquake guide(s) (and questionnaire), environmental hazards booklet, and home energy rating pamphlet; **(ii)** disclose if the Property is located in a Special Flood Hazard Area; Potential Flooding (Inundation) Area; Very High Fire Hazard Zone; State Fire Responsibility Area; Earthquake Fault Zone; and Seismic Hazard Zone; and **(iii)** disclose any other zone as required by Law and provide any other information required for those zones.

C. **WITHHOLDING TAXES:** Within the time specified in paragraph 14A, to avoid required withholding, Seller shall Deliver to Buyer or qualified substitute, an affidavit sufficient to comply with federal (FIRPTA) and California withholding Law (C.A.R. Form AS or QS).

D. **MEGAN'S LAW DATABASE DISCLOSURE:** Notice: Pursuant to Section 290.46 of the Penal Code, information about specified registered sex offenders is made available to the public via an Internet Web site maintained by the Department of Justice at **www.meganslaw.ca.gov**. Depending on an offender's criminal history, this information will include either the address at which the offender resides or the community of residence and ZIP Code in which he or she resides. (Neither Seller nor Brokers are required to check this website. If Buyer wants further information, Broker recommends that Buyer obtain information from this website during Buyer's inspection contingency period. Brokers do not have expertise in this area.)

E. **NOTICE REGARDING GAS AND HAZARDOUS LIQUID TRANSMISSION PIPELINES:** This notice is being provided simply to inform you that information about the general location of gas and hazardous liquid transmission pipelines is available to the public via the National Pipeline Mapping System (NPMS) Internet Web site maintained by the United States Department of Transportation at **http://www.npms.phmsa.dot.gov/**. To seek further information about possible transmission pipelines near the Property, you may contact your local gas utility or other pipeline operators in the area. Contact information for pipeline operators is searchable by ZIP Code and county on the NPMS Internet Web site.

F. **CONDOMINIUM/PLANNED DEVELOPMENT DISCLOSURES:**
(1) SELLER HAS: 7 (or ___) Days After Acceptance to disclose to Buyer if the Property is a condominium, or is located in a planned development or other common interest subdivision (C.A.R. Form SPQ or ESD).

Buyer's Initials (_____)(_____)   Seller's Initials (_____)(_____)

RPA-CA REVISED 12/15 (PAGE 4 OF 10) Print Date
CALIFORNIA RESIDENTIAL PURCHASE AGREEMENT (RPA-CA PAGE 4 OF 10)

FIGURE 7.1:   Residential Purchase Agreement (continued)

Property Address: _____ Date: _____

(2) If the Property is a condominium or is located in a planned development or other common interest subdivision, Seller has **3 (or ___) Days** After Acceptance to request from the HOA (C.A.R. Form HOA1): **(i)** Copies of any documents required by Law; **(ii)** disclosure of any pending or anticipated claim or litigation by or against the HOA; **(iii)** a statement containing the location and number of designated parking and storage spaces; **(iv)** Copies of the most recent 12 months of HOA minutes for regular and special meetings; **(v)** the names and contact information of all HOAs governing the Property (collectively, "CI Disclosures"); **(vi)** private transfer fees; **(vii)** Pet fee restrictions; and **(viii)** smoking restrictions. Seller shall itemize and Deliver to Buyer all CI Disclosures received from the HOA and any CI Disclosures in Seller's possession. Buyer's approval of CI Disclosures is a contingency of this Agreement as specified in paragraph 14B(3). The Party specified in paragraph 7, as directed by escrow, shall deposit funds into escrow or direct to HOA or management company to pay for any of the above.

11. **CONDITION OF PROPERTY:** Unless otherwise agreed in writing: **(i)** the Property is sold (a) "AS-IS" in its PRESENT physical condition as of the date of Acceptance and (b) subject to Buyer's Investigation rights; **(ii)** the Property, including pool, spa, landscaping and grounds, is to be maintained in substantially the same condition as on the date of Acceptance; and **(iii)** all debris and personal property not included in the sale shall be removed by Close Of Escrow.

 A. Seller shall, within the time specified in paragraph 14A, DISCLOSE KNOWN MATERIAL FACTS AND DEFECTS affecting the Property, including known insurance claims within the past five years, and make any and all other disclosures required by law.

 B. Buyer has the right to conduct Buyer Investigations of the Property and, as specified in paragraph 14B, based upon information discovered in those investigations: (i) cancel this Agreement; or (ii) request that Seller make Repairs or take other action.

 C. **Buyer is strongly advised to conduct investigations of the entire Property in order to determine its present condition. Seller may not be aware of all defects affecting the Property or other factors that Buyer considers important. Property improvements may not be built according to code, in compliance with current Law, or have had permits issued.**

12. **BUYER'S INVESTIGATION OF PROPERTY AND MATTERS AFFECTING PROPERTY:**

 A. Buyer's acceptance of the condition of, and any other matter affecting the Property, is a contingency of this Agreement as specified in this paragraph and paragraph 14B. Within the time specified in paragraph 14B(1), Buyer shall have the right, at Buyer's expense unless otherwise agreed, to conduct inspections, investigations, tests, surveys and other studies ("Buyer Investigations"), including, but not limited to: **(i)** a general physical inspection; **(ii)** an inspection specifically for wood destroying pests and organisms. Any inspection for wood destroying pests and organisms shall be prepared by a registered Structural Pest Control company; shall cover the main building and attached structures; may cover detached structures; shall NOT include water tests of shower pans on upper level units unless the owners of property below the shower consent; shall NOT include roof coverings; and, if the Property is a unit in a condominium or other common interest subdivision, the inspection shall include only the separate interest and any exclusive-use areas being transferred, and shall NOT include common areas; and shall include a report ("Pest Control Report") showing the findings of the company which shall be separated into sections for evident infestation or infections (Section 1) and for conditions likely to lead to infestation or infection (Section 2); **(iii)** inspect for lead-based paint and other lead-based paint hazards; **(iv)** satisfy Buyer as to any matter specified in the attached Buyer's Inspection Advisory (C.A.R. Form BIA); **(v)** review the registered sex offender database; **(vi)** confirm the insurability of Buyer and the Property including the availability and cost of flood and fire insurance; and **(vii)** review and seek approval of leases that may need to be assumed by Buyer. Without Seller's prior written consent, Buyer shall neither make nor cause to be made: invasive or destructive Buyer Investigations, except for minimally invasive testing required to prepare a Pest Control Report; or inspections by any governmental building or zoning inspector or government employee, unless required by Law.

 B. Seller shall make the Property available for all Buyer Investigations. Buyer shall **(i)** as specified in paragraph 14B, complete Buyer Investigations and either remove the contingency or cancel this Agreement, and **(ii)** give Seller, at no cost, complete Copies of all such Investigation reports obtained by Buyer, which obligation shall survive the termination of this Agreement.

 C. Seller shall have water, gas, electricity and all operable pilot lights on for Buyer's Investigations and through the date possession is made available to Buyer.

 D. **Buyer indemnity and seller protection for entry upon property:** Buyer shall: **(i)** keep the Property free and clear of liens; **(ii)** repair all damage arising from Buyer Investigations; and **(iii)** indemnify and hold Seller harmless from all resulting liability, claims, demands, damages and costs. Buyer shall carry, or Buyer shall require anyone acting on Buyer's behalf to carry, policies of liability, workers' compensation and other applicable insurance, defending and protecting Seller from liability for any injuries to persons or property occurring during any Buyer Investigations or work done on the Property at Buyer's direction prior to Close Of Escrow. Seller is advised that certain protections may be afforded Seller by recording a "Notice of Non-Responsibility" (C.A.R. Form NNR) for Buyer Investigations and work done on the Property at Buyer's direction. Buyer's obligations under this paragraph shall survive the termination of this Agreement.

13. **TITLE AND VESTING:**

 A. Within the time specified in paragraph 14, Buyer shall be provided a current preliminary title report ("Preliminary Report"). The Preliminary Report is only an offer by the title insurer to issue a policy of title insurance and may not contain every item affecting title. Buyer's review of the Preliminary Report and any other matters which may affect title are a contingency of this Agreement as specified in paragraph 14B. The company providing the Preliminary Report shall, prior to issuing a Preliminary Report, conduct a search of the General Index for all Sellers except banks or other institutional lenders selling properties they acquired through foreclosure (REOs), corporations, and government entities. Seller shall within 7 Days After Acceptance, give Escrow Holder a completed Statement of Information.

 B. Title is taken in its present condition subject to all encumbrances, easements, covenants, conditions, restrictions, rights and other matters, whether of record or not, as of the date of Acceptance except for: (i) monetary liens of record (which Seller is obligated to pay off) unless Buyer is assuming those obligations or taking the Property subject to those obligations; and (ii) those matters which Seller has agreed to remove in writing.

 C. Within the time specified in paragraph 14A, Seller has a duty to disclose to Buyer all matters known to Seller affecting title, whether of record or not.

 D. At Close Of Escrow, Buyer shall receive a grant deed conveying title (or, for stock cooperative or long-term lease, an assignment of stock certificate or of Seller's leasehold interest), including oil, mineral and water rights if currently owned by Seller. Title shall vest as designated in Buyer's supplemental escrow instructions. THE MANNER OF TAKING TITLE MAY HAVE SIGNIFICANT LEGAL AND TAX CONSEQUENCES. CONSULT AN APPROPRIATE PROFESSIONAL.

 E. Buyer shall receive a CLTA/ALTA "Homeowner's Policy of Title Insurance", if applicable to the type of property and buyer. If not, Escrow Holder shall notify Buyer. A title company can provide information about the availability, coverage, and cost of other title policies and endorsements. If the Homeowner's Policy is not available, Buyer shall choose another policy, instruct Escrow Holder in writing and shall pay any increase in cost.

Buyer's Initials (_____)(_____)   Seller's Initials (_____)(_____)

RPA-CA REVISED 12/15 (PAGE 5 OF 10) Print Date
CALIFORNIA RESIDENTIAL PURCHASE AGREEMENT (RPA-CA PAGE 5 OF 10)

FIGURE 7.1: **Residential Purchase Agreement (continued)**

Property Address: _____ Date: _____

14. **TIME PERIODS; REMOVAL OF CONTINGENCIES; CANCELLATION RIGHTS: The following time periods may only be extended, altered, modified or changed by mutual written agreement. Any removal of contingencies or cancellation under this paragraph by either Buyer or Seller must be exercised in good faith and in writing (C.A.R. Form CR or CC).**

A. **SELLER HAS: 7 (or ___) Days** After Acceptance to Deliver to Buyer all Reports, disclosures and information for which Seller is responsible under paragraphs 5, 6, 7, 8B(5), 10A, B, C, and F, 11A and 13A. If, by the time specified, Seller has not Delivered any such item, Buyer after first Delivering to Seller a Notice to Seller to Perform (C.A.R. Form NSP) may cancel this Agreement.

B. **(1) BUYER HAS: 17 (or ___) Days** After Acceptance, unless otherwise agreed in writing, to:
  (i) complete all Buyer Investigations; review all disclosures, reports, lease documents to be assumed by Buyer pursuant to paragraph 8B(5), and other applicable information, which Buyer receives from Seller; and approve all matters affecting the Property; and **(ii)** Deliver to Seller Signed Copies of Statutory and Lead Disclosures and other disclosures Delivered by Seller in accordance with paragraph 10A.
  (2) Within the time specified in paragraph 14B(1), Buyer may request that Seller make repairs or take any other action regarding the Property (C.A.R. Form RR). Seller has no obligation to agree to or respond to (C.A.R. Form RRRR) Buyer's requests.
  (3) By the end of the time specified in paragraph 14B(1) (or as otherwise specified in this Agreement), Buyer shall Deliver to Seller a removal of the applicable contingency or cancellation (C.A.R. Form CR or CC) of this Agreement. However, if any report, disclosure or information for which Seller is responsible is not Delivered within the time specified in paragraph 14A, then Buyer has **5 (or ___) Days** After Delivery of any such items, or the time specified in paragraph 14B(1), whichever is later, to Deliver to Seller a removal of the applicable contingency or cancellation of this Agreement.
  (4) Continuation of Contingency: Even after the end of the time specified in paragraph 14B(1) and before Seller cancels, if at all, pursuant to paragraph 14D, Buyer retains the right, in writing, to either (i) remove remaining contingencies, or (ii) cancel this Agreement based on a remaining contingency. Once Buyer's written removal of all contingencies is Delivered to Seller, Seller may not cancel this Agreement pursuant to paragraph 14D(1).
  (5) Access to Property: Buyer shall have access to the Property to conduct inspections and investigations for **17 (or ___) Days** After Acceptance, whether or not any part of the Buyer's Investigation Contingency has been waived or removed.

C. ☐ **REMOVAL OF CONTINGENCIES WITH OFFER: Buyer removes the contingencies specified in the attached Contingency Removal form (C.A.R. Form CR). If Buyer removes any contingency without an adequate understanding of the Property's condition or Buyer's ability to purchase, Buyer is acting against the advice of Broker.**

D. **SELLER RIGHT TO CANCEL:**
  (1) Seller right to Cancel; Buyer Contingencies: If, by the time specified in this Agreement, Buyer does not Deliver to Seller a removal of the applicable contingency or cancellation of this Agreement, then Seller, after first Delivering to Buyer a Notice to Buyer to Perform (C.A.R. Form NBP), may cancel this Agreement. In such event, Seller shall authorize the return of Buyer's deposit, except for fees incurred by Buyer.
  (2) Seller right to Cancel; Buyer Contract Obligations: Seller, after first delivering to Buyer a NBP, may cancel this Agreement if, by the time specified in this Agreement, Buyer does not take the following action(s): **(i)** Deposit funds as required by paragraph 3A, or 3B or if the funds deposited pursuant to paragraph 3A or 3B are not good when deposited; **(ii)** Deliver a notice of FHA or VA costs or terms as required by paragraph 3D(3) (C.A.R. Form FVA); **(iii)** Deliver a letter as required by paragraph 3J(1); **(iv)** Deliver verification, or a satisfactory verification if Seller reasonably disapproves of the verification already provided, as required by paragraph 3C or 3H; **(v)** In writing assume or accept leases or liens specified in 8B5; **(vi)** Return Statutory and Lead Disclosures as required by paragraph 10A(5); or **(vii)** Sign or initial a separate liquidated damages form for an increased deposit as required by paragraphs 3B and 21B; or **(viii)** Provide evidence of authority to sign in a representative capacity as specified in paragraph 19. In such event, Seller shall authorize the return of Buyer's deposit, except for fees incurred by Buyer.

E. **NOTICE TO BUYER OR SELLER TO PERFORM:** The NBP or NSP shall: **(i)** be in writing; **(ii)** be signed by the applicable Buyer or Seller; and **(iii)** give the other Party at least **2 (or ___) Days** After Delivery (or until the time specified in the applicable paragraph, whichever occurs last) to take the applicable action. A NBP or NSP may not be Delivered any earlier than **2 Days** Prior to the expiration of the applicable time for the other Party to remove a contingency or cancel this Agreement or meet an obligation specified in paragraph 14.

F. **EFFECT OF BUYER'S REMOVAL OF CONTINGENCIES:** If Buyer removes, in writing, any contingency or cancellation rights, unless otherwise specified in writing, Buyer shall conclusively be deemed to have: **(i)** completed all Buyer Investigations, and review of reports and other applicable information and disclosures pertaining to that contingency or cancellation right; **(ii)** elected to proceed with the transaction; and **(iii)** assumed all liability, responsibility and expense for Repairs or corrections pertaining to that contingency or cancellation right, or for the inability to obtain financing.

G. **CLOSE OF ESCROW:** Before Buyer or Seller may cancel this Agreement for failure of the other Party to close escrow pursuant to this Agreement, Buyer or Seller must first Deliver to the other Party a demand to close escrow (C.A.R. Form DCE). The DCE shall: **(i)** be signed by the applicable Buyer or Seller; and **(ii)** give the other Party at least **3 (or ___) Days** After Delivery to close escrow. A DCE may not be Delivered any earlier than **3 Days** Prior to the scheduled close of escrow.

H. **EFFECT OF CANCELLATION ON DEPOSITS:** If Buyer or Seller gives written notice of cancellation pursuant to rights duly exercised under the terms of this Agreement, the Parties agree to Sign mutual instructions to cancel the sale and escrow and release deposits, if any, to the party entitled to the funds, less fees and costs incurred by that party. Fees and costs may be payable to service providers and vendors for services and products provided during escrow. Except as specified below, **release of funds will require mutual Signed release instructions from the Parties, judicial decision or arbitration award.** If either Party fails to execute mutual instructions to cancel escrow, one Party may make a written demand to Escrow Holder for the deposit (C.A.R. Form BDRD or SDRD). Escrow Holder, upon receipt, shall promptly deliver notice of the demand to the other Party. If, within 10 Days After Escrow Holder's notice, the other Party does not object to the demand, Escrow Holder shall disburse the deposit to the Party making the demand. If Escrow Holder complies with the preceding process, each Party shall be deemed to have released Escrow Holder from any and all claims or liability related to the disbursal of the deposit. Escrow Holder, at its discretion, may nonetheless require mutual cancellation instructions. **A Party may be subject to a civil penalty of up to $1,000 for refusal to sign cancellation instructions if no good faith dispute exists as to who is entitled to the deposited funds (Civil Code §1057.3).**

Buyer's Initials (_____)(_____)   Seller's Initials (_____)(_____)

RPA-CA REVISED 12/15 (PAGE 6 OF 10) Print Date

CALIFORNIA RESIDENTIAL PURCHASE AGREEMENT (RPA-CA PAGE 6 OF 10)

FIGURE 7.1:   Residential Purchase Agreement (continued)

Property Address: _____   Date: _____

15. **FINAL VERIFICATION OF CONDITION:** Buyer shall have the right to make a final verification of the Property within **5 (or ☐ ___) Days** Prior to Close Of Escrow, NOT AS A CONTINGENCY OF THE SALE, but solely to confirm: **(i)** the Property is maintained pursuant to paragraph 11; **(ii)** Repairs have been completed as agreed; and **(iii)** Seller has complied with Seller's other obligations under this Agreement (C.A.R. Form VP).

16. **REPAIRS:** Repairs shall be completed prior to final verification of condition unless otherwise agreed in writing. Repairs to be performed at Seller's expense may be performed by Seller or through others, provided that the work complies with applicable Law, including governmental permit, inspection and approval requirements. Repairs shall be performed in a good, skillful manner with materials of quality and appearance comparable to existing materials. It is understood that exact restoration of appearance or cosmetic items following all Repairs may not be possible. Seller shall: **(i)** obtain invoices and paid receipts for Repairs performed by others; **(ii)** prepare a written statement indicating the Repairs performed by Seller and the date of such Repairs; and **(iii)** provide Copies of invoices and paid receipts and statements to Buyer prior to final verification of condition.

17. **PRORATIONS OF PROPERTY TAXES AND OTHER ITEMS:** Unless otherwise agreed in writing, the following items shall be PAID CURRENT and prorated between Buyer and Seller as of Close Of Escrow: real property taxes and assessments, interest, rents, HOA regular, special, and emergency dues and assessments imposed prior to Close Of Escrow, premiums on insurance assumed by Buyer, payments on bonds and assessments assumed by Buyer, and payments on Mello-Roos and other Special Assessment District bonds and assessments that are now a lien. The following items shall be assumed by Buyer WITHOUT CREDIT toward the purchase price: prorated payments on Mello-Roos and other Special Assessment District bonds and assessments and HOA special assessments that are now a lien but not yet due. Property will be reassessed upon change of ownership. Any supplemental tax bills shall be paid as follows: **(i)** for periods after Close Of Escrow, by Buyer; and **(ii)** for periods prior to Close Of Escrow, by Seller (see C.A.R. Form SPT or SBSA for further information). TAX BILLS ISSUED AFTER CLOSE OF ESCROW SHALL BE HANDLED DIRECTLY BETWEEN BUYER AND SELLER. Prorations shall be made based on a 30-day month.

18. **BROKERS:**
   A.   COMPENSATION: Seller or Buyer, or both, as applicable, agree to pay compensation to Broker as specified in a separate written agreement between Broker and that Seller or Buyer. Compensation is payable upon Close Of Escrow, or if escrow does not close, as otherwise specified in the agreement between Broker and that Seller or Buyer.
   B.   SCOPE OF DUTY: Buyer and Seller acknowledge and agree that Broker: **(i)** Does not decide what price Buyer should pay or Seller should accept; **(ii)** Does not guarantee the condition of the Property; **(iii)** Does not guarantee the performance, adequacy or completeness of inspections, services, products or repairs provided or made by Seller or others; **(iv)** Does not have an obligation to conduct an inspection of common areas or areas off the site of the Property; **(v)** Shall not be responsible for identifying defects on the Property, in common areas, or offsite unless such defects are visually observable by an inspection of reasonably accessible areas of the Property or are known to Broker; **(vi)** Shall not be responsible for inspecting public records or permits concerning the title or use of Property; **(vii)** Shall not be responsible for identifying the location of boundary lines or other items affecting title; **(viii)** Shall not be responsible for verifying square footage, representations of others or information contained in Investigation reports, Multiple Listing Service, advertisements, flyers or other promotional material; **(ix)** Shall not be responsible for determining the fair market value of the Property or any personal property included in the sale; **(x)** Shall not be responsible for providing legal or tax advice regarding any aspect of a transaction entered into by Buyer or Seller; and **(xi)** Shall not be responsible for providing other advice or information that exceeds the knowledge, education and experience required to perform real estate licensed activity. Buyer and Seller agree to seek legal, tax, insurance, title and other desired assistance from appropriate professionals.

19. **REPRESENTATIVE CAPACITY:** If one or more Parties is signing this Agreement in a representative capacity and not for him/herself as an individual then that Party shall so indicate in paragraph 31 or 32 and attach a Representative Capacity Signature Disclosure (C.A.R. Form RCSD). Wherever the signature or initials of the representative identified in the RCSD appear on this Agreement or any related documents, it shall be deemed to be in a representative capacity for the entity described and not in an individual capacity, unless otherwise indicated. The Party acting in a representative capacity **(i)** represents that the entity for which that party is acting already exists and **(ii)** shall Deliver to the other Party and Escrow Holder, within **3 Days** After Acceptance, evidence of authority to act in that capacity (such as but not limited to: applicable portion of the trust or Certification Of Trust (Probate Code §18100.5), letters testamentary, court order, power of attorney, corporate resolution, or formation documents of the business entity).

20. **JOINT ESCROW INSTRUCTIONS TO ESCROW HOLDER:**
   A.   The following paragraphs, or applicable portions thereof, of this Agreement constitute the joint escrow instructions of Buyer and Seller to Escrow Holder, which Escrow Holder is to use along with any related counter offers and addenda, and any additional mutual instructions to close the escrow: paragraphs 1, 3, 4B, 5A, 6, 7, 10C, 13, 14G, 17, 18A, 19, 20, 26, 29, 30, 31, 32 and paragraph D of the section titled Real Estate Brokers on page 10. If a Copy of the separate compensation agreement(s) provided for in paragraph 18A, or paragraph D of the section titled Real Estate Brokers on page 10 is deposited with Escrow Holder by Broker, Escrow Holder shall accept such agreement(s) and pay out from Buyer's or Seller's funds, or both, as applicable, the Broker's compensation provided for in such agreement(s). The terms and conditions of this Agreement not set forth in the specified paragraphs are additional matters for the information of Escrow Holder, but about which Escrow Holder need not be concerned. Buyer and Seller will receive Escrow Holder's general provisions, if any, directly from Escrow Holder and will execute such provisions within the time specified in paragraph 7C(1)(c). To the extent the general provisions are inconsistent or conflict with this Agreement, the general provisions will control as to the duties and obligations of Escrow Holder only. Buyer and Seller will execute additional instructions, documents and forms provided by Escrow Holder that are reasonably necessary to close the escrow and, as directed by Escrow Holder, within **3 (or ___) Days**, shall pay to Escrow Holder or HOA or HOA management company or others any fee required by paragraphs 7, 10 or elsewhere in this Agreement.
   B.   A Copy of this Agreement including any counter offer(s) and addenda shall be delivered to Escrow Holder within **3 Days After Acceptance (or _____). Buyer and Seller authorize Escrow Holder to accept and rely on Copies and Signatures as defined in this Agreement as originals, to open escrow and for other purposes of escrow. The validity of this Agreement as between Buyer and Seller is not affected by whether or when Escrow Holder Signs this Agreement. Escrow Holder shall provide Seller's Statement of Information to Title company when received from Seller. If Seller delivers an affidavit to Escrow Holder to satisfy Seller's FIRPTA obligation under paragraph 10C, Escrow Holder shall deliver to Buyer a Qualified Substitute statement that complies with federal Law.

Buyer's Initials (_____)(_____)   Seller's Initials (_____)(_____)
RPA-CA REVISED 12/15 (PAGE 7 OF 10) Print Date
CALIFORNIA RESIDENTIAL PURCHASE AGREEMENT (RPA-CA PAGE 7 OF 10)

EQUAL HOUSING OPPORTUNITY

FIGURE 7.1: **Residential Purchase Agreement (continued)**

Property Address: _____ Date: _____

C. Brokers are a party to the escrow for the sole purpose of compensation pursuant to paragraph 18A and paragraph D of the section titled Real Estate Brokers on page 10. Buyer and Seller irrevocably assign to Brokers compensation specified in paragraph 18A, and irrevocably instruct Escrow Holder to disburse those funds to Brokers at Close Of Escrow or pursuant to any other mutually executed cancellation agreement. Compensation instructions can be amended or revoked only with the written consent of Brokers. Buyer and Seller shall release and hold harmless Escrow Holder from any liability resulting from Escrow Holder's payment to Broker(s) of compensation pursuant to this Agreement.

D. Upon receipt, Escrow Holder shall provide Seller and Seller's Broker verification of Buyer's deposit of funds pursuant to paragraph 3A and 3B. Once Escrow Holder becomes aware of any of the following, Escrow Holder shall immediately notify all Brokers: **(i)** if Buyer's initial or any additional deposit or down payment is not made pursuant to this Agreement, or is not good at time of deposit with Escrow Holder; or **(ii)** if Buyer and Seller instruct Escrow Holder to cancel escrow.

E. A Copy of any amendment that affects any paragraph of this Agreement for which Escrow Holder is responsible shall be delivered to Escrow Holder within **3** Days after mutual execution of the amendment.

21. **REMEDIES FOR BUYER'S BREACH OF CONTRACT:**

A. **Any clause added by the Parties specifying a remedy (such as release or forfeiture of deposit or making a deposit non-refundable) for failure of Buyer to complete the purchase in violation of this Agreement shall be deemed invalid unless the clause independently satisfies the statutory liquidated damages requirements set forth in the Civil Code.**

B. **LIQUIDATED DAMAGES: If Buyer fails to complete this purchase because of Buyer's default, Seller shall retain, as liquidated damages, the deposit actually paid. If the Property is a dwelling with no more than four units, one of which Buyer intends to occupy, then the amount retained shall be no more than 3% of the purchase price. Any excess shall be returned to Buyer. Except as provided in paragraph 14G, release of funds will require mutual, Signed release instructions from both Buyer and Seller, judicial decision or arbitration award. AT THE TIME OF ANY INCREASED DEPOSIT BUYER AND SELLER SHALL SIGN A SEPARATE LIQUIDATED DAMAGES PROVISION INCORPORATING THE INCREASED DEPOSIT AS LIQUIDATED DAMAGES (C.A.R. FORM RID).**

Buyer's Initials _____/_____   Seller's Initials _____/_____

22. **DISPUTE RESOLUTION:**

A. **MEDIATION:** The Parties agree to mediate any dispute or claim arising between them out of this Agreement, or any resulting transaction, before resorting to arbitration or court action through the C.A.R. Real Estate Mediation Center for Consumers (www.consumermediation.org) or through any other mediation provider or service mutually agreed to by the Parties. The Parties **also agree to mediate any disputes or claims with Broker(s), who, in writing, agree to such mediation prior to, or within a reasonable time after, the dispute or claim is presented to the Broker.** Mediation fees, if any, shall be divided equally among the Parties involved. If, for any dispute or claim to which this paragraph applies, any Party (i) commences an action without first attempting to resolve the matter through mediation, or (ii) before commencement of an action, refuses to mediate after a request has been made, then that Party shall not be entitled to recover attorney fees, even if they would otherwise be available to that Party in any such action. THIS MEDIATION PROVISION APPLIES WHETHER OR NOT THE ARBITRATION PROVISION IS INITIALED. **Exclusions from this mediation agreement are specified in paragraph 22C.**

B. **ARBITRATION OF DISPUTES:**
The Parties agree that any dispute or claim in Law or equity arising between them out of this Agreement or any resulting transaction, which is not settled through mediation, shall be decided by neutral, binding arbitration. The Parties also agree to arbitrate any disputes or claims with Broker(s), who, in writing, agree to such arbitration prior to, or within a reasonable time after, the dispute or claim is presented to the Broker. The arbitrator shall be a retired judge or justice, or an attorney with at least 5 years of residential real estate Law experience, unless the parties mutually agree to a different arbitrator. The Parties shall have the right to discovery in accordance with Code of Civil Procedure §1283.05. In all other respects, the arbitration shall be conducted in accordance with Title 9 of Part 3 of the Code of Civil Procedure. Judgment upon the award of the arbitrator(s) may be entered into any court having jurisdiction. Enforcement of this agreement to arbitrate shall be governed by the Federal Arbitration Act. Exclusions from this arbitration agreement are specified in paragraph 22C.
"NOTICE: BY INITIALING IN THE SPACE BELOW YOU ARE AGREEING TO HAVE ANY DISPUTE ARISING OUT OF THE MATTERS INCLUDED IN THE 'ARBITRATION OF DISPUTES' PROVISION DECIDED BY NEUTRAL ARBITRATION AS PROVIDED BY CALIFORNIA LAW AND YOU ARE GIVING UP ANY RIGHTS YOU MIGHT POSSESS TO HAVE THE DISPUTE LITIGATED IN A COURT OR JURY TRIAL. BY INITIALING IN THE SPACE BELOW YOU ARE GIVING UP YOUR JUDICIAL RIGHTS TO DISCOVERY AND APPEAL, UNLESS THOSE RIGHTS ARE SPECIFICALLY INCLUDED IN THE 'ARBITRATION OF DISPUTES' PROVISION. IF YOU REFUSE TO SUBMIT TO ARBITRATION AFTER AGREEING TO THIS PROVISION, YOU MAY BE COMPELLED TO ARBITRATE UNDER THE AUTHORITY OF THE CALIFORNIA CODE OF CIVIL PROCEDURE. YOUR AGREEMENT TO THIS ARBITRATION PROVISION IS VOLUNTARY."
"WE HAVE READ AND UNDERSTAND THE FOREGOING AND AGREE TO SUBMIT DISPUTES ARISING OUT OF THE MATTERS INCLUDED IN THE 'ARBITRATION OF DISPUTES' PROVISION TO NEUTRAL ARBITRATION."

Buyer's Initials _____/_____   Seller's Initials _____/_____

C. **ADDITIONAL MEDIATION AND ARBITRATION TERMS:**
(1) **EXCLUSIONS: The following matters are excluded from mediation and arbitration: (i) a judicial or non-judicial foreclosure or other action or proceeding to enforce a deed of trust, mortgage or installment land sale contract as defined in Civil Code §2985; (ii) an unlawful detainer action; and (iii) any matter that is within the jurisdiction of a probate, small claims or bankruptcy court.**

Buyer's Initials (_____)(_____)   Seller's Initials (_____)(_____)
RPA-CA REVISED 12/15 (PAGE 8 of 10) Print Date
CALIFORNIA RESIDENTIAL PURCHASE AGREEMENT (RPA-CA PAGE 8 OF 10)

FIGURE 7.1:   **Residential Purchase Agreement (continued)**

Property Address: _____   Date: _____

(2) PRESERVATION OF ACTIONS: The following shall not constitute a waiver nor violation of the mediation and arbitration provisions: (i) the filing of a court action to preserve a statute of limitations; (ii) the filing of a court action to enable the recording of a notice of pending action, for order of attachment, receivership, injunction, or other provisional remedies; or (iii) the filing of a mechanic's lien.

(3) BROKERS: Brokers shall not be obligated nor compelled to mediate or arbitrate unless they agree to do so in writing. Any Broker(s) participating in mediation or arbitration shall not be deemed a party to this Agreement.

23. **SELECTION OF SERVICE PROVIDERS:** Brokers do not guarantee the performance of any vendors, service or product providers ("Providers"), whether referred by Broker or selected by Buyer, Seller or other person. Buyer and Seller may select ANY Providers of their own choosing.

24. **MULTIPLE LISTING SERVICE ("MLS"):** Brokers are authorized to report to the MLS a pending sale and, upon Close Of Escrow, the sales price and other terms of this transaction shall be provided to the MLS to be published and disseminated to persons and entities authorized to use the information on terms approved by the MLS.

25. **ATTORNEY FEES:** In any action, proceeding, or arbitration between Buyer and Seller arising out of this Agreement, the prevailing Buyer or Seller shall be entitled to reasonable attorney fees and costs from the non-prevailing Buyer or Seller, except as provided in paragraph 22A.

26. **ASSIGNMENT:** Buyer shall not assign all or any part of Buyer's interest in this Agreement without first having obtained the separate written consent of Seller to a specified assignee. Such consent shall not be unreasonably withheld. Any total or partial assignment shall not relieve Buyer of Buyer's obligations pursuant to this Agreement unless otherwise agreed in writing by Seller (C.A.R. Form AOAA).

27. **EQUAL HOUSING OPPORTUNITY:** The Property is sold in compliance with federal, state and local anti-discrimination Laws.

28. **TERMS AND CONDITIONS OF OFFER:**
This is an offer to purchase the Property on the above terms and conditions. The liquidated damages paragraph or the arbitration of disputes paragraph is incorporated in this Agreement if initialed by all Parties or if incorporated by mutual agreement in a counter offer or addendum. If at least one but not all Parties initial, a counter offer is required until agreement is reached. Seller has the right to continue to offer the Property for sale and to accept any other offer at any time prior to notification of Acceptance. The Parties have read and acknowledge receipt of a Copy of the offer and agree to the confirmation of agency relationships. If this offer is accepted and Buyer subsequently defaults, Buyer may be responsible for payment of Brokers' compensation. This Agreement and any supplement, addendum or modification, including any Copy, may be Signed in two or more counterparts, all of which shall constitute one and the same writing.

29. **TIME OF ESSENCE; ENTIRE CONTRACT; CHANGES:** Time is of the essence. All understandings between the Parties are incorporated in this Agreement. Its terms are intended by the Parties as a final, complete and exclusive expression of their Agreement with respect to its subject matter, and may not be contradicted by evidence of any prior agreement or contemporaneous oral agreement. If any provision of this Agreement is held to be ineffective or invalid, the remaining provisions will nevertheless be given full force and effect. Except as otherwise specified, this Agreement shall be interpreted and disputes shall be resolved in accordance with the Laws of the State of California. **Neither this Agreement nor any provision in it may be extended, amended, modified, altered or changed, except in writing Signed by Buyer and Seller.**

30. **DEFINITIONS:** As used in this Agreement:
   A. **"Acceptance"** means the time the offer or final counter offer is accepted in writing by a Party and is delivered to and personally received by the other Party or that Party's authorized agent in accordance with the terms of this offer or a final counter offer.
   B. **"Agreement"** means this document and any counter offers and any incorporated addenda, collectively forming the binding agreement between the Parties. Addenda are incorporated only when Signed by all Parties.
   C. **"C.A.R. Form"** means the most current version of the specific form referenced or another comparable form agreed to by the parties.
   D. **"Close Of Escrow"**, including "COE", means the date the grant deed, or other evidence of transfer of title, is recorded.
   E. **"Copy"** means copy by any means including photocopy, NCR, facsimile and electronic.
   F. **"Days"** means calendar days. However, after Acceptance, the last **Day** for performance of any act required by this Agreement (including Close Of Escrow) shall not include any Saturday, Sunday, or legal holiday and shall instead be the next Day.
   G. **"Days After"** means the specified number of calendar days after the occurrence of the event specified, not counting the calendar date on which the specified event occurs, and ending at 11:59 PM on the final day.
   H. **"Days Prior"** means the specified number of calendar days before the occurrence of the event specified, not counting the calendar date on which the specified event is scheduled to occur.
   I. **"Deliver"**, **"Delivered"** or **"Delivery"**, unless otherwise specified in writing, means and shall be effective upon: personal receipt by Buyer or Seller or the individual Real Estate Licensee for that principal as specified in the section titled Real Estate Brokers on page 10, regardless of the method used (i.e., messenger, mail, email, fax, other).
   J. **"Electronic Copy"** or **"Electronic Signature"** means, as applicable, an electronic copy or signature complying with California Law. Buyer and Seller agree that electronic means will not be used by either Party to modify or alter the content or integrity of this Agreement without the knowledge and consent of the other Party.
   K. **"Law"** means any law, code, statute, ordinance, regulation, rule or order, which is adopted by a controlling city, county, state or federal legislative, judicial or executive body or agency.
   L. **"Repairs"** means any repairs (including pest control), alterations, replacements, modifications or retrofitting of the Property provided for under this Agreement.
   M. **"Signed"** means either a handwritten or electronic signature on an original document, Copy or any counterpart.

31. **EXPIRATION OF OFFER:** This offer shall be deemed revoked and the deposit, if any, shall be returned to Buyer unless the offer is Signed by Seller and a Copy of the Signed offer is personally received by Buyer, or by _____,
who is authorized to receive it, by 5:00 PM on the third Day after this offer is signed by Buyer (or by ☐ _____ ☐AM/☐PM,
on _____(date)).

☐ One or more Buyers is signing this Agreement in a representative capacity and not for him/herself as an individual. See attached Representative Capacity Signature Disclosure (C.A.R. Form RCSD-B) for additional terms.

Date _____   BUYER _____

(Print name) _____

Date _____   BUYER _____

(Print name) _____

☐ Additional Signature Addendum attached (C.A.R. Form ASA).

RPA-CA REVISED 12/15 (PAGE 9 of 10)   Print Date   Seller's Initials (_____)(_____)

CALIFORNIA RESIDENTIAL PURCHASE AGREEMENT   (RPA-CA PAGE 9 OF 10)

FIGURE 7.1: **Residential Purchase Agreement (continued)**

Property Address: _____   Date: _____

32. ACCEPTANCE OF OFFER: Seller warrants that Seller is the owner of the Property, or has the authority to execute this Agreement. Seller accepts the above offer and agrees to sell the Property on the above terms and conditions. Seller has read and acknowledges receipt of a Copy of this Agreement, and authorizes Broker to Deliver a Signed Copy to Buyer.

☐ (If checked) SELLER'S ACCEPTANCE IS **SUBJECT TO ATTACHED COUNTER OFFER (C.A.R. Form SCO or SMCO) DATED:**
_____.

☐ One or more Sellers is signing this Agreement in a representative capacity and not for him/herself as an individual. See attached Representative Capacity Signature Disclosure (C.A.R. Form RCSD-S) for additional terms.

Date _____ SELLER _____

(Print name) _____

Date _____ SELLER _____

(Print name) _____

☐ Additional Signature Addendum attached (C.A.R. Form ASA).

(____/____) **(Do not initial if making a counter offer.) CONFIRMATION OF ACCEPTANCE:** A Copy of Signed Acceptance was
(Initials)   personally received by Buyer or Buyer's authorized agent on (date) _____ at _____
☐AM/☐PM. **A binding Agreement is created when a Copy of Signed Acceptance is personally received by Buyer or Buyer's authorized agent whether or not confirmed in this document. Completion of this confirmation is not legally required in order to create a binding Agreement; it is solely intended to evidence the date that Confirmation of Acceptance has occurred.**

REAL ESTATE BROKERS:
A. **Real Estate Brokers are not parties to the Agreement between Buyer and Seller.**
B. **Agency relationships are confirmed as stated in paragraph 2.**
C. If specified in paragraph 3A(2), Agent who submitted the offer for Buyer acknowledges receipt of deposit.
D. **COOPERATING BROKER COMPENSATION:** Listing Broker agrees to pay Cooperating Broker **(Selling Firm)** and Cooperating Broker agrees to accept, out of Listing Broker's proceeds in escrow, the amount specified in the MLS, provided Cooperating Broker is a Participant of the MLS in which the Property is offered for sale or a reciprocal MLS. If Listing Broker and Cooperating Broker are not both Participants of the MLS, or a reciprocal MLS, in which the Property is offered for sale, then compensation must be specified in a separate written agreement (C.A.R. Form CBC). Declaration of License and Tax (C.A.R. Form DLT) may be used to document that tax reporting will be required or that an exemption exists.

Real Estate Broker (Selling Firm) _____ CalBRE Lic. # _____
By _____ CalBRE Lic. # _____ Date _____
By _____ CalBRE Lic. # _____ Date _____
Address _____ City _____ State _____ Zip _____
Telephone _____ Fax _____ E-mail _____
Real Estate Broker (Listing Firm) _____ CalBRE Lic. # _____
By _____ CalBRE Lic. # _____ Date _____
By _____ CalBRE Lic. # _____ Date _____
Address _____ City _____ State _____ Zip _____
Telephone _____ Fax _____ E-mail _____

ESCROW HOLDER ACKNOWLEDGMENT:
Escrow Holder acknowledges receipt of a Copy of this Agreement, (if checked, ☐ a deposit in the amount of $ _____),
counter offer numbers _____ ☐ Seller's Statement of Information and _____
_____, and agrees to act as Escrow Holder subject to paragraph 20 of this Agreement, any
supplemental escrow instructions and the terms of Escrow Holder's general provisions.

Escrow Holder is advised that the date of Confirmation of Acceptance of the Agreement as between Buyer and Seller is _____

Escrow Holder _____ Escrow # _____
By _____ Date _____
Address _____
Phone/Fax/E-mail _____
Escrow Holder has the following license number # _____
☐ Department of Business Oversight, ☐ Department of Insurance, ☐ Bureau of Real Estate.

PRESENTATION OF OFFER: (_____) Listing Broker presented this offer to Seller on _____ (date).
Broker or Designee Initials

REJECTION OF OFFER: (_____)(_____) No counter offer is being made. This offer was rejected by Seller on _____ (date).
Seller's Initials

Buyer Acknowledges that page 10 is part of this Agreement (_____)(_____)
Buyer's Initials

Published and Distributed by:
REAL ESTATE BUSINESS SERVICES, INC.
a subsidiary of the CALIFORNIA ASSOCIATION OF REALTORS®
525 South Virgil Avenue, Los Angeles, California 90020

Reviewed by _____
Broker or Designee _____

RPA-CA REVISED 12/15 (PAGE 10 of 10) **Print Date**

CALIFORNIA RESIDENTIAL PURCHASE AGREEMENT (RPA-CA PAGE 10 OF 10)

Source: Reprinted with permission, California Association of REALTORS®. Endorsement not implied.

FIGURE 7.2:   Buyer's Inspection Advisory

CALIFORNIA
ASSOCIATION
OF REALTORS®

BUYER'S INSPECTION ADVISORY
(C.A.R. Form BIA, Revised 10/02)

Property Address: _____ ("Property").

A. IMPORTANCE OF PROPERTY INVESTIGATION: The physical condition of the land and improvements being purchased is not guaranteed by either Seller or Brokers. For this reason, you should conduct thorough investigations of the Property personally and with professionals who should provide written reports of their investigations. A general physical inspection typically does not cover all aspects of the Property nor items affecting the Property that are not physically located on the Property. If the professionals recommend further investigations, including a recommendation by a pest control operator to inspect inaccessible areas of the Property, you should contact qualified experts to conduct such additional investigations.

B. BUYER RIGHTS AND DUTIES: You have an affirmative duty to exercise reasonable care to protect yourself, including discovery of the legal, practical and technical implications of disclosed facts, and the investigation and verification of information and facts that you know or that are within your diligent attention and observation.   The purchase agreement gives you the right to investigate the Property. If you exercise this right, and you should, you must do so in accordance with the terms of that agreement. This is the best way for you to protect yourself. It is extremely important for you to read all written reports provided by professionals and to discuss the results of inspections with the professional who conducted the inspection. You have the right to request that Seller make repairs, corrections or take other action based upon items discovered in your investigations or disclosed by Seller. If Seller is unwilling or unable to satisfy your requests, or you do not want to purchase the Property in its disclosed and discovered condition, you have the right to cancel the agreement if you act within specific time periods. If you do not cancel the agreement in a timely and proper manner, you may be in breach of contract.

C. SELLER RIGHTS AND DUTIES: Seller is required to disclose to you material facts known to him/her that affect the value or desirability of the Property. However, Seller may not be aware of some Property defects or conditions. Seller does not have an obligation to inspect the Property for your benefit nor is Seller obligated to repair, correct or otherwise cure known defects that are disclosed to you or previously unknown defects that are discovered by you or your inspectors during escrow. The purchase agreement obligates Seller to make the Property available to you for investigations.

D. BROKER OBLIGATIONS: Brokers do not have expertise in all areas and therefore cannot advise you on many items, such as soil stability, geologic or environmental conditions, hazardous or illegal controlled substances, structural conditions of the foundation or other improvements, or the condition of the roof, plumbing, heating, air conditioning, electrical, sewer, septic, waste disposal, or other system. The only way to accurately determine the condition of the Property is through an inspection by an appropriate professional selected by you. If Broker gives you referrals to such professionals, Broker does not guarantee their performance. You may select any professional of your choosing. In sales involving residential dwellings with no more than four units, Brokers have a duty to make a diligent visual inspection of the accessible areas of the Property and to disclose the results of that inspection. However, as some Property defects or conditions may not be discoverable from a visual inspection, it is possible Brokers are not aware of them. If you have entered into a written agreement with a Broker, the specific terms of that agreement will determine the nature and extent of that Broker's duty to you. **YOU ARE STRONGLY ADVISED TO INVESTIGATE THE CONDITION AND SUITABILITY OF ALL ASPECTS OF THE PROPERTY. IF YOU DO NOT DO SO, YOU ARE ACTING AGAINST THE ADVICE OF BROKERS.**

E. YOU ARE ADVISED TO CONDUCT INVESTIGATIONS OF THE ENTIRE PROPERTY, INCLUDING, BUT NOT LIMITED TO THE FOLLOWING:
   1. **GENERAL CONDITION OF THE PROPERTY, ITS SYSTEMS AND COMPONENTS:** Foundation, roof, plumbing, heating, air conditioning, electrical, mechanical, security, pool/spa, other structural and non-structural systems and components, fixtures, built-in appliances, any personal property included in the sale, and energy efficiency of the Property. (Structural engineers are best suited to determine possible design or construction defects, and whether improvements are structurally sound.)
   2. **SQUARE FOOTAGE, AGE, BOUNDARIES:** Square footage, room dimensions, lot size, age of improvements and boundaries. Any numerical statements regarding these items are APPROXIMATIONS ONLY and have not been verified by Seller and cannot be verified by Brokers. Fences, hedges, walls, retaining walls and other natural or constructed barriers or markers do not necessarily identify true Property boundaries. (Professionals such as appraisers, architects, surveyors and civil engineers are best suited to determine square footage, dimensions and boundaries of the Property.)
   3. **WOOD DESTROYING PESTS:** Presence of, or conditions likely to lead to the presence of wood destroying pests and organisms and other infestation or infection. Inspection reports covering these items can be separated into two sections: Section 1 identifies areas where infestation or infection is evident. Section 2 identifies areas where there are conditions likely to lead to infestation or infection. A registered structural pest control company is best suited to perform these inspections.
   4. **SOIL STABILITY:** Existence of fill or compacted soil, expansive or contracting soil, susceptibility to slippage, settling or movement, and the adequacy of drainage. (Geotechnical engineers are best suited to determine such conditions, causes and remedies.)

Buyer's Initials (_____)(_____)
Seller's Initials (_____)(_____)

Reviewed by _____ Date _____

BIA REVISED 10/02 (PAGE 1 OF 2) Print Date

BUYER'S INSPECTION ADVISORY (BIA PAGE 1 OF 2)

Source: Reprinted with permission, California Association of REALTORS®. Endorsement not implied.

FIGURE 7.2: **Buyer's Inspection Advisory (continued)**

Property Address: _____ Date: _____

5. **ROOF:** Present condition, age, leaks, and remaining useful life. (Roofing contractors are best suited to determine these conditions.)
6. **POOL/SPA:** Cracks, leaks or operational problems. (Pool contractors are best suited to determine these conditions.)
7. **WASTE DISPOSAL:** Type, size, adequacy, capacity and condition of sewer and septic systems and components, connection to sewer, and applicable fees.
8. **WATER AND UTILITIES; WELL SYSTEMS AND COMPONENTS:** Water and utility availability, use restrictions and costs. Water quality, adequacy, condition, and performance of well systems and components.
9. **ENVIRONMENTAL HAZARDS:** Potential environmental hazards, including, but not limited to, asbestos, lead-based paint and other lead contamination, radon, methane, other gases, fuel oil or chemical storage tanks, contaminated soil or water, hazardous waste, waste disposal sites, electromagnetic fields, nuclear sources, and other substances, materials, products, or conditions (including mold (airborne, toxic or otherwise), fungus or similar contaminants). (For more in formation on these items, you may consult an appropriate professional or read the booklets "Environmental Hazards: A Guide for Homeowners, Buyers, Landlords and Tenants," "Protect Your Family From Lead in Your Home" or both.)
10. **EARTHQUAKES AND FLOODING:** Susceptibility of the Property to earthquake/seismic hazards and propensity of the Property to flood. (A Geologist or Geotechnical Engineer is best suited to provide information on these conditions.)
11. **FIRE, HAZARD AND OTHER INSURANCE:** The availability and cost of necessary or desired insurance may vary. The location of the Property in a seismic, flood or fire hazard zone, and other conditions, such as the age of the Property and the claims history of the Property and Buyer, may affect the availability and need for certain types of insurance. Buyer should explore insurance options early as this information may affect other decisions, including the removal of loan and inspection contingencies. (An insurance agent is best suited to provide information on these conditions.)
12. **BUILDING PERMITS, ZONING AND GOVERNMENTAL REQUIREMENTS:** Permits, inspections, certificates, zoning, other governmental limitations, restrictions, and requirements affecting the current or future use of the Property, its development or size. (Such information is available from appropriate governmental agencies and private information providers. Brokers are not qualified to review or interpret any such information.)
13. **RENTAL PROPERTY RESTRICTIONS:** Some cities and counties impose restrictions that limit the amount of rent that can be charged, the maximum number of occupants; and the right of a landlord to terminate a tenancy. Deadbolt or other locks and security systems for doors and windows, including window bars, should be examined to determine whether they satisfy legal requirements. (Government agencies can provide information about these restrictions and other requirements.)
14. **SECURITY AND SAFETY:** State and local Law may require the installation of barriers, access alarms, self-latching mechanisms and/or other measures to decrease the risk to children and other persons of existing swimming pools and hot tubs, as well as various fire safety and other measures concerning other features of the Property. Compliance requirements differ from city to city and county to county. Unless specifically agreed, the Property may not be in compliance with these requirements. (Local government agencies can provide information about these restrictions and other requirements.)
15. **NEIGHBORHOOD, AREA, SUBDIVISION CONDITIONS; PERSONAL FACTORS:** Neighborhood or area conditions, including schools, proximity and adequacy of law enforcement, crime statistics, the proximity of registered felons or offenders, fire protection, other government services, availability, adequacy and cost of any speed-wired, wireless internet connections or other telecommunications or other technology services and installations, proximity to commercial, industrial or agricultural activities, existing and proposed transportation, construction and development that may affect noise, view, or traffic, airport noise, noise or odor from any source, wild and domestic animals, other nuisances, hazards, or circumstances, protected species, wetland properties, botanical diseases, historic or other governmentally protected sites or improvements, cemeteries, facilities and condition of common areas of common interest subdivisions, and possible lack of compliance with any governing documents or Homeowners' Association requirements, conditions and influences of significance to certain cultures and/or religions, and personal needs, requirements and preferences of Buyer.

Buyer and Seller acknowledge and agree that Broker: **(i)** Does not decide what price Buyer should pay or Seller should accept; **(ii)** Does not guarantee the condition of the Property; **(iii)** Does not guarantee the performance, adequacy or completeness of inspections, services, products or repairs provided or made by Seller or others; **(iv)** Does not have an obligation to conduct an inspection of common areas or areas off the site of the Property; **(v)** Shall not be responsible for identifying defects on the Property, in common areas, or offsite unless such defects are visually observable by an inspection of reasonably accessible areas of the Property or are known to Broker; **(vi)** Shall not be responsible for inspecting public records or permits concerning the title or use of Property; **(vii)** Shall not be responsible for identifying the location of boundary lines or other items affecting title; **(viii)** Shall not be responsible for verifying square footage, representations of others or information contained in Investigation reports, Multiple Listing Service, advertisements, flyers or other promotional material; **(ix)** Shall not be responsible for providing legal or tax advice regarding any aspect of a transaction entered into by Buyer or Seller; and **(x)** Shall not be responsible for providing other advice or information that exceeds the knowledge, education and experience required to perform real estate licensed activity. Buyer and Seller agree to seek legal, tax, insurance, title and other desired assistance from appropriate professionals.

By signing below, Buyer and Seller each acknowledge that they have read, understand, accept and have received a Copy of this Advisory. Buyer is encouraged to read it carefully.

Buyer Signature _____ Date _____ Buyer Signature _____ Date _____

Seller Signature _____ Date _____ Seller Signature _____ Date _____

Published and Distributed by:
REAL ESTATE BUSINESS SERVICES, INC.
a subsidiary of the California Association of REALTORS®
525 South Virgil Avenue, Los Angeles, California 90020

Reviewed by _____ Date _____

BIA REVISED 10/02 (PAGE 2 OF 2)

BUYER'S INSPECTION ADVISORY (BIA PAGE 2 OF 2)

Remember, until the purchase contract is signed by the seller, it is an offer only and can be withdrawn by the buyer at any time before acceptance. Because such a contract is long and quite detailed, it is likely to contain corrections and written additions. The general rule regarding preprinted forms is as follows:

- *Typed* insertions take precedence over *preprinted* material.

- *Handwritten* insertions take precedence over both *typed* and *preprinted* material.

- *Specific information* takes precedence over *general information*.

Duties of the broker   A real estate broker (or associate licensee) may guide the buyer through the contract provisions and fill in the required information. Then, the broker will present the offer to the seller in the presence of the listing broker, if that is a different person from the selling broker.

The broker who prepares the contract *is not allowed to give legal advice* but can explain the meaning and purpose of the contract terms to the buyer and seller. The *listing* broker, if there is one, has primary responsibility for dealing with the *seller*. If there is a different selling broker, the listing broker most often will discuss the contract terms privately with the seller after the offer has been presented by the selling broker.

Contract terms   The Residential Purchase Agreement and Joint Escrow Instructions shown in Figure 7.1 first requires insertion of the date on which the buyer is signing the offer and the city where it is signed, with no abbreviations. Other features of this contract are discussed starting after Figure 7.1. The numbered paragraphs refer to the numbered sections of the contract.

> The property must be adequately identified.

1. **Offer.** The buyer's full name is entered. The city and county in which the property is located are provided, followed by a legal description of the property. A street address may be sufficient for city property, but a formal legal description (metes and bounds or lot and block) could be used in addition and is required for rural property. The exact acreage need not be specified, but if it is and a survey reveals a significant discrepancy (for instance, 165 acres surveyed when 185 acres are specified in the contract), a problem may arise later. If a lengthy legal description is needed, it is better to make a photocopy of the description from a reliable document and attach that to the contract, rather than risk an error in transcribing. The amount of the purchase price is supplied in both words and figures. The date for close of escrow (COE) is provided.

2. **Agency.** All agency relationships between the parties and broker(s) involved in the transaction are confirmed.

> How will the buyer pay for the property?

3. **Finance Terms.** The buyer indicates how the entire purchase price is to be paid. Terms of payment usually are expressed as conditions or contingencies to the buyer's purchase. If the buyer is unable to obtain the type of loan specified (after reasonably diligent efforts), the buyer could back out of the contract.

4. **Sale of buyer's property.** The contingent sale provision may be used when the buyer owns other property that must be sold before the buyer can complete this transaction.

5. **Addenda and Advisories.** Specific disclosures to be made by the seller are identified. The buyer's inspection is so important that it is the subject of a separate Buyer's Inspection Advisory form (Figure 7.2).

6. **Other terms.** Any contract terms not included elsewhere on the form can be added here.

7. **Allocation of costs.** The buyer may require the seller to provide a pest inspection and report. Allocation of the cost of property inspections as well as other costs associated with the transaction, such as transfer tax, is subject to the negotiation of the parties. In a strong buyer's market, the seller may bear more of these costs. In a strong seller's market, the buyer may offer to pay more of these costs as an inducement to the seller. Local custom and practice also may be followed.

8. **Items included in and excluded from sale.** Fixtures, as defined in Unit 1, are included in the sale of the real estate. A flat-panel television attached to a wall of the property by a bracket is not considered a fixture.

   Any item of personal property that will be included in the sale must be specified. Better practice is to sell such items separately so that their value is not added to the property's value for property tax purposes.

| Will the property be the buyer's primary residence? |

9. **Closing and possession.** Will the buyer live in the residence? Buyers should understand that this is an important question for a number of reasons, including loan financing. The date on which possession will be turned over to the buyer must be indicated. The property should be vacant at the time possession is transferred. The seller has responsibility for terminating any existing tenancy and complying with applicable rent control laws.

   If there are any assignable warranties on any item transferred as part of the sale, the seller will provide copies of the warranties to the buyer.

   All keys, electronic opening devices, security codes, or other devices will be provided to the buyer at the time of possession. If applicable, the buyer may need to make a deposit for keys to common areas.

10. **Statutory disclosures.** All legally mandated disclosures must be made whenever applicable, including federal lead-based paint disclosures. The first two pages of the Real Estate Transfer Disclosure Statement (shown in Figure 6.6) must be completed by a seller of a residence of one to four units. Property located in a very high fire hazard severity zone must be identified. The Foreign Investment in Real Property Tax Act (FIRPTA) and California laws must be complied with. All written contracts for sale or lease of residential real property must contain a specified notice regarding the database (www.meganslaw.ca.gov) maintained by the California Department of Justice, containing information on registered sex offenders. The form also includes a notice regarding the location of gas and hazardous liquid transmission pipelines.

www.meganslaw.ca.gov

10F. **Condominium/planned development disclosures.** Limitations on property located in a condominium or common interest subdivision must be disclosed, including provision for vehicle parking and a copy of the most recent 12 months of minutes of meetings of the homeowners association. As of July 1, 2016, the annual budget report of a condominium project must indicate the status of the common interest development as a Federal Housing Administration (FHA)-approved condominium project and as a Department of Veterans Affairs (VA)-approved condominium project.

11. **Condition of property.** A seller may make an "as-is" sale but still must maintain the property, disclose any known material defects, and make other disclosures required by law.

> Even in an "as-is" sale, the seller must make the required property disclosures.

12. **Buyer's investigation of property and matters affecting property.** The buyer has the right to conduct investigations or tests of the property, including tests for lead-based paint. The seller is not liable for any harm to the buyer and any inspectors or other workers acting on behalf of the buyer.

13. **Title and vesting.** Title insurance is the norm in California to protect the buyer's ownership interest.

14. **Time periods/removal of contingencies/cancellation rights.** All parties need to act promptly on all contract requirements.

15. **Final verification of condition.** A final walk-through inspection of the property by the buyer a day or two before closing is always advisable.

16. **Repairs.** Necessary property repairs must be made before closing.

17. **Prorations of property taxes and other items.** Expenses of ownership usually will be prorated so that seller and buyer pay only the amount attributable to their separate periods of ownership.

18. **Broker compensation.** A separate written agreement specifies how the broker is to be compensated, and by whom.

> Is there a buyer broker agreement?

19. **Representative capacity.** The authority of any person acting for one of the parties to the agreement must be verified.

20. **Joint escrow instructions to escrow holder.** The terms of this agreement also serve as instructions to the escrow holder. This provision was included so that the escrow officer will not have to duplicate the language from the purchase agreement in the escrow instructions.

21. **Remedies for buyer's breach of contract.** Civil Code Section 1675 sets the amount of **liquidated damages** (automatic damages) on the buyer's default that is presumed to be valid at 3% of the purchase price. An amount greater than 3% is presumed to be invalid unless it can be shown to be reasonable. If the property is a newly constructed attached condominium unit in a structure of 10 or more such units, and the amount paid to the seller as liquidated damages exceeds 3% of the purchase price, the seller must make an accounting to the defaulting purchaser of the actual costs and revenues related to the property within 60 days of the closing

> If the buyer defaults, will the seller be entitled to liquidated damages?

of the eventual sale of the unit, refunding any difference, if less than the amount of the liquidated damages paid, to the defaulting purchaser.

> Do buyer and seller agree to arbitrate any dispute not resolved through mediation?

22. **Dispute resolution.** Buyer and seller agree to submit any dispute or claim stemming from this contract to mediation, before resorting to arbitration or court action. Arbitration may be agreed on as the next step following an unsuccessful attempt at mediation. Certain legal matters (such as a mechanic's lien or probate) may require specific legal action. As mentioned in Unit 6, any predispute contractual waiver of the right to a jury trial is constitutionally invalid.

23. **Selection of service providers.** Brokers cannot serve as guarantors of the quality of service of any company or individual that they may be asked to name.

24. **Multiple listing service (MLS).** Use of the MLS is authorized.

25. **Attorney fees.** In a legal action, the losing party will pay the other side's legal expenses.

26. **Assignment.** Seller's written consent is required for the buyer's assignment of all or part of the contract.

27. **Equal housing opportunity.** The sale must comply with all applicable fair housing or equal opportunity laws.

28. **Terms and conditions of offer.** The buyer and seller must understand that the offer to purchase is not a binding agreement until it is accepted by the seller. If the buyer defaults after acceptance by the seller, the buyer may be required to compensate his broker.

29. **Time of essence; entire contract; changes.** This writing supersedes all earlier written or oral agreements.

30. **Definitions.** Important terms are defined.

31. **Expiration of offer.** This section specifies how long the offer will be open and how it can be accepted.

32. **Acceptance of offer.** The seller, by signing the contract, claims to be the owner of the property or to be acting with the owner's permission.

The agreement serves as a confirmation of the agency relationships specified in paragraph 2. The agreement also serves as an acknowledgment that the escrow holder has received it and agrees to serve as escrow as directed.

The **Natural Hazard Disclosure Statement** (Figure 7.3) must be provided in residential transactions of one to four dwelling units. Exceptions for spouses, co-owners, and others are found in Civil Code 1103.1. Other items may be covered in addenda to the purchase agreement.

The possible presence of mold in a property has become an important topic, as has the possible presence of radon gas. While it is not the responsibility of the seller (or the seller's agent) to test for either mold or radon, if either is known to exist on the property, it must be revealed to a prospective buyer. The Radon Gas and Mold Notice and Release Agreement prepared by the California Association of

REALTORS® to meet HUD requirements appears in Figure 14.8. The San Diego Association of REALTORS® (SDAR) has developed a mold disclosure form that is available at its website, www.sdar.com, in the forms section of its risk management department. Any disclosure form adopted by a real estate brokerage should be reviewed by legal counsel.

> Every counteroffer rejects the offer that preceded it.

Counteroffer   If the seller changes any of the contract terms, the seller makes a **counteroffer**. Any change by the seller rejects the buyer's offer as originally written. The seller can change terms only by, in effect, creating a brand new offer that replaces the buyer's original offer.

The seller attaches a counteroffer to the original offer, indicating in the counteroffer the changed or additional terms. In the contract in Figure 7.1, the seller would check the box in paragraph 30, the acceptance paragraph of the purchase contract, indicating that the contract is accepted "subject to attached counteroffer." The total number of pages then will include the counteroffer.

Figure 7.4 is a typical form of seller counteroffer. This counteroffer form leaves room for the seller to include any change or addition to the buyer's terms that the seller wishes. The form should be dated and the parties named. The seller should place a time limit on the buyer's acceptance of the counteroffer. One or two days may be sufficient. The seller signs and dates the counteroffer before giving it to the buyer.

If the terms are now acceptable to the buyer, the buyer also signs and dates the counteroffer and a binding contract is created. The buyer could instead counter the counteroffer by making a correction or addition to the terms of the counteroffer, and executing a new counteroffer. The CAR Buyer Counter Offer form is comparable to the Seller Counter Offer form, but does not include the seller's provision for marketing to other buyers.

FIGURE 7.3: **Natural Hazard Disclosure Statement**

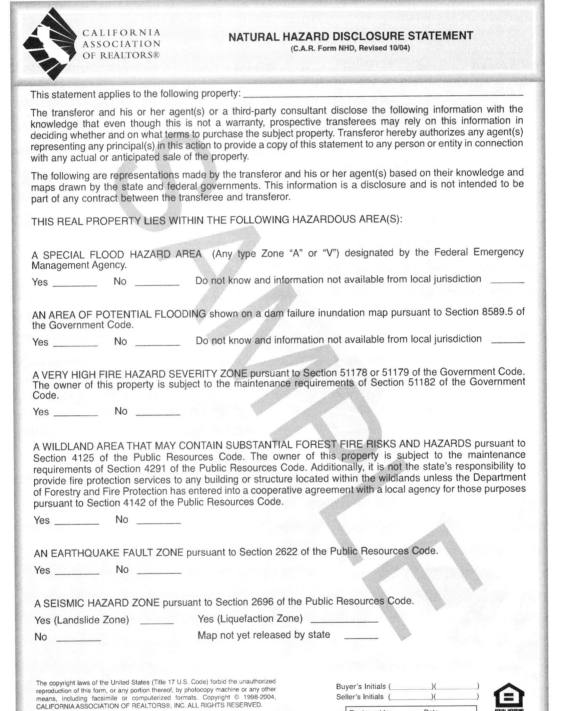

Source: Reprinted with permission, California Association of REALTORS®. Endorsement not implied.

FIGURE 7.4: **Counteroffer Form**

CALIFORNIA
ASSOCIATION
OF REALTORS®

SELLER COUNTER OFFER No. _____
May not be used as a multiple counter offer.
(C.A.R. Form SCO, 11/14)

Date _____

This is a counter offer to the: ☐ Purchase Agreement, ☐ Buyer Counter Offer No.___, or ☐ Other _____ ("Offer"),
dated _____, on property known as _____ ("Property"),
between _____ ("Buyer") and _____ ("Seller").

1. **TERMS:** The terms and conditions of the above referenced document are accepted subject to the following:
   A. **Paragraphs in the Offer that require initials by all parties, but are not initialed by all parties, are excluded from the final agreement unless specifically referenced for inclusion in paragraph 1C of this or another Counter Offer or an addendum.**
   B. **Unless otherwise agreed in writing, down payment and loan amount(s) will be adjusted in the same proportion as in the original Offer.**
   C. **OTHER TERMS:** _____
   _____
   _____
   _____
   _____
   _____
   _____
   _____
   _____
   _____

   D. **The following attached addenda are incorporated into this Seller Counter offer:** ☐ Addendum No. _____
   ☐ _____   ☐ _____

2. **EXPIRATION:** This Seller Counter Offer shall be deemed revoked and the deposits, if any, shall be returned:
   A. Unless by 5:00pm on the third Day After the date it is signed in paragraph 4 (if more than one signature then, the last signature date)(or by _____ ☐ AM ☐ PM on _____ (date)) (i) it is signed in paragraph 5 by Buyer and (ii) a copy of the signed Seller Counter Offer is personally received by Seller or _____, who is authorized to receive it.
   OR B. If Seller withdraws it anytime prior to Acceptance (CAR Form WOO may be used).
   OR C. If Seller accepts another offer prior to Buyer's Acceptance of this counter offer.

3. **MARKETING TO OTHER BUYERS:** Seller has the right to continue to offer the Property for sale. Seller has the right to accept any other offer received, prior to Acceptance of this Counter Offer by Buyer as specified in 2A and 5. In such event, Seller is advised to withdraw this Seller Counter Offer before accepting another offer.

4. **OFFER: SELLER MAKES THIS COUNTER OFFER ON THE TERMS ABOVE AND ACKNOWLEDGES RECEIPT OF A COPY.**
   Seller _____ Date _____
   Seller _____ Date _____

5. **ACCEPTANCE: I/WE** accept the above Seller Counter Offer **(If checked ☐ SUBJECT TO THE ATTACHED COUNTER OFFER)** and acknowledge receipt of a Copy.
   Buyer _____ Date _____ Time _____ AM/PM
   Buyer _____ Date _____ Time _____ AM/PM

CONFIRMATION OF ACCEPTANCE:

(_____/_____) (Initials) **Confirmation of Acceptance:** A Copy of Signed Acceptance was personally received by Seller, or Seller's authorized agent as specified in paragraph 2A on (date) _____ at _____ AM/PM. **A binding Agreement is created when a Copy of Signed Acceptance is personally received by Seller or Seller's authorized agent whether or not confirmed in this document.**

Published and Distributed by:
REAL ESTATE BUSINESS SERVICES, INC.
a subsidiary of the California Association of REALTORS®
525 South Virgil Avenue, Los Angeles, California 90020

Reviewed by _____ Date _____

EQUAL HOUSING
OPPORTUNITY

SCO 11/14 (PAGE 1 OF 1) Print Date

SELLER COUNTER OFFER (SCO PAGE 1 OF 1)

Source: Reprinted with permission, California Association of REALTORS®. Endorsement not implied.

Other Real Estate Contracts

Option   The right to buy property at some time in the future at an agreed-on price is called an **option**. Some form of payment (consideration) is required for an option. The person who acquires the right to purchase (the **optionee**) pays the **optionor** (the property owner) for the privilege of holding the option. The option agreement is unique because it provides the right to exercise or not exercise the option, while preventing the property owner from canceling the option during its term. The buyer of the option is, in effect, buying time to make a decision. The option right also may be assignable.

An option is frequently combined with a lease in the expectation that the lessee will want to stay in possession of the property at the end of the lease term by exercising the option and purchasing the property.

Exchange   In an **exchange**, owners of different properties transfer title to each other. The exchange may be a tax-deferred transaction if it involves properties held for business or investment purposes. An exchange may be accompanied by additional consideration if one property owner has a higher equity value than the other. The additional consideration, called *boot*, is taxable to the party receiving it.

Who Bears the Risk?

What happens if a house burns down while a sale is pending? Or what happens if a tree is knocked down in a storm and damages part of a building? Does the buyer still have to buy the property? Does the seller have to repair it?

California has answered those questions by adopting the **Uniform Vendor and Purchaser Risk Act**, which is found in the Civil Code. The answers depend on whether the buyer has already taken possession of the property or taken title to it. The law states that every contract for the purchase and sale of real property will be treated as if it included the following provisions:

1. If a material part of the real property is destroyed without fault of the *buyer* (or is taken by eminent domain), and

   ■ neither the legal title nor possession of the property has been transferred to the buyer,

   ■ the *seller* (vendor) cannot enforce the contract and the buyer is entitled to recover any part of the purchase price that has already been paid.

2. If either legal title or possession has been transferred, and

   ■ all or part of the property is then destroyed (or taken by eminent domain) without fault of the *seller*,

   ■ the buyer must still complete the terms of the contract and is not entitled to recover any part of the purchase price already paid.

Exchanges often involve loan assumptions, cash payments, and other forms of financing. Because of this—and also because of the possible tax consequences—handling an exchange can require a high level of expertise on the part of the licensee. An exchange should always be reviewed by the principal's tax preparer.

Exercise 7-3

You are to complete the Residential Purchase Agreement that appears as Figure 7.1, using the information that follows. The Buyer's Inspection Advisory will be checked off but is not reproduced here.

You are the broker of ABC Realty handling the listing for sale of a single-family residence belonging to Jim and Mary Ivers. The asking price for the Iverses' three-bedroom, one-bathroom home at 3840 Monroe Street, in Concord, Contra Costa County, is $323,000. The loan balance is not assumable. On January 11, you meet Kenneth A. and Peggy M. Plummer at an open house of the Ivers residence, and the Plummers indicate they want to make an offer.

You discuss the nature of agency relationships with the Plummers and present a copy of the agency disclosure form to them. After a few minutes of private discussion, Kenneth Plummer states that they have decided to make an offer on the Ivers property, and they would like you to assist them in making the offer as their agent. You point out the types of conflict that a dual agency representation creates, but the Plummers indicate that they still are willing to proceed on that basis.

You have a purchase agreement form with you and go through the form with the Plummers. After completing the form as the Plummers indicate, you present it to them for their signatures.

The Plummers are offering $317,000 for the Ivers house. Peggy Plummer writes a personal check for $2,000 as the deposit, which she gives to you. Monroe Street is not far from a branch office of First City Title Company, so the Plummers decide on First City to handle the escrow account and closing of the sale. The deposit check is made out to First City Title Company.

The Plummers will make a total cash down payment of $63,400, including the deposit. The buyers will not increase the deposit. The balance of the down payment will be deposited into the escrow account on or before closing. The remaining $253,600 will be financed by a note secured by a first deed of trust on the subject property. The agreement is contingent on both buyers and property qualifying for a conventional loan in that amount. The buyers are to be lender qualified within 10 calendar days for a 30-year, fixed-rate loan at an interest rate not to exceed 6%, with a loan fee of no more than two points.

The offer is contingent on the buyers' receipt of a property information disclosure statement from the sellers within two days after acceptance.

The buyers and sellers will deliver instructions on the closing of the sale to the escrow holder within five calendar days from the sellers' acceptance. The closing will take place within 60 calendar days from the sellers' acceptance. The escrow fee will be paid by the buyers, as will the transfer tax.

The buyers will use the house as their primary residence. The buyers will receive possession of the property no later than 6:00 pm, two days after the close of escrow.

The sellers will pay for a CLTA title report from First City Title Company, and the buyers will have three days after receiving the report to disapprove it. An ALTA insurance policy from the same company will be paid by the buyers. Prorations will be made as of close of escrow. Any liens on the property are to be paid by the sellers. The buyers will take title as specified in the escrow instructions.

The sellers will install a smoke detector and water heater bracing. They must also comply with all other requirements of state and local law.

No personal property is included in the sale. The sellers warrant that the roof does not leak and all appliances and building systems are in working order. There is no septic system. No geological inspection is necessary, and the property is not in a flood hazard zone or a special studies zone. No other special property condition disclosures are necessary. Energy conservation compliance is the responsibility of the sellers. The sellers are to provide a Home Protection Plan from Home Plan, Inc., at a cost of $350.

The sellers are to pay for a pest control report of all structures, to be conducted by Pest Away, Inc., within 20 days of acceptance. The buyers have five days to review reports, disclosures, and other information provided by the sellers except for reports on lead-based paint and lead-based paint hazards, which the buyers have 20 days to review. The buyers will inspect the property and report any defects within 20 calendar days of the sellers' acceptance. The "passive removal" clause will apply, with the sellers having a three-day response time and the buyers having a two-day right of cancellation. The buyers will have a final walk-through within two days before closing. The buyers agree to the provision regarding arbitration of disputes, and they also agree to the liquidated damages clause. The broker will be able to present the offer to the sellers on the same day it is drawn up, and the buyers will expect an acceptance within three days.

Your office address is 3844 Overview Drive, Concord; your telephone number is 1-510-555-6079; fax is 1-555-6080.

SUMMARY

A **contract** is a promise to do something or to refrain from doing something. A **tender** is an offer to perform a **contractual obligation**. A contract is **executory** as long as some contract obligation remains to be performed. A contract is **executed** when the transaction has been completed. A contract may be **express** or **implied**, **bilateral** (if both parties are bound), or **unilateral** (if only one party is obligated).

A **void contract** has no legal effect, and a **voidable contract** can be disavowed by its maker. A contract could also be **unenforceable**.

A **minor** cannot make a contract concerning real estate. Other contracts by a minor may be voidable. An **emancipated minor** can contract as an adult.

A contract requires an **offer** made by someone who has the **legal capacity** to enter a contract, sufficiently *definite contract terms*, *acceptance* by the offeree (who also must have contractual capacity), a **lawful object**, and **consideration**. An offer may be revoked before acceptance. A **counteroffer** rejects the previous offer and creates a new offer. The offeree must not act under threat of harm, undue influence, mistake, or on the basis of a **fraudulent misrepresentation**, whether the fraud is **actual** or **constructive**.

The **statute of frauds** specifies the types of contracts that must be written to be legally enforceable. The **statute of limitations** specifies the time period within which a legal action can be brought.

A contract can be **discharged** by **performance, rescission, release,** or **novation**. A contract also will be terminated if performance is impossible or perhaps impractical. A contract is modified by **reformation**. Most contracts can be **assigned** to someone else. A breach of the contract terms may **discharge** the contract, but the nonbreaching party may sue for *money damages* or **specific performance**. A lawsuit must be brought within the time period set by the *statute of limitations*.

An *offer to purchase* may be made and accepted through a **real estate purchase contract and receipt for deposit**. Such an agreement will include any *contingencies* that, if not met, may enable one party to terminate the contract. An **option** is a useful way to retain the right to purchase property for an extended period. An **exchange** agreement may benefit both parties and provide tax advantages.

OPEN FOR DISCUSSION

1. Have real estate contracts gotten too long?

2. What do you suggest to improve the readability of sales contracts?

REVIEW QUESTIONS

1. A 17-year-old can contract as an adult if she
   a. is living away from her parents.
   b. is emancipated.
   c. is an orphan.
   d. has an adult cosign with her.

2. The owner of a one-person shoe repair shop is
   a. a sole proprietor.
   b. a partner.
   c. an executor.
   d. an administrator.

3. Mary persuaded her elderly Aunt Agnes to buy a grossly overpriced condominium. Mary knew the price was too high, but she received a commission on the sale from the seller. Aunt Agnes may complain of
   a. actual fraud and undue influence.
   b. negligent misrepresentation.
   c. constructive fraud.
   d. commercial frustration.

4. The contract Haji Ababe accepted states a purchase price "as appraised on May 12, 2016, by Mike Morton, MAI." Based on this provision, the contract is
   a. void.
   b. voidable.
   c. unenforceable.
   d. enforceable.

5. Can a broker enforce an oral listing agreement for his neighbor's home?
   a. Yes
   b. No
   c. Possibly
   d. Only if he did not have a contract form handy

6. When both parties agree to cancel a contract, they effect
   a. a rescission.
   b. a release.
   c. a novation.
   d. a reformation.

7. Todd made an offer for the Brown residence, and the Browns accepted the offer. On reconsidering, Todd decided to back out of the deal, and the Browns agreed to let him do so. Todd and the Browns then signed
   a. a novation of the purchase contract.
   b. an agreement rescinding the purchase contract.
   c. an assignment of the purchase contract.
   d. an agreement reforming the purchase contract.

8. Which is *NOT* a way to terminate a contract?
   a. Rescission
   b. Release
   c. Verification
   d. Novation

9. Lonnie and Karen have a contract to buy the Santos house. Following a four-day rainstorm, the Santos house was pushed off its foundation by a mudslide and is now resting about halfway over a ravine. The contract probably is
   a. discharged because performance is impractical.
   b. still in effect.
   c. discharged because performance is impossible.
   d. renegotiable at the discretion of the seller.

10. If a buyer's performance of her sales contract becomes economically impractical, she should
    a. cancel the contract unilaterally.
    b. ask that the contract be terminated.
    c. claim the purchase is a mistake.
    d. tear up the contract.

11. Failure to perform a contract is
    a. a rescission.
    b. a breach.
    c. a novation.
    d. a reformation.

12. Drew signed a contract to sell his farm to George. Drew had second thoughts and refused to sell, but the sale went through anyway. How did this happen?
    a. George threatened Drew.
    b. George received a court order for specific performance of the contract.
    c. Once signed, a contract cannot be terminated.
    d. Drew increased the purchase price.

13. The time period in which a lawsuit can be brought is set by
    a. the equal dignities rule.
    b. the statute of frauds.
    c. the statute of limitations.
    d. the probate court.

14. The statute of limitations for an action based on a written real estate contract is
    a. unlimited.
    b. 2 years.
    c. 4 years.
    d. 20 years.

15. The rule for preprinted contracts is
    a. handwriting takes precedence only over printing.
    b. printing takes precedence over typing.
    c. handwriting takes precedence over both typing and printing.
    d. typing takes precedence over handwriting.

16. A property description including the words "250 acres, more or less" is
    a. fatally defective.
    b. not definite enough.
    c. sufficient if reasonably close to the exact acreage.
    d. incomplete without a metes and bounds description.

17. A well-drafted real estate purchase contract will include provision for
    a. the buyer's possession of the property.
    b. the financing terms.
    c. proration of property expenses.
    d. all of these.

18. Unless the seller provides the necessary documentation, part of the proceeds of a sale of real property must be withheld for federal tax purposes as provided by
    a. the FHA.
    b. Fannie Mae.
    c. FIRPTA.
    d. the IRS.

19. Liquidated damages paid on default by the buyer of a single-family residence who intended to occupy the dwelling cannot exceed what percentage of the purchase price?
    a. 1%
    b. 3%
    c. 7%
    d. 10%

20. A seller received an offer of $610,000 for his house. His asking price is $635,000. The seller countered with $625,000. If the buyer rejects the counteroffer, may the seller accept the $610,000 offer?
    a. Yes
    b. No
    c. Yes, if he does so within 24 hours
    d. Only if he redrafts the original offer

UNIT EIGHT

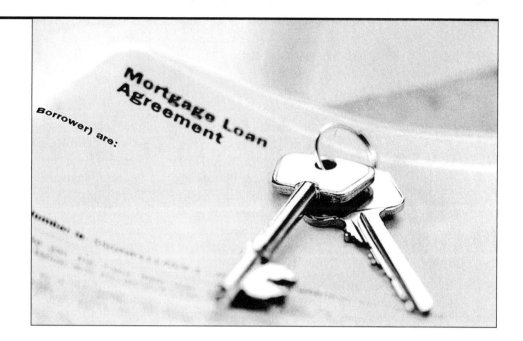

FINANCING REAL ESTATE

LEARNING OBJECTIVES

When you have completed this unit, you will be able to

■ **understand** the concept of leverage and its role in most real estate purchases;

■ **explain** how the various federal agencies help regulate the cost and availability of credit;

■ **identify** the documents used in the purchase and financing of real estate;

■ **describe** the impact of California's antideficiency protection for homeowners;

■ **explain** the foreclosure process under a mortgage and deed of trust, and how they differ;

■ **identify** the lenders who are part of the primary mortgage market;

■ **define** common mortgage plans; and

■ **explain** California's restrictions on mortgage brokers and state and federal disclosure requirements.

KEY TERMS

acceleration clause
adjustable-rate
    mortgage (ARM)
adjustable-rate note
alienation or due-on-
    sale clause
American Recovery
    and Reinvestment
    Act of 2009
    (ARRA)
amortized loan
annual percentage rate
    (APR)
assumption
balloon payment
basis point
beneficiary
California finance
    lender
California Finance
    Lenders Law
California Residential
    Mortgage Lending
    Act
certificate of discharge
construction loan
credit-bid
declaration of default
deed of reconveyance
deficiency judgment
Department of
    Housing and Urban
    Development
    (HUD)
discount rate
Equal Credit
    Opportunity Act
Fair and Accurate
    Credit Transactions
    Act of 2003
    (FACTA)
Fair Credit Reporting
    Act (FCRA)
federal funds rate
Federal Housing
    Finance Agency
    (FHFA)
Federal Reserve Bank
    System (the Fed)

FICO score
Financial Institutions
    Reform, Recovery,
    and Enforcement
    Act of 1989
    (FIRREA)
fixed-rate mortgage
graduated payment
    adjustable-rate
    mortgage (GPARM)
graduated payment
    mortgage (GPM)
growing equity
    mortgage (GEM)
holder in due course
Home Affordable
    Refinance Program
    (HARP)
home equity sales
    contract
Home Loan Toolkit
hypothecation
impound account
installment note
institutional lenders
interest rate
interim loan
joint and several
    liability
judicial foreclosure
junior lienor
kickback
leverage
loan-to-value ratio
lock-in clause
mortgage bankers
mortgagee
mortgagor
negative amortization
negotiable instrument
nominal rate
nonamortized
notice of default
notice of trustee's sale
open-ended mortgage
pledged
points
power of sale

power-of-sale clause
prime rate
principal
private mortgage
    insurance (PMI)
promissory note
Real Estate Settlement
    Procedures Act
    (RESPA)
Real Property Loan
    Law
redemption period
Regulation Z
reinstatement
renegotiable-rate
    mortgage (RRM)
reverse annuity
    mortgage (RAM)
right of redemption
right to rescind
satisfaction
Secure and Fair
    Enforcement for
    Mortgage Licensing
    Act (SAFE Act)
security instrument
shared appreciation
    mortgage (SAM)
standby commitment
standby fee
straight note
subject to
take-out loan
TILA-RESPA
    Integrated Disclosure
    (TRID)
trustee
trustee's sale
trustor
Truth in Lending Act
    (TILA)
Uniform Residential
    Loan Application
unlawful detainer
Unruh Civil Rights
    Act
usury

PURPOSES OF FINANCING REAL ESTATE

Affordable financing benefits both businesses and consumers. When funds are readily available for borrowing at reasonable terms, businesses can grow and prosper. For individuals, access to financing means the dream of home ownership can become a reality. Across the country, over $10 trillion in loans on one- to four-unit residences were held in 2016.

It is easy to understand why a homeowner or an investor would want to own property. Real estate has tended to grow in value over the years because of its scarcity and desirability. Real estate values can still be volatile, however, as they reflect the general state of the economy as well as demand for a limited supply of properties. As reported by the California Association of REALTORS®, the median price of a single-family detached home in California reached an all-time high of $594,530 in May 2007, before beginning a downturn to a low of $245,230 in February 2009, reflecting the nationwide recession. Home prices, aided by a growing economy and record-low interest rates, have recovered dramatically since then. In the second quarter of 2016, the median California single-family detached home price was $516,220, with San Jose, at $1,085,000, the first U.S. city to have a median existing single-family home price over $1 million.

Often the greatest financial benefit of real estate ownership is that it can be used as security for a loan. By borrowing money against the value of the property, home purchasers benefit from *present use* and, unless property values are stagnant or declining, *future appreciation* (increase in value), and *forced saving* by paying down the amount owed. There may also be *tax advantages*, as discussed in Unit 11.

> Most home purchases would be impossible without the use of leverage.

Of course, the purchaser who relies on a loan to finance the purchase must have enough income to make the loan payments. But that income generally is far less than the cash that would be needed to buy most property outright. The purchaser thus uses the leverage of a relatively small initial cash outlay to finance purchase of a property worth many times that amount. By reducing the amount of cash that a buyer has at risk, a leveraged purchase can also help protect the buyer if market values go down.

FOR EXAMPLE The Sanchezes are buying a suburban house. The purchase price of $500,000 is being financed by the seller. The Sanchezes will pay $100,000 cash and make a payment of $2,308.95, which includes interest and part of the principal (the balance of the loan), each month. At the end of 30 years, the Sanchezes will own their home outright and will have no further loan payments to make.

$100,000 Plus
$2,308.95 Per Month
for 30 Years

$500,000 House

Some of the most valuable benefits of home ownership are realized when the property is sold, even if it is sold well before the end of the loan term.

FOR EXAMPLE The Sanchezes decide to sell their home after 12 years of ownership. The selling price is $880,000. By that time, they have paid down the principal of their $400,000 debt by approximately $70,000 but they incur expenses of $50,000 in commission and costs on the sale. So, they net $500,000 at the close of escrow. After paying themselves back the initial $100,000 they used for their down payment, they receive a profit of $400,000. Thus, the Sanchezes have leveraged $100,000 to make $400,000.

The previous example is a very simplified one, of course. It fails to take into account the year-to-year benefit of home ownership that the Sanchezes may realize thanks to the tax deductions their real estate ownership generates. They should also take into account the cost of renting comparable housing (which may be more or less than the cost of ownership), as well as the intangible value of being owners and not renters.

COST OF CREDIT

A purchaser of real estate who defers part or all of the purchase price uses some form of *credit*. When the purchaser receives credit from the seller, the cost of that credit is usually the **interest rate** charged to the purchaser. The purchaser may borrow money from another source to finance the purchase or borrow money using property already owned outright as collateral. In either case, the cost of those funds typically is expressed as interest. The cost of using money also may include loan fees or **points** paid at the time of closing, with one point equal to 1% of the amount borrowed.

Note: When interest rates are quoted by regulatory agencies and financial institutions, they often are expressed as *basis points*. One **basis point** is $\frac{1}{100}$ of 1%, so 25 basis points are the same as 0.25%.

Just as there is a market for real estate, there also is a market for the money used to finance real estate. Lenders compete for borrowers by trying to make their loans as attractive as possible. They do so by lowering interest rates and making other loan terms, such as fees and time needed for processing, as attractive as possible.

Most lenders rely on outside sources from which they receive the funds that they loan out to purchasers of real estate. If the supply of funds is diminished, or if funds become more expensive for lenders to acquire, the result will be higher interest rates and less favorable terms for borrowers.

The Money Supply

Money is a medium of exchange as well as a measure of value. In exchange for our work efforts, we earn *income* in the form of money. Income also comes from the following:

■ Investments

- Rents
- Royalties
- Interest on amounts owed to us

We exchange our income for products and services, invest it, or save it. Income is taxed to provide funds for government to carry out the services it provides. Businesses also receive income and in turn make payments for taxes, salaries, and other costs of production, as well as investments.

The production of income is *cyclical*. (See Figure 8.1.) As consumer demand for goods and services increases, the elements of production flourish.

FIGURE 8.1:   Economic Cycles

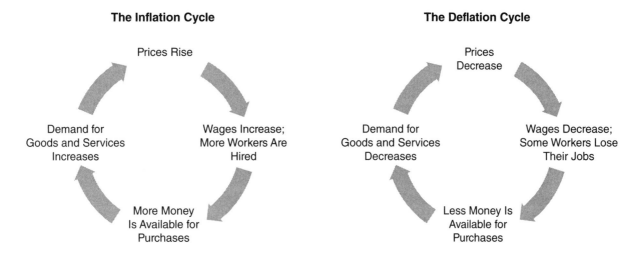

The Inflation Cycle

Prices Rise

Demand for Goods and Services Increases

Wages Increase; More Workers Are Hired

More Money Is Available for Purchases

The Deflation Cycle

Prices Decrease

Demand for Goods and Services Decreases

Wages Decrease; Some Workers Lose Their Jobs

Less Money Is Available for Purchases

Factories are built, products are made, and employees are paid. These activities, in turn, pump more money into the economy.

The income diverted to taxes is used to buy the goods and services that support government programs. Taxes also subsidize individuals and businesses through a variety of direct and indirect payments.

Investment funds and savings provide the capital needed for the industry to grow and prosper. Savings also form the basis of the funds loaned to purchasers and developers of real estate. Savers are paid interest by lending institutions, which in turn charge a higher rate of interest to borrowers of those savings.

The federal government is actively involved in the financial marketplace for both commercial and residential loans.

www.federalreserve.gov

Federal Reserve Bank System   The **Federal Reserve Bank System** (the Fed) was created by Congress in 1913 to serve as the central bank of the United States. Information on the history of the Fed, as well as links to related sites, can be found at the website, www.federalreserve.gov.

The Fed regulates the flow of money and the cost of credit to help stabilize the market fluctuations that create inflation or recession. The 12 regional Federal Reserve Banks follow the policies set by a seven-member Board of Governors. Members of the board are appointed by the President of the United States and confirmed by the Senate for 14-year terms. California, Alaska, Arizona, Hawaii, Idaho, Nevada, Oregon, Utah, and Washington are in the 12th Federal Reserve District, headquartered in San Francisco.

> When the chairman of the Federal Reserve Board announces a change in the Fed's interest rate, the whole world pays attention.

The Fed makes its own decisions but reports to Congress, and its power can be revoked by Congress. The main activities of the Fed are accomplished by

- raising or lowering *reserve requirements* (cash on hand) of member banks, which decreases or increases the amount of money allowed to circulate;

- establishing the **discount rate** (interest rate) that member banks must pay to borrow money from the Fed, which affects the **federal funds rate** that member banks charge each other for borrowing funds they maintain with the Fed, the **prime rate** that banks charge their most favorably rated commercial borrowers (usually—but not always—3% above the federal funds rate), and, ultimately, the rate consumers are charged; and

- buying and selling *government securities* to affect the amount of funds available for savings and other investment, and thus the amount available for borrowing.

Since 1980, even banks that are not members of the Fed have been required to comply with its reserve requirements.

> www.fhfa.gov

Federal Home Loan Banks   The Federal Home Loan Bank System (FHLB system) was authorized by Congress in 1932. There are 12 regional Federal Home Loan Banks and they are now regulated by the **Federal Housing Finance Agency (FHFA)**. The *Federal Home Loan Bank of San Francisco* covers the 11th Federal Home Loan Bank District, which includes California, Nevada, and Arizona.

Member institutions, such as federally or state-chartered savings and loan associations, must own capital stock in the regional Federal Home Loan Banks, which in turn lend money to member institutions. In 1989, commercial banks and federally insured credit unions became eligible for membership in the FHLB system. In 1999, Congress made membership in the FHLB system voluntary for all types of eligible institutions. By 2016, the FHLB system included 7,200 lenders.

Federal Deposit Insurance Corporation   The **Federal Deposit Insurance Corporation** (FDIC) was created by Congress in 1933 to insure individual accounts in participating banks and (as of 1989) savings and loan associations, currently up to $250,000 per depositor, per insured bank, for each ownership category.

Many other federal and state agencies and departments affect the availability and cost of credit. Some of them are discussed below, and others will be discussed in the next unit. Recent legislation has had far-reaching consequences.

Legislation intended to place thrifts (savings and loan associations) on equal footing with commercial banks had some unfortunate consequences, including the failure of many institutions. The Depository Institutions Deregulation and Monetary Control Act of 1980 began the process by greatly expanding the ability of depository institutions to offer services and yields competitive with market rates.

The Road to FIRREA and the Subprime Lending Crisis

With deregulation came many abuses by thrift associations that were poorly managed. Improperly documented loans, inept or falsified property appraisals, and outright theft of association funds were some abuses that led to the downfall of many institutions. Congress attempted to overhaul the thrift industry by passing the **Financial Institutions Reform, Recovery, and Enforcement Act of 1989** (FIRREA).

FIRREA established the *Office of Thrift Supervision* and the *Federal Housing Finance Board* to take over the savings and loan supervisory responsibilities that formerly had belonged to the Federal Home Loan Bank Board (FHLBB). The FDIC was given the additional responsibility of insuring deposits in all federally chartered banks and savings institutions, as well as the bank deposits it already insured. Savings and loan deposits had previously been insured by the Federal Savings and Loan Insurance Corporation (FSLIC), which ceased operation.

With one crisis under control, the seeds were sown for another. Continuing low interest rates and relatively easy access to funds inevitably led to the real estate market boom of the first years of the 21st century that also attracted investors who flocked to real estate as a safe haven from the stock market's booms and busts, particularly those involving the technology stocks. Wall Street played a role in the increasingly frenetic real estate market by creating securities based on the value of real estate used as collateral in increasingly risky loans. Many loans required little or no down payment, and borrowers were able to take advantage of no-doc loans in which the borrower's "stated income" was not verified.

Under such market conditions, subprime borrowers (based on their credit histories) who formerly would have been denied a loan, or offered a loan only at a high interest rate, found ready sources of funds. Low "teaser" interest rates attracted borrowers who failed to notice—or understand—the likely future jump in payment amounts when the initial rate period ended. The 2-28 adjustable-rate mortgage, for example, offered a low rate for the first two years of the loan term, followed by an adjustment to the index-plus-margin rate for the remaining 28 years. Perhaps even scarier were the "option ARMs" that allowed a borrower to make a minimal payment, adding part of the interest owed to the remaining loan balance, thus evaporating what little equity might have been built up, and in some cases making the loan balance greater than the market value of the property.

When the first of the adjustable subprime loans taken out at the height of the buying frenzy hit the readjustment point in mid-2006, a wave of loan defaults and foreclosures began to sweep across the country—a virtual financial tsunami for the housing market. As the number of properties on the market grew, prices began to fall. Buyers still hesitated to pick up a bargain, in part because there was no way of knowing if the market had reached bottom, but also because of tightening of underwriting criteria by lenders. With fewer clients, many mortgage brokers laid off employees and some closed their doors for good.

The subprime lenders—and the buyers of the *collateralized debt obligations* (CDOs) that were backed by real estate assets of greatly diminished value—took enormous losses. The crisis showed how far-reaching the residential mortgage market had become when financial institutions in Europe and Asia announced the devastating impacts of the American subprime lending crisis, with losses measured in the billions of dollars.

In January 2008, Congress passed the **Economic Stimulus Act of 2008** that, among other things, raised the limits on both conforming loans and those insured by FHA or guaranteed by VA. With the prospect of the U.S. government's involvement, it was hoped that the market for the affected loans would stabilize, and that borrowers would be able to refinance existing loans and also make new purchases.

HERA   The **Housing and Economic Recovery Act of 2008** (HERA) was signed by President Bush on July 30, 2008; some of its provisions were modified and additional provisions added by the **American Recovery and Reinvestment Act of 2009** (ARRA), signed by President Obama on February 17, 2009. In November 2009, Congress further modified the legislation. Following is the latest status of some of the major provisions of the laws. Additional provisions are discussed in Unit 9, Government-Sponsored and Other Financing, and Unit 11, Real Estate Taxation.

- New regulatory agency. The Federal Housing Finance Agency has replaced the Federal Housing Finance Board as regulator of the Federal Home Loan Banks.

- Low-income housing grants. This provision of ARRA allows states to trade in a portion of their 2009 low-income housing tax credits for Treasury grants to finance the construction or acquisition and rehabilitation of low-income housing, including those with or without tax credit allocations.

- Mortgage revenue bonds. HERA authorized $10 billion in mortgage revenue bonds for refinancing subprime mortgages.

- Neighborhood stabilization. HERA and ARRA authorized a total of $6 billion in funding for the Neighborhood Stabilization Program, which provides grants through the Community Development Block Grant program (CDBG) to states and localities to address the problems that can be created when whole neighborhoods are decimated by foreclosures. The funds can be used to purchase, manage, repair, and resell foreclosed and abandoned properties and to establish financing methods for the purchase and redevelopment of foreclosed properties. Homes purchased must be used to assist individuals and families with incomes at or below 120% of area median income. At least 25% of the funds must be used for households with incomes at or below 50% of area median income.

HERA has imposed reporting requirements on mortgage brokers that are to be enacted and enforced by the states. California Senate Bill 36 was signed into law in October 2009 to comply with the federal **Secure and Fair Enforcement for Mortgage Licensing Act** (SAFE Act), which is part of HERA. The reporting requirements regarding mortgage brokerage activities were added to the Business and Professions Code.

The law requires all real estate brokers (and salespersons acting under the supervision of a broker) who make, arrange, or service loans secured by real property to report that fact to the California Bureau of Real Estate by January 31, 2010 (or within 30 days of commencing the activity, whichever is later), using Form RE 866, Mortgage Loan Activity Notification, which is available at https://secure .dre.ca.gov/elicensing/nmls.asp and must be completed online. Identifying information required includes the licensee's name and real estate license number; if the licensee is a real estate corporation, the name and license number of the designated officer must also be provided. The form must identify the mortgage loan activities (including loan originations) being performed. The requirement applies to both residential and commercial businesses, and future business activity reporting will also be required. The penalty for failure to submit the required notification is $50 per day for the first 30 days the report is not filed and $100 per day for every day thereafter, not to exceed a maximum of $10,000.

| https://secure.dre.ca.gov /elicensing/nmls.asp |

SB 36 and the SAFE Act impose additional requirements on any licensee who conducts activities as a **residential mortgage loan originator** (MLO). The licensee must do the following:

| www.nationwidelicensing system.org |

- Register on the Nationwide Mortgage Licensing System and Registry (NMLS), www.nationwidelicensingsystem.org. The NMLS contains a single license record ("base record") for each mortgage loan lender, broker, branch, and MLO. There is no fee to register.

- Satisfy the federal requirements for MLO licensure, which include new qualification assessments, federal and state examinations, and background checks. There are no exceptions to or exemptions from these requirements for existing licensees.

- Be issued an MLO endorsement on the individual's real estate license. Endorsement applications for qualified MLO registrants must be submitted electronically to the NMLS.

MLO endorsements are issued annually and expire December 31 of each year. The endorsement carries a nationwide identification number ("unique identifier") assigned by the NMLS. Each California real estate licensee is responsible for filing the necessary renewal and record update requirements to maintain the four-year real estate license, apart from the requirements for the MLO endorsement.

Penalty fees for failure to obtain a license endorsement are $50 per day for the first 30 days the report is not filed and $100 per day for every day thereafter up to a maximum of $10,000.

Dodd-Frank Bill In response to the mortgage lending crisis and subsequent upheaval in financial markets, the Dodd-Frank Wall Street Reform and Consumer Protection Act (**Financial Stability Act of 2010**), was signed into law by President Obama on July 21, 2010. The Act created the *Financial Stability Oversight Council* and the *Office of Financial Research*, both as part of the Treasury Department. The Act also made the Office of Thrift Supervision (OTS) part of the Office of the Comptroller of the Currency (OCC); the merger was completed as of July 21, 2011, and the OTS no longer exists. The OCC now has supervisory responsibility for federal savings and loans and federal savings banks.

www.harp.gov

HARP The **Home Affordable Refinance Program** (HARP), introduced in March 2009, and later extended through September 30, 2017, has been made available to borrowers with little or no equity in their home. HARP allows such a borrower to refinance their mortgage with no new or additional mortgage insurance. No minimum credit score is needed and the borrower can get a lower interest rate, a shorter loan term, or a change from a fixed to an adjustable-rate mortgage. Information on the program can be found at www.harp.gov.

Appraisals With FIRREA, the federal government introduced minimum requirements for appraisals, as well as appraiser licensing and certification. As of January 1, 1993, a property appraisal in a *federally related transaction* (such as a loan insured or guaranteed by a federal agency or a loan sold on the secondary mortgage market) should be performed only by an appraiser licensed or certified by the state in which the property is located, as discussed in Unit 13.

The type of property and its estimated value determine whether appraiser licensing or certification is necessary. In addition, the appraisal itself must meet or exceed certain minimum standards. Property below a stated minimum value is exempt from the requirements.

REAL ESTATE AS SECURITY

Why would anyone lend as much money as most real estate transactions require? Because the loan can be backed by the property.

Real estate loans in California generally are made using two instruments:

- The **promissory note** is the borrower's promise to pay the amount borrowed. The promissory note is evidence of the debt. It establishes the underlying obligation of the loan transaction.

- The **security instrument** is used to identify the real estate that serves as assurance that the loan will be repaid.

With a security instrument, a property owner *hypothecates* the described real estate. **Hypothecation** means the real property will be forfeited to the holder of the security instrument if the underlying debt is not paid.

Usury

Usury is the charging of an exorbitant amount or rate of interest and is the subject of both state and federal law.

State Law

In 1979, California voters passed Proposition 2, which exempted from usury laws any loan made or arranged by a real estate broker and secured by real property. California law also exempts loans made by banks and savings and loan associations. Loans of credit unions, personal finance companies, and pawnbrokers are exempt unless the loan falls in one of the statutory categories mentioned below:

1. The maximum statutory interest rate that may be charged for consumer loans (money, goods, or other things intended for personal, family, or household purposes), other than loans for the purchase, construction, or improvement of real property, is 10% per year.

2. Money, goods, or other things intended for the purchase, construction, or improvement of real property are subject to a maximum rate of 10% or the prevailing Federal Reserve Bank discount rate plus 5%, whichever is higher.

3. Business loans are subject to a ceiling of the Federal Reserve Bank discount rate plus 5%.

4. The refinancing of a loan is subject to the same maximum rate as the original loan.

Federal Law

When they cover the same subject, federal law preempts state law. Federal law exempts federally related residential first mortgage loans made after March 31, 1980, from state interest limitations. This includes loans used to finance manufactured housing (mobile-homes) and the acquisition of stock in a cooperative housing corporation.

The federal act effectively limits the California usury laws to private lenders.

Seller Financing

When a seller of real property extends credit for part or all of the purchase price, it is not considered a loan for purposes of the usury laws, but merely an *extension of credit*. The seller must act in good faith, however, or the transaction can be questioned.

The process of hypothecation is similar to what occurs when personal property is **pledged** to secure payment of a loan. One important difference is that with a pledge, *possession* of the pledged property is turned over to the *lender* until the debt is paid. (Think of the jewelry on display in a pawn shop window.) The *borrower* typically retains possession of hypothecated real property, making it possible to enjoy the benefits of property ownership even when property is heavily mortgaged.

The security instrument is what is commonly referred to as a *mortgage*. As you will learn, however, the legal document that serves as the security instrument can take the form of either a mortgage or a *deed of trust*, with very different results.

Promissory Note

The *promissory note* is a promise to pay money according to specified terms. The payment may be by installments that include both interest and principal (the **amortized loan**) or by installments of interest only with the principal due in a lump sum (a **straight note**).

A combination of loan types also may be used, with a lump-sum *balloon payment* due at the end of a specified term, during which only part of the principal is paid. A **balloon payment** is defined by the Real Estate Law as an installment that is at least twice the amount of the smallest installment.

Interest rates are allowed to reflect market trends by use of an **adjustable-rate note**, described later in this unit. A loan can also call for payment of the entire amount due on demand of the holder of the note. An example of an **installment note** that specifies equal payments of both principal and interest appears in Figure 8.2.

Joint and several liability   When more than one person signs a promissory note, there will probably be language in the note (such as the phrase "jointly and severally") indicating that each cosigner is liable for the entire financial obligation imposed by the note. This **joint and several liability** means that, if one cosigner defaults in payment on the note, the note holder can demand full payment from any other cosigner. Obviously, careful consideration should be given to any request to serve as cosigner on a note or other financial obligation. Cosigning a note also will affect the cosigner's credit record.

Negotiable instrument   To qualify as a **negotiable instrument**, a promissory note must be

- an unconditional promise made by one person to another,
- in writing,
- an agreement to pay a specified amount of money on demand or at a fixed or determinable future time,
- payable on the order of a designated person or the bearer of the note, and
- signed by its maker.

FIGURE 8.2: **Installment Note–Interest Included**

DO NOT DESTROY THIS NOTE: When paid, said original note, together with the Deed of Trust securing same, must be surrendered to Trustee for cancellation before reconveyance will be made.

NOTE SECURED BY DEED OF TRUST
(INSTALLMENT-INTEREST INCLUDED)

$ 388,000.00 _____ Walnut Creek _____, California, October 24, 20_ _ _____

In installments as herein stated, for value received, I promise to pay to Local Savings and Loan Association _____

_____, or order,

at 7800 North Main Street Riverside, California _____

the sum of three hundred eighty-eight thousand (388,000) _____DOLLARS,

with interest from October 24, 20_ _ _____ on unpaid principal at the

rate of 5¾ _____ per cent per annum; principal and interest payable in installments of

three thousand two hundred twenty-one and $91/100$ _____DOLLARS,

or more on the 1st _____ day of each and every _____ month, beginning

on the 1st _____ day of November, 20_ _ _____

_____

_____

_____and continuing until said principal sum and interest

have been paid _____.

Each payment shall be credited first on interest then due and the remainder on principal; and interest shall thereupon cease upon the principal so credited. Should interest not be so paid it shall thereafter bear like interest as the principal, but such unpaid interest so compounded shall not exceed and amount equal to simple interest on the unpaid principal at the maximum rate permitted by law. Should default be made in payment of any installment of principal or interest when due the whole sum of principal and interest shall become immediately due at the option of the holder of this note. Principal and interest payable in lawful money of the United States. If action be instituted on this note I promise to pay such sum as the Court may fix as attorney's fees. This note is secured by a deed of trust to **STEWART TITLE OF CALIFORNIA, INC., as Trustee.**

Charles S. Buyer _____   *Marilyn H. Buyer* _____

_____   _____

DO NOT DESTROY THIS NOTE

DOCUMENT PROVIDED BY STEWART TITLE OF CALIFORNIA, INC.   NOTEIImod.DOC

Source: Reprinted courtesy of Stewart Title of California, Inc.

If a promissory note qualifies as a negotiable instrument, the *holder* of the note (the one to whom the money is to be paid) can sell the note, give it away, or transfer the rights it represents in some other way. With a single instrument, an obligation to pay a large sum of money can thus change hands efficiently.

The person who receives an assignment is the assignee or transferee.

A promissory note is a contract that may be enforced by the holder of the note or anyone to whom the holder assigns or transfers the right of payment. The person to whom the assignment is made is called the *assignee* or *transferee*. If all requirements for a negotiable instrument have *not* been met, the assignee or transferee has only the rights of the original holder of the note. If a promissory note meets all the requirements of a negotiable instrument, it attains a special status. Then a transferee or an assignee may be placed in a better position than the person from whom the note was received, *if* the transferee or assignee qualifies as a *holder in due course*, as described next.

Holder in due course   A holder in due course is someone who takes a negotiable instrument

- *for value,*
- *in good faith*, and
- *without notice of any defense* against its enforcement that might be made by any person.

A *defense* that a note maker could use to *prevent* enforcement of a negotiable instrument could be

- *lack of consideration* (the note maker never received the promised funds or property in exchange for the note);
- *prior payment* (the note already has been paid off);
- *cancellation* (the original note holder agreed to cancel the note obligation);
- *setoff* (the original holder owes money to the note maker that should be applied to the note debt); or
- *fraud in the inducement* (the note maker created the note based on fraudulent representation by the payee).

Consumer Credit

The Federal Trade Commission has limited the rights of a **holder in due course** in consumer credit contracts for goods or services. Subsequent holders of such contracts are subject to all of the same defenses the maker could bring against the original holder. This provision applies to real estate *only* in the case of contracts for particular building improvements added after initial construction, such as siding.

The holder in due course (or anyone who acquires a negotiable instrument from a holder in due course) is not bound by the above defenses. A holder in due course can insist on collecting on the note, even if the note maker can claim one of the above defenses against the original note holder.

A holder in due course still may not be able to enforce the instrument, however, *if*

- the note maker lacked the legal capacity to make a legal agreement;
- the note was forged;

■ the instrument involves an illegal activity; or

■ there has been a material alteration in the terms of the note (although a subsequent holder in due course can claim payment according to the note's original terms).

FOR EXAMPLE Ben Phillips has purchased the Simon residence, giving a promissory note for $292,000 to his Aunt Fran, who lent him the money to buy the house. Ben promised to pay 7% interest on the loan. Aunt Fran gave the note to her niece Marjorie, who altered the note to read 17% interest. Marjorie then sold the note to an investor, who had no knowledge of the alteration.

The investor informed Ben of the address to which the monthly payments should be sent. When Ben's monthly payments fell short of the 17% interest rate, the investor sent a reminder of the discrepancy. Does Ben have to pay the 17%? What does Ben have to do?

Even though the investor probably qualifies as a holder in due course, Ben can claim that the note was materially altered and refuse to pay 17%. Ben still must keep up the payments at the original rate of 7%, however.

MATH CONCEPTS

Real estate loan interest payments can be computed in two steps:

1. Principal × Rate = Annual interest

   The **principal** is the unpaid balance of the loan. The **rate** is the percentage rate of interest paid.

2. Interest on a loan ordinarily is calculated monthly. To find interest per month, divide the annual interest by 12.

Example: Calculate the interest to be paid for one month on a loan with a remaining balance of $176,000, when the interest rate is 6%.

   Principal × Rate = Annual interest

   $176,000 × .06 = $10,560

   $10,560 ÷ 12 = $880 Monthly interest

To find interest for a number of days, find the daily interest by dividing the annual interest by 360 days in the year (unless the exact number of days in the year is required). Then, multiply the interest per day by the number of days for which interest is owed.

Example: Calculate the interest to be paid for 17 days on a loan with a remaining balance of $176,000, when the interest rate is 6%.

   $176,000 × .06 = $10,560 Annual interest

   $10,560 ÷ 360 = $29.33 Daily interest

   $29.33 × 17 = $498.67 Interest for 17 days

Another way to find daily interest is to divide the annual interest by 12 and then divide that number by 30. If you don't have a calculator, that may be easier than dividing the annual interest by 360.

Security Instrument

The security instrument *hypothecates* the property that serves as the lender's assurance that the underlying debt will be repaid. The process of hypothecation, as described earlier, is similar to a pledge, but the property owner retains possession of the property.

> The security instrument usually is referred to as a mortgage, even when it is a deed of trust.

The security instrument is commonly referred to as a *mortgage*, although it may take one of several forms, only one of which technically is a mortgage. It is not commonly used in California, even though the mortgage was the first security instrument used in the state. The *deed of trust* now is the preferred security instrument in California.

Whether it takes the form of a mortgage or deed of trust, the security instrument will be recorded to provide constructive notice of the lien rights of the lender.

Mortgage   A *mortgage* is an instrument by which property is hypothecated to secure the payment of a debt or an obligation. A lien on the property is given by the **mortgagor** (borrower and property owner) to the **mortgagee** (lender). In the event of the mortgagor's default before final payment, the mortgagee's remedy is judicial (court-ordered) foreclosure. As an alternative, the mortgage instrument could contain a power-of-sale provision. A mortgage with a **power-of-sale clause** operates as a trust deed does when property is sold at a trustee's sale (discussed later in this unit).

The procedure for **judicial foreclosure** changed as of July 1, 1983. Instruments that originated before that date follow the old rules, and instruments as of that date follow the new rules. If you are involved in any foreclosure matter, always consult an attorney.

In a judicial foreclosure the court orders the property sold to the highest bidder at public auction in the county where at least part of the property is located. The court appoints a commissioner or orders the sheriff to carry out the sale. Statutory notice requirements must be met.

If the bid price exceeds $5,000, the successful bidder has the option of depositing the greater of $5,000 or 10% of the amount bid and paying the balance within 10 days of the sale. If this option is chosen, the bidder also must pay additional costs and interest that accrue between the sale and the date of payment. If full payment is not made within 10 days of the sale, a new sale is conducted and the *defaulting buyer* is liable for costs of the original sale and resale, interest, attorney's fees, and the amount of the original bid less the amount bid for the property in the subsequent sale. If no acceptable bid is received, the sale can be postponed.

The commissioner or sheriff delivers to the purchaser a *certificate of sale*, which should be recorded immediately.

The Old Rule

On sales stemming from instruments that originated before July 1, 1983, a **junior lienor** (such as a second-mortgage holder) also has a right of redemption. The redemption period is three months following the sale if the sale proceeds were sufficient to cover the remaining indebtedness plus interest and costs of foreclosure. Otherwise, the redemption period is one year, unless the mortgagee waives or is prohibited from obtaining a deficiency judgment. The buyer must consider the risk of redemption when deciding how much to bid for the property. Obviously, there are relatively few outstanding mortgages that originated before July 1, 1983; nevertheless, a buyer at a foreclosure sale should be interested in the date of origination of all liens on the property.

The proceeds of a foreclosure are used to pay off the remaining indebtedness on the property. Any funds left over go to other lienholders in order of priority; the last recipient is the mortgagor. If the sale proceeds do not cover the indebtedness plus court costs and sale fees, the mortgagee can obtain a **deficiency judgment** for the remaining debt against the mortgagor personally, *unless*

- the mortgage was a purchase-money debt (the mortgagee was the seller of the property); or

- the loan was to pay all or part of the purchase price of an owner-occupied residential dwelling of no more than four units.

Antideficiency—The Homeowner's Safety Net California Code of Civil Procedure 580b

As long as market demand exceeds supply and prices continue to rise, California homeowners usually don't need to worry about foreclosure. Even when an individual has difficulty making loan payments, the sale of the property will relieve the owner of the payment burden and most likely will provide a profit over the purchase price.

But what happens when the market takes a turn for the worse? And what about the worst-case scenario—the current market value of the property is less than the remaining loan balance? That's when California's antideficiency protection provides the ultimate safety net for homeowners. If a homeowner can no longer continue to make payments on a loan secured by a mortgage or deed of trust on the home, the only recourse for the lender is to take back the property. *Even if the current market value of the property is less than the outstanding loan balance, the lender cannot seek a judgment against the defaulting homeowner for the difference.*

This protection is automatic, so long as the loan is the one that the owner used to purchase the property. It even extends to situations in which a chattel mortgage is given for the purchase of personal property (such as furnishings) as part of the original home acquisition. In that case, the antideficiency protection covers both loans.

SB931, which applies to loans secured by a first lien and which took effect on January 1, 2011, and SB458, which applies to loans secured by a second lien and which took effect July 15, 2011, have clarified the borrower protection in the event of a short sale (sale for less than the amount of the remaining loan balance). Section 580e now provides that "No judgment shall be rendered for any deficiency under a note secured by a deed of trust or mortgage for a dwelling of not more than four units, in any case in which the trustor or mortgagor sells the dwelling for less than the remaining amount of the indebtedness due at the time of sale with the written consent of the holder..." The protection does not apply, however, if the original home loan was refinanced. It also does not apply to any home equity loan taken out after the original purchase. The potential benefit of the law is thus greatest for homeowners who incur the maximum indebtedness at the time the property is first acquired and resist refinancing the purchase loan and/or taking out a home equity loan.

Before a foreclosure sale, the mortgagor or anyone with a subordinate lien or encumbrance on the property may cure the default by paying all delinquencies, including court costs and fees that result from the foreclosure. The mortgage thus is placed back in effect in a process called **reinstatement**.

The least desirable aspect of judicial foreclosure is that it is time-consuming. Not only does it take many months for the sale to take place, the purchaser at a foreclosure sale receives only a certificate of sale. The purchaser does not receive possession until after the statutory **redemption period**, a period following the sale during which the judgment debtor or the judgment debtor's successor in interest can buy back the property.

When a mortgage debt has been satisfied, the *mortgagee* must execute a **certificate of discharge**, which is recorded with the county recorder. Otherwise, the mortgage lien may act as a cloud on the owner's title.

Deed of trust   It will soon become obvious, as we go over the characteristics of the deed of trust, why this is the security instrument preferred by lenders who make loans in California.

A deed of trust (or *trust deed*) is an instrument by which real property is *hypothecated* to secure *payment* of a debt or an obligation. The title to the property is transferred by the **trustor** (owner and borrower) to the **trustee** (a neutral third party) to hold on behalf of the **beneficiary** (lender) until the debt is repaid, even though the borrower retains possession. In the event the trustor defaults on the underlying debt, the trustee is instructed to sell the property and transfer the money obtained at the sale to the beneficiary as payment of the debt. An example of a deed of trust appears in Figure 8.3.

Someone other than the borrower could place title to property in trust to secure the borrower's loan, but the trustor is usually the borrower. For example, a loan made to a business could be secured by a mortgage on the home of one of its officers.

On the trustor's *default*, the beneficiary has the option of requesting a *trustee's sale* or a *judicial foreclosure* (the same remedy available with a mortgage). Neither choice prevents the other from ultimately being used before the sale is carried out, although the four-year statute of limitations will be applied to a judicial foreclosure. A **trustee's sale** is made possible by the provisions of the trust instrument. On default by the trustor, the beneficiary informs the trustee of that fact by a **declaration of default**, which states the reason for the default. The beneficiary includes the original note and trust deed with the declaration.

The form of **notice of default** that appears in Figure 8.4 became effective June 1, 1985. The first statement in the notice must be printed in bold type. *The notice must be in Spanish if the trustor so requested or if the contract was negotiated in Spanish.* The beneficiary or trustee must state that the entire debt is due because of the default, or it cannot be collected at the sale.

FIGURE 8.3: **Short Form Deed of Trust and Assignment of Rents**

RECORDING REQUESTED BY

AND WHEN RECORDED MAIL TO

NAME

ADDRESS

CITY
STATE & ZIP

TITLE ORDER NO. _____ ESCROW NO. _____ APN NO. _____

SHORT FORM DEED OF TRUST AND ASSIGNMENT OF RENTS (INDIVIDUAL)

This Deed of Trust, made this _____ day of _____ , between

_____ , herein called Trustor,

whose address is _____

Stewart Title of California, Inc., herein called Trustee, and

_____ , herein called Beneficiary,

Witnesseth: That Trustor **IRREVOCABLY GRANTS, TRANSFERS AND ASSIGNS TO TRUSTEE IN TRUST, WITH POWER OF SALE,** that property in _____ County, California, described as:

TOGETHER WITH the rents, issues and profits thereof, SUBJECT, HOWEVER, to the right, power and authority given to and conferred upon Beneficiary by paragraph (10) of the provisions incorporated herein by reference to collect and apply such rents, issues and profits.
For the Purpose of Securing: 1. Performance of each agreement of Trustor incorporated by reference or contained herein. 2. Payment of the indebtedness evidenced by one promissory note of even date herewith, and any extension or renewal thereof, in the principal sum of $_____ executed by Trustor in favor of Beneficiary or order. 3. Payment of such further sums as the then record owner of said property may borrow from Beneficiary, when evidenced by another note (or notes) reciting it is so secured.
    To Protect the Security of This Deed of Trust, Trustor Agrees: By the execution and delivery of this Deed of Trust and the rate secured hereby, that provisions (1) to (14), inclusive, of the fictitious deed of trust recorded October 23, 1961, in the book and at the page of Official Records in the office of the county recorder of the county where said property is located, noted below opposite the name of such county, viz.:

COUNTY	DATE	BOOK	PAGE	COUNTY	DATE	BOOK	PAGE	COUNTY	DATE	BOOK	PAGE	COUNTY	DATE	BOOK	PAGE
IMPERIAL	9/10/68	1267	574	ORANGE	9/6/68	8714	147	SAN BERNARDINO	9/6/98	7090	14	SANTA BARBARA	9/6/68	2244	922
KERN	9/6/68	4195	363	VENTURA	9/6/68	3363	84	SAN LUIS OBISPO	9/10/68	1489	429	LOS ANGELES	8/28/68	T5910	842
RIVERSIDE	9/10/68		ACCOUNT = 87097 YEAR 1968					SAN DIEGO	9/10/68			SERIES 9 BOOK 1968 PAGE 155820			

(which provisions, identical in all counties, are printed on the reverse hereof) hereby are adopted and incorporated herein and made a part hereof as fully as though set forth herein at length; that he will observe and perform said provisions; and that the references to property, obligations, and parties in said provisions shall be construed to refer to the property, obligations, and parties set forth in this Deed of Trust.
    The undersigned Trustor requests that a copy of any Notice of Default and of any Notice of Sale hereunder be mailed to him at his address hereinbefore set forth.

_____   _____

_____   _____

STATE OF CALIFORNIA
COUNTY OF _____ } SS.

On _____ before me, _____ ,
personally appeared _____
personally known to me (or proved to me on the basis of satisfactory evidence) to be the person(s) whose name(s) is/are subscribed to the within instrument and acknowledged to me that he/she/they executed the same in his/her/their authorized capacity(ies), and that by his/her/their signature(s) on the instrument the person(s), or the entity upon behalf of which the person(s) acted, executed the instrument.

WITNESS my hand and official seal.

Signature_____   (This area for official notarial seal)

DO NOT RECORD

Source: Reprinted courtesy of Stewart Title of California, Inc.

FIGURE 8.3:   Short Form Deed of Trust and Assignment of Rents (continued)

The following is a copy of provisions (1) to (14), inclusive, of the fictitious deed of trust, recorded in each county in California, as stated in the foregoing Deed of Trust and incorporated by reference in said Deed of Trust as being a part thereof as if set forth at length therein

To Protect the Security of This Deed of Trust, Trustor Agrees:

(1) To keep said property in good condition and repair, not to remove or demolish any building thereon, to complete or restore promptly and in good and workmanlike manner any building which may be constructed, damaged or destroyed thereon and to pay when due all claims for labor performed and materials furnished therefor, to comply with all laws affecting said property or requiring any alterations or improvements to be made thereon, not to commit or permit waste thereof, not to commit, suffer or permit any act upon said property in violations of law to cultivate, irrigate, fertilize, fumigate, prune and do all other acts which from the character or use of said property may be reasonably necessary, the specific enumerations herein not excluding the general

(2) To provide maintain and deliver to Beneficiary fire insurance satisfactory to and with loss payable to Beneficiary. The amount collected under any fire or other insurance policy may be applied by Beneficiary upon indebtedness secured hereby and in such order as Beneficiary may determine, or at option of Beneficiary the entire amount so collected or any part thereof may be released to Trustor. Such application or release shall not cure or waive any default or notice of default hereunder or invalidate any act done pursuant to such notice

(3) To appear in and defend any action or proceeding purporting to affect the security hereof or the rights or powers of Beneficiary or Trustee, and to pay all costs and expenses including cost of evidence of title and attorney's fees in a reasonable sum, in any such action or proceeding in which Beneficiary or Trustee may appear, and in any suit brought by Beneficiary to foreclose this Deed

(4) To pay at least ten days before delinquency all taxes and assessments affecting said property, including assessments on appurtenant water stock, when due, all encumbrances, charges and liens, with interest, on said property or any part thereof, which appear to be prior or superior hereto, all costs, fees and expenses of this Trust

Should Trustor fail to make any payment or to do any act as herein provided, then Beneficiary or Trustee, but without obligation so to do and without notice to or demand upon Trustor and without releasing Trustor from any obligation hereof, may make or do the same in such manner and to such extent as either may deem necessary to protect the security hereof Beneficiary or Trustee being authorized to enter upon said property for such purposes; appear in and defend any action or proceeding purporting to affect the security hereof or the rights or powers of Beneficiary or Trustee, pay, purchase, contest or compromise any encumbrance, charge or lien which in the judgment of either appears to be prior or superior hereto, and in exercising any such powers, pay necessary expenses, employ counsel and pay his reasonable fees

(5) To pay immediately and without demand all sums so expended by Beneficiary or Trustee, with interest from date of expenditure at the amount allowed by law in effect at the date hereof, and to pay for any statement provided for by law in effect at the date hereof regarding the obligation secured hereby any amount demanded by the Beneficiary not to exceed the maximum allowed by law at the time when said statement is demanded

(6) That any award of damages in connection with any condemnation for public use of or injury to said property or any part thereof is hereby assigned and shall be paid to Beneficiary who may apply or release such moneys received by him in the same manner and with the same effect as above provided for disposition of proceeds of fire or other insurance.

(7) That by accepting payment of any sum secured hereby after its due date, Beneficiary does not waive his rights either to require prompt payment when due of all other sums so secured or to declare default for failure so to pay.

(8) That at any time or from time to time, without liability therefor and without notice, upon written request of Beneficiary and presentation of this Deed and said note for endorsement, and without affecting the personal liability of any person for payment of the indebtedness secured hereby, Trustee may reconvey any part of said property, consent to the making of any map or plot thereof; join in granting any easement thereon; or join in any extension agreement or any agreement subordinating the lien or charge hereof.

(9) That upon written request of Beneficiary state that all sums secured hereby have been paid, and upon surrender of this Deed and said note to Trustee for cancellation and retention and upon payment of its fees, Trustee shall reconvey, without warranty, the property then held hereunder. The recitals in such reconveyance of any matters or facts shall be conclusive proof of the truthfulness thereof. The grantee in such reconveyance may be described as "The person or persons legally entitled thereto." Five years after issuance of such full reconveyance, Trustee may destroy said note and this Deed (unless directed in such request to retain them)

(10) That as additional security, Trustor hereby give to and confers upon Beneficiary the right, power and authority, during the continuance of these Trusts, to collect the rents, issues and profits of said property, reserving unto Trustor the right, prior to any default by Trustor in payment of any indebtedness secured hereby or in performance of any agreement hereunder, to collect the rents, issues and profits of said property, reserving unto Trustor the right, prior to any default by Trustor in payment of any indebtedness secured hereby or in performance of any agreement hereunder, to collect and retain such rents, issues and profits as they become due and payable. Upon any such default, Beneficiary may at any time without notice, either in person , by agent, or by a receiver to be appointed by a court, and without regard to the adequacy of any security for the indebtedness hereby secured, enter upon and take possession of said property or any part thereof, in his own name sue for or otherwise collect such rents, issues and profits, including those past due and unpaid, and apply the same, less costs and expenses of operation and collection, including reasonable attorney's fees. Upon any indebtedness secured hereby, and in such order as Beneficiary may determine. The entering upon and taking possession of said property, the collection of such rents, issues and profits and the application thereof as aforesaid, shall not cure or waive any default or notice of default hereunder or invalidate any act done pursuant to such notice.

(11) That upon default by Trustor in payment of any indebtedness secured hereby or in performance of any agreement hereunder. Beneficiary may declare all sums secured hereby immediately due and payable by delivery to Trustee of written declaration of default and demand for sale and of written notice of default and of election to cause to be sold said property which notice Trustee shall cause to be filed for record. Beneficiary also shall deposit with Trustee this Deed, said note and all documents evidencing expenditures secured hereby .

After the lapse of such time as may then be required by law following the recordation of said notice of default, and notice of sale having been given as then required by law, Trustee, without demand on Trustor, shall sell said property at the time and place fixed by it in said notice of sale, either as a whole or in separate parcels, and in such order as it may determine, at public auction to the highest bidder for cash in lawful money of the United States, payable at time of sale. Trustee may postpone sale of all or any portion of said property by public announcement at such time and place of sale, and from time to time thereafter may postpone such sale by public announcement at the time fixed by the preceding postponement Trustee shall deliver to such purchaser its deed conveying the property so sold, but without any covenant or warranty, express or implied. The recitals in such deed of any matters or facts shall be conclusive proof of the truthfulness thereof. Any person, including Trustor, Trustee, or Beneficiary as hereinafter defined, may purchase at such sale.

After deducting all costs, fees and expenses of Trustee and of this Trust, including cost of evidence of title in connection with sale, Trustee shall apply the proceeds of sale to payment of all sums expended under the terms hereof, not then repaid, with accrued interest at the amount allowed by law in effect at the date hereof, all other sums then secured hereby, and the remainder, if any, to the person or persons legally entitled thereto.

(12) Beneficiary, or any successor in ownership of any indebtedness secured hereby, may from time to time, by instrument in writing, substitute a successor or successors to any Trustee named herein or acting hereunder, which instrument, executed by the Beneficiary and duly acknowledged and recorded in the office of the recorder of the county or counties where said property is situated, shall be conclusive proof of proper substitution of such successor Trustee or Trustees, who shall, without conveyance from the Trustee predecessor, succeed to all its title, estate, rights, powers and duties. Said instrument must contain the name of the original Trustor, Trustee and Beneficiary hereunder, the book and page where this Deed is recorded and the name and address of the new Trustee.

(13) That this Deed applies to, inures to the benefit of, and binds all parties hereto, their heirs, legatees, devisees, administrators, executors, successors and assigns. The term Beneficiary shall mean the owner and holder, including pledgees, of the note secured hereby whether or not named as Beneficiary herein in this Deed, whenever the context so requires, the masculine gender includes the feminine and/or neuter, and the singular number includes the plural.

(14) That Trustee accepts this Trust when this Deed, duly executed and acknowledged, is made a public record as provided by law. Trustee is not obligated to notify any party hereto of pending sale under any other Deed of Trust or of any action or proceeding in which Trustor, Beneficiary or Trustee shall be a party unless brought by Trustee.

DO NOT RECORD
REQUEST FOR FULL RECONVEYANCE
To be used only when note has been paid:

To Stewart Title of California, Inc., Trustee: Dated _____

The undersigned is the legal owner and holder of all indebtedness secured by the within Deed of Trust. All sums secured by said Deed of Trust have been fully paid and satisfied; and you are hereby requested and directed, on payment to you of any sums owing to you under the terms of said Deed of Trust, to cancel all evidences of indebtedness, secured by said Deed of Trust, delivered to you herewith together with said Deed of Trust, and to reconvey, without warranty, to the parties designated by the terms of said Deed of Trust, the estate now held by you under the same.

MAIL RECONVEYANCE TO:

By _____   _____

By _____   _____

_____

Do not lose or destroy this Deed of Trust OR THE NOTE which it secures. Both must be delivered to the Trustee for cancellation before reconveyance will be made.

DOCUMENT PROVIDED BY STEWART TITLE OF CALIFORNIA, INC.   SHTFRMDT.DOC

Source: Reprinted courtesy of Stewart Title of California, Inc.

FIGURE 8.4:   Notice of Default

Notice of Default and Election to Sell Under Deed of Trust
IMPORTANT NOTICE

IF YOUR PROPERTY IS IN FORECLOSURE BECAUSE YOU ARE BEHIND IN YOUR PAYMENTS, IT MAY BE SOLD WITHOUT ANY COURT ACTION, and you may have the legal right to bring your account in good standing by paying all of your past due payments plus permitted costs and expenses within the time permitted by law for reinstatement of your account, which is normally five business days prior to the date set for the sale of your property. No sale date may be set until three months from the date this notice of default may be recorded (which date of recordation appears on this notice). This amount is _____

as of _____, and will increase until your account becomes current.
(Date)

You may not have to pay the entire unpaid portion of your account, even though full payment was demanded, but you must pay the amount stated above. However, you and your beneficiary or mortgagee may mutually agree in writing prior to the time the notice of sale is posted (which may not be earlier than the end of the three-month period stated above) to, among other things, (1) provide additional time in which to cure the default by transfer of the property or otherwise: (2) establish a schedule of payments in order to cure your default; or both (1) and (2).

Following the expiration of the time period referred to in the first paragraph of this notice, unless the obligation being foreclosed upon or a separate written agreement between you and your creditor permits a longer period, you have only the legal right to stop the sale of your property by paying the entire amount demanded by your creditor.

To find the amount you must pay, or to arrange for payment to stop the foreclosure, or if your property is in foreclosure for any other reason, contact:

_____
(Name of beneficiary or mortgagee)

_____
(Mailing address)

_____
(Telephone)

If you have any questions, you should contact a lawyer or the government agency which may have insured your loan.

Notwithstanding the fact that your property is in foreclosure, you may offer your property for sale, provided the sale is concluded prior to the conclusion of the foreclosure.

Remember, **YOU MAY LOSE LEGAL RIGHTS IF YOU DO NOT TAKE PROMPT ACTION.**

NOTICE IS HEREBY GIVEN, THAT _____ a corporation, is duly appointed Trustee under a Deed of Trust dated _____ executed by _____ as Trustor, to secure certain obligations

in favor of

_____, as beneficiary,
recorded _____, as instrument no. _____, in book _____, page _____, of Official Records
in the Office of the
Recorder of _____ County, California, describing land
therein as:
including _____ note _____ for the _____ sum of $ _____ said obligations

that the beneficial interest under such Deed of Trust and the obligations secured thereby are presently held by the undersigned; that a breach of, and default in, the obligations for which such Deed of Trust is security has occurred in that payment has not been made of:

that by reason thereof, the undersigned, present beneficiary under such Deed of Trust, has executed and delivered to said duly appointed Trustee, a written Declaration of Default and Demand for Sale, and has deposited with said duly appointed Trustee, such Deed of Trust and all documents evidencing obligations secured thereby, and has declared and does hereby declare all sums secured thereby immediately due and payable and has elected and does hereby elect to cause the trust property to be sold to satisfy the obligations secured thereby.

_____

_____

Dated _____

The notice of default is sent by registered or certified mail to

- the trustor,
- any successor in interest to the trustor,
- junior lienholders,
- the State Controller (if there is a tax lien on the property), *and*
- anyone who has filed a *request for notice* with the county recorder.

If any parties other than the original trustor are involved, notice is also published in a newspaper of general circulation once a week for four weeks. The California Foreclosure Prevention Act has extended the waiting period between filing of the notice of default and filing of the subsequent **notice of sale** from 90 days to 180 days, effective June 15, 2009, but the Act exempts from the extension lenders with comprehensive loan modification programs.

Notice must be made to the borrower at least 20 days before a foreclosure sale by mail to the defaulting borrower, as well as by posting at the property that is the subject of the foreclosure and in a public place in the county where the sale is to occur. A debt under a trust deed or mortgage can be reinstated if payment of the overdue amount is made at any time after the notice of default is recorded, but no later than five business days before the date of sale. Some deed-of-trust forms provide for a longer period of reinstatement—if so, the longer period will apply. A junior lienholder can pay the amount in arrears, which would then be added to the debt owed under that obligation.

The trustor always has the opportunity to prevent a sale by paying the entire debt owed, plus the costs and fees accumulated. At the sale itself, the beneficiary lender can **credit-bid** up to the amount of the debt owed. Otherwise, payment is by cash, cashier's check from a qualified lender, or a cash equivalent designated in the notice of trustee's sale as acceptable to the trustee.

Postponement of the Trustee's Sale

If no acceptable bid is received, or if more than one sale has been scheduled for the same time, the trustee's sale can be postponed. Postponement of the sale revives the right of reinstatement as of the date the new notice of sale is recorded, and it continues until five business days before the new date of sale. The same rule applies to any further postponement. There is no limitation on the number of postponements, but if the sale does not occur within 365 days of the notice of sale, a new notice of sale must be given before any further sale proceedings may be scheduled.

The most significant difference between a mortgage and a trust deed (or mortgage with power of sale) is that there is no **right of redemption** following a trustee's sale. The sale is absolutely final, and the purchaser can take possession immediately. A bidder at such a sale will understandably be willing to offer a higher price than if the sale were a judicial foreclosure.

Being entitled to possession is small comfort to the purchaser if the former owner refuses to vacate the premises. An **unlawful detainer** is the legal action by which the court orders the sheriff to evict the present occupant. The purchaser at a trustee's sale must also take such an eventuality into account.

The fact that there is no right of redemption helps minimize the lender's risk, for there is a greater chance that if the borrower defaults, the debt will be repaid in full by a trustee's sale. This is true even though sale by exercise of the **power of sale** by the beneficiary or mortgagee, rather than sale by judicial foreclosure, automatically *bars* any *deficiency judgment* in the event the sale proceeds fail to cover the unpaid balance of the debt plus interest, court costs, and sale fees.

| When the debt is repaid, title is deeded back to the trustor. |

Following a **satisfaction** (payoff) of the debt or obligation underlying a deed of trust, the beneficiary (or assignee or transferee of the beneficiary) delivers the original note and deed to the trustee and requests a reconveyance to the trustor. The reconveyance of title to the trustor by the trustee is accomplished by the trustee's executing to the trustor a **deed of reconveyance**, which is recorded in the county recorder's office. The original note and deed of trust can then be delivered to the trustor on the trustor's written request.

On satisfaction of the debt, the beneficiary (mortgagee) is obligated to clear the trustor's (mortgagor's) title. Failure to do so can subject the beneficiary (mortgagee) to civil or criminal penalties. The trustee also can be penalized for failure to comply with statutory requirements.

Deed in Lieu of Foreclosure

A *deed* may be used to transfer property to the beneficiary of a trust deed with the beneficiary's consent, to prevent a forced sale. Transfer of the property to the beneficiary may be to the beneficiary's advantage if the property is worth at least the amount of the remaining debt. The trustor benefits by avoiding the publicity of a public foreclosure sale. A danger arises when the property is worth more than the outstanding debt owed to the beneficiary. In that case, the beneficiary should pay the difference to the trustor, or the transfer could be challenged later in court.

Conclusion   To summarize, the differences between mortgage and trust deed lie in the

- number of parties,
- conveyance of title,
- statute of limitations,
- available remedies on default,
- period of reinstatement,
- availability of redemption,
- availability of deficiency judgment, and
- procedure following satisfaction of the debt.

Most important is that the trust deed offers the lender a relatively *faster* and *cheaper* means of protecting the security interest. Sale of the encumbered property is a last resort, however, no matter what form the sale takes. The lender may very well be the only bidder at the sale, and owning the property is an alternative most lenders do not welcome.

> ## When a Mortgage Is Really a Deed of Trust
>
> The term *mortgage* is used generically to refer to any security device. In California, that device (instrument) most often takes the form of a *deed of trust.* The trustor (borrower), trustee (third party holding title), and beneficiary (lender) are the parties involved in a deed of trust. When we refer to a mortgage in the rest of this and the next unit, however, we will mean any real property security instrument. By *mortgagor* we will mean the *borrower* under any form of security instrument, and by *mortgagee* we will mean the *lender* under any form of security instrument. In the same way, the term *foreclosure* most often means a *trustee's sale.* The use of what may appear to be the wrong terminology simply is recognition of the fact that for most of the country, those are the correct terms.

California Foreclosure Reduction Act

The California Foreclosure Reduction Act, also known as the California Homeowner Bill of Rights, took effect on January 1, 2013, and makes changes to nonjudicial foreclosures in California. Much of the law concerns mortgage servicers that have foreclosed on more than 175 homes during the preceding calendar year. The law has many important provisions, including the possibility of civil penalties and criminal prosecution, which include the following:

- The mortgage servicer is prohibited from commencing or continuing a foreclosure while a loan modification application submitted by a borrower is pending.

- The mortgage servicer must provide a single point of contact for a borrower who has requested a foreclosure prevention alternative.

- The borrower must be provided a written acknowledgment of receipt of a completed loan modification application or related documents within five business days; the initial acknowledgment of the loan modification application must describe the modification process, note any deficiencies in the application, and provide an estimate of when a decision will be made, the length of time the borrower will have to consider an offer, and any deadlines or expiration dates for submitting documents.

- Written notice is required if a loan modification application is denied and a notice of default cannot be recorded (or the notice of sale cannot be recorded, if the notice of default has already been recorded) until the later of 31 days after the borrower is provided with the notice of denial; or, if the borrower appeals, the later of 15 days after denial of the appeal or 14 days after a loan modification is offered after appeal but declined by the borrower; or, if a loan modification is offered after appeal and accepted, the date on which the borrower defaults or breaches the terms of the offer.

- Before beginning the foreclosure process, the mortgage servicer must review competent and reliable evidence to substantiate the default. All parts of the process must be supported by competent and reliable evidence. A lender that records and files multiple unverified documents will be subject to a civil penalty of up to $7,500 per loan. A lender who is in violation is also subject to enforcement by a licensing agency, including the California Department of Business Oversight and the California Bureau of Real Estate.

- A borrower can seek redress in the event of "material" violations of the new foreclosure process protections. Injunctive relief is available before a foreclosure sale, and damages can be recovered after a sale.

- The statute of limitations to prosecute mortgage-related crimes is extended from one to three years, and the attorney general's office can use a statewide grand jury to investigate and indict the perpetrators of financial crimes involving victims in multiple counties.

- In addition, a purchaser of a foreclosed home must give tenants at least 90 days before starting eviction proceedings. If the tenant has a fixed-term lease that began before the transfer of title at the foreclosure sale, the new owner must honor the lease unless the new owner can prove that an exception intended to prevent fraudulent leases applies.

www.dbo.ca.gov
/Laws_&_Regs/legislation
/ca_foreclosure_reduction
_act.asp

A list of the mortgage servicers licensed and regulated by the Department of Business Oversight with more than 175 foreclosures in calendar year 2012 is posted online at www.dbo.ca.gov/Laws_&_Regs/legislation/ca_ foreclosure_reduction _act.asp.

Unruh Act Mortgages and Deeds of Trust

California's **Unruh Civil Rights Act** covers contracts for goods and services. If a mortgage with a *power-of-sale clause* or *deed of trust* on a single-family owner-occupied residence stems from a contract that falls within the Unruh Act, even more explicit notice must be given to a trustor or mortgagor in default. The act also prohibits discriminatory language in real property instruments for the purpose of restricting the conveyance, encumbrance, lease, mortgage, use, or occupation of property.

The object of this special provision is to prevent a homeowner from unwittingly losing the home as the result of a retail installment purchase. The requirements for imposing a mortgage or deed of trust, as well as the requirements on default, can be found in the Civil Code.

Home Equity Sales Contracts

The high rate of overall property appreciation in recent decades greatly increased the equity of owners of real estate throughout the state. Increased equity has made properties attractive to unscrupulous individuals seeking to take advantage of homeowners whose property is in foreclosure. By use of a **home equity sales contract**, the property owner in foreclosure may be persuaded to sell the equity in a home for far less than its true value. The problem became severe enough to warrant legislation now included in the Civil Code. The law provides the following:

- A home equity sales contract must be in letters equal to 10-point bold type. **This sentence is printed in 10-point bold type.**

- The contract must include notices of the equity seller's *right of cancellation*.

- The contract may be *canceled* by the equity seller at any time up to midnight of the fifth business day following the contract signing, or 8:00 am on the day set for sale under a deed of trust, whichever comes first.

There are exceptions to these requirements for properties sold for use as a personal residence, by deed in lieu of foreclosure, trustee's sale, foreclosure sale, as authorized by statute or a court, or between blood relatives or their spouses.

Penalties for violation of the law include a fine of up to $10,000, imprisonment for up to one year in the county jail or state prison, or both. The equity seller can recover damages, attorneys' fees, and costs.

Finally, any transaction involving residential real property in foreclosure in which any person initiating, entering into, negotiating, or consummating the transaction takes *unconscionable advantage* of the property owner is *voidable* and can be rescinded within two years after the sale.

Other foreclosure abuses   The California Civil Code also covers the abuses of *mortgage foreclosure consultants*. In Section 2945(a), the legislature states that "homeowners whose residences are in foreclosure are subject to fraud, deception, harassment, and unfair dealing by foreclosure consultants..." To combat these practices, the law specifies notice and other requirements that must be scrupulously followed by anyone (other than those exempted from the provision) who offers to

- stop or postpone a foreclosure sale,

- assist in obtaining a loan or an extension for payment, or

- perform other activities involving property in foreclosure.

Though attorneys and real estate licensees are generally exempted from these requirements, SB 94 (effective until January 1, 2013) bans all foreclosure consultants, including loan modification attorneys and firms, from asking for any advance fees before fully completing the services contracted, whether successful or denied by the loan servicer. In 2010, AB 2325 expanded the foreclosure consultant restrictions to anyone who performs a forensic audit (an audit performed as part of a legal action) of a residential mortgage loan.

Abuses by mortgage foreclosure consultants are taken very seriously. Violation of the law could result in both civil and criminal penalties, including fine, imprisonment, or both.

> Penalties for misuse of a home equity sales contract are severe.

Exercise 8-1

Identify the security instrument described in each of the following situations:

1. Harvey and Helen Headstrong have purchased Whiteacre. If they default on their loan payments, they can have the loan reinstated or redeem their property if it is sold at the lender's request.

2. Bernice Bosh has purchased Blackacre. She holds title to Blackacre. If she defaults on her loan payments and Blackacre is sold at the lender's request, she cannot redeem it.

3. Mel and Millie Mendez have purchased Greenacre and are living there, even though they have conveyed title to someone else.

4. Alan Adema bought Redacre. He defaulted in his loan payments and received notice that Redacre would be sold. The day before the sale, Alan offered to pay the overdue installments and costs but was surprised when the lender demanded that the entire loan balance be paid to stop the sale.

REAL ESTATE LENDERS—THE PRIMARY MORTGAGE MARKET

Lenders who *initiate* loans with borrowers are part of what is called the *primary mortgage market*. There are both *institutional* and *noninstitutional lenders* in the primary mortgage market.

Institutional Lenders

Institutional lenders make most of the loans used by home and business owners. *Depository institutions* include those that lend money for the purchase or refinancing of real estate or for the construction of improvements. Such institutions act as intermediaries between the borrowers and the sources of the funds the institution has available to lend. As discussed previously, those funds are typically savings or investments.

Savings and loan associations Most California savings and loan associations (S&Ls) are federally chartered. All are required by state law to insure accounts through the FDIC.

Loan-to-Value Ratio and PMI

The **loan-to-value ratio** is the percentage of the current appraised market value represented by the amount of the loan. In other words, what percentage of the value does the loan represent? If the loan-to-value ratio exceeds 80%, the borrower must obtain insurance for the loan amount over 80%.

Private mortgage insurance (PMI), typically added to the monthly loan payment, will automatically be discontinued after the loan has been paid down to 78% of the original sales price, as required by the federal **Homeowner's Protection Act of 1998** (HPA). The borrower has the right to request cancellation of PMI when the loan balance is no more than 80% of the original purchase price or appraised value at the time of purchase, whichever is less.

The deductibility of PMI payments was approved by Congress for policies issued in 2007, and was later extended for PMI payments made through 2013.

Federally chartered S&Ls (also called *thrift and loans* or just *thrifts*) are members of the Federal Home Loan Bank System. The Board of Governors of the Federal Reserve System establishes minimum reserve requirements.

A loan is an **open-ended mortgage** if it permits the mortgagor to borrow additional money at will without further financial qualification, on the original loan terms. A **lock-in clause** in a promissory note or land contract prohibits the promissor from paying off the debt before the date set forth in the contract.

Home loan payment terms may be described as

- *fully amortized* (equal payments including both interest and principal are made over the loan term);

- *partially amortized* (most of the principal remains to be paid in the last payment);

- **nonamortized** (the *straight note*, typically interest only, with the entire amount of principal due at the end of the loan term); or as having

- **negative amortization** (loan payments do not cover all of the interest due, which is then added to the remaining loan balance).

Figure 8.5 summarizes important features of some of the most widely used real estate loans.

Commercial banks   All banks must be members of the Federal Reserve System. The National Bank Act covers national banks; the California Banking Law covers state banks.

> Banks make the greatest number of different types of loans.

Commercial banks make the broadest range of loans, including those for real estate purchase, construction, and interim financing (before a building under construction is completed), and even consumer loans for home improvements. Commercial banks also make many business and short-term credit loans, including automobile financing. Bank credit cards represent a growing portion of commercial banks' activity.

There are no restrictions on loan-to-value ratios or amortization schedules or limitations on the amount of funds that can be loaned on real estate by national banks. This is one reason why this form of institution is becoming increasingly popular. Commercial banks are supervised by the U.S. Comptroller of the Currency.

Insurance companies   With the exception of single-family homes, insurance companies invest in most types of real estate by making mortgage loans. Insurance companies are governed by the laws of the state of their incorporation as well as by the laws of the state in which they do business.

Insurance companies typically finance large commercial projects but also buy loans from mortgage companies (discussed later in this unit) and invest in government-insured or -guaranteed loans.

Mutual savings banks   A mutual savings and loan association distributes its earnings to depositors (after providing for expenses, reserves, and other costs of operation) as dividends, rather than interest. Originally found in the New England states and relatively new to California, both mutual and stock savings and loan associations have reformed as mutual savings banks. They can retain federal deposit insurance and follow federal regulations. They can also be state chartered.

Credit unions   Of growing importance are the loan-making functions of credit unions, which are organized under the National Credit Union Administration, a federal agency. Credit unions receive the savings of members, frequently through payroll deductions, which they use to make loans to members. Loans may be unsecured but more often are secured by a home, an automobile, a boat, or other asset purchased.

Credit unions typically have relatively low overhead expenses. As a result, many credit unions can offer loans at competitive interest rates while also offering interest rates on savings accounts and other investments that may be better than those offered by commercial banks and savings and loans. Participation is restricted to the defined group of prospective members, such as federal employees.

Noninstitutional Lenders

Noninstitutional lenders include

- mortgage companies,
- private individuals, and
- organizations that are not financial institutions.

FIGURE 8.5:   Common Mortgage Plans

LOANS FROM FEDERAL INSTITUTIONS ON BORROWER-OCCUPIED HOMES		
Loan Type	**Description**	**Advantages/Disadvantages**
Fixed-rate mortgage	Fixed interest rate; equal monthly payments of principal and interest until debt is paid in full	Stable, with long-term tax advantages; rarely assumable
Adjustable-rate mortgage (ARM) (also called flexible-rate or variable-rate mortgage)	Interest rate changes based on index; could increase payments, term, or principal; could have rate cap or payment cap	Very popular with lenders; rate cap of no more than 5% advisable; with payment cap, negative amortization possible; usually assumable
Graduated payment mortgage (GPM)	Lower monthly payments rise gradually over 5 to 10 years, then level off for remainder of term	Easier to qualify for
Graduated payment adjustable-rate mortgage (GPARM)	Same as GPM, but additional payment change possible if index changes	Easier to qualify for; could be negative amortization
Growing equity mortgage (GEM) (also called rapid payoff mortgage)	Fixed interest rate; payments vary by index or schedule	Rapid payoff as payout increases; income must also increase
Reverse annuity mortgage (RAM) (also called equity conversion mortgage)	One-time or monthly payment(s) are made to borrowers age 62 or older using property as collateral	Provides cash to homeowner; loan amount plus accrued interest is due when property is sold or at homeowner's death; high closing costs require independent loan counseling for homeowner
Renegotiable-rate mortgage (RRM) (also called rollover mortgage)	Rate and payments constant for three- to five-year intervals; can change based on FHLBB index; rate cap of 5% over maximum 30-year term	Fair stable payments due to less-frequent changes in rate
Shared appreciation mortgage (SAM)	Below-market rate and lower payments in exchange for losing some equity	Loss of equity makes investment more expensive

Mortgage companies   Mortgage companies, or **mortgage bankers,** make real estate loans, then sell those loans to investors. The mortgage company will service the loans it has sold on a contractual basis. Servicing a loan includes receiving payments on behalf of the investor and otherwise handling the day-to-day supervision of the investment.

Mortgage companies are a prime source of government-insured and guaranteed loan funds as well as conventional loans (loans that do not involve government cooperation). State laws regarding mortgage companies historically have been much broader than those governing banks and S&Ls. Many mortgage companies invest their own funds or borrow investment funds themselves from commercial banks.

Mortgage Bankers vs. Mortgage Loan Brokers

Even though the *mortgage banker* often serves as a middleman between investor and borrower, the mortgage banker is not necessarily a mortgage broker. In California, mortgage bankers are licensed by the California Department of Business Oversight and are subject to the California Residential Mortgage Lending Act (CRMLA), found in the California Financial Code. *Mortgage loan brokers* are licensed as real estate brokers by the California Bureau of Real Estate and are governed by the California Real Estate Law. They bring borrower and lender together but typically do not invest their own funds, and they do not service loans.

Private individuals Nonfinancial institutions and private individuals hold one-quarter of all mortgage debt. Private individuals are the largest source of second-mortgage funds (junior loans).

When the lender is an individual, rather than a bank or mortgage company, there won't be a loan committee or arduous qualification process. In addition, an individual may offer lower loan costs and a better interest rate. When individuals make direct loans (as opposed to extending purchase-money credit), they are subject to the usury laws, unless a broker has arranged the loan.

Nonfinancial institutions Real estate loans make up some of the most important assets of nonfinancial institutions. These include

- pension funds,
- colleges and universities,
- trusts,
- estates,
- mortgage investment companies, and
- other groups.

As with individuals, nonfinancial institutions may make fewer demands in terms of borrower qualifications. Such investors are also unlikely to be part of the primary mortgage market for single-family homes.

Mortgage Loan Brokers

California's **Real Property Loan Law** (a part of the Real Estate Law) allows a real estate broker to

- solicit borrowers or lenders or
- negotiate loans for real property.

FIGURE 8.6:   **Maximum Mortgage Loan Broker Commission**

Type of Security	Loan Amount	Loan Term	Maximum Commission
First deed of trust	Less than $30,000 $30,000 or more	Three years or more Less than three years	10% of loan amount 5%
Second deed of trust	Less than $20,000 $20,000 or more	Three years or more Two to less than three years Less than two years	15% of loan amount 10% 5%

The Real Property Loan Law applies to loans secured by equity in real property, but it does not apply to purchase-money loans. Put another way, the law applies to "hard money" (cash-out) as opposed to "soft money" loans (those used to buy the property). A broker can loan his own funds if the borrower is informed of the source of the funds. If funds from a family member of the broker are loaned, the relationship also must be disclosed.

The maximum commission that a broker can charge for negotiating or making a loan depends on

- the amount of the loan,
- the length of the loan term, and
- whether the loan is secured by a first or second deed of trust.

Maximum commission amounts are summarized in Figure 8.6.

Costs and expenses, such as appraisal fees, credit investigation fees, notary fees, and escrow fees, can be charged in addition to the commission or broker's fee. The maximum that can be charged for such costs and expenses (excluding title charges and recording fees) is shown in Figure 8.7.

If a loan is negotiated or made by a broker, a mortgage loan disclosure statement must be completed and presented to the borrower for the borrower's signature before the loan transaction is completed and the borrower becomes obligated under the terms of the agreement. This statement is separate from any other required disclosure statement.

FIGURE 8.7:   **Maximum Chargeable Mortgage Loan Broker Costs and Expenses**

Loan Amount	Maximum Costs and Expenses
Up to $7,800	Actual costs or $390, whichever is less
$7,800 to $14,000	Actual costs or 5% of loan amount, whichever is less
More than $14,000	Actual costs, but not more than $700

As of January 1, 2004, the Real Estate Law allows brokers to arrange multilender loans that are secured by more than one parcel of real property. Form revisions effective as of January 2004 are RE 851A Lender/Purchaser Disclosure Statement (Loan Origination); RE 851B Lender/Purchaser Disclosure Statement (Sale of Existing Note); and RE 851D Lender/Purchaser Disclosure Statement—Multi-Property (Cross Collateralization) Addendum. All of the new forms are available at www.bre.ca.gov. A sample Lender/Purchaser Disclosure Statement is shown in Figure 8.8.

www.bre.ca.gov

Advertising by a mortgage loan broker must include a statement that the broker is licensed by the California Bureau of Real Estate.

Other Restrictions on Mortgage Loan Brokers

There are other restrictions on loans made by brokers that are not greater than $30,000 for a first mortgage or $20,000 for a second mortgage. They include the following:

- No balloon payment (a payment more than twice the amount of the smallest payment) is required on an owner-occupied dwelling if the loan term is less than six years (three years for property not owner-occupied), unless the loan is taken back by the seller as part of the purchase price.

- No borrower-paid loan servicing or loan collection fees are assessed.

- Borrower may not be required to obtain credit life or disability insurance as a loan condition; if the broker provides such insurance, only one premium may be collected, and only a borrower who might be expected to contribute to loan payments (such as a wage earner) may be insured.

- The penalty for late payment of an installment is limited to 10% of the principal and interest payment.

- Payments may be made within 10 days of the date due without penalty.

- On loans of any amount secured by a borrower-occupied dwelling, no prepayment penalty is allowed after seven years from the date the loan was made. In the first six years of the loan, 20% of the loan principal can be paid off per year without penalty. Otherwise, the maximum prepayment penalty is six months' interest on prepayments of principal that are greater than 20% of the unpaid principal balance.

FIGURE 8.8:   **Lender/Purchaser Disclosure Statement**

STATE OF CALIFORNIA
BUREAU OF REAL ESTATE

LENDER/PURCHASER DISCLOSURE STATEMENT
(LOAN ORIGINATION)

RE 851A (Rev. 8/16)   MORTGAGE LENDING

DISCLOSURE STATEMENT SUMMARY		

Note: If this is a multi-lender transaction and more than one property secures the loan, you should also refer to the
attached Lender/Purchaser Disclosure Statement Multi-Property (Cross Collateralization) Addendum (RE 851D).

AMOUNT OF THIS LOAN *(SEE PART 3)*	MARKET VALUE OF PROPERTY (SEE PART 9)	TOTAL AMOUNT OF ENCUMBRANCES SENIOR TO THIS LOAN *(SEE PART 10)*
$	$	$
TOTAL AMOUNT OF ENCUMBRANCES ANTICIPATED OR EXPECTED TO BE JUNIOR TO THIS LOAN *(SEE PART 10)*	PROTECTIVE EQUITY (MARKET VALUE MINUS THIS LOAN AND TOTAL SENIOR ENCUMBRANCES)	TOTAL LOAN TO VALUE (SEE PART 11G)
$	$	%

PART 1	BROKER INFORMATION	

NAME OF BROKER	REAL ESTATE LICENSE ID#
BUSINESS ADDRESS	TELEPHONE NUMBER
NAME OF BROKERS REPRESENTATIVE	

PART 2	BROKER CAPACITY IN TRANSACTION	

THE BROKER IDENTIFIED IN PART 1 OF THIS STATEMENT IS ACTING IN THE FOLLOWING CAPACITY IN THIS TRANSACTION: (CHECK AS APPLIES)

☐   A. Agent in arranging a loan on behalf of another

☐   B. Principal as a borrower on funds from which broker will directly or indirectly benefit other than through the receipt of
commissions, fees and costs and expenses as provided by law for services as an agent.

☐   C. Funding a portion of this loan. *(Multi-lender transactions are subject to Business and Professions Code §10238.)*

IF MORE THAN ONE CAPACITY HAS BEEN CHECKED, PROVIDE AN EXPLANATION HERE.

IF "B" HAS BEEN CHECKED, THE BROKER INTENDS TO USE FUNDS FROM THE LENDER/PURCHASER IN THIS TRANSACTION FOR:

PART 3	TRANSACTION INFORMATION	

(CHECK IF APPLICABLE)

☐   THERE IS MORE THAN ONE PROPERTY SECURING THE LOAN. IF MULTI-LENDER LOAN, YOU SHOULD ALSO REFER TO ATTACHED RE 851D.

TERM OF LOAN	PRIORITY OF THIS LOAN (1ST, 2ND, ETC.)	PRINCIPAL AMOUNT	YOUR SHARE IF MULTI-LENDER TRANS.
		$	$

INTEREST RATE	(CHECK ONE)		
% ☐ VARIABLE ☐ FIXED	☐ AMORTIZED ☐ PARTIALLY AMORTIZED	☐ INTEREST ONLY	***THE TRUST DEED WILL BE RECORDED.***

PAYMENT FREQUENCY	APPROXIMATE PAYMENT DUE DATE	AMOUNT OF PAYMENT	YOUR SHARE IF MULTI-LENDER TRANS.
☐ MONTHLY ☐ WEEKLY		$	$

BALLOON PAYMENT	APPROX. BALLOON PAYMENT DUE DATE	AMOUNT OF BALLOON PAYMENT	YOUR SHARE IF MULTI-LENDER TRANS.
☐ YES ☐ NO		$	$

Balloon Payment — A balloon payment is any installment payment (usually the payment due at maturity) which is greater than twice the amount of the smallest installment payment under the terms of the promissory note or sales contract.

The borrower/vendee may have to obtain a new loan or sell the property to make the balloon payment. If the effort is not successful it may be necessary for the holder of the note/contract to foreclose on the property as a means of collecting the amount owed.

There are subordination provisions. ....   ☐ Yes   ☐ No
If YES, explain here or on an attachment.

FIGURE 8.8: **Lender/Purchaser Disclosure Statement (continued)**

RE 851A *Page 2 of 6*

PART 4	MULTI-LENDER TRANSACTIONS	

NAME OF ESCROW HOLDER | ANTICIPATED CLOSING DATE

ADDRESS OF ESCROW HOLDER

ESTIMATED LENDER COSTS

ESTIMATED BORROWER COSTS —
Broker will provide you a copy of the "mortgage loan disclosure statement" given to the borrower or a separate itemization of borrower's costs.

_____ $ _____

_____ $ _____

_____ $ _____

TOTAL $ _____

TOTAL $ _____

Servicing

You will be a joint beneficiary with others on this note and you should request a list of names and addresses of the beneficiaries as of the close of escrow from the broker or servicing agent. The beneficiary(ies) holding more than 50% interest in the note may govern the actions to be taken on behalf of all holders in the event of default or other matters. See Civil Code §2941.9.

PART 5	LOAN TO VALUE	

GENERALLY the aggregate principal amount of the notes or interests sold, together with the unpaid principal amount of any encumbrances upon the real property senior thereto, shall not exceed the following percentages of the current market value of the real property as determined in writing by the broker or qualified appraiser.

Single-family residence, owner-occupied...80%

Single-family residence, not owner-occupied 75%

Commercial and income-producing properties 65%

Single-family residentially zoned lot or parcel which has installed off-site improvements including drainage, curbs, gutters, sidewalks, paved roads, and utilities as mandated by the political subdivision having jurisdiction over the lot or parcel...65%

Land that produces income from crops, timber, or minerals 60%

Land that is not income producing but has been zoned for (and if required, approved for subdivision as) commercial or residential development 50%

Other real property...35%

The percentage amounts specified above may be exceeded when and to the extent that the broker determines that the encumbrance of the property in excess of these percentages is reasonable and prudent considering all relevant factors pertaining to the real property. However, in no event shall the aggregate principal amount of the notes or interests sold, together with the unpaid principal amount of any encumbrances upon the property senior thereto, exceed 80 percent of the current fair market value of improved real property or 50 percent of the current fair market value of unimproved real property, except in the case of a single-family residentially zoned lot or parcel as defined above, which shall not exceed 65% of current fair market value of that lot or parcel. A written statement shall be prepared by the broker that sets forth the material considerations and facts that the broker relies upon for his or her determination which shall be disclosed to the lender or note purchaser(s) and retained as a part of the broker's record of the transaction.

NOTE: If more than one property secures this loan, you should also refer to attached RE 851D.

FIGURE 8.8:   **Lender/Purchaser Disclosure Statement (continued)**

RE 851A   *Page 3 of 6*

PART 6	SERVICING ARRANGEMENTS

If the loan is to be serviced by a real estate broker you must be notified within ten (10) days if the broker makes any advances on senior encumbrances to protect the security of your note. Depending on the terms and conditions of the servicing contract, you may be obligated to repay any such advances made by the broker. (Note: There must be a servicing agent on multi-lender transactions.) The broker may not guarantee, or imply to guarantee, or advance any payments to you unless a securities permit is obtained from the Department of Business Oversight.

CHECK APPROPRIATE STATEMENTS

☐ THERE ARE NO SERVICING ARRANGEMENTS *(Does not apply to multi-lender transactions.)*   ☐ BROKER IS THE SERVICING AGENT

☐ ANOTHER QUALIFIED PARTY WILL SERVICE THE LOAN   ☐ COPY OF THE SERVICING CONTRACT IS ATTACHED

IF BROKER IS NOT THE SERVICING AGENT, WHAT IS THE RELATIONSHIP BETWEEN THE BROKER AND SERVICER?	COST TO LENDER FOR SERVICING ARRANGEMENTS *(EXPRESS AS DOLLAR AMOUNT OR PERCENTAGE)*

PER ☐ MONTH ☐ YEAR   PAYABLE ☐ MONTHLY ☐ ANNUALLY

NAME OF AUTHORIZED SERVICER, IF ANY

BUSINESS ADDRESS   TELEPHONE NUMBER

PART 7	BORROWER INFORMATION

SOURCE OF INFORMATION

☐ BORROWER   ☐ BROKER INQUIRY   ☐ CREDIT REPORT   ☐ OTHER (DESCRIBE)

NAME	CO-BORROWER'S NAME
RESIDENCE ADDRESS	CO-BORROWER'S RESIDENCE ADDRESS
OCCUPATION OR PROFESSION	CO-BORROWER'S OCCUPATION OR PROFESSION
CURRENT EMPLOYER	CO-BORROWER'S CURRENT EMPLOYER
HOW LONG EMPLOYED? AGE	HOW LONG EMPLOYED? CO-BORROWER'S AGE

SOURCES OF GROSS INCOME *(LIST AND IDENTIFY EACH SOURCE SEPARATELY.)*	MONTHLY AMOUNT	CO-BORROWER SOURCES OF GROSS INCOME (LIST AND IDENTIFY EACH SOURCE SEPARATELY.)	MONTHLY AMOUNT
Gross Salary	$	Gross Salary	$
OTHER INCOME INCLUDING: Interest	$	OTHER INCOME INCLUDING: Interest	$
Dividends	$	Dividends	$
Gross Rental Income	$	Gross Rental Income	$
Miscellaneous Income	$	Miscellaneous Income	$

TOTAL EXPENSES OF ALL BORROWERS *(DO NOT COMPLETE IF BORROWER IS A CORPORATION)*

Payment of Loan being obtained	$	Spousal/Child Support	$
Rent	$	Insurance	$
Charge Account/Credit Cards	$	Vehicle Loan(s)	$
Mortgage Payments *(include taxes and property insurance)*	$	Other *(federal & state income taxes, etc.)*	$
TOTAL GROSS MONTHLY INCOME OF BORROWER(S) $		TOTAL MONTHLY EXPENSES OF BORROWER(S) $	

FIGURE 8.8: **Lender/Purchaser Disclosure Statement (continued)**

RE 851A   *Page 4 of 6*

The borrower has filed for bankruptcy in the past 12 months.. ☐ Yes   ☐ No

If YES, the bankruptcy has been discharged or dismissed.. ☐ Yes   ☐ No

❖ *THE FOLLOWING STATEMENTS ONLY APPLY IF THE BORROWER IS A CORPORATION, PARTNERSHIP OR SOME OTHER FORM OF OPERATING BUSINESS ENTITY.*

Copies of a balance sheet of the entity and income statement covering the indicated period have been supplied by the borrower/obligor and are attached. If no, explain on addendum. .... ☐ Yes   ☐ No

If YES, Date of balance sheet.. _____

Income statement period *(from-to)*.. _____

Financial Statements have been audited by CPA or PA. .... ☐ Yes   ☐ No

Additional information is included on an attached addendum .... ☐ Yes   ☐ No

PART 8	PROPERTY INFORMATION

Identification of property that is the security for note. *(If no street address, the assessor's parcel number or legal description and a means for locating the property is attached.)*

(CHECK IF APPLICABLE)

☐ THERE IS MORE THAN ONE PROPERTY SECURING THE LOAN. IF MULTI-LENDER LOAN, YOU SHOULD REFER TO ATTACHED RE 851D.

STREET ADDRESS	OWNER OCCUPIED
	☐ NO ☐ YES

ANNUAL PROPERTY TAXES	ARE TAXES DELINQUENT?	IF YES, AMT. REQUIRED TO BRING CURRENT
$ ☐ ACTUAL ☐ ESTIMATED	☐ NO ☐ YES	$

SOURCE OF TAX INFORMATION

PART 9	APPRAISAL INFORMATION

Estimate of fair market value is to be determined by an independent appraisal, copy of which must be provided to you prior to your obligating funds to make the loan. Note: You may waive the requirement of an independent appraisal, in writing, on a case-by-case basis, in which case the broker must provide a written estimate of fair market value. The broker must provide you, the investor, with the objective data upon which the broker's estimate is based. **In the case of a construction or rehabilitation loan, an appraisal must be completed by an independent, qualified appraiser in accordance with the Uniform Standards of Professional Appraisal Practice (USPAP).**

(CHECK IF APPLICABLE)

☐ THERE IS MORE THAN ONE PROPERTY SECURING THE LOAN. IF A MULTI-LENDER LOAN REFER TO ATTACHED RE 851D.

FAIR MARKET VALUE (ACCORDING TO APPRAISER) *(Place this figure or brokers estimate of fair market value on line "F" of Part 11.)*	DATE OF APPRAISAL
$	
NAME OF APPRAISER (IF KNOWN TO BROKER)	PAST AND/OR CURRENT RELATIONSHIP OF APPRAISER TO BROKER (EMPLOYEE, AGENT, INDEPENDENT CONTRACTOR, ETC.)

ADDRESS OF APPRAISER

DESCRIPTION OF PROPERTY/IMPROVEMENT	IS THERE ADDITIONAL SECURING PROPERTY?
	☐ YES IF YES, SEE ADDENDUM.
	☐ NO

AGE	SQUARE FEET	TYPE OF CONSTRUCTION

IF THE PROPERTY IS CURRENTLY GENERATING INCOME FOR THE BORROWER/OBLIGOR: ESTIMATED GROSS ANNUAL INCOME	ESTIMATED NET ANNUAL INCOME
$	$

FIGURE 8.8:   **Lender/Purchaser Disclosure Statement (continued)**

PART 10	ENCUMBRANCE INFORMATION

Information is being provided concerning senior encumbrances against the property, to the extent reasonably available from customary sources (excluding the note described on page 1, Part 3). **Note:** You have the option to purchase a policy of title insurance or an endorsement to an existing policy of title insurance to insure your interest. You are entitled to a copy of a written loan application and a credit report to obtain information concerning all encumbrances which constitute liens against the property. This information may help determine financial standing and creditworthiness of the borrower.

(CHECK IF APPLICABLE)

☐ THERE IS MORE THAN ONE PROPERTY SECURING THE LOAN. IF MULTI-LENDER LOAN, YOU SHOULD REFER TO ATTACHED RE 851D.

SOURCE OF INFORMATION

☐ BROKER INQUIRY   ☐ BORROWER   ☐ OTHER *(EXPLAIN):* _____

Are there any encumbrances of record against the securing property at this time?. .... ☐ YES   ☐ NO

A. Over the last 12 months were any payments more than 60 days late? .... ☐ YES   ☐ NO

B. If YES, how many?.. _____

C. Do any of these payments remain unpaid? .... ☐ YES   ☐ NO

D. If YES, will the proceeds of subject loan be used to cure the delinquency?.......................... ☐ YES   ☐ NO

E. If NO, source of funds to bring the loan current.. _____

Encumbrances remaining and/or expected to be placed against the property by the borrower/obligor after the close of escrow (excluding the note described on page 1).

ENCUMBRANCE(S) REMAINING *(AS REPRESENTED BY THE BORROWER)*

PRIORITY (1ST, 2ND, ETC.)	INTEREST RATE %	PRIORITY (1ST, 2ND, ETC.)	INTEREST RATE %
BENEFICIARY		BENEFICIARY	
ORIGINAL AMOUNT $	APPROXIMATE PRINCIPAL BALANCE $	ORIGINAL AMOUNT $	APPROXIMATE PRINCIPAL BALANCE $
MONTHLY PAYMENT $	MATURITY DATE	MONTHLY PAYMENT $	MATURITY DATE
BALLOON PAYMENT ☐ YES ☐ NO ☐ UNKNOWN	IF YES, AMOUNT $	BALLOON PAYMENT ☐ YES ☐ NO ☐ UNKNOWN	IF YES, AMOUNT $

ENCUMBRANCES EXPECTED OR ANTICIPATED *(AS REPRESENTED BY THE BORROWER)*

PRIORITY (1ST, 2ND, ETC.)	INTEREST RATE %	PRIORITY (1ST, 2ND, ETC.)	INTEREST RATE %
BENEFICIARY		BENEFICIARY	
ORIGINAL AMOUNT $	MATURITY DATE	ORIGINAL AMOUNT $	MATURITY DATE
MONTHLY PAYMENT $		MONTHLY PAYMENT $	
BALLOON PAYMENT ☐ YES ☐ NO ☐ UNKNOWN	IF YES, AMOUNT $	BALLOON PAYMENT ☐ YES ☐ NO ☐ UNKNOWN	IF YES, AMOUNT $

Additional remaining, expected or anticipated encumbrances are set forth in an attachment to this statement. .... ☐ Yes   ☐ No

FIGURE 8.8:   Lender/Purchaser Disclosure Statement (continued)

RE 851A   *Page 6 of 6*

| PART 11 | LOAN TO VALUE RATIO | ← |

(CHECK IF APPLICABLE)

☐ THERE IS MORE THAN ONE PROPERTY SECURING THE LOAN. IF A MULTI-LENDER LOAN, YOU SHOULD REFER TO ATTACHED RE 851D.

A. Remaining encumbrances senior to this loan *(from part 9)* .... $_____

B. Encumbrances expected or anticipated senior to this loan
    (from part 10)...   + $_____

C. Total remaining and expected or anticipated encumbrances senior to this loan................   = $_____

D. Principal amount of this loan from page 1 part 3 ....   + $_____

E. Total all senior encumbrances and this loan...   = $_____

F. Fair market value from page 4 part 9...   + $_____

G. Loan to value ratio ....   = _____%

Note: See Part 4 if multi-lender transaction.

| NOTICE |

The broker has a responsibility to make reasonable efforts to determine that the loan/investment is suitable and appropriate for the lender/purchaser based on information provided by the lender/purchaser regarding the lender/purchaser's financial situation and investment objectives.

| ADDITIONAL DISCLOSURES |

- Investments in notes secured by trust deeds and real property sales contracts are subject to risk of loss of principal and monthly income. If the borrower stops making payments on any investments you make, you will not receive income; therefore, you cannot rely on this income.

- If your investment is secured by a junior lien and the borrower defaults on a senior lien, it may be necessary for you to meet the obligations of the senior lien in order to protect your security interests, which may include making the senior loan current or paying the senior loan balance in full.

- If your investment is in a multi-lender note and the borrower defaults, foreclosure proceedings will require consensus of a majority of the beneficiaries on the note.

- The trust deed investments that you will make will either name you and your percentage interest in the investment or will be assigned to you. Your trust deed investments are not secured by the real estate collateral unless your interests in those investments are recorded.

- Since trust deed and real property sales contract investments have a maturity date, borrowers are under no obligation to pay off the loan prior to the maturity date. Further, in the case of a balloon payment, there is potential risk that the borrower may not be able to make the balloon payment.

| BROKER VERIFICATION |

The information in this statement and in the attachments hereto is true and correct to the best of my knowledge and belief.

| SIGNATURE OF BROKER OR DESIGNATED REPRESENTATIVE | BROKER/CORPORATION ID# | DATE |
| ➢ | | |

| ACKNOWLEDGEMENT OF RECEIPT |

I, The prospective lender/purchaser, acknowledge receipt of a copy of this statement signed by or on behalf of the broker.

NAME OF PROSPECTIVE LENDER/PURCHASER

| SIGNATURE OF PROSPECTIVE LENDER/PURCHASER | DATE |
| ➢ | |

The California Bureau of Real Estate does not endorse or offer any opinions regarding the suitability of any proposed or existing real estate investments.

Bureau of Real Estate license information telephone number: 877-373-4542, or check license status at www.calbre.ca.gov.

A guide to trust deed investments entitled "Trust Deed Investments - What You Should Know!!" (RE35) is available on the Bureau's Web site at www.calbre.ca.gov under the Publications menu.

FOR EXAMPLE   Mortgage loan broker Mary Miller arranges a $20,000 loan secured by a second deed of trust for a homeowner who wants extra cash to pay off some credit cards. The loan term is 15 years. Mary's commission is 10% of the loan amount, and loan expenses include an appraisal fee of $350, a credit report of $40, and notary fees of $50. What is the total maximum fee that Mary can charge on this loan, including brokerage commission and expenses?

Mary's commission is

$20,000 × 10% = $2,000

Expenses are

$350 + $40 + $50 = $44 0

Both Mary's commission and the expenses come within the limitations of the Real Property Loan Law. The total maximum fee thus is $2,000 + $440, or $2,440.

California Residential Mortgage Lending Act

www.dbo.ca.gov

Some lending activities are conducted under the rules of the **California Residential Mortgage Lending Act**. The law applies to those involved in making or servicing mortgage loans on one- to four-family dwellings. The Department of Business Oversight, www.dbo.ca.gov, issues licenses for the activities covered by the law, but the following are exempt:

- *Real estate brokers* licensed in California
- Institutional and noninstitutional lenders already licensed by the state or federal government, such as banks, savings and loan associations, trust companies, and insurance companies
- An individual or company making residential mortgage loans with his, her, or its own money
- Government and pension plan employees
- Court-appointed estate or other representatives
- A trustee under a deed of trust

The law also exempts a **California finance lender** licensed under the **California Finance Lenders Law**. A *finance lender* is someone who is in the business of making consumer loans or commercial loans in which personal property may be used as collateral.

Exercise 8-2

Loan charges usually include not only the interest rate but also a loan origination fee, points, and other costs. Make a survey of loan charges by at least three online lenders who make loans in California. Base your comparisons on both a fixed-rate and an adjustable-rate loan of $320,000, representing 80% of the value of a home selling for $400,000, with a down payment of 20%. As a further comparison, use loan terms of both 15 and 30 years. You can begin your survey by entering the search term "home loan" in one of the internet search engines, such as Google or Yahoo. You could also check out some of the online property listing services, which include www.realtor.com, www.homegain.com, www.realestate.com, and www.zillow.com.

www.google.com
www.yahoo.com
www.realtor.com
www.homegain.com
www.realestate.com
www.zillow.com

FEDERAL DISCLOSURE REQUIREMENTS

What Is TRID?

The **TILA-RESPA Integrated Disclosure Rule** (TRID) consolidates four existing disclosures required under the **Truth in Lending Act** (TILA) and the **Real Estate Settlement Procedures Act** (RESPA) for closed-end credit transactions secured by real property into two forms: a *Loan Estimate* that must be delivered or placed in the mail no later than the third business day after receiving the consumer's application, and a *Closing Disclosure* that must be provided to the consumer at least three business days before consummation.

What Transactions Does TRID Cover?

TRID applies to most closed-end consumer credit transactions secured by real property. It does not apply to

- HELOCs,
- reverse mortgages, or
- chattel-dwelling loans, such as loans secured by a mobilehome or by a dwelling that is not attached to real property (i.e., land).

Consistent with the current rules under TILA, the rule also does not apply to loans made by a person or an entity that makes five or fewer mortgages in a calendar year.

However, certain types of loans that are currently subject to TILA but not RESPA are subject to TRID's requirements, including

- construction-only loans and
- loans secured by vacant land or by 25 or more acres.

What Are the TRID Record Retention Requirements?

The creditor must retain copies of the Closing Disclosure for five years after consummation. For evidence of compliance with the integrated disclosure provisions of Regulation Z, including the Loan Estimate, creditors must maintain records for three years after consummation of the transaction.

What Are the General Requirements for the Loan Estimate?

For closed-end credit transactions secured by real property (other than reverse mortgages), the creditor must provide the consumer with good-faith estimates of credit costs and transaction terms on a new form called the **Loan Estimate** (see Figure 8.9). This form integrates and replaces the existing Good-Faith Estimate (GFE) and the initial truth-in-lending disclosure for these transactions. The creditor is generally required to provide the Loan Estimate within three business days of the receipt of the consumer's loan application.

A *business day* is any day except Sundays and federal holidays. Some state-chartered lenders also recognize state holidays.

The Loan Estimate must also be delivered or placed in the mail no later than the seventh business day before consummation of the transaction. The consumer may modify or waive the seven-business-day waiting period after receiving the Loan Estimate if the consumer has a bona fide personal financial emergency that necessitates consummating the credit transaction before the end of the waiting period.

What Are the General Requirements for the Closing Disclosure?

For loans that require a Loan Estimate and that proceed to closing, creditors must provide a new final disclosure reflecting the actual terms of the transaction called the **Closing Disclosure**. The form integrates and replaces the existing Settlement Statement (HUD-1) and the final truth-in-lending disclosure for these transactions. The creditor is generally required to ensure that the consumer receives the Closing Disclosure no later than three business days before consummation of the loan. The Closing Disclosure form is described in detail in Unit 10.

New three-day waiting period   If the creditor provides a corrected disclosure, it may also be required to provide the consumer with an additional three-business-day waiting period before consummation.

May a Consumer Waive the Three-Business-Day Waiting Period?

Yes. Like the seven-business-day waiting period after receiving the Loan Estimate, consumers may waive or modify the three-business-day waiting period when

- the extension of credit is needed to meet a bona fide personal financial emergency;
- the consumer has received the Closing Disclosure; and
- the consumer gives the creditor a dated written statement that describes the emergency, specifically modifies or waives the waiting period, and bears the signature of all consumers who are primarily liable on the legal obligation.

FIGURE 8.9:   Loan Estimate

Save this Loan Estimate to compare with your Closing Disclosure.

Loan Estimate

DATE ISSUED
APPLICANTS

PROPERTY
SALE PRICE

LOAN TERM
PURPOSE
PRODUCT
LOAN TYPE   ☐ Conventional ☐ FHA ☐ VA ☐ _____
LOAN ID #
RATE LOCK   ☐ NO ☐ YES, until

Before closing, your interest rate, points, and lender credits can change unless you lock the interest rate. All other estimated closing costs expire on

Loan Terms	Can this amount increase after closing?
Loan Amount	
Interest Rate	
Monthly Principal & Interest *See Projected Payments below for your Estimated Total Monthly Payment*	
	Does the loan have these features?
Prepayment Penalty	
Balloon Payment	

Projected Payments

Payment Calculation	
Principal & Interest	
Mortgage Insurance	
Estimated Escrow *Amount can increase over time*	
Estimated Total Monthly Payment	
Estimated Taxes, Insurance & Assessments *Amount can increase over time*	**This estimate includes** **In escrow?** ☐ Property Taxes ☐ Homeowner's Insurance ☐ Other: *See Section G on page 2 for escrowed property costs. You must pay for other property costs separately.*

Costs at Closing

Estimated Closing Costs	Includes in Loan Costs + in Other Costs – in Lender Credits. *See page 2 for details.*
Estimated Cash to Close	Includes Closing Costs. *See Calculating Cash to Close on page 2 for details.*

Visit **www.consumerfinance.gov/mortgage-estimate** for general information and tools.

FIGURE 8.9:   Loan Estimate (continued)

Closing Cost Details

Loan Costs

A. Origination Charges

% of Loan Amount (Points)

B. Services You Cannot Shop For

C. Services You Can Shop For

D. TOTAL LOAN COSTS (A + B + C)

Other Costs

E. Taxes and Other Government Fees

Recording Fees and Other Taxes
Transfer Taxes

F. Prepaids

Homeowner's Insurance Premium (months)
Mortgage Insurance Premium (months)
Prepaid Interest (per day for   days @   )
Property Taxes (months)

G. Initial Escrow Payment at Closing

Homeowner's Insurance	per month for	mo.
Mortgage Insurance	per month for	mo.
Property Taxes	per month for	mo.

H. Other

I. TOTAL OTHER COSTS (E + F + G + H)

J. TOTAL CLOSING COSTS

D + I
Lender Credits

Calculating Cash to Close

Total Closing Costs (J)

Closing Costs Financed (Paid from your Loan Amount)

Down Payment/Funds from Borrower

Deposit

Funds for Borrower

Seller Credits

Adjustments and Other Credits

Estimated Cash to Close

Adjustable Payment (AP) Table

Interest Only Payments?	
Optional Payments?	
Step Payments?	
Seasonal Payments?	
Monthly Principal and Interest Payments	
First Change/Amount	
Subsequent Changes	
Maximum Payment	

Adjustable Interest Rate (AIR) Table

Index + Margin	
Initial Interest Rate	
Minimum/Maximum Interest Rate	
Change Frequency	
First Change	
Subsequent Changes	
Limits on Interest Rate Changes	
First Change	
Subsequent Changes	

FIGURE 8.9:   Loan Estimate (continued)

Additional Information About This Loan

LENDER	MORTGAGE BROKER
NMLS/___ LICENSE ID	NMLS/___ LICENSE ID
LOAN OFFICER	LOAN OFFICER
NMLS/___ LICENSE ID	NMLS/___ LICENSE ID
EMAIL	EMAIL
PHONE	PHONE

Comparisons	Use these measures to compare this loan with other loans.
In 5 Years	Total you will have paid in principal, interest, mortgage insurance, and loan costs. Principal you will have paid off.
Annual Percentage Rate (APR)	Your costs over the loan term expressed as a rate. This is not your interest rate.
Total Interest Percentage (TIP)	The total amount of interest that you will pay over the loan term as a percentage of your loan amount.

Other Considerations

Appraisal	We may order an appraisal to determine the property's value and charge you for this appraisal. We will promptly give you a copy of any appraisal, even if your loan does not close. You can pay for an additional appraisal for your own use at your own cost.
Assumption	If you sell or transfer this property to another person, we ☐ will allow, under certain conditions, this person to assume this loan on the original terms. ☐ will not allow assumption of this loan on the original terms.
Homeowner's Insurance	This loan requires homeowner's insurance on the property, which you may obtain from a company of your choice that we find acceptable.
Late Payment	If your payment is more than ___ days late, we will charge a late fee of _____
Refinance	Refinancing this loan will depend on your future financial situation, the property value, and market conditions. You may not be able to refinance this loan.
Servicing	We intend ☐ to service your loan. If so, you will make your payments to us. ☐ to transfer servicing of your loan.

Confirm Receipt

By signing, you are only confirming that you have received this form. You do not have to accept this loan because you have signed or received this form.

_____   _____   _____   _____
Applicant Signature   Date   Co-Applicant Signature   Date

The creditor is prohibited from providing the consumer with a preprinted waiver form.

When Must the Settlement Agent Provide the Closing Disclosure to the Seller?

The settlement agent must provide the seller its copy of the Closing Disclosure no later than the day of consummation.

When Must Creditors Deliver the Home Loan Toolkit?

Creditors must provide a copy of "Your Home Loan Toolkit: A Step-by-Step Guide" to consumers who apply for a consumer credit transaction secured by real property, except in certain circumstances (see below). This booklet is published by the Consumer Finance Protection Bureau to help consumers applying for federally related mortgage loans understand real estate transactions. The creditor need not provide the booklet if the consumer is applying for a real property-secured consumer credit transaction that does not have the purpose of purchasing a one-to four-family residential property (for example, refinancing, a closed-end loan secured by a subordinate lien, or a reverse mortgage).

Creditors must deliver the booklet or place it in the mail no later than three business days after receiving the consumer's loan application. When two or more persons apply together for a loan, the creditor may provide a copy of the booklet to just one of them.

Does TRID Require Any Other New Disclosures?

In addition to the disclosures discussed above, TRID also changes some other post-consummation disclosures provided to consumers by creditors and servicers: the *Escrow Closing Notice* and mortgage servicing transfer and partial payment notices.

For loans subject to the Escrow Closing Notice requirement, the creditor or servicer must provide consumers with a notice no later than three business days before the consumer's escrow account is canceled.

The Escrow Closing Notice must be provided before canceling an escrow account to any consumers for whom an escrow account was established in connection with a closed-end consumer credit transaction secured by a first lien on real property or a dwelling, except for reverse mortgages.

Impound Accounts

The lender may require that an **impound account** be established for the benefit of the borrower, to accumulate reserves for future recurring costs, such as property taxes and hazard insurance. The borrower's mortgage payments will be increased to cover contributions to the impound account, which is held in trust for the borrower's benefit by the lender.

An impound account may be *required* by a lender in California as a condition of loan approval on a loan secured by a single-family, owner-occupied dwelling, *only when*

- the loan amount is 90% or more of property value;

- combined loan amounts exceed 80% of property value;

- it is required by a state or federal regulatory authority;

- the loan is made, guaranteed, or insured by a state or federal governmental lending or insuring agency; or

- the borrower has failed to pay two consecutive tax installments on the property before the delinquency date for the payments (Civil Code Section 2954).

If both lender and borrower agree, an impound account can be established in other circumstances as well, but cannot be made a condition of loan approval. Homeowners who make use of an impound account should verify that amounts withheld are not excessive and also that property tax and other payments are made on time to avoid late payment penalties.

A **kickback** is an illegal fee paid by a nonlicensee (such as a loan officer) to a salesperson or broker.

The lender is not allowed to charge a fee for preparation or distribution of RESPA or TILA documents. The lender is also prohibited from paying a fee, kickback, rebate, or other thing of value to any person who does not provide loan services. (The same prohibitions also apply to title and escrow companies.)

Examples of loan services that may be compensated include counseling the borrower, comparing borrower housing needs with available mortgage loans, and keying information into a computerized loan origination system.

Consumer Communications

http://files.consumerfinance
.gov/f/201301_cfpb
_mortgage-servicing
-rules_what-it-means-for
-consumers.pdf

The Consumer Financial Protection Bureau (CFPB), created by the Dodd-Frank Act, has issued new mortgage disclosure rules that took effect January 10, 2014. A consumer information pamphlet, found at http://files.consumerfinance.gov/f/201301_cfpb_mortgage-servicing-rules_what-it-means-for-consumers.pdf, must be provided to the borrower. The pamphlet explains the information that the lender must provide to the borrower and also explains how the borrower can initiate a complaint if the lender is not following the rules. The lender must

- provide billing information in writing;

- give the borrower two months' warning if an adjustable-rate mortgage will have a rate change;

- promptly credit the borrower's payments;

- respond quickly when the borrower asks about paying off the loan;

- not charge for insurance the borrower doesn't need, or overcharge for insurance the lender provides if the borrower fails to do so ("force-placed insurance");

- quickly resolve complaints, generally within 30 to 45 business days, and share information;
- contact the borrower to help if the borrower is having trouble making payments and work with the borrower before starting or continuing fore-closure; and
- allow the borrower to seek review of the decision about a loan workout request.

OTHER LOAN CONSIDERATIONS

Loan Assumptions and "Subject To"

When property is sold or transferred, the existing loan may be *paid off* by the seller or *assumed* by the new owner (if the loan agreement allows). Another possibility is for the property to be taken *subject to* the loan (if the loan agreement allows).

In a loan **assumption**, the new borrower is substituted for the old borrower (the seller), releasing the seller from further obligation under the note. If a property is taken **subject to** the note, the seller will technically still be liable for the remaining indebtedness. If the buyer defaults, the lender can look to the seller (the former owner) for payment.

Taking possession subject to an existing loan benefits the buyer, who cannot be held liable for any deficiency judgment that might stem from a default on the loan. Loan costs are usually lower than what would be paid to obtain a new loan.

Loan Assignment

www.federalreserve.gov
/boarddocs/supmanual/cch
/til.pdf

The Helping Families Save Their Homes Act amended TILA in 2009 by requiring that consumers be notified of the sale or transfer of their mortgage loans. The party acquiring the loan, whether a purchaser or assignee, must provide the required disclosures no later than 30 days after the date on which the loan was acquired. The regularly updated *Consumer Compliance Handbook for Regulation Z* can be found at www.federalreserve.gov/boarddocs/supmanual/cch/til.pdf.

Acceleration and Due-on-Sale Clause

Most mortgages and trust deeds contain a provision that allows the lender to declare the remaining indebtedness due and payable on the happening of certain conditions. The loan can be "called" (the lender can demand full payment) if the borrower defaults by

- missing a payment,
- failing to pay taxes,
- committing waste by failing to maintain the property that is used for security, or
- using the property for an illegal purpose.

An **acceleration clause** may also be put into effect when the borrower relinquishes possession of the secured property by sale or transfer, preventing an assumption by a new owner. Use of such an **alienation or due-on-sale clause** has been the subject of much case law and legislation. At present, due-on-sale clauses are enforceable. Generally, loan agreements provide that fixed-rate mortgage loans are not assumable, but variable-interest-rate loans (which allow an increase of income to lenders if market conditions warrant) are assumable.

Construction Lending

The length and expense of the housing development process has resulted in several types of specialized loans. A **construction loan** (also called an **interim loan**) is one made to finance building construction or other improvements to land. Loan funds are usually made available to the builder in increments as the construction progresses. The builder may arrange for permanent financing for the property buyer in the form of a **take-out loan** for the buyer. The proceeds of the take-out loan are used to pay off the builder's construction loan.

To ensure that funds are available for prospective purchasers of the completed properties, a mortgage banker may make a **standby commitment** to a builder, agreeing to make mortgage loans at a stated price for a future time. The builder pays a **standby fee** for this privilege.

The Loan Application

A copy of the Uniform Residential Loan Application can be downloaded from www.fanniemae.com.

The **Uniform Residential Loan Application** (Form 1003) typically is used to qualify a prospective borrower purchasing a single-family residence. Form 1003 was prepared by Freddie Mac (formerly the Federal Home Loan Mortgage Corporation, or FHLMC) and Fannie Mae (FNMA, formerly the Federal National Mortgage Association), which are discussed in the next unit.

www.Equifax.com
www.experian.com
www.TransUnion.com

Use of a carefully drafted form helps ensure that the federal **Equal Credit Opportunity Act** is not violated. That act prohibits discrimination based on age, sex, race, color, marital status, religion, or national origin. All applicants must be considered in light of their income, the stability of the source of that income, total assets and liabilities, and their credit rating. The three major credit reporting agencies are Equifax, Experian, and TransUnion. Several companies have created methods of analyzing a borrower's credit reports to produce a credit score. One of these companies is Fair Isaac Corporation, headquartered in San Rafael, California, which produces a credit rating known as the **FICO score**. A borrower whose FICO score is in the highest range will be able to obtain financing at a lower interest rate than someone who has a FICO score in a lower range. Someone with a FICO score in the range of 760–850 is considered an excellent credit risk. An individual with a score below 620 is considered a very poor risk and will pay a much higher interest rate, assuming a loan can be obtained. More information about credit scoring, and how a credit score can be improved, can be found at www.myfico.com.

www.myfico.com

If a loan is rejected, the federal **Fair Credit Reporting Act** (FCRA) and state law require that the lender provide a statement to the loan applicant within 30 days detailing the reasons for the refusal. The loan applicant also has the right to a free copy of any credit report that was considered in the loan application process. California Civil Code Section 1785 provides credit reporting protections for victims of identity theft. If a victim of identity theft provides a police report or valid DMV investigative report of the violation to a consumer credit reporting agency, the victim is entitled to receive, free of charge, up to 12 copies of her credit file during a consecutive 12-month period, not to exceed one copy per month. The federal **Fair and Accurate Credit Transactions Act of 2003** (FACTA) amended FCRA by creating a procedure for victims of identity theft to include a *fraud alert* on their consumer credit reports. Numerous provisions of FACTA apply to lenders, insurers, landlords, and others. The text of the law is available at www.ftc.gov /os/statutes/031224fcra.pdf.

www.ftc.gov/os
/statutes/031224fcra.pdf

The loan application usually follows an interview with a loan officer of the lending institution. The interview is useful in explaining the loan procedure and initially qualifying the loan applicant. The next step is the loan officer's analysis, which includes the property being considered for purchase. An appraisal is made to ensure that the property will provide good security for the amount borrowed.

After the loan is approved, the necessary paperwork and funding are usually handled through an *escrow agent*, who makes sure that all parties have fulfilled their obligations before the transaction is closed. There is a detailed description of the obligations of buyer, seller, and escrow agent in Unit 10.

California Restrictions on Predatory Lending and Products

California's Covered Loan Law, found in Financial Code sections 4970-4979.8, applies to loans that do not exceed the maximum conforming limit established by Fannie Mae for owner-occupied one- to four-unit properties. The law restricts fees and points that may be charged to and paid by a borrower to no greater than 6% of the total loan amount, restricts prepayment penalties to no greater a term than 36 months, places limitations on loans that allow negative amortization, and includes additional restrictions against certain specific abusive lending practices, including prohibiting the origination for refinancing of any loan that fails to offer any benefit to the borrower. Effective January 1, 2010, three new restrictions designed to protect California homebuyers and borrowers from predatory lending practices were implemented. These provisions include the following:

- Mortgage brokers shall not steer, counsel, or direct a borrower to accept a loan at a higher cost than that for which the borrower could qualify based upon the loan programs regularly available to the broker.

- A mortgage broker who provides mortgage brokerage services for a borrower shall not receive compensation, including a yield spread premium, fee, commission, or any other compensation, for arranging a higher-priced mortgage loan with a prepayment penalty that exceeds the compensation that the mortgage broker would otherwise receive for arranging the higher-priced mortgage loan without a prepayment penalty.

- When providing mortgage brokerage services for a borrower, a mortgage broker shall receive the same compensation for providing those services whether paid by the lender, borrower, or a third party.

- No licensed person shall recommend or encourage default on an existing loan or other debt prior to and in connection with the closing or planned closing of a higher-priced mortgage loan that refinances all or any portion of the existing loan or debt.

- Negative amortization loans are banned for higher-priced mortgage loans (HPML), which are made to borrowers who do not qualify financially for other loans.

- Prepayment penalties are limited to no more than 2% of the loan balance.

- State regulators are allowed to enforce federal lending laws.

Combating Mortgage Fraud

Under its mandate from FACTA, the FTC has instituted an anti-fraud regulation called the *Red Flags Rule* that requires creditors and financial institutions to implement programs to identify, detect, and respond to the warning signs that could indicate identity theft. The financial regulatory agencies, including the FTC, developed the rule, which took effect on March 1, 2011. More information can be found at www.ftc.gov/redflagsrule.

www.ftc.gov/redflagsrule

The **Fraud Enforcement and Recovery Act of 2009** provides federal authorities with expanded legal powers against individuals and mortgage operations that previously have only been overseen at the state or local levels. The law has created a Financial Crisis Inquiry Commission with broad powers to investigate such topics as the subprime boom, Wall Street influence, and bank failures. The law devotes $650 million over two years to hire fraud prosecutors and investigators at the Justice Department; $140 million to increase the number of FBI officials for the agency's mortgage fraud task forces; $100 million to expand the staff of the U.S.

Attorney's office, and $80 million to expand the Justice Department's criminal, civil, and tax divisions.

www.PreventLoanScams.org

HUD, in partnership with the Loan Modification Scam Prevention Network, a national coalition of public and private enterprises, has created a website, www.PreventLoanScams.org, to which homeowners can report questionable practices. The site is designed to help establish a national complaint database for federal, state, and local governments. Information available at the site includes a state-by-state breakdown of resources available to consumers.

SUMMARY

Buyers use the **leverage** afforded by credit to finance the purchase of all forms of real estate. The availability of loan funds is influenced by the cyclical nature of our economy and regulated by the Federal Reserve Board.

The Office of Thrift Supervision (OTS) regulates the savings and loan industry. The **Federal Housing Finance Agency** (FHFA) oversees the Federal Home Loan Banks, which lend funds to member institutions.

Recent legislation to promote recovery from the recent economic (and housing) downturn includes the **Housing and Economic Recovery Act of 2008** (HERA) and the **American Recovery and Reinvestment Act of 2009** (ARRA). HERA includes the **Secure and Fair Enforcement for Mortgage Licensing Act** (SAFE Act), which requires reporting and recordation of those who make, arrange, or service loans secured by real property. California and federal laws impose special requirements on the **residential mortgage loan originator** (MLO).

Usury laws prohibit the charging of exorbitant rates of interest. Proposition 2 and the deregulation act exempt from the usury laws loans secured by real estate and made by most lenders.

Real estate financing is made possible by use of a **promissory note** in conjunction with a **security instrument** that *hypothecates* the real estate against which money is borrowed. Cosigners on a promissory note may have **joint and several liability**. A promissory note can be sold or transferred. If a promissory note meets the requirements for a **negotiable instrument**, a subsequent **holder in due course** can defeat most defenses to its enforcement.

The *deed of trust* is the security instrument of choice in California, although the *mortgage* also may be used. Notice must be given in the event of the borrower's default. The **judicial foreclosure** of a mortgage is a longer process than a **trustee's sale**, and there is no **right of redemption** following a trustee's sale. A mortgage with a **power-of-sale clause** also will avoid a judicial foreclosure.

The primary mortgage market consists of both institutional and noninstitutional lenders. **Institutional lenders** include thrifts, commercial banks, mutual savings banks, credit unions, and insurance companies. Noninstitutional lenders include mortgage companies and private individuals. Nonfinancial institutions, such as colleges and universities, pension funds, and trusts, also carry real estate loans, although not usually as part of the primary mortgage market.

Mortgage brokers are subject to the **Real Property Loan Law**. They must complete and deliver a mortgage loan disclosure statement to borrowers for signature before the transaction is completed.

The **Truth in Lending Act (Regulation Z)** imposes disclosure requirements on consumer credit transactions and restricts advertising of credit terms. The required disclosure statement includes all details of financing, including the **annual percentage rate** (APR), which may be much higher than the **nominal rate**. A consumer has the right to cancel a credit transaction involving a security interest in the consumer's principal dwelling within a three-business-day period, or longer if the interest rate changes before closing.

TRID requires a **Home Loan Toolkit** and a **Loan Estimate** detailing estimated closing costs. A **Closing Disclosure** must be supplied no later than three business days before consummation of the loan.

Some loans may be **assumed** or property may be sold **subject to** the loan. **Acceleration or due-on-sale clauses** are enforceable by lenders. Loan application policies must comply with the **Equal Credit Opportunity Act** and the **Fair Credit Reporting Act**, as well as state law.

OPEN FOR DISCUSSION

When property values rose to dizzying heights in Japan, lenders began to make loans with up to 100-year terms.

1. Do you see such loans in California's future?
2. In what ways can lenders help keep loan costs down?

REVIEW QUESTIONS

1. A $450,000 house can be purchased with a $90,000 down payment using the principle of
   a. borrowed funds.
   b. leveraging.
   c. partial financing.
   d. home equity.

2. The Fed can increase or decrease the amount of money in circulation by all of the following EXCEPT
   a. establishing the discount rate.
   b. issuing government securities.
   c. raising or lowering reserve requirements.
   d. buying and selling government securities.

3. Federal savings and loan activities are overseen by
   a. the FHLMC.
   b. the Office of the Comptroller of the Currency.
   c. the Federal Reserve Board.
   d. the FDIC.

4. California usury laws apply primarily to
   a. financial institutions.
   b. all lenders.
   c. nonfinancial institutions.
   d. private lenders.

5. Real estate is hypothecated by use of
   a. a promissory note.
   b. a negotiable instrument.
   c. a security instrument.
   d. a pledge.

6. To be a negotiable instrument, a promissory note must be
   a. a promise to pay money to the bearer.
   b. an oral agreement.
   c. payable at an indefinite future time.
   d. signed by the bearer.

7. A holder in due course must take a negotiable instrument
   a. within 90 days of its execution.
   b. with knowledge of all defenses against it.
   c. without notice of any defense against its enforcement.
   d. for cash.

8. In a mortgage, the lender is
   a. the mortgagor.
   b. the mortgagee.
   c. the maker.
   d. the holder.

9. The highest bidder at a judicial foreclosure receives
   a. a deed.
   b. a contract.
   c. a title.
   d. a certificate of sale.

10. In a deed of trust, the borrower is
    a. the trustor.
    b. the trustee.
    c. the beneficiary.
    d. the holder.

11. In a deed of trust, the lender is
    a. the trustor.
    b. the trustee.
    c. the beneficiary.
    d. the holder.

12. The first step in bringing about a trustee's sale is to prepare
    a. a declaration of default.
    b. a notice of levy.
    c. a request for notice.
    d. a notice of default.

13. There is no right of redemption following
    a. a strict foreclosure.
    b. a trustee's sale.
    c. a judicial foreclosure.
    d. a mortgage foreclosure.

14. An ARM is
    a. a graduated payment mortgage.
    b. a growing equity mortgage.
    c. a mortgage in which the interest rate changes periodically based on an index.
    d. a reverse annuity mortgage.

15. MOST adjustable-rate loans are
    a. assumable.
    b. not assumable.
    c. held by sellers.
    d. not allowed for federal institutions.

16. Interest rate and payment can change every three to five years in
    a. a graduated payment mortgage.
    b. a renegotiable-rate mortgage.
    c. a growing equity mortgage.
    d. a reverse annuity mortgage.

17. TRID applies to
    a. HELOCs.
    b. construction-only loans.
    c. loans made by a person who makes five or fewer mortgages in a calendar year.
    d. reverse mortgages.

18. RESPA covers
    a. the listing agreement.
    b. the broker's commission.
    c. the Closing Disclosure form.
    d. the loan application form.

19. David Yoo bought Whiteacre and is making the former owner's original loan payments. If David defaults, the seller will be obligated on the loan. Which statement is *TRUE*?
    a. David bought the loan.
    b. David bought the property subject to the loan.
    c. David is subject to a due-on-sale clause.
    d. David does not have title to Whiteacre.

20. A lender that discriminates against a loan applicant because of race has violated
    a. the Equal Dignities Rule.
    b. the Truth in Lending Act.
    c. the Equal Credit Opportunity Act.
    d. the Lender's Law.

UNIT NINE

GOVERNMENT-SPONSORED AND OTHER FINANCING

LEARNING OBJECTIVES

When you have completed this unit, you will be able to

- **state** the eligibility requirements for an FHA-insured, VA-guaranteed, and CalVet home loan;

- **list** the loan fees involved with the FHA-insured, VA-guaranteed, and CalVet home loan;

- **describe** the forms of creative financing;

- **explain** how the secondary mortgage market aids homebuyers; and

- **describe** several ways in which the Economic Stimulus Act of 2008 helped homebuyers.

KEY TERMS

all-inclusive trust deed
  (AITD)
California Housing
  Finance Agency
  (CalHFA)
California Veterans
  Farm and Home
  Purchase Program
  (CalVet)
certificate of eligibility
conforming loan
conventional loans
creative financing
Department of
  Housing and Urban
  Development
  (HUD)
Department of
  Veterans Affairs
  (VA)

Direct Endorsement
  Plan
discount points
Economic Stimulus
  Act of 2008
Electronic Signatures
  in Global and
  National Commerce
  Act
Fannie Mae
Farmer Mac
Federal Housing
  Administration
  (FHA)
Federal Housing
  Finance Agency
  (FHFA)
Freddie Mac
Ginnie Mae
installment sales
  contract

interest rate reduction
  refinancing loan
  (IRRRL)
land contract
leaseback
mortgage-backed
  securities
mortgage insurance
  premium
overriding trust deed
purchase-money
  mortgage
purchase-money trust
  deed
sale-leaseback
secondary mortgage
  market
veteran's entitlement
wraparound mortgage
wraparound trust deed

GOVERNMENT-SPONSORED FINANCING

Loans that do *not* involve government cooperation are called **conventional loans**. Loans that are created or financed with the help of a government source are *nonconventional loans*, and they are the focus of this unit. Both federal and state programs are discussed.

Federal Housing Administration

The **National Housing Act** was passed in 1934 in response to the numerous foreclosures brought about by the Depression and has been amended many times since. One of the agencies created by the National Housing Act was the **Federal Housing Administration** (FHA), a division of the **Department of Housing and Urban Development** (HUD). FHA does not make loans, but it *insures* loans made by lending institutions such as thrifts, banks, life insurance companies, mortgage companies, and others. For 60 years, FHA has been a major force in determining how lending practices are carried out. Information about HUD and FHA programs can be found at www.hud.gov, www.fha.com, or by calling 1-800-CALLFHA. The HOPE Hotline, 1-888-995-HOPE or www.995HOPE.org, provides free mortgage counseling in English and other languages, 24 hours a day, seven days a week.

www.hud.gov
www.fha.com
www.995HOPE.org

Section 203 *Section 203* of Title II of the National Housing Act specifies eligibility requirements for federal mortgage insurance for housing construction and finance. *Section 203(b)* covers mortgages on one- to four-family homes. *Section*

203(k) covers loans for property renovation. FHA insures approximately seven million loans valued at almost $400 billion through this and its other programs.

FHA-insured loan limits Insured loan amounts are adjusted annually to reflect changes to the maximum amount allowed for loans that are held or backed by the organizations, such as Fannie Mae and Freddie Mac, which comprise the secondary mortgage market, discussed later in this unit. FHA-insured loan limits are set at 65%–150% of the limit for loans purchased on the secondary market, with the higher loan limits available for higher-cost areas. For 2017, the maximum FHA-insured loan on a California single-family home range from $275,665 to $636,150, as shown in Figure 9.1. The maximum also is higher for property in Alaska, Hawaii, Guam, and the U.S. Virgin Islands. The selling price of a home can be higher than the maximum amount stated, but FHA insurance will not cover the excess. *Condominium* loan limits are approximately the same as those for single-family residences in the same county. Higher limits apply to two- to four-unit properties. Current loan limits can be found at www.fha.com /lending_limits_state?state=CALIFORNIA.

www.fha.com
/lending_limits
_state?state=CALIFORNIA

Legislation raising FHA loan limits created the FHA Forward program. FHA also has the Home Equity Conversion Mortgage (HECM), a reverse mortgage program for homeowners age 62 or older, and loans available through the HOPE for Homeowners program, a refinancing plan for homeowners having difficulty making mortgage payments but who can afford a new FHA-insured loan.

Total cash investment The minimum cash investment made by a borrower on an FHA-insured loan must be at least 3.5% of the sales price, provided the borrower has a credit score of at least 580. If the borrower has a credit score of 500 to 579, the required down payment is 10%, although other factors, such as late payments on existing debts, may result in denial of the loan application by FHA. A borrower with a credit score of less than 500 is ineligible for FHA-insured financing.

Mortgage insurance premium and monthly fee FHA-insured loans have both an up-front **mortgage insurance premium** (MIP) that is paid to FHA at closing as well as an annual renewal fee, which is paid on a monthly basis. The up-front MIP is not considered an acquisition cost of the loan in computing down payment. The premium may be paid by the borrower or someone else, or it may be included in the loan amount. Presently, the FHA MIP is 1.75% of the loan amount for all purchase loans and 2% for home equity loans. The MIP is refunded if a loan is prepaid (paid in full before the end of the loan term).

FIGURE 9.1: FHA Loan Limits for 2017

County Name	One-Family	Two-Family	Three-Family	Four-Family
ALAMEDA	$636,150	$814,500	$984,525	$1,223,475
ALPINE	$463,450	$593,300	$717,150	$891,250
AMADOR	$332,350	$425,450	$514,300	$639,150
BUTTE	$293,250	$375,400	$453,750	$563,950
CALAVERAS	$373,750	$478,450	$578,350	$718,750

FIGURE 9.1: **FHA Loan Limits for 2017 (continued)**

County Name	One-Family	Two-Family	Three-Family	Four-Family
COLUSA	$275,665	$352,950	$426,625	$530,150
CONTRA COSTA	$636,150	$814,500	$984,525	$1,223,475
DEL NORTE	$275,665	$352,950	$426,625	$530,150
EL DORADO	$488,750	$625,700	$756,300	$939,900
FRESNO	$281,750	$360,700	$436,000	$541,800
GLENN	$275,665	$352,950	$426,625	$530,150
HUMBOLDT	$327,750	$419,550	$507,150	$630,300
IMPERIAL	$275,665	$352,950	$426,625	$530,150
INYO	$369,150	$472,550	$571,250	$709,900
KERN	$275,665	$352,950	$426,625	$530,150
KINGS	$275,665	$352,950	$426,625	$530,150
LAKE	$275,665	$352,950	$426,625	$530,150
LASSEN	$275,665	$352,950	$426,625	$530,150
LOS ANGELES	$636,150	$814,500	$984,525	$1,223,475
MADERA	$275,665	$352,950	$426,625	$530,150
MARIN	$636,150	$814,500	$984,525	$1,223,475
MARIPOSA	$322,000	$412,200	$498,250	$619,250
MENDOCINO	$373,750	$478,450	$578,350	$718,750
MERCED	$275,665	$352,950	$426,625	$530,150
MODOC	$275,665	$352,950	$426,625	$530,150
MONO	$529,000	$677,200	$818,600	$1,017,300
MONTEREY	$575,000	$736,100	$889,800	$1,105,800
NAPA	$636,150	$814,500	$984,525	$1,223,475
NEVADA	$477,250	$610,950	$738,500	$917,800
ORANGE	$636,150	$814,500	$984,525	$1,223,475
PLACER	$488,750	$625,700	$756,300	$939,900
PLUMAS	$336,950	$431,350	$521,400	$648,000
RIVERSIDE	$379,500	$485,800	$587,250	$729,800
SACRAMENTO	$488,750	$625,700	$756,300	$939,900
SAN BENITO	$636,150	$814,500	$984,525	$1,223,475
SAN BERNARDINO	$379,500	$485,800	$587,250	$729,800
SAN DIEGO	$612,950	$784,700	$948,500	$1,178,750
SAN FRANCISCO	$636,150	$814,500	$984,525	$1,223,475
SAN JOAQUIN	$362,250	$463,750	$560,550	$696,650
SAN LUIS OBISPO	$586,500	$750,800	$907,550	$1,127,900
SAN MATEO	$636,150	$814,500	$984,525	$1,223,475
SANTA BARBARA	$636,150	$814,500	$984,525	$1,223,475
SANTA CLARA	$636,150	$814,500	$984,525	$1,223,475
SANTA CRUZ	$636,150	$814,500	$984,525	$1,223,475
SHASTA	$275,665	$352,950	$426,625	$530,150
SIERRA	$304,750	$390,100	$471,550	$586,050

FIGURE 9.1:   FHA Loan Limits for 2017 (continued)

County Name	One-Family	Two-Family	Three-Family	Four-Family
SISKIYOU	$275,665	$352,950	$426,625	$530,150
SOLANO	$431,250	$552,050	$667,350	$829,350
SONOMA	$595,700	$762,600	$921,800	$1,145,600
STANISLAUS	$299,000	$382,750	$462,650	$575,000
SUTTER	$276,000	$353,300	$427,100	$530,750
TEHAMA	$275,665	$352,950	$426,625	$530,150
TRINITY	$275,665	$352,950	$426,625	$530,150
TULARE	$275,665	$352,950	$426,625	$530,150
TUOLUMNE	$331,200	$424,000	$512,500	$636,900
VENTURA	$603,750	$772,900	$934,250	$1,161,050
YOLO	$488,750	$625,700	$756,300	$939,900
YUBA	$276,000	$353,300	$427,100	$530,750

Source: Federal Housing Administration

The annual insurance charge, which is paid in monthly increments, depends on the loan amount, loan term, and the loan-to-value ratio (LTV).

The following table shows the current annual MIP rates by amortization term, base loan amount and loan-to-value (LTV) ratio. These MIP amounts became effective for FHA loans originated on or after January 26, 2015. Rates will remain in effect until and unless revised by FHA as authorized by Congress.

Loan Terms Greater Than 15 Years		
Base Loan Amount	**LTV**	**MIP**
$625,500 or less	95.0% or less	0.80%
$625,500 or less	Over 95.0%	0.85%
Over $625,500	95.0% or less	1.00%
Over $625,500	Over 95.0%	1.05%

Loan Terms 15 Years or Less		
Base Loan Amount	**LTV**	**MIP**
$625,500 or less	90.0% or less	0.45%
$625,500 or less	Over 90.0%	0.70%
Over $625,500	78.0% or less	0.45%
Over $625,500	78.01% - 90.00%	0.70%
Over $625,500	Over 90.0%	0.95%

FHA insurance may be canceled for loans originated after January 1, 2001. For loans that originated before June 3, 2013, the FHA monthly mortgage insurance payments automatically terminate when one of these conditions is met:

- If the mortgage term is 15 years or less and the loan-to-value ratio was 90% at the time of origination, the annual premium will be canceled when the loan-to-value ratio reaches 78%, regardless of the amount of time the borrower has paid the premiums.

■ If the mortgage term is more than 15 years, the annual premium will be canceled when the loan-to-value ratio reaches 78%, provided the borrower has paid the annual premium for at least five years.

For loans that originated on June 3, 2013, or later, the following apply:

■ If the original mortgage term was 15 years or less and the original LTV was 78% or less, the mortgage insurance premium will be terminated after 11 years. If the original LTV was greater than 90%, the mortgage insurance premium will continue for the loan term.

■ If the original loan term was greater than 15 years and the original LTV was not greater than 90%, the mortgage insurance premium will be terminated after 11 years. If the original LTV was greater than 90% the mortgage insurance premium will continue for the loan term.

Interest rate and loan term   The interest rate may rise or fall with prevailing market rates. The *loan term* may not be longer than 35 years if the loan is approved before construction, or 30 years otherwise. The 30-year term has been the most popular with lenders and borrowers, but shorter-term loans are beginning to gain favor. Generally, loans must be fully amortized in equal monthly payments that include both principal and interest. Monthly payments also include impounds for taxes, special assessments, and fire or other hazard insurance.

Prepayment penalty   FHA-insured loans have *no* prepayment penalties.

| One discount point is 1% of the loan amount paid up front. |

Points   A lender can charge **discount points** (prepaid interest) to the borrower in addition to the 1% loan fee. Discount points are the lender's way of increasing loan income while keeping the interest rate at a competitive level. One discount point equals one percentage point of the loan amount.

Discount points are paid at closing by the borrower or someone else. Usually the seller pays discount points to increase the lender's effective yield, even though the borrower may be offered a lower-than-market interest rate. On loans of the same amount and term, one discount point increases the overall yield on a loan by approximately 1/8%. Thus, a loan at 7% and three discount points effectively earns 73/8% for the lender.

F O R   E X A M P L E   Joe Dash is selling his single-family residence in Solano County. Harold Maloney and Barbara Clark have offered $159,000, contingent on their securing FHA-insured financing. Joe accepts the offer. A lender approached by Maloney and Clark is willing to make a loan of the maximum FHA-insurable amount of $151,725, to carry an interest rate of 7½%, with two discount points to be paid at closing, when the loan is funded. What is the amount of the discount points, and who will pay them?

The discount points are valued at $3,035 ($151,725 × 2%) and are payable as stipulated in the agreement between the buyers and Joe Dash.

Discount points are a matter for negotiation between buyer and seller. Regardless of who pays, the contract of sale should stipulate who will pay and set a limit on the number of discount points that will be paid.

Seller-funded down payment assistance programs   Effective October 1, 2008, FHA prohibits the use of down payment assistance programs funded by those who have a financial interest in the sale, such as the property seller. Programs provided by nonprofits or funded by other sources, such as churches, employers, or family members, are still allowed. Allowable seller concessions, such as payment of discount points, cannot exceed 6% of the home purchase price.

Types of loans available   In addition to the traditional fixed-rate amortized loan, FHA allows use of a *graduated payment mortgage (GPM)*. The GPM is available for families who expect income to increase over the loan term and who otherwise would not qualify for a mortgage loan. Only single-family residences are eligible. With a GPM, monthly payments do *not* cover all of the interest due. The unpaid interest is added to the remaining balance of principal owed. This *negative amortization* process continues for five to ten years, depending on which of five different GPM plans is used. At that point, monthly payments stay the same to the end of the loan term and are fully amortized. Because interest is paid on interest, the statute specifically preempts any state usury laws that might be violated.

FHA allows an *adjustable-rate mortgage (ARM)* for owner-occupied residences of no more than four units. The rate of interest charged is adjusted by increases in monthly payment, outstanding principal balance, loan term, or a combination of the three. Maximum loan term is 40 years. Adjustment of the interest rate must correspond to a specified national interest rate index. Adjustments of no more than 1% of the outstanding loan balance may be made annually, with an increase of no more than 5% over the initial contract interest rate over the life of the loan. At the time of application, the borrower must be given a written explanation of the loan features and possible rate and payment increases over the loan term. FHA also allows a *shared appreciation mortgage (SAM)* for a dwelling of one to four units.

Buyer Qualification for an FHA Loan

The following rules are aimed at reducing the number of defaults on FHA-insured loans, in addition to preventing defaulting borrowers from acquiring more credit:

- Total *seller* contributions, including discounts, buydown costs, and closing costs, cannot exceed 6% of acquisition cost.

- The *borrower* must be qualified at the *full note rate,* rather than the buydown rate.

The borrower's *Social Security number* must be supplied on the loan application to assist in reporting of delinquent and foreclosed loans to other federal agencies and to credit bureaus.

HUD Direct Endorsement Plan   Under HUD's **Direct Endorsement Plan,** qualified lenders may process a loan without prior HUD review, except for construction projects. This program thus eliminates the lengthy processing time that is one of the major drawbacks of the federally insured loan.

National Housing Trust Fund The Housing and Economic Recovery Act of 2008 (HERA) created the National Housing Trust Fund (NHTF), to be funded by a percentage of profits from the government-sponsored enterprises mentioned later in this unit. The NHTF is intended to provide revenue to communities to build, preserve, and rehabilitate affordable rental homes for extremely and very low-income households. The first state allocations, to be made in 2016, total $173.6 million; California's allocation is $10,128,143, to be administered by the California Department of Housing and Community Development. More information on NHTF is at www.nlihc.org /issues/nhtf.

www.nlihc.org/issues/nhtf

Department of Veterans Affairs

The *Servicemember's Readjustment Act of 1944* (the GI Bill of Rights) helped ease the transition into civilian life of World War II veterans. The programs later were expanded to include veterans of subsequent conflicts. The GI Bill also covers the surviving spouse of an eligible person who died as the result of a service-connected injury, and the surviving spouse of a person missing in action or listed as a prisoner of war for more than 90 days. Benefits are available as long as the surviving spouse remains unmarried. Information on the GI Bill is at www.gibill.va.gov.

www.gibill.va.gov

The **Department of Veterans Affairs** (VA) presently authorizes first mortgage loans as well as second-mortgage loans of less than 40% of property value. The VA *guarantees* payment of the remaining mortgage indebtedness, up to a maximum amount. If the borrower defaults, the VA will pay the lender's net loss up to the amount of the guarantee, which is decreased proportionately as the loan amount is repaid. There is no cost to the borrower for the VA guarantee.

www.va.gov
www.benefits.va.gov
/homeloans/

The VA also makes loans to veterans directly in areas where there are few mortgage lenders. Because of the abundance of financing sources in this state, there are no direct VA loans to veterans in California.

Borrower qualifications VA-guaranteed loans are available to those men and women who served in the U.S. armed forces and were other than dishonorably discharged and to their spouses, as mentioned above. The period of active duty required varies, depending on the date of service—90 days during wartime and 181 days otherwise for those who served up to September 7, 1980 (enlisted) or October 16, 1981 (officer). Veterans who served after those dates must have completed 24 months of continuous active duty or the full period (at least 181 days) for which they were called to duty, or have been discharged for a service-connected disability or in certain other cases. Veterans with service during the Gulf War period and subsequent conflicts (August 2, 1990, to a date yet to be determined) must have completed 24 months of continuous active duty or the full period (at least 90 days) for which they were called to active duty or have been discharged for a service-connected disability or in certain other cases.

Lending institutions are able to screen VA loan applicants for eligibility as part of the loan qualification process. Supervised lenders verify the veteran's entitlement, then process the loan as usual. There is no need for VA review and approval.

The certificate of eligibility shows the veteran's entitlement.

An interested veteran should request a **certificate of eligibility** from the nearest VA regional office in advance of loan application. The certificate will indicate the amount of loan guarantee, called the **veteran's entitlement**, available to the veteran. If VA records indicate sufficient data on the veteran, an automated certificate of eligibility (ACE) can be obtained by a lender using the internet, and the certificate will be issued online within a few seconds.

The Native American Direct Loan (NADL) program helps Native American Veterans purchase, construct, improve, or refinance a home on Native American trust lands. The veteran's tribal organization must participate in the VA direct loan program and the veteran must have a valid certificate of eligibility.

Loan guarantee amount   VA-guaranteed loans can be made for purchase, construction, repair, or improvement of a veteran's dwelling, which can be a building of one to four units or a condominium. The basic veteran's entitlement is $36,000. For loans in excess of $144,000 to purchase or construct a home, the entitlement is up to 25% of the loan limit set by the VA for a single-family home. In California, for loans closed in the calendar year 2016, the limit ranges from $417,000 up to $1,202,925 for a four-unit dwelling, based on the median sales price of the county. For 2017, the limit ranges from $431,250 to $636,150 for a single-family home, with corresponding increases on two- to four-unit dwellings.

The VA makes a Specially Adapted Housing (SAH) or Special Housing Adaptation (SHA) grant available to service people and veterans with certain total and permanent disabilities related to their military service. The maximum amount allowable for an SAH grant in 2016 is $73,768. The maximum amount allowable for an SHA grant in 2016 is $14,754. The maximum is subject to adjustment upward annually based on a cost-of-construction index. No individual may use the grant benefit more than three times, up to the maximum amount.

Restoration of entitlement   The amount of a veteran's entitlement can be restored once, if the veteran refinances a VA loan with a conventional loan. The veteran's entitlement is increased to the *full* amount if

- the property is disposed of and VA-guaranteed loan is paid in full;
- the VA is released from liability on the original loan;
- any loss suffered by the VA has been repaid in full; or
- the property is transferred to another veteran who is entitled to VA home loan guarantee benefits.

There must be a *release* from personal liability to the government on a VA loan *before* an assumption of the loan by a purchaser of the property. Otherwise, the veteran remains liable under the original terms of the guarantee. *Such a release should be a condition of the sale, specified in the contract.* If the property is *foreclosed* and there has been no act of fraud, misrepresentation, or bad faith by the veteran, the VA can release the veteran from further liability.

> The NOV sets the maximum loan amount the VA will guarantee.

Notice of value The lender will request a determination of reasonable value from one of a panel of VA-recommended appraisers, who will provide a notice of value (NOV), formerly called a certificate of reasonable value, for the subject property. The veteran must be given a copy of the NOV *before* signing a contract of sale, *or* the contract should include a contingency that the veteran be able to either affirm or withdraw from the transaction without penalty if the NOV value is less than the purchase price.

Types of loans available Veterans have had a choice of four payment plans:

- *Fixed-term* is a fully amortized mortgage for up to 30 years and 32 days.

- *Adjustable-rate mortgage (ARM)* is similar to the FHA program but based on the Treasury Securities index on loans initiated before October 1, 1995. These loans are no longer available.

- *Growing equity mortgage (GEM)* is tied to an index and results in increases in payments with the increases applied to the principal balance. The GEM is a formalized way of making additional principal payments, which increases the accumulation of equity and shortens the overall loan term.

- *Graduated payment mortgage (GPM)* provides for lower initial monthly payments, increasing at a rate of 7% annually for the first five years. From the sixth year to the end of the loan term, the payments remain the same. Unlike FHA, which allows four other variations of the GPM, the VA allows only this one form of graduated payment.

Some restrictions apply on *manufactured home loans*. The manufactured home must be at least 40 feet long and 10 feet wide, with a minimum of 400 square feet, and installed on a permanent foundation. The maximum loan term for the purchase of a single-wide manufactured home, with or without a lot, is 15 years and 32 days. The maximum loan term for the purchase of a double-wide manufactured home, with or without a lot, is 20 years and 32 days.

Interest rate The VA now allows borrowers to negotiate the interest rate on a VA-guaranteed loan with the lender.

Down payment and closing costs As long as the estimate of reasonable value does not exceed the amount of the VA loan guarantee, the VA does not require a down payment, although the lender may. The VA loan guarantee can never be more than the estimate of reasonable value, but a higher purchase price may be negotiated *if* the veteran pays the difference between the reasonable value and the purchase price in cash at the closing. The cash must come from the personal resources of the veteran and not from secondary financing.

On the first use of a VA-guaranteed loan with a down payment of less than 5%, a funding fee of 2.15% of the loan amount is charged (2.4% for veterans of the reserves or National Guard) on loans closed on or after November 22, 2011, through September 29, 2024. With a down payment of at least 5% but less than 10%, the fee is 1.50% (or 1.75%). With a down payment of 10% or more, the fee is reduced to 1.25% (or 1.50%). Subsequent use of a VA-guaranteed loan carries a higher funding fee, presently 3.3% for all veterans making a down payment of less than 5%, 1.5% (or 1.75%) with a down payment of at least 5% but less than 10%, and 1.25% (or 1.5%) with a down payment of 10% or more.

There is a funding fee of 1% for all manufactured home loans.

The veteran can pay *discount points,* which are subject to negotiation with the lender. Veterans are permitted to finance discount points.

Refinancing   An existing VA loan can be *refinanced* with a VA-guaranteed **interest rate reduction refinance loan** (IRRRL). The reasons for the refinancing, which must be acceptable to the lender, can include repairs or improvements to the property or providing the veteran with funds for educational purposes.

A veteran can refinance an existing VA loan *if* the new loan will carry a lower interest rate. The amount refinanced cannot exceed the remaining balance of the existing loan *plus* allowable closing costs (which may include discount points). The amount financed cannot be greater than the original amount guaranteed, and the overall loan term must remain the same. No additional amount will be charged against the veteran's entitlement.

On a refinancing loan, the funding fee is .5% in all cases.

Loan servicing   The VA is available to help a veteran even after a loan is secured if the veteran is having a problem making loan payments. If a loan is delinquent three months, a *notice of default* alerts the VA to the situation. Financial counseling is provided to help the veteran pay arrearages and avoid future missed payments.

FHA vs. VA Loans

At present, there are fewer distinctions between FHA-insured and VA-guaranteed loans than there have been in the past. The differences that still exist involve the following factors.

Loan purpose   Both FHA-insured and VA-guaranteed loans are available for first mortgages of owner-occupied property. VA loans also include junior liens for repairs or improvements. Although FHA technically allows some types of secondary financing, for all practical purposes the FHA market is first mortgages only.

Loan amount   VA guarantee limits do not set the upper limit of the loan amount. FHA loan maximums are exactly that.

Interest rate   Both VA and FHA allow lenders and borrowers to negotiate the interest rate offered, which can vary from lender to lender. Both FHA and VA allow a variety of loan types.

Down payment   VA generally does not require a down payment, although the lender may. FHA requires a down payment of at least 3.5% of the sales price or appraised value, whichever is less.

Down payment and closing costs usually are lower on a VA-guaranteed loan than on an FHA-insured loan.

Service charges FHA allows a service charge of 1% on loans involving existing buildings and 2% on loans for buildings to be constructed. Buyers can be charged discount points, which are a subject for buyer-seller negotiation. Seller contributions cannot be more than 6% of acquisition cost as of March 2012. The buyer also can be charged an FHA application fee and fees for credit report, appraisal, and other closing costs.

VA allows lenders to charge reasonable costs, including credit report, survey, title evidence, and recording fees. The VA does not have a charge for mortgage insurance, but loan origination costs can be included in a flat charge that cannot exceed 1% of the loan amount for most properties. In certain cases, the veteran may be charged discount points. The VA funding fee depends on the down payment and origination date.

Loan prepayment Both agencies allow full or partial prepayment of principal at any time. The VA does require that any prepayment be at least $100 or the amount of one installment.

Refinancing to avoid default Both FHA and VA loans can be refinanced to avoid imminent default, so that payments may be extended beyond the initial loan term. VA loans can be refinanced only if 80% or more of the new loan will be paid within the original loan term limit. The FHA loan term on refinancing can be no more than three-quarters of the remaining economic life of the building. HERA has provided a refinancing program for homebuyers with problematic subprime loans, allowing lenders to write down qualified mortgages to 90% of current appraised value and providing qualified borrowers a new FHA 30-year fixed-rate mortgage at 90% of appraised value, up to a maximum loan amount of $550,440. Borrowers share 50% of all future appreciation with FHA.

The *Helping Families Save Their Homes Act*, which was signed into law by President Obama on May 20, 2009, gives FHA more enforcement capabilities against lenders who use false or misleading marketing tactics.

RESPA Note one final similarity between FHA-insured and VA-guaranteed loans. Because both are federally related, both fall within the requirements of the Real Estate Settlement Procedures Act (RESPA), discussed in Unit 8, in addition to all other disclosure requirements. A HUD settlement statement noting transaction charges for both buyer and seller appears in Unit 10.

California Veterans Farm and Home Purchase Program

The **California Veterans Farm and Home Purchase Program** (CalVet) was created in 1921 to assist California veterans in acquiring home or farm property. The program is included in Division 4, Unit 6, of the Military and Veterans Code.

www.cdva.ca.gov

CalVet loans are administered by the California Department of Veterans Affairs (CDVA), found at www.cdva.ca.gov. CDVA authorizes, processes, funds, and services the loans. No outside lenders are involved, because the program is totally self-supporting. Funds for CalVet loans come from voter-approved State General Obligation Bonds and Revenue Bonds issued by the legislature.

CDVA buys the selected property from the seller and resells the property to the veteran on a land contract (explained later in this unit). CDVA holds title until the veteran has repaid the amount owed, although the veteran has the right to possession of the property as his personal residence.

CalVet loans can be used to

- purchase an existing home,

- finance a lot purchase and new construction,

- rehabilitate a home purchased "as-is," and

- make home improvements.

All properties purchased with a CalVet contract (except for mobilehomes and condominiums) are covered under the fire and hazard insurance program. In addition, a master disaster indemnity policy provides insurance coverage for losses due to flood and earthquake.

Eligibility requirements   CalVet loans are available to most veterans planning to buy a home in California. Prior or current California residency is no longer a requirement. CalVet loans are available to any veteran who

- served a minimum of 90 days on active duty (not including active duty for training purposes only); or

- was discharged due to a service-connected disability; or

- is eligible to receive a U.S. campaign or expeditionary medal; or

- was called to active duty from the reserves or National Guard due to a Presidential Executive Order.

CalVet loans are available to currently active duty personnel. The applicant or a member of the applicant's immediate family must occupy the home within 60 days of close of escrow and continue to occupy the home until the loan is paid in full. A current member of the reserves or California National Guard who has served a minimum of one year of a six-year obligation is also eligible provided the applicant is a first-time homebuyer or purchases a property located in a targeted area. In some instances, *unremarried spouses* of veterans are also eligible.

If funds are in short supply (which is not usually the case), *preference* will be given to

- wounded or disabled veterans, then

- former prisoners of war and unremarried spouses of those missing in action or prisoners of war, then

- Vietnam-era veterans and Native American Veterans applying for loans on reservation or trust land, then

- all other eligible veterans.

Information on CalVet loans is available at www.cdva.ca.gov/CalVetloans/ or by calling 1-800-952-5626.

Loan qualifying   *Loan application* must be made before purchase. The veteran must meet ordinary standards of creditworthiness.

Interest rate and loan term   The loan term is always 30 years, but prepayment of principal can be made at any time, which can shorten the loan term. The interest rate on all loans may change *annually*, depending on the cost of bonds to fund the program. Monthly loan installments will increase to cover additional interest charges. CDVA offers three funding/interest rate programs. A veteran's eligibility for each program may vary based on income or purchase price limits, prior home ownership, and wartime service. The rates posted for these programs for 2016 for a 30-year loan are

- 5.5%/5.71% APR (with an additional 1% added for loans on mobilehomes in parks) for loans made from unrestricted funds, with wartime service not required and the veteran must apply within 25 years of release from active duty;

- 3.5%/3.69% APR (3%/3.26% APR for a 20-year term) for loans made from Qualified Veterans' Mortgage Bonds, with wartime service required and the veteran must apply within 25 years of release from active duty; and

- 3.45%/3.64% APR for loans made from Qualified Mortgage Bonds subject to income and purchase price limits but with no wartime service requirement. There is a 0.5% cap on increases during the term of the loan.

The APR is based on a $200,000 sales price, 10% down payment, financing the VA funding fee under the CalVet/VA loan program, and a one-year premium for disaster insurance.

Prepayment   CalVet loans may be prepaid at any time without penalty.

Loan amount/down payment   The maximum CalVet loan amount, minimum down payment, and loan fees are shown in Figure 9.2. The maximum CalVet loan amount for 2016 varies by county and is 125% of the maximum Fannie Mae loan limit (150% for farm loans). A home improvement loan can be made for up to $150,000.

Change of residence   A veteran can obtain a new CalVet loan as long as the first loan is paid in full or awarded in a divorce to a nonveteran spouse.

As with all government loan programs, CalVet loan requirements are subject to change at any time. Anyone interested in such a loan should contact the closest office of the California Department of Veterans Affairs via the website or telephone.

Mortgage assistance   The California Military Families Financial Relief Act allows for the deferral of mortgage payments secured by the principal residence of a member of the reserves or National Guard who is called to active duty. The loan does not have to be a CalVet loan.

FIGURE 9.2:   CalVet Loan Programs

Loan Program	CalVet / VA	CalVet 97	CalVet 80/20
Maximum Loan	$781,875 (including funding fee, if financed) for all programs, depending upon county)		
Property/Program	New or existing homes (incl. VA-approved condos) PUDs Mobilehomes on land	New or existing homes Condominiums PUDs Construction loans Rehabilitation loans Mobilehomes on land	New or existing homes Condominiums PUDs Construction loans Rehabilitation loans Mobilehomes on land Mobilehomes in parks
		(Maximum loan on mobilehomes in parks is $175,000 and interest rate is 1% higher; max. loan on farm properties is $938,250, depending upon county.)	
Down Payment	None	3%	20%
Funding Fee	1.25%–3.3% Waived for vets with disability ratings of 10% or higher; may be financed	1.25%–3.3% Must be paid in escrow	1.25%
Loan Origination Fee	1%	1%	1%
Other Requirements	VA certificate of eligibility required for full entitlement		

Except for mobilehomes and condominiums, CalVet home loans are covered for fire and hazard insurance. Veterans should contact GAB Robins at 1-800-626-1613, ext. 5.

California Housing Finance Agency

The **California Housing Finance Agency** (CalHFA) was chartered in 1975 as a self-supported affordable housing bank to make low-interest loans funded by the sale of tax-exempt bonds. CalHFA bonds are repaid by mortgage loan revenue.

The CalHFA conventional loan program offers a fully amortized 30-year fixed-rate first mortgage loan. As an added benefit, the CalHFA loan can be combined with either the MyHome Assistance Program (MyHome) or the Extra Credit Teacher Program (ECTP).

www.calhfa.ca.gov

Information on current CalHFA borrower requirements and loan programs can be found at www.calhfa.ca.gov.

Exercise 9-1

Refer to the information discussed in this unit to answer the following questions:

1. Could the same individual be eligible for an FHA, a VA, and a CalVet loan?

2. Mary Smith is eligible for a CalVet loan and would like to make the minimum down payment. What will be the maximum loan amount that she will be allowed?

3. Is a borrower's down payment likely to be lower with an FHA-insured or a VA-guaranteed loan?

CREATIVE FINANCING

When interest rates are high, there is an oversupply of properties for sale, or rising prices make housing less affordable, sellers frequently help to finance property purchases. Seller financing and other techniques can bring down the effective interest rate paid by buyers and make property purchases more attractive. Some of those **creative financing** techniques are discussed next.

Purchase-Money Trust Deeds and Mortgages

The **purchase-money trust deed** or **purchase-money mortgage** is given by *buyer* to *seller* at the time of purchase to secure all or part of the purchase price. The purchase money may come from either a third party (such as an institutional lender) or in the form of credit from the seller.

Typically, the seller who is willing to *take back (carry back)* a purchase-money mortgage or trust deed will set a rate lower than market interest to attract a greater number of qualified buyers without having to reduce the selling price drastically. The concept of seller financing certainly is not new, and it has been used to a considerable extent in California. The seller can finance a first or second mortgage or deed of trust. Without the availability of the "seller-financed second," many buyers would lack sufficient funds for the ever-increasing down payments necessitated by rising property values.

Land Contract

A land contract appeals to people who don't want to deal with a bank or other institutional lender, or who may have difficulty qualifying for a loan.

The **land contract**, also referred to as a *contract for deed* or **installment sales contract**, should not be confused with what we have referred to as the *contract of sale* between the parties.

A *land contract* is a form of seller financing in which the buyer takes possession of property and makes payments on its purchase but does not receive legal title to the property for *at least one year* from the date of possession. The sales contract specifies the amount of the purchase price that must be paid before legal title is conveyed. A land contract is one alternative for a buyer who does not qualify for a regular mortgage loan.

A land contract usually requires little or no down payment. The buyer takes possession of the property but, because the seller retains title, it may be less risky for the seller than other forms of financing. The seller cannot automatically eliminate the buyer's interest on default, however. Courts and legislature have rejected "harsh" remedies that could prevent a defaulting buyer from realizing any buildup of equity in the property. The land contract also must follow strict notice and other requirements. *Any seller contemplating such a sale should not do so without first consulting an attorney to ensure that all legal requirements are met.*

Wraparound Mortgage or Trust Deed

> A wraparound mortgage makes sense only when interest rates are rising.

The **wraparound mortgage** or **wraparound trust deed** is also called an **overriding trust deed** or **all-inclusive trust deed** (AITD). An AITD is a way to take advantage of a seller's existing loan with a relatively low rate of interest. The existing loan is unchanged, but the buyer receives additional funds (using the property as collateral) to make the purchase, and the lender of those new funds receives payment sufficient to cover both old and new loans. The new loan "wraps around" the existing loan.

The advantage to the buyer is that an overall less-than-market rate of interest is paid on the new loan balance. The lender benefits by receiving interest based on the entire loan balance at a rate higher than the original loan rate. The lender not only earns interest on the additional loan amount but may keep the excess earned at the new rate on the old balance as well.

A buyer could give a wraparound trust deed or mortgage to a seller, who then would make payments on the first loan. *It is important to note that a wraparound loan is possible only if the original loan documents permit such a refinancing. An alienation clause in the original loan documents would prevent a sale under such terms. An attorney should be consulted before entering into any such transaction.*

FOR EXAMPLE Present market interest rate on a home mortgage loan of $100,000 is 6%. A money market account earns 1.5%. The seller of Greenacre will hold a wraparound mortgage on his home priced at $100,000, with $20,000 down, for 20 years, at only 5% interest. The seller has an existing mortgage loan balance of $50,000 at 6% interest for 20 years. On those terms, what will be the rate of return to the seller on his remaining equity?

The seller receives $20,000 immediately, leaving an equity interest in the property of $30,000. The seller is owed yearly interest of 5% on $80,000, or $4,000, and owes 6% on $50,000, or $3,000.

The seller's yearly return is thus $1,000 ($4,000 – $3,000). That return divided by the amount "invested" ($30,000) indicates a rate of return of 3.33%. The buyer benefits from a lower-than-market interest rate, and the seller benefits from a return that is higher than the prevailing money market rate.

Sale-Leaseback

The **sale-leaseback,** or just **leaseback,** is a method of property transfer. It is mentioned here because it is a useful way for a financially sound but cash-poor business to gain needed capital while keeping office or other space.

By selling property it owns and uses, a business gets cash. By leasing the same space back from the buyer, the business can deduct the entire lease payment from income. Not all of the property need be sold—the land alone could be sold for the same tax reasons, but buildings on the land could be kept for depreciation deductions.

The buyer in a leaseback benefits by the typically higher payments of a lease over a mortgage and the property's appreciation (among other benefits). The lease term probably would be much longer (99 years, for instance) than the standard mortgage term (perhaps 25 years), assuring the buyer of a steady income stream.

Exercise 9-2

Identify each of the following financing transactions:

1. Lizumi built a small medical clinic on her own land. After 15 years, Lizumi sold the clinic. She still maintains her practice in the clinic building and plans to do so for many more years.

2. Ray Washington is making monthly payments on the house in which he lives with his son. Ray is buying the house but has never had legal title.

3. Debra Harold has held legal title to Blackacre for six months, since she took possession. She is making monthly payments of principal and interest to the former owner.

4. Juan Aldana, a veteran, pays a lower-than-market rate of interest on his home loan, which he pays directly to the government agency that funded the loan.

THE SECONDARY MORTGAGE MARKET

> Don't confuse the secondary mortgage market with secondary financing, which is a second (junior) lien on already-mortgaged property.

The initial mortgage lender may be the borrower's only source of contact regarding the loan. The borrower may make all mortgage payments to the original lender and receive periodic statements of interest paid and remaining principal owed from the same source. Yet in today's mortgage marketplace, chances are that the initial lender has sold the promissory note that is the underlying obligation and is only servicing it for someone else.

The sale and purchase of such obligations constitutes the **secondary mortgage market**. Real estate securities are a substantial source of investment opportunities for those who otherwise might seek alternate markets. This section will review the federally originated agencies that dominate the secondary mortgage market and are called **government-sponsored enterprises** (GSEs).

Fannie Mae

Fannie Mae (formerly the Federal National Mortgage Association) was created in 1938 as a subsidiary of the Reconstruction Finance Corporation. Authorized by the National Housing Act of 1934, the organization was to have been privately backed, but became a government agency when no private enterprise was willing to back it, given the continuing financial challenges brought on by the Great Depression. Information about Fannie Mae can be found at www.fanniemae.com /singlefamily. Fannie Mae has a 15-member board of directors. Ten members are elected by shareholders, and five members are appointed by the President of the United States.

www.fanniemae.com
/singlefamily

From its original mandate to serve as a secondary market for FHA-insured and VA-guaranteed loans, Fannie Mae's authority has been expanded to take in *conventional* mortgage loans as well. Fannie Mae currently buys FHA and VA graduated payment mortgages, adjustable-rate mortgages, and conventional fixed-rate first and some qualifying second mortgages on dwellings of one to four units.

A conforming loan meets
Fannie Mae's criteria.

A loan that meets Fannie Mae's underwriting criteria and dollar amount is called a **conforming loan**. Loans purchased by Fannie Mae cannot exceed the limits established each year using the formula prescribed in the Housing and Community Development Act of 1980. For 2017, the limit has been set at $424,100 for a loan on a single-family residence ($208,500 for a second mortgage); $543,000 for a two-family loan; $676,350 for a three-family loan; and $815,650 for a loan secured by a four-family residence. Limits are 50% higher for properties in Alaska, Hawaii, the U.S. Virgin Islands, and Guam.

Loan limits for other high-cost areas, including those in California, are $636,150 for a single-family home; $814,500 for a two-family home; $984,525 for a three-family home; and $1,223,475 for a loan secured by a four-family residence. The increases have enabled many more California homeowners to qualify for a loan within the conforming limit and avoid the increase in interest rates typically paid for a "jumbo" (nonconforming) loan. Fannie Mae calls loans that are over the regular limit, but within the high-cost area limit, *jumbo conforming loans*.

Fannie Mae will buy a block (pool) of mortgages from a lender in exchange for **mortgage-backed securities** that represent undivided interests in the group of loans. The securities may be sold or kept by the lender. Fannie Mae *guarantees* payment of all interest and principal to the holder of the securities.

In 1968, Fannie Mae was divided into a corporation owned by private shareholders (which retained the original name) and an organization called the Government National Mortgage Association (now called *Ginnie Mae*), which is discussed below. Fannie Mae now issues its own *common stock*, and it also obtains capital from borrowing, selling notes and debentures, selling mortgage-backed securities, and money earned from its own mortgage portfolio.

Ginnie Mae

Ginnie Mae (created as the Government National Mortgage Association) has brought many investors into the residential mortgage market by offering high-yield, risk-free, guaranteed securities. These securities also have none of the servicing obligations of a regular mortgage loan portfolio. Information about Ginnie Mae can be found at www.ginniemae.gov.

www.ginniemae.gov

Unlike Fannie Mae, Ginnie Mae does not buy securities. Instead, Ginnie Mae *guarantees* securities issued by FHA-approved home mortgage lenders. Ginnie Mae guarantees that the purchaser of privately issued securities backed by a pool of residential mortgages will receive timely payment of interest and principal, less servicing and Ginnie Mae fees. In the event of late payment by the borrower, the securities issuer advances the payment to the securities holder.

Ginnie Mae securities are backed by FHA-insured and VA-guaranteed mortgages, as well as those guaranteed by **Farmer Mac**, including single-family fixed-rate, graduated payment, growing equity, and manufactured home mortgage loans.

Freddie Mac

Freddie Mac (originally the Federal Home Loan Mortgage Corporation) was created in 1970 in direct response to the scarcity of mortgage funds. Freddie Mac provides a secondary market for residential conventional mortgage loans by buying such loans and reselling them to individual investors and financial institutions. Maximum loan amounts are the same as those set for Fannie Mae.

Freddie Mac was funded initially by the sale of nonvoting common stock to the Federal Home Loan Banks. Freddie Mac now issues preferred stock to the general public. You can learn more about Freddie Mac at its website, www.freddiemac .com.

www.freddiemac.com

www.makinghomeaffordable .gov

- Since 2009, Freddie Mac has been authorized by the government to conduct a number of programs to ease the home foreclosure crisis. Descriptions of current programs are at www.makinghomeaffordable.gov.

The most recent programs include the following:

- *Hardest Hit Fund (HHF)* programs in 18 states (including California) and the District of Columbia were created to assist homeowners through loan modification, mortgage payment assistance, including funding to eliminate second lien loans, and transition to more affordable housing. Some states have already closed program applications; no new applications will be accepted in any jurisdiction after December 31, 2020.

- The *Home Affordable Modification Program (HAMP)* provides eligible homeowners the opportunity to modify their mortgages to make them more affordable. Eligible homeowners must live in an owner-occupied principal residence, have a mortgage balance less than $729,750, owe monthly mortgage payments that are not affordable (greater than 31% of the homeowner's income), and demonstrate a financial hardship. This program originally terminated for both Fannie Mae and Freddie Mac loans on December 31, 2012, but was extended for participating non-GSE-serviced loans. Application deadline is December 31, 2016.

- The *Home Affordable Foreclosure Alternatives Program (HAFA)*, which is a part of HAMP, applies to loans not owned or guaranteed by Fannie Mae or Freddie Mac. HAFA provides opportunities for homeowners who can no longer afford to stay in their home, but want to avoid foreclosure, to transition to more affordable housing through a short sale or deed in lieu of foreclosure. Homeowners must submit an application with an executed purchase agreement on or before December 31, 2016, with escrow to close on or before September 30, 2017.

■ The *Home Affordable Refinance Program* gives homeowners with loans owned or guaranteed by Fannie Mae or Freddie Mac an opportunity to refinance into more affordable monthly payments. This program expires September 30, 2017.

Congressional Oversight

The Office of Federal Housing Enterprise Oversight (OFHEO) was created by Congress in the Federal Housing Enterprises Financial Safety and Soundness Act of 1992. OFHEO was charged with making legislative recommendations that are designed to enhance the financial safety and soundness of Fannie Mae and Freddie Mac. Under the Housing and Economic Recovery Act of 2008 (HERA), OFHEO was merged with the Federal Housing Finance Board (FHFB) to create the Federal Housing Finance Agency (FHFA). The website of FHFA, www.fhfa.gov, has a great deal of useful information, including a house price index for all 50 states and the District of Columbia.

www.fhfa.gov

Electronic Signatures

A growing number of loan originations accomplished via the internet. This trend has undoubtedly benefited from the passage by Congress of the **Electronic Signatures in Global and National Commerce Act**, which took effect October 1, 2000. Many states, including California, had already adopted the Uniform Electronic Transactions Act. The new federal law gives electronic signatures and records the same legal validity as written contracts and documents in every state. The law makes it possible for a mortgage loan to be applied for, approved, and made without a single piece of paper changing hands. Not every transaction can be carried out electronically, however. The law makes exceptions for certain documents of critical nature, such as court orders, mortgage foreclosures, termination of health insurance, utility cancellations, wills, and adoptions, which will still require written documentation on paper.

Federal Housing Finance Agency (FHFA)

The effort to insure the stability of the housing market has resulted in stronger federal control over the GSEs. Fannie Mae and Freddie Mac were placed into conservatorship by the Director of the Federal Housing Finance Agency (FHFA) on September 7, 2008, in accordance with the Housing and Economic Recovery Act of 2008 (HERA).

In an agreement with the U.S. Treasury that was reached in September 2008 and amended in December 2009, the Treasury was to provide Fannie Mae with the capital needed to correct any net worth deficiencies recorded in any quarter through 2012. After 2012, the Treasury's remaining funding commitment would be $124.8 billion, less any positive net worth Fannie May may have had as of December 31, 2012.

As the housing market has improved, so have the fortunes of Fannie Mae, which has not received funds from the Treasury since the first quarter of 2012. Fannie Mae reported that it would pay taxpayers $2.9 billion in dividends in September 2016, for a total of about $151.4 billion in dividends paid to the Treasury. Nevertheless, proposed legislation may replace Fannie and Freddie with federally insured mortgage securities that would require private insurers to cover initial losses before a government guarantee would kick in.

Exercise 9-3

How does a secondary market for real estate mortgage loans benefit borrowers?

SUMMARY

Nonconventional real estate loans include those insured by the **Federal Housing Administration** (FHA) or guaranteed by the **Department of Veterans Affairs** (VA). Through a variety of loan plans, these agencies use approved lenders to make lower-interest, low-down-payment loans available for owner-occupied dwellings. Recent increases in FHA-insured loan limits should help homebuyers in high-cost areas such as California.

The **California Veterans Farm and Home Purchase Program** (CalVet) has for many years purchased and resold residences and farms to veterans. This self-supporting program is run by the **California Department of Veterans Affairs** (CDVA).

In a time of expensive credit, seller financing through **purchase-money mortgages** and **trust deeds** can be a boon. *Sales* or **land contracts** can be tricky but may be useful if undertaken with the proper legal advice. The **wraparound mortgage**, when allowed, can benefit both buyer and seller.

The **sale-leaseback** is a way to free up capital for a financially sound property owner.

Fannie Mae has encouraged the growth of a strong **secondary mortgage market** by guaranteeing payment of interest and principal to holders of the **mortgage-backed securities** it creates by buying mortgages from lenders. **Ginnie Mae** guarantees securities issued by FHA-approved home mortgage lenders. **Freddie Mac** buys conventional residential mortgage loans for resale to investors and financial institutions. Increased limits on loans purchased by Fannie Mae and Freddie Mac should help homeowners in high-cost areas such as California, who can now qualify for conforming loan interest rates. Fannie and Freddie are now under the conservatorship of the Federal Housing Finance Agency.

OPEN FOR DISCUSSION

Once property is encumbered by debt, it becomes much more difficult to transfer title. One way to simplify real estate transactions would be to have a loan stay with the borrower, with the security interest transferred to the borrower's next property (assuming that the borrower purchases property equal to or greater in value than the property sold).

1. What do you think of this concept?

REVIEW QUESTIONS

1. A California veteran might have a home loan *insured* by
   a. FHA.
   b. VA.
   c. CalVet.
   d. Fannie Mae.

2. FHA appraisal value is used to set the upper limit of
   a. the purchase price.
   b. the loan amount.
   c. the construction cost.
   d. the seller contributions.

3. In addition to a monthly charge, FHA mortgage insurance includes a one-time payment on a purchase loan that is
   a. 1.75% of the loan amount.
   b. variable.
   c. negotiable.
   d. determined by the lender.

4. For an existing structure, the maximum FHA mortgage loan term is
   a. 15 years and 32 days.
   b. 25 years.
   c. 30 years.
   d. 40 years.

5. One discount point will increase a lender's effective yield by approximately
   a. ¼%.
   b. ⅛%.
   c. ½%.
   d. 1%.

6. Four discount points will increase a lender's effective yield by approximately
   a. ¼%.
   b. ⅛%.
   c. ½%.
   d. 4%.

7. On FHA loans, seller contributions, including discounts and closing costs, cannot exceed
   a. $5,000.
   b. 4%.
   c. five points.
   d. 6% of acquisition cost.

8. Five different graduated payment mortgages are approved by
   a. FHA.
   b. VA.
   c. CalVet.
   d. Ginnie Mae.

9. A veteran can have a home loan *guaranteed* by
   a. FHA.
   b. VA.
   c. CalVet.
   d. Fannie Mae.

10. The notice of value sets the upper limit of value for
    a. the purchase price.
    b. the loan.
    c. the guarantee.
    d. none of the above

11. Using the benefits of the GI Bill, a veteran *cannot* buy
    a. a house.
    b. a condominium.
    c. a farm.
    d. a manufactured home.

12. A veteran can be given a home loan on property *owned* by
    a. FHA.
    b. VA.
    c. CalVet.
    d. Fannie Mae.

13. A CalVet purchase loan must be applied for
    a. within one year of property purchase.
    b. before closing.
    c. before a contract of sale is signed.
    d. before talking to a property seller.

14. CalVet loans are *NOT* available for
   a. single-family homes.
   b. manufactured homes.
   c. working farms.
   d. commercial property.

15. Many seller-financed purchases are examples of
   a. institutional lending.
   b. creative financing.
   c. mortgage-backed securities.
   d. blended-rate mortgages.

16. An installment sales contract also is called
   a. a GEM.
   b. a GPM.
   c. a land contract.
   d. a bill of sale.

17. In a sale-leaseback
   a. land is never sold.
   b. buildings are always sold.
   c. both land and buildings can be sold.
   d. only a leasehold interest is sold.

18. The secondary mortgage market does *NOT* deal in
   a. primary mortgage market instruments.
   b. junior liens.
   c. issuing loans.
   d. mortgage-backed securities.

19. Which is *NOT* a part of the primary mortgage market?
   a. FHA
   b. VA
   c. CalVet
   d. Fannie Mae

20. Ginnie Mae securities are *NOT* backed by
   a. FHA-insured loans.
   b. VA-guaranteed loans.
   c. Farmer Mac-guaranteed loans.
   d. CalVet loans.

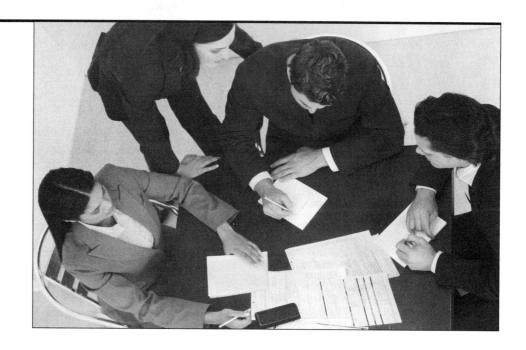

UNIT TEN

10

ESCROW AND TITLE INSURANCE

LEARNING OBJECTIVES

When you have completed this unit, you will be able to

- **list** the requirements to create a valid escrow for a real estate sale;
- **identify** escrow practices that differ from Northern to Southern California;
- **describe** the Escrow Law and its exemptions;
- **list** the requirements for a real estate broker to serve as an escrow agent;
- **identify** the stages of the escrow process, and the duties of the participants;
- **describe** the contents of a Closing Disclosure form; and
- **define** the various types of title insurance used in California.

KEY TERMS

abstract of title
beneficiary statement
binding contract
certificate of title
close of escrow
conditional delivery
demand for payoff
escrow
escrow agent

escrow holder
escrow instructions
escrow officer
extended-coverage
 policy
general indexes
guarantee of title
interpleader
loan commitment

lot books
preliminary report
settlement statement
standard policy
title insurance
title insurance
 company
title plant

ESCROW

An **escrow** is the possession by a *neutral third person* of money, a written instrument, evidence of title, or another thing of value that is received from *one party to a transaction* for delivery to the *other party to the transaction* on the performance of one or more conditions at a specified time.

An escrow can involve the sale, transfer, encumbering, or leasing of *real property,* such as a house or an office building. An escrow also can help in a transaction involving *personal property,* including what is known as a **bulk sale,** which involves the transfer of a business or a business license or permit. The emphasis in this unit is on the use of an escrow in the sale of real estate.

The person who performs escrow duties is called an **escrow agent** or **escrow holder.** As an agent of both buyer and seller, the escrow holder receives and dispenses the required money or documents and carries out whatever paperwork is needed to facilitate their transfer. The escrow holder's task is not to force the parties to fulfill their obligations but to ensure that those obligations are fulfilled before the sale is closed, the funds are released, and the buyer takes title.

The escrow holder in a sale of real estate usually combines the following two separate functions in one transaction:

- The sale itself
- The loan that finances the sale

The escrow holder is instructed to collect all necessary funds and documents with proper execution and required acknowledgments. The typical residential sales transaction may involve a dozen or more separate documents, from the transfer deed to the promissory note and security instrument, a title report, and some disclosure statements.

The escrow holder's duties may include

- preparation of the necessary documents;
- calculation of the prorations, adjustments, and charges to be assessed against each party; and
- verification that all required documents and funds are on hand before the necessary transfers are made.

When all conditions to the sale have been met, the escrow agent can *close* (complete) the transaction by transferring the relevant documents and funds. At **close of escrow,** the escrow agent provides each party with a **settlement statement** that itemizes all receipts and disbursements. The closing itself may take more than one day. Buyer and seller do not need to be present for closing. Because funds and documents are collected before closing, buyer and seller may never meet.

Creating an Escrow

To create a valid escrow for a real estate sale, two requirements must be met: a binding contract and conditional delivery of the necessary documents and funds.

Binding contract   There must be a **binding contract** between the buyer and seller. The contract can be

- a purchase contract and receipt for deposit,

- an agreement of sale,

- an option,

- an exchange agreement, or

- any other legally binding document.

Between the buyer and lender, the agreement usually is in the form of a **loan commitment** specifying the loan terms.

Conditional delivery   There also must be a **conditional delivery** of the instruments of transfer to the escrow holder. Instruments of transfer include

- money,

- the deed transferring title from grantor to grantee,

- loan documents, and

- other required paperwork.

The delivery of all instruments of transfer is conditioned on the successful fulfillment of both the contract terms and any new terms imposed by the agreement establishing the escrow.

Escrow Instructions

The escrow agent is given written **escrow instructions** to carry out the terms of the contract that is the basis of the transaction. If the escrow instructions differ from the terms of the underlying agreement, such as a purchase contract, the most recent in time controls. The escrow holder must follow the escrow instructions and can be held liable for failing to do so.

Escrow instructions are called *bilateral* when they are given by both parties jointly. The escrow instructions are *unilateral* when they are given separately by each of the parties.

North vs. South

In Northern California, the general practice is to use *unilateral* escrow instructions.

In Southern California, the general practice is to use *bilateral* escrow instructions.

After instructions to the escrow holder have been signed by the parties, neither can change the instructions unilaterally. If both parties agree, they may amend the escrow instructions at any time. It is necessary to have the agreement of both parties on every matter affecting the transaction, even if it is a condition that is to be waived by only one party.

The Escrow as Agent

The escrow holder acts as an agent only in a very limited capacity.

A limited *agency relationship* is established between the escrow holder and the principals to the transaction, defined by the responsibilities set out in the escrow instructions. When escrow is first established, the escrow holder is the agent of both parties. As the conditions to the transaction are performed, the escrow holder acts as the agent of each party as necessary to complete the transaction.

F O R   E X A M P L E   The escrow holder acts as the **agent of the grantor** when the deed is delivered to the grantee. The escrow holder acts as the **agent of the grantee** in delivering the purchase price to the grantor.

Ordinarily, the escrow holder should not be a party to the transaction. (There is an exception for licensed real estate brokers, as you will learn later in this unit.) Unless an exception applies, the escrow holder should not give advice on any part of the transaction and should remain impartial.

Who May Be an Escrow

www.dbo.ca.gov

The California Financial Code contains the *Escrow Law*. It describes the legal requirements to act as an escrow agent. An escrow agent must be licensed by the Department of Business Oversight (www.dbo.ca.gov), unless entitled to an exemption from licensing.

Exemptions from escrow licensing   There are *exemptions* from escrow licensing requirements for

- banks,
- savings and loan associations,
- title insurance companies,
- attorneys, and
- real estate brokers.

Section 12389 of the California Insurance Code was amended in 2015 to include rules governing what are termed "underwritten title companies" that are similar to the rules governing independent escrow companies. Real estate brokers who act as escrow agents are subject to special rules (discussed in the section "The Real Estate Broker as Escrow Agent").

North vs. South

In Northern California, escrow typically is handled by the title insurance company.

In Southern California, separately licensed escrow companies often are used, and financial institutions also perform many escrows.

General requirements A *license* to act as an escrow agent can be held *only* by a *corporation*. An individual cannot receive such a license. The licensed corporation must be solvent and furnish a $25,000 surety bond. There are also certain liquidity and tangible net worth requirements.

An escrow agent must keep *accurate records and accounts*, which may be audited by the Department of Business Oversight. Every fiscal year, the escrow agent (at the escrow agent's expense) must submit an independent audit prepared by a public accountant or certified public accountant to the department.

An escrow agent is *not* allowed to do the following:

■ Pay a referral fee, a commission, or any other compensation (including gifts of merchandise) to anyone other than employees of the escrow agent

■ Disclose any information concerning the transaction to outside parties (Each party to the transaction may be informed of instructions of another party only when those instructions form a part of the original contract.)

■ Solicit or accept escrow instructions or amendments that contain blanks to be filled in after the escrow instructions are signed

■ Give advice in tax and legal matters (The escrow agent is not a supervisor or guarantor of the soundness or advisability of the transaction.)

The Real Estate Broker as Escrow Agent

As already noted, a real estate broker need not be licensed as an escrow agent to perform the duties of an escrow. There are, however, strict requirements established by both the Department of Business Oversight and Bureau of Real Estate to govern brokers acting as escrows:

■ The license exemption is personal and applies only to the broker. The broker may delegate any duties to be performed under the broker's supervision, such as clerical functions.

■ The broker must be the selling or listing broker in the transaction or a party to the transaction.

■ Escrows must be only an incidental part of the broker's real estate business.

■ The broker may not form an association with other brokers for the purpose of conducting an escrow business.

■ The broker can advertise services as an escrow only in the context of the real estate brokerage. The broker cannot use a fictitious business name or one with the word *escrow* in the title or do anything to mislead the public as to the general nature of the brokerage.

■ All escrow funds must be kept in a trust account subject to inspection by the Real Estate Commissioner.

FOR EXAMPLE Sally Salt, a licensed real estate broker, has decided that she can supplement her income nicely by handling escrows for other real estate brokers. Can she?

No. Unless she becomes licensed as an escrow agent, broker Salt can act as an escrow only for transactions in which she is a party or the agent of one of the parties.

Other Principles and Prohibitions

Impartiality The escrow holder should be *impartial* to all parties to a transaction. If the escrow holder receives conflicting instructions from the parties, neither instruction should be followed. Only written instructions signed by all parties should direct the escrow. *Oral instructions alone should never be followed.*

Interpleader A conflict may arise between the parties as to the contract terms and resulting escrow instructions. If so, the escrow holder can bring a legal action known as **interpleader**. By this action the escrow holder forces the parties to have their rights and obligations clarified in court.

Above all, the escrow holder should *not* act as arbitrator or mediator or attempt to advise the parties on a course of action. It follows that an escrow holder should not give legal advice or speak to the parties on a matter that should be handled by the real estate broker.

Disclosure of material facts Because of the escrow holder's position, *material facts* concerning the transaction that are unknown to the parties may come to the escrow holder's attention. If the escrow holder does receive any such information, it should be disclosed immediately to the relevant parties. On the other hand, the escrow agent is not a guarantor of the soundness of a transaction. There is no duty to conduct an independent investigation or to warn a party that a deal is not in that person's best interest.

The escrow holder should be aware of the agency relationship and treat the information in its possession accordingly. As stated earlier, there may be information to which only one principal is entitled, such as the dealings of buyer and lender. *Under no circumstances is information concerning the escrow to be released to nonparties.*

Record keeping Accurate, up-to-date *records and accounts* are absolutely essential. Escrow files should be added to or revised daily if necessary. Likewise, an account never should be overdrawn. If documents or funds that were not part of the escrow instructions are submitted to the escrow holder, they should not be accepted.

Full and clear information It is in the best interests of the escrow holder, as well as the parties, to make the *settlement statements* that are supplied at the conclusion of the transaction as clear and easy to follow as possible. There should never be ambiguities or missing information.

FOR EXAMPLE Betty Buyer and Sam Seller are in escrow. Betty finds out that her loan will take longer to process than initially expected. She informs Sam, who agrees to a two-week extension of the closing of the sale. Sam phones Reliance Escrow to relay the information. What date will the escrow holder treat as the termination date of the contract of sale?

Unless both Betty and Sam sign a written amendment to the escrow instructions (drawn up by the escrow holder), the escrow holder must treat the original termination date as still in effect.

Exercise 10-1

1. After a much-delayed sale closing, the parties are waiting only for the proration of all of the expenses associated with the property, an apartment building. The seller, anxious to complete the sale, phones the escrow agent, telling the person handling the transaction to "just charge all expenses for this month to me, to expedite things." Can the agent do so? Why?

2. Tom Takahashi handles escrows for Sunny Acres Title Insurance Company. Tom receives signed escrow instructions from the seller and buyer of a tract of vacant land in Sunny Acres Heights. The day before closing, Tom learns that the property has suffered severe mud slide damage. Should Tom do anything with that information?

ESCROW PROCEDURES

After an offer to purchase has been accepted by a seller of real estate, it is important for buyer, seller, and broker(s) to make sure that all necessary details have been covered. If there are no vague or ambiguous provisions between the parties, the escrow process will be that much smoother. *Remember that an agent is considered to be involved in a transaction even if the agent will not receive a commission or fee.*

Transaction Checklist

Both buyer and seller will be concerned that all of the points discussed in the negotiations are included in the final contract terms. The real estate agent, also, must make sure that certain information is known to the parties. Has the broker made the appropriate inspection of the property? Is the buyer fully informed of all material facts concerning the property? Have the appropriate disclosures been made regarding the broker's agency relationship to seller and buyer? Have seller and buyer confirmed their understanding of the broker's role in the transaction? Have all other necessary disclosures been made? The use of a checklist, such as the one in Figure 10.1, will help ensure a successful sale closing. Once the requirements of the transaction are clearly established, the escrow holder knows what to expect from buyer and seller.

> A checklist is a necessity to make sure all details (especially disclosures) have been covered.

Some of the important elements of a successful transaction are included in the items listed in Figure 10.1, such as a property appraisal acceptable to the lender. If the lender isn't satisfied that the property is sufficient collateral for the loan, the loan will not be granted and the borrower will make use of the loan contingency clause.

FIGURE 10.1: Transaction Checklist

Transaction Checklist

_____ Date and place of signing of contract by buyer(s).

_____ Full name, address, and marital status of each buyer. If a business, the type of business (corporation, general partnership, etc.) should be specified.

_____ Purchase price, amount of deposit, and how the deposit will be made (such as by personal check or cashier's check). The person who will hold the deposit prior to closing (the escrow holder, for instance) also should be named.

_____ Financing terms. The buyer may be required to obtain a loan commitment by a certain date. The buyer should always have the protection of a loan contingency clause in the purchase contract, such as "This offer is subject to and conditioned upon the buyer and property qualifying for and the buyer obtaining said loan within X days of opening of escrow." Without such protection, the buyer could risk forfeiting the deposit if the sale were frustrated by the buyer's or property's failure to qualify for the loan. If the buyer will assume an existing loan, some provision should be made for the buyer's approval of the existing loan's terms.

_____ Encumbrances that affect title, such as restrictions and easements. These should be clarified as acceptable to the buyer, or a time period should be given in which a preliminary title report is to be received and accepted by the buyer. If the seller will retain any interest in the property, such as an easement, that interest should be specified, as should rights of any person (such as tenants) currently in possession.

_____ Required property inspections and who will pay for them. The person who will pay for necessary repairs also should be named. The buyer usually will want a final "walk-through" of the property just before closing to ensure it has been properly maintained and repaired (if necessary).

_____ Names of escrow holder and title company, as well as who is to pay the escrow fee, title insurance premium, and applicable county and city documentary transfer taxes and other fees.

_____ Description of any other documents required from either party.

_____ Names of all real estate brokers and salespeople involved, as well as the agency role of each in the transaction, the negotiated sales commission, and who will pay the commission.

_____ Contract termination date, how long the buyer's offer is open, and when the buyer will take possession.

_____ Signatures of all parties, including broker(s). If a salesperson signs on behalf of a broker, the broker must review the contract within five days, initialing and dating it. The Real Estate Law provides for delegation of the broker's responsibility in certain instances.

Responsibilities of the Buyer

The *buyer* will

- sign escrow instructions;

- provide a copy of any contract of the buyer that will affect the escrow, such as a buyer broker agreement;

- review the preliminary report and any encumbrances of record;

- review all loan documents, including new loans, loans to be assumed, loans buyer is taking title "subject to," and disclosure information if the seller is taking back a purchase-money mortgage;

- obtain hazard insurance coverage;

- review and approve all property inspection reports and arrange for a final property inspection before closing;

- examine the bill of sale covering any items of personal property to be conveyed separately at closing; and

- deposit the cash needed to cover down payment, closing costs, and other expenses, such as revolving debt and collection accounts, if any, to be paid off at closing.

Usually, expenses may be negotiated between buyer and seller. (An exception may be a government-backed loan.) The buyer typically pays for

- buyer's share of escrow fees,

- loan fees,

- appraisal fee,

- credit report,

- lender's title insurance,

- recording fees for documents prepared on the buyer's behalf,

- notary fees for documents prepared on the buyer's behalf,

- prepayment of loan interest,

- assumption fee (if applicable),

- new fire or other hazard insurance premiums,

- FHA mortgage insurance, and

- any prorated expenses the seller already has paid.

Responsibilities of the Seller

The *seller* will

- sign escrow instructions;

- provide a copy of any contract of the seller that will affect the escrow, such as the listing agreement, and any required disclosure statement(s);

- include the seller's deed and title insurance policy and any unrecorded instruments affecting title;

- provide information on the present status of existing loans, including consent to the submission of a beneficiary statement or demand for payoff, as required, and financing disclosure information if the seller is taking back a purchase-money mortgage;

■ provide certificates or releases on any mortgage, judgment, mechanic's lien, or other encumbrance to be paid off through escrow;

■ provide any existing hazard insurance policies to be assigned to the buyer;

■ provide any subordination agreement required by the contract;

■ provide tenant information, including their names, rent and deposit information, assignment of all leases to buyer, and the fact that tenants have been notified of the change of ownership;

■ provide executed deed on real property to the buyer;

■ provide executed bill of sale on any items of personal property, or security agreement if purchase is by installments; and

■ make available any other documents or approvals needed to close the sale.

Again, most sale expenses are open to negotiation. The seller typically pays for

■ seller's share of escrow fees,

■ title insurance,

■ home warranty plan (if any),

■ structural pest control report and clearance (if needed),

■ the beneficiary statement,

■ existing loan payoff and prepayment fee (if any),

■ mortgage discount points and nonallowable fees on behalf of the buyer in FHA transactions,

■ all fees in VA transactions,

■ notary fees on documents prepared primarily on the seller's behalf,

■ various transfer fees,

■ cost of required disclosure reports, and

■ any arrearages for taxes or other prorated items.

Responsibilities of the Real Estate Agent

When a real estate agent represents a party in a transaction, there are steps the agent can take to ensure that the transaction is successfully completed. In general, a real estate agent's responsibilities are to keep informed of the progress of the escrow and assist the escrow officer when necessary. The *agent* usually will

■ deliver copies of the executed (signed) purchase contract to the parties;

■ deliver and explain the escrow instructions to the parties in the transaction, and ensure that the parties have signed and returned the instructions (it may be best to have the parties go to the escrow office for signatures);

■ provide all necessary property and transfer disclosure reports;

■ provide the escrow officer with copies of the seller's payment coupons on any loans, a property profile or copy of the grant deed indicating the present owner(s), tax information, and any other items that will assist the escrow officer;

■ advise the buyer(s) (particularly a married couple) to obtain legal advice on how to take title (agents and escrow officers, unless licensed to practice law, may not give this advice);

■ remind the seller to continue to make all payments on loans during escrow and maintain the property as required by the purchase agreement;

■ advise the parties (buyer and seller) to notify the escrow officer if they have plans to be traveling during the escrow period, especially if they plan to be out of the country (If so, an arrangement, such as a power of attorney, must be made to ensure that the transaction is not delayed);

■ review the preliminary report as soon as it is available and explain its contents to the buyer;

■ assist the buyer in obtaining any necessary loans and place the lender in contact with the escrow officer;

■ assist the buyer in obtaining an inspection of the property and review the inspection with the buyer afterward;

■ assist the seller in ordering a timely pest control report and review the required corrective work;

■ make sure that the parties deliver the required documents and funds to escrow; and

■ provide any assistance the parties request or require that is within the agent's abilities, to ensure that the parties fulfill their obligations and are fully informed of the progress of the transaction.

FIGURE 10.2: **Cooperating Broker Compensation Agreement and Escrow Instruction**

CALIFORNIA
ASSOCIATION
OF REALTORS ®

**COOPERATING BROKER COMPENSATION AGREEMENT
AND ESCROW INSTRUCTION**
(C.A.R. Form CBC, Revised 4/09)

1. **IDENTITY OF LISTING BROKER, PROPERTY AND SELLER:**
_____ ("Listing Broker") is a real estate broker who has entered
into a written agreement for the marketing and sale or lease of the real property, manufactured home, or business opportunity
described as _____, Assessor's Parcel No. _____,
situated in _____, County of _____, California
("Property") for _____ ("Seller").

2. **IDENTITY OF COOPERATING (SELLING) BROKER AND BUYER:**
_____ ("Cooperating Broker") is a real estate broker
licensed to practice real estate in California (or ☐ if checked _____) and
represents _____ ("Buyer")
who has offered, is contemplating making an offer, or has entered into a contract, to purchase or lease the Property.

3. **LISTING BROKER COMPENSATION TO COOPERATING BROKER:**
Provided the transaction between the principals closes or Listing Broker receives compensation for the transaction,
Listing Broker agrees to pay Cooperating Broker, and Cooperating Broker agrees to accept, compensation as follows:
   A. **PROPERTY LISTED WITH THE** _____ **MULTIPLE LISTING SERVICE ("MLS"):**
      (i) ☐ **Confirmation of Compensation in MLS:** Cooperating Broker is a participant in the MLS or reciprocal MLS and accepts the
      offer of compensation published in the MLS as: _____% of the selling (or leasing) price or $_____ ☐ and/or _____.
      OR (ii) ☐ **Modification of Compensation in MLS:** Cooperating Broker is a participant in the MLS or reciprocal MLS and accepts the
      offer of compensation published in the MLS as modified herein: _____% of the selling (or leasing) price or $_____
      ☐ and/or _____.
      OR (iii) ☐ **Cooperating Broker Not a Member of the MLS or Reciprocal MLS:** Cooperating Broker compensation shall be _____%
      of the selling (or leasing) price or $_____ ☐ and/or _____. Listing Broker and Cooperating Broker agree to resolve
      disputes arising out of this agreement by arbitration conducted by the Association of Realtors® (or if none, the MLS) to which
      the Listing Broker belongs.
      OR (iv) ☐ **Short Sale Confirmation of Compensation in MLS:** Cooperating Broker (i) is a participant in the MLS or a reciprocal
      MLS; (ii) accepts the offer of compensation published in the MLS; and (iii) if the amount or method of reduction of commission
      upon Lender approval is specified in the MLS, agrees to such reduction.
   B. **PROPERTY NOT LISTED WITH ANY MULTIPLE LISTING SERVICE ("MLS"):**
      ☐ Cooperating Broker compensation shall be _____% of the selling (or leasing) price or $_____ ☐ and/or _____.
   C. **COOPERATING BROKER HAS PROCURED A TENANT FOR THE PROPERTY LISTED FOR LEASE,
      AND THAT TENANT ACQUIRES THE PROPERTY DURING THE TERM OF THE LEASE OR ANY EXTENSION:**
      ☐ Cooperating Broker compensation on the sale shall be _____% of the selling price or $_____ ☐ and/or _____.

4. **BROKER INSTRUCTION TO ESCROW HOLDER:**
Listing Broker and Cooperating Broker instruct Escrow Holder to disburse to Cooperating Broker the amount specified in paragraph 3,
out of Listing Broker's proceeds in escrow, and upon Close Of Escrow of the Property. This compensation instruction can be amended
or revoked only with the written consent of both Brokers. Escrow Holder shall immediately notify Brokers if either Broker instructs
Escrow Holder to change the terms of this instruction.

5. **MANAGEMENT APPROVAL:**
If Paragraph 3A(ii), 3A(iii), or 3B is checked, this Agreement is not binding until the Broker or office manager for the Listing Broker
firm has signed below.

6. **ACKNOWLEDGMENT:**
By signing below, the undersigned acknowledge that each has read, understands, accepts and has received a Copy of this Agreement.

Listing Broker (Firm) _____ DRE Lic. # _____
By (Agent) _____ DRE Lic. # _____ Date _____
Address _____ City _____ State _____ Zip _____
Telephone _____ Fax _____ E-mail _____

If paragraph 3A(ii), 3A(iii), or 3 B is checked:

Listing Broker/Office Manager: _____, _____ Date _____
  (Name)   (Signature)

Cooperating Broker (Firm) _____ DRE Lic. # _____
By (Agent) _____ DRE Lic. # _____ Date _____
Address _____ City _____ State _____ Zip _____
Telephone _____ Fax _____ E-mail _____

Published and Distributed by:
REAL ESTATE BUSINESS SERVICES, INC.
a subsidiary of the California Association of REALTORS®
525 South Virgil Avenue, Los Angeles, California 90020

Reviewed by _____ Date _____

EQUAL HOUSING OPPORTUNITY

CBC 4/09 (PAGE 1 OF 1)

COOPERATING BROKER COMPENSATION AGREEMENT AND ESCROW INSTRUCTION (CBC PAGE 1 OF 1)

Source: Reprinted with permission, California Association of REALTORS®. Endorsement not implied.

The real estate broker for the seller may share the sales commission with a cooperating broker who brings the buyer to the transaction. An agreement between the two brokers will ensure that both understand the compensation that will be paid at the closing of the transaction. The Cooperating Broker Compensation Agreement and Escrow Instruction shown in Figure 10.2 can be used both to clarify the compensation that the cooperating broker will receive and to provide for payment of the compensation by the escrow holder.

Responsibilities of the Escrow Holder

Although local practices may vary somewhat, the duties of the *escrow holder* generally include those listed below and in the flowchart shown in Figure 10.3. Throughout this section, we refer to the **escrow officer**, someone employed by an escrow company or escrow holder to handle escrow transactions. The escrow officer follows the specific procedures required by the escrow company or escrow holder, which vary from company to company and may be quite detailed.

Escrow instructions   The escrow holder in a residential property sale typically uses a printed form of escrow instructions listing what buyer and seller must do. Both buyer and seller *must* sign the instructions. The instructions will include such items as the

- purchase price,
- terms,
- financing provisions,
- how buyer's title is to vest,
- encumbrances that will affect the buyer's title,
- conditions affecting the transaction,
- date of closing,
- required inspections and other reports,
- expenses to be prorated,
- date on which buyer will take possession of the property,
- documents involved, and
- disbursements to be made and who will pay for them.

Since 1999, the CAR Residential Purchase Agreement (Form RPA-CA, described in Unit 7) has included joint basic escrow instructions. Most escrow companies now send out instructions that serve as a supplement/addendum to the contract, stipulating their additional general provisions of escrow practice and providing disclosures required by federal and state laws applicable to escrow agents.

FIGURE 10.3:   The Escrow Process

Title search Following a request by the escrow officer, the title company named by the parties searches the title records and provides a **preliminary report**. The preliminary report should identify the property and current owner of record, as well as any recorded liens or other encumbrances. The escrow holder reads the report to verify the legal description and to determine if there are any child support liens, taxes, or judgments for which a release will be required before the close of escrow. The buyer and the buyer's agent should review the preliminary report.

Lenders' statements   If the property is encumbered by any loans, the escrow officer contacts all lenders. Each is asked to provide either a **demand for payoff** (if the loan is to be paid in full through escrow) or a **beneficiary statement** (if the buyer will take title subject to loans of record).

Termite and other reports   The escrow officer receives all reports authorized by the escrow instructions and obtains the necessary *approvals* of those reports by the parties. Such reports might include a structural pest control report or a roof, an electrical, a foundation, or a soil report. If the seller has agreed to pay for indicated repairs through escrow, provision for that payment at closing must be made.

New loan package   Most often, the buyer obtains new financing. In that case, the escrow officer receives the appropriate loan documents and instructions, obtains the buyer's signature of approval, and makes sure all conditions are met before funds are disbursed at closing.

Hazard insurance policies   Prudent buyers arrange to insure property they purchase, effective as soon as they take title. Lenders will insist on a policy that adequately covers the cost to repair or replace the improvements. The escrow officer must obtain a copy of the *policy commitment*.

Other information and statements   The closing may require information on property taxes, assessments for improvements such as sewers, utility payments, and other property expenses that will require an accounting at the time of closing. If the property is rented, rent payments and security deposits also may be part of the computations. Other statements, such as the FHA appraisal value required in an FHA-insured sale, are required as indicated in Unit 9.

Prorations and adjustments

The escrow holder, who has received all of the required information, then computes the necessary **prorations** of items charged to buyer and seller. These may include insurance, taxes, assessments, utilities, and security deposits and rents.

> Tax prorations will depend on whether the tax has been paid. Prepaid taxes from the day of closing will be a credit to the seller and debit to the buyer. If current tax due has not been paid, the seller will be debited and the buyer credited the amount of tax owed up to the day of closing.

Taxes are prorated as of July 1, the first day of the tax year, or January 1, the beginning of the second half of the tax year. The escrow holder also prorates the buyer's mortgage interest as of the date funds are disbursed. Because interest payments always are made in arrears (that is, for the month just past), interest for the number of days from closing to the start of the first full month must be computed.

In most prorations, a *30-day month* is used. (In interest prorations, the lender sometimes insists on the actual number of days in the month—31 days, for instance.) Prorations typically assume that the buyer's rights and obligations begin on the day of closing. The buyer is responsible for any payments to be made for that day, such as property taxes and homeowners association dues. The buyer will receive credit for any proceeds, such as rent income, that have been received for that day.

MATH CONCEPTS

Proration is the allocation of property expenses and other charges to seller or buyer. Rents, taxes, insurance premiums, and interest on loans are only some of the expenses prorated at the time of closing a real estate transaction. Unless otherwise agreed, the standard term of 360 days per year (30 days per month) is used.

Usually, property expenses up to the day of closing are the responsibility of the seller. Depending on local custom, expenses as of the day of closing usually are the responsibility of the buyer.

F O R   E X A M P L E Ben Phillips is buying a four-unit apartment building. Monthly rents total $2,350 and are due on the first day of the month, and the date of closing is October 18. What part of the October rents is Ben entitled to receive?

Using a 30-day month, rental payments are $78.33 per day ($2,350 ÷ 30). Ben will receive rents for 13 days (October 18 through October 30). Ben would thus be credited with $1,018.29 for October rents at closing ($78.33 × 13 days).

Using a 31-day month, rental payments are $75.81 ($2,350 ÷ 31) per day. Ben then would be credited with rents for 14 days, or $1,061.34 ($75.81 ×14).

If the actual number of calendar days is required, a table such as the one below can be used to calculate the number of days quickly.

To use the chart, add the applicable number of days in the month to the nearest full preceding month. For example, the period from June 1 to February 15 would be 260 days—245 days from June 1 to February 1, and 15 days in February. The chart does not include February 29, the extra day in the leap year every four years. In a leap year, add an extra day to all calculations that include the last day of February.

For the First Day of	To the First Day of											
	Jan.	Feb.	March	April	May	June	July	Aug.	Sept.	Oct.	Nov.	Dec.
Jan.	365	31	59	90	120	151	181	212	243	273	304	334
Feb.	334	365	28	59	89	120	150	181	212	242	273	303
March	306	337	365	31	61	92	122	153	184	214	245	275
April	275	306	334	365	30	61	91	122	153	183	214	244
May	245	276	304	335	365	31	61	92	123	153	184	214
June	214	245	273	304	334	365	30	61	92	122	153	183
July	184	215	243	274	304	335	365	31	62	92	123	153
Aug.	153	184	212	243	273	304	334	365	31	62	92	122
Sept.	122	153	181	212	242	273	303	334	365	30	61	91
Oct.	92	123	151	182	212	243	273	304	335	365	31	61
Nov.	61	92	120	151	181	212	242	273	304	334	365	30
Dec.	31	62	90	121	151	182	212	243	274	304	335	365

FOR EXAMPLE   Jim and Janet Razer are buying the Landy house. The date of closing is June 16, and the key will be given to the Razers that day. The Landys have already paid both installments of the fiscal year's tax bill of $1,987.20. What amount will be charged to the Razers?

The date of closing is June 16. The Razers must pay for property taxes from June 16 to the end of the fiscal year, June 30. They thus will be charged for 15 days, or $82.80. The yearly payment of $1,987.20 is divided by 360 and that number is multiplied by 15.

Funding   The escrow officer requests the appropriate party to deposit the required funds in the escrow account. The *lender* provides the committed percentage of the purchase price. The *buyer* (borrower) will provide whatever amount is necessary to cover the remainder of the purchase price, taking into account any deposits already made as well as costs of closing, such as fees and prorations.

Audit of the file   The escrow officer *double-checks* that all conditions before closing have been met, including all necessary funding.

Final title review   The escrow officer orders the title company to make a final check of the *seller's title* as of the close of business of the escrow completion date. This is done to verify that the title has not changed or been encumbered since the time of the preliminary report. If no change has occurred, the title company *records* all transaction documents.

Closing of the sale   After the escrow officer has confirmed the recording of the transaction documents, the escrow is considered *closed*. The escrow holder will send settlements to buyer and seller, disburse funds, and deliver documents as soon as possible. *Note:* California law permits the lender to charge interest for no more than one day before the date that the loan proceeds are disbursed out of escrow or disbursed to the borrower or another party on behalf of the borrower. The law applies to notes secured by a mortgage or deed of trust on property of one to four residential units.

Settlement statements detailing transaction costs to buyers and sellers of dwellings of one to four units are required by the Real Estate Settlement Procedures Act (RESPA), discussed in Unit 8. A Closing Disclosure form appears in Figure 10.4.

Exercise 10-2

Using the first three pages of the Closing Disclosure form that appears in Figure 10.4, enter the details of the following residential sale transaction.

Michael Jones and Mary Stone are purchasing the single-family house of Steve Cole and Amy Doe located at 456 Somewhere Avenue, Anytown, CA Michael and Mary live at 123 Anywhere Street, Anytown, CA 12345. Steve and Amy live at 321 Somewhere Drive, Anytown, CA 12345.

FIGURE 10.4: Closing Disclosure

Closing Disclosure

This form is a statement of final loan terms and closing costs. Compare this document with your Loan Estimate.

Closing Information	Transaction Information	Loan Information
Date Issued	**Borrower**	**Loan Term**
Closing Date		**Purpose**
Disbursement Date		**Product**
Settlement Agent	**Seller**	
File #		**Loan Type** ☐ Conventional ☐ FHA
Property		☐ VA ☐ _____
	Lender	**Loan ID #**
Sale Price		**MIC #**

Loan Terms

	Can this amount increase after closing?
Loan Amount	
Interest Rate	
Monthly Principal & Interest *See Projected Payments below for your Estimated Total Monthly Payment*	
	Does the loan have these features?
Prepayment Penalty	
Balloon Payment	

Projected Payments

Payment Calculation	
Principal & Interest	
Mortgage Insurance	
Estimated Escrow *Amount can increase over time*	
Estimated Total Monthly Payment	
Estimated Taxes, Insurance & Assessments *Amount can increase over time* *See page 4 for details*	**This estimate includes** **In escrow?** ☐ Property Taxes ☐ Homeowner's Insurance ☐ Other: *See Escrow Account on page 4 for details. You must pay for other property costs separately.*

Costs at Closing

Closing Costs	Includes in Loan Costs + in Other Costs − in Lender Credits. *See page 2 for details.*
Cash to Close	Includes Closing Costs. *See Calculating Cash to Close on page 3 for details.*

FIGURE 10.4:   Closing Disclosure (continued)

Closing Cost Details

Loan Costs	Borrower-Paid		Seller-Paid		Paid by Others
	At Closing	Before Closing	At Closing	Before Closing	
A. Origination Charges					
01 % of Loan Amount (Points)					
02					
03					
04					
05					
06					
07					
08					
B. Services Borrower Did Not Shop For					
01					
02					
03					
04					
05					
06					
07					
08					
09					
10					
C. Services Borrower Did Shop For					
01					
02					
03					
04					
05					
06					
07					
08					
D. TOTAL LOAN COSTS (Borrower-Paid)					
Loan Costs Subtotals (A + B + C)					

Other Costs					
E. Taxes and Other Government Fees					
01 Recording Fees Deed: Mortgage:					
02					
F. Prepaids					
01 Homeowner's Insurance Premium (mo.)					
02 Mortgage Insurance Premium (mo.)					
03 Prepaid Interest (per day from to)					
04 Property Taxes (mo.)					
05					
G. Initial Escrow Payment at Closing					
01 Homeowner's Insurance per month for mo.					
02 Mortgage Insurance per month for mo.					
03 Property Taxes per month for mo.					
04					
05					
06					
07					
08 Aggregate Adjustment					
H. Other					
01					
02					
03					
04					
05					
06					
07					
08					
I. TOTAL OTHER COSTS (Borrower-Paid)					
Other Costs Subtotals (E + F + G + H)					

J. TOTAL CLOSING COSTS (Borrower-Paid)					
Closing Costs Subtotals (D + I)					
Lender Credits					

FIGURE 10.4: Closing Disclosure (continued)

Calculating Cash to Close Use this table to see what has changed from your Loan Estimate.

	Loan Estimate	Final	Did this change?
Total Closing Costs (J)			
Closing Costs Paid Before Closing			
Closing Costs Financed (Paid from your Loan Amount)			
Down Payment/Funds from Borrower			
Deposit			
Funds for Borrower			
Seller Credits			
Adjustments and Other Credits			
Cash to Close			

Summaries of Transactions Use this table to see a summary of your transaction.

BORROWER'S TRANSACTION

K. Due from Borrower at Closing
01 Sale Price of Property
02 Sale Price of Any Personal Property Included in Sale
03 Closing Costs Paid at Closing (J)
04
Adjustments
05
06
07
Adjustments for Items Paid by Seller in Advance
08 City/Town Taxes   to
09 County Taxes   to
10 Assessments   to
11
12
13
14
15

L. Paid Already by or on Behalf of Borrower at Closing
01 Deposit
02 Loan Amount
03 Existing Loan(s) Assumed or Taken Subject to
04
05 Seller Credit
Other Credits
06
07
Adjustments
08
09
10
11
Adjustments for Items Unpaid by Seller
12 City/Town Taxes   to
13 County Taxes   to
14 Assessments   to
15
16
17

CALCULATION
Total Due from Borrower at Closing (K)
Total Paid Already by or on Behalf of Borrower at Closing (L)
Cash to Close ☐ From ☐ To Borrower

SELLER'S TRANSACTION

M. Due to Seller at Closing
01 Sale Price of Property
02 Sale Price of Any Personal Property Included in Sale
03
04
05
06
07
08
Adjustments for Items Paid by Seller in Advance
09 City/Town Taxes   to
10 County Taxes   to
11 Assessments   to
12
13
14
15
16

N. Due from Seller at Closing
01 Excess Deposit
02 Closing Costs Paid at Closing (J)
03 Existing Loan(s) Assumed or Taken Subject to
04 Payoff of First Mortgage Loan
05 Payoff of Second Mortgage Loan
06
07
08 Seller Credit
09
10
11
12
13
Adjustments for Items Unpaid by Seller
14 City/Town Taxes   to
15 County Taxes   to
16 Assessments   to
17
18
19

CALCULATION
Total Due to Seller at Closing (M)
Total Due from Seller at Closing (N)
Cash ☐ From ☐ To Seller

FIGURE 10.4:   Closing Disclosure (continued)

Additional Information About This Loan

Loan Disclosures

Assumption

If you sell or transfer this property to another person, your lender

☐ will allow, under certain conditions, this person to assume this loan on the original terms.

☐ will not allow assumption of this loan on the original terms.

Demand Feature

Your loan

☐ has a demand feature, which permits your lender to require early repayment of the loan. You should review your note for details.

☐ does not have a demand feature.

Late Payment

If your payment is more than ___ days late, your lender will charge a late fee of _____

Negative Amortization (Increase in Loan Amount)

Under your loan terms, you

☐ are scheduled to make monthly payments that do not pay all of the interest due that month. As a result, your loan amount will increase (negatively amortize), and your loan amount will likely become larger than your original loan amount. Increases in your loan amount lower the equity you have in this property.

☐ may have monthly payments that do not pay all of the interest due that month. If you do, your loan amount will increase (negatively amortize), and, as a result, your loan amount may become larger than your original loan amount. Increases in your loan amount lower the equity you have in this property.

☐ do not have a negative amortization feature.

Partial Payments

Your lender

☐ may accept payments that are less than the full amount due (partial payments) and apply them to your loan.

☐ may hold them in a separate account until you pay the rest of the payment, and then apply the full payment to your loan.

☐ does not accept any partial payments.

If this loan is sold, your new lender may have a different policy.

Security Interest

You are granting a security interest in _____

_____

_____

You may lose this property if you do not make your payments or satisfy other obligations for this loan.

Escrow Account

For now, your loan

☐ will have an escrow account (also called an "impound" or "trust" account) to pay the property costs listed below. Without an escrow account, you would pay them directly, possibly in one or two large payments a year. Your lender may be liable for penalties and interest for failing to make a payment.

Escrow		
Escrowed Property Costs over Year 1		Estimated total amount over year 1 for your escrowed property costs:
Non-Escrowed Property Costs over Year 1		Estimated total amount over year 1 for your non-escrowed property costs: You may have other property costs.
Initial Escrow Payment		A cushion for the escrow account you pay at closing. See Section G on page 2.
Monthly Escrow Payment		The amount included in your total monthly payment.

☐ will not have an escrow account because ☐ you declined it ☐ your lender does not offer one. You must directly pay your property costs, such as taxes and homeowner's insurance. Contact your lender to ask if your loan can have an escrow account.

No Escrow		
Estimated Property Costs over Year 1		Estimated total amount over year 1. You must pay these costs directly, possibly in one or two large payments a year.
Escrow Waiver Fee		

In the future,

Your property costs may change and, as a result, your escrow payment may change. You may be able to cancel your escrow account, but if you do, you must pay your property costs directly. If you fail to pay your property taxes, your state or local government may (1) impose fines and penalties or (2) place a tax lien on this property. If you fail to pay any of your property costs, your lender may (1) add the amounts to your loan balance, (2) add an escrow account to your loan, or (3) require you to pay for property insurance that the lender buys on your behalf, which likely would cost more and provide fewer benefits than what you could buy on your own.

FIGURE 10.4:   Closing Disclosure (continued)

Loan Calculations

Total of Payments. Total you will have paid after you make all payments of principal, interest, mortgage insurance, and loan costs, as scheduled.

Finance Charge. The dollar amount the loan will cost you.

Amount Financed. The loan amount available after paying your upfront finance charge.

Annual Percentage Rate (APR). Your costs over the loan term expressed as a rate. This is not your interest rate.

Total Interest Percentage (TIP). The total amount of interest that you will pay over the loan term as a percentage of your loan amount.

Questions? If you have questions about the loan terms or costs on this form, use the contact information below. To get more information or make a complaint, contact the Consumer Financial Protection Bureau at **www.consumerfinance.gov/mortgage-closing**

Other Disclosures

Appraisal
If the property was appraised for your loan, your lender is required to give you a copy at no additional cost at least 3 days before closing. If you have not yet received it, please contact your lender at the information listed below.

Contract Details
See your note and security instrument for information about
  • what happens if you fail to make your payments,
  • what is a default on the loan,
  • situations in which your lender can require early repayment of the loan, and
  • the rules for making payments before they are due.

Liability after Foreclosure
If your lender forecloses on this property and the foreclosure does not cover the amount of unpaid balance on this loan,
☐ state law may protect you from liability for the unpaid balance. If you refinance or take on any additional debt on this property, you may lose this protection and have to pay any debt remaining even after foreclosure. You may want to consult a lawyer for more information.
☐ state law does not protect you from liability for the unpaid balance.

Refinance
Refinancing this loan will depend on your future financial situation, the property value, and market conditions. You may not be able to refinance this loan.

Tax Deductions
If you borrow more than this property is worth, the interest on the loan amount above this property's fair market value is not deductible from your federal income taxes. You should consult a tax advisor for more information.

Contact Information

	Lender	Mortgage Broker	Real Estate Broker (B)	Real Estate Broker (S)	Settlement Agent
Name					
Address					
NMLS ID					
__ License ID					
Contact					
Contact NMLS ID					
Contact __ License ID					
Email					
Phone					

Confirm Receipt

By signing, you are only confirming that you have received this form. You do not have to accept this loan because you have signed or received this form.

_____   _____   _____   _____
Applicant Signature   Date   Co-Applicant Signature   Date

The lender is Ficus Bank. The settlement agent is Epsilon Title Company. The date the closing information was issued is April 15, 2013. The closing date and disbursement date is April 15, 2013. The file number is 12-3456. The sales price is $180,000. There is a conventional 30-year loan of $162,000 with a fixed interest rate of 3.875% and monthly principal and interest payments of $761.78. The loan ID number is 123456789, and the MIC number is 000654321. The loan has a prepayment penalty that can go as high as $3,240 if the loan is paid off during the first two years. The loan is amortized, and there is no balloon payment. Because the loan is a 90% loan, private mortgage insurance is required for the first seven years at a cost of $82.35 per month; it is terminated after the first seven years. Escrow amounts that can increase over time for property taxes and homeowners in the amount of $206.13 are required over the 30-year period of the loan. The estimated monthly payments for the first seven years total $1,050.26; the estimated monthly payments for years 8–30 total $967.91. The total estimated amount for monthly property taxes, homeowners insurance, and homeowners association (HOA) assessments is $356.13. Property taxes and homeowners insurance is paid in advance in escrow. HOA dues are not paid in escrow but are paid directly by the borrower to the HOA. The total closing costs paid by the borrower total $9,712.10. The total cash to close from the borrower totals $14,147.26.

The following loan costs are paid from the borrowers' funds at settlement:

- The total loan origination charges totaled $1,802
    - 0.25% of loan amount (points): $405
    - Application fee of $300
    - Underwriting fee of $1,097
- Services the borrower did not shop for totaled $236.55 and included
    - An appraisal fee to John Smith Appraisers, Inc., that was paid by others in the amount of $405 and amounts that the borrower paid, including a credit report fee to Information, Inc., that was paid before closing for $29.80
    - The following fees that are to be paid at closing
    - A flood determination fee to Info Co. for $20
    - A flood monitoring fee to Info Co. for $31.75
    - A tax monitoring fee to Info Co. for $75
    - A tax status research fee to Info Co. for $80
- Services the borrower did shop for totaled $2,655.50 and included
    - A pest inspection fee to Pests Co. for $120
    - A survey fee to Surveys Co. for $85
    - A title insurance binder to Epsilon Title Co. for $650
    - Lenders title insurance to Epsilon Title Co. for $500
    - Settlement agent fee to Epsilon Title Co. for $500
    - A title search to Epsilon Title Co. for $800

Thus the total loan costs that the borrower paid were $4,694.05, of which $4,664.25 was to be paid by the borrower at closing and $29.80 was paid before closing.

Taxes and other government fees totaled $85 and included $40 for recording the deed and $45 for recording the mortgage, for a total of $85 to be paid by the borrower at closing.

The buyer had $2,120.80 in prepaid amounts that included

- a homeowners insurance premium for 12 months to Insurance Co. of $1,209.96;

- prepaid interest at $17.44 per day from April 15, 2013, to May 1, 2013, for a total of $279.04; and

- six months of property taxes to Any County, USA, for $631.80.

The borrower paid an initial escrow account payment at closing of a total of $412.25 for the following:

- $201.66 for homeowners insurance for two months at $100.83 per month

- $210.60 for property taxes for two months at $105.30 per month

There was also an aggregate adjustment for expenses at closing for initial escrow payments of $.01.

Other payments by the borrower at closing totaled $2,400 and included

- an HOA capital contribution to HOA Acre, Inc., of $500,

- an HOA processing fee to HOA Acre, Inc., of $150,

- a home inspection fee to Engineers, Inc., of $750, and

- $1,000 to Epsilon Title Co. for an owners title insurance policy.

This resulted in total other costs paid by the borrower of $5,018.05. The total closing costs paid by the borrower were $9,712.10, consisting of $9,682.30 paid by the borrower at closing and $29.80 paid before closing.

The mandatory Loan Estimate form indicated the following loan estimates:

- Total closing costs of $8,054

- Down payment/funds from borrower of $28,000

- Deposit of $18,000

The total cash to close totaled $16,054. The final amounts equaled

- total closing costs of $9,712.10;

- closing costs paid before closing of $29.80;

- down payment/funds from the borrower of $18,000;

- a deposit of $10,000;

- a seller credit to buyer of $2,500; and

- adjustments and other credits of $1,035.04 for a total of $14,147.26.

The summaries of the borrower's transactions consisted of money due from the borrower at closing totaling $289,762.30, which included

- $180,000 for the sale price of the property;
- $9,682.30 in closing costs paid at closing; and
- HOA dues from April 1, 2013, to April 30, 2013.

Amounts already paid by or on behalf of the borrower at closing totaled $175,615.04 and included

- a deposit of $10,000;
- a loan amount of $162,000;
- a seller credit of $2,500; and
- other credits, including a rebate from Epsilon Title Co. of $750 and an adjustment for an item that was unpaid by the seller for city taxes from January 1, 2013, to April 14, 2013, of $365.04.

The calculation of the total due from the borrower at closing totaled $189,762.30, of which the total already paid by or on behalf of the borrower at closing was $175,615.04, leaving a cash to close from borrower in the amount of $14,147.26.

The other costs paid by the seller at closing included

- transfer tax to Any State of $950 (Section E); and
- other expenses (Section H), including
  - a home inspection fee to Engineers, Inc., before closing of $750; and
  - the following amounts to be paid at closing:
    - A home warranty fee to XYZ Warranty, Inc., of $450
    - A real estate commission to Alpha Real Estate Broker of $5,700
    - A real estate commission to Omega Real Estate Broker of $5,700

The total amount of closing costs to be paid by the seller at closing totals $12,800, and the total amount paid by the seller before closing is $750.

The summaries of the seller's transaction consisted of money due to the seller at closing totaling $180,080, including a sale price of the property of $180,000 and an adjust for items paid by the seller in advance for HOA dues from April 15, 2013, to April 30, 2013, of $80. It also amounted to a total due from the seller at closing of a total of $115,665.04, including

- closing costs paid at closing (J) of $12,800;
- payoff of a first mortgage loan of $100,00;
- a seller credit to the borrower of $2,500; and
- an adjustment for an item unpaid by the seller consisting of city taxes from January 1, 2013, to April 14, 2013, of $365.04.

Thus, the total due to the seller at closing is $180,080, and the total due from the seller at closing is $115,665.04, resulting in total cash to the seller of $64,414.96.

Cancellation of the escrow   Not every transaction reaches a successful closing. The escrow can be canceled and the deposit returned to the buyer, only if both parties provide written instructions to the escrow holder. The Cancellation of Contract, Release of Deposit, and Cancellation of Escrow form that appears in Figure 10.5 provides for both buyer and seller to authorize the escrow holder to cancel the escrow. The agent(s) should check with the escrow officer for cancellation fees before having buyer and seller complete the form to ensure that all costs are accounted for.

FIGURE 10.5:   Cancellation of Contract, Release of Deposit, and Joint Escrow Instructions

CALIFORNIA
ASSOCIATION
OF REALTORS®

**CANCELLATION OF CONTRACT,
RELEASE OF DEPOSIT
AND CANCELLATION OF ESCROW**
(C.A.R. Form CC, Revised 11/14)

In accordance with the terms and conditions of the: ☐ California Residential Purchase Agreement; or ☐ Other _____ ("Agreement"), dated _____, including all amendments and related documents, on property known as _____ ("Property"), between _____ ("Buyer") and _____ ("Seller").

Paragraphs 1 and 2 below constitute escrow instructions to Escrow Holder. Release of funds (pursuant to paragraph 2) requires mutually Signed release instructions from Buyer and Seller, judicial decision or arbitration award. A party may be subject to a civil penalty of up to $1,000 for refusal to sign such instructions if no good faith dispute exists as to who is entitled to the deposited funds (Civil Code §1057.3).

1. **CANCELLATION OF CONTRACT:** ☐ Buyer ☐ Seller ☐ both Buyer and Seller cancel(s) the Agreement for the following reason:
   A. ☐ As permitted by the good faith exercise of paragraph(s) _____ of the Agreement.
   OR B. ☐ Buyer has failed to remove the applicable contingency after being given a Notice to Buyer to Perform (C.A.R. Form NBP).
   OR C. ☐ Buyer has failed to take the applicable contractual action after being given a Notice to Buyer to Perform (C.A.R. Form NBP).
   OR D. ☐ Seller has failed to take the applicable contractual action after being given a Notice to Seller to Perform (C.A.R. Form NSP).
   OR E. ☐ Seller has failed to remove the applicable contingency after being given a Notice to Seller to Perform (C.A.R. Form NSP).
   OR F. ☐ Per mutual agreement.
   OR G. ☐ Other _____.

   _____   _____
   Buyer's or Seller's Signature (party cancelling the contract)   Date

   _____   _____
   Buyer's or Seller's Signature (party cancelling the contract)   Date

2. **RELEASE OF DEPOSIT and CANCELLATION OF ESCROW**
   Buyer and Seller cancel escrow # _____ with _____ and
   A. ☐ Seller authorizes release of Buyer's deposit, less Buyer's fees and costs, to Buyer.

   OR B. ☐ Buyer authorizes release of Buyer's deposit, less Seller's fees and costs, to Seller. (☐ Pursuant to a properly executed liquidated damages clause, Buyer's authorization of release of deposit to Seller is limited to no more than 3% of the purchase price. Any additional deposit shall be returned to Buyer.)

   OR C. ☐ Both Buyer and Seller acknowledge mutual cancellation of the Agreement and authorize Escrow Holder to continue to hold the deposit until receiving subsequent mutual instructions, judicial decision or arbitration award.

   OR D. ☐ Other: _____.

   Unless otherwise specified, Buyer and Seller (i) mutually release each other from all obligation to buy, sell or exchange the Property under the Agreement, and from all claims, actions and demands that each may have against the other(s) by reason of the Agreement; and (ii) intend that all rights and obligations arising out of the Agreement are null and void.
   Date _____   Date _____
   Buyer _____   Seller _____
   Buyer _____   Seller _____

Published and Distributed by:
REAL ESTATE BUSINESS SERVICES, INC.
a subsidiary of the California Association of REALTORS®
525 South Virgil Avenue, Los Angeles, California 90020

Reviewed by _____ Date _____

EQUAL HOUSING
OPPORTUNITY

CC REVISED 11/14 (PAGE 1 OF 1) Print Date

CANCELLATION OF CONTRACT, RELEASE OF DEPOSIT AND CANCELLATION OF ESCROW (CC PAGE 1 OF 1)

Source: Reprinted with permission, California Association of REALTORS®. Endorsement not implied.

TITLE INSURANCE

In several earlier units, we have referred to the concept of *marketability of title*. Real estate has value when it can be marketed (sold). It will be easiest to sell when there are no *clouds on the title*.

Land may change hands many times over the years of documented ownership. During that time, many parties may have property rights in the land, including water and mineral rights. Heirs of deceased owners may not come forward. A spouse may not join in a conveyance. How can a purchaser be sure the seller owns all of the rights of ownership being sold, whatever those are?

Various forms of title inspection have developed in response to the need for some guarantee that the seller has *good title*—title that a reasonably prudent person would accept.

Abstract of Title

In Unit 4, we mentioned the *chain of title* from one property owner to the next. By laboriously going back through all pertinent records, including tax records and court judgments, an abstract of title can be prepared. An **abstract of title** lists every recorded change of ownership or claim on the property being examined. The abstract is accompanied by a *lawyer's opinion of title*, which comments on the present validity of any claims of lien or ownership. This way of ensuring marketability of title is usually a lengthy, expensive process.

Certificate of Title

When title abstractors began to perform quantities of title research, their own records became significant sources of title information. Abstract companies compiled that information into **lot books** referencing documents by property location, and **general indexes** listing names of owners alphabetically along with documents affecting their property interests. Eventually, title examiners needed to check only their company's **title plant** containing the lot books and indexes. They then could prepare a **certificate of title** stating the property's owner of record and listing any present encumbrances, usually without an attorney's opinion. The certificate of title is not often used today.

Guarantee of Title

The **guarantee of title** was next made available; it not only provided for examination of title but *guaranteed* the title as described. The title examiners using this device thus took on the responsibilities of insurers, which led to the next step in the formation of the modern title insurance industry.

Title Insurance Policies

Although the guarantee of title was useful, it was based (as were the earlier forms of title inspection) on examination of the public records. Unfortunately, there can be impediments to good title, such as forgeries or documents procured through fraud, that aren't revealed by examining public records. And not all documents may have been recorded. How, then, could the buyer be protected? The solution was the development of **title insurance**. Title insurance is available in several forms of coverage but basically insures against possible unrecorded risks.

Title insurance can be for the benefit of either *property owner* or *lender* and takes effect as of the day of closing.

Title insurance companies   Title insurance companies in California are regulated by the state. A **title insurance company** must provide a "guarantee fund" to the Insurance Commissioner and set aside a certain amount from premiums each year as a **title insurance surplus fund**. Fee schedules must be available to the public.

Referral Fees for Title Business Are Illegal

No referral fees may be paid by any title insurer, underwritten title company, or escrow company as an inducement for the placement or referral of title business. This prohibition includes both direct and indirect payments, in any form, whether or not the payment results in actual placement or referral of title business. It is part of both state law (California Insurance Code 12404) and federal law (Real Estate Settlement Procedures Act).

Standard policy   The **standard policy** of title insurance assumes that the policyholder is able to inspect the property before purchase and determine how the land is being used and by whom. The standard policy covers FRIC: forgery, recording defects, improper delivery of a document of title, and incapacity of the grantor. The standard policy of title insurance excludes

- rights or claims of persons in actual physical possession of the property (even though not shown in the public records);
- easements and liens not shown in the public records;
- any title defects known to the policyholder at the time of insurance or that would be shown by a survey;
- mining claims;
- reservations;
- water rights; or
- changes in land use dictated by zoning ordinances.

The *California Land Title Association (CLTA)*, the trade association of the state's title companies, has a standard form of title insurance that its members use. Part of one of those policies, listing covered title defects as well as exceptions, appears in Figure 10.6.

In practice, the standard policy of title insurance also includes a legal description of the property and lists encumbrances currently of record. If more thorough coverage than that provided in a standard policy is desired, another form of policy is available.

Extended-coverage policy   There is an **extended-coverage policy** that is intended primarily for the benefit of *lenders*. The lender may be located some distance from the property, even out-of-state, and may have no easy or inexpensive method of examining the property being encumbered. The *American Land Title Association (ALTA)* has a variety of policies, including one that extends coverage to insure property against

- rights or claims of persons in physical possession of the property (even by virtue of an unrecorded instrument);
- unrecorded easements and liens;
- rights or claims that a survey would reveal;
- mining claims;
- reservations; and
- water rights.

The property owner also can be insured by such a policy, although the ALTA extended-coverage policy will exclude any title defects known to the buyer at the time of purchase.

Note: The ALTA extended-coverage policy, like the CLTA policy, excludes changes in land use brought about by zoning ordinances, unless there is a recorded notice of enforcement of the specified zoning.

For an additional charge, a title insurance policy will also include protection against such occurrences as post-policy issuance forgeries and forced removal of an existing structure due to prior building permit violations.

FIGURE 10.6: Policy of Title Insurance

EAGLE POLICY

Form No. 1490 EAGLE (6/98)
CLTA Homeowner's Policy of Title Insurance (6/2/98)

Policy Page 1

Policy of Title Insurance

ISSUED BY

First American Title Insurance Company
EAGLE Protection Owner's Policy
FOR A ONE-TO-FOUR FAMILY RESIDENCE

OWNER'S COVERAGE STATEMENT

This Policy insures You against actual loss, including any costs, attorneys' fees and expenses provided under this Policy, resulting from the Covered Risks set forth below, if the Land is an improved residential lot on which there is located a one-to-four family residence and each insured named in Schedule A is a Natural Person.

Your insurance is effective on the Policy Date. This Policy covers Your actual loss from any risk described under Covered Risks if the event creating the risk exists on the Policy Date or, to the extent expressly stated, after the Policy Date.

Your insurance is limited by all of the following:

- The Policy Amount shown in Schedule A
- For Covered Risk 14, 15, 16 and 18, Your Deductible Amount and Our Maximum Dollar Limit of Liability shown in Schedule A
- Exceptions in Schedule B
- Our Duty To Defend Against Legal Actions
- Exclusions on page 2
- Conditions on page 2 and 3.

COVERED RISKS

The Covered Risks are:

1. Someone else owns an interest in Your Title.
2. Someone else has rights affecting Your Title arising out of leases, contracts, or options.
3. Someone else claims to have rights affecting Your Title arising out of forgery or impersonation.
4. Someone else has an easement on the Land.
5. Someone else has a right to limit Your use of the Land.
6. Your Title is defective.
7. Any of Covered Risks 1 through 6 occurring after the Policy Date.
8. Someone else has a lien on Your Title, including a:
   a. Mortgage;
   b. judgment, state or federal tax lien, or special assessment;
   c. charge by a homeowner's or condominium association; or
   d. lien, occurring before or after the Policy Date, for labor and material furnished before the Policy Date.
9. Someone else has an encumbrance on Your Title.
10. Someone else claims to have rights affecting Your Title arising out of fraud, duress, incompetency or incapacity.
11. You do not have both actual vehicular and pedestrian access to and from the Land, based upon a legal right.
12. You are forced to correct or remove an existing violation of any covenant, condition or restriction affecting the Land, even if the covenant, condition or restriction is excepted in Schedule B.
13. Your Title is lost or taken because of a violation of any covenant, condition or restriction, which occurred before You acquired Your Title, even if the covenant, condition or restriction is excepted in Schedule B.
14. Because of an existing violation of a subdivision law or regulation affecting the Land:
    a. You are unable to obtain a building permit;
    b. You are forced to correct or remove the violation; or
    c. someone else has a legal right to, and does, refuse to perform a contract to purchase the Land, lease it or make a Mortgage loan on it.

    The amount of Your insurance for this Covered Risk is subject to Your Deductible Amount and Our Maximum Dollar Limit of Liability shown in Schedule A.
15. You are forced to remove or remedy Your existing structures, or any part of them — other than boundary walls or fences — because any portion was built without obtaining a building permit from the proper government office. The amount of Your insurance for this Covered Risk is subject to Your Deductible Amount and Our Maximum Dollar Limit of Liability shown in Schedule A.

16. You are forced to remove or remedy Your existing structures, or any part of them, because they violate an existing zoning law or zoning regulation. If You are required to remedy any portion of Your existing structures, the amount of Your insurance for this Covered Risk is subject to Your Deductible Amount and Our Maximum Dollar Limit of Liability shown in Schedule A.
17. You cannot use the Land because use as a single-family residence violates an existing zoning law or zoning regulation.
18. You are forced to remove Your existing structures because they encroach onto Your neighbor's Land. If the encroaching structures are boundary walls or fences, the amount of Your insurance for this Covered Risk is subject to Your Deductible Amount and Our Maximum Dollar Limit of Liability shown in Schedule A.
19. Someone else has a legal right to, and does, refuse to perform a contract to purchase the Land, lease it or make a Mortgage loan on it because Your neighbor's existing structures encroach onto the Land.
20. You are forced to remove Your existing structures because they encroach onto an easement or over a building set-back line, even if the easement or building set-back line is excepted in Schedule B.
21. Your existing structures are damaged because of the exercise of a right to maintain or use any easement affecting the Land, even if the easement is excepted in Schedule B.
22. Your existing improvements (or a replacement or modification made to them after the Policy Date), including lawns, shrubbery or trees, are damaged because of the future exercise of a right to use the surface of the Land for the extraction or development of minerals, water or any other substance, even if those rights are excepted or reserved from the description of the Land or excepted in Schedule B.
23. Someone else tries to enforce a discriminatory covenant, condition or restriction that they claim affects Your Title which is based upon race, color, religion, sex, handicap, familial status, or national origin.
24. A taxing authority assesses supplemental real estate taxes not previously assessed against the Land for any period before the Policy Date because of construction or a change of ownership or use that occurred before the Policy Date.
25. Your neighbor builds any structures after the Policy Date — other than boundary walls or fences — which encroach onto the Land.
26. Your Title is unmarketable, which allows someone else to refuse to perform a contract to purchase the Land, lease it or make a Mortgage loan on it.
27. A document upon which Your Title is based is invalid because it was not properly signed, sealed, acknowledged, delivered or recorded.
28. The residence with the address shown in Schedule A is not located on the Land at the Policy Date.
29. The map, if any, attached to this Policy does not show the correct location of the Land according to the Public Records.

OUR DUTY TO DEFEND AGAINST LEGAL ACTIONS

We will defend Your Title in any legal action only as to that part of the action which is based on a Covered Risk and which is not excepted or excluded from coverage in this Policy. We will pay the costs, attorneys' fees, and expenses We incur in that defense.

We will not pay for any part of the legal action which is not based on a Covered Risk or which is excepted or excluded from coverage in this Policy.

We can end Our duty to defend Your Title under paragraph 4 of the Conditions.

This Policy is not complete without Schedules A and B.

FIRST AMERICAN TITLE INSURANCE COMPANY INCORPORATED SEPTEMBER 24, 1968 CALIFORNIA

CEO

FIGURE 10.6: **Policy of Title Insurance (continued)**

EXCLUSIONS

In addition to the Exceptions in Schedule B, You are not insured against loss, costs, attorneys' fees, and expenses resulting from:

1. Governmental police power, and the existence or violation of any law or government regulation. This includes ordinances, laws and regulations concerning:
   a. building
   b. zoning
   c. land use
   d. improvements on the Land
   e. land division
   f. environmental protection

   This Exclusion does not apply to violations or the enforcement of these matters if notice of the violation or enforcement appears in the Public Records at the Policy Date.

   This Exclusion does not limit the coverage described in Covered Risk 14, 15, 16, 17 or 24.

2. The failure of Your existing structures, or any part of them, to be constructed in accordance with applicable building codes. This Exclusion does not apply to violations of building codes if notice of the violation appears in the Public Records at the Policy Date.

3. The right to take the Land by condemning it, unless:
   a. a notice of exercising the right appears in the Public Records at the Policy Date; or
   b. the taking happened before the Policy Date and is binding on You if You bought the Land without Knowing of the taking.

4. Risks:
   a. that are created, allowed, or agreed to by You, whether or not they appear in the Public Records;
   b. that are Known to You at the Policy Date, but not to Us, unless they appear in the Public Records at the Policy Date;
   c. that result in no loss to You; or
   d. that first occur after the Policy Date - this does not limit the coverage described in Covered Risk 7, 8.d, 22, 23, 24 or 25.

5. Failure to pay value for Your Title.

6. Lack of a right:
   a. to any Land outside the area specifically described and referred to in paragraph 3 of Schedule A; and
   b. in streets, alleys, or waterways that touch the Land.

   This Exclusion does not limit the coverage described in Covered Risk 11 or 18.

CONDITIONS

1. DEFINITIONS:

a. **Easement** - the right of someone else to use the Land for a special purpose.

b. **Known** - things about which You have actual knowledge. The words "Know" and "Knowing" have the same meaning as Known.

c. **Land** - the Land or condominium unit described in paragraph 3 of Schedule A and any improvements on the Land which are real property.

d. **Mortgage** - a mortgage, deed of trust, trust deed or other security instrument.

e. **Natural Person** - a human being, not a commercial or legal organization or entity. Natural Person includes a trustee of a Trust even if the trustee is not a human being.

f. **Policy Date** - the date and time shown in Schedule A. If the insured named in Schedule A first acquires the interest shown in Schedule A by an instrument recorded in the Public Records later than the date and time shown in Schedule A, the Policy Date is the date and time the instrument is recorded.

g. **Public Records** - records that give constructive notice of matters affecting Your Title, according to the state statutes where the Land is located.

h. **Title** - the ownership of Your interest in the Land, as shown in Schedule A.

i. **Trust** - a living trust established by a human being for estate planning.

j. **We/Our/Us** - First American Title Insurance Company.

k. **You/Your** - the insured named in Schedule A and also those identified in paragraph 2.b. of these Conditions.

2. CONTINUATION OF COVERAGE:

a. This Policy insures You forever, even after You no longer have Your Title. You cannot assign this Policy to anyone else.

b. This Policy also insures:
   (1) anyone who inherits Your Title because of Your death;
   (2) Your spouse who receives Your Title because of dissolution of Your marriage;
   (3) the trustee or successor trustee of a Trust to whom You transfer Your Title after the Policy Date; or
   (4) the beneficiaries of Your Trust upon Your death.

c. We may assert against the insureds identified in paragraph 2.b. any rights and defenses that We have against any previous insured under this Policy.

3. HOW TO MAKE A CLAIM

a. Prompt Notice Of Your Claim
   (1) As soon as You Know of anything that might be covered by this Policy, You must notify Us promptly in writing.
   (2) Send Your notice to First American Title Insurance Company, 114 East Fifth Street, Santa Ana, California, 92701, Attention: Claims Department. Please include the Policy number shown in Schedule A , and the county and state where the Land is located. Please enclose a copy of Your policy, if available.
   (3) If You do not give Us prompt notice, Your coverage will be reduced or ended, but only to the extent Your failure affects Our ability to resolve the claim or defend You.

b. Proof Of Your Loss
   (1) We may require You to give Us a written statement signed by You describing Your loss which includes:
      (a) the basis of Your claim;
      (b) the Covered Risks which resulted in Your loss;
      (c) the dollar amount of Your loss; and
      (d) the method You used to compute the amount of Your loss.
   (2) We may require You to make available to Us records, checks, letters, contracts, insurance policies and other papers which relate to Your claim. We may make copies of these papers.
   (3) We may require You to answer questions about Your claim under oath.
   (4) If You fail or refuse to give Us a statement of loss, answer Our questions under oath, or make available to Us the papers We request, Your coverage will be reduced or ended, but only to the extent Your failure or refusal affects Our ability to resolve the claim or defend You.

4. OUR CHOICES WHEN WE LEARN OF A CLAIM

a. After We receive Your notice, or otherwise learn, of a claim that is covered by this Policy, Our choices include one or more of the following:
   (1) Pay the claim.
   (2) Negotiate a settlement.
   (3) Bring or defend a legal action related to the claim.
   (4) Pay You the amount required by this Policy.
   (5) End the coverage of this Policy for the claim by paying You Your actual loss resulting from the Covered Risk, and those costs, attorneys' fees and expenses incurred up to that time which We are obligated to pay.
   (6) End the coverage described in Covered Risk 14, 15, 16 or 18 by paying You the amount of Your insurance then in force for the particular Covered Risk, and those costs, attorneys' fees and expenses incurred up to that time which We are obligated to pay.
   (7) End all coverage of this Policy by paying You the Policy Amount then in force and all those costs, attorneys' fees and expenses incurred up to that time which We are obligated to pay.
   (8) Take other appropriate action.

FIGURE 10.6:   Policy of Title Insurance (continued)

b. When We choose the options in paragraphs 4.a. (5), (6) or (7), all Our obligations for the claim end, including Our obligation to defend, or continue to defend, any legal action.

c. Even if We do not think that the Policy covers the claim, We may choose one or more of the options above. By doing so, We do not give up any rights.

5. HANDLING A CLAIM OR LEGAL ACTION

a. You must cooperate with Us in handling any claim or legal action and give Us all relevant information.

b. If You fail or refuse to cooperate with Us, Your coverage will be reduced or ended, but only to the extent Your failure or refusal affects Our ability to resolve the claim or defend You.

c. We are required to repay You only for those settlement costs, attorneys' fees and expenses that We approve in advance.

d. We have the right to choose the attorney when We bring or defend a legal action on Your behalf. We can appeal any decision to the highest level. We do not have to pay Your claim until the legal action is finally decided.

e. Whether or not We agree there is coverage, We can bring or defend a legal action, or take other appropriate action under this Policy. By doing so, We do not give up any rights.

6. LIMITATION OF OUR LIABILITY

a. After subtracting Your Deductible Amount if it applies, We will pay no more than the least of:

(1) Your actual loss,

(2) Our Maximum Dollar Limit of Liability then in force for the particular Covered Risk, for claims covered only under Covered Risk 14, 15, 16 or 18, or

(3) the Policy Amount then in force,

and any costs, attorneys' fees and expenses which We are obligated to pay under this Policy.

b. (1) If We remove the cause of the claim with reasonable diligence after receiving notice of it, all Our obligations for the claim end, including any obligation for loss You had while We were removing the cause of the claim.

(2) Regardless of 6.b. (1) above, if You cannot use the Land because of a claim covered by this Policy:

(a) You may rent a reasonably equivalent substitute residence and We will repay You for the actual rent You pay, until the earlier of:

(1) the cause of the claim is removed; or

(2) We pay You the amount required by this Policy. If Your claim is covered only under Covered Risk 14, 15, 16 or 18, that payment is the amount of Your insurance then in force for the particular Covered Risk.

(b) We will pay reasonable costs You pay to relocate any personal property You have the right to remove from the Land, including transportation of that personal property for up to twenty-five (25) miles from the Land, and repair of any damage to that personal property because of the relocation. The amount We will pay You under this paragraph is limited to the value of the personal property before You relocate it.

c. All payments We make under this Policy reduce the Policy Amount, except for costs, attorneys' fees and expenses. All payments we make for claims which are covered only under Covered Risk 14, 15, 16 or 18 also reduce Our Maximum Dollar Limit of Liability for the particular Covered Risk, except for costs, attorneys' fees and expenses.

d. If We issue, or have issued, a policy to the owner of a Mortgage on Your Title and We have not given You any coverage against the Mortgage, then:

(1) We have the right to pay any amount due You under this Policy to the owner of the Mortgage to reduce the amount of the Mortgage, and any amount paid shall be treated as a payment to You under this Policy, including under paragraph 4.a.of these Conditions;

(2) Any amount paid to the owner of the Mortgage shall be subtracted from the Policy Amount of this Policy; and

(3) If Your claim is covered only under Covered Risk 14, 15, 16 or 18, any amount paid to the owner of the Mortgage shall also be subtracted from Our Maximum Dollar Limit of Liability for the particular Covered Risk.

e. If You do anything to affect any right of recovery You may have against someone else, We can subtract from Our liability the amount by which You reduced the value of that right.

7. TRANSFER OF YOUR RIGHTS TO US

a. When We settle Your claim, We have all the rights You have against any person or property related to the claim. You must transfer these rights to Us when We ask, and You must not do anything to affect these rights. You must let Us use Your name in enforcing these rights.

b. We will not be liable to You if We do not pursue these rights or if We do not recover any amount that might be recoverable.

c. We will pay any money We collect from enforcing these rights in the following order

(1) to Us for the costs, attorneys' fees and expenses We paid to enforce these rights;

(2) to You for Your loss that You have not already collected;

(3) to Us for any money We paid out under this Policy on account of Your claim; and

(4) to You whatever is left.

d. If You have rights under contracts (such as indemnities, guaranties, bonds or other policies of insurance) to recover all or part of Your loss, then We have all of those rights, even if those contracts provide that those obligated have all of Your rights under this Policy.

8. ENTIRE CONTRACT

This Policy, with any endorsements, is the entire contract between You and Us. To determine the meaning of any part of this Policy, You must read the entire Policy. Any changes to this Policy must be agreed to in writing by Us. Any claim You make against Us must be made under this Policy and is subject to its terms.

9. INCREASED POLICY AMOUNT

The Policy Amount will increase by ten percent (10%) of the Policy Amount shown in Schedule A each year for the first five years following the policy date shown in Schedule A up to one hundred fifty percent (150%) of the Policy Amount shown in Schedule A. The increase each year will happen on the anniversary of the policy date shown in Schedule A.

10. SEVERABILITY

If any part of this Policy is held to be legally unenforceable, both You and We can still enforce the rest of this Policy.

11. ARBITRATION

a. If permitted in the state where the Land is located You or We may demand arbitration.

b. The arbitration shall be binding on both You and Us. The arbitration shall decide any matter in dispute between You and Us.

c. The arbitration award may be entered as a judgment in the proper court.

d. The arbitration shall be under the Title Insurance Arbitration Rules of the American Arbitration Association. You may choose current Rules or Rules in existence on the Policy Date.

e. The law used in the arbitration is the law of the place where the Land is located.

f. You can get a copy of the Rules from Us.

Preliminary report   After the title insurance policy is ordered and before the sale closes, the title insurer submits a **preliminary report** to the purchaser through the escrow holder. The preliminary report

- describes the property and names the owner of record;

- indicates any outstanding taxes, bonds, and assessments;

- identifies any conditions and restrictions on the property; and

- lists any recorded encumbrances or other items that will be exceptions to the title insurance coverage. (Encumbrances need to be cleared before the loan can be made, because the title insurance will not protect the lender's interest against them.)

Title insurance fees   Title insurance is paid for in a single payment. The expense of title insurance can be paid by either buyer or seller, as the parties negotiate:

- The policy fee for title insurance benefiting the *lender* typically is paid by the borrower (buyer).

- Title insurance benefiting the *buyer* could be paid for by either buyer or seller.

North vs. South

In Northern California, the customary practice is for the owner's title insurance policy to be paid by the buyer.

In Southern California, the customary practice is for the owner's title insurance policy to be paid by the seller.

Except for the normal compensation paid to employees, no person acting as an escrow agent in California is permitted to pay any commission, fee, or other consideration to anyone in exchange for referring, soliciting, handling, or servicing escrow customers or accounts. This provision (Civil Code 1057.5) also prohibits the use of any such compensation arrangement with any person acting in a dual capacity, or having a direct or indirect interest in the escrow.

Title companies as escrows   Because use of title insurance is so common in California, title companies frequently serve as escrow agents, particularly in Northern California.

Notice If No Title Insurance

Title insurance has become such a necessary and accepted part of real estate transactions that California law (Civil Code 1057.6) requires notice to be given if title insurance will *not* be provided. If title insurance will not be issued in an escrow transaction for the purchase or simultaneous exchange of real property, the purchaser or exchange parties must receive the following notice in a separate document that must be signed and acknowledged by them.

IMPORTANT: IN A PURCHASE OR EXCHANGE OF REAL PROPERTY, IT MAY BE ADVISABLE TO OBTAIN TITLE INSURANCE IN CONNECTION WITH THE CLOSE OF ESCROW SINCE THERE MAY BE PRIOR RECORDED LIENS AND ENCUMBRANCES WHICH AFFECT YOUR INTEREST IN THE PROPERTY BEING ACQUIRED. A NEW POLICY OF TITLE INSURANCE SHOULD BE OBTAINED TO ENSURE YOUR INTEREST IN THE PROPERTY THAT YOU ARE ACQUIRING.

Exercise 10-3

State the form of title protection that has each of the following characteristics:

1. Statement of ownership of property, using the title company's own records

2. Statement of ownership of property, backed by the title company's guarantee

3. Title insurance excluding water rights

4. Title insurance including water rights

5. Complete documentation of all recorded rights and claims of property ownership

6. Title insurance excluding changes in land use brought about by zoning ordinances, with or without recorded notice

SUMMARY

The many steps involved in carrying out a real estate transaction proceed most efficiently when an **escrow agent** is appointed by the parties. The escrow, as an impartial third party, can collect the necessary paperwork and funds and make the required distribution only when all preconditions have been met. The interests of both buyer and seller can thus be protected.

To create a valid escrow there must be a **binding contract** and **conditional delivery** of instruments of transfer to the escrow holder. An escrow agent must be licensed by the state, with certain exceptions. If the parties cannot agree on terms, the escrow holder can bring a legal action known as **interpleader** to have a court determine the rights of the parties.

The lender of the seller will make a **demand for payoff** or submit a **beneficiary statement** if title is to be taken subject to an existing loan. The lender of the buyer will submit a loan package requiring an *appraisal* and *hazard insurance*, among other items. A **preliminary report** will indicate the current owner of record of the property and any encumbrances of record. A structural pest control report may indicate needed repairs. When all conditions have been met, the escrow is complete. A **settlement statement** summarizes the collection and distribution of the proceeds of the sale.

Above all, the buyer wants a *marketable title*—one a prudent person would accept. Through various forms of title examination and verification the present system of **title insurance** has been devised. A **standard policy** insures against certain risks. An **extended-coverage policy** provides more extensive coverage and is particularly useful to lenders. Referral fees for placement or referral of title business are never allowed.

If title insurance will not be issued as part of the escrow for the purchase or simultaneous exchange of real property, notice must be given to the purchaser or parties to the exchange.

OPEN FOR DISCUSSION

As you learned in this unit, the details of the escrow process vary throughout the state. The number of documents produced during even a modest home purchase can be staggering.

1. Suggest ways in which the escrow process might be simplified.

REVIEW QUESTIONS

1. To create an escrow, there must be
   a. a binding contract.
   b. unconditional delivery.
   c. real property.
   d. all of these.

2. Escrow instructions can be
   a. changed by oral agreement.
   b. only unilateral.
   c. changed only by written agreement of both parties.
   d. all of these.

3. The escrow holder acts in the capacity of
   a. mediator.
   b. agent of both parties.
   c. adviser on the transaction.
   d. surety.

4. Which must be licensed as escrow agents to perform such services?
   a. Attorneys
   b. Title insurance companies
   c. Banks
   d. Escrow companies

5. In Southern California, escrows are MOST often held by
   a. savings and loan associations.
   b. escrow companies.
   c. title insurance companies.
   d. attorneys.

6. By law a licensed escrow agent must
   a. pay a referral fee to a real estate agent.
   b. disclose information concerning the transaction to outside parties.
   c. be a corporation.
   d. have a real estate broker's license.

7. A real estate broker can serve as an escrow
   a. through associates.
   b. with other brokers.
   c. when she represents one of the parties to the transaction.
   d. under a fictitious business name.

8. The legal action that may be brought by an escrow holder is
   a. quiet title.
   b. interpleader.
   c. adverse possession.
   d. injunction.

9. Providing a copy of any buyer broker agreement is the responsibility of
   a. the buyer.
   b. the seller.
   c. the escrow agent.
   d. the real estate agent.

10. Providing tenant information is the responsibility of
    a. the buyer.
    b. the seller.
    c. the escrow agent.
    d. the real estate agent.

11. Prorations at closing on amounts other than interest payments usually are based on
    a. a 30-day month.
    b. a 31-day month.
    c. the actual calendar number of days.
    d. the number of days indicated by the buyer.

12. If closing is on May 19, what amount will be charged to the buyers on a total property tax of $4,320 paid by the sellers for the current tax year? Remember to use the standard number of days in the month.
    a. $492
    b. $504
    c. $1,584
    d. $1,728

13. Closing is on June 15, and rent of $2,400 has been prepaid for the current month. What amount will the seller be debited at closing if the buyer receives credit for the day of closing?
    a. $1,280
    b. $1,200
    c. $1,350
    d. $2,200

14. A buyer's settlement statement includes
    a. only prorations chargeable to the buyer.
    b. the borrower's loan application.
    c. loan origination fees.
    d. all encumbrances of record.

15. The MOST thorough method of title check results in
    a. an abstract of title.
    b. a certificate of title.
    c. a guarantee of title.
    d. a policy of title insurance.

16. A title plant consists of
    a. all possible title records.
    b. a title company's lot books and general indexes.
    c. recorded and unrecorded title information.
    d. duplicates of county recorder's records.

17. Title insurance is paid as of the day
    a. escrow opens.
    b. the sales contract is executed.
    c. of closing.
    d. the buyer takes possession.

18. Title insurance protects a buyer against
    a. all claims from any source.
    b. all claims except those excluded by the policy.
    c. claims arising from the buyer's future actions.
    d. any claims the buyer already knows about.

19. Water rights are excluded from coverage in
    a. a standard policy of title insurance.
    b. an extended-coverage policy of title insurance.
    c. a warranty deed.
    d. all residential title insurance policies.

20. Lender's title insurance typically is paid by
    a. the buyer.
    b. the seller.
    c. the lender.
    d. the broker.

11

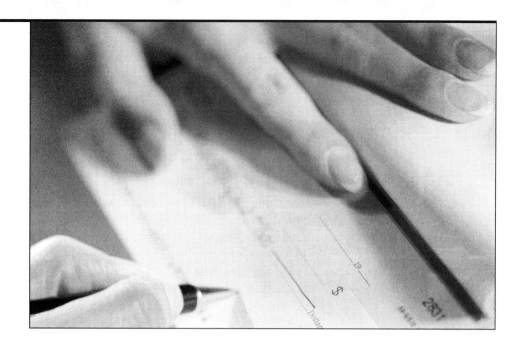

REAL ESTATE TAXATION

LEARNING OBJECTIVES

When you have completed this unit, you will be able to

- **describe** how the real property tax rate is determined;

- **define** base value, assessed value, and a reassessment event;

- **identify** the important dates in the property tax year;

- **compute** a documentary transfer tax;

- **name** the tax considerations that affect homeowners;

- **describe** the general provisions of a tax-deferred exchange; and

- **determine** whether or not the California rules on tax withholding apply in a transaction.

KEY TERMS

ad valorem	documentary transfer	property tax year
adjusted cost basis	tax	Proposition 13
adjusted gross income	donee	reassessment event
assessed value	donor	recovery property
base value	estate tax	sales tax
basis	franchise tax	special assessment
benefit assessment	gift	straight-line method
boot	gift tax	supplemental
California Franchise	homeowner's	assessment
Tax Board	exemption	taxable income
capital asset	inheritance tax	tax bracket
capital gain	installment sale	tax credit
certificate of	Mello-Roos	tax deed
redemption	Community	tax-deferred exchange
change in ownership	Facilities Act	Taxpayer Advocate's
statement	Morgan Property	Office
county assessor	Taxpayers' Bill	tax rate
deductions	of Rights	use tax
depreciation	ordinary income	veteran's exemption

PROPERTY TAXATION

Property taxes usually are **ad valorem** taxes. They are charged in relation to the value of the property taxed (Assessed Value x Tax Rate = Actual Tax). Real property provides an easily measured source of wealth for purposes of taxation. The average homeowner might not feel wealthy, but California real estate historically has been a good investment.

Proposition 13

In 1978, California voters passed **Proposition 13**, an amendment to the California Constitution that is now Section 110.1 of the Revenue and Taxation Code. A summary of the major provisions of Proposition 13 and subsequent voter initiatives follows.

Tax rate The *maximum* annual tax on real property set by the board of supervisors of each county can be no more than

- 1% of base year value, *plus*

- an additional amount to pay for indebtedness (such as transit bonds) that was already approved by voters before passage of Proposition 13, which generally ranges from one-quarter to one-fifth of 1% of property value, *and*

- bonded indebtedness approved by voters after July 1, 1978.

Property value The **base value** of a property is its full cash value (market value) as of February 28, 1975, or the date of a subsequent **reassessment event**.

Assessed value, for property tax purposes, is the property value to which the tax rate is applied. The rules are as follows:

- If there has been no change in the property (addition, remodeling, or other improvement) *or* its ownership since February 28, 1975, assessed value is base value as of that date *plus* an annual inflation factor of no more than 2%.

- If the property has been sold or has changed ownership since February 28, 1975, assessed value is the full cash value as of the date of sale or change of ownership (the base value) *plus* an inflation factor of no more than 2% annually in subsequent years.

- For new construction since February 28, 1975, the assessed value is the full cash value as of completion of construction (the base value) *plus* an inflation factor of no more than 2% annually in subsequent years.

- If existing or new property has been improved since February 28, 1975, assessed value is the base value *plus* the value of the improvement *plus* an inflation factor of no more than 2% annually in subsequent years.

Assessed values do not always go up, even though there is no change in ownership. For the tax year 2010, assessed values in California were reduced for the first time because of a negative inflation (deflation) factor of 0.237% for 2009. The resulting decline in taxes owed was about $2.60 per $100,000 of assessed value. A property's assessed value can also decrease if the property's market value falls below its assessed value.

Special rules   When there is a reassessment event (property is sold or remodeled), the result may be a substantial increase in the property tax base value. Taxpayers thus have passed numerous propositions to limit the effect of Proposition 13. Now the terms *purchase* and *change of ownership* do *not* include

- the transfer of real property between spouses and

- the transfer of a principal residence and the first $1 million in assessed value of other real property between parents and children.

Homeowners over age 55 may be able to transfer a low assessed value to a new home.

Proposition 60 provides that homeowners older than age 55 who buy or build another residence *within the same county* can transfer the assessed value of the previous residence to the new residence. Proposition 90 provides that homeowners older than age 55 may transfer assessed value to a new residence in another county, *if allowed by the new county*. An application form must be submitted within three years of the purchase of the replacement property.

Severely disabled homeowners can transfer their present assessed valuation to a replacement home in the same manner available to those older than age 55. In addition, property improvements that enhance the usability of a home by a severely disabled person are not subject to reassessment. From the 1999–2000 tax year to the 2008–2009 tax year, inclusive, construction or addition of an active solar energy system is excluded from determination of assessed value.

Property Tax Collection

The **county assessor** is the elected official responsible for determining assessed values and preparing the tax roll. Anyone who acquires an interest in real property must file a **change in ownership statement** with the county recorder or assessor *within 45 days* of the date the transfer is recorded. If the transfer is not recorded, the statement must be filed within 45 days of the date of the change in ownership. The penalty for failure to file within 45 days of a written request by the assessor is $100 or 10% of the tax computed on the new base property value, whichever is greater. The penalty also applies if complete information is not supplied following a second request.

www.boe.ca.gov
www.lacounty.gov
http://assessor.lacounty.gov

Taxpayer Rights

The **Morgan Property Taxpayers' Bill of Rights** requires the county assessor to allow inspection and copying of documents related to an assessed property, including an auditor's work papers.

Information on property taxpayer rights can be found at the State Board of Equalization's website, www.boe.ca.gov, as well as from:

State Board of Equalization
Taxpayers' Rights Advocate's Office
PO Box 942879
Sacramento, CA 94279-0070
Phone: 1-888-324-2798

Tax bill information for Los Angeles County is available at www.lacounty.gov. Assessment information, including forms, can be found at the Los Angeles County Assessor Online Public Service, http://assessor.lacounty.gov.

A taxpayer who disagrees with the assessor's opinion of value may *appeal* that decision by contacting the local assessor's office or appeals board office. Time limitations apply on bringing an appeal, so the taxpayer should do so as quickly as possible and be prepared to offer *appraisal data* refuting the assessor's estimate and substantiating the taxpayer's valuation.

FOR EXAMPLE The Smiths decide to add a few rooms to their home. They get a building permit for their planned addition of 1,500 square feet and hire a contractor. While the work is under way, an appraiser from the assessor's office comes by to look at the extent of the property improvement. When the work is finished, the appraiser comes by again, but the Smiths refuse to allow the appraiser to see the finished improvement. Judging from the outside of the property the appraiser estimates that the finished addition is 2,100 square feet. Based on that estimate, the property is reassessed and the Smiths' property tax bill increased accordingly. The Smiths then appeal the assessment, claiming that the finished addition is no more than 1,650 square feet and the assessment should be reduced to reflect that fact.

In this case, the court held that the assessor's estimate is the only reasonable basis on which the reassessment can be made. The Smiths' statement of the square footage of the addition is self-serving and, therefore, cannot serve as the basis for reassessment. The Smiths cannot complain that the estimate is inexact because they themselves refused the assessor's appraiser access to the property.

Exemptions

The general rule is that all real property and tangible personal property (except business inventory) is taxable. Property that is *exempt* from taxation includes

- intangible property (such as stocks and promissory notes);

- personal property and household furnishings of individuals;

- property owned by a government, unless the property is outside the jurisdiction of the public entity and was taxable before acquisition, or it is new construction replacing property that was taxable when acquired;

- property used exclusively for religious, charitable, or hospital purposes; and

- property owned by nonprofit organizations, such as private schools and colleges.

In addition, many boats and seagoing vessels, as well as agricultural products (such as growing crops, fruit and nut-bearing trees less than five years old, and grapevines less than three years old) are exempt.

Homeowner's exemption   An owner-occupied residence, including a condominium or duplex unit, qualifies for a **homeowner's exemption** of the first $7,000 of full cash value. The residence must be occupied by the lien date (January 1). A form available from the county tax assessor must be completed by the owner and filed by 5:00 pm on February 15 of the tax year to receive the exemption.

If the owner's occupancy ceases, the county tax assessor must be notified, or an assessment plus 25% penalty will be made.

> Multiply the exemption amount by four to find its full value.

Veteran's exemption   Qualified California war veterans are entitled to a $4,000 **veteran's exemption** on property not already subject to the homeowner's exemption. A veteran owning more than $5,000 of any type of property ($10,000 if owned by spouses) is ineligible. One-quarter of the value of taxable property and the full value of exempt property are included in calculating the total property owned. The $4,000 exemption also is available for the unmarried surviving spouse or pensioned father or mother of a qualified deceased veteran.

Qualified *disabled* veterans are entitled to a separate exemption. For 2013, the principal residence of a qualified disabled veteran is entitled to an exemption amount of $119,285, or $178,929 if the veteran's annual income is no more than $54,842, with exemption and income limit adjusted annually for inflation. An unremarried surviving spouse of a qualified veteran also is entitled to the exemption. Two qualified disabled veterans who share a residence can each qualify for the exemption amount to the extent of each person's property interest.

How to Compute the Basic Tax Rate

The **property tax year**, as shown in Figure 11.1, runs from July 1 through the following June 30. Property tax is payable in two installments due November 1 and February 1. The November payment is delinquent after 5:00 pm on December 10, and the February payment is delinquent after 5:00 pm on April 10. If those dates fall on a weekend or legal holiday, the deadline is 5:00 pm of the next business day.

A 10% *penalty* is added to delinquent installments. After the second delinquent installment, a $10 fee is charged for adding the property to the delinquent roll.

FOR EXAMPLE Cara and Jose Ortiz have owned their home in Valley Meadow since 1974. The assessor's appraised value of the Ortizes' home in 1975 at the time Proposition 13 went into effect was $62,000, and the Ortizes receive a homeowner's exemption. There are no additional assessments, although there has been an annual increase of 2% in assessed valuation due to inflation. The current assessed value of the Ortizes' home is approximately $119,300. What tax do the Ortizes currently pay? What amount is due in the first installment? What amount will be due if that installment is paid after December 10?

Assessor's appraised value	$119,300.00
Less homeowner's exemption	7,000.00
Taxable amount	$112,300.00
Tax rate	.01
Tax	$1,123.00
Installment	$561.50
Delinquent payment	$617.65

FIGURE 11.1: **Important Dates in the Property Tax Year**

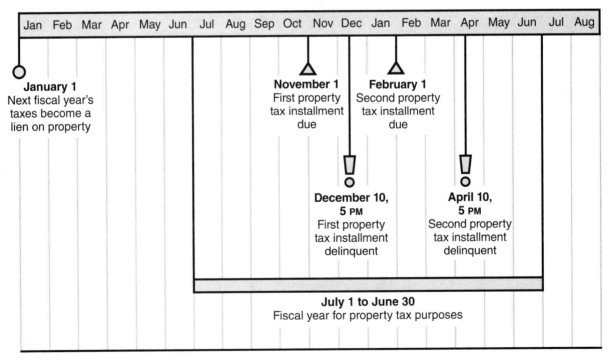

The impact of Proposition 13 is apparent when comparing its effect on similar properties when one has undergone a reassessment event and the other has not.

FOR EXAMPLE   John and Mildred Marsh, neighbors of Cara and Jose Ortiz, moved to their home in Valley Meadow in 1998. The purchase price of their home was $308,000. With the 2% inflation factor applied each year since, the assessed value of the Marsh home in 2006 was $360,871. The Marshes received a homeowner's exemption. What was the Marshes' total tax for the next tax year? The first installment? The delinquent payment on the first installment?

Base value	$360,871.00
Less homeowner's exemption	7,000.00
Taxable amount	$353,871.00
Tax rate	.01
Tax	$3,538.71
Installment	$1,769.36
Delinquent payment	$1,946.29

Exercise 11-1

A home in Valley Meadow was purchased on July 1, 2016. The purchase price was $695,000, and the new owner is entitled to a homeowner's exemption. Compute the new owner's first year property tax bill, the amount of each installment, and the amount of the delinquent payment.

Supplemental Assessments

Few people take possession of real estate on July 1, the first day of the tax year. For the first few years after Proposition 13 took effect, reassessments following property purchase, transfer, construction, or improvement were made only on the next January 1, even if the reassessment event occurred earlier.

As of July 1, 1983, new procedures were put into effect to make sure property is reassessed as quickly as possible. Now if the reassessment event takes place between January 1 and May 31, there are two **supplemental assessments** to adjust for any increase in tax liability. If the reassessment event takes place between June 1 and the last day of December, there is one supplemental assessment. A Notice of Supplemental Assessment may be appealed within 60 days of issuance of the notice.

Tax Lien

When a lien is created   On January 1, when the assessment roll takes effect for the next tax year, a *lien* is placed on all assessed real property in the amount of the tax due.

Real property can also serve as security for personal property taxes.

Taxes on personal property also may be liens on secured real property if they are listed with or cross-referenced to real property on the secured assessment roll. The assessor determines whether the real property is sufficient security for the personal property tax. At the taxpayer's request, real property owned by the taxpayer elsewhere in the county also may secure the personal property tax lien. Before the lien date, the assessor issues and records a certificate to that effect. The real and personal property are cross-referenced in the tax rolls.

Priority of state tax lien   The *state tax lien* takes priority over all others, with some exceptions. The exceptions are for the following:

- Holders of a security interest or mechanic's lien

- Someone who bought the property or took title to it without knowledge of the lien

- A judgment lien creditor who acquired a right, title, or interest before the recording of the lien

Redemption

On June 8 of the tax year, the delinquent tax list is published in a local newspaper of general circulation. *Unpaid taxes* are subject to delinquency penalties. Over time, the amount owed also is increased by additional costs, interest, and redemption penalties. If a taxpayer begins making currently due payments, such arrearages may be paid in five annual installments. At the time all past-due amounts have been paid, the county tax collector issues a **certificate of redemption**.

Tax Sale

If residential property is not redeemed by its owner within *five years* it may be sold. If the property is damaged by a disaster and is located in an area declared to be a disaster area by local, state, or federal officials, the five-year period runs from the date of the damage. After the applicable five-year period, the tax collector has two years to sell the property. The former owner's right to redeem the property is in effect until the close of business on the last business day before a sale occurs. The redemption period for nonresidential commercial property is three years, unless a county elects to apply a five-year redemption to those properties as well.

The tax collector can sell the property to a taxing agency, revenue district, or certain nonprofit organizations. A nonprofit organization purchasing residential property must rehabilitate the property and sell it to low-income persons. If the property is vacant, the organization can dedicate it to public use or construct housing for low-income purchasers. The tax collector also can sell the property to the highest bidder at *public auction*. The County Board of Supervisors approves the minimum bid. The sales price at auction must equal at least 50% of the property's fair market value as determined by the county assessor within one year before the auction date. The high bid must be paid in cash or negotiable paper, or a combination of the two, as the tax collector decides. The purchaser at a tax sale receives a **tax deed**.

Tax Relief for Renters

www.ftb.ca.gov

Renters pay property taxes, in effect, when they pay rent. In recognition of this fact, there is a state income tax credit available to qualified renters meeting income limits. Details of the Renter Assistance Program can be found at the website of the Franchise Tax Board, www.ftb.ca.gov.

Property Tax Postponement and Homeowner Assistance

A senior citizen is a person aged 62 or older.

The state has recognized that many older people on fixed incomes are property owners but have little funds to set aside for taxes. Property tax postponement allows a senior citizen (person aged 62 or older) to postpone payment of taxes on a personal residence. Postponement also is possible by persons who are blind or disabled, as defined in the law. The individual applying for postponement must have at least a 20% equity interest in the property, based on its assessed value, and have an annual total household income of no more than the stipulated amount, currently $35,000.

For those who successfully file a claim for this program, the deferral of property tax creates a lien on the property in favor of the state. Interest on the amount of tax postponed is charged at the rate earned by California's Pooled Money Investment Fund. There is no time limit on the deferral amount and interest, which are recovered by the state when

- the property is *sold*,
- the claimant *dies* or *no longer occupies* the property,
- the claimant *no longer qualifies*, or
- the claimant allows any tax or special assessment to become *delinquent*.

On February 20, 2009, the Senior Citizens and Disabled Citizens Property Tax Postponement Law was suspended, but reinstated as of July 1, 2016.

Special Assessments

A **special assessment** can be imposed on real property for a specific local purpose, such as street construction or repair. A special assessment appears as a separate entry on the property tax bill. Special assessments are made on an ad valorem basis (according to property value) and are liens on the property until paid.

Special assessments require approval of *two-thirds of voters*. Assessments are proposed by a local governing body or by an improvement district created by a city or county, as provided by state law. An assessment for a particular project can be made in one tax period or spread out over a number of years.

Improvement districts may also secure financing by issuing *bonds* that are repaid by assessments.

Benefit Assessments

A **benefit assessment** also may be called a *local assessment, levy based on other than assessed value, special benefit assessment,* or *special assessment.* It is different in form and effect from a true special assessment, however.

A benefit assessment differs from a special assessment in that its tax base is only the properties benefited. Also, a benefit assessment is *not* a deductible tax for federal and state income tax purposes. A benefit assessment is considered a nondeductible assessment to finance a property improvement, rather than a deductible assessment to finance maintenance.

Benefit assessments have been specifically authorized by the state through various measures since 1885. An *improvement area* is created to assess only the property benefited by the improvement. Examples of improvements include grading and finishing of streets, construction of sewers, and acquisition of public utilities. As with special assessments, bonds may be issued for benefit assessments and repaid by tax levy.

Mello-Roos and Other Disclosures

A special form of property assessment is that created by the **Mello-Roos Community Facilities Act**. This law expanded the type of facilities and services that could be provided by improvement bonds and also eliminated the requirement that improvements specifically benefit individual properties. Mello-Roos assessments still are a lien on property, but amounts owed are billed and collected separately from other property taxes.

Because of confusion over the nature of Mello-Roos assessments and the fact that they may not appear on the property tax bill, a seller of a one- to four-unit dwelling subject to a Mello-Roos assessment (or the seller's agent) must *disclose* that fact to a prospective purchaser.

Disclosure must also be made if there are any fixed lien assessments on the property to pay bonds issued under the Improvement Bond Act of 1915 (Streets and Highways Code 8500 and following). A prospective purchaser must be given a mandatory Notice of Your Supplemental Property Tax Bill explaining supplemental property tax assessments, printed in an easy-to-read format (at least 12-point type).

Documentary Transfer Tax

California allows a city or county to impose a **documentary transfer tax** on all transfers of real property located in the jurisdiction. Notice of payment of the documentary transfer tax usually appears on the face of the deed transferring title, but it also can appear on a separate paper filed with the deed. If a *county* has adopted a transfer tax, a *city* within the county may adopt a similar ordinance.

Transfer tax is $.55 per $500 of new money changing hands. It does not include any loan being assumed.

The **tax rate** is 55 cents per $500 or fraction of $500 of the consideration (price) paid for the property. There is no tax if the total consideration is $100 or less (such as the "love and affection" stated as consideration in a gift deed). In computing transfer tax, the consideration paid for the property excludes any preexisting liens or encumbrances that were not removed by the sale (such as an assumed loan).

If a portion of the sales price is not subject to the documentary transfer tax, that information must be provided on the deed or a separate paper filed with the deed. The declaration of the amount of tax due must state whether the property consideration or value was or was not exclusive of the value of any remaining lien or encumbrance.

FOR EXAMPLE The 1200 Via Loca house is sold for $687,575. An existing first trust deed of $524,000 is assumed by the purchaser. What amount of documentary transfer tax may be charged?

$687,575 − $524,000 = $163,575

$163,575 ÷ $500 = $327.15, rounded up to $328

$328 × $.55 = $180.40 transfer tax

Cities sometimes impose documentary transfer tax far in excess of the minimum charged by most counties. For example, the following cities have passed ordinances imposing the indicated transfer tax per $1,000 of value transferred:

Alameda County	
Alameda	$12.00
Berkeley	$15.00
Hayward	$4.50
Oakland	$15.00
Piedmont	$13.00

Los Angeles County	
Culver City	$4.50
Los Angeles	$4.50
Pomona	$2.20
Redondo Beach	$2.20
Santa Monica	$3.00

FOR EXAMPLE The 1200 Via Loca house in the last example is located in Los Angeles. If the sales price and assumed loan amount are the same, what is the total amount of documentary transfer tax that will be charged?

$163,575 ÷ $1,000 = $163.575, rounded to $164

$164 × $4.50 = $738

$738 + $180.40 = $918.40 transfer tax

Taxation of Manufactured Homes

Manufactured can be either personal property or real property. As *personal property*, a manufactured home is subject to vehicle license fee status. Vehicle license fee status means that title to the manufactured home is registered with the Departhttp://housing.hcd.ca.gov

ment of Housing and Community Development (HCD). HCD's website can be found at http://housing.hcd.ca.gov. If treated as *real property*, a manufactured home is subject to local real property taxation.

Qualification as real property   A manufactured home qualifies as *real property* under the Health and Safety Code if

- a building permit is obtained,
- the home is attached to a foundation,
- a certificate of occupancy is obtained, and
- a document stating that the home is attached to a foundation is recorded.

The manufactured home is then treated as a fixture or an improvement to the real estate. HCD cancels its title registration, and title is registered with the county recorder where the manufactured home is located.

There are specific conditions for *removal* of a manufactured home from its foundation. All property owners must give written consent, supplied to HCD, and the local assessor must be notified by 30 days in advance of the move. A transportation permit or mobilehome registration is issued by HCD, as appropriate.

After removal from its foundation, a manufactured home becomes personal property until it again qualifies as real property.

Other State Taxes

Sales tax and use tax   Information concerning sales tax and use tax is available from the local office of the State Board of Equalization.

California Sales Tax

The *minimum* sales tax charged in California, as of January 1, 2013, is 7.5% of gross receipts. That amount is divided between the state, county, and local taxing authorities.

In addition to the minimum sales tax rate, individual counties can add charges and many do so to cover transportation or water district costs. San Francisco has an 8.75% sales tax rate; Los Angeles has a 9% sales tax rate. A complete list of counties and sales tax rates is available at the State Board of Equalization's website, www.boe.ca.gov.

www.boe.ca.gov

State **sales tax** is owed by retailers of tangible personal property regardless of whether the tax was paid by a customer. There are exceptions. Sales of food, for instance, are *not* taxed. The retailer can add sales tax to the product price paid by the customer or pay the tax separately. Buildings removed from land by a seller may be subject to sales tax. Buildings removed by a buyer as part of a transaction are not subject to sales tax. When a business is sold, *fixtures* are subject to sales tax, but *inventory* is not.

Use tax is charged to the purchaser for storage, use, or other consumption of certain purchased or leased tangible personal property. The purchaser is not liable for the tax if the tax was paid to a retailer who has a *seller's permit* to collect it.

If a business requiring a seller's permit is sold, the buyer may be liable for tax owed by the seller. The sale of any business that requires a seller's permit should include provision for an amount to be held in escrow until the State Board of Equalization provides a *tax clearance*.

Broker sales of manufactured homes   A real estate broker selling manufactured homes as a *retailer* must obtain a seller's permit and report applicable sales or use tax.

New manufactured homes sold as dwellings on or after July 1, 1980, are subject to sales tax on 75% of selling price, in addition to property tax. Unattached furnishings are subject to the regular full retail sales tax. Used manufactured homes subject to property tax are exempt from sales tax (except for unattached furnishings). Sales tax applies to manufactured homes that are subject to license fees.

A real estate broker may act as an agent in the sale of a manufactured home, rather than as a dealer. As an agent, the broker should be aware that the sale of a manufactured home that is subject to *property tax* will involve neither sales tax nor use tax. The purchaser of a manufactured home that is *not* subject to property tax will be charged use tax on the purchase price.

State Inheritance and Estate Taxes

To take advantage of federal inheritance tax credits, the California **inheritance tax** and **gift tax** were repealed by voters on June 8, 1982, and no longer apply to estates of decedents who died or to gifts made after that date. The California estate tax was repealed as of January 1, 2005, and requires voter approval to be reinstated.

Federal Gift Tax

A **gift** is a voluntary transfer by an individual of any type of property for less than full consideration. The giver is the **donor**; the recipient of the gift is the **donee**. No gift tax return need be made on a gift to one donee, in one year, of a *present interest* valued, as of 2013, at $14,000 or less. (A married couple could give $14,000 each, for a total of $28,000 to one donee in one year.) For every year after that, the maximum gift allowed before a gift tax return must be made will be $14,000 per donee plus an adjustment for inflation, although the exclusion will remain at $14,000 for 2014. If the gift is a *future interest*, a return always must be made.

Payments made on behalf of someone else as tuition to an educational organization or to a person who provides medical care are *not* considered gifts, no matter what the amount.

Federal gift tax returns must be filed by April 15 of the year following the gift. Even though a return must be filed, there may be a *credit* or an *exemption* available to reduce or eliminate any tax liability. Transfers between spouses, for instance, are not taxed.

Federal Estate Tax

The American Taxpayer Relief Act of 2012 established a federal estate tax exemption of $5 million per person, indexed for inflation. The estate is taxed at a 40% rate on any estate value over that amount. The exemption was $5.25 million for 2013 and is $5.34 million for 2014. The exemption is reduced by any large gifts (those subject to gift tax) made during the decedent's lifetime.

There is no limit on the amount of property that can be left to a spouse. For estates of decedents dying after 1997, the executor can elect to exclude the adjusted value of a qualified family-owned business interest, up to a limited amount, as set out in Section 2033A of the Internal Revenue Code. A *federal estate tax return* must be filed within nine months of death, even if there is no tax due. The *Internal Revenue Service (IRS)* makes pamphlets available that explain the applicable rules.

www.irs.gov

Under the Internal Revenue Code, unpaid federal taxes become a *lien* on all property and rights to property belonging to the taxpayer during the lien period, even if acquired *after* the lien arises. *Notice* of a lien against *real property* must be filed in the county recorder's office where the property is located for the lien to be effective against purchasers, mortgagees of any type, mechanics' lienors, and judgment lien creditors.

Federal Tax Liens

An *estate tax lien*, which is not recorded, attaches to all of the deceased's property at the moment of death. Even though unrecorded, the estate tax lien is valid against later purchasers. Two kinds of recorded estate tax liens are used when tax payments are made in installments or when real property is used in a closely held family business.

A *gift tax lien* is unrecorded. A lien in the amount of the tax is imposed on all gifts made during the year. Gift tax unpaid by the donor becomes a personal liability of the donee.

FEDERAL INCOME TAXES

A *federal income tax return* must be filed by April 15 for the preceding calendar year if adjusted gross income is high enough or federal income tax has been withheld and a refund is due. Both individuals and corporations are taxed, but the discussion that follows deals primarily with individuals.

The amount of *gross income* required before a tax is imposed on an individual depends on

- whether the income earner is married or single (including the divorced or legally separated),

- whether there are any dependent children, and

- if there is a spouse, whether the income earner is living with the spouse and whether income earner and spouse are filing jointly or separately.

The various tax law revisions and clarifications passed by Congress are sometimes phased in over a number of years. Bear in mind that future tax law revisions are inevitable. Your local IRS office has complete details on the current law.

> Awareness of issues of concern does not mean that one becomes a tax advisor.

The real estate licensee should not serve as a tax advisor. But it may be in a real estate broker's or salesperson's best interest to be as familiar as possible with the tax ramifications of real estate transactions. Virtually all important decisions affecting tax liability must be made *before* a transaction is negotiated. The terms of sale will have serious implications for most taxpayers, for whom the purchase of a home is the most important investment of a lifetime. For the investor the transaction becomes even more complex. Unless a real estate licensee is qualified as an income tax or investment counselor, advice on tax and economic factors should be left to the client's tax preparer or advisor.

The following is only a partial list of the many tax concepts covered by the Internal Revenue Code, but it will serve as a general introduction.

Tax Terms

Adjusted gross income   **Adjusted gross income** is the taxpayer's total income. Not all income is taxable. Child support payments are nontaxable income, for example, while alimony payments are considered taxable income in the year received. Contributions to certain retirement accounts, such as 401(k) plans, are not taxed.

Taxable income   A taxpayer's **taxable income** is found by taking allowed exemptions and deductions from *adjusted gross income*. An exemption is allowed for the taxpayer, spouse, and eligible dependents. Taxpayers then choose to take the standard deduction or to itemize deductions separately using the required form. Homeowners may find that the home mortgage interest and property taxes they pay, in addition to charitable and other allowed deductions, provide a greater reduction of taxable income than the standard deduction.

Tax bracket   The **tax bracket** is the tax rate applicable to a taxpayer's taxable income. The higher the taxable income, the higher the rate. At present, income up to a certain level is taxed at 10%, with income above that level taxed at a higher percentage. At very high income levels (more than $378,350 for 2013), individual taxpayers are taxed at a 39.6% rate.

Ordinary income   **Ordinary income** is included in adjusted gross income for tax purposes and includes wages, business income, profits, interest, dividends, rents, and royalties, among other items.

Capital asset   A **capital asset** is all property except business inventory or other property held for sale in the ordinary course of one's business. Capital assets include a personal residence, land held for investment, stocks, bonds, and machinery and equipment used in business.

Depreciation Depreciation is a way to spread the cost of acquiring property used in a trade or business over its useful life and is a deduction from adjusted gross income. An owner-occupied residence, even though purchased for its appreciation potential, is *not* considered a depreciable investment. The cost of improvements to investment (non-owner-occupied) real property can be depreciated over a certain number of years. Land is not depreciable. Later in this unit we discuss one of the ways in which depreciation is determined.

Basis The **basis** of property generally is its cost when acquired, also known as *book value*. Certain business property can be *depreciated*—that is, its cost can be deducted from income, spread out over a number of years. The property's basis is reduced by the amount of depreciation already claimed, but it also can be increased by the cost of any improvements made. The result is an **adjusted cost basis**.

Capital gain **Capital gain** is the difference between the sales price of a capital asset less selling costs and its adjusted cost basis.

The holding period for long-term capital gains tax treatment is 12 months. Gains on investment real estate are taxed generally at 10% or 20%. There is a depreciation recapture rate (tax on prior depreciation deductions) of 25%.

Tax Considerations for the Homeowner

Improvements to real estate that is owned as a personal residence, whether it is a house, condominium, or stock in a cooperative apartment, cannot be depreciated. Homeowners receive other forms of preferential treatment, however. As of August 5, 1997, homeowners are allowed an exclusion from federal income taxation of up to $250,000 (for single taxpayers) or $500,000 (for a couple who are married at the time of sale) of the profit on the sale of the principal residence. The exemption will be allowed if the home was owned and occupied for two of the last five years before the sale.

The full $250,000 single/$500,000 married exemption is available every two years. Under certain circumstances, if qualified property is owned for less than two years, a proportionate share of the exemption can be taken. For example, if a residence is occupied for only one year, then sold as a result of a qualifying job relocation, 50% of the applicable exemption can be used. Effective January 1, 2008, if a married person's spouse dies, the surviving spouse can take advantage of the full $500,000 exclusion on a sale of the principal residence within two years of the date of the spouse's death.

FOR EXAMPLE Penelope Pilot owns her home, for which she paid $372,000, and has occupied it as her principal residence for seven years. If Penelope sells her home for $595,000, must she pay any federal income tax on her profit?

No. Penelope's profit of $223,000 (which will be even lower after it is reduced by expenses of sale, such as a real estate commission) is less than the $250,000 profit she is allowed to receive free from federal income tax.

The Housing Economic Recovery Act of 2008 (HERA) modified the $250,000/$500,000 tax exclusion for gain on the sale of a second home or rental property that is converted to a principal residence. When the second home (or rental property) is sold, any gain attributable to its use as a second home (or rental property) will be taxed at capital gains rates. Any gain attributable to use of the property as the taxpayer's principal residence will be excludable, up to the applicable limit of $250,000 or $500,000.

Deductions   *Mortgage interest payments* on first and second homes are *deductible* from taxable income on an original acquisition loan or a loan to substantially improve the property up to $1,000,000. Interest on loans secured by a personal residence but not used to purchase the residence (home equity loans) is deductible on loan amounts up to $100,000. Local property taxes are also deductible. For many homebuyers, such **deductions** make the difference between an affordable home payment and one that is not. Any state, local, or foreign taxes levied on real property for the general public welfare are deductible. Local benefits taxes are deductible if they are for maintenance or repair, or interest charges to those benefits.

In 2007, for the first time, private mortgage insurance (PMI) payments were made deductible for loans originated in that year. The PMI deduction was extended by Congress through the Mortgage Forgiveness Debt Relief Act of 2007 and later extensions to loans originating between January 1, 2007, and December 31, 2013.

Tax credits   A **tax credit** is a direct deduction, not from income but from tax owed. HERA offered an incentive for first-time home buyers that provided impetus to the housing market. As subsequently modified by the American Recovery and Reinvestment Act of 2009 (ARRA) and other legislation, an $8,000 tax credit was provided for first-time homebuyers who purchased a home by April 30, 2010, or who were under contract to purchase a home by April 30, 2010, and completed the purchase by June 30, 2010. The deadline was April, 2011, for military personnel. Existing homeowners were eligible for a $6,500 tax credit for the purchase of a new home by April 30 if they had sold a home that was the principal residence for five consecutive years out of the preceding eight years. A state tax credit available to California homebuyers is discussed later in this unit.

Note: Homeowners who took advantage of the federal tax credit in 2008 must repay the amount of the credit over 15 years, starting with the tax return for 2010. The remaining balance must be repaid in full if the property is sold within the 15-year payback period. No matter when the credit was taken, if the home is no longer the buyer's principal residence within 36 months of the purchase, the credit taken must be repaid in full. If the property is sold within the first year of ownership, the entire credit is disallowed.

ARRA provided state and local governments with $6 billion in energy efficiency and conservation grants for energy audits, retrofits, and financial incentives. Through 2013, homeowners could claim a 30% tax credit (up from 10%) for purchases of new furnaces, windows, and insulation. Another $5 billion was made available for weatherization assistance for low-income households and $2 billion for energy efficiency projects for federally assisted housing (Section 8).

Tax Considerations for the Investor

An *investor* is someone who buys property for its appreciation or income potential and who does not plan to occupy it personally. An investor *cannot* take advantage of the homeowner's exemption from federal income taxation but receives other benefits of property ownership.

Mortgage interest and property taxes are deductible from property income. Property income also can be reduced by expenses of operation, such as maintenance, utilities, and property management.

Depreciation   One of the most important tax benefits for the real estate investor involves the **depreciation** of property improvements.

Real property that can be depreciated, which includes buildings used in business or for rental or other income-producing activities, is called **recovery property**. The cost of real estate (after subtracting nondepreciating land value) is recovered through deductions from taxable income over a certain number of years. The depreciable value of real estate owned as of January 1, 1987, can be deducted over 27½ years (residential rental property) or 39 years (most other commercial real property), in equal amounts each year. This is called the **straight-line method** of computing depreciation.

FOR EXAMPLE   An investor purchased an apartment building for $7,500,000. The land is valued at $800,000 and the improvements are valued at $6,700,000. What is the amount of the yearly depreciation deduction available to the investor?

The depreciation deduction is $243,636 per year ($6,700,000 ÷ 27.5).

Investors in a real estate partnership may take allowable deductions, but only up to the amount at risk—that is, the amount invested. Losses from partnership investments cannot be used to offset wages and other income.

> Those in the real estate business can deduct rental property losses from other income without limitation.

A person who is *actively* involved in managing her rental real estate and who earns less than $100,000 per year can offset up to $25,000 of losses against that income per year. The allowable deduction is phased out as income rises, and there is no deduction when income is $150,000 or more. As of January 1, 1994, a taxpayer whose primary business is real estate (and spouse, if filing a joint return) can deduct rental property losses from "active" income, including real estate commissions, without limitation.

The longer depreciation term currently in effect has forced many would-be investors to carefully examine the *cash flow* (income-producing) potential of investment property. With the tax advantages of property ownership of somewhat less importance, the property buyer must consider the traditional goal of investment—the ability to generate profit through income or long-term appreciation.

Tax-Deferred Exchanges

Property held for productive use in a trade or business or for investment may be exchanged between owners and qualify for deferral of taxation. To be a **tax-deferred exchange**, as defined in Section 1031 of the Internal Revenue Code, the properties exchanged must be of *like kind* in nature or character. Most real property can be exchanged for other real property, such as an office building for vacant land. Property held for personal use cannot be exchanged for investment property; for example, a personal residence cannot be exchanged for a house that will be rented. Also, property received in an exchange must be held for the required minimum period before being sold.

Related-party exchanges   IRC Section 1031(f) applies to exchanges between parties with a familial or business relationship. Related parties include spouses, brothers, sisters, ancestors such as parents and grandparents, and lineal descendants such as children and grandchildren; a corporation and an individual who owns more than 50% of the value of the stock of the corporation; and two partnerships in which the same person owns more than 50% of the capital or profit interests.

If a taxpayer exchanges property with a related party, and either party disposes of the replacement property within *two years* of the exchange, the Section 1031 nonrecognition of gain does not apply. In other words, the transaction is treated as a sale by each party of the formerly owned property and the proceeds are taxed.

The two-year rule does *not* apply if the property disposition occurs because of the death of the taxpayer or related party, or as a result of a compulsory or voluntary conversion of the property (such as a foreclosure or bankruptcy sale), or if the taxpayer can establish that one of the principal purposes of the exchange or subsequent disposition of the property was *not* the avoidance of federal income tax.

Delayed exchanges   The *Starker* case set the precedent for delayed (nonsimultaneous) exchanges. Property is sold, with the proceeds held by a third party (called a qualified intermediary) until a new property is identified (within 45 days) and purchased (within 180 days).

In a *reverse-Starker*, the replacement property is purchased before the relinquished property is sold. *Caution:* Strict legal requirements mean that legal/tax counsel should be involved in planning and execution of an exchange.

Taxable gain from an exchange   Property received in an exchange has the same *cost basis* for the recipient as the property transferred, provided that no money or other additional consideration accompanies the transfer. Additional consideration, or **boot**, is reportable gain for tax purposes in the amount of the cash value of the boot received.

FOR EXAMPLE An investor exchanged her eight-unit apartment building for a six-store strip shopping center owned by the River Valley Trust. Both properties were owned free and clear, but the investor paid $500,000 in cash in addition to turning over the deed to the apartment building. Disregarding any commission or other expenses of sale, what is the tax impact of the transaction for each party?

The investor's tax basis in her new property is the tax basis of her old property, plus $500,000. She owes no tax on the transaction.

The trust's tax basis in its new property is the tax basis of its old property if the trust's gain is greater than $500,000. In addition, the trust will be taxed on the $500,000 in boot that it received as part of the transaction.

Calculation of gain becomes more difficult when there is a mortgage on one or both properties. The taxpayer then is considered to have received income equal to the relief from indebtedness on the property transferred (the amount of the mortgage). Such *mortgage relief* is offset, however, by any indebtedness on the property received.

A real estate dealer may not elect to take part in a tax-deferred exchange of property held for sale to customers since it is held for resale and not for investment purposes.

Installment Sales

In an **installment sale**, a taxpayer sells property and receives payments over a term that extends beyond the present tax year. The taxpayer can elect to report any profit on the transaction at the time of sale *or* as installment payments are received. The taxpayer's basis in the property plus costs of sale are totaled and deducted from the purchase price (if reported in the year of sale) or deducted proportionately from each tax year's principal payments, with the remainder reported as taxable income. Interest income is always taxable.

Spreading out the reporting of income usually favors the taxpayer/seller, who may avoid a step up to a higher tax bracket or who may not want to pay the required tax in the year of sale. Investment property probably will have been depreciated by the taxpayer, and the taxpayer's cost basis in the property reduced accordingly. To the extent that the installment contract price exceeds the property's reduced basis, it must be reported as gain in the year of sale.

FOR EXAMPLE A homeowner is about to close on the sale of his home. After paying sale expenses, he will receive $125,000 in cash from the equity in the home. If the seller takes the $125,000 cash and places the funds in a five-year U.S. Treasury note, he will receive 4.5% annual interest on his money, or $5,625, which will be compounded (added to principal each year). Instead, the seller may decide to lend the buyers of the home the $125,000 by taking a second trust deed and accepting payments that include interest of 6.5%, the same rate the buyers are paying to the lender on the first deed of trust. If the seller accepts payments of interest only, he will receive interest income of $8,125 per year ($125,000 × 6.5%), or $677.08 per month ($8,125 ÷ 12). If he chooses, the seller can place the interest income in a savings or money market account and receive future interest on that money as well.

STATE INCOME TAX

In general, California income tax law conforms to the federal tax law because both use the same basic computational methods. Information on both individual and business taxes, including tax forms, can be obtained at the **California Franchise Tax Board's** website, www.ftb.ca.gov. You will also find information about the **Taxpayer Advocate's Office**, as well as the text of the *California Taxpayers' Bill of Rights*.

Who Must File

www.ftb.ca.gov

Generally a *state income tax return* must be filed by persons who have been residents of California for the entire year if they have gross income that exceeds the minimum requirement of the tax law. Information and downloadable tax forms can be found at www.ftb.ca.gov/forms. Persons who are nonresidents for part of the year and have income from sources in California file a nonresident or part-year resident tax return regardless of sources of income.

Estates, trusts, and partnerships report income as under federal law. Corporations incorporated in or doing business in California are subject to the *California franchise tax*.

Tax Withholding

Unless an exemption applies, a buyer of California real property must withhold and remit to the Franchise Tax Board funds equal to $3\frac{1}{3}\%$ of the property's sales price, if the seller is an individual. The tax withholding does not apply to a(n)

- seller that is a tax-exempt entity,
- insurance company,
- individual retirement account,
- qualified pension/profit sharing plan,
- charitable remainder trust,
- corporation,
- partnership, or
- limited liability company classified as a partnership for federal and state income tax purposes.

Other exemptions apply to

- the sale of property for $100,000 or less;
- the sale of a principal residence;

- an IRC Section 1031 tax-deferred exchange, although withholding will be required on any cash or cash equivalent the seller receives that exceeds $1,500;

- an involuntary conversion under IRC Section 1033; and

- the sale of property at a loss or zero gain for California income tax purposes.

The seller can claim an exemption by completing Form 593-C, Real Estate Withholding Certificate, and presenting it to the escrow holder before the close of escrow. Real estate agents have no responsibility regarding withholding.

Full details of the tax withholding rules are available at the Franchise Tax Board website.

Exercise 11-2

Matt and Irene Clock are considering purchasing the Folsom house as their principal residence. They never have owned a home and are not sure they can afford one. Their combined gross income is $9,800 per month. They have saved $145,000 and have no outstanding debts. The rent on their present two-bedroom, two-bath apartment is $1,875 per month, and they pay utility bills of $186 per month, averaged over the year. They anticipate yearly rent increases of 5%. Their landlord is holding their security deposit of $1,655.

The three-bedroom, two-bathroom Folsom house could be purchased for $575,000, requiring a down payment of $115,000 and monthly principal and interest payments of $2,757.93 on a loan of $460,000, with a 6% fixed interest rate and a 30-year term. During the first year of the loan, only $5,648.85 in principal would be paid; in the fifth year, $7,176.81 in principal would be paid. The yearly property tax bill would be $5,865, and annual fire insurance would be $1,400. The Folsoms have paid utility bills averaging $225 per month, and the Clocks use that figure.

1. What are the Clocks' present and anticipated total apartment rental expenses before taxes? After taxes, assuming a 28% tax rate? In five years?

2. What would be the Clocks' total monthly expenses as homeowners, before taxes? After taxes, assuming a 28% tax rate? In five years?

3. What other factors should the Clocks take into account in determining the financial advantages and disadvantages of home ownership?

SUMMARY

Proposition 13, approved by California voters, amended the California Constitution to limit the state's ability to increase property tax assessments over 1975 base values. Now there must be a **reassessment event**—transfer of title, new construction, or a property improvement—or assessed valuation may be raised only by an inflation factor of no more than 2% annually. Assessed value could be reduced following a year of negative inflation (deflation) or if a property's market value drops below its assessed value.

The **property tax year** runs from July 1 through the following June 30, with tax due in two installments on November 1 (delinquent after 5:00 pm on December 10) and February 1 (delinquent after 5:00 pm on April 10). A state tax lien that will take priority over most creditors takes effect on January 1 of the tax year.

Residential property not *redeemed* by a *delinquent taxpayer* after five years may be sold at public auction. Nonresidential commercial property must be redeemed within three years or five years, if the county elects.

Special assessments and **benefit assessments** are additional means by which local governing bodies or improvement districts can increase property taxes for a specific purpose. A **documentary transfer tax** (with notice of payment usually shown on the face of a deed) may be required by a city or county.

Manufactured are subject to either *vehicle license fee* status or *real property taxation*. The form of taxation depends on how title is registered and whether the home is permanently attached to a foundation. A real estate broker selling manufactured homes as a retailer must obtain a seller's permit.

Sales tax paid on retail purchases benefits both the state and individual counties. **Use tax** is charged on storage, use, or other consumption of certain purchased or leased tangible personal property.

California no longer imposes an **estate tax**. Federal **gift tax** is currently imposed on gifts of more than $14,000 to one recipient in one year. Federal *estate tax* is imposed on estates of more than the amount set for the tax year.

Unpaid federal taxes become a *lien* on all property of the taxpayer, even if acquired after the lien arises. Notice of a lien against real property must be recorded, but estate and gift tax liens need not be recorded.

Homeowners now can take advantage of the tax *exclusion* of up to $250,000 in profit on the sale of the principal residence if single, or $500,000 in profit if married.

The **tax-deferred exchange** may postpone recognition of taxable gain. An **installment sale** may enable a taxpayer to report gain only when received.

California state *income tax* is paid by individuals. Corporations in California pay **franchise tax**.

OPEN FOR DISCUSSION

The United States is an unusual country in that it provides generous tax incentives for home ownership, such as allowing interest payments on home loans to be deducted from taxable income.

1. Make an argument for continuing this practice.
2. Make an argument for discontinuing this practice.

REVIEW QUESTIONS

1. Property taxes are ad valorem taxes, which means that they are
   a. charged in relation to the value of the property taxed.
   b. charged once at the time of a property transfer.
   c. use taxes.
   d. sales taxes.

2. The Smiths' sale of their residence is
   a. a release of equity.
   b. a reassessment event.
   c. a local assessment.
   d. a notice of change of ownership.

3. The property tax year runs from
   a. January 1 through December 31.
   b. April 10 through December 10.
   c. July 1 through June 30.
   d. December 10 through December 9.

4. A lien in the amount of tax due is placed on all assessed real property on
   a. April 15.
   b. December 10.
   c. January 1.
   d. July 1.

5. When all past-due property taxes are paid, the county tax collector issues
   a. a receipt for unpaid taxes.
   b. a letter of credit.
   c. a certificate of redemption.
   d. a release of equity.

6. The buyer of property at an auction by the tax collector receives
   a. a certificate of sale.
   b. a release of equity.
   c. a quitclaim deed.
   d. a tax deed.

7. A benefit assessment also may be called
   a. a tax credit.
   b. a special assessment.
   c. a community assessment.
   d. a documentary transfer tax.

8. The use of property assessments was expanded by
   a. the Senior Citizens' Tax Act.
   b. the Mello-Roos Community Facilities Act.
   c. the State Board of Equalization.
   d. the Housing Economic Recovery Act.

9. A deed may show on its face that which of the following taxes was paid?
   a. Release of equity
   b. Gift tax
   c. Deed tax
   d. Documentary transfer tax

10. Sales and use taxes are the responsibility of
    a. the Internal Revenue Service.
    b. the Franchise Tax Board.
    c. the State Board of Equalization.
    d. the Department of Housing and Community Development.

11. In California there is a state sales tax on
    a. food.
    b. buildings to be removed from land by the buyer as part of a transaction.
    c. fixtures sold as part of a business.
    d. inventory sold as part of a business.

12. The State of California collects
    a. federal income tax.
    b. gift tax.
    c. state income tax.
    d. inheritance tax.

13. A gift is made
    a. by a donor to a beneficiary.
    b. when an individual voluntarily transfers property for anything less than its fair market value.
    c. any time property is transferred between parent and child.
    d. when like-kind property is exchanged.

14. Gift tax is payable when the total value of gifts to an individual in one year is more than
    a. $8,000.
    b. $14,000.
    c. $15,000.
    d. $28,000.

15. Sam gave his friend Joe $15,000 for his tuition at Old Ivy, sending the money directly to the school. Must a gift tax return be filed?
    a. Yes, because this is a gift
    b. No, because this gift has an exemption
    c. Yes, so that the exemption can be claimed
    d. No, because this is not considered a gift

16. Mario died in 2014, leaving only his separate property estate valued at $500,000. Must an estate tax return be filed?
    a. Yes
    b. No
    c. Only if Mario was a widower
    d. Only if the estate is probated

17. The rate of federal income tax paid depends on the taxpayer's
    a. tax bracket.
    b. state income tax paid.
    c. location.
    d. source of income.

18. Property that can be depreciated for income tax purposes is called
    a. recovery property.
    b. tax basis.
    c. boot.
    d. like-kind property.

19. With respect to investment property, an investor can make use of
    a. the residence replacement rule.
    b. exclusion from taxation.
    c. property tax postponement.
    d. mortgage interest deductions from property income.

20. For 2016, all of the following were deductions from a homeowner's gross income for purposes of federal income taxation *EXCEPT*
    a. mortgage interest on a loan of $750,000.
    b. local property tax.
    c. mortgage interest on combined first- and second-home loans totaling $935,000.
    d. depreciation based on a 39-year schedule.

12

LANDLORD AND TENANT

LEARNING OBJECTIVES

When you have completed this unit, you will be able to

- **define** the types of leasehold estate;
- **describe** how to create a leasehold, and when a written agreement is necessary;
- **explain** the essential terms of a residential lease;
- **list** the obligations of landlord and tenant, and remedies available to each;
- **identify** two of the California laws that prohibit housing discrimination;
- **describe** how a lease is terminated;
- **identify** the important elements of a rent control law; and
- **list** the duties of a property manager.

KEY TERMS

abandonment	Fair Credit Reporting Act (FCRA)	net lease
Civil Rights Housing Act of 2006	Fair Employment and Housing Act (FEHA)	notice to pay or quit
constructive eviction		percentage lease
Costa-Hawkins Rental Housing Act	Fair Housing Amendments Act of 1988	periodic tenancy
covenant of quiet enjoyment	gross lease	property management
covenant to repair	holdover tenancy	rent
escalator clause	landlord	rent control
estate at sufferance	lease	resident apartment manager
estate at will	lease assignment	right of entry
estate for years	leasehold	sandwich lease
estate from period to period	lease option	security deposit
eviction	lessee	tenant
Fair and Accurate Credit Transactions Act of 2003 (FACTA)	lessor	unlawful detainer
	Mobilehome Residency Law (MRL)	Unruh Civil Rights Act
		untenantable dwelling
		warranty of habitability

THE LEASEHOLD

A **lease** is a contract that conveys an interest in real property from one person to another. Any form of real estate ownership can be leased. Most frequently, a lease transfers the *use* of property without transferring outright ownership. The use can be occupancy only, or it can include the right to remove such property assets as oil, gas, or other minerals from the surface or subsurface of the land. The California Civil Code, beginning at Section 1940, governs situations in which a person "hires" real property. *Tenants, lessees, boarders, lodgers,* and others (but not guests at hotels) are included in those provisions, which will be mentioned throughout this unit.

The owner of a **leasehold** has *exclusive* right of possession of the real estate (land, buildings, or both) during the lease term. The lease is the instrument that sets the conditions of the occupancy:

- The **lessor** (**landlord**, the property owner) is someone who owns an interest in real property.

- The **lessee** (**tenant**) is someone who acquires use and possession of the property for a fixed period.

- **Rent** is the consideration paid by the tenant to the landlord in exchange for use of the property.

(Because they are more familiar to most people, the terms *landlord* and *tenant* will be used throughout the rest of this unit, instead of the terms *lessor* and *lessee.*)

The Leasehold as Property

Historically, a leasehold estate was considered *personal property*. Even though a leasehold estate conveyed possession of real estate, it was a personal property right rather than a real property right. This meant that important protections available to real property owners, such as that provided by what is referred to as the "anti-deficiency law," were not available to holders of a leasehold estate.

California law now provides that an estate for years (leasehold) generally is treated as *real property* in

- giving constructive notice of the existence of a leasehold by *recording*;

- determining the *priority* of lien claimants;

- determining the legal *rights* and *remedies* of the parties when an estate for years is hypothecated by a mortgage or trust deed; and

- applying the *antideficiency* law.

Types of Leasehold Estates

> A lease for six months still qualifies as an estate for years.

Estate for years   An **estate for years** is a leasehold created by landlord and tenant for a particular period. The period could be a fixed number of years, months, weeks, or even days. An estate for years always will have a definite termination date that the parties agree to before the lease begins. No termination notice is required.

Estate from period to period   An **estate from period to period** is also called a **periodic tenancy**. At the end of the lease term, if the tenant offers an additional rent payment and the landlord accepts the payment, the lease is renewed for an identical period. The lease continues from period to period until one of the parties gives notice of termination.

Periodic tenancies usually have month-to-month terms. If no lease term has been specified by landlord and tenant, a month-to-month tenancy will be presumed for most real property. Exceptions are lodgings and dwelling houses, if there is no local custom as to lease term. Other exceptions are agricultural or grazing land, where a one-year term is presumed.

Estate at will   In the early days of the common law, an **estate at will** was one that could be terminated by either landlord or tenant at any time, without the consent of the other party. California and other states now have statutory notice requirements that must be met by either landlord or tenant to terminate a tenancy. In addition, the landlord's acceptance of rent creates a periodic tenancy. For these reasons, a true tenancy at will now is uncommon.

Estate at sufferance   An **estate at sufferance** is created when a tenant remains in possession at the end of the agreed-on lease term, without consent of the landlord. An estate at sufferance is also created when a tenant gives notice of intent to vacate but stays on after the date specified in the notice, again, without prior consent of the landlord. Unless the tenant pays rent that is accepted by the landlord, creating a periodic tenancy, the landlord can give notice of termination under an estate at sufferance at any time. For this reason, the estate at sufferance is considered the lowest (least valuable) estate of tenancy.

Creating a Leasehold

An *agreement* to create a leasehold estate that is to terminate *more than one year following the date of the agreement*, even if the lease term is for less than one year, must be *in writing*.

Practically speaking, both landlord and tenant benefit from a written lease agreement, no matter how long the term. Even though only the landlord (or the property manager) need sign the lease (the tenant can accept the lease terms by occupying the property), both parties should sign to avoid misunderstandings.

www.caanet.org

A typical form of *residential* lease, prepared by the California Association of REALTORS®, appears in Figure 12.1. A variety of lease and other forms are available to members of the California Apartment Association through its website, www.caanet.org. It is important to remember the following characteristics of every lease:

- A lease, whether oral or written, is a *contract*. As such, it must follow the contract formalities outlined in Unit 7.
- Parties to the contract must have *legal capacity*, and there must be an *offer* by one party that is *accepted* by the other.
- The contract must have *definite terms* and a *lawful object* and must be supported by sufficient *consideration*.
- If the contract is written, it cannot be changed by oral agreement of the parties. A contract *modification* does take place, however, if both parties *perform* in accordance with orally agreed-on changes.

As mentioned in Units 6 and 7, any predispute contractual waiver of the right to a jury trial is constitutionally invalid.

A carefully drawn lease agreement covers the subjects discussed next. You can remember them as the four *P* 's:

- Parties
- Property
- Period of time
- Payment

Parties   The lease should *identify* the landlord and tenant, as well as any other persons expected to occupy the leased premises.

Property   The property should be adequately *described* and its allowable *use* specified.

Clause 12 of the lease form, shown in Figure 12.1, concerns neighborhood conditions. As of July 1, 1999, all written leases and rental agreements and contracts for sale of residential real property must contain a specified notice regarding the database maintained by law enforcement authorities that contains the locations of registered sex offenders and other related provisions, which is provided in clause 27 of this form.

Period of time (lease term)   The *date* on which the lease is to commence and the *length* of the lease term always should be mentioned. By law, property located in a city or town *cannot* have a lease term longer than 99 years. The 99-year limitation also applies to land leased for the production of oil, gas, or other hydrocarbons. Lands used for agricultural or horticultural purposes cannot be leased for longer than 51 years. The probate court determines the maximum lease term for property belonging to a minor or an incompetent person.

If no lease term is specified for a dwelling, the length of time for which rent is paid is considered the lease term. A weekly rent payment implies a weekly term. If there is no specified time to which the rent applies, a month-to-month tenancy is presumed.

The tenant must receive a copy of the lease or rental agreement within 15 days of executing the agreement. Annually after that, the landlord must provide the tenant with a copy of the lease or rental agreement within 15 days of the tenant's request. If the rental agreement is oral, the landlord must provide the tenant with a written statement setting forth the information required under the new law.

Payment   Rent is the usual consideration paid for possession and use of leased property. A tenant is obligated to pay rent after taking possession or after the period of the lease term begins. Rent can be made payable in advance of the actual possession or beginning of the lease term, or at any other agreed-on time. If the parties fail to stipulate when rent is due, California law provides that it will be payable at the *end* of the lease term if the term is one year or less (or as local custom dictates).

All residential leases and rental agreements must include the name, telephone number, and address of the person or entity to whom rent payments are to be made, and if rent may be paid personally, the usual days and hours the person will be available to receive rent payments. The landlord can choose not to include this information, but only if the landlord expressly includes in the lease or rental agreement specific information that will allow the tenant to pay by direct deposit into the landlord's account or by electronic funds transfer. The lease or rental agreement must also include the form by which rent payments are to be made.

FIGURE 12.1:   Residential Lease or Month-to-Month Rental Agreement

CALIFORNIA ASSOCIATION OF REALTORS ®

RESIDENTIAL LEASE OR MONTH-TO-MONTH RENTAL AGREEMENT
(C.A.R. Form LR, Revised 12/15)

Date _____, _____ ("Landlord") and
_____ ("Tenant") agree as follows:

1. **PROPERTY:**
   A.   Landlord rents to Tenant and Tenant rents from Landlord, the real property and improvements described as:_____
        _____ ("Premises").
   B.   The Premises are for the sole use as a personal residence by the following named person(s) **only:** _____
        _____.
   C.   The following personal property, maintained pursuant to paragraph 11, is included: _____
        _____ or ☐ (if checked) the personal property on the attached addendum.
   D.   The Premises may be subject to a local rent control ordinance _____.
2. **TERM:** The term begins on (date) _____ ("Commencement Date"), **(Check A or B):**
   ☐   A. **Month-to-Month:** and continues as a month-to-month tenancy. Tenant may terminate the tenancy by giving written notice at
        least 30 days prior to the intended termination date. Landlord may terminate the tenancy by giving written notice as provided by
        law. Such notices may be given on any date.
   ☐   B. **Lease:** and shall terminate on (date) _____ at _____ ☐ AM/☐ PM. Tenant
        shall vacate the Premises upon termination of the Agreement, unless: **(i)** Landlord and Tenant have extended this Agreement
        in writing or signed a new agreement; **(ii)** mandated by local rent control law; or **(iii)** Landlord accepts Rent from Tenant (other
        than past due Rent), in which case a month-to-month tenancy shall be created which either party may terminate as specified in
        paragraph 2A. Rent shall be at a rate agreed to by Landlord and Tenant, or as allowed by law. All other terms and conditions of
        this Agreement shall remain in full force and effect.
3. **RENT:** "Rent" shall mean all monetary obligations of Tenant to Landlord under the terms of the Agreement, except security deposit.
   A.   Tenant agrees to pay $ _____ per month for the term of the Agreement.
   B.   Rent is payable in advance on the **1st (or ☐ _____) day** of each calendar month, and is delinquent on the next day.
   C.   If Commencement Date falls on any day other than the day Rent is payable under paragraph 3B, and Tenant has paid one full
        month's Rent in advance of Commencement Date, Rent for the second calendar month shall be prorated and Tenant shall pay
        1/30th of the monthly rent per day for each day remaining in prorated second month.
   D.   PAYMENT: Rent shall be paid by ☐ personal check, ☐ money order, ☐ cashier's check, or ☐ other _____, to
        (name) _____ (phone) _____ at (address) _____
        _____, (or at any other location subsequently
        specified by Landlord in writing to Tenant) (and ☐ if checked, rent may be paid personally, between the hours of _____ and _____
        on the following days _____). If any payment is returned for non-sufficient
        funds ("NSF") or because tenant stops payment, then, after that: (i) Landlord may, in writing, require Tenant to pay Rent in cash for
        three months and (ii) all future Rent shall be paid by ☐ money order, or ☐ cashier's check.
   E.   Rent payments received by Landlord shall be applied to the earliest amount(s) due or past due.
4. **SECURITY DEPOSIT:**
   A.   Tenant agrees to pay $ _____ as a security deposit. Security deposit will be
        ☐ transferred to and held by the Owner of the Premises, or ☐ held in Owner's Broker's trust account.
   B.   All or any portion of the security deposit may be used, as reasonably necessary, to: **(i)** cure Tenant's default in payment of Rent (which
        includes Late Charges, NSF fees or other sums due); **(ii)** repair damage, excluding ordinary wear and tear, caused by Tenant or by a guest
        or licensee of Tenant; **(iii)** clean Premises, if necessary, upon termination of the tenancy; and **(iv)** replace or return personal property or
        appurtenances. **SECURITY DEPOSIT SHALL NOT BE USED BY TENANT IN LIEU OF PAYMENT OF LAST MONTH'S RENT.**
        If all or any portion of the security deposit is used during the tenancy, Tenant agrees to reinstate the total security deposit within five
        days after written notice is delivered to Tenant. Within 21 days after Tenant vacates the Premises, Landlord shall: **(1)** furnish Tenant
        an itemized statement indicating the amount of any security deposit received and the basis for its disposition and supporting
        documentation as required by California Civil Code § 1950.5(g); and **(2)** return any remaining portion of the security deposit to Tenant.
   C.   **Security deposit will not be returned until all Tenants have vacated the Premises and all keys returned. Any security
        deposit returned by check shall be made out to all Tenants named on this Agreement, or as subsequently modified.**
   D.   No interest will be paid on security deposit unless required by local law.
   E.   If the security deposit is held by Owner, Tenant agrees not to hold Broker responsible for its return. If the security deposit is held
        in Owner's Broker's trust account, **and** Broker's authority is terminated before expiration of this Agreement, **and** security deposit is
        released to someone other than Tenant, **then** Broker shall notify Tenant, in writing, where and to whom security deposit has been
        released. Once Tenant has been provided such notice, Tenant agrees not to hold Broker responsible for the security deposit.
5. **MOVE-IN COSTS RECEIVED/DUE:** Move-in funds made payable to _____ shall be
   paid by ☐ personal check, ☐ money order, or ☐ cashier's check.

Category	Total Due	Payment Received	Balance Due	Date Due
Rent from _____ to _____ (date)				
*Security Deposit				
Other _____				
Other _____				
Total				

*The maximum amount Landlord may receive as security deposit, however designated, cannot exceed two months' Rent for unfurnished
premises, or three months' Rent for furnished premises.

Tenant's Initials (_____)(_____)   Landlord's Initials (_____)(_____)

© 2015, California Association of REALTORS®, Inc.
LR REVISED 12/15 (PAGE 1 OF 6) Print Date

EQUAL HOUSING OPPORTUNITY

RESIDENTIAL LEASE OR MONTH-TO-MONTH RENTAL AGREEMENT (LR PAGE 1 OF 6)

Source: Reprinted with permission, California Association of REALTORS®. Endorsement not implied.

FIGURE 12.1:   Residential Lease or Month-to-Month Rental Agreement (continued)

Premises: _____   Date: _____

6. **LATE CHARGE; RETURNED CHECKS:**
   A. Tenant acknowledges either late payment of Rent or issuance of a returned check may cause Landlord to incur costs and expenses, the exact amounts of which are extremely difficult and impractical to determine. These costs may include, but are not limited to, processing, enforcement and accounting expenses, and late charges imposed on Landlord. If any installment of Rent due from Tenant is not received by Landlord within **5 (or ☐ _____) calendar days** after the date due, or if a check is returned, Tenant shall pay to Landlord, respectively, an additional sum of $ _____ or _____% of the Rent due as a Late Charge and $25.00 as a NSF fee for the first returned check and $35.00 as a NSF fee for each additional returned check, either or both of which shall be deemed additional Rent.
   B. Landlord and Tenant agree that these charges represent a fair and reasonable estimate of the costs Landlord may incur by reason of Tenant's late or NSF payment. Any Late Charge or NSF fee due shall be paid with the current installment of Rent. Landlord's acceptance of any Late Charge or NSF fee shall not constitute a waiver as to any default of Tenant. Landlord's right to collect a Late Charge or NSF fee shall not be deemed an extension of the date Rent is due under paragraph 3 or prevent Landlord from exercising any other rights and remedies under this Agreement and as provided by law.

7. **PARKING: (Check A or B)**
   ☐ **A.** Parking is permitted as follows: _____
      _____.
      The right to parking ☐ is ☐ is not included in the Rent charged pursuant to paragraph 3. If not included in the Rent, the parking rental fee shall be an additional $ _____ per month. Parking space(s) are to be used for parking properly licensed and operable motor vehicles, except for trailers, boats, campers, buses or trucks (other than pick-up trucks). Tenant shall park in assigned space(s) only. Parking space(s) are to be kept clean. Vehicles leaking oil, gas or other motor vehicle fluids shall not be parked on the Premises. Mechanical work or storage of inoperable vehicles is not permitted in parking space(s) or elsewhere on the Premises.
  OR ☐ **B.** Parking is not permitted on the Premises.

8. **STORAGE: (Check A or B)**
   ☐ **A.** Storage is permitted as follows:
      The right to separate storage space ☐ is, ☐ is not, included in the Rent charged pursuant to paragraph 3. If not included in the Rent, storage space fee shall be an additional $ _____ per month. Tenant shall store only personal property Tenant owns, and shall not store property claimed by another or in which another has any right, title or interest. Tenant shall not store any improperly packaged food or perishable goods, flammable materials, explosives, hazardous waste or other inherently dangerous material, or illegal substances.
  OR ☐ **B.** Except for Tenant's personal property, contained entirely within the Premises, storage is not permitted on the Premises.

9. **UTILITIES:** Tenant agrees to pay for all utilities and services, and the following charges: _____ except _____, which shall be paid for by Landlord. If any utilities are not separately metered, Tenant shall pay Tenant's proportional share, as reasonably determined and directed by Landlord. If utilities are separately metered, Tenant shall place utilities in Tenant's name as of the Commencement Date. Landlord is only responsible for installing and maintaining one usable telephone jack and one telephone line to the Premises. Tenant shall pay any cost for conversion from existing utilities service provider.

10. **CONDITION OF PREMISES:** Tenant has examined Premises and, if any, all furniture, furnishings, appliances, landscaping and fixtures, including smoke detector(s).
   (Check all that apply:)
   ☐ **A.** Tenant acknowledges these items are clean and in operable condition, with the following exceptions: _____
      _____
   ☐ **B.** Tenant's acknowledgment of the condition of these items is contained in an attached statement of condition (C.A.R. Form MIMO).
   ☐ **C. (i)** Landlord will Deliver to Tenant a statement of condition (C.A.R. Form MIMO) ☐ within **3 days** after execution of this Agreement; ☐ prior to the Commencement Date; ☐ within **3 days** after the Commencement Date.
      (ii) Tenant shall complete and return the MIMO to Landlord within **3 (or ☐ _____) days** after Delivery. Tenant's failure to return the MIMO within that time shall conclusively be deemed Tenant's Acknowledgement of the condition as stated in the MIMO.
   ☐ **D.** Tenant will provide Landlord a list of items that are damaged or not in operable condition within **3 (or ☐ _____) days** after Commencement Date, not as a contingency of this Agreement but rather as an acknowledgment of the condition of the Premises.
   ☐ **E.** Other:_____.

11. **MAINTENANCE USE AND REPORTING:**
   A. Tenant shall properly use, operate and safeguard Premises, including if applicable, any landscaping, furniture, furnishings and appliances, and all mechanical, electrical, gas and plumbing fixtures, carbon monoxide devices and smoke alarms, and keep them and the Premises clean, sanitary and well ventilated. Tenant shall be responsible for checking and maintaining all carbon monoxide detectors and any additional phone lines beyond the one line and jack that Landlord shall provide and maintain. Tenant shall immediately notify Landlord, in writing, of any problem, malfunction or damage with any item including carbon monoxide devices and smoke alarms on the property. Tenant shall be charged for all repairs or replacements caused by Tenant, pets, guests or licensees of Tenant, excluding ordinary wear and tear. Tenant shall be charged for all damage to Premises as a result of failure to report a problem in a timely manner. Tenant shall be charged for repair of drain blockages or stoppages, unless caused by defective plumbing parts or tree roots invading sewer lines.
   B. ☐ Landlord ☐ Tenant shall water the garden, landscaping, trees and shrubs, except: _____
      _____.
   C. ☐ Landlord ☐ Tenant shall maintain the garden, landscaping, trees and shrubs, except: _____
      _____.
   D. ☐ Landlord ☐ Tenant shall maintain _____.
   E. Landlord and Tenant agree that State or local water use restrictions shall supersede any obligation of Landlord or Tenant to water or maintain any garden, landscaping, trees or shrubs pursuant to 11B, 11C, and 11D.
   F. Tenant's failure to maintain any item for which Tenant is responsible shall give Landlord the right to hire someone to perform such maintenance and charge Tenant to cover the cost of such maintenance.
   G. The following items of personal property are included in the Premises without warranty and Landlord will not maintain, repair or replace them: _____.

Tenant's Initials (_____)(_____)   Landlord's Initials (_____)(_____)

LR REVISED 12/15 (PAGE 2 OF 6)

RESIDENTIAL LEASE OR MONTH-TO-MONTH RENTAL AGREEMENT (LR PAGE 2 OF 6)

FIGURE 12.1: Residential Lease or Month-to-Month Rental Agreement (continued)

Premises: _____ Date: _____

12. **NEIGHBORHOOD CONDITIONS:** Tenant is advised to satisfy him or herself as to neighborhood or area conditions, including schools, proximity and adequacy of law enforcement, crime statistics, proximity of registered felons or offenders, fire protection, other governmental services, availability, adequacy and cost of any wired, wireless internet connections or other telecommunications or other technology services and installations, proximity to commercial, industrial or agricultural activities, existing and proposed transportation, construction and development that may affect noise, view, or traffic, airport noise, noise or odor from any source, wild and domestic animals, other nuisances, hazards, or circumstances, cemeteries, facilities and condition of common areas, conditions and influences of significance to certain cultures and/or religions, and personal needs, requirements and preferences of Tenant.

13. **PETS:** Unless otherwise provided in California Civil Code § 54.2, no animal or pet shall be kept on or about the Premises without Landlord's prior written consent, ☐ except as agreed to in the attached Pet Addendum (C.A.R. Form PET).

14. ☐ (If checked) **NO SMOKING:** No smoking of any substance is allowed on the Premises or common areas. If smoking does occur on the Premises or common areas, (i) Tenant is responsible for all damage caused by the smoking including, but not limited to stains, burns, odors and removal of debris; (ii) Tenant is in breach of this Agreement; (iii) Tenant, guests, and all others may be required to leave the Premises; and (iv) Tenant acknowledges that in order to remove odor caused by smoking, Landlord may need to replace carpet and drapes and paint the entire premises regardless of when these items were last cleaned, replaced. or repainted. Such actions and other necessary steps will impact the return of any security deposit. The Premises or common areas may be subject to a local non-smoking ordinance.

15. **RULES/REGULATIONS:**
    A. Tenant agrees to comply with all Landlord rules and regulations that are at any time posted on the Premises or delivered to Tenant. Tenant shall not, and shall ensure that guests and licensees of Tenant shall not, disturb, annoy, endanger or interfere with other tenants of the building or neighbors, or use the Premises for any unlawful purposes, including, but not limited to, using, manufacturing, selling, storing or transporting illicit drugs or other contraband, or violate any law or ordinance, or commit a waste or nuisance on or about the Premises.
    B. (If applicable, check one)
      ☐ **1.** Landlord shall provide Tenant with a copy of the rules and regulations within _____ days
        or _____.
    OR ☐ **2.** Tenant has been provided with, and acknowledges receipt of, a copy of the rules and regulations.

16. ☐ (If checked) **CONDOMINIUM;PLANNED UNIT DEVELOPMENT:**
    A. The Premises are a unit in a condominium, planned unit development, common interest subdivision or other development governed by a homeowners' association ("HOA"). The name of the HOA is _____
      Tenant agrees to comply with all HOA covenants, conditions and restrictions, bylaws, rules and regulations and decisions ("HOA Rules"). Landlord shall provide Tenant copies of HOA Rules, if any. Tenant shall reimburse Landlord for any fines or charges imposed by HOA or other authorities, due to any violation by Tenant, or the guests or licensees of Tenant.
    B. (Check one)
      ☐ **1.** Landlord shall provide Tenant with a copy of the HOA Rules within _____ days
        or _____.
    OR ☐ **2.** Tenant has been provided with, and acknowledges receipt of, a copy of the HOA Rules.

17. **ALTERATIONS; REPAIRS:** Unless otherwise specified by law or paragraph 29C, without Landlord's prior written consent, **(i)** Tenant shall not make any repairs, alterations or improvements in or about the Premises including: painting, wallpapering, adding or changing locks, installing antenna or satellite dish(es), placing signs, displays or exhibits, or using screws, fastening devices, large nails or adhesive materials; **(ii)** Landlord shall not be responsible for the costs of alterations or repairs made by Tenant; **(iii)** Tenant shall not deduct from Rent the costs of any repairs, alterations or improvements; and **(iv)** any deduction made by Tenant shall be considered unpaid Rent.

18. **KEYS; LOCKS:**
    A. Tenant acknowledges receipt of (or Tenant will receive ☐ prior to the Commencement Date, or ☐ _____):
      ☐ _____ key(s) to Premises,   ☐ _____ remote control device(s) for garage door/gate opener(s),
      ☐ _____ key(s) to mailbox,   ☐ _____,
      ☐ _____ key(s) to common area(s),   ☐ _____
    B. Tenant acknowledges that locks to the Premises ☐ have, ☐ have not, been re-keyed.
    C. If Tenant re-keys existing locks or opening devices, Tenant shall immediately deliver copies of all keys to Landlord. Tenant shall pay all costs and charges related to loss of any keys or opening devices. Tenant may not remove locks, even if installed by Tenant.

19. **ENTRY:**
    A. Tenant shall make Premises available to Landlord or Landlord's representative for the purpose of entering to make necessary or agreed repairs (including, but not limited to, installing, repairing, testing, and maintaining smoke detectors and carbon monoxide devices, and bracing, anchoring or strapping water heaters), decorations, alterations, or improvements, or to supply necessary or agreed services, or to show Premises to prospective or actual purchasers, tenants, mortgagees, lenders, appraisers, or contractors.
    B. Landlord and Tenant agree that 24-hour written notice shall be reasonable and sufficient notice, except as follows: (1) 48-hour written notice is required to conduct an inspection of the Premises prior to the Tenant moving out, unless the Tenant waives the right to such notice. (2) If Landlord has in writing informed Tenant that the Premises are for sale and that Tenant will be notified orally to show the premises (C.A.R. Form NSE), then, for the next 120 days following the delivery of the NSE, notice may be given orally to show the Premises to actual or prospective purchasers. (3) No written notice is required if Landlord and Tenant orally agree to an entry for agreed services or repairs if the date and time of entry are within one week of the oral agreement. (4) No notice is required: **(i)** to enter in case of an emergency; **(ii)** if the Tenant is present and consents at the time of entry; or **(iii)** if the Tenant has abandoned or surrendered the Premises.
    C. ☐ (If checked) Tenant authorizes the use of a keysafe/lockbox to allow entry into the Premises and agrees to sign a keysafe/lockbox addendum (C.A.R. Form KLA).

20. **SIGNS:** Tenant authorizes Landlord to place FOR SALE/LEASE signs on the Premises.

21. **ASSIGNMENT; SUBLETTING:** Tenant shall not sublet all or any part of Premises, or assign or transfer this Agreement or any interest in it, without Landlord's prior written consent. Unless such consent is obtained, any assignment, transfer or subletting of Premises or this Agreement or tenancy, by voluntary act of Tenant, operation of law or otherwise, shall, at the option of Landlord, terminate this Agreement. Any proposed assignee, transferee or sublessee shall submit to Landlord an application and credit information for Landlord's approval and, if approved, sign a separate written agreement with Landlord and Tenant. Landlord's consent to any one assignment, transfer or sublease, shall not be construed as consent to any subsequent assignment, transfer or sublease and does not release Tenant of Tenant's obligations under this Agreement.

Tenant's Initials (_____)(_____)   Landlord's Initials (_____)(_____)

LR REVISED 12/15 (PAGE 3 OF 6)

RESIDENTIAL LEASE OR MONTH-TO-MONTH RENTAL AGREEMENT (LR PAGE 3 OF 6)

FIGURE 12.1:   Residential Lease or Month-to-Month Rental Agreement (continued)

Premises: _____ Date: _____

22. **JOINT AND INDIVIDUAL OBLIGATIONS:** If there is more than one Tenant, each one shall be individually and completely responsible for the performance of all obligations of Tenant under this Agreement, jointly with every other Tenant, and individually, whether or not in possession.

23. ☐ **LEAD-BASED PAINT (If checked):** Premises were constructed prior to 1978. In accordance with federal law, Landlord gives and Tenant acknowledges receipt of the disclosures on the attached form (C.A.R. Form FLD) and a federally approved lead pamphlet.

24. ☐ **MILITARY ORDNANCE DISCLOSURE:** (If applicable and known to Landlord) Premises are located within one mile of an area once used for military training, and may contain potentially explosive munitions.

25. ☐ **PERIODIC PEST CONTROL:** Landlord has entered into a contract for periodic pest control treatment of the Premises and shall give Tenant a copy of the notice originally given to Landlord by the pest control company.

26. ☐ **METHAMPHETAMINE CONTAMINATION:** Prior to signing this Agreement, Landlord has given Tenant a notice that a health official has issued an order prohibiting occupancy of the property because of methamphetamine contamination. A copy of the notice and order are attached.

27. **MEGAN'S LAW DATABASE DISCLOSURE:** Notice: Pursuant to Section 290.46 of the Penal Code, information about specified registered sex offenders is made available to the public via an Internet Web site maintained by the Department of Justice at www. meganslaw.ca.gov. Depending on an offender's criminal history, this information will include either the address at which the offender resides or the community of residence and ZIP Code in which he or she resides. (Neither Landlord nor Brokers, if any, are required to check this website. If Tenant wants further information, Tenant should obtain information directly from this website.)

28. **POSSESSION:**
   A. Tenant is not in possession of the Premises. If Landlord is unable to deliver possession of Premises on Commencement Date, such Date shall be extended to the date on which possession is made available to Tenant. If Landlord is unable to deliver possession within 5 (or ☐ _____) **calendar days** after agreed Commencement Date, Tenant may terminate this Agreement by giving written notice to Landlord, and shall be refunded all Rent and security deposit paid. Possession is deemed terminated when Tenant has returned all keys to the Premises to Landlord.
   B. ☐ Tenant is already in possession of the Premises.

29. **TENANT'S OBLIGATIONS UPON VACATING PREMISES:**
   A. Upon termination of this Agreement, Tenant shall: **(i)** give Landlord all copies of all keys or opening devices to Premises, including any common areas; **(ii)** vacate and surrender Premises to Landlord, empty of all persons; **(iii)** vacate any/all parking and/or storage space; **(iv)** clean and deliver Premises, as specified in paragraph C below, to Landlord in the same condition as referenced in paragraph 10; **(v)** remove all debris; **(vi)** give written notice to Landlord of Tenant's forwarding address; and **(vii)**
   _____.
   B. All alterations/improvements made by or caused to be made by Tenant, with or without Landlord's consent, become the property of Landlord upon termination. Landlord may charge Tenant for restoration of the Premises to the condition it was in prior to any alterations/improvements.
   C. **Right to Pre-Move-Out Inspection and Repairs: (i)** After giving or receiving notice of termination of a tenancy (C.A.R. Form NTT), or before the end of a lease, Tenant has the right to request that an inspection of the Premises take place prior to termination of the lease or rental (C.A.R. Form NRI). If Tenant requests such an inspection, Tenant shall be given an opportunity to remedy identified deficiencies prior to termination, consistent with the terms of this Agreement. **(ii)** Any repairs or alterations made to the Premises as a result of this inspection (collectively, "Repairs") shall be made at Tenant's expense. Repairs may be performed by Tenant or through others, who have adequate insurance and licenses and are approved by Landlord. The work shall comply with applicable law, including governmental permit, inspection and approval requirements. Repairs shall be performed in a good, skillful manner with materials of quality and appearance comparable to existing materials. It is understood that exact restoration of appearance or cosmetic items following all Repairs may not be possible. **(iii)** Tenant shall: **(a)** obtain receipts for Repairs performed by others; **(b)** prepare a written statement indicating the Repairs performed by Tenant and the date of such Repairs; and **(c)** provide copies of receipts and statements to Landlord prior to termination. Paragraph 29C does not apply when the tenancy is terminated pursuant to California Code of Civil Procedure § 1161(2), (3) or (4).

30. **BREACH OF CONTRACT; EARLY TERMINATION:** In addition to any obligations established by paragraph 29, in the event of termination by Tenant prior to completion of the original term of the Agreement, Tenant shall also be responsible for lost Rent, rental commissions, advertising expenses and painting costs necessary to ready Premises for re-rental. Landlord may withhold any such amounts from Tenant's security deposit.

31. **TEMPORARY RELOCATION:** Subject to local law, Tenant agrees, upon demand of Landlord, to temporarily vacate Premises for a reasonable period, to allow for fumigation (or other methods) to control wood destroying pests or organisms, or other repairs to Premises. Tenant agrees to comply with all instructions and requirements necessary to prepare Premises to accommodate pest control, fumigation or other work, including bagging or storage of food and medicine, and removal of perishables and valuables. Tenant shall only be entitled to a credit of Rent equal to the per diem Rent for the period of time Tenant is required to vacate Premises.

32. **DAMAGE TO PREMISES:** If, by no fault of Tenant, Premises are totally or partially damaged or destroyed by fire, earthquake, accident or other casualty that render Premises totally or partially uninhabitable, either Landlord or Tenant may terminate this Agreement by giving the other written notice. Rent shall be abated as of the date Premises become totally or partially uninhabitable. The abated amount shall be the current monthly Rent prorated on a 30-day period. If the Agreement is not terminated, Landlord shall promptly repair the damage, and Rent shall be reduced based on the extent to which the damage interferes with Tenant's reasonable use of Premises. If damage occurs as a result of an act of Tenant or Tenant's guests, only Landlord shall have the right of termination, and no reduction in Rent shall be made.

33. **INSURANCE:** Tenant's or guest's personal property and vehicles are not insured by Landlord, manager or, if applicable, HOA, against loss or damage due to fire, theft, vandalism, rain, water, criminal or negligent acts of others, or any other cause. **Tenant is advised to carry Tenant's own insurance (renter's insurance) to protect Tenant from any such loss or damage.** Tenant shall comply with any requirement imposed on Tenant by Landlord's insurer to avoid: **(i)** an increase in Landlord's insurance premium (or Tenant shall pay for the increase in premium); or **(ii)** loss of insurance.

34. **WATERBEDS/PORTABLE WASHERS:** Tenant shall not use or have waterbeds on the Premises unless: **(i)** Tenant obtains a valid waterbed insurance policy; **(ii)** Tenant increases the security deposit in an amount equal to one-half of one month's Rent; and **(iii)** the bed conforms to the floor load capacity of Premises. Tenant shall not use on the Premises ☐ Portable Dishwasher ☐ Portable Washing Machine.

35. **WAIVER:** The waiver of any breach shall not be construed as a continuing waiver of the same or any subsequent breach.

Tenant's Initials (_____)(_____)   Landlord's Initials (_____)(_____)

FIGURE 12.1: Residential Lease or Month-to-Month Rental Agreement (continued)

Premises: _____ Date: _____

36. **NOTICE:** Notices may be served at the following address, or at any other location subsequently designated:
Landlord: _____ Tenant: _____
_____ _____
_____ _____

37. **TENANT ESTOPPEL CERTIFICATE:** Tenant shall execute and return a tenant estoppel certificate delivered to Tenant by Landlord or Landlord's agent within **3 days** after its receipt. Failure to comply with this requirement shall be deemed Tenant's acknowledgment that the tenant estoppel certificate is true and correct, and may be relied upon by a lender or purchaser.

38. **REPRESENTATION**
   A. TENANT REPRESENTATION; OBLIGATIONS REGARDING OCCUPANTS; CREDIT: Tenant warrants that all statements in Tenant's rental application are accurate. Landlord requires all occupants 18 years of age or older and all emancipated minors to complete a lease rental application. Tenant acknowledges this requirement and agrees to notify Landlord when any occupant of the Premises reaches the age of 18 or becomes an emancipated minor. Tenant authorizes Landlord and Broker(s) to obtain Tenant's credit report periodically during the tenancy in connection with the modification or enforcement of this Agreement. Landlord may cancel this Agreement: **(i)** before occupancy begins; **(ii)** upon disapproval of the credit report(s); or **(iii)** at any time, upon discovering that information in Tenant's application is false. A negative credit report reflecting on Tenant's record may be submitted to a credit reporting agency if Tenant fails to fulfill the terms of payment and other obligations under this Agreement.
   B. LANDLORD REPRESENTATIONS: Landlord warrants that, unless otherwise specified in writing, Landlord is unaware of **(i)** any recorded Notices of Default affecting the Premise; **(ii)** any delinquent amounts due under any loan secured by the Premises; and **(iii)** any bankruptcy proceeding affecting the Premises.

39. **MEDIATION:**
   A. Consistent with paragraphs B and C below, Landlord and Tenant agree to mediate any dispute or claim arising between them out of this Agreement, or any resulting transaction, before resorting to court action. Mediation fees, if any, shall be divided equally among the parties involved. If, for any dispute or claim to which this paragraph applies, any party commences an action without first attempting to resolve the matter through mediation, or refuses to mediate after a request has been made, then that party shall not be entitled to recover attorney fees, even if they would otherwise be available to that party in any such action.
   B. The following matters are excluded from mediation: **(i)** an unlawful detainer action; **(ii)** the filing or enforcement of a mechanic's lien; and **(iii)** any matter within the jurisdiction of a probate, small claims or bankruptcy court. The filing of a court action to enable the recording of a notice of pending action, for order of attachment, receivership, injunction, or other provisional remedies, shall not constitute a waiver of the mediation provision.
   C. Landlord and Tenant agree to mediate disputes or claims involving Listing Agent, Leasing Agent or property manager ("Broker"), provided Broker shall have agreed to such mediation prior to, or within a reasonable time after, the dispute or claim is presented to such Broker. Any election by Broker to participate in mediation shall not result in Broker being deemed a party to this Agreement.

40. **ATTORNEY FEES:** In any action or proceeding arising out of this Agreement, the prevailing party between Landlord and Tenant shall be entitled to reasonable attorney fees and costs collectively not to exceed $1,000 (or $_____), except as provided in paragraph 39A.

41. **C.A.R. FORM:** C.A.R. Form means the specific form referenced or another comparable form agreed to by the parties.

42. **OTHER TERMS AND CONDITIONS;SUPPLEMENTS:** ☐ Interpreter/Translator Agreement (C.A.R. Form ITA); _____
☐ Keysafe/Lockbox Addendum (C.A.R. Form KLA); ☐ Lead-Based Paint and Lead-Based Paint Hazards Disclosure (C.A.R. Form FLD);
☐ Landlord in Default Addendum (C.A.R. For LID) _____
_____
The following ATTACHED supplements are incorporated in this Agreement: _____
_____
_____

43. **TIME OF ESSENCE; ENTIRE CONTRACT; CHANGES:** Time is of the essence. All understandings between the parties are incorporated in this Agreement. Its terms are intended by the parties as a final, complete and exclusive expression of their Agreement with respect to its subject matter, and may not be contradicted by evidence of any prior agreement or contemporaneous oral agreement. If any provision of this Agreement is held to be ineffective or invalid, the remaining provisions will nevertheless be given full force and effect. Neither this Agreement nor any provision in it may be extended, amended, modified, altered or changed except in writing. This Agreement is subject to California landlord-tenant law and shall incorporate all changes required by amendment or successors to such law. This Agreement and any supplement, addendum or modification, including any copy, may be signed in two or more counterparts, all of which shall constitute one and the same writing.

44. **AGENCY:**
   A. CONFIRMATION: The following agency relationship(s) are hereby confirmed for this transaction:
   Listing Agent: (Print firm name) _____ is the agent of
   (check one): ☐ the Landlord exclusively; or ☐ both the Landlord and Tenant.
   Leasing Agent: (Print firm name) _____ (if not same as Listing Agent) is
   the agent of (check one): ☐ the Tenant exclusively; or ☐ the Landlord exclusively; or ☐ both the Tenant and Landlord.
   B. DISCLOSURE: ☐ (If checked): The term of this lease exceeds one year. A disclosure regarding real estate agency relationships (C.A.R. Form AD) has been provided to Landlord and Tenant, who each acknowledge its receipt.

45. ☐ **TENANT COMPENSATION TO BROKER:** Upon execution of this Agreement, Tenant agrees to pay compensation to Broker as specified in a separate written agreement between Tenant and Broker.

46. ☐ **INTERPRETER/TRANSLATOR:** The terms of this Agreement have been interpreted for Tenant into the following language: _____. Landlord and Tenant acknowledge receipt of the attached interpreter/translator agreement (C.A.R. Form ITA).

Tenant's Initials (_____)(_____)   Landlord's Initials (_____)(_____)

LR REVISED 12/15 (PAGE 5 OF 6)

RESIDENTIAL LEASE OR MONTH-TO-MONTH RENTAL AGREEMENT (LR PAGE 5 OF 6)

FIGURE 12.1:   Residential Lease or Month-to-Month Rental Agreement (continued)

Premises: _____   Date: _____

47. NOTICE OF RIGHT TO RECEIVE FOREIGN LANGUAGE TRANSLATION OF LEASE/RENTAL AGREEMENTS: California Civil Code requires a landlord or property manager to provide a tenant with a foreign language translation copy of a lease or rental agreement. If the agreement was negotiated primarily in Spanish, Chinese, Korean, Tagalog or Vietnamese. If aplicable, every term of the lease/rental needs to be translated except for, among others, names, dollar amounts and dates written as numerals, and words with no generally accepted non-English translation.

48. OWNER COMPENSATION TO BROKER: Upon execution of this Agreement, Owner agrees to pay compensation to Broker as specified in a separate written agreement between Owner and Broker (C.A.R. Form LL or LCA).

49. RECEIPT: If specified in paragraph 5, Landlord or Broker, acknowledges receipt of move-in funds.

> Landlord and Tenant acknowledge and agree Brokers: **(a)** do not guarantee the condition of the Premises; **(b)** cannot verify representations made by others; **(c)** cannot provide legal or tax advice; **(d)** will not provide other advice or information that exceeds the knowledge, education or experience required to obtain a real estate license. Furthermore, if Brokers are not also acting as Landlord in this Agreement, Brokers: **(e)** do not decide what rental rate a Tenant should pay or Landlord should accept; and **(f)** do not decide upon the length or other terms of tenancy. Landlord and Tenant agree that they will seek legal, tax, insurance and other desired assistance from appropriate professionals.

Tenant agrees to rent the Premises on the above terms and conditions.

Tenant _____   Date _____
Address _____ City _____ State _____ Zip _____
Telephone _____ Fax _____ E-mail _____
Tenant _____   Date _____
Address _____ City _____ State _____ Zip _____
Telephone _____ Fax _____ E-mail _____

☐ **GUARANTEE:** In consideration of the execution of this Agreement by and between Landlord and Tenant and for valuable consideration, receipt of which is hereby acknowledged, the undersigned ("Guarantor") does hereby: **(i)** guarantee unconditionally to Landlord and Landlord's agents, successors and assigns, the prompt payment of Rent or other sums that become due pursuant to this Agreement, including any and all court costs and attorney fees included in enforcing the Agreement; **(ii)** consent to any changes, modifications or alterations of any term in this Agreement agreed to by Landlord and Tenant; and **(iii)** waive any right to require Landlord and/or Landlord's agents to proceed against Tenant for any default occurring under this Agreement before seeking to enforce this Guarantee.

Guarantor (Print Name) _____
Guarantor _____   Date _____
Address _____ City _____ State _____ Zip _____
Telephone _____ Fax _____ E-mail _____

Landlord agrees to rent the Premises on the above terms and conditions.

Landlord _____ Date _____ Landlord _____ Date _____
Address _____
Telephone _____ Fax _____ E-mail _____

> **REAL ESTATE BROKERS:**
> **A.** Real estate brokers who are not also Landlord under this Agreement are not parties to the Agreement between Landlord and Tenant.
> **B.** Agency relationships are confirmed in paragraph 44.
> **C.** **COOPERATING BROKER COMPENSATION:** Listing Broker agrees to pay Cooperating Broker (Leasing Firm) and Cooperating Broker agrees to accept: **(i)** the amount specified in the MLS, provided Cooperating Broker is a Participant of the MLS in which the Property is offered for sale or lease or a reciprocal MLS; or **(ii)** ☐ (if checked) the amount specified in a separate written agreement between Listing Broker and Cooperating Broker.

Real Estate Broker (Listing Firm) _____ CalBRE Lic. # _____
By (Agent) _____ CalBRE Lic. # _____ Date _____
Address _____ City _____ State _____ Zip _____
Telephone _____ Fax _____ E-mail _____

Real Estate Broker (Leasing Firm) _____ CalBRE Lic. # _____
By (Agent) _____ CalBRE Lic. # _____ Date _____
Address _____ City _____ State _____ Zip _____
Telephone _____ Fax _____ E-mail _____

Published and Distributed by:
REAL ESTATE BUSINESS SERVICES, INC.
a subsidiary of the California Association of REALTORS®
525 South Virgil Avenue, Los Angeles, California 90020

LR REVISED 12/15 (PAGE 6 OF 6)

Reviewed by _____ Date _____   EQUAL HOUSING OPPORTUNITY

RESIDENTIAL LEASE OR MONTH-TO-MONTH RENTAL AGREEMENT (LR PAGE 6 OF 6)

Source: Reprinted with permission, California Association of REALTORS®. Endorsement not implied.

If the address provided by the landlord does not allow for personal delivery, it is conclusively presumed that the landlord received the rent on the date posted, if the tenant provides proof of mailing to the name and address provided by the landlord.

Price Gouging Is a Crime

Penal Code Section 396 makes it a misdemeanor to sell certain goods and services for a price that exceeds by 10% the price charged for the good or service immediately prior to the proclamation of a state of emergency by the President of the United States or the governor, or the declaration of a local emergency by the executive officer of a city or county, resulting from an earthquake, flood, fire, riot, storm, or natural or manmade disaster.

The law applies for a period of 30 days following the declaration and includes rental housing with an initial lease term of no longer than one year. The 30-day period may be extended for additional 30-day periods, as needed, by the official or governing body, if necessary to protect the lives, property, or welfare of citizens.

Violation of the law is punishable by imprisonment in a county jail for up to one year, a fine of up to $10,000, or both. In addition, violation of the law will be considered an unlawful business practice and an act of unfair competition which can result in additional, cumulative remedies under the Business and Professions Code or other laws.

Security deposit   A **security deposit** is an amount paid at the *start* of the lease term and retained by the landlord until the tenant vacates the premises. All or part of the security deposit may be kept by the landlord at the end of the lease term to cover costs of any *default in rent payments* by the tenant or *reasonable costs of repairs or cleaning* necessitated by the tenant's use of the premises.

The security required for a rental of residential property includes any charges imposed at the beginning of the tenancy, including costs associated with processing a new tenant and costs associated with cleaning the property. Application screening fees are not included. The landlord must notify the tenant in writing of the tenant's option to request an initial inspection on termination of the tenancy, and the tenant's right to be present at the inspection. If the tenant requests an initial inspection, the landlord must make that inspection before a final inspection, after the tenant vacates, and provide the tenant with an itemized list of potential deductions from the security. The tenant must have the opportunity to remedy identified deficiencies during the period from the initial inspection until the end of the tenancy. The maximum amount of a security deposit is

- two months' rent for an *unfurnished* residential property or
- three months' rent for a *furnished* residential property.

Within *21 days* after the tenant has vacated the premises, the landlord must mail the tenant either the full amount of the security deposit or an itemized statement of the basis for the disposition of any of the security deposit and a check for any remaining amount.

If the landlord's interest in the property is *transferred*, the security deposit also is transferred. The tenant is notified by personal delivery or certified mail of the transfer, any claims against the security deposit, and the transferee's name, address, and telephone number. *Alternatively,* the remaining security deposit can be returned to the tenant along with an itemized statement of the basis for the disposition of any amount not returned.

A landlord retaining any amount of the security deposit in bad faith is subject to damages of twice the amount of the security, in addition to the actual loss suffered by the tenant.

> A security deposit on residential property cannot be labeled nonrefundable.

If any question arises about the validity of a claim, the law presumes that the tenant is entitled to the return of the entire security deposit. The landlord has the burden of proving the reasonableness of the amounts claimed. In fact, the California Civil Code provides that in a lease or rental of *residential property*, a security deposit can *never* be labeled "nonrefundable."

Similar provisions apply in the case of nonresidential property, but

- the amount of the required security deposit is *not* limited,

- any portion of the security deposit in excess of one month's rent must be returned to the tenant within *two weeks* after the landlord receives possession of the premises, and

- the landlord has up to *30 days* after receiving possession to return the remaining deposit after deductions for repairs or cleaning (but not anticipated future damages).

The security deposit often is a substantial amount of money. It is in the tenant's best interest to inspect the premises being leased carefully at the time of first taking possession by completing a *statement of property condition*. If the tenant provides such a statement to the landlord at both the beginning and the end of the lease term, there should be fewer disputes later about repairs properly charged against the tenant's security deposit.

Possession by the tenant   The tenant's right to possession is ensured by the **covenant of quiet enjoyment** made by the landlord, which is implied by law. The covenant refers not to noise but to interference by the landlord in the tenant's possession or use of the property. The landlord could interfere with the tenant's possession by removing the tenant from the property by the eviction process discussed later in this unit.

The landlord also could bring about a **constructive eviction** of the tenant by

- failing to make necessary repairs, after notice from the tenant;

- interfering with the tenant's legitimate use of the property;

- threatening to remove the tenant;

- making unwarranted alterations to the property; or

- attempting to lease the property to someone else.

Landlord's right of entry The landlord has the right to enter the premises if necessary. The California Civil Code permits such **right of entry** in the following cases:

- An *emergency*
- When the tenant has *abandoned* the premises
- Pursuant to a *court order*
- So that the landlord can make necessary or agreed-on *repairs* or perform other required *services*
- So that the landlord can *show* the property to prospective tenants, mortgagees, purchasers, workers, or contractors

The landlord must give the tenant *notice* of the intended entry unless there is an emergency (and then must notify the tenant immediately afterward), or the tenant has abandoned the premises, or it is impractical to do so. Notice of *at least 24 hours* is presumed to be sufficient.

Tenant improvements A residential lease usually requires prior approval by the landlord before the tenant makes any alterations to the premises. Subject to negotiation, a commercial lease is likely to require that the tenant make property alterations, called "tenant improvements," and also may require that the tenant return the property to its original condition on termination.

What If a Tenant Has Installed a Fixture?

If the lease mentions fixtures installed by the tenant, then the lease terms apply.

If no prior agreement was made regarding fixtures installed by the tenant and removal of a fixture would damage the property, the tenant may not remove the fixture, even at the conclusion of the lease term.

If there is no prior agreement regarding fixtures and the fixture can be removed without injury to the property, the tenant may do so if the fixture was installed by the tenant for the purpose of trade, manufacture, ornamental, or domestic use.

The best way to avoid conflict is to clarify the status of such items before they are brought onto the property.

Transferability The tenant may need to vacate the premises before the end of the lease term. The landlord may agree to *terminate* the lease (to increase the rent paid by a new tenant, for instance).

A tenant also can transfer possession of leased property by *sublease* or *assignment*, unless prohibited from doing so by the lease terms. The lease could require landlord approval before a sublease or an assignment. The landlord's decision on approval must be *reasonable*.

In a *sublease* the tenant transfers possession of the property to another party for only part of the remaining lease term. The original tenant then has a reversion, which is the right to possess the property when it is vacated by the sublessee. The original tenant's interest is also called a **sandwich lease**. *Primary responsibility for payment of rent remains with the original tenant.*

Internet Private Residence Rental Listings

The use of an internet listing platform, such as Airbnb, by a tenant is considered a short-term property sublease and must comply with the tenant's lease terms. Legislation, beginning with Section 22590, has been added to Division 8 of the Business and Professions Code, to clarify the obligations of the "hosting platform", which must provide notice to occupants listing a residence for a short-term rental that, if the occupant is a tenant, the rental contract or lease may contain restrictions on the occupant's ability to list the property and the possibility of legal action by the landlord that may include eviction. There must be an affirmative acknowledgment by the occupant of having read the notice before the property can be listed on the hosting platform's internet site.

Alternatively, the tenant can make a **lease assignment** of the entire remaining lease term to another party. In an assignment, the first tenant retains no interest in the property but is secondarily liable for lease obligations, unless the landlord agrees to release the first tenant from further liability.

Renewal of the lease   The lease usually specifies the procedure for its renewal. It is preferable to have a new lease drawn up for the new term, although the old lease could be extended on the original terms.

A lease could provide for an *automatic renewal* or extension of the lease term if the tenant were to remain in possession after the termination date. All such provisions in residential leases are now *voidable* by the party who did not prepare the lease unless

- the automatic renewal clause is printed in at least eight-point *boldface type* and

- the existence of the automatic renewal provision is noted *directly above* the space provided for the tenant's signature, again in at least eight-point *boldface type*.

Exercise 12-1

1. Sue Parker rents a one-bedroom apartment in Walnut Grove for $450 per month. Sue's rent probably will increase in three months, when her lease term ends. What kind of leasehold estate does Sue have?

2. The lease on Jim Smith's apartment ended last month. The landlord has not offered to renew the lease, and Jim has not made another rent payment. What kind of leasehold estate does Jim have?

3. When must a lease agreement be in writing?

4. Jim Smith rented an office in which to conduct his bookmaking operation from his good friend Sam, who liked the convenience of placing bets in

his own building. Jim was arrested before the lease term expired and will not be returning for some time. Can Sam collect the remaining rent payments?

5. Sue Parker is considering a move to a new one-bedroom unfurnished apartment. The monthly rent is $650, and the landlord expects a security deposit of $2,000. That amount seems excessive to Sue. Is she right?

6. Sue will rent the apartment of a friend who is going abroad for nine months, then return it to her friend. What will Sue have?

7. While Sue was at work, her landlord went into her apartment without her knowledge to turn off the gas line, which was leaking somewhere in the building. Should Sue object?

Landlord's Obligations

As a minimum the landlord must follow all applicable housing or building standards. Even if there is no express provision in a lease agreement, there is a legally implied **warranty of habitability**. The California legislature has specified in the Civil Code the conditions under which a dwelling will be considered *untenantable*.

Covenant to repair   In most lease agreements the landlord expressly covenants (promises) to make necessary repairs to the premises. If there is no express promise to repair, a court may find an implied **covenant to repair**, depending on the nature of the work required.

FOR EXAMPLE   The Jolly Arms apartment complex has a tennis court for the exclusive use of residents. The tennis court is not mentioned in the lease that the apartment management firm uses, however. Part of the tennis court is destroyed in a small mud slide, and the tennis court is fenced off and not repaired. The tenants bring suit against the owner of the complex and the management firm, claiming breach of the covenant to repair. Will they be successful?

Unless repairs to the tennis court are specifically mentioned in the lease, a tennis court may not be considered an element of habitability that automatically will impose an implied covenant to repair.

Residential tenant's remedies   To whom can a tenant complain? The local Building Inspection Department, Health Department, or Fire Department will receive tenant complaints on applicable violations of state or local building, fire and safety, and other standards. The tenant's complaint will be investigated, and the landlord will be required to make necessary repairs.

If a residential landlord won't make repairs that are necessary to make the property *tenantable* (livable), the tenant is allowed to make repairs to the property. The tenant must give written or oral notice of the needed repairs to the landlord or the landlord's agent, then wait a reasonable time (30 days, for example, depending on the circumstances) for the landlord to act. After that time, if the landlord has not acted, the tenant can spend up to one month's rent on repairs. The tenant may not *repair and deduct* more than twice in any 12-month period.

> A landlord is not allowed to retaliate against a tenant who complains.

A landlord is not allowed to penalize a tenant who complains to an appropriate agency about the condition of the premises or who uses rent money for repairs. Actions considered "penalties" include retaliatory eviction, increasing rent, or decreasing services. If the landlord does retaliate against the tenant and the tenant is not in default in payment of rent, the landlord may *not* recover possession of the premises, cause the tenant to quit the premises, increase rent, or decrease services, for *180 days* from notice of the complaint or needed repair.

If the landlord fails to make a necessary repair, the tenant also may sue the landlord for *breach of the warranty of habitability*. Or the tenant could simply *abandon* the premises with no further obligation to pay rent or otherwise comply with the lease terms. The tenant should seek competent professional advice before taking either action, however.

An Untenantable Dwelling

California law defines an **untenantable dwelling** as one that substantially *lacks* any of the following:

- Dead bolt lock on each swinging entry door
- Security or locking device on every window designed to open
- Adequate weatherproofing, including unbroken windows and doors
- Plumbing or gas lines that conformed to local building codes when installed and have been maintained in good working order
- Hot and cold running water, with fixtures and sewage disposal system approved under applicable law
- Heating facilities that conformed to applicable law when installed and have been maintained in good working order
- Electrical lighting, with equipment and wiring that conform to local building codes and are maintained in good working order
- Building and grounds clean, sanitary, and free of debris, rubbish, rodents, and vermin at the time the lease term begins, with areas under the control of the landlord to be so maintained during the lease term
- Adequate trash receptacles provided in clean condition and good repair and so maintained by the landlord when under the landlord's control
- Floors, stairways, and railings maintained in good repair

Commercial tenant's remedies   There are important exceptions to a commercial tenant's remedies, for a commercial tenant is regarded as being in a better bargaining position than a residential tenant.

At present, the courts generally do *not* allow a commercial tenant to *repair and deduct*. A commercial tenant can bring a *lawsuit* against the landlord for breach of warranty, rather than use the breach as a reason for nonpayment of rent. The commercial tenant also may treat the breach as a *constructive eviction*, vacate the premises, and sue for damages.

Tenant's Obligations

In addition to paying rent, the *tenant* must care for the leased property and use it appropriately. The tenant's duties are specified in the California Civil Code:

- The tenant must keep the premises as clean and sanitary as conditions permit. Rubbish and other waste must be disposed of in a clean and sanitary manner. (The landlord could agree in writing to undertake the duties of maintenance and waste disposal.)

- The tenant must use all electrical, gas, and plumbing fixtures properly and keep them as clean and sanitary as conditions permit.

- Neither the tenant nor any person on the premises with the tenant's permission may deface, impair, or remove any part of the structure or its equipment.

- With regard to a dwelling place, different portions of the property may be used by the tenant only for the purposes for which they were designed and intended. For instance, only the kitchen may be used for cooking.

Landlord's remedies   If a tenant is in substantial violation of his obligation to use *ordinary care* to maintain the premises, a residential landlord has no duty to make resulting necessary repairs. The lease could give the tenant the *duty to repair*, but if such repairs are not reasonable the landlord will be unable to sue for damages if the repairs are not made.

Breach of lease terms also may give the landlord grounds for terminating the lease and evicting the tenant if necessary.

Liability of Landlord and Tenant

A guest in a leased building trips on a piece of loose tile flooring, falls, and breaks his arm. Who is liable for damages arising from the *defective condition* of the premises? Under certain conditions, the *landlord, tenant, or both* could be liable for injuries suffered on the premises by anyone, whether tenant, an invited guest, someone permitted on the premises (such as a meter reader), or even a trespasser.

The **landlord** of *residential* property may be liable under a negligence theory for injuries to tenants that result from the defective condition of the premises at the time the tenant takes possession, if the landlord failed to correct the defect. The landlord's liability generally extends to damages that arise from injuries caused by *defective conditions* in the leased real estate that the landlord knew or should, with reasonable diligence, have known about. Even after the tenant takes possession, the landlord must repair defects that are brought to the landlord's attention. The landlord also is charged with the condition of public areas or areas over which the landlord retains control, such as hallways, stairways, and elevators.

F O R   E X A M P L E   An apartment tenant suffered serious injuries after falling in a slippery bathtub. The landlord had received complaints about bathtubs but did nothing to rectify the problem. Is the landlord liable for the tenant's injuries?

In this case, yes, because the landlord should have treated the bathtub to make it safer for residents.

The tenant should notify the landlord of a dangerous condition.

The landlord is not allowed to hide a defect in the property or simply post a warning sign. On the other hand, if the tenant is *aware* of a property defect that arises after taking possession and fails to notify the landlord, the landlord will *not* be liable for any subsequent injury.

The landlord is *not* liable to a *trespasser* who is injured on the property if the landlord did not know and could not be expected to know of an unsafe condition.

The *tenant's* liability extends to injuries on the premises as a result of the tenant's lack of ordinary care in maintaining the premises.

FOR EXAMPLE   A trespasser entered the premises of an automobile paint stripping company through a hole in a fence. The trespasser noticed a vat of a smelly liquid next to a business building. The vat was partially covered with a piece of plywood. The trespasser climbed onto the plywood to look through one of the building's windows. The plywood broke, and the trespasser fell into the vat, which contained highly corrosive acid used in stripping paint from cars. The landlord did not know of the hole in the fence, which was not there when the property was originally leased. The landlord was aware of the purpose for which the property had been leased, however. Is the landlord liable for the severe burns suffered by the trespasser?

No, the landlord is not liable for the trespasser's injuries. The property was used for its expected ordinary business purpose, and the landlord was unaware of the hole in the fence. The tenant may be liable to the trespasser if the tenant knew, or should have known, about the hole in the fence.

Exercise 12-2

Who usually bears responsibility for each of the following in a residential apartment building?

1. Termite infestation

2. Hole in plaster wall made by guest of tenant

3. Injury suffered by guest who trips over tenant's coffee table

4. Insufficient lighting in common hallway

5. Broken main entry door to building

6. Window broken by present tenant

7. Window broken by previous tenant

8. Trash pickup from outside receptacles

9. Removing trash from premises

10. Injuries to trespasser who falls through floorboard weakened by tenant's bathtub overflow that was never reported to the landlord

Discriminatory Acts

California's **Fair Employment and Housing Act** (FEHA), found in the Government Code, prohibits housing discrimination based on marital status as well as race, color, religion, sex (including gender identity), sexual orientation, national origin, ancestry, familial status (age), disability (physical or mental), medical condition, or source of income. The *Department of Fair Employment and Housing* enforces the law, which is based on the former Rumford Fair Housing Act.

FOR EXAMPLE Some years ago, Len Lessor tried to evict Alice Tenant because Alice, an unmarried woman, was living with an unrelated adult male. Len was unsuccessful because his intended action violated what was then the Rumford Act. Len recently decided to require that each member of an unrelated couple living together in one of his apartments meet his rental financial requirements, even though married couples can aggregate their income to meet the financial requirements. Can Len do that?

No. The Fair Employment and Housing Act bans discrimination based on marital status.

Note: "Discrimination" under FEHA does *not* include refusal to rent part of a single-family, owner-occupied dwelling to only one individual. All notices and advertisements must comply with FEHA, except for those expressing a preference for applicants of one sex for the sharing of living areas in a single dwelling unit.

California's **Civil Rights Housing Act of 2006** provides that, as of January 1, 2007, all of the protected classifications of FEHA are extended automatically to all other nondiscrimination laws; this includes the Unruh Civil Rights Act, discussed next.

The **Unruh Civil Rights Act**, found in the California Civil Code, now forbids discrimination as to race, color, religion, ancestry, national origin, familial status (age), disability (physical or mental), medical condition, marital status, sex (including gender identity), sexual orientation, and source of income in *accommodations* and *business establishments*. Under the Unruh Act, there can be no arbitrary eviction, rent increase, or withholding of services by virtually any landlord, including the owner of a non-owner-occupied single-family dwelling that is sold or leased for income or gain. An exception to the prohibition of discrimination based on age is made for housing designed to meet the physical and social needs of senior citizens.

FOR EXAMPLE Len Lessor brings an action to evict Adam Lessee from one of his rental properties because Adam has numerous tattoos, receives public assistance, and is a student.

Len will not be successful because all of those "reasons" are arbitrary and fail to establish good cause for an eviction.

The same act of discrimination can violate both state and federal law. Since 1968, *federal law* has expressly prohibited public and private discrimination based on race, religion, or national origin or ancestry in the sale, rental, or lease of housing.

Discrimination based on sex was prohibited in 1974. With the passage of the **Fair Housing Amendments Act of 1988**, discrimination on the basis of handicap or familial status (age) is also prohibited. These and other federal prohibitions against discrimination in housing will be covered further in Unit 15.

Termination of the Lease

There are various ways by which a lease may be terminated, both with and without the consent of both parties.

Expiration of the lease term   The lease should specify a termination date or the length of any notice that must be given to the other party before termination.

| Landlord and tenant are free to agree on a termination date. |

A *lease for a definite term* terminates at the end of that term, even without notice. A *periodic tenancy* (usually month-to-month) may be terminated by the landlord or tenant on notice equal to the lease period but not more than 30 days before the date of termination. If a tenant fails to give adequate notice of termination, additional rent may be owed even if the premises are vacated as of the end of the lease term. If both parties agree, notice to vacate may be shorter than 30 days.

A residential tenancy requires a 60-day notice if the tenant has resided in the dwelling for one year or more. A *tenant at sufferance* need not be given advance notice. The *death* of landlord or tenant automatically terminates a tenancy at will or tenancy at sufferance. It does not terminate a tenancy for a definite term unless the lease provides otherwise.

FOR EXAMPLE   Jane Dough rented an apartment on a month-to-month basis as of the first of each month. On April 15, after six months, she notified her landlord that she would vacate the apartment on April 30. Jane Dough is liable for rent up to May 15. If Jane gives notice on April 15 of her intent to vacate on May 15, she still will owe rent only through May 15.

Under Section 1946.7 of the Civil Code, special notice requirements apply if a residential tenant who intends to terminate a tenancy is a victim of domestic violence or sexual assault. The notice requirement is just 14 days if the tenant attaches to the written notice to terminate

- a copy of either a temporary restraining order or a protective order that protects the tenant or household member from further domestic violence or sexual assault,

- a report by a peace officer stating that the tenant or household member has filed a report alleging that person or the household member has filed a report alleging the person or household member is a victim of domestic violence or sexual assault, or

- documentation from a qualified third party, based on information received while the third party was acting in a professional capacity, indicating that the tenant or household member is seeking assistance for physical or mental injuries or abuse resulting from an act of domestic violence, sexual assault, stalking, human trafficking, elder abuse, or dependent adult abuse.

Surrender of the leasehold estate   The lease interest can be given up by a *surrender* of the leasehold. This will happen if both parties consent to it, or if one of them acts in a manner inconsistent with the existence of the lease (such as the landlord leasing the property to someone else).

Grounds for unilateral termination   Either landlord or tenant may have grounds for *termination* of the lease without the other's consent.

A lease may be terminated by a *tenant* in the following situations:

- The landlord has violated the tenant's right to *quiet enjoyment* (possession).
- The landlord has violated the *duty to repair*.
- The landlord otherwise has failed to keep the premises *habitable*.
- The landlord *evicts* the tenant.
- The landlord *breaches* a condition of the lease.
- The premises are *destroyed* and there is no covenant to repair.
- The property is taken by *eminent domain*. (If only part of the property is taken, the lease will be effective as to the rest unless a court determines the remaining property is unsuitable for its leased purpose.)

A lease may be terminated by a *landlord* in the following situations:

- The tenant uses the premises for an *unauthorized purpose*.
- The tenant *abandons* the premises.
- The tenant *breaches* a condition of the lease.
- The premises are *destroyed* and there is no covenant to repair.

Request for demolition   California requires the owner of a residential dwelling unit (or the owner's agent) who applies to any public agency for a permit to demolish the unit to give written notice of the request to current tenants before applying for the permit. Notice of the request must be given to prospective tenants before entering into or initiating a rental agreement. The notice must include the earliest possible approximate date the owner expects the demolition to occur as well as the approximate date the owner will terminate the tenancy. If a landlord fails to provide the required notice, a court may award a tenant actual damages and moving expenses, in addition to a civil penalty not to exceed $2,500 and reasonable attorney's fees.

Abandonment   Abandonment is the tenant's voluntary relinquishment of the premises without the landlord's express or implied consent and with no intention to perform future lease obligations. (The landlord's express or implied consent would make the relinquishment a surrender rather than an abandonment.)

If rent is owed for at least 14 days and the landlord reasonably believes the tenant has abandoned the premises, the landlord can establish the fact of abandonment by giving *written notice* of that belief. The tenant must respond in writing within 15 days after personal service of the notice, or 18 days after receiving a mailed notice, denying any intent to abandon the property and giving the landlord a forwarding address where he can be reached. Notice is not strictly necessary, but it is a wise precaution that will protect the landlord if the tenant shows up later. Abandonment notice can be given in addition to any other notice and may be the fastest way to establish the landlord's right to retake possession of property.

Eviction

Eviction is the process by which a tenant can be removed from the leased premises. The landlord must first *notify* the tenant of the breach of the lease or other unfulfilled obligation.

Notice   If the tenant has not paid the required rent, the lessor must first give three days' written **notice to pay or quit**, requesting compliance with the lease terms or property relinquishment. An example of such a notice appears in Figure 12.2. Similar notice is given if the tenant has breached some other lease provision. If an illegal sale of a controlled substance has occurred on the premises, the landlord can give a three-day *notice to quit* without providing for the option to cure the misconduct. If drug activity can be proven, city attorneys and district attorneys can evict tenants within the cities of Long Beach, Los Angeles, Oakland, and San Diego.

If notice to terminate is given as discussed earlier, the notice period will be the period specified in the lease, the period of tenancy, or 30 days. In a periodic tenancy the notice period is 30 days, unless the lease specifies a shorter period, which must be at least seven days. Even when a tenant has breached such a lease (by not paying rent, for instance), the landlord may choose to use the 30-day notice to prevent the tenant from paying the rent and curing the breach. The landlord also could give both forms of notice.

FIGURE 12.2:   Notice to Pay Rent or Quit

**CALIFORNIA
ASSOCIATION
OF REALTORS®**

NOTICE TO PAY RENT OR QUIT

(C.A.R. Form PRQ, Revised 11/11)

To: _____ ("Tenant")
and any other occupant(s) in possession of the premises located at: _____
_____ (Street Address) _____ (Unit/Apartment #)
_____ (City) _____ (State) _____ (Zip Code) ("Premises").

Other notice address if different from Premises above: _____
_____.

Notice to the above-named person(s) and any other occupants of the above-referenced Premises:

WITHIN 3 (OR ☐ _____ (BUT NOT LESS THAN 3)) DAYS from service of this Notice you are required to either:
1.   Pay rent for the Premises in the following amount, which is past due, to _____
_____ (Name) _____ (Phone)
at _____
_____ (Address)
between the hours of _____ on the following days: _____.

Past Due Rent: $ _____ for the period _____ to _____
$ _____ for the period _____ to _____
$ _____ for the period _____ to _____
Total Due: $ _____.

OR 2.   Vacate the Premises and surrender possession.

If you do not pay the past due amount or give up possession by the required time, a legal action will be filed seeking not only damages and possession, but also a statutory damage penalty of up to $600.00 (California Code of Civil Procedure § 1174). Landlord declares a forfeiture of the lease if past due rent is not paid and you continue to occupy the Premises. As required by law, you are hereby notified that a negative credit report reflecting on your credit record may be submitted to a credit reporting agency if you fail to pay your rent.

Landlord _____ Date _____
(Owner or Agent)
Address _____ City _____ State _____ Zip _____
Telephone _____ Fax _____ E-mail _____

(Keep a copy for your records.)

This Notice was served by:

1.   ☐   **Personal service.** A copy of the Notice was personally delivered to the above named Tenant.

2.   ☐   **Substituted service.** A copy of the Notice was left with a person of suitable age and discretion at the Tenant's residence or usual place of business and a copy was mailed to the Tenant at Tenant's residence.

3.   ☐   **Post and mail.** A copy of the Notice was affixed to a conspicuous place on the Premises and a copy was mailed to the Tenant at the Premises.

Published and Distributed by:
REAL ESTATE BUSINESS SERVICES, INC.
a subsidiary of the California Association of REALTORS®
525 South Virgil Avenue, Los Angeles, California 90020

11/11

Reviewed by _____ Date _____

EQUAL HOUSING
OPPORTUNITY

NOTICE TO PAY RENT OR QUIT (PRQ PAGE 1 OF 1)

Source: Reprinted with permission, California Association of REALTORS®. Endorsement not implied.

Notice must be *written* and *personally served* on the other party or, in the tenant's absence, on a suitable person at the tenant's residence or place of business. If served on a third party, notice also must be mailed to the tenant at the tenant's residence address. If no residence or business address is known, notice must be placed in a conspicuous place on the leased property and also mailed to the tenant at the property location.

Government-Owned or Subsidized Housing

Special notice requirements apply for rental housing owned or subsidized by a government agency. In 2005, the California Supreme Court held in *Wasatch Property Mgt. v. Degrate* that Section 8/ public housing tenants are entitled to a 90-day notice of lease termination. An action to evict such a tenant requires good cause to evict or an administrative hearing to determine whether there is good cause to evict. At the hearing, the tenant can be represented by an attorney. The tenant also has the right to have the hearing conducted in private.

Unlawful detainer If the tenant fails to comply after notice to pay or quit has been given, the landlord can *sue* for rent owed (which does not terminate the lease). The landlord also can request an *order of eviction* from the court by a legal proceeding called **unlawful detainer**. If the court decides in favor of the landlord and if the notice to the tenant stated the landlord's intention to declare a forfeiture of the lease, the lease will be forfeited.

The tenant will be liable for damages (such as rent owed) up to the date of the court's judgment or the date the landlord retakes possession of the premises. If the landlord failed to include a statement of intention to declare a forfeiture in the notice, the tenant's liability for damages is up to the court's determination.

A landlord of residential property may not cause disruption or termination of the tenant's utility service, even if the right of eviction has been granted.

Tenant's response The tenant can defeat the unlawful detainer action if

- proper notice was not given,
- the landlord's action is retaliatory,
- the alleged facts are not true,
- the landlord's action is arbitrary (without good cause), or
- there is some other legal barrier to the eviction, such as a violation of the Unruh Act.

A tenant may *willfully* and *maliciously* remain in possession of leased premises after the expiration or termination of the lease term, in what is called a **holdover tenancy**. In that case, the tenant is liable to the landlord for *three times* the amount of rent and any damages due, as punitive damages.

An unlawful detainer action is given priority over all other civil cases.

An unlawful detainer is not the only legal action that can be brought by a landlord against a tenant, but it may be the *quickest* way to regain possession of leased premises. Courts must give unlawful detainer suits precedence over all other cases—except criminal cases—in setting a court date.

Lessor and lessee frequently settle their differences before a trial. The landlord may forgive part or all of the rent owed, or even pay the tenant's moving expenses, in exchange for a prompt vacancy. If the tenant has proof of some breach by the landlord, it is more likely that concessions will be made.

Writ of possession   The landlord who succeeds in an unlawful detainer suit can be awarded *rent arrearages*, *damages* caused by the unlawful detention, and *possession* of the leased premises. If possession is granted, the clerk of the court issues a *writ of possession* that directs the sheriff or marshal to take all legal steps necessary to remove the tenant(s) from the premises.

The sheriff or marshal executes the writ by *serving* it on one occupant of the property. Service is accomplished by leaving a copy of the writ with the occupant or an employee or agent of the occupant or a suitable member of the occupant's household. If that is not possible, a copy of the writ is *posted* in a conspicuous place on the premises, and another copy is served *personally* or *by mail* to the judgment debtor.

Five days after the service, the sheriff or marshal may remove any occupant still on the premises, *unless* the occupant

- is *not* named in the writ and
- claims possession or a right to possession that stems from *before* the time at which the unlawful detainer action was filed with the court.

Stay of execution   The tenant may receive a *stay of execution* of a judgment in favor of the landlord for *five days* to pay back rent and have legal possession restored *if*

- the reason for the eviction is nonpayment of rent,
- the lease would not have expired otherwise, and
- the termination notice did not declare the forfeiture of the tenant's lease rights.

The trial court also can stay execution of the judgment under its own authority.

Tenant's personal possessions   An *inventory* must be made of any of the tenant's personal possessions left behind when the tenant vacates the premises. The inventory is made or verified by the sheriff or marshal. The landlord must store the possessions for 15 days from the date notice is personally delivered or 18 days after mailing, during which time they can be reclaimed on payment of reasonable storage fees. If unclaimed, they may be sold at public auction and the proceeds applied to storage and sale costs. Any remaining sale proceeds and security or other deposits must be returned to the tenant.

FOR EXAMPLE   A tenant was evicted from an apartment at the Jolly Arms. The tenant never responded to any of the notices that were sent. When the property manager took possession of the apartment, a sheriff's deputy was present to inventory the clothing and furnishings the tenant had left behind. The items then were stored in a locked basement area inaccessible to tenants. The landlord also changed the locks to the apartment. One week later, the tenant showed up and demanded the key to her apartment. She said he had been called out of the country on a very important assignment and had simply been too busy to send word back to the property manager. Does the tenant have the right to reclaim the apartment?

No. It was the tenant's responsibility to make sure that her absence was understood and not misinterpreted as an abandonment of the apartment. By failing to contact the property manager, the tenant forfeited her right to the apartment. She can reclaim the belongings she left in the apartment, but she must pay any reasonable storage fees. She also will receive any part of her security deposit to which she is entitled.

MOBILEHOME TENANCIES

Laws applying to mobilehomes appear in many California code sections. Some of the most important provisions are mentioned here.

Mobilehome Residency Law

The **Mobilehome Residency Law** (MRL) (Civil Code Sections 798–799) regulates manufactured home (mobilehome) rental agreements, charges, grounds for eviction, and eviction procedures.

The MRL defines a *mobilehome, mobilehome park, homeowner, resident,* and *tenancy* to which the law is applicable. General landlord-tenant laws apply to manufactured housing, except where they are preempted by specific laws regarding such homes.

Applicability   The MRL applies to agreements between (1) mobilehome park management and the resident of an owner-occupied home and (2) mobilehome park management and a nonresident owner who rents a home to someone else. In the latter case, the agreement could include provision for subletting.

Agreements between park management and the resident of a park-owned home are not included in the MRL, although for the sake of uniformity similar provisions should be used.

Parks are subject to the same provisions against discrimination that apply to other residential landlords, although the type and size of homes within a park can be controlled.

Fees   The *prescribed lease form* includes any fees to be paid by the tenant, although an additional fee can be imposed after 60 days' written notice. Fees are *limited* to rent, utilities, and incidental reasonable service charges.

Termination   The MRL states the following as the *only* permitted reasons for termination of a lease by mobilehome park management:

- Nonpayment of rent, utility charges, or reasonable incidental service charges

■ Failure to comply with reasonable park rules or regulations as set out in the rental agreement or amendments

■ Conduct by the homeowner or resident on park premises that is a "substantial annoyance" to other homeowners or residents

■ Failure of homeowner or resident to comply with applicable laws and ordinances within a reasonable time

■ Condemnation of the park

■ Change of use of the park

Notice If a tenant has not paid rent, utility bills, or other fees for at least five days from their due date, termination proceedings may begin. A written *notice to pay or quit* must be made, allowing *three days* for payment to be made. Written *notice of termination* must be given *60 days* before the termination date. A copy of the notice must be sent to the registered mobilehome owner and junior lienholders within 10 days of service on the homeowner.

> A notice of termination can be defeated by payment, but only twice in a 12-month period.

Notice of termination can be given at the same time as notice to pay or quit, but payment within the three-day period will satisfy both. The registered homeowner (if not the same as the resident), the legal owner (if there is a deed of trust on the property), and any junior lienholders have *30 days* after the notice of termination is mailed in which to cure the default but may do so no more than twice during a 12-month period.

If the homeowner or resident has not complied with reasonable park rules, a *seven-day* written *notice to comply* must precede the 60-day notice of termination, *unless* three such notices already have been given within a 12-month period.

Other notice provisions apply if the termination is due to a change of use of the park in which the home is located.

Exercise 12-3

What is the minimum notice or other time requirement for each of the following?

1. Notice by the tenant to terminate a month-to-month tenancy

2. Tenant's denial of abandonment of premises

3. Notice to pay or quit

4. Enforcement of writ of possession

5. Storage of tenant's personal belongings after eviction

6. Notice to pay or quit under MRL

7. Notice to terminate under MRL

OTHER LEASE ARRANGEMENTS

Lease Option

A lease can serve many purposes. A **lease option**, unlike an option alone, conveys the *right of possession* as well as the option right. In residential transactions especially, the lease option can be a way to ensure a subsequent purchase, particularly if part of each lease payment is applied to the eventual down payment.

FOR EXAMPLE   A prospective home purchaser has only $9,000, not enough for an adequate down payment on the kind of house she would like to buy. An owner who wants to sell his property agrees to give her a one-year lease with option to purchase on his single-family residence if she makes a monthly payment of $2,000 in consideration for the lease and option. This is somewhat more than the average rental in the area of $1,400 for a comparable home, but $600 of every payment will be credited to the renter in the event she chooses to buy the property at the end of the lease term at an agreed purchase price of $170,000.

At the end of the lease term the renter will have a credit of $7,200, which, added to her savings of $9,000 (plus interest), will give her enough for the down payment she wants to make. If the property appreciates in value over the term of the lease, the renter also will benefit from the already agreed-on purchase price. The owner, who has seen other property in his area take many months to sell and needs to move to take a new job, is happy to have the house rented for the time being at a higher-than-market payment. He also is reasonably confident the renter will buy the house at the end of the lease term.

Commercial Leases

In the typical **gross lease** the tenant pays a fixed amount for rent over the lease term. In turn, the landlord pays all expenses of ownership, such as taxes, assessments, and insurance.

An **escalator clause** in a lease may provide for an increase in payments based on an increase in an index such as the *consumer price index (CPI)* or the *wholesale price index (WPI)*. This type of lease is called a *graduated lease*.

> With a percentage lease, both landlord and tenant share in the success of the tenant's business.

Commercial lease rent payments also may be based on the income earned on the leased premises. In a **percentage lease**, the rent is a percentage of the tenant's *gross income*, usually with a minimum base amount. As income increases, the percentage typically decreases.

FOR EXAMPLE   Pam's Pins and Needles Shop pays a base monthly rent of $1,000 plus 4% of gross income over $20,000 per month and 2% of gross income over $40,000 per month. If proceeds for February are $32,000, what is the required rent payment for that month?

The required payment is $1,480, which is the base rent of $1,000 plus 4% of $12,000 ($32,000 – $20,000).

With a **net lease**, the landlord is guaranteed a specific (net) income because the tenant pays that amount plus some or all of the operating and other expenses, such as taxes, insurance, assessments, maintenance, and other charges. The tenant's obligations are stipulated in the lease agreement. A net lease also can be referred to as a *triple-net lease*, or *3N lease*, because the tenant pays the taxes, insurance, maintenance, and other charges.

Other lease terms   As a result of the terrorist attacks of September 11, 2001, issues that are now of concern, particularly with well-known buildings, include access control and security, including admittance to the building, parking, and mail and other deliveries. They are subject to negotiation between landlord and tenant but should be covered.

PROPERTY MANAGEMENT

Any type of property, from a single-family residence to a 1,000-unit office building, can be managed by an agent of the owner. The size of modern structures and widespread holdings of some investors have made **property management** a growing specialty in the real estate field.

The Resident Property Manager

In California, every building with 16 or more dwelling units must have a **resident apartment manager**. By living on the premises, the resident manager helps ensure that tenant complaints are handled promptly.

Duties of the Property Manager

An on-site resident property manager, or professional management firm or individual with a real estate broker's license, can act as the owner's agent to

- lease units,
- collect rents,
- maintain communication with tenants, and
- conduct all day-to-day business necessary to maintain the property.

The property manager ordinarily earns a fee based on the income the property produces in rents. The property manager also may receive a separate fee for such activities as supervising alterations or remodeling. A typical form of *property management agreement* is shown in Figure 12.3.

Qualifications of the Property Manager

Real estate brokers can be property managers, but sound business practice as well as ethical considerations require that they be adequately prepared before offering their services as property managers. Knowledge of contracts, lease requirements, building operation, maintenance, and other aspects of property management, including the "people skills" necessary to deal with tenants, must be learned by training, study, or experience.

RENT CONTROL

Rent control is imposed by ordinance of a local governing body to protect tenants from relatively high rent increases over the occupancy period of a lease. In the past, as many as one-quarter of California's residential units were subject to some form of rent control.

Types of Rent Control

There are two types of rent control in California, based on whether a new tenant benefits from existing rent protection. There is also a state law that eliminates rent control on new units, single-family homes, and other properties.

Ordinances with vacancy decontrol   If an ordinance contains a vacancy decontrol provision, when a unit becomes vacant there is no restriction on the rent set for a new tenant. After the premises have been leased again, the new rent becomes the new base amount and is again subject to controls.

Ordinances without vacancy decontrol   Ordinances *without* a vacancy decontrol provision limit rent increases for new tenants as well as for existing ones.

State Law

State law has greatly reduced the impact of rent control.

The **Costa-Hawkins Rental Housing Act** preempts local rent control laws on the following:

- New units with a certificate of occupancy issued after February 1, 1995
- Single-family detached houses and condominiums
- Multiunit dwellings in areas with vacancy control, except where the tenancy is terminated by the landlord's service of a termination notice or a change in the tenancy's terms

From January 1, 1996, through December 31, 1998, after a voluntary vacancy, abandonment, or eviction based on nonpayment of rent on one of these units, landlords were allowed to increase rents by the greater of 15% or up to 70% of the prevailing market rate for a comparable unit. Two rent increases were allowed during the initial three-year period.

As of January 1, 1999, there are no limits on allowable rent increases for new tenancies *and* tenancies created on or after January 1, 1996.

FIGURE 12.3: Property Management Agreement

PROPERTY MANAGEMENT AGREEMENT
(C.A.R. Form PMA, Revised 12/15)

_____ ("Owner"), and
_____ ("Broker"), agree as follows:

1. **APPOINTMENT OF BROKER:** Owner hereby appoints and grants Broker (hereinafter "Property Manager") the exclusive right to rent, lease, operate and manage the property(ies) known as _____
    _____ and any additional property that may later be added to this Agreement ("Property"), upon the terms below,
    for the period beginning (date) _____ and ending (date) _____, at 11:59 PM.
    (If checked:) ☐ Either party may terminate this Property Management Agreement ("Agreement") on at least 30 days written notice _____
    months after the original commencement date of this Agreement. After the exclusive term expires, this Agreement shall continue as a non-exclusive agreement that either party may terminate by giving at least 30 days written notice to the other.

2. **PROPERTY MANAGER ACCEPTANCE:** Property Manager accepts the appointment and grant, and agrees to:
    A. Use due diligence in the performance of this Agreement.
    B. Furnish the services of its firm for the rental, leasing, operation and management of the Property.

3. **AUTHORITY AND POWERS:** Owner grants Property Manager the authority and power, at Owner's expense, to:
    A. **ADVERTISING:** Display FOR RENT/LEASE and similar signs on the Property. Advertise the availability of the Property, or any part thereof, for rental or lease in the Multiple Listing Service and other online media.
    B. **RENTAL; LEASING:** Initiate, sign, renew, modify or cancel rental agreements and leases for the Property, or any part thereof; collect and give receipts for rents, other fees, charges and security deposits. Any lease or rental agreement executed by Property Manager for Owner shall not exceed _____ year(s) or ☐ shall be month-to-month. Unless Owner authorizes a lower amount, rent shall be: ☐ at market rate; OR ☐ a minimum of $ _____ per _____; OR ☐ see attachment.
    C. **TENANCY TERMINATION:** Sign and serve in Owner's name notices that are required or appropriate; commence and prosecute actions to evict tenants; recover possession of the Property in Owner's name; recover rents and other sums due; and, when expedient, settle, compromise and release claims, actions and suits and/or reinstate tenancies.
    D. **REPAIR; MAINTENANCE:** Make, cause to be made, and/or supervise repairs, improvements, alterations and decorations to the Property; purchase, and pay bills for, services and supplies. Owner agrees that state and local water use restrictions will supersede any obligation by Property Manager or any Tenant to water/maintain gardens, landscaping trees or shrubs. Property Manager shall obtain prior approval of Owner for all expenditures over $ _____ for any one item. Prior approval shall not be required for monthly or recurring operating charges or, if in Property Manager's opinion, emergency expenditures over the maximum are needed to protect the Property or other property(ies) from damage, prevent injury to persons, avoid suspension of necessary services, avoid penalties or fines, or suspension of services to tenants required by a lease or rental agreement or by law, including, but not limited to, maintaining the Property in a condition fit for human habitation as required by Civil Code §§1941 and 1941.1 and Health and Safety Code §§17920.3 and 17920.10.
    E. **REPORTS, NOTICES AND SIGNS:** Comply with federal, state or local law requiring delivery of reports or notices and/or posting of signs or notices.
    F. **CONTRACTS; SERVICES:** Contract, hire, supervise and/or discharge firms and persons, including utilities, required for the operation and maintenance of the Property. Property Manager may perform any of Property Manager's duties through attorneys, agents, employees, or independent contractors and, except for persons working in Property Manager's firm, shall not be responsible for their acts, omissions, defaults, negligence and/or costs of same.
    G. **EXPENSE PAYMENTS:** Pay expenses and costs for the Property from Owner's funds held by Property Manager, unless otherwise directed by Owner. Expenses and costs may include, but are not limited to, property management compensation, fees and charges, expenses for goods and services, property taxes and other taxes, Owner's Association dues, assessments, loan payments and insurance premiums.
    H. **SECURITY DEPOSITS:** Receive security deposits from tenants, which deposits shall be ☐ given to Owner, or ☐ placed in Property Manager's trust account and, if held in Property Manager's trust account, pay from Owner's funds all interest on tenants' security deposits if required by local law or ordinance. Owner shall be responsible to tenants for return of security deposits and all interest due on security deposits held by Owner.
    I. **TRUST FUNDS:** Deposit all receipts collected for Owner, less any sums properly deducted or disbursed, in a financial institution whose deposits are insured by an agency of the United States government. The funds shall be held in a trust account separate from Property Manager's personal accounts. Property Manager shall not be liable in event of bankruptcy or failure of a financial institution.
    J. **RESERVES:** Maintain a reserve in Property Manager's trust account of $ _____
    K. **DISBURSEMENTS:** Disburse Owner's funds held in Property Manager's trust account in the following order:
        (1) Compensation due Property Manager under paragraph 8.
        (2) All other operating expenses, costs and disbursements payable from Owner's funds held by Property Manager.
        (3) Reserves and security deposits held by Property Manager.
        (4) Balance to Owner.
    L. **OWNER DISTRIBUTION:** Remit funds, if any are available, monthly (or ☐ _____), to Owner.

Owner's Initials (_____)(_____)   Property Manager's Initials (_____)(_____)

PMA REVISED 12/15 (PAGE 1 OF 4)

EQUAL HOUSING
OPPORTUNITY

PROPERTY MANAGEMENT AGREEMENT (PMA PAGE 1 OF 4)

Source: Reprinted with permission, California Association of REALTORS®. Endorsement not implied.

FIGURE 12.3:   Property Management Agreement (continued)

Owner Name: _____   Date:_____

M.   OWNER STATEMENTS: Render monthly (or ☐ Quarterly or ☐ _____), and year-end statements of receipts, expenses and charges for each Property.

N.   PROPERTY MANAGER FUNDS: Property Manager shall not advance Property Manager's own funds in connection with the Property or this Agreement.

O.   KEYSAFE/LOCKBOX: ☐ (If checked) Owner authorizes the use of a keysafe/lockbox to allow entry into the Property and agrees to sign a keysafe/ lockbox addendum (C.A.R., Form KLA).

4.   OWNER RESPONSIBILITIES: Owner shall:

A.   Provide all documentation, records and disclosures as required by law or required by Property Manager to manage and operate the Property, and immediately notify Property Manager if Owner becomes aware of any change in such documentation, records or disclosures, or any matter affecting the habitability of the Property.

B.   Indemnify, defend and hold harmless Property Manager, and all persons in Property Manager's firm, as permitted by law, from all costs, expenses, suits, liabilities, damages, attorney fees and claims of every type, including but not limited to those arising out of injury or death of any person, or damage to any real or personal property of any person, including Owner, for: **(i)** any repairs performed by Owner or by others hired directly by Owner; or **(ii)** those relating to the management, leasing, rental, security deposits, or operation of the Property by Property Manager, or any person in Property Manager's firm, or the performance or exercise of any of the duties, powers or authorities granted to Property Manager.

C.   Maintain the Property in a condition fit for human habitation as required by Civil Code §§ 1941 and 1941.1 and Health and Safety Code §§ 17920.3 and 17920.10 and other applicable law.

D.   Pay all interest on tenants' security deposits if required by local law or ordinance.

E.   Carry and pay for: **(i)** public and premises liability insurance in an amount of no less than $1,000,000; and **(ii)** property damage and worker's compensation insurance adequate to protect the interests of Owner and Property Manager. Property Manager shall be, and Owner authorizes Property Manager to be, named as an additional insured party on Owner's policies.

F.   Pay any late charges, penalties and/or interest imposed by lenders or other parties for failure to make payment to those parties, if the failure is due to insufficient funds in Property Manager's trust account available for such payment.

G.   Immediately replace any funds required if there are insufficient funds in Property Manager's trust account to cover Owner's responsibilities.

5.   OWNER REPRESENTATIONS: Owner represents that, unless otherwise specified in writing, Owner is unaware of: **(i)** any recorded Notice of Default affecting the Property; **(ii)** any delinquent amounts due under any loan secured by, or other obligation affecting, the Property; **(iii)** any bankruptcy, insolvency or similar proceeding affecting the Property; **(iv)** any litigation, arbitration, administrative action, government investigation, or other pending or threatened action that does or may affect the Property or Owner's ability to transfer it; and **(v)** any current, pending or proposed special assessments affecting the Property. Owner shall promptly notify Property Manager in writing if Owner becomes aware of any of these items during the term of this Agreement.

6.   TAX WITHHOLDING:

A.   If Owner is not a California Resident or a corporation or LLC qualified to conduct business in California, Owner authorizes Property Manager to withhold and transmit to California Franchise Tax Board ("FTB") 7% of the GROSS payments to Owner that exceed $1,500 received by Property Manager, unless Owner completes and transmits to Property Manager FTB form 589, nonresident reduced withholding request, FTB form 588, nonresident withholding waiver, or FTB form 590, withholding exemption certificate.

B.   If Owner is a nonresident alien individual, a foreign entity, or other non-U.S. person (Foreign Investor) Owner authorizes Property Manager to withhold and transmit to the Internal Revenue Service (IRS) 30% of the GROSS rental receipts unless Owner elects to treat rental income as "effectively connected income" by submitting to Property Manager a fully completed IRS form W-8ECI, Certificate of Foreign Person's Claim for Exemption From Withholding on Income Effectively Connected With the Conduct of a Trade of Business in the United States. A Foreign investor Owner will need to obtain a U.S. tax payer identification number and file a declaration with the IRS regarding effectively connected income in order to complete the form given to Property Manager. Further, the Foreign Investor Owner will be responsible for making any necessary estimated tax payments.

7.   DISCLOSURE:

A.   LEAD-BASED PAINT

(1) ☐ The Property was constructed on or after January 1, 1978.

OR (2) ☐ The Property was constructed prior to 1978.

(i) Owner has no knowledge of lead-based paint or lead-based paint hazards in the housing except:_____

_____

(ii) Owner has no reports or records pertaining to lead-based paint or lead-based paint hazards in the housing, except the following, which Owner shall provide to Property Manager: _____

B.   POOL/SPA DRAIN

Any pool or spa on the property does (or, ☐ does not) have an approved anti-entrapment drain cover, device or system.

8.   COMPENSATION:

A.   Owner agrees to pay Property Manager fees in the amounts indicated below for:

(1) Management: _____

(2) Renting or Leasing: _____

(3) Evictions: _____

(4) Preparing Property for rental or lease: _____

(5) Managing Property during extended periods of vacancy: _____

(6) An overhead and service fee added to the cost of all work performed by, or at the direction of, Property Manager: _____

(7) Other: _____

Owner's Initials (_____)(_____)   Property Manager's Initials (_____)(_____)

PROPERTY MANAGEMENT AGREEMENT (PMA PAGE 2 OF 4)

FIGURE 12.3: **Property Management Agreement (continued)**

Owner Name: _____ Date:_____

B. This Agreement does not include providing on-site management services, property sales, refinancing, preparing Property for sale or refinancing, modernization, fire or major damage restoration, rehabilitation, obtaining income tax, accounting or legal advice, representation before public agencies, advising on proposed new construction, debt collection, counseling, attending Owner's Association meetings or_____

If Owner requests Property Manager to perform services not included in this Agreement, a fee shall be agreed upon before these services are performed.

C. Property Manager may divide compensation, fees and charges due under this Agreement in any manner acceptable to Property Manager.

D. Owner further agrees that:

(1) Property Manager may receive and keep fees and charges from tenants for: **(i)** requesting an assignment of lease or sublease of the Property; **(ii)** processing credit applications; **(iii)** any returned checks and/or (☐ if checked) late payments; and **(iv)** any other services that are not in conflict with this Agreement.

(2) Property Manager may perform any of Property Manager's duties, and obtain necessary products and services, through affiliated companies or organizations in which Property Manager may own an interest. Property Manager may receive fees, commissions and/or profits from these affiliated companies or organizations. Property Manager has an ownership interest in the following affiliated companies or organizations:

_____

Property Manager shall disclose to Owner any other such relationships as they occur. Property Manager shall not receive any fees, commissions or profits from unaffiliated companies or organizations in the performance of this Agreement, without prior disclosure to Owner.

(3) Other: _____

9. **AGENCY RELATIONSHIPS:** Property Manager may act, and Owner hereby consents to Property Manager acting, as dual agent for Owner and tenant(s) in any resulting transaction. If the Property includes residential property with one-to-four dwelling units and this Agreement permits a tenancy in excess of one year, Owner acknowledges receipt of the "Disclosure Regarding Agency Relationships" (C.A.R. Form AD). Owner understands that Property Manager may have or obtain property management agreements on other property, and that potential tenants may consider, make offers on, or lease through Property Manager, property the same as or similar to Owner's Property. Owner consents to Property Manager's representation of other owners' properties before, during and after the expiration of this Agreement.

10. **NOTICES:** Any written notice to Owner or Property Manager required under this Agreement shall be served by sending such notice by first class mail or other agreed-to delivery method to that party at the address below, or at any different address the parties may later designate for this purpose. Notice shall be deemed received three (3) calendar days after deposit into the United States mail OR ☐ _____

11. **DISPUTE RESOLUTION:**

A. **MEDIATION:** Owner and Property Manager agree to mediate any dispute or claim arising between them out of this Agreement, or any resulting transaction, before resorting to arbitration or court action. Mediation fees, if any, shall be divided equally among the parties involved. If, for any dispute or claim to which this paragraph applies, any party (i) commences an action without first attempting to resolve the matter through mediation, or (ii) before commencement of an action, refuses to mediate after a request has been made, then that party shall not be entitled to recover attorney fees, even if they would otherwise be available to that party in any such action. THIS MEDIATION PROVISION APPLIES WHETHER OR NOT THE ARBITRATION PROVISION IS INITIALED. **Exclusions from this mediation agreement are specified in paragraph 11C.**

B. **ARBITRATION OF DISPUTES:**
Owner and Property Manager agree that any dispute or claim in Law or equity arising between them out of this Agreement or any resulting transaction, which is not settled through mediation, shall be decided by neutral, binding arbitration. The arbitrator shall be a retired judge or justice, or an attorney with at least 5 years of residential real estate Law experience, unless the parties mutually agree to a different arbitrator. The parties shall have the right to discovery in accordance with Code of Civil Procedure §1283.05. In all other respects, the arbitration shall be conducted in accordance with Title 9 of Part 3 of the Code of Civil Procedure. Judgment upon the award of the arbitrator(s) may be entered into any court having jurisdiction. Enforcement of this agreement to arbitrate shall be governed by the Federal Arbitration Act. Exclusions from this arbitration agreement are specified in paragraph 11C.
"NOTICE: BY INITIALING IN THE SPACE BELOW YOU ARE AGREEING TO HAVE ANY DISPUTE ARISING OUT OF THE MATTERS INCLUDED IN THE 'ARBITRATION OF DISPUTES' PROVISION DECIDED BY NEUTRAL ARBITRATION AS PROVIDED BY CALIFORNIA LAW AND YOU ARE GIVING UP ANY RIGHTS YOU MIGHT POSSESS TO HAVE THE DISPUTE LITIGATED IN A COURT OR JURY TRIAL. BY INITIALING IN THE SPACE BELOW YOU ARE GIVING UP YOUR JUDICIAL RIGHTS TO DISCOVERY AND APPEAL, UNLESS THOSE RIGHTS ARE SPECIFICALLY INCLUDED IN THE 'ARBITRATION OF DISPUTES' PROVISION. IF YOU REFUSE TO SUBMIT TO ARBITRATION AFTER AGREEING TO THIS PROVISION, YOU MAY BE COMPELLED TO ARBITRATE UNDER THE AUTHORITY OF THE CALIFORNIA CODE OF CIVIL PROCEDURE. YOUR AGREEMENT TO THIS ARBITRATION PROVISION IS VOLUNTARY."
"WE HAVE READ AND UNDERSTAND THE FOREGOING AND AGREE TO SUBMIT DISPUTES ARISING OUT OF THE MATTERS INCLUDED IN THE 'ARBITRATION OF DISPUTES' PROVISION TO NEUTRAL ARBITRATION." | Owner's Initials _____/_____ Property Manager's Initials _____/_____ |

Owner's Initials (_____)(_____)   Property Manager's Initials (_____)(_____)

PMA REVISED 12/15 (PAGE 3 OF 4)

PROPERTY MANAGEMENT AGREEMENT (PMA PAGE 3 OF 4)

FIGURE 12.3:   Property Management Agreement (continued)

Owner Name: _____   Date: _____

C.   **ADDITIONAL MEDIATION AND ARBITRATION TERMS:** The following matters shall be excluded from mediation and arbitration: **(i) a judicial or non-judicial foreclosure or other action or proceeding to enforce a deed of trust, mortgage or installment land sale contract as defined in Civil Code §2985; (ii) an unlawful detainer action; (iii) the filing or enforcement of a mechanic's lien; and (iv) any matter that is within the jurisdiction of a probate, small claims or bankruptcy court. The filing of a court action to enable the recording of a notice of pending action, for order of attachment, receivership, injunction, or other provisional remedies, shall not constitute a waiver or violation of the mediation and arbitration provisions.**

12.   **EQUAL HOUSING OPPORTUNITY:** The Property is offered in compliance with federal, state and local anti-discrimination laws.

13.   **ATTORNEY FEES:** In any action, proceeding or arbitration between Owner and Property Manager regarding the obligation to pay compensation under this Agreement, the prevailing Owner or Property Manager shall be entitled to reasonable attorney fees and costs from the non-prevailing Owner or Property Manager, except as provided in paragraph 11A.

14.   **ADDITIONAL TERMS:**   ☐ Keysafe/Lockbox Addendum (C.A.R. Form KLA); ☐ Lead-Based Paint and Lead-Based Paint Hazards Disclosure (C.A.R. Form FLD) _____
_____
_____
_____

15.   **TIME OF ESSENCE; ENTIRE CONTRACT; CHANGES:** Time is of the essence. All understandings between the parties are incorporated in this Agreement. Its terms are intended by the parties as a final, complete and exclusive expression of their Agreement with respect to its subject matter, and may not be contradicted by evidence of any prior agreement or contemporaneous oral agreement. If any provision of this Agreement is held to be ineffective or invalid, the remaining provisions will nevertheless be given full force and effect. Neither this Agreement nor any provision in it may be extended, amended, modified, altered or changed except in writing. This Agreement and any supplement, addendum or modification, including any copy, may be signed in two or more counterparts, all of which shall constitute one and the same writing.

Owner warrants that Owner is the owner of the Property or has the authority to execute this Agreement. Owner acknowledges Owner has read, understands, accepts and has received a copy of the Agreement.

Owner _____   Date _____
Owner _____   _____
          Print Name   Social Security/Tax ID # (for tax reporting purposes)
Address _____ City _____ State _____ Zip _____
Telephone _____ Fax _____ Email _____

Owner _____   Date _____
Owner _____   _____
          Print Name   Social Security/Tax ID # (for tax reporting purposes)
Address _____ City _____ State _____ Zip _____
Telephone _____ Fax _____ Email _____

Real Estate Broker (Firm) _____ CalBRE Lic. #: _____
By (Agent) _____ CalBRE Lic. #: _____ Date _____
Address _____ City _____ State _____ Zip _____
Telephone _____ Fax _____ Email _____

R E B S / I N C
Published and Distributed by:
REAL ESTATE BUSINESS SERVICES, INC.
a subsidiary of the California Association of REALTORS®
525 South Virgil Avenue, Los Angeles, California 90020

PMA REVISED 12/15 (PAGE 4 OF 4) | Reviewed by _____ Date _____ | EQUAL HOUSING OPPORTUNITY

PROPERTY MANAGEMENT AGREEMENT (PMA PAGE 4 OF 4)

CREDIT REPORTING

Permission for the landlord to obtain a prospective tenant's credit report is usually a requirement of a lease application. The requirements of both state and federal law must be followed with regard to the use of the report, as well as information on tenants provided to credit bureaus by the landlord. The federal **Fair Credit Reporting Act** (FCRA) was amended by the **Fair and Accurate Credit Transactions Act of 2003** (FACTA) to include protections for those whose identity is stolen. If an identity theft report has been made by a tenant, for example, a landlord is not allowed to report delinquent rent to a credit bureau. FACTA is available at www.ftc.gov/os/statutes/031224fcra.pdf. State law is found in California Civil Code Section 1785.

www.ftc.gov/os
/statutes/031224fcra.pdf

Exercise 12-4

Carl Class, a computer technician, wants to lease a storefront for his new business, Classy Computers. In addition to selling computers, he will also be conducting classes in computer and internet use.

Carl approaches the owner of a vacant unit in a small strip shopping center in a high-traffic area near a community college. The owner is impressed by Carl's business plan and agrees to lease space to him. She is interested in helping him become established and also in benefiting from the expected growth of his business.

What kind of lease would best accomplish the aims of both parties?

SUMMARY

A **lease** is a form of contract transferring a less-than-freehold estate—the right to property possession and use but not ownership. The **lessor (landlord)** conveys the leased premises to the **lessee (tenant)**. The tenant pays **rent** in consideration for the lease. A **security deposit** may also be required. If rent is unpaid, the landlord has the ultimate remedy of **eviction**.

A written lease agreement may be required by law, and it always is preferable. A lease follows the same formalities as any other contract. A statement of property condition at the time the lease begins will help when the tenant vacates the premises.

If the tenant's **right to quiet enjoyment** of the premises is interfered with by the landlord, the tenant may complain of a **constructive eviction**. The landlord has only a limited **right of entry** to the leased premises and usually must give notice to the tenant first.

The tenant may be able to *sublease* or *assign* the right of possession granted by the lease. There are strict requirements for *automatic renewal* of leases.

The landlord makes an *implied* **warranty of habitability** and an *express* or *implied* **covenant to repair** the premises. Certain minimal requirements must be met or the property will be considered an **untenantable dwelling**. If the landlord fails to meet those responsibilities, the tenant can complain to the appropriate authorities, withhold rent to make necessary repairs the landlord has not made, sue the landlord, or abandon the premises. The tenant must also maintain the premises and cannot expect repairs from the landlord for damage resulting from the tenant's own *negligence*.

Both landlord and tenant may be liable to persons injured on the premises if the premises are under their control and they fail to exercise *ordinary care*. A landlord may be liable for injuries to a tenant of residential property caused by the *defective condition* of the premises.

Discrimination in accommodations and business establishments is forbidden by the **Unruh Civil Rights Act**. Discrimination in housing is forbidden by the **California Fair Employment and Housing Act**. Federal prohibitions against housing discrimination also apply. California's **Civil Rights Housing Act of 2006** extends all of the protected classes of FEHA to all other nondiscrimination laws, including the Unruh Civil Rights Act.

Notice may be required to *terminate* a lease. The leasehold estate could be surrendered by agreement of the parties. There are specific grounds for termination before the lease term ends, and the tenant could abandon the premises. **Eviction** can be carried out only by a prescribed procedure, including notice to the tenant. An **unlawful detainer** is the legal action that can result in a *writ of possession* directing the sheriff or marshal to remove the tenant(s) from the premises.

Manufactured home rentals have certain unique requirements, although they basically follow general landlord-tenant law. Other types of leases can range from the **lease option** to the **net lease** used in commercial transactions.

Property management is an important and growing area of real estate professionalism. **Rent control** in several forms exists in communities throughout the state. Legal counsel must be consulted for particular requirements of individual ordinances as well as state law.

Credit reporting practices have come under increasing regulation, particularly with the growing threat of identity theft.

OPEN FOR DISCUSSION

Lack of affordable housing continues to be a problem in California and is a deterrent to business entry and growth.

1. Suggest ways in which decent housing can be provided for all citizens, particularly the "working poor."

REVIEW QUESTIONS

1. An apartment in San Francisco can be leased for a term of no more than
   a. 150 years.
   b. a reasonable time.
   c. 99 years.
   d. 51 years.

2. An office in Los Angeles can be leased for a term of no more than
   a. 150 years.
   b. a reasonable time.
   c. 99 years.
   d. 51 years.

3. Agricultural land can be leased for a term of no more than
   a. 150 years.
   b. a reasonable time.
   c. 99 years.
   d. 51 years.

4. A security deposit on furnished residential property can be no more than
   a. two months' rent.
   b. three months' rent.
   c. a reasonable amount.
   d. $2,000.

5. If a question arises as to the validity of a landlord's claim against a tenant's security deposit,
   a. the landlord is presumed to be entitled to the security deposit.
   b. the tenant is presumed to be entitled to the security deposit.
   c. the security deposit is forfeited to the state.
   d. there is no presumption regarding ownership of the security deposit.

6. A landlord wants to give a tenant's apartment to her nephew. The landlord tries to drive the tenant out by constantly phoning him, visiting him, and insisting that his apartment be used to show prospective tenants for other units what the building is like. The landlord is violating the tenant's
   a. right to use the property without interference.
   b. covenant to repair.
   c. covenant of quiet enjoyment.
   d. warranty of habitability.

7. A landlord has a right of entry
   a. in an emergency.
   b. only to show the premises to prospective tenants.
   c. only when the tenant agrees.
   d. any time.

8. Transfer of all of a tenant's rights under a lease is
   a. an assignment.
   b. a sublease.
   c. a freehold estate.
   d. an estate at will.

9. A lease may be renewed automatically only if
   a. the landlord prepared the lease.
   b. the tenant and landlord are unable to agree on any other term.
   c. the automatic renewal provision is noted in a separate document referenced in the lease.
   d. all of the statutory requirements are met.

10. A dwelling is untenantable if it substantially lacks
    a. a heating unit.
    b. windows in every room.
    c. a trash compactor.
    d. freeway access.

11. Because a tenant complains about the condition of the building, the landlord may
    a. evict the tenant.
    b. raise the tenant's rent.
    c. shut off the tenant's utilities.
    d. investigate the complaint.

12. Which may be considered in choosing a tenant?
    a. Marital status
    b. National ancestry
    c. Whether the prospective tenant is on welfare
    d. Tenant's income

13. On May 15, a business owner notified her landlord that she would be vacating her retail store location on June 30. The business owner has a month-to-month periodic tenancy. Until what date will she incur rent?
    a. June 15
    b. June 30
    c. July 15
    d. July 30

14. A landlord must follow the legal requirements for an eviction
    a. from leased premises.
    b. but can shorten the notice required if the tenant agrees.
    c. unless the tenant can be physically removed.
    d. unless the housing is government subsidized.

15. A landlord may begin eviction proceedings with
    a. a notice of termination.
    b. a notice of abandonment.
    c. a notice to pay or quit.
    d. an order of eviction.

16. The sheriff or marshal can forcibly remove a tenant by
    a. a judgment of eviction.
    b. a writ of possession.
    c. a notice of eviction.
    d. a notice to pay or quit.

17. A retail business has a percentage lease based on 5% of gross income of up to $25,000 per month and 2½% of gross income above that amount. The minimum to be paid is $1,000 per month. For a month in which the business has a gross income of $47,000, what will be the rent payment?
    a. $1,800
    b. $4,675
    c. $2,800
    d. $3,675

18. The owner of 417 Main, an office building, receives a guaranteed monthly income from her tenants and pays no expenses. She has
    a. a gross lease.
    b. a trust lease.
    c. a percentage lease.
    d. a net lease.

19. A property manager
    a. must be a real estate broker.
    b. is the property owner's agent.
    c. is the tenant's agent.
    d. is not an agent.

20. A tenant moved out of his apartment at the end of the lease term. The landlord will be allowed to increase the rent for a new tenant to reflect the current market value because the local rent control ordinance
    a. provides for vacancy control.
    b. provides for vacancy decontrol.
    c. is based on an index.
    d. is favorable to the tenant.

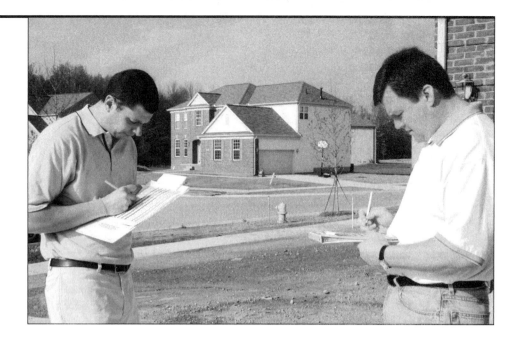

REAL ESTATE APPRAISING

LEARNING OBJECTIVES

When you have completed this unit, you will be able to

- **state** the requirements to become licensed as an appraiser in California;

- **define** what an appraisal is and explain how an appraisal may be used;

- **list** the basic economic principles that affect market value;

- **recognize** how a comparative market analysis can assist a seller or buyer in estimating market value;

- **describe** the three basic methods of appraising real estate;

- **explain** how the appraiser reconciles the values reached by each of the appraisal approaches; and

- **list** the ways in which the appraiser's final opinion of market value is reported.

KEY TERMS

anticipation	equilibrium	regression
appraisal	external obsolescence	replacement cost
arm's-length transaction	federally related transaction	reproduction cost
balance	functional obsolescence	restricted use report
broker's price opinion (BPO)	gentrification	revitalization
Bureau of Real Estate Appraisers (BREA)	gross income multiplier (GIM)	sales comparison approach
capitalization ("cap") rate	growth	scarcity
change	highest and best use	self-contained report
comparative market analysis (CMA)	income capitalization approach	site value
competition	index method	square-foot method
comps	market rent	straight-line method
conformity	market value	substitution
contract rent	net operating income	summary report
contribution	observed condition method	supply and demand
cost approach	physical deterioration	transferability
decline	potential gross income	Uniform Residential Appraisal Report (URAR)
depreciation	progression	unit-in-place method
effective gross income	quantity survey method	utility
	reconciliation	value in exchange
		value in use

APPRAISER LICENSING

Perhaps the most important step in selling real estate is pricing it right. This means that the asking price must reflect what buyers in the marketplace are willing to pay for property of that type. And that is where a property appraisal—an estimate of a property's market value—comes in. This unit will discuss the qualifications of an appraiser and the requirements for an appraisal, but there is a less formal valuation process that is frequently performed by real estate licensees called a *broker's price opinion* (BPO), which is discussed later in the unit.

The Financial Institutions Reform, Recovery, and Enforcement Act of 1989 (FIRREA) requires that as of January 1, 1993, all property appraisals that are part of *federally related transactions* be performed only by appraisers licensed by the state in which the property is located. Individual federal agencies are allowed to set a minimum property value, and appraiser licensing is not required below that value.

State qualifications for a licensed appraiser and a licensing examination should meet or exceed those produced by the Appraiser Qualifications Board of the Appraisal Foundation. In addition, each state should set standards for an acceptable appraisal report that meet or exceed those developed by the Appraisal Standards Board of the Appraisal Foundation. The Appraisal Foundation is a nonprofit association of trade groups, including appraisers, lenders, educators, and others, located in Washington, D.C.

Appraisals came under renewed scrutiny with the drop in home values initiated with the subprime mortgage crisis. As a result, Freddie Mac, the Federal Housing Finance Agency (FHFA), and the New York State Attorney agreed in March 2008, to develop the **Home Valuation Code of Conduct (Code)**. Following opportunity for public comments, the Code was adopted by Freddie Mac. Effective May 1, 2009, Freddie Mac no longer purchased mortgages from sellers (lenders) that did not adopt the Code with respect to single-family mortgages delivered to Freddie Mac. For single-family mortgages with loan application dates on or after May 1, 2009, Freddie Mac sellers/servicers were required to represent and warrant that the appraisal reports were obtained in a manner consistent with the Code. Freddie Mac exempted from the requirements FHA/VA, Section 184 Native American, and Section 502 Guaranteed Rural Housing mortgages.

Among other provisions, the Code prohibited lenders and third parties from influencing or attempting to influence the development, result, or review of an appraisal report. The Code also required lenders to ensure that borrowers were provided a copy of the appraisal report no less than three business days before closing, unless the borrower waived the requirement. More information about the Code can be found at www.freddiemac.com.

www.freddiemac.com

The Dodd-Frank Wall Street Reform and Consumer Protection Act of 2010 (Dodd-Frank Act) superseded the Code, effective April 1, 2011. The Dodd-Frank Act stresses that lending institutions should provide for the independence of the persons ordering, performing, and reviewing appraisals or evaluations. The Act does not apply to appraisals of property when the transaction value is $250,000 or less, the transaction is a business loan with a value of $1 million or less, or the transaction is any extension of credit at the lending institution.

Federally Related Transactions

A **federally related transaction** is any real estate-related financial transaction involving or identified as such by a federal institution's regulatory agency. Because this definition includes all loans made by federally chartered banks and savings and loans, it includes most residential mortgage loans.

California Law

www.brea.ca.gov

California's appraiser regulations went into effect November 1, 1992. Enforcement is the responsibility of the Bureau of Real Estate Appraisers (BREA) (formerly called the Office of Real Estate Appraisers), which is now part of the Department of Consumer Affairs, and can be found at www.brea.ca.gov. As of January 1, 1998, four categories of appraiser credentials are issued. All of the following are *minimum* requirements; additional requirements that took effect on January 1, 2015, for all new applicants, as well as those wishing to upgrade a license, are also mentioned:

- **Trainee license**, requiring 150 classroom hours of instruction, for a prospective appraiser to work under the technical supervision of a licensed appraiser to gain the experience to qualify for a residential license

- **Residential license**, requiring 150 classroom hours of instruction and 2,000 hours of acceptable appraisal experience acquired in no fewer than 12 months, for appraisals of noncomplex one- to four-unit residential property up to a transaction value of $1 million, and nonresidential property up to a transaction value of $250,000; as of January 1, 2015, requires 30 semester credit hours of college-level education or an associate's degree or higher in any field

- **Certified residential license**, requiring 200 classroom hours of instruction, an associate's degree or 21 semester credit hours in specified subjects, and a minimum of 2,500 hours of acceptable appraisal experience acquired in no fewer than 30 months, for appraisals of all one- to four-unit residential property and nonresidential property up to a transaction value of $250,000; as of January 1, 2015, requires a bachelor's degree or higher in any field

- **Certified general license**, requiring 300 classroom hours of instruction, a bachelor's degree or 30 semester credit hours in specified subjects, and a minimum of 3,000 hours of acceptable appraisal experience acquired in no fewer than 30 months, with at least 1,500 hours of the experience in nonresidential properties, for appraisals of all real estate; as of January 1, 2015, requires a bachelor's degree or higher in any field

All applicants must complete the 15-hour national USPAP (*Uniform Standards of Professional Appraisal Practice*) course as part of the required classroom hours. In addition, every renewal applicant must complete the seven-hour national USPAP update course every two years as part of the continuing education requirements.

In addition to successfully completing education requirements, applicants for licensing must pass the appropriate examination. A license is valid for four years, and continuing education requirements must be met to qualify for renewal. Information on appraiser licensing requirements can be obtained from BREA at 1-916-552-9000 or www.brea.ca.gov. The Appraisal Foundation's website, www.appraisalfoundation.org, provides information on the federal requirements; the latest edition of USPAP can be found at www.uspap.org.

www.brea.ca.gov
www.appraisalfoundation.org
www.uspap.org

As of January 1, 2010, California requires registration with BREA of all appraisal management companies (AMC) doing business in the state. AMC requirements are separate from licensing requirements and can be found at www.orea.ca.gov /html/AmcInfo.html. By using an AMC, a lender can avoid direct hiring of the appraiser who completes an appraisal assignment, helping to insure the independence required by the Dodd-Frank Act.

www.orea.ca.gov/html
/AmcInfo.html

The largest trade association of appraisal professionals in the United States is the Appraisal Institute. Its website, www.appraisalinstitute.org, has a directory of appraisers and links to an extensive list of real estate-related websites. The site also provides access to the Appraisal Institute's Lum Library of publications, which provides search and copying services free of charge to members and for a fee to nonmembers.

www.appraisalinstitute.org

WHAT IS A REAL ESTATE APPRAISAL?

Most often, a *real estate appraisal* is the appraiser's opinion of a property's monetary value on the open market as of a specified date. In addition to market value, an appraisal can also be made for a variety of other purposes, such as to find insurance or investment value. An appraisal also can indicate a property's type and condition, its utility for a given purpose, or its *highest and best use* (a concept that will be discussed in this unit). The term **appraisal** is used to refer to both

- the *process* by which the appraiser arrives at an opinion of value and

- the *written report* in which the appraiser explains how the opinion of value was achieved.

Any of the property interests discussed in Unit 3, such as a life estate or remainder, can be appraised. Usually, though, the property interest being appraised is a *fee simple estate*.

The appraiser

- identifies the *scope of work* required by the appraisal assignment;

- compiles a variety of *data*, including information on the subject property and comparables; and

- considers *market forces* and *local market conditions* to arrive at an opinion of the property's value.

The data and factors considered will vary somewhat, depending on the method of appraisal used.

The appraiser's *final value conclusion* will be a dollar value. Most often, the value conclusion is the appraiser's opinion of the property's market value as of the date of the property inspection. An appraisal can provide an opinion of value as of some other date, however, such as the date property was taken in a condemnation proceeding.

Market Value

The value of an item can be defined as the amount of money or goods or services that will be accepted in exchange for it. This **value in exchange** is not the only type of value, however. Real estate is described as having a **value in use**, which refers to its value when used for a particular purpose. This value is subjective because it depends on the needs of a unique user.

> Market value is the appraiser's opinion of what a typical buyer would pay.

The value most often sought in a real estate appraisal is *market value*. **Market value** is the most probable price a property would bring in an **arm's-length transaction** under normal conditions on the open market. This value is *objective*, because it is not based on the requirements of a particular owner. In an arm's-length transaction

- *neither* buyer nor seller is acting under duress;

- the real estate has been on the market a *reasonable* length of time for property of its type;

- buyer and seller have *full knowledge* of the property's assets and defects;

- *no unusual circumstances* exist, such as a sale involving related parties; and

- the price represents the *normal consideration* for the property sold, unaffected by creative financing or sales concessions.

Elements of Market Value

Demand
Utility
Scarcity
Transferability

Four basic elements (that you can remember by the word *DUST*) must be present before any product has a market value. A market exists only when **demand** has been created by a product's **utility**, or usefulness, coupled with its relative **scarcity**. The product must also have the quality of **transferability**; that is, there must be no impediment to its sale, such as a lien or other encumbrance.

In the case of real estate, a fifth element also is usually necessary. Due to the relative high cost of real estate, and the tax benefits and other advantages of leveraging the purchase with a modest down payment, most purchases are made primarily with borrowed funds, which means that the buyer must be able to secure suitable *financing*. The market for real estate, then, is determined by

- the property's possible uses,

- the availability of similar property and suitable financing,

- the number of potential purchasers, and

- the ability of the seller to convey good title to the buyer.

Basic Value Principles

It is the appraiser's task to recognize the factors that influence market value as early and as thoroughly as possible. As you study the basic value principles defined in this section, keep in mind that new concepts are constantly making an appearance. For example, many neighborhoods are now undergoing what is termed **gentrification** as buyers return to close-in urban and suburban areas, acquiring older buildings and investing money and labor in restoring their purchases.

Highest and best use   The **highest and best use** of real estate is its

- most profitable,

- *physically possible*, and

- *legally permissible* use.

A *highest and best use study* can be made of a vacant site or a site to be redeveloped. If a structure exists on the property, the cost of renovating or demolishing that structure is considered.

Balance   In general, a **balance** of varying land uses results in the highest property values overall. For example, housing should benefit from its proximity to places of employment and shopping areas.

Supply and demand   The principle of **supply and demand** reflects the relationship between the number of properties on the market at a given time and the number of potential buyers. All other factors being equal, prices tend to rise if demand is greater than supply. Prices tend to fall if supply exceeds demand.

Real estate markets tend to be most stable when there is a moderate oversupply of properties on the market relative to demand. To some extent, this reflects the fact that the marketplace usually includes sellers who can "wait out" a slow market or take their properties off the market for a time (rather than lower the asking price).

Conformity   Buildings exhibit **conformity** when they are similar in design, construction, and age. Particularly in residential neighborhoods, all property owners usually will benefit when there is consistency in the quality of design and construction, even when architectural styles vary.

Progression and regression   The value of a building is enhanced if buildings around it have a higher value, typically because they are better maintained, better quality construction, larger, or a combination of such factors. This is an example of the principle of **progression**.

According to the principle of **regression**, a building's value declines if the buildings around it have a lower value. For example, no matter how beautiful or extravagant a house is, it will not realize its full market potential if it is in a neighborhood of smaller, lower-quality (and thus less valuable) houses.

An improvement adds value only if it is what buyers want.

Contribution   A property improvement may or may not increase the property's overall market value, regardless of the cost of the improvement. In an appraisal, a property improvement is valued at only its **contribution** to the property's market value. The addition of a second bathroom, for instance, probably will contribute more of its cost to the market value of a house than a finished basement. The contribution to value of individual improvements will depend on market demand for those improvements. The National Association of Home Builders (NAHB) tracks the market value of common home remodeling projects in various regions of the country. Check www.nahb.org for the latest home remodeling cost survey.

www.nahb.org

Competition   Commercial properties are affected by **competition**, both positively and negatively. As businesses are attracted to a particular area, interest in the area generally increases. At a certain point, however, the market will become saturated and some businesses will suffer. In Silicon Valley, for example, office construction often falls behind market demand. Competition has brought attention to the benefits offered by the area (such as a skilled work force) and enabled property owners to profit. In a booming market, it may be difficult to remember that there can also be times in which "see-throughs" (vacant new office buildings) are common.

Change   As residents of California are well aware, real estate—land—is subject to a wide range of natural and other influences. Real estate undergoes constant **change** from

- *physical,*
- *economic,*

■ *social*, and

■ *political* forces.

A change may be subtle or catastrophic. Physical changes include the gradual accretion of soil along a riverbank that increases a property's size, as well as the earthquake that renders a structure uninhabitable within seconds. Economic forces include the availability of jobs, transportation, and credit. Social forces include subjective factors that influence our decisions on lifestyle, family planning, education, leisure, and retirement. Zoning, building codes, rent control, and other restrictions on property use are political forces that can be used to encourage, discourage, or even prohibit land development.

Life cycle   Both buildings and neighborhoods go through *life cycles*. As they are developed, they achieve **growth**, attain a period of **equilibrium** (or stability) in which little change is evident, then **decline** as properties deteriorate. By the time the first three stages of the cycle have been completed, the properties involved will show the effects of wear and tear, even when they have been adequately maintained. If otherwise well located, they will attract the investment needed to keep up increased maintenance and undergo a fourth stage, **revitalization**, before they begin another cycle of gradual deterioration.

Anticipation   Real estate is purchased for its expected future benefits. Because real estate values historically have increased, the expectation or **anticipation** of purchasers usually is that values will continue to rise. Purchases based on that anticipation add to market demand, which helps fulfill the expectation. Real estate values are still affected by property affordability and tend to do best when first-time homebuyers are able to enter the market.

Substitution   The principle of **substitution** is that value tends to be decided by the cost of acquiring an equally desirable property. This principle provides the basis of most residential real estate appraisals. The appraiser determines the value of a property that is *comparable* to the one being appraised and applies that value to the subject property. If there are two comparable properties, the one with the lower price will attract the greatest demand.

Exercise 13-1

Which basic value principle(s) does each of the following case examples illustrate?

1. Jeff Powell has finally remodeled his extra bedroom as the den of his dreams. The rosewood wainscoting is set off by hand-painted reproduction antique wallpaper and by light fixtures that Jeff salvaged from the wreck of a yacht. The den was expensive, but Jeff is philosophical, believing that he will always be able to recoup his expenses if he has to sell his house.

2. Baez began her dentistry practice in a small office building in a tiny farm community many miles from the city, surrounded by nothing but flat,

unproductive farmland and three major freeways. Baez now owns that building, several apartment complexes, a strip shopping center, and a condo on Maui.

3. Papa Joe has owned his corner grocery store for 40 years. He grew up only a few blocks from the store, in a house that is still his home. He remembers the way the neighborhood looked when he was a boy and there were still many open spaces to explore. When he took over the store, a vacant lot was hard to find. Papa Joe was happy with his business, even when his friends began moving to the suburbs and he had fewer customers. The neighborhood became rundown and there were quite a few vacant buildings. Lately though, he has noticed quite a few young people moving in and working hard to fix up their houses. New businesses are also opening. Papa Joe has decided to stay and has even put in a gourmet takeout deli counter.

4. The Blairs own a five-bedroom, three-bathroom house in a well-kept but modest section of town. The Blairs' house is the largest in their neighborhood. They have decided to sell their home and have asked Deborah Dollar, a real estate agent, for her estimate of what sales price they can expect. Deborah knows that a house very similar to the Blairs' was sold a few weeks ago, but that house is about a mile away and only a block from an elementary school. Deborah goes over her data on that sale and others in the neighborhood very carefully before she explains to the Blairs why she thinks their house should sell for somewhat less than the one most similar to theirs.

THE APPRAISAL PROCESS

The flowchart in Figure 13.1 shows the steps an appraiser takes in identifying the scope of work required to complete the appraisal assignment, and then gathering, recording, and analyzing the many types of data that contribute to the final opinion of value.

The appraiser becomes familiar with the national, regional, city, and neighborhood factors that affect the subject property (the property being appraised). Then, the appraiser's focus shifts to the subject itself.

What effect does the location of the property have? Is the subject property located in the direction of growth of the city in which it is located or of a nearby city? Will building restrictions and zoning ordinances impede or aid its value? Is the property's size an optimum one for its highest and best use? Does the topography of the area lend itself to that use? Is the property located on a major thoroughfare that will help or hinder its desirability? These are only some of the appraiser's concerns.

> The right data forms the basis of an accurate appraisal.

After a thorough description of the subject property, and in light of all the other information compiled, the appraiser is ready to gather the data needed for the specific *appraisal techniques*. You can remember them by the three Cs—comparison, cost, and capitalization:

- The **sales comparison approach** requires descriptions of comparable properties that have sold recently.

- The **cost approach** requires building cost data.

- The **income capitalization approach** requires income and expense data on the subject, comparable properties, or both.

FIGURE 13.1: The Appraisal Process

Although we have provided only the briefest coverage of the data collection process, we must stress that the appraiser's thorough knowledge of the subject, market area, and other pertinent facts provides the substance of an accurate appraisal. *The most valuable component of an appraisal is the competence and experience of the appraiser.*

All three appraisal methods may not be used in every appraisal. The appraiser uses the most appropriate method(s), then determines the value that (in the appraiser's opinion) is the most reliable indicator of value. The final value selection process is called **reconciliation** and will be discussed later in this unit.

SALES COMPARISON APPROACH

The method that usually is the most significant in appraising residential property is the **sales comparison approach**. The reasoning behind it is easy to understand, and the data required to apply it usually is readily available. The sales comparison approach is also called the *market data approach*, *market comparison approach*, or *paired sales approach*. Following is a summary of this approach:

- The appraiser finds three to five (or more) recently sold properties that are similar in basic characteristics to the property that is the subject of the appraisal. These *comparable properties* are referred to as **comps**. Ideally, the sales should have occurred within the last six months, and each comp should offer *amenities* (special features, such as a swimming pool) similar to those offered by the subject property.

- The appraiser analyzes each sale and notes significant *differences* between the comps and the subject property.

- The appraiser then *adjusts* the sales price of each comp to more accurately reflect the features of the subject property. The appraiser can also make an adjustment to compensate for a sale that occurred earlier than six months before the date of the appraisal.

- The appraiser's final step is to analyze the resulting figures and choose the one that best represents the value of the subject property.

This process can be expressed as a formula:

$$\text{Sales price of comparable property} \pm \text{Adjustments} = \text{Indicated value of subject property}$$

The appraiser *adds* to the sales price of the comparable property the value of any feature that is present in the subject property but not in the comp. The appraiser *subtracts* from the sales price of the comparable property the value of any feature that is present in the comp but not in the subject property.

FOR EXAMPLE   House A is being appraised. House B is comparable to A. House B, which has a three-car garage, sold for $396,000. House A has only a two-car garage. The extra garage space is valued by the appraiser at $8,500, based on recent sales.

Using the formula for the sales comparison approach, the value of the extra garage space is subtracted from the price of B, as follows:

$$\$396,000 - \$8,500 = \$387,500$$

The adjusted price of B is $387,500. This adjusted price will be compared to that of other properties to determine a market value for A.

Comparable properties ideally should be located in the same neighborhood as the subject property. They also should be substantially similar to the subject property in style, age, number and type of rooms, size of lot and building, type of construction, and general condition. The financing terms under which the property was sold should be typical of financing in the area, without special consideration for either buyer or seller. The sales should be fairly recent, ideally no more than six months before the date of appraisal, or an adjustment will have to be made. Current listings should be examined to reveal any downward trend in seller expectations. This is an especially important consideration at a time of slowing market demand.

> A forced sale usually places the seller at a disadvantage and the transaction will not be a good comparable.

Any variation in the previously listed specifications would be treated as an adjustment to the sales price of the comp. The one variable that would be difficult, if not impossible, to treat as an adjustment would be a sale that was not an arm's-length transaction. Perhaps the seller acted under the duress of an impending foreclosure, divorce action, or immediate job transfer. In such a case, the property probably should be disqualified as a comparable. What if the only recent sales in the neighborhood are foreclosure sales? In that event, property condition will be a critical factor. Foreclosure sales that best reflect the overall characteristics and condition of the subject property may be the most appropriate to use. If the area is a strong rental market, the income approach, discussed later in this unit, may be a good indicator of property value.

Real estate agents who perform market analyses for prospective clients and customers have ready sources of sales information—their own files. They also can obtain sales information from multiple listing services and can exchange data on transactions that have closed with other agents. Once a transaction has been recorded in the county clerk's office, the county assessor also is a source of sales information.

Exercise 13-2 takes you through a very simplified version of an appraisal of a single-family residence using the sales comparison approach. Read all of the information given, then supply the necessary calculations in the chart. When you have finished, decide which of the indicated values appears to come closest to the market value of the subject property. Isolate the high and low figures and find the value that most closely represents the entire range of values.

Exercise 13-2

You are to provide an opinion of the current market value of house X.

House X is a one-story, single-family residence with wood siding. It has a living room, a formal dining room, a kitchen, a family room with a fireplace, four bedrooms, two bathrooms, and an attached two-car garage.

Appliances are in good condition, and the seller will pay for a home warranty to cover repairs to major mechanical systems for one year.

House X is in a neighborhood of similar homes, all landscaped and well maintained, and presents an attractive streetside appearance. House X has an in-ground swimming pool with well-established landscaping.

House A also has a swimming pool and is comparable to X but has an extra half-bath off the family room.

House B has a swimming pool and is comparable to X but has no fireplace.

House C is comparable to X, but has no swimming pool.

House A sold for $551,000, B sold for $538,000, and C sold for $499,000.

In this price range, an extra half-bath is valued at $8,000, a fireplace is valued at $6,200, and an in-ground swimming pool with mature landscaping is a desirable amenity valued at $25,000.

Complete the following chart, using the figures above.

	Comparables		
	A	**B**	**C**
Sales price			
Adjustment variables			
Extra half-bath			
No fireplace			
No swimming pool			
Total adjustments			
Adjusted value			

Comparative Market Analysis

Many real estate agents who are not appraisers will supply the information necessary for a **comparative market analysis** (CMA), also sometimes called a competitive market analysis or a **broker's price opinion** (BPO). The agent's purpose is to assist the seller or buyer in determining the property's fair market value. A CMA ordinarily is more limited in scope than an appraisal and does not include an opinion of value by the agent.

The most frequently used source of data for a CMA is the bank of properties handled through the agent's *multiple listing service*. Sales, asking prices, and length of time on the market will be examined for the following three categories of property in a defined area:

> Properties that failed to sell may reveal more than properties that sold.

- Property that was sold recently
- Property that is for sale now
- Property that was previously listed for sale, but the listing has expired or the property was withdrawn from the market

The sales and/or asking prices, when examined together, indicate to the *seller* a range of values that includes the listing or asking price as well as the sales price of the subject property. Such data also indicate the number of days the property may be expected to be on the market before it sells.

For the *buyer*, the market analysis suggests a price range from which to select an offer to purchase and the maximum price that should be paid.

COST APPROACH

In the **cost approach** for establishing value, the appraiser determines what it would cost to duplicate the subject property:

1. The appraiser begins with the *present cost* of improvements on the subject property.

2. The appraiser then *subtracts* the amount by which those improvements have depreciated.

3. Finally, the appraiser *adds* in the value of the land to arrive at an indicated value.

The formula for the cost approach is as follows:

$$\text{Reproduction or replacement cost of improvement(s)} - \text{Accrued depreciation} + \text{Site value}$$

Reproduction cost is the cost of a new building of exactly the same design and materials as the subject property. **Replacement cost** is the cost of a new building using modern methods, design, and materials and having the same use as the subject property but without the identical specifications. The replacement cost of a building is appropriate when the structure's design or construction is not *economically feasible* to reproduce today. Certain design features could be impossible to duplicate at any price. Because skilled craftspeople may not be available to produce special building features, such as ornate cornices, moldings, or ceilings, the closest modern substitutes are evaluated instead.

Site value is determined by the sales comparison approach or other appropriate method. The records of the county tax assessor show a land-to-improvements ratio that can be useful in evaluating comparable properties to derive land value alone. Many lenders making government-backed loans do not accept other valuation sources for their appraisals.

Local labor costs are probably the biggest construction cost variable.

The cost approach has the drawback of relying on construction cost estimates that differ greatly from region to region, even within a state. Builders' costs vary and often depend on the number of units under construction. Construction techniques also affect cost; for example, prefabricated roof trusses lower on-site labor costs. National and regional *cost manuals* help the appraiser keep cost estimates up-to-date. Such manuals are revised frequently, and the better ones have online services that update price changes weekly or even daily.

Finally, the cost approach assumes that the building(s) already on the site represents its highest and best use. As mentioned earlier in this unit, the **value in use** of a property is its value to its present owner and, thus, is a *subjective* value. **Market**

value, on the other hand, should be an *objective* determination. A property with no utility to anyone but its present owner will not be evaluated fairly by the cost approach. In the same way, a property that is not put to its highest and best use is not an appropriate subject for the cost approach. Local preferences also must be considered. For example, an ornate but little-used movie theater may have great sentimental value but probably would be better appraised for the redevelopment value of its site rather than as a structure maintaining its present use. If it is declared a historical landmark, however, and redevelopment is prohibited, its present use may be the only available option.

The cost approach method is ideal for special purpose properties—those that have no comparables in the area or which produce no income. Examples are museums, schools, and churches.

Finding Reproduction or Replacement Cost

The appraiser can use any one or more of the following four methods to find the reproduction or replacement cost of property improvements:

- Square-foot method
- Unit-in-place method
- Quantity survey method
- Index method

Square-foot method   Using the **square-foot method**, the appraiser multiplies the current cost per square foot of a comparable building by the number of square feet in the subject building. This is the method most frequently used by appraisers. A similar approach is the *cubic-foot method*, most commonly used for nonresidential properties such as warehouses. Cost data services, such as those found at www.rsmeans.com and www.marshallswift.com, can be used to find the cost per square or cubic foot of a property with the same specifications as the subject building.

www.rsmeans.com
www.marshallswift.com

Unit-in-place method   The **unit-in-place method** makes use of the construction cost per unit of measure of each of the component parts of the subject property, such as walls, plumbing units, heating units, and so on. Each unit cost includes material, labor, overhead, and builder's profit. The cost per unit is multiplied by the number of units of each component part, and the individual unit costs are then totaled. Most measurements will be in square feet, although mechanical and plumbing systems will be estimated as complete units.

Quantity survey method   The **quantity survey method** requires a thorough itemization of all construction costs, both direct (materials and labor) and indirect (permits, taxes, profits, insurance, and other overhead). Every material, labor, and indirect cost is estimated separately, and the individual costs are totaled. The quantity survey method can be used only by someone familiar with all facets of building construction. It is very accurate but time-consuming.

Index method   In the **index method**, the appraiser multiplies the original cost of the subject property by a factor that represents the percentage increase (or decrease) of construction costs generally from the time of construction to the present time. Cost reporting or indexing services, such as those mentioned previously, provide information on cost changes over time as well as from area to area.

If the original cost of the subject structure is known, the index method is the simplest way to estimate present cost. It is a very imprecise method, however, and for that reason it should be used only as a check on the value arrived at by one of the other methods.

Depreciation

Tax depreciation is not the same as appraisal depreciation.

Depreciation is a loss in value from any cause. Note that depreciation for appraisal purposes is *not* the depreciation that Uncle Sam allows investors to deduct from income in computing taxes. Depreciation for tax purposes is meant to encourage investment, and it may have absolutely no relation to the loss in value to a structure brought about by physical deterioration and other causes. The appraiser's job is to estimate the *actual* loss in value from depreciation and reduce the replacement cost of the subject property accordingly.

There are three main types of depreciation. Some forms of depreciation are considered *curable* because they can be remedied by a repair or an addition to the property at relatively low cost. In other words, the property's value after the repair or improvement is increased by an amount greater than or at least equal to the cost of the work.

Other forms of depreciation are considered *incurable* because there is no easy or economical way to remedy them. Many buildings damaged by earthquakes or mudslides could be repaired but at too great an expense to make the repairs feasible as a practical matter.

The three forms of depreciation are as follows:

- Physical deterioration
- Functional obsolescence
- External obsolescence

Physical deterioration   **Physical deterioration** includes damage or destruction to a building as well as the more subtle effects of ordinary wear and tear. Examples of physical deterioration include windows destroyed by vandals, roof damage caused by a violent storm, and wood siding that has cracked and separated over time.

Functional obsolescence   **Functional obsolescence** occurs when a building's design, layout, or utility is no longer desirable. Functional obsolescence reflects the changing requirements of the marketplace and may be observed in both houses and commercial structures.

The suburban house with only one bathroom and the gas station forced out of business because the owner cannot afford to upgrade the underground holding tanks, as required by law, are both examples of functional obsolescence. The selling price of the house will suffer. The gas station will remain vacant until another use for the property is found or it is sold for the value of its site, which will take into account the cost of removing the underground tanks and performing the necessary environmental remediation.

External obsolescence   External obsolescence, also called *environmental obsolescence* or *economic obsolescence*, is the loss in a property's value due to *outside* causes. Changes in nearby land use through development, rezoning, or transfer of ownership may bring about a loss in value. Ironically, rezoning may increase the value of the rezoned property while decreasing the value of adjacent property. Property on a residential street rezoned to allow commercial uses most likely will *increase* in value. Adjacent property, which must remain residential, may *decline* in value due to greater noise and traffic.

Economic factors tend to have a ripple effect and eventually affect property values. For example, if a major employer moves to a distant location, there may be more homes on the market as transferred employees move to the new location, which will lower prices. As the population decreases and unemployment rises, both the housing market and businesses dependent on consumer spending will suffer.

External obsolescence generally is *incurable*, because by definition it is caused by outside forces.

Computing Depreciation

The two most widely used direct methods of computing depreciation are the

- straight-line method and
- observed condition method.

Straight-line method   The **straight-line method** of computing depreciation is the easiest to understand and the least complicated to use. Every building has an *economic life*, which is the period of years in which it may be used for its originally intended purpose.

If the value of the building is divided by the number of years of its estimated economic (useful) life, the resulting figure is the amount by which the building can be expected to depreciate every year. If property is well maintained, however, its rate of depreciation may be slowed. In that case, its *effective age* will be less than its age in actual calendar years.

FOR EXAMPLE A storage warehouse is constructed at a cost of $425,000 and has an estimated economic life of 50 years. After 30 years of good maintenance, the building has an effective age of only 20 years. By how much will the building have depreciated?

$$\frac{\$425,000}{50 \text{ years}} = \$8,500 \text{ depreciation each year}$$

$$\$8,500 \times 20 = \$170,000 \text{ total depreciation}$$

Or

$$\frac{100\%}{50 \text{ years}} = 2\% \text{ depreciation per year}$$

$$20 \text{ years} \times 2\% = 40\% \text{ depreciation}$$

$$\$425,000 \times 40\% = \$170,000 \text{ total depreciation}$$

The straight-line method is one that the Internal Revenue Service uses. The number of years prescribed by the IRS is not necessarily the number of years the appraiser will use, however.

Observed condition method The **observed condition method** of computing depreciation is also called the *breakdown method*. It requires the appraiser to estimate the loss in value caused by every individual item of depreciation, whether curable or incurable.

The appraiser determines the effect on value of each item in every category of depreciation (physical deterioration, functional obsolescence, and external obsolescence). The appraiser then deducts the loss in value in each category from the reproduction cost of the subject building. Computing depreciation in a very old building by the breakdown method might be an overwhelming task, and another approach would be advisable.

FOR EXAMPLE The reproduction cost of a building is $670,000. Its depreciation is estimated as follows:

Physical deterioration	
Curable	$84,000
Incurable	67,000
Functional obsolescence	
Curable	43,000
Incurable	0
External obsolescence	
Curable	0
Incurable	0
Total	$194,000

Depreciated building cost is reproduction cost less depreciation:

$$\$670,000 - \$194,000 = \$476,000$$

Land value would be added to the depreciated building cost to find total property value.

Remember that a cost estimate of value usually determines the upper limit of a property's value. A buyer ordinarily does not want to pay more for an existing building than it would cost to build a new one.

Exercise 13-3

Find the current market value of house X using the square-foot method of estimating value by the cost approach.

House X has a living area of 25 feet by 60 feet, with an attached garage of 25 feet by 25 feet. Current cost per square foot of a residence with the specifications of X is $125 per square foot of living area and $75 per square foot of garage space. House X had an original useful life of 40 years and is now four years old.

A few lots are still available in house X's subdivision. A lot comparable to the one on which X is built is valued at $56,000.

Living area = _____ square feet @ _____ per square foot = _____

Garage area = _____ square feet @ _____ per square foot = _____

Total reproduction cost = _____

$$\frac{\text{Total reproduction cost}}{\text{Years of useful life}} = \$ \_\_\_\_ \text{ Yearly depreciation}$$

Yearly depreciation × _____ years = $_____ Total depreciation

Reproduction cost − Total depreciation + Land value = _____

The estimate of value of house X by the cost approach is _____.

INCOME CAPITALIZATION APPROACH

In estimating value by the **income capitalization approach**, the appraiser first determines the property's potential gross income. **Potential gross income** is a property's maximum income from all sources. An office or apartment building might produce income from vending machines or a laundry room in addition to rental income. A single-family residence probably would have only a base monthly rent.

The "going rate" for a property is its market rent.

The appraiser estimates what is called the property's *market rent* or *economic rent*. **Market rent** is an estimate of the property's rent potential—what it could rent for if available for rental on today's market. The rent received by the current property owner is called the property's *contract rent* or *scheduled rent*. **Contract rent** may be higher or lower than *market rent*.

The appraiser next makes an allowance for *vacancy and collection losses*. Not every unit in the building will be continuously occupied, and sometimes a tenant is delinquent in rent payments. The appraiser estimates and then subtracts these anticipated losses from gross income to derive **effective gross income**.

Yearly *operating expenses* are then subtracted from effective gross income to arrive at **net operating income**. By applying a *capitalization rate* to net operating income, the appraiser arrives at an estimate of market value.

The **capitalization ("cap") rate** is the property owner's annual expected rate of return. The capitalization rate can be expressed as the relationship between the net operating income the property produces and its market value, as in the following equation:

$$\frac{\text{Net operating income}}{\text{Value}} = \text{Capitalization rate}$$

We can also derive two corollaries from that equation:

Capitalization rate × Value = Net operating income

$$\frac{\text{Net operating income}}{\text{Capitalization rate}} = \text{Value}$$

The capitalization rate can be developed by analyzing net income and sales prices of comparable properties.

FOR EXAMPLE   Building Y produces a yearly net operating income of $32,000. What is the market value of Y?

Building D has a net operating income of $35,000 per year, and it sold two months ago for $389,000. Building E has a net operating income of $31,000 per year, and it sold last week for $345,000.

Building D and E are otherwise comparable to Y. They are in the same area and are also six-unit apartment buildings of the same age and general physical condition as Y. Using the equation for the capitalization rate:

$$\frac{\$35,000}{\$389,000} = 9\% \qquad\qquad \frac{\$31,000}{\$345,000} = 9\%$$

The capitalization rates for building D and E support the assigning of a capitalization rate of 9% to Y. Using the equation for value:

$$\frac{\$32,000}{.09} = \$355,555.56$$

The indicated market value of Y, rounded to the nearest hundred dollars, is $355,600.

The better the investment (the more stable its projected income stream), the lower the cap rate that the investor will demand. Conversely, an investor will expect a higher rate of return on a riskier investment.

Note: Financing costs have not been included in this discussion of net operating income. Financing costs will vary, depending on the individual property buyer's financial position and negotiating power with a lender. Thus, interest and principal payments are considered costs associated with a particular buyer rather than with operating expenses of the property. In short, how a property is financed does not affect its value. All property is treated as if it is held free and clear.

Gross Income Multipliers

Many properties, including single-family residences, are not purchased primarily for their income-producing potential. For those properties, a simpler method of determining value based on income may be used.

The gross income multiplier is sometimes referred to as the "gross multiplier."

Begin by dividing the *sales price* of a rented, comparable property by the *gross income* the property produces to arrive at a factor called the **gross income multiplier** (GIM):

$$\frac{\text{Sales price}}{\text{Gross income}} = \text{GIM}$$

An *annual GIM* is more likely to be used for industrial or commercial property. A *monthly GIM* generally is used for residential property. Because its income is generally limited to rent, the multiplier for a single-family residence is usually termed a *gross rent multiplier (GRM)*.

F O R   E X A M P L E   A commercial building with an annual gross income of $48,000 sold two months ago for $535,000. What is that building's gross income multiplier? Using the equation:

$$\frac{\$535,000}{\$48,000} = 11.1$$

The building's gross income multiplier is 11.1, rounding to the nearest tenth.

The appraiser compares the GIM of at least four comparable properties to determine the multiplier most applicable to the subject property. The GIM selected for the subject property then is multiplied by the actual or projected rental of the subject to find its market value:

$$\text{Gross income} \times \text{GIM} = \text{Market value}$$

F O R   E X A M P L E   Building Y has an annual gross income of $63,000. What is its market value, using the gross income multiplier method?

Of four comparable properties, one has a GIM of 10.0, one has a GIM of 8.5, and the other two each have a GIM of 9.5. Discounting the high and low figures, we arrive at a gross income multiplier for the subject property of 9.5.

$$\$63,000 \times 9.5 = \$598,500$$

Building Y has a market value of $598,500.

The gross income multiplier method is not accurate enough to serve as the sole means of determining market value. It fails to take into account the many variables that contribute to gross income. It also fails to consider the many property expenses that can reduce effective net income. Because it is relatively easy to use, however, it may be a useful check of the value reached by another appraisal method.

Exercise 13-4

You are appraising a single-family residence that may be purchased as a rental property. Complete the following chart to determine the property's gross income multiplier. Then estimate its market value.

Sale No.	Market Value	Monthly Gross Income	Gross Income Multiplier
1	$585,000	$2,845	205.6
2	$582,000	$2,810	207.1
3	$575,000	$2,775	207.2
4	$565,000	$2,775	203.6
5	$568,000	$2,600	218.5
Subject	_____	$2,800	_____

RECONCILIATION AND THE APPRAISAL REPORT

The appraiser begins the final step in the appraisal process with as many as three different values for the subject property, one for each of the approaches used—sales comparison, cost, or income capitalization.

To determine the most appropriate estimate of value for the subject property, the appraiser reconsiders each of the values in light of

- the type of property being appraised,
- the purpose of the appraisal, and
- any other factors that may be unique to the appraisal.

The process of weighing the differing values by their relevance to the appraisal problem is called **reconciliation**, or *correlation*. The goal of the analysis is to select the value that is *most likely* to be an accurate reflection of market value. The appraiser's *final opinion of value* can then be presented and explained in the report to the client.

To comply with the *Uniform Standards of Professional Appraisal Practice (USPAP)*, the appraiser must identify an appraisal report as a

- self-contained report;
- summary report; or
- restricted use report.

Self-Contained Report

The **self-contained report**, also called a *narrative report*, is the most comprehensive report the appraiser can make. It includes a complete statement of the appraiser's credentials. It provides a thorough description of the property being appraised, the purpose of the appraisal, and a summary of the background data supporting each opinion of value. It will include a full description of all data considered and all techniques used in the appraisal process.

The self-contained report provides an overview of the subject property's region, city, and neighborhood. It may total 30 pages or more, even for a single-family residence. It is used most often in a legal proceeding, such as the probate of an estate, a divorce settlement, litigation, or a condemnation action where extensive detail is necessary.

Summary Form Report

A **summary report** will provide the most important details of the appraiser's analysis, including a brief version of pertinent data and a shortened discussion of the appraisal techniques used. A summary report is commonly used by government agencies and the lenders with which they do business, typically by means of a standardized form. The type of property and the purpose of the appraisal dictate the exact form used. The first three pages of the **Uniform Residential Appraisal Report** (URAR), Form 1004, used by Fannie Mae, Freddie Mac, and many other agencies, appears in Figure 13.2. The last three pages of the form include definitions of terms and the appraiser's certification. A copy of the complete form is available at www.efanniemae.com.

www.efanniemae.com

Restricted Use Report

A **restricted use report** will be limited in either the method of valuation used or the property interests valued. The limitation must be stated in the appraisal and the client must be the only intended user.

FIGURE 13.2: Uniform Residential Appraisal Report

Complete Appraisal Analysis - Summary Appraisal Report

Uniform Residential Appraisal Report
File # 05060001

The purpose of this summary appraisal report is to provide the lender/client with an accurate, and adequately supported, opinion of the market value of the subject property.

SUBJECT

Property Address 4807 Catalpa Road	City Woodview	State CA	Zip Code 90000
Borrower David and Rachel Phillips	Owner of Public Record Thomas Tsao		County Delta

Legal Description Lot 174, Block 13, Woodview Heights Subdivision, recorded in Plat 7, Book 3, Delta County Recorder of Deeds

Assessor's Parcel # 6412-028-007 — Tax Year 20-- — R.E. Taxes $ Prop 13

Neighborhood Name Woodview Heights — Map Reference 17H — Census Tract 8888

Occupant [X] Owner [ ] Tenant [ ] Vacant — Special Assessments $ 1,250 — [X] PUD — HOA $ 136 [ ] per year [X] per month

Property Rights Appraised [X] Fee Simple [ ] Leasehold [ ] Other (describe)

Assignment Type [X] Purchase Transaction [ ] Refinance Transaction [ ] Other (describe)

Lender/Client Woodview Federal Bank — Address 1887 Main Street, Woodview, CA 90000

Is the subject property currently offered for sale or has it been offered for sale in the twelve months prior to the effective date of the appraisal? [X] Yes [ ] No

Report data source(s) used, offering price(s), and date(s). Listed July 5, 20-- at $779,000, according to listing agent Marie Moreno.

CONTRACT

I [X] did [ ] did not analyze the contract for sale for the subject purchase transaction. Explain the results of the analysis of the contract for sale or why the analysis was not performed. Conventional financing, with no seller concessions.

Contract Price $ 775,000 Date of Contract 7-12-20-- Is the property seller the owner of public record? [X] Yes [ ] No Data Source(s)

Is there any financial assistance (loan charges, sale concessions, gift or downpayment assistance, etc.) to be paid by any party on behalf of the borrower? [ ] Yes [X] No

If Yes, report the total dollar amount and describe the items to be paid:

NEIGHBORHOOD

Note: Race and the racial composition of the neighborhood are not appraisal factors.

Neighborhood Characteristics	One-Unit Housing Trends	One-Unit Housing	Percent Land Use %
Location [ ] Urban [X] Suburban [ ] Rural	Property Values [X] Increasing [ ] Stable [ ] Declining	PRICE $(000) / AGE (yrs)	One-Unit 100 %
Built-Up [X] Over 75% [ ] 25-75% [ ] Under 25%	Demand/Supply [ ] Shortage [X] In Balance [ ] Over Supply	680 Low 22	2-4 Unit %
Growth [ ] Rapid [X] Stable [ ] Slow	Marketing Time [X] Under 3 mths [ ] 3-6 mths [ ] Over 6 mths	950 High 22	Multi-Family %
		800 Pred. 22	Commercial %
			Other %

Neighborhood Boundaries Washington Boulevard to north; Lake Avenue to east; Bay Street to south; Harbor Avenue to west

Neighborhood Description Gently rolling hills 15 miles from Bay City, accessible by interstate highway and commuter train. Location of Woodview Heights makes it one of the most desirable suburbs in the area.

Market Conditions (including support for the above conclusions) Steady demand for housing in the Bay City area, and lack of new development, has resulted in record prices for existing homes. Despite recent rise in interest rates, offers usually are close to asking prices.

SITE

Dimensions 75Fx125LSx72Rx130RS — Area 9371 +/- sq. ft. — Shape Rectangular — View Residential; hills

Specific Zoning Classification R-2 — Zoning Description Single-family residential

Zoning Compliance [X] Legal [ ] Legal Nonconforming (Grandfathered Use) [ ] No Zoning [ ] Illegal (describe)

Is the highest and best use of the subject property as improved (or as proposed per plans and specifications) the present use? [X] Yes [ ] No If No, describe

Utilities	Public	Other (describe)		Public	Other (describe)	Off-site Improvements--Type	Public	Private
Electricity	[X]		Water	[X]		Street Asphalt	[X]	
Gas			Sanitary Sewer			Alley None		

FEMA Special Flood Hazard Area [ ] Yes [X] No FEMA Flood Zone — FEMA Map No. — FEMA Map Date

Are the utilities and off-site improvements typical for the market area? [X] Yes [ ] No. If No, describe

Are there any adverse site conditions or external factors (easements, encroachments, environmental conditions, land uses, etc.)? [ ] Yes [X] No If Yes, describe

IMPROVEMENTS

General Description	Foundation	Exterior Description materials/condition	Interior materials/condition
Units [X] One [ ] One with Accessory Unit	[ ] Concrete Slab [X] Crawl Space	Foundation Walls Poured concrete	Floors Hardwood
# of Stories 2	[ ] Full Basement [ ] Partial Basement	Exterior Walls Stucco	Walls Drywall/paint
Type [X] Det. [ ] Att. [ ] S-Det/End Unit	Basement Area sq. ft.	Roof Surface Tile	Trim/Finish Wood/paint
[X] Existing [ ] Proposed [ ] Under Const.	Basement Finish %	Gutters & Downspouts Aluminum	Bath Floor Ceramic tile
Design (Style) Mission	[ ] Outside Entry/Exit [ ] Sump Pump	Window Type Aluminum	Bath Wainscot Ceramic tile
Year Built 1979	Evidence of [ ] Infestation	Storm Sash/Insulated	Car Storage [ ] None
Effective Age (Yrs) 15	[ ] Dampness [ ] Settlement	Screens Aluminum	[ ] Driveway # of Cars
Attic [X] None	Heating [X] FWA [ ] HWBB [ ] Radiant	Amenities	Driveway Surface Concrete
[ ] Drop Stair [ ] Stairs	[ ] Other Fuel	[X] Fireplace(s) # 1 [X] Fence	[X] Garage # of Cars 2
[ ] Floor [ ] Scuttle	Cooling [X] Central Air Conditioning	[X] Patio/Deck [ ] Porch	[ ] Carport # of Cars
[ ] Finished [ ] Heated	[ ] Individual [ ] Other	[ ] Pool [ ] Other	[X] Att. [ ] Det. [ ] Built-in

Appliances [X] Refrigerator [X] Range/Oven [X] Dishwasher [X] Disposal [X] Microwave [ ] Washer/Dryer [ ] Other (describe)

Finished area **above grade** contains: 8 Rooms 4 Bedrooms 2.50 Bath(s) 2,014 Square Feet of Gross Living Area Above Grade

Additional features (special energy efficient items, etc.) 6" insulation in ceiling and exterior walls

Describe the condition of the property (including needed repairs, deterioration, renovations, remodeling, etc.). Property has been well maintained, with newer paint. Appliances are original; in working order, but due for replacement. Landscaping is mature, but not overgrown.

Are there any physical deficiencies or adverse conditions that affect the livability, soundness, or structural integrity of the property? [ ] Yes [ ] No If Yes, describe
No adverse conditions noted.

Does the property generally conform to the neighborhood (functional utility, style, condition, use, construction, etc.)? [X] Yes [ ] No If No, describe

Freddie Mac Form 70 March 2005 — Page 1 of 6 — Fannie Mae Form 1004 March 2005

Fundamentals of Real Estate Appraisal

FIGURE 13.2: Uniform Residential Appraisal Report (continued)

Complete Appraisal Analysis - Summary Appraisal Report

Uniform Residential Appraisal Report

File # 05060001

There are **4** comparable properties in the subject neighborhood ranging in price from $ 725,000.00 to $ 925,000.00 .

There are **5** comparable sales in the subject neighborhood within the past twelve months ranging in sale price from $ 700,000.00 to $ 940,000.00 .

FEATURE	SUBJECT	COMPARABLE SALE # 1		COMPARABLE SALE # 2		COMPARABLE SALE # 3	
Address	4807 Catalpa Road Woodview	1516 Mayfield Avenue		5208 Bainbridge Road		1324 North Avenue	
Proximity to Subject		1/4 mile		1/2 mile		1/4 mile	
Sale Price	$ 775,000	$ 749,900		$ 790,000		$ 769,000	
Sale Price/Gross Liv. Area	$ 384.81 sq. ft.	$ 390.57 sq. ft.		$ 383.50 sq. ft.		$ 381.83 sq. ft.	
Data Source(s)							
Verification Source(s)							
VALUE ADJUSTMENTS	DESCRIPTION	DESCRIPTION	+(-)$ Adjustment	DESCRIPTION	+(-)$ Adjustment	DESCRIPTION	+(-)$ Adjustment
Sale or Financing Concessions		Conv. mort.		Conv. mort.		Conv. mort.	
Date of Sale/Time		6-17-20--		5-25-20--		5-18-20--	
Location	Suburban	Suburban		Suburban		Suburban	
Leasehold/Fee Simple	Fee Simple	Fee Simple		Fee Simple		Fee Simple	
Site	9371 +/- sq. ft.	9,200 +/- sq.ft.		9,400 +/- sq.ft.		9,350 +/- sq.ft.	
View	Nbhd./avg.	Nbhd./equal		Nbhd./equal		Nbhd./equal	
Design (Style)	Mission	Mission		Mission		Mission	
Quality of Construction	Good	Good		Good		Good	
Actual Age	22	22		22		22	
Condition	Good	Good		Good		Good	
Above Grade	Total Bdrms. Baths	Total Bdrms. Baths		Total Bdrms. Baths		Total Bdrms. Baths	
Room Count	8 4 2.50	7 3 2.5	+20,000	8 5 3	-25,000	8 4 2.5	
Gross Living Area	2,014 sq. ft.	1,920 sq. ft.		2,060 sq. ft.		2,014 sq. ft.	
Basement & Finished Rooms Below Grade	Crawlspace	Crawlspace		Crawlspace		Crawlspace	
Functional Utility	Good	Good		Good		Good	
Heating/Cooling	Central	Central		Central		Central	
Energy Efficient Items	Extra insul.	Extra insul.		Extra insul.		Extra insul.	
Garage/Carport	Gar 2 att.	Gar 2 att.		Gar 2 att.		Gar 2 att.	
Porch/Patio/Deck	Patio	Patio		Patio		Patio	
Fireplace	Fireplace	No firepl.	+4,000	Fireplace		Fireplace	
Fence	Fence	Fence		Fence		Fence	
Storage building						Storage bldg.	+6,000
Net Adjustment (Total)		X + ☐ -	$ 24,000	☐ + X -	$ -25,000	X + ☐ -	$ 6,000
Adjusted Sale Price of Comparables		Net Adj. 3.20 % Gross Adj. 3.20 %	$ 773,900	Net Adj. -3.20 % Gross Adj. 3.20 %	$ 765,000	Net Adj. 0.80 % Gross Adj. 0.80 %	$ 775,000

I ☒ did ☐ did not research the sale or transfer history of the subject property and comparable sales. If not, explain T

My research ☐ did ☒ did not reveal any prior sales or transfers of the subject property for the three years prior to the effective date of this appraisal.

Data Source(s)

My research ☒ did ☐ did not reveal any prior sales or transfers of the comparable sales for the prior year to the date of sale of the comparibe sale.

Data Source(s) Comp. #2 sold in September, 20-- for $689,000, according to MLS records.

Report the results of the research and analysis of the prior sale or transfer history of the subject property and comparable sales (report additional prior sales on page 3).

ITEM	SUBJECT	COMPARABLE SALE # 1	COMPARABLE SALE # 2	COMPARABLE SALE # 3
Date of Prior Sale/Transfer			Nov. 8, 20--	
Price of Prior Sale/Transfer			689,000	
Data Source(s)			MLS	
Effective Date of Data Source(s)			Sept. 29, 20--	

Analysis of prior sale or transfer history of the subject property and comparable sales Sale of comp. #2 two years ago for $689,000 and for $790,000 in May of this year, an increase of 15%, is consistent with recent rates of appreciation in the Bay City area.

Summary of Sales Comparison Approach The subject property conforms to the condition and quality of other property in the neighborhood. The frequency of sales in Woodview Heights, and steady increase in property values, support a market valuation by sales comparison approach. Because comp. #3 is closest to the subject in size and amenities, its adjusted value of $775,000 supports the appraiser's opinion of the market value of the subject property.

Indicated Value by Sales Comparison Approach $ 775,000

Indicated Value by: Sales Comparison Approach $ 775,000 Cost Approach (if developed) $ Income Approach (if developed) $ 532,800

This appraisal is made ☒ "as is," ☐ subject to completion per plans and specifications on the basis of a hypothetical condition that the improvements have been completed, ☐ subject to the following repairs or alterations on the basis of a hypothetical condition that the repairs or alterations have been completed, or ☐ subject to the following required inspection based on the extraordinary assumption that the condition or deficiency does not require alteration or repair:

Based on a complete visual inspection of the interior and exterior areas of the subject property, defined scope of work, statement of assumptions and limiting conditions, and appraiser's certification, my (our) opinion of the market value, as defined, of the real property that is the subject of this report is $ 775,000 , as of 7-26-20-- , which is the date of inspection and the effective date of this appraisal.

Freddie Mac Form 70 March 2005 Page 2 of 6 Fannie Mae Form 1004 March 2005

Fundamentals of Real Estate Appraisal

FIGURE 13.2: **Uniform Residential Appraisal Report (continued)**

Complete Appraisal Analysis - Summary Appraisal Report

Uniform Residential Appraisal Report File # 05060001

ADDITIONAL COMMENTS

COST APPROACH TO VALUE (not required by Fannie Mae)

Provide adequate information for the lender/client to replicate the below cost figures and calculations.

Support for the opinion of site value (summary of comparable land sales or other methods for estimating site value)

Due to lack of vacant land for building in this area, the cost approach was not used.

ESTIMATED	REPRODUCTION OR	REPLACEMENT COST NEW	OPINION OF SITE VALUE.......................................=$
Source of cost data			Dwelling Sq. Ft. @ $ ....=$
Quality rating from cost service		Effective date of cost data	Sq. Ft. @ $ ....=$
Comments on Cost Approach (gross living area calculations, depreciation, etc.)			
			Garage/Carport Sq. Ft. @ $ ....=$
			Total Estimate of Cost-New ....=$
			Less Physical Functional External
			Depreciation =$ ( )
			Depreciated Cost of Improvements.........................=$
			'As-is' Value of Site Improvements........................=$
			..................=$
Estimated Remaining Economic Life (HUD and VA only) 45 Years			Indicated Value By Cost Approach..........................=$

INCOME APPROACH TO VALUE (not required by Fannie Mae)

Estimated Monthly Market Rent $ 3,600 X Gross Rent Multiplier 148 = $ 532,800 Indicated Value by Income Approach

Summary of Income Approach (including support for market rent and GRM) Current rentals in Woodview Heights are low in relation to sales prices because of recent high rates of appreciation of properties sold, and are not indicative of market value of subject property.

PROJECT INFORMATION FOR PUDs (if applicable)

Is the developer/builder in control of the Homeowners' Association (HOA)? ☐ Yes ☐ No Unit type(s) ☐ Detached ☐ Attached

Provide the following information for PUDs ONLY if the developer/builder is in control of the HOA and the subject property is an attached dwelling unit.

Legal name of project

Total number of phases Total number of units Total number of units sold

Total number of units rented Total number of units for sale Data Source(s)

Was the project created by the conversion of existing building(s) into a PUD? ☐ Yes ☐ No If Yes, date of conversion

Does the project contain any multi-dwelling units? ☐ Yes ☐ No Data Source(s)

Are the units, common elements, and recreation facilities complete? ☐ Yes ☐ No If No, describe the status of completion.

Are the common elements leased to or by the Homeowners' Association? ☐ Yes ☐ No If Yes, describe the rental terms and options.

Describe common elements and recreational facilities

Freddie Mac Form 70 March 2005 Page 3 of 6 Fannie Mae Form 1004 March 2005

Fundamentals of Real Estate Appraisal

SUMMARY

An accurate **appraisal** is a necessary and very important part of the real estate transaction. An appraisal by a licensed or certified **appraiser** is also useful for many other purposes, from acquiring insurance to determining a property's **highest and best use**.

An appraiser's *opinion of value* can be determined as of the date on which the appraiser inspects the subject property or any time in the past. The value most often sought is **market value**, which is a result of **demand, utility, scarcity, transferability**, and the availability of suitable financing.

The appraiser follows certain valuation principles that provide a way to define and examine forces at work in the marketplace, such as **competition, growth, anticipation**, and **supply and demand**.

Using the **sales comparison approach**, the appraiser analyzes data regarding the subject property and comparable properties (**comps**) to determine *market value*.

Using the **cost approach**, the appraiser determines what it would cost to construct a new building having the same utility as the subject property. The value of the site without improvements is added to the **reproduction cost** or **replacement cost** of the improvements, less the amount by which they have **depreciated**. Computing **reproduction cost** requires knowledge of current construction methods and costs, particularly if the **unit-in-place method** or **quantity survey method** is used.

Depreciation can be **physical, functional**, or **external**. Items of *curable depreciation* can be corrected economically. Items of *incurable depreciation* cannot be corrected economically.

Using the **income capitalization approach**, the appraiser develops the appropriate **capitalization rate** for the subject property. The appraiser then applies that rate to the property's **net operating income** to find property value. For some properties, a better approach is to use a **gross income multiplier**.

All three approaches to value may be used in an appraisal. The appraiser will choose the value most appropriate for the property being appraised. In this process, called **reconciliation**, the appraiser uses the other values to support the final opinion of value or explain variances.

The **sales comparison approach** usually is the best indicator of value for residential property. The **cost approach** is the most reliable indicator for newly constructed or special purpose property. The **income capitalization approach** is the best indicator of value for commercial/industrial property and apartment buildings of five units or more.

OPEN FOR DISCUSSION

Organizations such as the Appraisal Institute are creating national databases of property information, including sales and appraisal data.

1. Do you think such databases will eventually replace the work of professional appraisers?

2. What are some of the reasons why the appraiser may still be a necessary part of the transaction?

REVIEW QUESTIONS

1. A house is appraised at $423,000, even though it cost $435,000 to build three years earlier. Which factor could *NOT* have contributed to the loss in value?
   a. Regression
   b. Gentrification
   c. Functional obsolescence
   d. Supply and demand

2. Trevor owns a vacant lot and employs an appraiser to determine the property's
   a. growth.
   b. reproduction cost.
   c. replacement cost.
   d. highest and best use.

3. Since the Riverside factory closed, houses in Sunny Acres are taking longer to sell, and prices have gone down. This is a result of
   a. highest and best use.
   b. supply and demand.
   c. contribution.
   d. conformity.

4. A house that benefits from the desirability of its neighboring properties is an example of the principle of
   a. balance.
   b. contribution.
   c. progression.
   d. regression.

5. A homeowner's deluxe five-bedroom house is in a neighborhood of modest three-bedroom houses. The value of the five-bedroom house will be affected because of the principle of
   a. substitution.
   b. scarcity.
   c. progression.
   d. regression.

6. An improvement to a house may or may not create a corresponding increase in the house's market value. This is an example of
   a. balance.
   b. progression.
   c. contribution.
   d. regression.

7. The Miejas are looking forward to eventually retiring on the profit they will make from selling their house. Their attitude is an example of
   a. progression.
   b. growth.
   c. acquisition.
   d. anticipation.

8. House A sold for $867,000 and is comparable to the house being appraised, but it has an extra garage valued at $47,000. What is the adjusted value of house A?
   a. $767,000
   b. $813,000
   c. $820,000
   d. $914,000

9. To calculate the market value of a 19th-century San Francisco Victorian-style mansion using the cost approach, you probably would use
   a. reproduction cost.
   b. replacement cost.
   c. historical building cost.
   d. cost averaging.

10. The cubic-foot method of estimating construction cost is *BEST* used for
    a. single-family residences.
    b. manufactured homes.
    c. industrial properties.
    d. multifamily residential properties.

11. Appraiser Hansen estimated all direct and indirect construction costs of the Harley Building separately, then totaled them. She used
    a. the unit-in-place method.
    b. the index method.
    c. the quantity survey method.
    d. the cost averaging method.

12. A single-family residence with a one-car garage may be an example of
    a. external obsolescence.
    b. functional obsolescence.
    c. economic obsolescence.
    d. environmental obsolescence.

13. Houses adjacent to a new highway will probably suffer from
    a. curable external obsolescence.
    b. incurable functional obsolescence.
    c. curable functional obsolescence.
    d. incurable external obsolescence.

14. Which is *NOT* a form of depreciation?
    a. Physical deterioration
    b. Straight-line method
    c. Economic obsolescence
    d. Functional obsolescence

15. The upper limit of a property's value usually is determined by
    a. the market comparison approach.
    b. the cost approach.
    c. the income approach.
    d. the sales comparison approach.

16. Vacancy and collection losses are subtracted from potential gross income to derive
    a. net operating income.
    b. gross operating income.
    c. effective gross income.
    d. capitalization rate.

17. An office building with an annual gross income of $70,175 sold for $800,000. What is the building's gross income multiplier?
    a. 11.4
    b. 1.147
    c. .0877
    d. 12

18. The gross rent multiplier for most single-family residences in the Northside neighborhood is 268. What is the market value of a house using that GRM, if the house rents for $1,975 per month?
    a. $736,940
    b. $525,350
    c. $529,300
    d. $568,800

19. The step in which the appraiser arrives at a final opinion of value is called
    a. equilibrium.
    b. reconciliation.
    c. substitution.
    d. equalization.

20. The MOST comprehensive method of conveying the result of an appraisal is
    a. the self-contained report.
    b. the form report.
    c. the restricted use report.
    d. the summary report.

UNIT FOURTEEN 14

RESIDENTIAL DESIGN AND CONSTRUCTION

LEARNING OBJECTIVES

When you have completed this unit, you will be able to

- **describe** the types of regulations that help ensure safe housing;

- **list** the types of construction work that can be performed without a contractor's license;

- **describe** the insurance protections for consumers created by the Homeowner's Bill of Rights of 2004;

- **identify** basic housing styles and building components; and

- **explain** some of the environmental hazards that are of concern to homeowners.

KEY TERMS

anchor bolts	energy-efficiency ratio (EER)	mold
asbestos		orientation
backfill	fire stops	perc test
bracing	flashing	plasterboard
brownfields	foundation	platform frame
building permit	frame	post-and-beam frame
California Department of Insurance	girders	radon
	gutter	rafters
California Department of Public Health	home energy rating program	ridge board
		R-value
California Solar Initiative (CSI)	Homeowner's Bill of Rights of 2004	sheathing
		siding
certificate of occupancy (CO)	insulation	sill
	joists	soffit
crawl space	lath and plaster	solar heating
Department of Housing and Community Development	lead-based paint	stucco
	manufactured home	studs
	masonry	uniform codes
downspout	minimum property requirements (MPRs)	urea-formaldehyde
drywall		wallboard
eave		

BUILDING CONSTRUCTION STANDARDS

Federal, state, and local standards of design and construction help ensure safe dwellings and workplaces. This section describes the standards that apply to housing in California. The emphasis is on the wood-frame structure, the most commonly used form of residential building.

Federal Regulations

On the national level, federally insured (FHA) or guaranteed (VA) loans require inspection and compliance with **minimum property requirements** (MPRs) first established in 1934. Since 1986, FHA has permitted local **building codes** to set the standard for most property specifications. Property that fails to meet the minimum requirements may have to undergo corrective work. Approval of the property (and loan) will be withheld until satisfactory completion of all necessary repairs or additions.

The term **manufactured home** is used by the federal government to describe a house constructed in a factory to comply with the Department of Housing and Urban Development (HUD) building code. Manufactured homes must meet the National Manufactured Home Construction and Safety Standards. The standards for "HUD-code" homes include design and construction, minimum room sizes, durability, fire resistance, insulation, weatherproofing, and energy efficiency. Buyers must be given a *homeowner's manual* that covers general maintenance, safety, and information on state agencies enforcing the federal standards.

State Regulations

The State of California regulates the building industry through building codes and by requiring building contractors to be licensed.

State Housing Law   The *Housing Law* sets minimum construction and occupancy requirements for all dwellings, including apartment houses and hotels. It is under the administration of the Codes and Standards Division of the **Department of Housing and Community Development**. Compliance with construction standards is the responsibility of the local building official and inspectors. Occupancy and sanitation standards are enforced by local health officers.

The *Commission of Housing and Community Development* is required by the legislature to adopt regulations that comply with the **uniform codes** that set construction standards for the industry. Local building codes must comply with state regulations.

All three major code organizations in the United States (including the former International Conference of Building Officials [ICBO] in Whittier, California) merged in 2000 to create the International Code Council (ICC). The International Building Code and the International Residential Building Code were adopted by ICC, revised in 2003 and every three years thereafter. They are now the standards being adopted across the United States as well as by other countries. The former ICBO office in Whittier is now a branch office of ICC, found at www.iccsafe.org. The California codes that are based on the ICC code but include property specifications unique to California can be ordered at the ICC website.

www.iccsafe.org

Building codes are enforced by the appropriate municipal or county governing authority. A **building permit** must be obtained before construction is allowed to begin. Application for a permit is made to the local building official, who also is supplied with plot plan and building plans and specifications for the proposed structure. Problem areas are pointed out and can be revised. The permit is issued only when the application is finally approved.

Periodic inspections during the construction process help ensure that code requirements are met. In addition, a completed building cannot be placed into service until the local building department issues a **certificate of occupancy** (CO). A *temporary* CO may be issued to allow occupancy while minor features of the work are still under way. All construction must be successfully completed by the date stated in the temporary certificate.

The **California Department of Public Health**, www.cdph.ca.gov, acts through county and city health officers and may halt construction if contamination of the water supply, the drainage system, or proper sewage disposal is threatened.

In addition, California's *Mobilehome Accommodation Structures Law* regulates buildings and other structures used with manufactured homes at grade level. The *Mobilehome Parks Act* regulates construction and operation of parks for manufactured homes as well as parks for recreational vehicles. Both laws are part of the Health and Safety Code.

Contractors' License Law Under the *Contractors' License Law*, the Contractors' State License Board licenses all building contractors working within the state. The current license status of all California contractors can be checked at www.cslb.ca.gov. *Criminal charges can be brought against any unlicensed individual who does the work of a contractor and is not exempt from the licensing law.*

www.cslb.ca.gov

No contractor's license is needed for the following:

- Work (including labor and materials) costing less than $500 (but the worker must disclose the lack of a contractor's license to the customer)
- Owner-performed work (unless the owner intends to offer the property for sale)
- Certain construction for agricultural purposes
- Oil and gas operations
- Work performed by public entities and public utilities

To be licensed, a contractor must meet both experience and knowledge qualifications. Various private schools throughout the state specialize in preparing students for the contractors' licensing exam. If the requirements are met, the applicant must post a *bond* or *cash deposit* with the state and must file with the Board a Certificate of Workers' Compensation Insurance or a Certificate of Self-Insurance. This fund is for the benefit of persons who might be damaged or defrauded by the contractor in the conduct of her business.

A contractor's license can be *suspended* or *revoked* for

- failing to follow plans and specifications,
- abandoning a project,
- diverting funds,
- violating building laws or work safety regulations, or
- breaching the construction contract in a material respect.

Department of Insurance

In Unit 10, we mentioned that a mortgage lender will require a homeowner to carry hazard insurance that will cover the repair or replacement cost of damage to the property. The **California Department of Insurance** regulates the provision of homeowners' insurance policies, including disclosure to the homeowner of the policy terms, as well as the insurance claim process. Following the major Southern California fires of 2003, the legislature added the **Homeowner's Bill of Rights of 2004** to the Insurance Code (not to be confused with the Homeowner Bill of Rights regarding foreclosure practices that took effect in 2013). The fires that occurred in 2007 reinforced the rationale behind the new requirements. They include the following indicated provisions of the Insurance Code:

- An insurer cannot use the fact that the primary residence is damaged as a basis for canceling insurance. *Section 675.1(b)*

- An insurer cannot cancel insurance for a primary residence when it is up for renewal and hasn't been rebuilt yet. *Section 675.1(a)*

- An insurer must renew an insurance policy at least once if a total loss to the primary residence was caused by a disaster and not by the homeowner's negligence. *Section 675.1(c)*

When the policy covers the actual cash value (depreciated value rather than replacement cost), the following rules apply:

- The amount of recovery for fire insurance that requires payment of actual cash value for the loss is the expense to the homeowner of replacing what was lost as of the time the fire began. *Section 2051(a)*

- For a total loss to a structure, the amount recovered by the insured is the policy limit or the fair market value of the structure, whichever is less. *Section 2051(b)*

- For a partial loss to a structure of loss to its contents, the amount recovered is what it costs to repair, rebuild, or replace the structure or contents minus a fair and reasonable deduction for depreciation, whichever is less. The depreciation only applies to the parts of the structure that are subject to repair and replacement during the useful life of the structure. *Section 2051(c)*

When a policy covers the "replacement cost" of the insured property, the following are required by Section 2051.5 of the Insurance Code:

- Replacement cost for a fire loss must be based on what it would cost the homeowner to repair, rebuild, or replace the home without a deduction for physical depreciation.

- The homeowner has at least 12 months to rebuild and receive replacement costs, with the possibility of a six-month extension. In a declared disaster (governor's state of emergency), the homeowner has at least 24 months in which to repair, rebuild, or replace the home.

- After a total loss, the homeowner can rebuild or replace the home at a location other than the original location of the total loss.

The *Homeowner's Mediation Program* provides that claims for residential property losses (other than from earthquakes) occurring after September 30, 2003, for which the governor has declared a state of emergency, may be referred by the Department of Insurance to its mediation program for discussion of possible payments over the policy limits. There are also other conditions on mediation. *Section 10089.70(b)*

Other new rules include the following:

- If a state of emergency has been declared, coverage for additional living expenses will be for a period of 24 months and the homeowner must be provided with a list of items that are covered by the "additional living expense" part of the insurance policy. *Section 2060*

- The insurer must inform the insured in writing of any increase or decrease in the annual premium for residential property insurance compared to the previous year, including the reasons for the change, and telephone numbers and information regarding the consumer complaint process. *Section 678*

- An insurer cannot cancel, fail to renew, or increase the premium amount based on the fact that the insured has asked questions about residential fire or property insurance policy limits, coverage, and so on. *Section 791.12*

- Notice for cancellation of property insurance must be at least 20 days, except if cancellation is for nonpayment of premiums, in which case it must be at least 10 days. *Section 677.4*

- A public insurance adjuster must not solicit business from a homeowner until seven days after a disaster (declared state of emergency or more than 25 dwellings are damaged or destroyed), unless the homeowner or the homeowner's representative contacts the adjuster directly. *Section 15027.1*

Finally, amendments were made to the *California Residential Property Insurance Disclosure* form that must be sent to insured homeowners and a new disclosure, known as the *California Residential Property Insurance Bill of Rights*, must be sent to the insured homeowner every other year. *Sections 10102, 10103, and 10103.5*

Local Regulations

Since 1970, local building codes have been required to follow the uniform codes adopted by the Commission of Housing and Community Development. Local variations necessitated by local conditions must be specifically approved. Local codes also may prohibit undesirable practices otherwise allowed by the uniform codes. An example is the "piggybacking" of copper wiring to a system with aluminum wiring.

Local codes do not apply to the *construction* of HUD-code (manufactured) homes but do apply to site improvements, such as grading, foundation work, and installation of utilities as well as placement and anchoring of the home on the site.

Local governments also initiate regulations regarding land use, fire safety, sanitation, density, building setbacks, and property line requirements. These are covered in Unit 15.

Exercise 14-1

Broker Bob wants to sell the Gray house, one of his listings, but knows that it needs some foundation repair work. With the Grays' approval, and for a small fee, Bob hires a work crew that places new support jacks under the Gray house and rebuilds some of the foundation walls. Bob supervises the entire job. Do you see any problems with this arrangement?

ARCHITECTURE

Present-day architects and builders may borrow parts of one or more of the classic designs. Design features are adapted, using modern materials and techniques, to make the resulting concept a workable one for current tastes and living patterns.

Roof Styles

The roof styles illustrated on in Figure 14.1 are referred to in the descriptions of architectural styles that follow. The variations are based on the direction, degree of pitch (steepness), and number of roof planes.

Architectural Styles

The architectural styles described and illustrated below typically have most, if not all, of the features listed.

Colonial American or Cape Cod

- Wood siding with shutters
- One to two or more stories
- Steep-pitched, wood-shingled roof
- Shed addition
- Dormer windows
- Multipaned glass windows, usually placed symmetrically in relation to front door

FIGURE 14.1:   Roof Designs

Dutch Colonial

- One and one-half or two and one-half stories
- Distinctive gambrel roof
- Dormers

Queen Anne Victorian

- Wood, with elaborate decoration
- More than one story
- White, pastel, or deep colors typical of the era
- High-ceilinged rooms
- Leaded and stained-glass windows
- Front porch, sometimes wrapping around side of house

Town House or Row House

- Adjoins or shares a common (party) wall with neighboring house
- Found in cities or as part of a suburban development
- Exterior style variations possible, limited to front expanse and roofline

French Provincial

- Large, with white brick or brick and stucco exterior
- Hip roof
- Two stories, possibly with dormers

Spanish

- White or pastel stucco exterior
- One story (two-story Santa Barbara or Monterey style)
- Brown or orange tile roof
- Courtyard
- Wrought-iron trim and fencing

California Ranch

- One story
- Wood or masonry exterior
- Built on concrete slab or shallow crawlspace
- Attached garage on concrete slab

Contemporary

- One or more stories
- Wood, stucco, or masonry exterior finish
- Roof low-pitched or flat
- Minimal decoration
- Open floor plan

Within the described range of styles, differences in floor level can affect both design and layout. The split-level house, illustrated below, can be useful both in conserving expensive foundation costs and in taking advantage of a sloping lot.

An extreme slope, whether uphill or downhill from the building site, also calls for special consideration. For very steep sites, a contemporary design often is most attractive.

The most common style of manufactured home is the ranch, as shown below. Some types of modular factory-built housing allow virtually unlimited design and size specifications and are indistinguishable from their site-built counterparts.

Exercise 14-2

Describe the architectural style and features of the house pictured below.

DESIGN AND FUNCTION

The design of a home includes all of the elements of the floor plan: number of rooms, their size, and their relation to one another. Design is influenced by aesthetic and functional concerns as well as by external factors such as placement of a house on its site to allow maximum sunlight, view, or both.

Orientation on the Site

The placement of a house on a site is called its **orientation**. Orientation is generally best when the greatest window expanse faces south. With a deep enough roof overhang, south-facing windows allow the winter sunlight in yet are shielded from the summer sun. This is particularly important in desert communities. Figure 14.2 shows this principle at work. During the winter months the sun's arc is much lower in the sky than it is in the summer months, allowing maximum use of the natural heating power of sunlight. In the summer, the sun's higher arc permits a roof overhang to block much or all of the sunlight from the interior of the structure.

In a region that has relatively mild winters, a southern exposure to the rear of the house may be desirable. Such an orientation allows maximum use of outdoor facilities, such as a patio or swimming pool.

Especially on a hillside lot, the view may be the primary consideration in orienting the house. Because contemporary designs do not require rigid placement of front entry and windows, those features can be placed to take maximum advantage of the site. Often a fence-enclosed outside patio can turn a part of the house with a poor view into an attractive oasis.

Many subdivisions are designed to allow homes to take maximum advantage of a common area. The common area may include a park, walkway, golf course, swimming pool, or clubhouse. The benefit of being near or adjacent to a common area must be balanced against any resulting loss of privacy, increased noise, or actual danger. Errant golf balls can be more than just a nuisance, and there must be adequate fencing to safeguard small children from hazards such as ponds.

Floor Plan

The floor plan of a house should provide for both easy *circulation* and convenient *access* to living areas. The old "railroad" concept of all rooms in a line, with entry from one to the next, is highly undesirable. Each bedroom should have a separate entry, and the most luxurious plan gives each bedroom its own adjoining (*en suite*) bathroom. As much as possible, bedrooms should be isolated from living areas.

The "great room" combining kitchen and family/living areas has become more popular than separate kitchen and family room, visually expanding the floor area of both spaces. Telecommuting and home computer use have created demand for a separate office space, with a separate outside entrance a useful feature. Traditional exterior styles often belie the open, high-ceilinged spaces within. Even the one-story ranch-style houses built throughout California by the thousands after World War II have proven their versatility. They are still in demand as expandable starter homes as well as homes that suit the needs of the growing number of seniors. Some, such as the distinctive homes built by Joseph Eichler, are valued even more highly today for their innovative use of glass and easy flow of indoor and outdoor spaces.

FIGURE 14.2: Solar Angles and Overhang

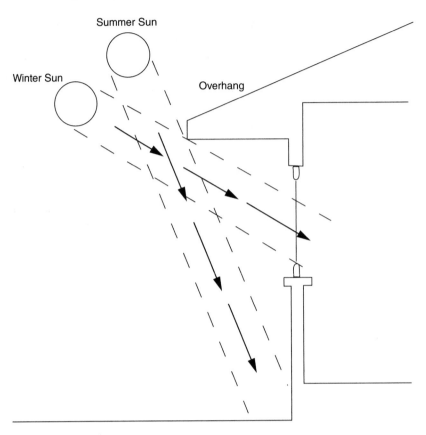

Most California single-family dwellings do not have *basements*—that is, rooms that are partly or entirely below ground level. Houses in some city areas, such as San Francisco, have what are called basements, but these are ground-level garage and storage spaces. Such buildings typically have outside stairway access to the main entrance on the second level of the building.

A house without a basement loses storage space but saves on the cost of the increased concrete needed for the deeper foundation walls and floor. Because there are few exceptionally cold areas in the state, the insulation value of a basement is not usually a factor. Hillside houses often make use of a lower level that is properly a basement but may have one or more walls above the surface of the slope. Such basement space may be counted in the home's living area, if typical of homes in the community.

Square Footage

The Board of Standards Review of the American National Standards Institute (ANSI) has adopted a voluntary national standard for measuring square footage in single-family detached and attached homes. A copy of the complete standard can be purchased at the website of the Research Center of the National Association of Home Builders, www.nahbrc.com.

The standard specifies that the person taking the measurement do the following:

- Measure from the exterior face of outside walls

- Measure to the nearest inch or tenth and report to the nearest whole square foot

- Include only finished areas

- Measure only space with a ceiling height of at least seven feet except under stairs, beams, and sloping ceilings

- Make a clear distinction between above-grade finished square footage and below-grade finished square footage and identify a level as below grade if any part of that level is below the grade line

- Not include openings in floors in square footage but do include stair treads

- Include accessory apartments and other finished areas not within the main house only if they are connected to the main house by finished hallways/ stairways

- Never consider a garage as finished space, although a garage can be calculated as unfinished square footage

---

Exercise 14-3

Label each space in the floor plan below according to its most likely best use.

CONSTRUCTION STAGES

You should be familiar with the names of the various construction stages and components of a house, particularly if you are taking the real estate licensing examination. Refer to the diagrams as you read through this section.

Site Preparation

Preparing a parcel of land for building requires much more than simply leveling it with a bulldozer. Before a building permit will be issued, the contractor will have to comply with all local, national, and federal requirements regarding site utilization. A soil engineer's report, **perc test** of the ability of water to drain (percolate) through the soil, seismic analysis, environmental impact report, and other studies may be necessary. The previous use of the site might dictate removal and replacement of soil if hazardous materials were stored or present on the property in the past. Sites identified as **brownfields** by the Environmental Protection Agency require extensive remediation.

Hillside locations, found throughout California, have their own unique requirements. Grading might require construction of retaining walls to prevent earth movement above or below the site. Seasonal water flow might necessitate extensive drainage systems and extraordinarily deep foundation supports.

Often, the lack of vacant building sites results in the "teardown" phenomenon in which an older home is purchased for the value of the underlying land, then torn down so that a new home can be built. The tendency to build huge new homes on such sites has not been well received in some communities, with the result that the approval process in such cases has become much more difficult.

Foundation

The wood-frame house typically rests on **foundation** walls of poured concrete. The site is excavated, the foundation walls are poured into wood forms, the wood forms are removed after the concrete has cured, and dirt (**backfill**) is moved back against the walls. The floor of the house also may be concrete, poured either at the same time as the foundation walls or after. More commonly used is the wood floor on concrete foundation walls, usually plywood panels over wood beams called **girders** and **joists**. This design leaves a **crawl space** beneath the home for ventilation and protection against termites. It is illustrated in Figure 14.3. Instead of continuous concrete foundation walls, some older homes have concrete or stone supports called *footings*.

FIGURE 14.3:   Foundation

Subfloor

Joist

Sill Plate

Anchor Bolt - 8' o.c.

Sill Sealer

Foundation Wall

A. With Sill Plate

Insect infestation is possible wherever wood comes into contact with earth. Termites also can build their earth tunnels from the ground to the wood structure along cement foundation walls or supports. The foundation itself should be chemically treated to poison termites, and any wood that must be in even indirect contact with earth, such as a fence post or deck support, also should be chemically treated and inspected regularly. As a general rule there should be no direct contact of wood with earth.

The **sill** is the wood member that is placed directly on the foundation wall. Since 1931, California building codes have required the use of **anchor bolts** through the sill and into the foundation wall as an earthquake safety measure. Nevertheless, the California legislature has estimated that *1.2 million* homes in the state have foundations that are not adequately secured (Government Code 8897).

Radon is a gas that occurs naturally in all parts of the country as a result of the breakdown of uranium in the soil. It is harmless when it dissipates into the atmosphere, but in the enclosed environment of a crawl space or basement, radon can accumulate to high-enough levels to increase the risk of lung cancer and other ailments for residents. The solution to a high level of radon is to add ventilation to the area of the building closest to ground level, such as the crawl space, to vent the gas and prevent it from accumulating to a dangerously high level. Information on radon and mitigation measures can be found at www.epa.gov.

www.epa.gov

Framework

After the foundation has been prepared, the house frame is erected. The **frame** is the skeleton to which the exterior and interior walls are attached. The frame consists of vertical supports called **studs**, which local building codes require to be *no more than 16 inches apart.* Short, horizontal pieces of wood are placed between the studs at intervals to act as **fire stops** by blocking air drafts.

In **platform frame** construction, the frame of a multistory house is built one story at a time, with each story supporting the next. Figure 14.4 shows the components of a platform frame system. The **post-and-beam frame**, used less frequently than the platform frame, allows great design flexibility. Ceiling boards are supported on beams that rest on posts placed within the house. Because the wall frame studs do not have to bear the full weight of the ceiling and roof, they can be spaced farther apart, allowing for greater room area.

As California earthquakes have demonstrated many times, ground movement can create tremendous forces that buildings withstand only if they are properly anchored and braced.

Exterior Walls

Insulating **sheathing** of plywood or drywall is applied to exterior walls, which are then ready for **siding**, whether wood, aluminum, brick, stone, or other material. **Stucco**, a type of plaster, requires wood furring strips to be nailed to the plywood, with metal lathing stretched over the wood strips as a base for the stucco.

> Plywood sheathing provides bracing needed for a building to ride out an earthquake.

Plywood sheathing is an excellent way to provide the **bracing** needed to protect a building in an earthquake. A sheet of plywood securely fastened to wall studs serves the same purpose as an X-shaped wall bracing system. Plywood sheathing allows a building to move with the movement of the earth yet keeps the structure intact so that it returns to its original shape.

Masonry, which refers to any use of brick or stone, is either solid or veneer. If veneer, it is a decorative finish and does not support the roof structure. The thickness of the walls is one way to tell whether masonry is veneer. With masonry veneer, the depth of the walls generally is 8 to 10 inches or less.

FIGURE 14.4: Wall Framing with Platform Construction

Unreinforced masonry is very susceptible to earthquake damage. The Government Code requires an owner who has actual or constructive knowledge that such a building is located in a Seismic Zone 4 to post a prescribed notice at the building's entrance. The notice is not required if the walls are non-load-bearing and have steel or concrete frames. If the building's buyer receives the required notice and fails to bring the building into code compliance within five years, the buyer cannot receive any state earthquake repair payment until all other applicants have been paid.

www.seismic.ca.gov/cog.html

Government Code Section 8875.6 requires the transferor (or the transferor's agent) of any unreinforced masonry building with wood-frame floors or roofs that was built before January 1, 1975, to deliver to the purchaser as soon as practicable before a sale, transfer, or exchange, a copy of the *Commercial Property Owner's Guide to Earthquake Safety* described in Section 10147 of the Code. The guide was updated in 2006 and is available on the Seismic Safety Commission website, www.seismic.ca.gov/cog.html. This requirement does not apply to transfers between spouses or co-owners, from an estate or trust administrator, from mortgagor to mortgagee, or pursuant to a court order.

Insulation

In the days of (relatively) cheap oil and gas energy, **insulation** of walls and ceiling was of less importance than it is today. The effectiveness of any of the various kinds of insulation is expressed by its **R-value**. When more than one layer of insulation is used, the R-values of the individual layers are added to each other to find the total R-value of all the layers. Thus, if insulation of R-9 is placed over insulation of R-11, the two layers provide a total insulation value of R-20. An R-1 value is equivalent to about 1½ inches of insulation.

Any hardware store customer has probably seen the bulky aluminum-foil-clad rolls of fiberglass or rockwool insulation that are sized to fit between wall studs. Such products are easy to install in a home with an exposed ceiling frame accessible through an attic. Unless walls are insulated before interior walls are finished, they require the services of a professional. Insulation can be blown into wall cavities, for instance, using the proper equipment. *Protective clothing, including mask and gloves, is necessary during any handling of insulation materials.*

Putting an insulating blanket on a water heater can save energy and money.

Other building components also can be insulated. A fiberglass "blanket" can be purchased for a water heater and installed by the homeowner. Water pipes can be wrapped to help prevent heat loss. Water pipes wrapped with insulation will be less likely to suffer from the effects of a sudden freeze, which could cause them to burst.

www.energy.ca.gov
/commission/

The California State Energy Resources Conservation and Development Commission, www.energy.ca.gov/commission/, has established a statewide **home energy rating program**, revised in December 2008. The residential dwelling seller (or agent) must provide a copy of an information booklet on the program to the buyer.

Until the mid-1970s, **asbestos** was frequently used in walls and sprayed on ceilings and other building components. Asbestos fibers, released when the material is handled or as it deteriorates, now are believed to be a potential cause of cancer if inhaled. Use of **urea-formaldehyde** is prohibited in most parts of the United States. Toxic fumes from this product may cause nausea and other adverse reactions. Urea-formaldehyde frequently is found in older manufactured homes, where its effects may be amplified by poor ventilation. Any building suspected of having lead-based paint, asbestos, or urea-formaldehyde in its construction should be inspected by a competent professional.

Roof

Basic roof styles were illustrated in Figure 14.1. The roof structure is shown in Figure 14.5. Roofs are formed by **rafters**, sheathing, and a finishing material. The rafters meet at the **ridge board**, the highest point of construction of a frame building. Sheathing is usually plywood. Spaced sheathing of one-inch by four-inch boards is used for a wood shake or shingle roof to allow better air circulation. A heavy waterproof paper called **building paper** goes over the sheathing first.

FIGURE 14.5: Rafter Framing

Ridge Board
Collar Beam
Rafter
End Stud
Ceiling Joist
Top Plates
Rafter
Block
Notch or Birdsmouth

Roof finishes can range from wood shakes or shingles to mineral fiber shingles, tile, or slate. Sheet metal, called **flashing**, surrounds openings cut in the roof for chimneys and vents. A flat roof, the hardest to waterproof because it allows water and snow to collect, is covered with tar, which must be renewed periodically.

> Wood roof coverings are prohibited in many parts of the state.

Wood-look, mineral-based shingles and shakes are now being made to simulate the attractiveness of wood yet provide the protection of a long-wearing, fireproof material. *Increasingly, the fire hazard posed by wood roof coverings has resulted in ordinances prohibiting their use either for new construction or to replace an existing roof.*

The roof **eave** is the part of a pitched roof that extends beyond the outer wall of the house. It may be enclosed by a **soffit** or left open. A better quality house has a **gutter** along the eave to direct rain run-off through a **downspout**.

Windows

Windows are available in many styles and materials. Aluminum framing is a low-cost alternative to wood, but the more expensive wood windows are also popular, particularly in remodeling. Some of the common window styles are pictured in Figure 14.6. The fixed type does not open, and some windows have both fixed and opening sections. Casement windows are unusual in that they open outward.

FIGURE 14.6: Types of Windows

| Fixed | Awning | Casement | Jalousie |

| Sliding | Hopper | Center Pivot | Double or Single-Hung |

Doors

There usually are three exterior doors to a house—the main entrance, the service door leading to garage or rear area, and the patio door leading to patio, deck, or garden. Although exterior doors usually are—or should be—made of solid wood, plywood, or wood filler, interior doors are often hollow core. Patio doors are most often sliding glass doors, although multipaned glass doors (called French doors) are popular.

Interior Walls

Interior walls can be finished with **plasterboard**, also referred to as **drywall** or **wallboard**. Plasterboard is a preformed layer of plaster sandwiched between layers of paper and cut into sheets that are typically four feet by eight feet. Its weight makes plasterboard difficult to handle, but it can be cut, if necessary, to fit around door and window openings, and it covers large areas quickly.

The seams between sections of plasterboard are covered with a special tape and a thin plaster referred to as *mud*. Most plaster finishes can be painted, and smooth finishes can be wallpapered. Plasterboard is a much cheaper alternative to the **lath and plaster** technique in which wet plaster is applied to the wall against a backing of wood and wire.

Lead-Based Paint

The presence of lead in paint used in housing is a major health concern. Deteriorating paint releases lead; renovations can release large amounts of lead into the home as well as the surrounding soil. The danger of lead exposure to adults includes high blood pressure, memory and concentration problems, and difficulty during pregnancy. The danger to children includes damage to the brain and nervous system, behavior and learning problems, slowed growth, and hearing loss. Encapsulation using special paints that prevent lead from leaching through to the surface may be the best preventative.

Since 1978, the use of **lead-based paint** in housing has been prohibited by the federal government. It has been estimated that 83% of homes built before 1978 (about 64 million homes) contain lead-based paint.

The *Residential Lead-Based Paint Hazard Reduction Act of 1992*, a federal law, requires disclosure of the possible presence of lead-based paint in homes built before 1978. Sellers and landlords of rental units must also comply with the law. The enforcement body is the *Environmental Protection Agency (EPA)*. Information on legal requirements is available from the *National Lead Information Center (NLIC),* 1-202-659-1192, as well as EPA branches and state health departments. The EPA has a website at www.epa.gov. NLIC can be found at www.epa.gov/lead/pubs/nlic.htm.

www.epa.gov
www.epa.gov/lead/pubs/nlic.htm

The law does not require a seller or landlord to conduct any testing or hazard reduction. The seller or landlord must disclose any known presence of lead and provide copies of available lead hazard evaluations and reports.

The prospective buyer or renter must

- receive an EPA disclosure pamphlet (or state-approved alternative),
- have 10 days in which to arrange a property inspection, and
- sign a lead warning statement and acknowledgment.

Real estate agents must

- inform the seller or landlord of the requirements,
- make sure that the buyer or renter has received the necessary documentation, and
- retain the signed disclosure/acknowledgment statement for three years.

As of April 22, 2010, a renovator of housing built before 1978 (other than the homeowner) must be trained and EPA-certified to perform safe work practices to prevent lead contamination. The renovator also must deliver EPA's lead renovation pamphlet to an occupant within 60 days (if mailed, at least seven days) before a project begins and obtain a signed acknowledgment of receipt from the occupant. A handbook summarizing the requirements can be found at the EPA website.

Interior walls also can be paneled with wood, either in boards or in lightweight sheets of wood veneer plywood, usually four feet by eight feet. There also are wood-look and marble-look panels.

Floor

Plywood floor *underlayment* or *subflooring* can be finished with wood boards, tile (wood parquet, ceramic, vinyl, or asphalt), or carpeting.

Wiring

In new homes, *telephone wiring* that allows installation of two separate lines is becoming standard. Urban areas now offer the advantages of fiber-optic cable connections to take maximum advantage of internet services.

Although 110-volt *electrical service* was once the norm, the electrical system of a house built today should be wired for 240-volt service to allow use of the widest range of appliances. Wiring in the average house also should be able to carry at least 100 amperes (amps) of electricity at the required voltage. Because of the steadily increasing number of household appliances, many contractors recommend a minimum of 150 amps.

Heating and Cooling

Both heating and air- conditioning units are found in many homes in California. An air-conditioning unit can be rated in terms of its energy consumption. The **energy-efficiency ratio** (EER) is found by dividing the unit's capacity measured in British thermal units (Btu) by the number of watts of electricity needed to run it. For example, a 36,000-Btu (three-ton) air conditioner that needs 6,000 watts to run has an EER of 6.0. A unit of the same capacity that needs 5,000 watts to run has an EER of 7.2. A higher EER means that less energy is consumed and the unit is more efficient.

Solar heating of both room air and water supply is enjoying increasing popularity. The simplest form of solar heat is the sunlight coming through a window. If water-filled tanks are placed inside the house at a place where the sun can shine on them, they absorb the heat of the sunlight and will help warm the house at night when that heat is dispersed. To some degree any heat-absorbing material, such as ceramic tile flooring, will produce the same effect. Such a solar-heating system is called *passive*, because it has no mechanical parts.

The Health and Safety Code provides that any city or county may permit windows required for light and ventilation of habitable rooms in dwellings to open into areas provided with natural light and ventilation that are designed and built to act as passive solar energy collectors. This provision allows the addition to a house of a greenhouse-style room with water-filled heat collectors, or a stone or tile floor serving the same purpose, designed to receive maximum sunlight during the day to retain heat to be released into the interior of the house (through window openings) at night.

There are also *active* solar-heating systems. Typically, a water-filled panel, or "collector," is placed on a surface facing the sun, usually the building roof. The water warmed by the sun flows to a storage tank in the house, and colder water is returned to the collector. A small pump operates the system. The warm water can be used directly, such as for bathing, and also warms the air as it passes through the pipes. A backup conventional heating system can be used on cloudy days. An active system also may be a cost-effective way to heat a swimming pool.

Tax incentives, including rebates of part of installation costs, have been used to encourage owners of homes as well as businesses to make use of solar-heating systems. As mentioned in Unit 11, the American Recovery and Reinvestment Act of 2009 (ARRA) provides state and local governments with funds for energy efficiency and conservation grants for energy audits, retrofits, and financial incentives.

Through 2010, homeowners could claim a 30% tax credit (increased from 10%) for purchases of new furnaces, windows, and insulation. The tax credit returned to 10% in 2011 for allowed improvements to an existing home that is the taxpayer's principal residence. The tax credit is 30% for allowed improvements to new and existing homes for geothermal heat pumps, small residential wind turbines, and solar energy systems, with no upper limit, and a $500 limit for qualified residential fuel cell and microturbine systems. Other funds are available for weatherization assistance for low-income households and for efficiency efforts for federally assisted housing. In addition, $5 billion was made available to modernize the nation's electricity grid and install smart meters on homes that help to save consumers money. *Note:* The tax basis of the home must be reduced by the amount of the tax credit taken.

www.gosolarcalifornia.ca.gov
/csi/index/php
www.gosolarcalifornia.org

The **California Solar Initiative** (CSI), which took effect in January 2008, requires municipal utilities to offer a solar incentive program to customers, in effect paying them for the output of their solar systems. Information on CSI is available at www.gosolarcalifornia.ca.gov/csi/index/php. Events for homeowners are posted at www.gosolarcalifornia.org.

www.sdcounty.ca.gov/dplu
/greenbuildings.html

Local jurisdictions are also offering incentives for construction of solar systems. San Diego County charges no fees for the building permit and plan check of residential photovoltaic systems. Information on this and other green building incentives is available at www.sdcounty.ca.gov/dplu/greenbuildings.html.

www.sfwater.org/index
.aspx?page=133

As of July 1, 2008, San Francisco's Solar Incentive Program, GoSolarSF, provides rebates for installation of solar systems. The program, described at www.sfwater.org/index.aspx?page=133, provides part of the cost of a photovoltaic system that produces at least one kilowatt of electricity. The local rebate, available to both residents and businesses, can be coupled with federal and state incentives.

Fixtures

Kitchen and bathroom   The kitchen requires special attention. *Cabinets*, usually of wood, can be custom-made on-site or prefabricated. Some *appliances* may be built-in, including dishwasher, range top, wall oven, and trash compactor. There may be a separate counter "island" in the kitchen with chopping block, sink, and self-exhausting broiler/range top. Natural and manufactured granite, marble, and glass countertops and backsplashes have joined ceramic tile as desirable counter and wall finishes around fixtures in kitchen and bathroom.

Plumbing fixtures—bathtubs, toilets, and sinks—can range from standard grade cast iron or pressed steel coated with enamel to molded fiberglass. Many homeowners consider the stainless-steel sink attractive, and it also is easier to maintain.

A double-basin sink is desirable for the kitchen. The newest trend is the farm-house sink, with a single deep, wide basin.

Smoke detectors California law requires that any single-family house (including factory-built houses) sold on or after January 1, 1986, have an operable smoke detector. A battery-operated unit is sufficient in most counties, but some (such as San Francisco) require a smoke detector to be wired to the home's electrical system to avoid the danger of an inoperable battery. The seller of the house is responsible for smoke-detector installation and must give the buyer a written statement indicating compliance with the law. If the seller does not do so, the buyer cannot rescind the contract of sale, but the seller may be liable for damages of $100 plus attorney's fees and court costs.

While not yet a state requirement, a carbon monoxide detector is an inexpensive way to warn a home's occupants of this odorless, colorless, potentially deadly by-product of fuel burning.

Carbon monoxide detectors Existing single-family homes with fossil fuel-burning appliances or heaters, an attached garage, or a fireplace were required to be equipped with carbon monoxide detectors by July 2011. Other dwellings, such as hotels, were given until 2013 to be equipped with carbon monoxide detectors.

Water heater bracing To help reduce earthquake-caused damage to dwellings, California law requires that all water heaters be braced, anchored, or strapped to resist falling or horizontal displacement. The seller of real property must certify to the buyer that the law has been complied with.

MANUFACTURED HOMES

Manufactured homes now account for one-third of all new single-family home purchases in the United States. For federal purposes, a manufactured home is one built off-site that meets HUD construction standards on or after June 15, 1976; before that date, the term mobilehome was used for any structure built off-site. California's Business and Professions Code defines what it still terms a "mobilehome" as a "structure transportable in one or more sections, designed and equipped to contain not more than two dwelling units to be used with or without a foundation system." The definition of a mobilehome does not include recreational vehicles, commercial coaches, or modular housing. The code defines a mobilehome park as "any area or tract of land where two or more mobilehome lots are rented or leased or held out for rent or lease."

Advantages of Manufactured Homes

Mass production of building components and assembly in factories make it possible for builders to ignore inclement weather. This results in homes that are constructed without exposure to the elements, avoiding delays and dangerous working conditions. They are also significantly cheaper than houses constructed on-site. The need to transport a manufactured home limits the maximum size of a single construction unit, but two or more units can be combined on-site, allowing a degree of flexibility in design.

California's mobilehome parks are often tailored to specific recreational or residential lifestyles (such as those of senior citizens). A well-planned mobilehome park with adequate space between units, limited access, and reduced speed limits contributes to the value of its homes.

PROPERTY CONDITION DISCLOSURES

The *Easton* case and subsequent legislation mentioned in Unit 6 require a real estate broker or salesperson to conduct a reasonably competent and diligent visual inspection of residential property and disclose to prospective purchasers all facts revealed by the investigation that materially affect the value or desirability of the property. The real estate agent is not expected to replace the role of a professional home inspector, however, and both seller and buyer should be made aware of that fact. It is thus in a real estate agent's best interests to not only make the appropriate property inspection and disclosure but also to be specific about what is *not* included in that inspection.

Figure 14.7 is the Agent Visual Inspection Disclosure form prepared by the California Association of REALTORS®. This form, or one similar to it prepared by the real estate brokerage, helps to make the parties to the transaction aware that, although the agent's inspection may reveal a fact that should be made known to the prospective buyer, the agent's inspection does not replace the type of inspection(s) that should be performed by competent specialists. The type of inspection necessary will depend on the type of property. Every property should have an inspection that includes the structure and mechanical systems. Some properties, such as those located on a hillside, may require an inspection and appropriate testing by a structural and/or soils engineer (the kind of inspections that should have been performed in the *Easton* case). Typically, the home inspector's report will reveal any areas requiring further investigation.

Certain inspections are necessitated by both seen and unseen hazards. Roofing problems or plumbing that has not been properly installed or maintained can be a source of leaks that can weaken ceilings or walls and also help create conditions in which **mold** can grow. The increased awareness of the respiratory distress that can be caused by high mold levels—and the even more severe physical symptoms caused by certain toxic molds—has created concern for property owners. As mentioned earlier in this unit, the presence of radon gas can create the need for a special ventilation system. In response to both of these potential problems, the Department of Housing and Urban Development (HUD) now requires notice to property buyers of the potential hazards of radon and mold when HUD-owned property is sold. Figure 14.8 is the CAR form that meets the HUD requirements. *Note:* This form can only be used when, in fact, there is no evidence of mold or radon on the property.

FIGURE 14.7:   Agent Visual Inspection Disclosure

AGENT VISUAL INSPECTION DISCLOSURE
(CALIFORNIA CIVIL CODE § 2079 ET SEQ.)
For use by an agent when a transfer disclosure statement is required or when a seller is exempt from completing a TDS
(C.A.R. Form AVID, Revised 11/13)

CALIFORNIA ASSOCIATION OF REALTORS®

This inspection disclosure concerns the residential property situated in the City of_____, County of_____, State of California, described as _____
_____ ("Property").

☐ This Property is a duplex, triplex, or fourplex. This AVID form is for unit # _____. Additional AVID forms required for other units.

Inspection Performed By (Real Estate Broker Firm Name) _____

California law requires, with limited exceptions, that a real estate broker or salesperson (collectively, "Agent") conduct a reasonably competent and diligent **visual** inspection of reasonably and normally accessible areas of certain properties offered for sale and then disclose to the prospective purchaser material facts affecting the value or desirability of that property that the inspection reveals. The duty applies regardless of whom that Agent represents. The duty applies to residential real properties containing one-to-four dwelling units, and manufactured homes (mobilehomes). The duty applies to a stand-alone detached dwelling (whether or not located in a subdivision or a planned development) or to an attached dwelling such as a condominium. The duty also applies to a lease with an option to purchase, a ground lease or a real property sales contract of one of those properties.

California law does not require the Agent to inspect the following:
• Areas that are not reasonably and normally accessible
• Areas off site of the property
• Public records or permits
• Common areas of planned developments, condominiums, stock cooperatives and the like.

Agent Inspection Limitations: Because the Agent's duty is limited to conducting a reasonably competent and diligent visual inspection of reasonably and normally accessible areas of only the Property being offered for sale, there are several things that the Agent will not do. What follows is a non-exclusive list of examples of limitations on the scope of the Agent's duty.

   Roof and Attic: Agent will not climb onto a roof or into an attic.

   Interior: Agent will not move or look under or behind furniture, pictures, wall hangings or floor coverings. Agent will not look up chimneys or into cabinets, or open locked doors.

   Exterior: Agent will not inspect beneath a house or other structure on the Property, climb up or down a hillside, move or look behind plants, bushes, shrubbery and other vegetation or fences, walls or other barriers.

   Appliances and Systems: Agent will not operate appliances or systems (such as, but not limited to, electrical, plumbing, pool or spa, heating, cooling, septic, sprinkler, communication, entertainment, well or water) to determine their functionality.

   Size of Property or Improvements: Agent will not measure square footage of lot or improvements, or identify or locate boundary lines, easements or encroachments.

   Environmental Hazards: Agent will not determine if the Property has mold, asbestos, lead or lead-based paint, radon, formaldehyde or any other hazardous substance or analyze soil or geologic condition.

   Off-Property Conditions: By statute, Agent is not obligated to pull permits or inspect public records. Agent will not guarantee views or zoning, identify proposed construction or development or changes or proximity to transportation, schools, or law enforcement.

   Analysis of Agent Disclosures: For any items disclosed as a result of Agent's visual inspection, or by others, Agent will not provide an analysis of or determine the cause or source of the disclosed matter, nor determine the cost of any possible repair.

What this means to you: An Agent's inspection is not intended to take the place of any other type of inspection, nor is it a substitute for a full and complete disclosure by a seller. Regardless of what the Agent's inspection reveals, or what disclosures are made by sellers, California Law specifies that a buyer has a duty to exercise reasonable care to protect himself or herself. This duty encompasses facts which are known to or within the diligent attention and observation of the buyer. Therefore, in order to determine for themselves whether or not the Property meets their needs and intended uses, as well as the cost to remedy any disclosed or discovered defect, **BUYER SHOULD: (1) REVIEW ANY DISCLOSURES OBTAINED FROM SELLER; (2) OBTAIN ADVICE ABOUT, AND INSPECTIONS OF, THE PROPERTY FROM OTHER APPROPRIATE PROFESSIONALS; AND (3) REVIEW ANY FINDINGS OF THOSE PROFESSIONALS WITH THE PERSONS WHO PREPARED THEM. IF BUYER FAILS TO DO SO, BUYER IS ACTING AGAINST THE ADVICE OF BROKER.**

Buyer's Initials (_____)(_____)   Seller's Initials (_____)(_____)

AVID REVISED 11/13 (PAGE 1 OF 3)   Print Date

Reviewed by _____ Date _____

EQUAL HOUSING OPPORTUNITY

AGENT VISUAL INSPECTION DISCLOSURE (AVID PAGE 1 OF 3)

FIGURE 14.7:   Agent Visual Inspection Disclosure (continued)

Property Address: _____ Date: _____

If this Property is a duplex, triplex, or fourplex, this AVID is for unit # _____.

Inspection Performed By (Real Estate Broker Firm Name) _____

Inspection Date/Time:_____ Weather conditions: _____

Other persons present: _____

THE UNDERSIGNED, BASED ON A REASONABLY COMPETENT AND DILIGENT VISUAL INSPECTION OF THE REASONABLY AND NORMALLY ACCESSIBLE AREAS OF THE PROPERTY, STATES THE FOLLOWING:

Entry (excluding common areas): _____

_____

_____

Living Room: _____

_____

_____

Dining Room: _____

_____

_____

Kitchen: _____

_____

_____

Other Room: _____

_____

_____

Hall/Stairs (excluding common areas): _____

_____

_____

Bedroom # __: _____

_____

_____

Bedroom # __: _____

_____

_____

Bedroom # __: _____

_____

_____

Bath # ____: _____

_____

_____

Bath # ____: _____

_____

_____

Bath # ____: _____

_____

_____

Other Room: _____

_____

_____

Buyer's Initials (_____)(_____)   Seller's Initials (_____)(_____)

Copyright © 2013, CALIFORNIA ASSOCIATION OF REALTORS®, INC.
AVID REVISED 11/13 (PAGE 2 OF 3)

| Reviewed by _____ Date _____ |

EQUAL HOUSING OPPORTUNITY

AGENT VISUAL INSPECTION DISCLOSURE (AVID PAGE 2 OF 3)

Source: Reprinted with permission, California Association of REALTORS®. Endorsement not implied.

FIGURE 14.7: Agent Visual Inspection Disclosure (continued)

Property Address: _____ Date: _____

If this Property is a duplex, triplex, or fourplex, this AVID is for unit # _____.

Other Room: _____
_____
_____
_____

Other: _____
_____
_____
_____

Other: _____
_____
_____
_____

Other: _____
_____
_____

Garage/Parking (excluding common areas): _____
_____
_____

Exterior Building and Yard - Front/Sides/Back: _____
_____
_____

Other Observed or Known Conditions Not Specified Above: _____
_____
_____

This disclosure is based on a reasonably competent and diligent visual inspection of reasonably and normally accessible areas of the Property on the date specified above.

Real Estate Broker (Firm who performed the Inspection)_____
By _____ Date _____
(Signature of Associate Licensee or Broker)

Reminder: Not all defects are observable by a real estate licensee conducting an inspection. The inspection does not include testing of any system or component. Real Estate Licensees are not home inspectors or contractors. BUYER SHOULD OBTAIN ADVICE ABOUT AND INSPECTIONS OF THE PROPERTY FROM OTHER APPROPRIATE PROFESSIONALS. IF BUYER FAILS TO DO SO, BUYER IS ACTING AGAINST THE ADVICE OF BROKER.

I/we acknowledge that I/we have read, understand and received a copy of this disclosure.

SELLER _____ Date _____
SELLER _____ Date _____
BUYER _____ Date _____
BUYER _____ Date _____
Real Estate Broker(FirmRepresentingSeller) _____

By _____ Date _____
(Associate Licensee or Broker Signature)

Real Estate Broker (Firm Representing Buyer) _____

By _____ Date _____

Published and Distributed by:
REAL ESTATE BUSINESS SERVICES, INC.
a subsidiary of the California Association of REALTORS®
525 South Virgil Avenue, Los Angeles, California 90020

Reviewed by _____ Date _____

AVID REVISED 11/13 (PAGE 3 OF 3)
AGENT VISUAL INSPECTION DISCLOSURE (AVID PAGE 3 OF 3)

Source: Reprinted with permission, California Association of REALTORS®. Endorsement not implied.

Exercise 14-4

Using the diagrams and definitions in this unit, label the indicated parts of the house shown below.

FIGURE 14.8: Radon Gas and Mold Notice and Release Agreement

CALIFORNIA ASSOCIATION OF REALTORS®

**RADON GAS AND MOLD NOTICE AND RELEASE AGREEMENT
U.S. DEPARTMENT OF HOUSING AND URBAN DEVELOPMENT**
OFFICE OF HOUSING, FEDERAL HOUSING COMMISSIONER
(C.A.R. Form RGM, 7/04)

Name of Buyer _____ ("Purchaser)
Property Case #: _____
Property address: _____
_____
_____

PURCHASERS ARE HEREBY NOTIFIED AND UNDERSTAND THAT RADON GAS AND SOME MOLDS HAVE THE POTENTIAL TO CAUSE SERIOUS HEALTH PROBLEMS.

Purchaser acknowledges and accepts that the HUD-owned property described above (the "Property") is being offered for sale **"AS IS"** with no representations as to the condition of the Property. The Secretary of the U.S. Department of Housing and Urban Development, his/her officers, employees, agents, successors and assigns (the "Seller") and _____ (name of M & M Contractor), an independent management and marketing contractor ("M & M Contractor") to the Seller, have no knowledge of radon or mold in, on, or around the Property other than what may have already been described on the web site of the Seller or M & M Contractor or otherwise made available to Purchaser by the Seller or M & M Contractor.

Radon is an invisible and odorless gaseous radioactive element. Mold is a general term for visible growth of fungus, whether it is visible directly or is visible when barriers, such as building components (for example, walls) or furnishings (for example, carpets), are removed.

Purchaser represents and warrants that Purchaser has not relied on the accuracy or completeness of any representations that have been made by the Seller and/or M & M Contractor as to the presence of radon or mold and that the Purchaser has not relied on the Seller's or M & M Contractor's failure to provide information regarding the presence or effects of any radon or mold found on the Property.

Real Estate Brokers and Agents are not generally qualified to advise purchasers on radon or mold treatment or its health and safety risks. **_PURCHASERS ARE ENCOURAGED TO OBTAIN THE SERVICES OF A QUALIFIED AND EXPERIENCED PROFESSIONAL TO CONDUCT INSPECTIONS AND TESTS REGARDING RADON AND MOLD PRIOR TO CLOSING._** Purchasers are hereby notified and agree that they are solely responsible for any required remediation and/or resulting damages, including, but not limited to, any effects on health, due to radon or mold in, on or around the property.

In consideration of the sale of the Property to the undersigned Purchaser, Purchaser does hereby release, indemnify, hold harmless and forever discharge the Seller, as owner of the Property and separately, M & M Contractor, as the independent contractor responsible for maintaining and marketing the Property, and its officers, employees, agents, successors and assigns, from any and all claims, liabilities, or causes of action of any kind that the Purchaser may now have or at any time in the future may have against the Seller and/or M & M Contractor resulting from the presence of radon or mold in, on or around the Property.

Purchaser has been given the opportunity to review this Release Agreement with Purchaser's attorney or other representatives of Purchaser's choosing, and hereby acknowledges reading and understanding this Release. Purchaser also understands that the promises, representations and warranties made by Purchaser in this Release are a material inducement for Seller entering into the contract to sell the Property to Purchaser.

Dated this _____ day of _____, 20_____.

Purchaser's Signature_____   Purchaser's Signature _____

_____   _____
(Print Name)   **(Print Name)**

Published and Distributed by:
REAL ESTATE BUSINESS SERVICES, INC.
a subsidiary of the California Association of REALTORS®
525 South Virgil Avenue, Los Angeles, California 90020

SURE TRAC
The System for Success®

Reviewed by _____ Date _____

EQUAL HOUSING OPPORTUNITY

RGM 7/04 (PAGE 1 OF 1) Print Date

RADON GAS AND MOLD NOTICE (RGM PAGE 1 OF 1)

Source: Reprinted with permission, California Association of REALTORS®. Endorsement not implied.

SUMMARY

Residential construction makes use of designs and techniques that have been available for many years. New concepts for both site-built and manufactured housing have made homebuilding more efficient, economical, and responsive to contemporary needs. Some innovations, such as smoke detectors, present low-cost ways to improve the safety of the home environment. Other innovations, such as solar-heating systems, promote the goal of making the best possible use of our natural resources.

Real estate is a dynamic industry—one that requires knowledge of where we are as well as where we are going. Technological advances and design trends both shape and mirror consumer desires. Federal, state, and local law-making bodies dictate requirements for acceptable housing. Awareness of how those desires and requirements are changing benefits consumers, as well as real estate brokers and salespeople, who in turn can do the best possible job for every client.

OPEN FOR DISCUSSION

Manufactured housing generally is perceived by the public as less desirable than site-built housing.

1. What are some of the reasons for this perception?
2. What can be done to change it?

REVIEW QUESTIONS

1. In contracting for any work on someone else's property, a contractor's license is *NOT* needed
   a. by an attorney.
   b. by a real estate broker.
   c. by a real estate salesperson.
   d. if the work costs less than $500.

2. A contractor's license can be suspended or revoked for
   a. abandoning a project.
   b. violating building laws.
   c. breaching a construction contract.
   d. all of these.

3. A type of roof with two steeply pitched planes is called
   a. a gambrel roof.
   b. a flat roof.
   c. a gable roof.
   d. a saltbox roof.

4. A Dutch colonial house is distinguished by
   a. a hip roof.
   b. a shed roof.
   c. a gable roof.
   d. a gambrel roof.

5. Ornate exterior woodwork is usually found on
   a. a Colonial American house.
   b. a Queen Anne Victorian house.
   c. a contemporary house.
   d. a California ranch house.

6. An architectural style in which homes share a common wall is called
   a. a Colonial American house.
   b. a Queen Anne Victorian house.
   c. a Spanish house.
   d. a town house.

7. The location of a house on its site is called its
   a. view.
   b. architecture.
   c. orientation.
   d. floor plan.

8. The sun's arc in the sky is highest in
   a. summer.
   b. fall.
   c. winter.
   d. spring.

9. A good floor plan has
   a. the kitchen near the garage.
   b. bedrooms near living areas.
   c. one bathroom for every three bedrooms.
   d. no closets in the bedrooms, to conserve space.

10. Earthquake protection is provided by
    a. anchor bolts.
    b. cross-bracing.
    c. plywood sheathing.
    d. all of these.

11. A two-story platform house is built
    a. with studs that extend from the first floor to the ceiling of the second story.
    b. one story at a time.
    c. with posts within the house that support beams.
    d. with no interior supporting walls.

12. The vertical supports in a wood-frame house are called
    a. studs.
    b. plates.
    c. joists.
    d. beams.

13. A post-and-beam frame house is built
    a. with studs that extend from the first floor to the ceiling of the second story.
    b. one story at a time.
    c. with posts within the house that support beams.
    d. with interior supporting walls.

14. A brick or stone exterior finish is called
    a. glazing.
    b. paneling.
    c. veneer.
    d. tile.

15. The main roof supports are
    a. the soffits.
    b. the rafters.
    c. the gutters.
    d. the eaves.

16. A window that opens out is called
    a. a double-hung window.
    b. a horizontal sliding window.
    c. a casement window.
    d. a fixed window.

17. A relatively inexpensive and easy-to-install interior wall finishing is
    a. plasterboard.
    b. drywall.
    c. wallboard.
    d. all of these.

18. Heat from sunlight reaching water-filled containers is used in
    a. active solar-heating systems only.
    b. passive solar-heating systems.
    c. most homes.
    d. air-conditioning systems.

19. Every house sold in California must have at LEAST
    a. three bedrooms.
    b. two bathrooms.
    c. one smoke detector.
    d. one garage.

20. All water heaters must be
    a. cemented in place.
    b. braced, anchored, or strapped.
    c. at least 80 gallons in capacity.
    d. warranted by the state.

GOVERNMENT CONTROL OF LAND USE

LEARNING OBJECTIVES

When you have completed this unit, you will be able to

- **identify** the ways in which the police power of government is used to regulate land use;

- **list** the required provisions of a general plan;

- **state** the purpose of a community redevelopment agency;

- **identify** the two major subdivision laws and **state** the purpose of each;

- **describe** the forms of common interest subdivisions; and

- **explain** the federal and state fair housing laws and how they apply to real estate practice.

KEY TERMS

city planning
Civil Rights Act of 1866
Civil Rights Housing Act of 2006
coastal zone
commercial acre
common interest subdivision
community apartment project
community redevelopment agency (CRA)
condemnation
conditional use permit
Department of Fair Employment and Housing
earthquake fault zone
eminent domain

environmental impact report (EIR)
Fair Employment and Housing Act (FEHA)
Fair Housing Act
form-based planning
general plan
Housing Financial Discrimination Act
inverse condemnation
Jones v. Mayer
limited equity housing cooperative
master plan
mortgage revenue bonds
negative declaration
nonconforming use
parcel map
planned development

planned unit development (PUD)
police power
public report
redlining
rezoning
seismic hazards zone
standard subdivision
Subdivided Lands Law
subdivision map
Subdivision Map Act
tax increment funding
time-share project
undivided interest subdivision
Unruh Civil Rights Act
zones
zoning
zoning ordinances
zoning variance

LAND-USE REGULATIONS

Police Power and Eminent Domain

Land-use controls are possible because of the government's **police power**. This power enables government bodies to regulate private activity by enacting laws that benefit the public health, safety, and general welfare. As a general rule, the owner of property is not compensated for any loss in property value that results from the government's exercise of its police power.

Some of the ways in which the use of real estate is regulated were included in earlier units. Unit 14 discussed building codes and other criteria that establish standards for safe housing. Additional government controls of the *use* of real estate are covered in this unit.

www.cacities.org
www.sandiego.gov

Information on many California cities can be found at the site of the League of California Cities, www.cacities.org. The most useful municipal sites, such as that of the City of San Diego (www.sandiego.gov), provide the city's charter, municipal code, agendas, and other information.

Taking a property by condemnation requires compensation to the property owner.

As discussed in Unit 4, government also may take all or some of the rights of *ownership* from private individuals by exercising its power of **eminent domain**. The government does compensate individuals when property is "taken" through the process called **condemnation**, as when buildings are torn down to make way for highway expansion.

The *fair market value* of the real estate is paid to compensate the willing or unwilling former owner. When only part of a property is taken, compensation generally is based on the difference between the value of the entire parcel before the taking and the value of the remaining part.

FOR EXAMPLE   Agricultural land zoned for residential use is purchased for development. The purchase price is much greater than it would be for land zoned for strictly agricultural use. The land then is rezoned to strictly agricultural use before the development begins. Should the landowner be compensated for the loss in market value caused by the change in zoning classification?

At present, the answer to that question is "No," unless the property owner is denied all reasonable use of the property. The U.S. Supreme Court is called on to consider such cases frequently, however, and eventually may decide that loss in land value resulting from any change in use is a *taking* and must be compensated.

Just compensation on the taking of all or part of a property may include not just the fair market value of the property but also

- moving costs,
- mortgage prepayment penalties, and even a
- "going out of business" payment.

Assistance in finding new housing is required when residential property is condemned. Tenants who must relocate also are entitled to relocation payments and services. These protections are the result of the *Uniform Relocation Assistance and Real Property Acquisition Policies Act of 1970*. The act applies to all federal agencies and those agencies using federal funds for property acquisition. This covers a great number of condemnation actions because it includes property taken as part of federally financed road improvements, such as a freeway.

Inverse condemnation is a proceeding brought by a landowner when government puts nearby land to a use that diminishes the value of the owner's property. The *Tucker Act of 1887*, another federal law, allows a landowner to bring such a suit against the federal government.

FOR EXAMPLE   A roadway is dredged for a canal, and the owner of adjacent property is deprived of reasonable access to his land. The property owner has a claim for damages based on inverse condemnation.

City Planning

When an area is first settled, there usually is abundant land for all purposes. Planning for the use of the land may be considered an unnecessary burden on development. At a certain point, however, there is demand from all sectors of society on ever-scarcer land and resources. **City planning** then becomes a useful tool to help ensure orderly, sensible growth and development.

Early city plans in California include that of the city of Paso Robles in San Luis Obispo County, which was planned in the late 1860s by Drury Woodson James.

A modern example is the City of Irvine, in Orange County, created on what was the 53,000-acre Irvine Ranch. Since the 1960s the Irvine Company has developed residential and business areas within the city and has even donated land for what is now the campus of the University of California at Irvine. More recently, development of the inland valleys has seen the creation of many new planned communities.

The General Plan

The Government Code requires that every general plan include provision for the following:

- *Land use*, including standards of population density and building intensity
- *Circulation*, including distribution of transportation facilities and public utilities
- *Housing* at all income levels
- *Conservation* of natural resources
- *Open space* to preserve natural resources in light of recreational needs and public health and safety
- *Noise* problems, both existing and foreseeable
- *Safety* from fire, seismic (earthquake), and geological hazards

Where applicable the general plan also provides for *coastal development*, protection of *mineral and forestry resources*, and development within *seismic zones*. The plan also may include local areas of concern, such as *historic preservation*.

Since 1982 counties have been required to have a *solid waste management plan* consistent with the county's general plan.

Finally, every county with a public airport served by a certified air carrier has an airport land-use commission that must prepare an airport land-use plan that is consistent with the general plan, unless a specific exception is allowed.

Community development goals are set out in the general plan.

The general plan   Every city and county within California now is required by state law to adopt a comprehensive, long-term **general plan** for development within its jurisdiction.

The general plan, also referred to as the **master plan**, is both a statement of policy and a means to enact that policy. It usually includes background information on the area economy, its development, population growth, and existing land uses. It states the goals and policies determining future development and gives one or more maps showing population distribution and designated land-use areas and density. In addition, the general plan presents a program designed to implement the stated policy.

The local *planning commission*, required by state law for counties but optional for cities, formulates the general plan, which then is adopted by resolution of the legislative body.

Form-Based Planning

Assembly Bill 1268, signed into law in July 2004, is an outgrowth of the *White Paper on Smart Growth Policy in California*, prepared for the Governor's Office of Planning and Research in February 2003. The new law expands on the traditional system of planning to allow a concept called **form-based planning**. In traditional planning, different specialists working apart from one another design separate components of the urban landscape, often leading to isolated land-use areas and "sprawl." Form-based planning provides for a mix of land uses, while taking into account the relationship of buildings and public areas, resulting in a much more "pedestrian-friendly" urban environment.

Procedure for adoption   The Government Code outlines the procedure for adoption of a general plan or an amendment to the general plan. If the jurisdiction has a planning commission, a public hearing is held before that group, and a majority of planning commissioners must vote in favor of the plan. Then another public hearing is held by the local governing body (city council or county board of supervisors), which can adopt the plan or amendment by resolution.

The specific plan   A *specific plan* can be formulated after a general plan has been adopted. The specific plan may be so detailed that no further land-use regulations (such as zoning) are required. In the specific plan, further attention is given to population growth as well as environmental, economic, and other considerations in particular areas. Locations of streets and utilities, projected population density, building construction requirements, and topographical information (terrain and physical features) can be provided.

Zoning

Zoning is the primary method of regulating property use.

Zoning is the dividing of a city into areas, or **zones**, limited to certain land uses, building requirements, or both. Zoning is the primary device for controlling land use and the principal tool for implementing the general plan.

Zoning is authorized by the California Constitution as an exercise of a city's *police power*. It must be consistent with the policies and long-range goals of the general plan. If there is a conflict, the general plan takes precedence over zoning. The state has established a procedure for citizen complaints regarding noncompliance with the general plan.

Zoning specifications   Zoning ordinances typically cover

- permitted uses,
- minimum parcel size,
- building height limitations,
- lot coverage limitations,
- required setbacks, and
- maximum density.

A zoning ordinance also typically provides for a **conditional use permit** that allows a **nonconforming use**, such as a church in a residential zone. An already existing use that does not conform to the current zoning may be "grandfathered" in and allowed to remain.

The zoning classifications used by the City of Los Angeles are shown here. Note that both property classifications and letter and number designations vary widely throughout the state. There is no uniform system of zone classification. An extensive listing of municipal codes, including zoning ordinances, for cities throughout the United States, can be found at www.municode.com/library/library.aspx.

www.municode.com/library /library.aspx

Zoning changes   The overall designated land use may be changed in the process called **rezoning**.

A **zoning variance** permits a change in the specifications required by the zoning ordinance, if a property owner is placed at a disadvantage by the prescribed zoning specifications. State law permits a zoning variance where "the strict application of the zoning ordinance deprives such property of privileges enjoyed by other property in the vicinity and under identical zoning classification." To expedite routine applications for permits, variances, and appeals, many jurisdictions have a *zoning administrator*, *zoning board*, or *board of zoning adjustment*.

FOR EXAMPLE   The Long family owns a home in Hundred Oaks and would like to build a deck behind their home. Because of the unusual configuration of their hillside lot, their home is closer to the rear property line than other homes in the subdivision. A deck similar in size to the ones built by their neighbors would violate the local zoning ordinance by being too close to the rear boundary line. What can the Longs do?

The Longs can seek a variance to the zoning ordinance to allow their backyard deck to be built closer to the rear lot line than the minimum setback stated in the ordinance. Because they are asking only to be allowed to enjoy their property in the same way that neighboring property owners are able to enjoy theirs, the Longs most likely will be allowed a variance.

Los Angeles Zoning Classifications

Los Angeles is divided into the following zones, from the most restrictive (OS) to the least restrictive (PF):

OS	Open Space Zone
A1	Agricultural Zone
A2	Agricultural Zone
RA	Suburban Zone
RE	Residential Zone
RS	Suburban Zone
R1	One-Family Zone
RU	Residential Urban Zone
RZ	Residential Zero Side Yard Zone
RW1	One-Family Residential Waterways Zone
R2	Two-Family Zone
RD	Restricted Density Multiple Dwelling Zone
RMP	Mobilehome Park Zone
RW2	Two-Family Residential Waterways Zone
R3	Multiple Dwelling Zone
RAS3	Residential/Accessory Services Zone
CA	Commercial and Artcraft District
POD	Pedestrian Oriented District
CDO	Community Design Overlay District
MU	Mixed Use District
FH	Fence Height District
SN	Sign District
R4	Multiple Dwelling Zone
RAS4	Residential/Accessory Services Zone
R5	Multiple Dwelling Zone
P	Automobile Parking Zone
PB	Parking Building Zone
CR	Limited Commercial Zone
C1	Limited Commercial Zone
C1.5	Limited Commercial Zone
C2	Commercial Zone
C4	Commercial Zone
C5	Commercial Zone
CM	Commercial Manufacturing Zone
MR1	Restricted Industrial Zone
M1	Limited Industrial Zone
MR2	Restricted Light Industrial Zone
M2	Light Industrial Zone
M3	Heavy Industrial Zone
PF	Public Facilities Zone
SL	Ocean-Submerged Land Zone

The following are Specific Plan Zones:

CCS	Century City South Studio Zone
CM (GM)	Commercial Manufacturing (Glencoe/Maxella) Zone
CW	Central City West Specific Plan Zone
WC	Warner Center Specific Plan Zone
ADP	Alameda District Specific Plan Zone
LASED	Los Angeles Sports and Entertainment District Specific Plan Zone
LAX	Los Angeles International Airport Specific Plan Zone

Certain portions of the city are also designated as being in one or more of the following districts:

O	Oil Drilling District
S	Animal Slaughtering
G	Surface Mining District
RPD	Residential Planned Development District
K	Equinekeeping District

Planned development The **planned development**, or **planned unit development** (PUD), is both a type of development and a zoning classification. A PUD usually allows individually owned residential property together with shared common areas. A PUD also may include commercial uses, industrial uses, or both.

Redevelopment

The deteriorating condition of some urban neighborhoods has served as the impetus for local redevelopment efforts. California's *Community Redevelopment Law* (found in the Health and Safety Code) allowed the formation of a **community redevelopment agency** (CRA). CRAs worked to rehabilitate existing structures or bring in new development both to provide low- and moderate-income housing and to employ low-income persons.

The governing board of a CRA often was composed of city council members. The redevelopment proposed was required to conform to the general plan but did not need to conform to zoning ordinances. Instead, the redevelopment plan contained its own building use limitations. The CRA used the power of *eminent domain* to acquire parcels, borrowed money from any source to finance purchase and construction, and generally acted as a developer would. Funding for CRA activities came from a variety of bond programs, some of which required voter approval. Repayment was through **tax increment funding**, using the additional taxes produced by the redevelopment property. Repayment also was made through the issuing of tax-exempt **mortgage revenue bonds**.

Legislation passed in 2011, and upheld by the California Supreme Court in *California Redevelopment Assn. v. Matosantos*, dissolved the state's redevelopment agencies as of February 1, 2012. At the time of the legislation, 400 CRAs were receiving 12% of the state's property taxes; the state's fiscal crisis prompted action to return that revenue to local governments and the general fund.

Exercise 15-1

Why should the following factors be taken into account in formulating a general plan for a newly incorporated suburban city?

- Proximity (20 miles) to city of 2 million population
- County plan encouraging commercial development
- No-growth initiative passed by voters of a neighboring city
- Generally hilly terrain with past mudslide problems

SUBDIVISIONS

Most land development involves the *subdividing* of a parcel of land for the purpose of sale, lease, or financing. Controlled land development is important, and subdivisions often involve sales to consumers. For these reasons there are two laws that specifically govern planning, design, site preparation, construction of improvements, and sales of subdivision land known as the following:

- Subdivided Lands Law
- Subdivision Map Act

www.bre.ca.gov/files/pdf
/ResidentialSubdivisionsGuide
.pdf

www.bre.ca.gov/files/pdf
/ResidentialSubdivisionBuyers
Guide.pdf

An overview of the subdivision process is provided in "A Guide to Understanding Residential Subdivisions in California," prepared by CalBRE along with California State University, Sacramento, in 2014. It is available at www.bre.ca.gov/files/pdf/ResidentialSubdivisionsGuide.pdf. The "Residential Subdivision Buyer's Guide," also from CalBRE and Sacramento State, can be found at www.bre.ca.gov/files/pdf/ResidentialSubdivisionBuyersGuide.pdf.

Subdivided Lands Law

The **Subdivided Lands Law** (found in the Business and Professions Code) describes the forms of ownership allowed in a subdivision of *five or more parcels* on up to 160 acres of land.

The Subdivided Lands Law also regulates the marketing and financing of the subdivision. For purposes of this law, the different parcels do not need to be adjacent or contiguous (touching).

The Subdivided Lands Law is administered by the Real Estate Commissioner. Its objective is to protect purchasers of property in new subdivisions from fraud, misrepresentation, or deceit in the marketing of the property.

Details of any subdivision offered for sale in California must be submitted to the Real Estate Commissioner, who prepares and issues a subdivision public report describing the property. Before issuing the report, the commissioner also receives information on the project's financial status. This is primarily to make sure that improvements to the land will be made as promised to purchasers.

Types of Subdivisions

The three basic types of subdivisions are the

- standard subdivision,
- common interest subdivision, and
- undivided interest subdivision.

Standard subdivision   In the **standard subdivision**, the owners of separate parcels have no shared interest in any part of the subdivided land. Subdivision lots can be sold unimproved—but with utilities installed—to individual owners or developers for building purposes. Subdivision lots also can be fully improved with completed homes and offered with or without seller-arranged financing.

If land is divided into parcels of 160 acres or more, it is not considered a subdivision as defined by the law. There is an exception to this general rule, however. If land is divided for sale for oil and gas purposes, it will be considered a subdivision no matter how large the individual parcels are.

Common interest subdivision   In the **common interest subdivision**, a separate ownership or leasehold interest in a parcel is accompanied by a shared interest in what are called the *common areas* of the subdivision. The common areas usually are governed by a *homeowners association*. Some of the different forms of common interest subdivisions are summarized below.

An important addition to the Common Interest Development Open Meeting Act took effect January 1, 2008. Civil Code 1363.05(i) requires that the agenda of *any* meeting of a homeowners association board be posted at least *four days* before the meeting. The law formerly required that notice of an upcoming meeting be given at least four days in advance of the meeting, but there was no requirement that the meeting agenda be posted in advance.

Common Interest Subdivisions

Planned development.   A planned development consists of individually owned parcels or lots as well as areas owned in common.

Community apartment project.   A community apartment project is one in which the owner has an individual interest in the land and exclusive right of occupancy of an apartment on the land. All owners are tenants in common. The project will receive one tax bill and any loan will be on the entire project and the responsibility of all tenants.

Condominium project.   The owner of a condominium has an exclusive ownership interest in the airspace of a particular portion of real property, as well as an interest in common in the land and structure. The condominium form of ownership has been used for apartments, offices, stores, and industrial space. A condominium can be purchased and financed like any other real property.

Stock cooperative project.   Most stock cooperatives are apartment buildings. Each owner in a stock cooperative project is a shareholder in a corporation that holds title to the property, and the individual shareholders receive a right of exclusive occupancy of a portion of the property.

Limited equity housing cooperative.   A limited equity housing cooperative is a stock cooperative financed by the California Housing Finance Agency.

Time-share project.   The latest type of primarily vacation-use property is the time-share. In a time-share project, a purchaser receives the right to exclusive use of a portion of the property for a particular period of time each year, in perpetuity or for a certain number of years. There must be 12 or more separate interests before the project will be subject to California Bureau of Real Estate regulation.

A time-share *estate* includes an estate interest in the property, but a time-share *use* does not. Time-share properties range from city apartments to campground spaces. There is a *seven-day right to rescind* an offer to purchase a time-share. Time-share plan development is subject to the Vacation Ownership and Time-Share Act of 2004, as amended in 2005.

Now the law provides that, if an item of business does not appear on an agenda posted at least four days in advance of the meeting, the board *cannot* discuss it. A nonagenda item can be brought up *only* if it concerns

- an emergency (as designated by a vote of a majority of the board), in which case it can be discussed and voted on;

- an item that a member speaks on in an open forum, in which case the board can answer questions;

- a clarification, announcement, or report on an ongoing activity; or

- a matter that the board refers to the property manager or a member of the manager's staff for action or for a report back to the board at a future meeting.

The law is clear that an emergency exists only if a majority of the board of directors present at the meeting determines that "there are circumstances that could not have been reasonably foreseen by the board, that require immediate attention and possible action by the board, and that, of necessity, make it impracticable to provide notice." And the board is not free to discuss and/or vote on a nonagenda item just because a member brings it up in an open forum. The board can answer questions but must schedule discussion of the item for a future meeting.

Undivided interest subdivision In an **undivided interest subdivision**, each owner is a tenant in common with all other owners. Each has the nonexclusive right to the use and occupancy of the property. An example of a common interest subdivision is a campground with shared facilities.

The Subdivision Public Report

Subdivisions must meet the requirements of the Subdivided Lands Law before the Real Estate Commissioner will issue the necessary **public report**. All prospective purchasers must be given a copy of the report and be allowed to read it.

In general, a notice of intention, a questionnaire, and an application must be filed. After a notice of intention has been filed or a public report has been made, any *material change* involving the subdivision must be reported to the commissioner. Examples of material changes include changes to lot size, deed restrictions, or financing terms.

The report requirements are stricter for common interest subdivisions (such as condominiums) than for standard subdivisions. The public report for a standard residential subdivision usually discloses the following:

- Project name, location, and size
- Subdivider's name
- Interest to be acquired by purchaser or lessee
- Procedure for handling all payments, taxes, and assessments
- Extraordinary expenses at closing or expected in the future
- Hazards or adverse environmental factors
- All conditions or restrictions on use of the property
- Unusual easements, rights-of-way, or setbacks
- Special building permit requirements

False or misleading advertising is always prohibited.

Guidelines for advertising or promoting a subdivision are provided in the Commissioner's Regulations. False or misleading advertising of any type is prohibited, regardless of whether it is specifically mentioned in the regulations.

Because the public report may take months to compile, the subdivider may begin taking reservations for future purchases on the basis of an approved *conditional public report*. No sales can be closed or transactions completed, however, until the *final public report* is received. All persons who make a property reservation agreement based on a conditional report *or* who make an offer to purchase based on a final public report must indicate in writing that they have received and read the applicable report. The signed receipt must be in the form required by the Commissioner's Regulations. The subdivider must make the receipt available for inspection by the commissioner for three years from the date it is signed.

Renewal   If all parcels have not been sold within five years of issuance of a final public report, it can be renewed for an additional five years.

> ### Right to Negotiate Property Inspections
>
> The public report for a residential subdivision must disclose that a prospective buyer has the right to negotiate with the seller to permit inspections of the property by the buyer (or someone designated by the buyer) under terms mutually agreeable to buyer and seller. (Business and Professions Code 11010.11)

Filing fees   The Subdivided Lands Law sets maximum filing fees, but the commissioner can charge less if administrative costs warrant it.

Subdivision Map Act

The **Subdivision Map Act** (found in the Government Code) establishes a statewide procedure for filing a subdivision plan when property is divided into two or more parcels. The different parcels generally must be contiguous (touching). Figure 15.1 shows the basic differences between the Subdivided Lands Law and the Subdivision Map Act.

The Subdivision Map Act is an *enabling act*. This means that it authorizes cities and counties to establish subdivision requirements by local ordinance. Its purpose is to give local governments direct control of all physical aspects of a subdivision, such as lot design, placement of streets and sewers, and so on. Although the act makes some procedural and other requirements, much of the content of the subdivision map will be dictated by the local authority.

The twofold objectives of the Subdivision Map Act are

- to coordinate subdivision design, including streets and utilities, with the general plan; and
- to ensure that areas of a subdivision dedicated to public use, such as public streets, will be properly improved initially.

The Subdivision Map

The **subdivision map** must take into account much more than just parcel division lines and street locations. The Subdivision Map Act provides for tentative, final, and parcel maps for most subdivisions.

Tentative map   The initial map is called the *tentative subdivision map*. It does not need to be based on a final, detailed survey of the property to be subdivided, unless that is required by local ordinance. A survey prepared by a registered civil engineer or licensed surveyor is always useful, however.

The tentative map typically is required by local ordinance to include the following:

- Legal description, including property boundaries of land and all parcels
- Widths and names of all existing streets

- Proposed street widths and grades and public areas
- Existing and proposed road, drainage, sewer, and other utility easements
- Source of water supply
- Storm water overflow and direction and flow of all watercourses
- Proposed property use

The developer (subdivider) is generally responsible for installing streets, curbs, and public utilities, and the government is responsible for maintaining them. From the developer's perspective, the most important consideration is the land remaining after accounting for streets, sidewalks, curbs, and so on. A **commercial acre** is the portion of an acre remaining after deducting the area required for streets and other improvements.

FIGURE 15.1: **Comparison of Subdivision Laws**

	Subdivision Map Act	Subdivided Lands Law
Number of Parcels	Two or more	Five or more
Size of Parcels	Any size	Exempt if 160 acres or larger, as surveyed
Residential Subdivisions Within City Limits	Included	Exempt
Parcels Contiguous	Yes	No
"Proposed Division"	Not included	Included
Condominiums	Included	Included
Community Apartments	Included	Included
Stock Cooperatives	Included only if five or more dwelling units converted	Included
Limited Equity Housing Cooperatives	Not included	May be exempt
Time-Shares	Not included	Included if 12 or more
Agricultural Leases	Not included	Included
Zoned Industrial or Commercial Subdivisions	Included	Exempt
Long-Term Leasing of Spaces in Mobilehome Parks or Trailer Parks	Not included	Included
Leasing of Space in Apartment, Industrial, or Commercial Building	Not included	Not included
Out-of-State Subdivisions	Not included	Included

Both state and local rules must be followed in preparing a subdivision map.

Final map Requirements specified by local ordinance must be met in preparing the *final map*. In addition, the Subdivision Map Act specifies certain requirements for a final subdivision map, beginning with the color of ink (black) and size of paper (18 by 26 inches) to be used.

Each parcel must be numbered, each block must be numbered or lettered, and each street must be named. The exact boundaries of the land must be shown. All soils reports are to be made part of the public record. If the subdivision will interfere with full and complete use of rights-of-way, easements, or other interests held by a public entity or public utility, the public entity or utility must be notified of the subdivision formation and given a chance to object to it.

A *dedication* or offer to dedicate any part of the land for public purposes must be made by a certificate signed by all parties having an interest of record in the land. Compliance with state law creates a *statutory dedication*. The clerk of each approving legislative body signs a *certificate of execution* indicating the acceptance or rejection of such dedicated property. The engineer or surveyor responsible for the map also signs a certificate that the survey is true and complete as shown.

Other certificates also may be required. If the property is within an unincorporated area, the county surveyor and, if applicable, the city engineer must certify that the map is technically correct and conforms to both the law and the tentative map.

Parcel map   Preparation of a **parcel map** may be waived by local ordinance. If not, the parcel map must meet both state and local requirements. The paper and ink specifications noted above also apply to parcel maps. Each parcel must be designated and all property boundaries shown. The subdivider must sign and acknowledge the parcel map by certificate. The engineer or surveyor conducting the field survey and preparing the map must certify its accuracy.

Procedure for Subdivision Map Approval

Approval of the subdivision map is the responsibility of the advisory agency designated by the city or county. Typically, this is the planning commission, but it could be any other official or official body so designated, such as the city council or a committee of city officials.

There are *notice, hearing, time limitation*, and other requirements involved in the subdivision map approval process. Notice and opportunity for hearing are *required* only when a map approval would constitute a *significant* deprivation of other landowners' property rights. The better practice, however, is to give notice and an opportunity for hearing before any subdivision approval.

Approval of the *tentative map* requires that it conform to the general or specific plan, as well as to local ordinances or actions regarding housing needs. It also must meet requirements for future passive or natural heating or cooling opportunities. The site must be physically suitable for the proposed use and not likely to cause substantial environmental damage or serious public health problems.

The *final map* must be filed before the tentative map expires, which is two years after its approval or conditional approval (three years for maps approved before May 16, 1996), plus any extension granted, with the total time not to exceed five years.

The final map must be in substantial compliance with the tentative map. Local ordinances determine the approval procedure, but notice and an opportunity for hearing must be given to adjoining property owners if the subdivision will result in significant deprivation of their property rights.

Other Subdivision Requirements

Environmental impact report   An **environmental impact report** (EIR), authorized by the *California Environmental Quality Act of 1970 (CEQA)*, may be required before subdivision approval.

CEQA requires any government agency that must approve a project (which may include the Real Estate Commissioner as well as a local governing body) to prepare an EIR if the project will have a *significant effect* on the environment. Subdivision approval must be denied if the design of either the project or its improvements is likely to

- *cause substantial environmental damage or*
- *substantially injure fish or wildlife or their habitat.*

CEQA requires an EIR or negative declaration.

It is in the best interest of a subdivision developer to determine whether an EIR is necessary even before a tentative subdivision map is prepared. The government agency is authorized to issue a **negative declaration** (a statement that there will be no impact on the environment significant enough to warrant preparation of an EIR) if that is the case.

www.conservation.ca.gov /CGS/RGHM/AP/Pages /Index.aspx

Alquist-Priolo Earthquake Fault Zoning Act   The *Alquist-Priolo Earthquake Fault Zoning Act* (formerly called the Alquist-Priolo Special Studies Zones Act) regulates development in earthquake fault areas. It is concerned solely with possible damage from fault ruptures, rather than from seismic (shaking) effects. Information on the law can be found at www.conservation.ca.gov/CGS/RGHM /AP/Pages/Index.aspx.

A geologic report must be obtained by local government for any new project initiated after May 4, 1975, involving improvements or structures in an **earthquake fault zone**, typically within a quarter of a mile or more of an active fault. If there are no undue hazards, the city or county can waive the report if the state geologist approves.

Any agent—or a seller acting without an agent—of real estate located within an earthquake fault zone identified as such in a reasonably available map must disclose that fact to any prospective buyer.

www.conservation.ca.gov /cgs/Pages/Index.aspx

California Geological Survey maps of earthquake fault zones can be obtained from one of the California Department of Conservation offices in Los Angeles, Menlo Park, and Sacramento. Maps can be ordered or downloaded from the CGS publications page at www.conservation.ca.gov/cgs/Pages/Index.aspx.

The *Seismic Hazards Mapping Act* requires the same type of disclosure for property located in a **seismic hazards zone**, if a map of the property's area is reasonably available. A map of the San Francisco area was released in 1995, with maps covering the rest of the state due for release over the next several years.

http://earthquake.usgs.gov

The United States Geologic Service provides information on earthquake preparation and recent earthquake activity at http://earthquake.usgs.gov.

California Coastal Act   The California Coastal Act defines **coastal zones**, which generally run the length of the state from the sea inland 1,000 or more yards, depending on terrain. The California coastal management program authorizes local governments to make policies providing for coastal conservation and to require permits from developers of such property or owners seeking to improve it. A copy of the law and other regulations can be found at www.coastal.ca.gov /ccatc.html.

www.coastal.ca.gov/ccatc .html

Rangeland, Grazing Land, and Grassland Protection Act   The Rangeland, Grazing Land, and Grassland Protection Act has established a program that provides grants for acquisition of conservation easements to protect, restore, or enhance California's rangeland, grazing land, and grasslands. Procedures and criteria for awarding of grants can be found in Division 10.4 of the California Public Resources Code.

Water Conservation   Recent years of prolonged drought have prompted the California governor and legislature to take action to reduce water demand. Governor Edmund G. Brown Jr. issued an executive order directing the State Water Resources Control Board to implement the first statewide mandatory water reductions to reduce water usage by 25%. One goal of the order is the replacement of 50 million square feet of lawns throughout the state with drought tolerant landscaping. With this goal in mind, Section 53087.7 was enacted to prohibit a city, including a charter city, county, or city and county, from enacting any new, or enforcing any existing, ordinance or regulation that prohibits the installation of drought tolerant landscaping, synthetic grass, or artificial turf on residential property. The governing body may impose reasonable restrictions on the type of drought tolerant landscaping, synthetic grass, or artificial turf that may be installed on residential property provided that those restrictions do not substantially increase the cost, effectively prohibit the installation, or significantly impede the installation of drought tolerant landscaping.

Exercise 15-2

1. Ernest Holmes is subdividing the Eagle Ranch property. Ernest's subdivision map was approved, and a notice of intention was filed with the Real Estate Commissioner. Ernest then decided to change the deeds to include more CC&Rs. Must Ernest notify the commissioner?

2. Describe the differences between the Subdivision Map Act and Subdivided Lands Law in the following areas:

	Subdivision Map Act	Subdivided Lands Law
Number of subdivision units or parcels		
Inclusion of undivided interests		
Inclusion of time-shares		
Inclusion of stock cooperatives		
Opportunity for notice and hearing		

FAIR HOUSING LAWS

Both the federal and the state governments have passed legislation to prohibit housing discrimination. This issue is so important, it is a mandatory subject of study for real estate license renewal.

Discrimination in Housing

Owners of housing are not to discriminate in the sale, rental, or lease of their property. *Real estate brokers* should not accept the listing of any property where such discrimination is attempted. Real estate property owners, brokers, salespeople, lenders, landlords, and hotel keepers are held to the same standard of conduct expected of all ethical citizens and professionals. Arbitrary discrimination, particularly in supplying housing, is strictly forbidden by both federal and state law.

Federal law   The **Civil Rights Act of 1866** prohibits racial discrimination in every property transaction. Although long ignored, the 1866 Civil Rights Act was upheld in 1968 by the U.S. Supreme Court in the case of *Jones v. Mayer*. The Court found a constitutional basis for the 1866 Act in the 13th Amendment to the U.S. Constitution prohibiting slavery. A private individual may file a lawsuit in federal court alleging discrimination under the 1866 Civil Rights Act.

Shortly before the Supreme Court decision in *Jones v. Mayer*, Congress enacted the federal **Fair Housing Act** (Title VIII of the Civil Rights Act of 1968), based on the goal of "fair housing throughout the United States." As since amended, it prohibits discrimination based on

- race,
- color,
- religion,
- sex,
- national origin,
- ancestry,
- handicap, or
- familial status.

The federal Fair Housing Act applies to a sale or lease of residential property, as well as to advertising, lending, real estate brokerage activities, and other services related to residential transactions. It is enforceable by individuals, the Department of Housing and Urban Development (HUD), and the U.S. Attorney General. An individual has one year in which to file a complaint alleging discrimination with HUD's Office of Equal Opportunity (OEO), or two years in which to file a lawsuit in federal or state court. Both steps also could be taken, within the separate deadlines.

Some properties are *exempt* from the prohibitions against discrimination based on familial status (households with children under the age of 18). The act exempts *adult communities*, provided that

- *all* residents are age 62 or older, or

- at least 80% of the units are occupied by people age 55 or older.

Some *transactions* exempt from the federal Fair Housing Act include those involving

- preference to members of religious organizations or societies or affiliated nonprofit organizations, when dealing with their own property, and as long as membership is not restricted on the basis of race, color, or national origin; and

- preference or limitation to members of private clubs with lodgings that are not open to the public and are not operated for a commercial purpose.

> No one is exempt from the 1866 Civil Rights Act that forbids racial discrimination.

Also exempt are transactions involving a single-family home sold or rented by its owner (if the owner owns no more than three such homes) or the rental of a room or unit in an owner-occupied dwelling of up to four units. Despite these exemptions, the property owner still would be subject to the 1866 Civil Rights Act. Also, being exempt from the federal Fair Housing Act does not serve as an exemption from state law.

State law   California's prohibitions against discrimination generally have been broader than the federal government's. In addition, local jurisdictions have passed a variety of antidiscrimination ordinances aimed at offering the widest housing choice to every resident of the state.

> www.dfeh.ca.gov
> /Publications_FEHADescr
> .htm

California's **Fair Employment and Housing Act** (FEHA), formerly the Rumford Fair Housing Act, www.dfeh.ca.gov/Publications_FEHADescr.htm, prohibits discrimination in employment, training, or compensation based on race, religion, creed, color, national origin, ancestry, physical or mental disability, medical condition, genetic information, marital status, sex, gender, gender identity, gender expression, age, or sexual orientation of any person (*Government Code Section 12940*). FEHA prohibits discrimination or harassment in all aspects of housing (including sale, rental, lease, or financing) against any person because of the race, color, religion, sex, gender, gender identity, gender expression, sexual orientation, marital status, national origin, ancestry, familial status, source of income, disability, or genetic information of that person (*Government Code Section 12955*). Housing that meets the legal definition of senior housing for older persons under federal or state law is exempt from the familial status provisions of FEHA.

Examples of discrimination include refusal to show property and arbitrary financing requirements. An individual may file a complaint alleging discrimination with the California **Department of Fair Employment and Housing**.

The **Civil Rights Housing Act of 2006** (AB 2800), which took effect January 1, 2007, extends the protected classifications of FEHA to all California laws prohibiting discrimination in housing and housing-related areas, including real estate licensure, mortgage lending, membership in clubs established by condominium homeowner associations and mobilehome parks, development projects, and community redevelopment. In addition, whenever additional protected classes are added to FEHA, the other nondiscrimination laws will also be updated automatically.

www.dfeh.ca.gov
/Publications_Unruh.htm

The **Unruh Civil Rights Act**, www.dfeh.ca.gov/Publications_Unruh.htm, prohibits discrimination in accommodations and business establishments and now includes all of the protected classifications that appear in FEHA. Section 51 of the California Civil Code was amended in 2015 to extend the protections of the Unruh Civil Rights Act to all individuals regardless of citizenship, primary language, or immigration status. The provision of services or documents in a language other than English is not specifically required by this law. Sections 54-55.1 of the California Civil Code prohibit discrimination in the rental, leasing, or sale of housing accommodations against anyone in one of the FEHA protected classifications.

Discrimination in Lending

The federal Fair Housing Act prohibits discrimination in mortgage lending based on certain classifications. Prohibited activities include

- refusal to make a mortgage loan;
- refusal to provide information regarding loans;
- imposing different conditions, fees, loan points, or interest rates;
- discrimination in appraising property; and
- refusal to purchase a loan or setting of different terms or conditions for purchasing a loan.

www.hud.gov

Information and a complaint form can be found at the HUD website, www.hud .gov, by entering "housing discrimination" in the search box at the top of the page.

In addition to federal requirements, state-licensed savings and loan associations are subject to state regulations and guidelines adopted in 1976 that prohibit redlining. **Redlining** is the practice of rejecting real estate loan applications because of the location of the property involved. The state prohibition applies to *all* loans for the financing of dwellings of one to four units, including conventional, FHA-insured, and VA-guaranteed loans.

As of January 1, 1978, California's **Housing Financial Discrimination Act** (the *Holden Act*) prohibits all financial institutions from discriminating in real estate loan decisions based on the geographic location, the neighborhood, or another characteristic of the property, unless such a decision can be shown to be based on sound business practice. *All* loans on owner-occupied dwellings of one to four units, whether for purchase, construction, repair, remodeling, or refinancing, are included. The law also applies to secured home improvement loans from a financial institution, even if the property is not to be owner occupied. Including the individuals protected by FEHA, the Holden Act provides that there may be no consideration of

- race,
- color,
- religion,
- sex,
- sexual orientation,
- marital status,
- national origin,
- ancestry,
- familial status,
- disability (physical or mental),
- medical condition,
- source of income, or
- conditions, characteristics, or trends in the neighborhood or geographic area surrounding the subject property.

Complaints of violations of the Housing Financial Discrimination Act may be brought to the Secretary of the California State Transportation Agency (formerly the Business, Transportation, and Housing Agency), who has 30 days to act on the complaint.

Various remedies are available in the event discrimination is found, including granting of the loan, granting of more favorable loan terms, or requiring payment of damages of up to $1,000. Decisions of the secretary may be appealed to the Office of Administrative Hearings and from that body to a court.

Lenders must notify loan applicants of both the existence of the law and the complaint procedure. Figure 15.2 shows the Fair Lending Notice that must be given to every loan applicant.

Exercise 15-3

The Smiths are selling their house without an agent. What forms of discrimination are acceptable in their consideration of prospective purchasers?

FIGURE 15.2: Fair Lending Notice

The Housing Financial Discrimination Act of 1977

FAIR LENDING NOTICE

It is illegal to discriminate in the provision of or in the availability of financial assistance because of the consideration of:

1. **Trends, characteristics or conditions in the neighborhood or geographic area surrounding a housing accommodation, unless the financial institution can demonstrate in the particular case that such consideration is required to avoid an unsafe and unsound business practice; or**

2. **Race, color, religion, sex, marital status, domestic partnership, national origin or ancestry.**

It is illegal to consider the racial, ethnic, religious or national origin composition of a neighborhood or geographic area surrounding a housing accommodation or whether or not such composition is undergoing change, or is expected to undergo change, in appraising a housing accommodation or in determining whether or not, or under what terms and conditions, to provide financial assistance.

These provisions govern financial assistance for the purpose of the purchase, construction, rehabilitation or refinancing of one- to four-unit family residences occupied by the owner and for the purpose of the home improvement of any one- to four-unit family residence.

If you have any questions about your rights, or if you wish to file a complaint, contact the management of this financial institution or the Bureau of Real Estate at one of the following locations:

2550 Mariposa Mall, Suite 3070
Fresno, CA 93721-2273

320 W. 4th Street, Suite 350
Los Angeles, CA 90013-1105

1515 Clay Street, Suite 702
Oakland, CA 94612-1462

1651 Exposition Boulevard
Sacramento, CA 95815
P.O. Box 137000 *(mailing address)*
Sacramento, CA 95813-7000

1350 Front Street, Suite 1063
San Diego, CA 92101-3608

ACKNOWLEDGMENT OF RECEIPT

I (we) received a copy of this notice.

_____   _____
Signature of Applicant   *Date*

_____   _____
Signature of Applicant   *Date*

Bureau of Real Estate — Mortgage Lending Unit   RE 867 (Rev. 11/16)

SUMMARY

Using its power of **eminent domain**, a government can procure property by condemnation in exchange for the property's *fair market value*. Federal involvement requires relocation assistance for displaced property owners and tenants.

In an **inverse condemnation** action, a property owner complains that the value of property is impaired by the government's use of other property.

The power of eminent domain involves a "taking" of property. A government can use its **police power** to regulate property use and is not required to compensate the owner for any resulting loss in value.

The **general plan**, or **master plan**, establishes the development policies and goals of a city or county. The *specific plan* goes even further in defining desired population density and building intensity.

Zoning is the primary form of land-use regulation. A **conditional use permit** or **zoning variance** may be sought if a **nonconforming use** is desired.

A **community redevelopment agency** was allowed to act as a developer would in refurbishing and rebuilding dilapidated residential buildings. Financing was repaid through **tax increment funding** or **mortgage revenue bonds**.

The **Subdivided Lands Law** provides for issuance by the Real Estate Commissioner of a **public report** on the *subdivision* and available financing. A *conditional public report* allows property reservations even before a *final public report* is issued by the commissioner.

The **Subdivision Map Act** establishes minimum subdivision approval standards, which are elaborated on by local ordinances. Besides the **subdivision map**, an **environmental impact report** may be necessary. Special consideration will be given to property in an **earthquake fault zone**, **seismic hazards zone**, or **coastal zone**.

Discrimination in housing and business establishments is strictly prohibited by both federal and state law. Fair housing protections also cover mortgage lending. Financing cannot be based on discriminatory practices such as the **redlining** of certain areas as unsuitable for loans.

OPEN FOR DISCUSSION

1. Find out the zoning classifications in your city or county and compare them with those of nearby areas.

2. If you could eliminate one regulation affecting land use, what would it be?

3. If you had to create one new regulation affecting land use, what would it be?

REVIEW QUESTIONS

1. Land-use policies and goals are established through
   a. the general plan.
   b. the subdivision report.
   c. the preliminary report.
   d. the notice of intention.

2. The general plan must consider
   a. housing at current market rates.
   b. only present land uses and hazards.
   c. the needs of all applicants for development permits.
   d. housing at all income levels.

3. Planning for future development does NOT include consideration of
   a. solid waste management.
   b. conservation of natural resources.
   c. safety.
   d. Contractors' License Law.

4. Zoning ordinances are an exercise of a government's
   a. power of eminent domain.
   b. power of condemnation.
   c. police power.
   d. judicial power.

5. A property owner deprived by a zoning ordinance of the privileges enjoyed by owners of other property in the vicinity may apply for
   a. a conditional use permit.
   b. a variance.
   c. a master plan exception.
   d. a nonconforming use permit.

6. Land may be subdivided for purposes of
   a. sale.
   b. lease.
   c. financing.
   d. all of these.

7. The Subdivided Lands Law applies to subdivisions of land into
   a. 2 or more parcels.
   b. 5 or more parcels.
   c. 12 or more parcels.
   d. 25 or more parcels.

8. An out-of-state subdivider of California land
   a. must procure a public report.
   b. need not procure a public report.
   c. can decide whether to procure a public report.
   d. needs a public report only to finance a California subdivision.

9. A standard subdivision includes
   a. single-family residences and condominiums.
   b. no common interests.
   c. only residential property.
   d. no irregularly shaped parcels.

10. A subdivision consisting of individually owned lots as well as areas owned in common is
    a. a planned development.
    b. a community apartment project.
    c. a condominium project.
    d. a stock cooperative project.

11. A subdivision consisting of individual ownership of airspace and areas owned in common is
    a. a planned development.
    b. a community apartment project.
    c. a condominium project.
    d. a stock cooperative project.

12. A corporation holds title to property and shareholders having a right of occupancy to part of the property own the corporation in
    a. a planned development.
    b. a community apartment project.
    c. a condominium project.
    d. a stock cooperative project.

13. The subdivision public report is issued by
    a. the advisory agency.
    b. the planning commission.
    c. the Real Estate Commissioner.
    d. the California Bureau of Real Estate.

14. A final subdivision public report has an initial term of
    a. one year.
    b. two years.
    c. four years.
    d. five years.

15. The Subdivision Map Act allows
    a. the state to have a say in how property is subdivided.
    b. local jurisdictions to determine whether a subdivision is desirable.
    c. developers to dictate how subdivision will take place.
    d. neighboring landowners to petition to have land subdivided.

16. A "proposed subdivision" is covered by
    a. the Subdivision Map Act.
    b. the Subdivided Lands Law.
    c. the Contractors' License Law.
    d. the Contractors' State License Board.

17. Disclosure of the fact that property is located in a special studies zone must be made by
    a. the city council or board of supervisors.
    b. the property buyer.
    c. the real estate agent who represents the seller.
    d. the seller, in addition to the real estate agent.

18. Discrimination in housing is prohibited by
    a. federal law.
    b. state law.
    c. both state and federal laws.
    d. neither state nor federal laws.

19. A homeowner whose property is exempt from the requirements of the federal Fair Housing Act will still be subject to
    a. the 1866 Civil Rights Act.
    b. the Housing Financial Discrimination Act.
    c. the Subdivision Map Act.
    d. the Subdivided Lands Law.

20. The broadest prohibition against all forms of discrimination in the sale of residential real estate is found in
    a. the federal Fair Housing Act.
    b. *Jones v. Mayer.*
    c. California law.
    d. the Civil Rights Act of 1968.

MATH

Every real estate transaction involves arithmetic. A real estate agent must know the principles of basic mathematics to determine square footage, loan payment amounts, closing costs, and other necessary parts of a transaction. Consumers and investors should understand how the computations that will affect their sale or purchase are being carried out.

If you plan to take a real estate licensing exam, you may face questions involving mathematical computations. If you do, you will be allowed to use a simple calculator (no tape printout or beeping sounds). Make sure you understand how your calculator works, before entering the exam room. Will you be able to *chain* steps of a problem in sequence by entering all of the information without stopping for a subtotal? For example, if you enter 15 + 5 × 7, will the answer be 140 (15 + 5 = 20 and 20 × 7 = 140)? Above all, you must have a basic understanding of the mathematics involved in the problems you are given.

DOLLARS AND DECIMALS

Some of the most important real estate calculations involve dollars and cents. What will be the asking price? What will be the offer? Which closing expenses will be prorated? What will be the commission—to the listing broker and the selling broker? You'll need to be comfortable working with decimals and percentages throughout a transaction.

A dollar contains 100 cents.

one cent = one-hundredth ($\frac{1}{100}$) of a dollar = $0.01

The decimal point divides the dollars and cents. We indicate one dollar and fifteen cents by $1.15. One hundred dollars and fifteen cents is $100.15. Every number to the *left* of the decimal point is *increased* by a factor of 10.

ten dollars = $10.00

one hundred dollars = $100.00

one thousand dollars = $1,000.00

Every number to the *right* of the decimal point is *decreased* by a factor of 10.

$$\text{ten cents} = \text{one-tenth } (\tfrac{1}{10}) \text{ of a dollar} = \$0.10$$

$$\text{one cent} = \text{one-hundredth } (\tfrac{1}{100}) \text{ of a dollar} = \$0.01$$

$$\text{one mill} = \text{one-thousandth } (\tfrac{1}{1000}) \text{ of a dollar} = \$0.001$$

Decimals aren't used only for money calculations. They are also used to indicate percentages.

Percentages

> One percent is one-hundredth or 0.01.

A *percentage* is another way of expressing a number that has been carried out to two decimal places. The number 0.02, which is the same as $\tfrac{2}{100}$, may also be written as 2%. The number 0.38 ($\tfrac{38}{100}$) is also 38%. A number carried out to more than two decimal places can also be expressed as a percentage. Thus, 0.698 can be written 69.8%. The important point to remember is that the percent sign has the effect of moving the decimal point two places to the *right*.

F O R   E X A M P L E   The Barlows intend to subdivide their suburban lot, keeping 5/8 of the lot for their own use. What percentage of their land will they keep?

$$\tfrac{5}{8} = 8\overline{)5.000}^{\,.625} = .625 = 62.5\%$$

The Barlows will keep 62.5% of their land.

Some fractions are commonly expressed as their decimal equivalents, and vice versa.

$\tfrac{1}{10}$	= .100	= 10%		$\tfrac{1}{2}$	= .50	= 50%
$\tfrac{1}{8}$	= .125	= 12.5% or 12½%		$\tfrac{3}{5}$	= .60	= 60%
$\tfrac{1}{6}$	= .167	= 16.7% or 16⅔%		$\tfrac{5}{8}$	= .625	= 62.5% or 62½%
$\tfrac{1}{5}$	= .20	= 20%		$\tfrac{2}{3}$	= .667	= 66.7% or 66⅔%
$\tfrac{1}{4}$	= .25	= 25%		$\tfrac{3}{4}$	= .75	= 75%
$\tfrac{1}{3}$	= .333	= 33.3% or 33⅓%		$\tfrac{4}{5}$	= .80	= 80%
$\tfrac{3}{8}$	= .375	= 37.5% or 37½%		$\tfrac{7}{8}$	= .875	= 87.5% or 87½%
$\tfrac{2}{5}$	= .40	= 40%				

When converting a percentage to its decimal equivalent, move the decimal point two places to the *left* and remove the percent sign. Thus 82% becomes 0.82, and 67.6% becomes 0.676.

Percentages are used in problem solving to express the relationship (**percentage rate**, or simply **rate**) between part of something (**part**) and all of that thing (**whole**). The rate, part, and whole can be expressed in formulas:

$$\text{Whole} \times \text{Rate} = \text{Part}$$

$$\text{Part} \div \text{Whole} = \text{Rate}$$

$$\text{Part} \div \text{Rate} = \text{Whole}$$

As a memory aid, the formulas can be illustrated as follows:

$$\frac{\text{Part}}{\text{Whole} \mid \text{Rate}}$$

The horizontal line indicates a division and the vertical line indicates a multiplication.

FOR EXAMPLE   A house and lot are priced at $388,000. The lot alone is valued at $87,600. What percentage of the total asking price is attributable to the value of the lot?

Because we are looking for the rate, we will use the formula

Part ÷ Whole = Rate

$$\overset{.2258}{\$388,000\,\overline{)\$87,600.0000}} = 23\% \text{ (rounded)}$$

The value of the lot represents 23% of the property's total asking price.

FOR EXAMPLE   If the broker's commission is 5% of the selling price, what will the commission be on the sale of property for $644,000?

Here we know the rate and the whole and we are looking for the part, so we use the formula:

Whole	×	Rate	=	Part
$644,000	×	5%	=	$32,200

The broker's commission for this sale is $32,200.

FOR EXAMPLE   The commission for the sale of Whiteacre was $14,400. The broker's commission rate was 6%. What was the selling price of Whiteacre?

Because we know the part paid to the broker and the rate, we use the formula:

Part ÷ Rate = Whole

$$\overset{240000.}{.06\,\overline{)\$14,4000.00.}} = \$240,000$$

Whiteacre's selling price was $240,000.

INTEREST AND LOAN FINANCE PROBLEMS

Interest is the cost of borrowing money. Real estate interest (interest on a loan secured by real estate) typically is simple interest based on a specified annual return. For example, a 6% annual interest payment on a loan of $100,000 is $100,000 ×.06, or $6,000. As a monthly payment, the interest is $6,000 ÷ 12, or $500. Interest is always calculated on the remaining principal balance.

The formula for computing real estate loan interest payments is:

Principal × Rate × Time = Interest

$$PRT = I$$

The **principal** is the unpaid balance of the loan. The **rate** is the percentage rate of interest to be paid. The **time** is the length of the period for which interest is to be paid.

Use a 360-day year unless a problem specifies a calendar year.

Ordinarily time is expressed in years or parts of a year. A year is considered to have 360 days and a month 30 days, unless the exact number of days in the year or month is required.

If interest is to be calculated for a number of days, time is expressed as a fraction in which the numerator is the number of days and the denominator is 360. Interest for 65 days thus becomes $\frac{65}{360}$. If interest is being computed for a number of months, the fractional part of a year may be used; for example, four months is $\frac{4}{12}$ or $\frac{1}{3}$ of a year.

FOR EXAMPLE Calculate the interest to be paid for one month on a home equity loan with a remaining balance of $92,000 when the interest rate is 6%.

Principal × Rate × Time = Interest

$92,000 × 0.06 × \frac{1}{12}$ = Interest

$5,520 × \frac{1}{12}$ = Interest

$460 = Interest

The formula for interest can also be used to find principal, rate, or time. So,

$$PRT = I$$

$$P = \frac{I}{RT}$$

$$R = \frac{I}{PT}$$

$$T = \frac{I}{PR}$$

Use the formulas to solve the following example problems. Note that all the problems deal with simple interest.

FOR EXAMPLE   A homeowner paid $840 as one month's interest at 7½% on the outstanding balance of his home loan. What is the current outstanding principal balance of the loan?

$$\text{Principal} = \frac{\text{Interest}}{\text{Rate} \times \text{Time}}$$

$$\text{Principal} = \frac{\$840}{7\frac{1}{2} \times \frac{1}{12}}$$

$$\text{Principal} = \frac{\$840}{.075 \times \frac{1}{12}}$$

$$\text{Principal} = \frac{\$840}{.00625}$$

$$\text{Principal} = \$134{,}400$$

FOR EXAMPLE   What rate would be paid if an interest payment of $6,800 was made on a loan amount of $85,000 for one year?

$$\text{Rate} = \frac{\text{Interest}}{\text{Principal} \times \text{Time}}$$

$$\text{Rate} = \frac{\$6{,}800}{\$85{,}000}$$

$$\text{Rate} = 8\%$$

FOR EXAMPLE   A homeowner just made an interest-only payment of $2,760 on a remaining home equity loan balance of $92,000. The interest rate on the loan is 9%. What period of time does the interest payment cover?

$$\text{Time} = \frac{\text{Interest}}{\text{Principal} \times \text{Rate}}$$

$$\text{Time} = \frac{\$2{,}760}{\$92{,}000 \times 9\%}$$

$$\text{Time} = \frac{\$2{,}760}{\$8{,}280}$$

$$\text{Time} = .333 = \tfrac{1}{3}\ \text{year} = 4\ \text{months}$$

Interest rate tables, such as the one in Table A.1, can be used to shortcut some of the steps involved in computing monthly payments of principal and interest. Such tables can be used to determine interest payments. They also can be used to tell the potential investor how much of the principal balance must be paid to pay down the loan balance over a given number of payments, referred to as **amortization**.

F O R E X A M P L E What will be the monthly payment on a loan of $600,000 for 15 years at 7% interest if the loan is to be fully amortized by the end of that time?

Using Table A.1, we see that a loan of $1,000 at 7% for 15 years requires a payment of $8.99 per month to be completely paid in that time. The monthly payment on a $600,000 loan is, thus,

$$\$8.99 \times 600 = \$5,394$$

A monthly payment of $5,394 will fully amortize a $600,000 loan payable at 7% for 15 years.

Prorations

The mathematics involved in computing prorations were mentioned in the "Escrow Procedures" section of Unit 10. **Prorations**, which indicate the allocation to seller and buyer of the expenses incurred during their relative periods of ownership, are usually handled as part of the escrow process.

TABLE A.1: Monthly Payments to Amortize a $1,000 Loan

Term of Years	Interest Rate														
	5%	5½%	6%	6½%	7%	7½%	8%	8½%	9%	9½%	10%	10½%	11%	11½%	12%
1	85.61	85.84	86.07	86.30	86.53	86.76	86.99	87.22	87.46	87.69	87.92	88.15	88.38	88.62	88.85
2	43.88	44.10	44.33	44.55	44.78	45.00	45.23	45.46	45.69	45.92	46.14	46.38	46.61	46.84	47.07
3	29.98	30.20	30.43	30.65	30.88	31.11	31.34	31.57	31.80	32.04	32.27	32.50	32.74	32.98	32.21
4	23.03	23.26	23.49	23.72	23.95	24.18	24.42	24.65	24.89	25.13	25.36	25.60	25.85	26.09	26.33
5	18.88	19.11	19.34	19.57	19.81	20.04	20.28	20.52	20.76	21.01	21.25	21.50	21.75	22.00	22.25
6	16.11	16.34	16.58	16.81	17.05	17.30	17.54	17.78	18.03	18.28	18.53	18.78	19.04	19.30	19.56
7	14.14	14.38	14.61	14.85	15.10	15.34	15.59	15.84	16.09	16.35	16.61	16.87	17.13	17.39	17.66
8	12.66	12.90	13.15	13.39	13.64	13.89	14.14	14.40	14.66	14.92	15.18	15.45	15.71	15.98	16.26
9	11.52	11.76	12.01	12.26	12.51	12.77	13.02	13.28	13.55	13.81	14.08	14.36	14.63	14.91	15.19
10	10.61	10.86	11.11	11.36	11.62	11.88	12.14	12.40	12.67	12.94	13.22	13.50	13.78	14.06	14.35
11	9.87	10.12	10.37	10.63	10.89	11.15	11.42	11.69	11.97	12.24	12.52	12.81	13.10	13.39	13.68
12	9.25	9.51	9.76	10.02	10.29	10.56	10.83	11.11	11.39	11.67	11.96	12.25	12.54	12.84	13.14
13	8.74	8.99	9.25	9.52	9.79	10.06	10.34	10.62	10.90	11.19	11.48	11.78	12.08	12.38	12.69
14	8.29	8.55	8.82	9.09	9.36	9.64	9.92	10.20	10.49	10.79	11.09	11.39	11.70	12.01	12.32
15	7.91	8.17	8.44	8.72	8.99	9.28	9.56	9.85	10.15	10.45	10.75	11.06	11.37	11.69	12.01
16	7.58	7.85	8.12	8.40	8.68	8.96	9.25	9.55	9.85	10.15	10.46	10.78	11.10	11.42	11.74
17	7.29	7.56	7.84	8.12	8.40	8.69	8.99	9.29	9.59	9.90	10.22	10.54	10.86	11.19	11.52
18	7.04	7.31	7.59	7.87	8.16	8.45	8.75	9.06	9.37	9.68	10.00	10.33	10.66	10.99	11.32
19	6.81	7.08	7.37	7.65	7.95	8.25	8.55	8.86	9.17	9.49	9.82	10.15	10.48	10.82	11.16
20	6.60	6.88	7.17	7.46	7.76	8.06	8.37	8.68	9.00	9.33	9.66	9.99	10.33	10.67	11.02
25	5.85	6.15	6.45	6.76	7.07	7.39	7.72	8.06	8.40	8.74	9.09	9.45	9.81	10.17	10.54
30	5.37	5.68	6.00	6.33	6.66	7.00	7.34	7.69	8.05	8.41	8.78	9.15	9.53	9.91	10.29
35	5.05	5.38	5.71	6.05	6.39	6.75	7.11	7.47	7.84	8.22	8.60	8.99	9.37	9.77	10.16
40	4.83	5.16	5.51	5.86	6.22	6.59	6.96	7.34	7.72	8.11	8.49	8.89	9.28	9.68	10.08

We assume that all expenses up to the day of closing are the responsibility of the seller. Expenses as of the day of closing are the responsibility of the buyer. The standard term of 360 days per year (30 days per month) is used. If the strict number of calendar days is required, a table such as the one found in the "Math Concepts" example may be used to calculate the number of days quickly.

The standard 30-day month formulation may favor either seller or buyer in a transaction, depending on whether it is a 31-day month and whether income or expense is being prorated.

AREA

The real estate professional often needs to determine the floor or ground area of property.

Square footage is floor ground area.

The **perimeter** of a building or parcel is the sum of the length of all of its sides. **Area**, or **square footage**, is a measurement of the floor or ground space within the perimeter. Square footage is arrived at by multiplying the length and width of a rectangular area or taking one-half of the base multiplied by the height of a triangular area.

A **rectangle** is a four-sided figure with all sides touching at a 90-degree angle (one-quarter of a circle, which has 360 degrees). If any sides meet at an angle greater or less than 90 degrees, another method of computing area must be used.

Area of rectangle = Length × Width

$$A = L \times W$$

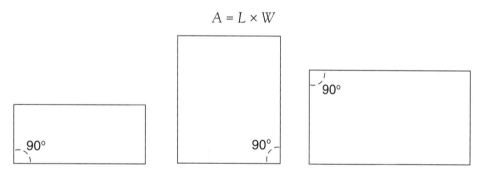

The area of a rectangle is found by multiplying its length by its width. Only units of like measure can be multiplied by each other in deriving area, and the answer will always be in square units of that measure. For example, if feet are multiplied by feet, the resulting area will be in square feet.

F O R   E X A M P L E   Find the area of the following rectangle.

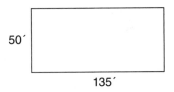

$A = L \times W$

$A = 50 \text{ ft.} \times 135 \text{ ft.}$

$A = 6{,}750 \text{ sq. ft.}$

F O R   E X A M P L E   A property owner is selling a small house that measures 25 feet by 40 feet. What is the square footage of the house?

$A = L \times W$

$A = 25 \text{ ft.} \times 40 \text{ ft.}$

$A = 1{,}000 \text{ sq. ft.}$

The house has 1,000 square feet.

A **triangle** is simply a three-sided figure. We find the area of a triangle by taking half of its base multiplied by its height.

F O R   E X A M P L E   Find the area of a triangle having a base of 80 feet and a height of 40 feet.

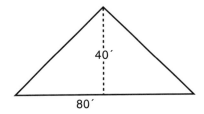

$\text{Area} = \frac{1}{2} (\text{Base} \times \text{Height})$

$A = \frac{1}{2} (BH)$

$A = \frac{1}{2} (80 \text{ feet} \times 40 \text{ feet})$

$A = 1{,}600 \text{ square feet}$

Remember that all units of measure of a given figure must be of the same kind—that is, inches, feet, yards, or whatever unit is used. The answer will always be given in *square* units.

F O R   E X A M P L E   A real estate brokerage is selling a triangular lot with a road frontage of 90 feet and a maximum depth of 600 feet. What is the area of the lot?

$A = \frac{1}{2} (BH)$

$A = \frac{1}{2} (90 \text{ ft.} \times 600 \text{ ft.})$

$A = 27{,}000 \text{ sq. ft.}$

Irregularly shaped property can be measured easily by a nonsurveyor only if its dimensions can be translated into rectangles and triangles.

FOR EXAMPLE The following diagram shows the measurements of a house that is being appraised. What is its square footage, exclusive of the garage space? What is the square footage of the garage space?

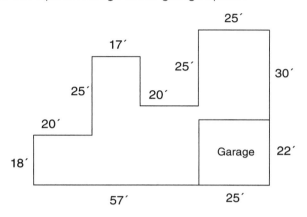

The house is a group of rectangles; the square footage of each of those rectangles can be found, then totaled to find the total square footage of the house.

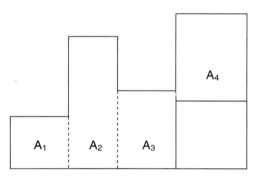

$A = L \times W$

$A_1 = 18 \text{ ft.} \times 20 \text{ ft.}$

$A_2 = 17 \text{ ft.} \times 43 \text{ ft.}$

$A_3 = 20 \text{ ft.} \times 27 \text{ ft.}$

$A_4 = 25 \text{ ft.} \times 30 \text{ ft.}$

$A = (360 + 731 + 540 + 750) \text{ sq. ft.}$

$A = 2,381 \text{ sq. ft. excluding garage}$

Garage area $= 22 \text{ ft.} \times 25 \text{ ft.}$

Garage area $= 550 \text{ sq. ft.}$

Computing Construction Costs

As you learned in Unit 13, there are several different ways to estimate building construction costs. The most basic is the *square-foot method,* using the type of calculations that were covered in the last section.

Ordinary homes and commercial buildings have a certain *cost per square foot,* depending on the quality of construction materials used. That cost may vary from region to region within the state and country, but experience and industry averages can give a fairly accurate figure to use.

FOR EXAMPLE A building contractor has been asked to estimate the cost to build a new house having the dimensions and quality of the house described in the last example. The contractor knows that this type of structure will cost approximately $112 per square foot, including labor and overhead. The garage area can be built for less, $65 per square foot if the ceiling and interior walls are left unfinished. Based on those figures, what is the cost of constructing a new house to the specifications of the existing house?

Living area = 2,381 sq. ft.

2,381 × $112 = $266,672

Garage area = 550 sq. ft.

550 × $65 = $35,750

Total cost = $302,422

In the previous example, total property value will also include land value.

SUMMARY

The mathematical calculations required in the average real estate transaction are not complicated, but they do require familiarity with a few basic concepts and formulas. After you have become comfortable working with percentages, interest, amortization, prorations, and finding area, you will have the groundwork for handling most of the necessary computations.

MATH REVIEW QUESTIONS

1. A sales associate found a buyer for the property located at 611 Prince Edward Road, listed with another firm. The sales associate worked as the buyer's agent in exchange for a commission to his brokerage firm of 2½% of the sales price. The sales associate's share of any commissions he earns is 70%. If the property sold for $756,000, what did he earn?

2. A couple is refinancing their home loan. Their new loan of $175,000 will be at a fixed interest rate of 6.625% for 30 years. The monthly payment is $1,120.54. How much of the first payment will be interest? How much will be principal?

3. Using Table A.1, compute the monthly payment on a loan of $260,000 at an interest rate of 7% for 15 years. Then, find the monthly payment on the same loan for a term of 30 years.

4. A parcel of land on the Old Sonoma Highway is for sale. The parcel is 1,150 feet by 2,400 feet. How many square feet does the parcel contain? How many acres is that?

5. Lois Lovely, a movie star, is building a house in Palm Springs. The house will have 7,200 square feet, and construction is estimated at $265 per square foot. What is the estimated construction cost of the house?

6. A buyer is shopping for a home mortgage loan on the condominium he is purchasing in Long Beach. The purchase price is $780,000 and the buyer will make a 20% down payment. He must choose either a 30-year loan at an interest rate of 6½% or a 15-year loan at an interest rate of 5½%. Which loan will require the smallest monthly payment? What will that payment be?

7. Property in Sunny Glen has appreciated at an average rate of 12% per year for the last four years. If a couple bought a house for $230,000 four years ago, and it appreciated at the average rate, how much is it worth today?

8. Using the facts in problem 7, if the couple made a 10% down payment on their home, and have paid down their mortgage by $8,000, how much equity do they have in their home?

9. The owner of Saguaro Saddles, a horse ranch in Shasta County, is planning to enlarge her facility by purchasing an adjoining parcel. The parcel is listed as "20 acres more or less" and is described as the East ½ of the Northwest ¼ of the Southeast ¼ of Section 15. Do the two descriptions match? If the parcel is priced at $26,600 per acre, what is the total asking price?

10. A vineyard in Temecula was sold for $2,325,000. The total commission on the sale was $116,250. What percentage of the sales price did this represent?

APPENDIX B

INTERNET RESOURCES

The following list contains internet resources that have been mentioned in this book and others that may be of interest to readers. You are encouraged to explore other resources, including the numerous online property listing services and lenders.

Alquist-Priolo Earthquake Fault Zoning Act
www.conservation.ca.gov/CGS/RGHM/AP/Pages/Index.aspx

Appraisal Foundation
www.appraisalfoundation.org

Appraisal Institute
www.appraisalinstitute.org

Association of Real Estate License Law Officials
www.arello.org

California Apartment Association
www.caanet.org

California Association of Business Brokers
www.californiabusinessbrokers.biz

California Association of Community Managers
www.cacm.org

California Association of Mortgage Professionals
www.ca-amp.org

California Association of REALTORS® (CAR)
Information on courses to obtain the GRI (Graduate, REALTOR® Institute) designation in California is available at www.eDesignations.com.
www.car.org

California Building Industry Association
www.cbia.org

California Bureau of Real Estate (BRE)
www.bre.ca.gov

California Bureau of Real Estate Appraisers (BREA)
www.brea.ca.gov

California Coastal Commission
www.coastal.ca.gov

California Department of Business Oversight
www.dbo.ca.gov

California Department of Conservation
www.conservation.ca.gov

California Department of Finance
www.dof.ca.gov

California Department of Housing and Community Development
www.hcd.ca.gov

California Department of Insurance
www.insurance.ca.gov

California Department of Veterans Affairs (CDVA)
www.cdva.ca.gov

California Energy Commission
www.energy.ca.gov

California Environmental Protection Agency
www.calepa.ca.gov

California Fair Employment and Housing Act
www.dfeh.ca.gov/Publications_FEHADescr.htm

California Housing Finance Agency (CalFHA)
www.calhfa.ca.gov

California Legislative Information
http://leginfo.legislature.ca.gov

California Mortgage Bankers Association
www.cmba.com

City of San Diego
www.sandiego.gov

Consumer Financial Protection Bureau
www.cfpb.gov

Contractors' State License Board
www.cslb.ca.gov

Department of Housing and Urban Development (HUD)
www.hud.gov

Department of Veterans Affairs (VA)
www.va.gov

Environmental Protection Agency (EPA)
www.epa.gov

Equifax
www.equifax.com

Executive Council of Homeowners
www.echo-ca.org

Experian
www.experian.com

Fannie Mae (FNMA)
www.fanniemae.com

Federal Home Loan Mortgage Corporation (FHLMC)
www.freddiemac.com

Federal Housing Finance Agency
www.fhfa.gov

Federal Reserve Bank System (the Fed)
www.federalreserve.gov

Franchise Tax Board
www.ftb.ca.gov

Ginnie Mae
www.ginniemae.gov

Inman Real Estate News Service
www.inman.com

Internal Revenue Service (IRS)
www.irs.gov

International Code Council (ICC)
www.iccsafe.org

League of California Cities
www.cacities.org

Los Angeles County
www.lacounty.gov

Los Angeles County Assessor Online Public Service
http://assessor.lacounty.gov

National Association of Home Builders
www.nahb.org

National Association of Real Estate Brokers, Inc. (NAREB)
www.nareb.com

National Association of Real Estate Investment Trusts
www.nareit.com

National Association of REALTORS® (NAR)
www.realtor.com
www.realtor.org

National Lead Information Center (NLIC)
www.epa.gov/lead/forms/lead-hotline-national-lead-information-center

Nationwide Mortgage Licensing System
www.nmls.org

Office of the Comptroller of the Currency
www.occ.gov

Real Estate Educators Association
www.reea.org

Realty Times
www.realtytimes.com

San Francisco Solar Incentive Program
www.sfwater.org/index.aspx?page=133

Secretary of State Business Service Center
www.sos.ca.gov/business/

Small Business Administration
www.sba.gov

State Bar of California
www.calbar.ca.gov

State Board of Equalization
www.boe.ca.gov

State Controller's Office
www.sco.ca.gov

State of California
www.ca.gov

TrueForms
www.trueforms.com

United States Geological Survey
www.usgs.gov

GLOSSARY

abandonment Giving up possession or ownership of property by nonuse, usually accompanied by some affirmative act, such as removing one's belongings from an apartment.

abstract of judgment Document stipulating the outcome of a legal action, which can be filed in any county where the judgment debtor has property.

abstract of title A summary or digest of all recorded transfers, conveyances, legal proceedings, and any other facts relied on as evidence of title to show continuity of ownership and indicate any possible impairments to title.

acceleration clause A provision in a real estate financing instrument that allows the lender to declare the remaining indebtedness due and payable on the happening of certain conditions, such as the sale of the property or the borrower's default in payment.

acceptance Indication by the person to whom an offer is made (the *offeree*) of agreement to the terms of the offer. If the offer requires a writing, the acceptance must also be in writing.

accession The process of manufactured or natural improvement or addition to property.

accounting The obligation to account for all money or property belonging to the principal.

accretion Accession by natural forces, such as alluvion.

acknowledgment A formal declaration made before an authorized person by a person who has executed a written instrument, stating that the execution of the instrument is the person's own act.

acquisition cost For FHA-insured loans, the price to procure property, including purchase price and all nonrecurring closing costs, including discount points, FHA application fee, service charge and credit report, FHA appraisal, escrow, document preparation, title insurance, termite inspection, reconveyance, and recording fees.

acre A measure of land equaling 160 square rods, 4,840 square yards, or 43,560 square feet, or a tract about 208.71 feet square.

action for declaratory relief Legal proceeding brought to determine the respective rights of the parties before a controversy arises.

action to quiet title A court proceeding brought to establish title to real property.

actual age The number of years since completion of a building; also called *historical* or *chronological* age.

actual authority The authority an agent has because it is specified in the agency agreement, or that the agent believes she has because of an unintentional or a careless act of the principal.

actual fraud A deliberate misrepresentation or a representation made in reckless disregard of its truth or falsity; the suppression of truth; a promise made without the intention to perform it; or any other act intended to deceive.

adjustable-rate mortgage (ARM) Finance instrument whose interest rate will vary according to the change in an identified index or rate, such as the 11th District Cost of Funds.

adjustable-rate note Promissory note that serves as evidence of a debt that carries an interest rate that will vary according to the change in an identified index or rate, such as the 11th District Cost of Funds.

adjusted cost basis Purchase price of property plus cost of specified improvements, less any depreciation deductions taken on the property.

adjusted gross income Income from all sources less deductions for taxes, depreciation, and other allowable deductions.

administrator Personal representative of the estate of a decedent, appointed by the probate court. *See also* executor.

ad valorem A Latin phrase meaning "according to value" that is used to describe a tax charged in relation to the value of the property taxed.

adverse possession A method of acquiring title to real property by occupying the property against the interests of the true owner and fulfilling other statutory requirements.

affirmative fraud A deliberate statement of a material fact that the speaker knows to be false and on which the speaker intends another person to rely to his detriment.

after-acquired title If title is acquired by a grantor only after a conveyance to a grantee, the deed to the grantee becomes effective at the time the grantor receives title.

agency The relationship between a principal and the agent of the principal that arises out of a contract, whether express or implied, written or oral, by which the agent is employed by the principal to do certain acts dealing with a third party.

agency confirmation form Written statement required for a residential transaction involving property of one to four residential units, in the wording required by the California Civil Code, and signed by the property seller as well as the listing agent and selling agent (if different from the listing agent), that indicates the seller's understanding of the relationship of the seller to the listing and selling agent in the transaction.

agency disclosure form Written statement required for a residential transaction involving property of one to four residential units, using the wording required by the California Civil Code, and signed by both buyer and seller in a transaction, that explains the various relationships of those involved in a residential property sale.

agent One who acts for and with authority from another person, called the *principal*; a *special* agent is appointed to carry out a particular act or transaction, and any other agent is a *general* agent.

air rights The real property right to the reasonable use of the airspace above the surface of the land.

alienation The transferring of property to another; an involuntary transfer of title.

alienation clause *See* due-on-sale clause.

all-inclusive trust deed *See* wraparound mortgage or trust deed.

alluvion Alluvium; the increase of soil along the bank of a body of water by natural forces.

amortized loan The payment of a financial obligation in installments; recovery over a period of cost or value. A loan has negative amortization when the loan payments do not cover all of the interest due, which then is added to the remaining loan balance.

anchor bolts Bolts that fasten the sill plate of a wood-frame house to the house's foundation, required in California since 1931 for all new construction as an earthquake safety measure.

annual percentage rate (APR) The relative cost of credit as determined in accordance with Regulation Z of the Consumer Financial Protection Bureau for implementing the federal Truth in Lending Act.

anticipation, principle of Expectation that property will offer future benefits, which tends to increase present value.

apparent authority Authority to act as an agent that someone appears to have but does not have, which will place no obligation on the party the agent claims to represent if that party is in no way responsible for the representation.

appraisal An estimate of a property's monetary value on the open market; an estimate of a property's type and condition, its utility for a given purpose, or its highest and best use.

appropriation, right of *See* right of appropriation.

appurtenance Anything affixed (attached) to or used with land for its benefit that is transferred with the land.

APR *See* annual percentage rate.

area Measure of the floor or ground space within the perimeter of a building or land parcel.

arm's-length transaction A transaction in which neither party acts under duress and both have full knowledge of the property's assets and defects, the property involved has been on the market a reasonable length of time, there are no unusual circumstances, and the price represents the normal consideration for the property sold, without unusual financing terms.

asbestos Naturally occurring fibrous silicate mineral linked with various forms of cancer if inhaled and which, until the mid-1970s, was used for its insulating properties in spray-on and batting applications in homes and commercial structures; remediation can be by containment or removal and requires following strict procedures. Information on asbestos detection and removal can be found at www.epa.gov/asbestos.

assessed value A valuation placed on a piece of property by a public authority as a basis for levying taxes on that property.

assessor The official responsible for determining assessed values.

assignee Party to whom an assignment of rights is made.

assignment Transfer of rights from one party to another, usually for compensation.

assignor Party making an assignment of rights to someone else.

associate licensee A real estate salesperson or broker who works as the employee of a real estate broker.

assumption An undertaking or adoption of a debt or an obligation resting primarily on another person.

attachment The process by which real or personal property of a party to a lawsuit is seized and retained in the custody of the court.

attorney-at-law Someone licensed by the state to practice law.

attorney-in-fact An agent who has been granted a power of attorney by a principal.

avulsion The tearing or washing away of land along the bank of a body of water by natural forces.

backfill Dirt placed against the foundation of a structure after the concrete used to create the foundation wall has cured and the wood forms in which the concrete was poured have been removed.

balance, principle of The combination of land uses that results in the highest property values overall.

balloon payment An installment payment on a promissory note—usually the final payment—that is significantly larger than the other installment payments.

bankruptcy A federal court proceeding in which the court takes possession of the assets of an insolvent debtor and sells the nonexempt assets to pay off creditors on a pro rata basis; title to the debtor's assets is held by a *trustee in bankruptcy*.

base lines Imaginary lines that run east-west and intersect meridians that run north-south to form the starting point for land measurement using the rectangular survey system of land description.

base value For property tax assessment purposes, the full cash value of a parcel of real estate as of February 28, 1975, or the date of a subsequent sale or other reassessment event.

basis Cost basis is the dollar amount assigned to property at the time of acquisition under provisions of the Internal Revenue Code for the purpose of determining gain, loss, and depreciation in calculating the income tax to be paid on the sale or exchange of the property; adjusted cost basis is derived after the application of certain additions, such as for improvements, and deductions, such as for depreciation.

basis point For financing and investment purposes, $z/z/l$ of 1%.

beneficiary One on whose behalf a trustee holds property conveyed by a trustor; the lender under a deed of trust.

beneficiary statement Document provided by the lender if the buyer of a property encumbered by an existing loan will take title to the property subject to that loan.

benefit assessment Amount owed by owners of property that is enhanced by the construction or renovation of improvements.

bequest Transfer of property, particularly personal property, called a legacy, by will. *See also* devise.

bilateral contract Agreement in which both parties make a promise to do something or to refrain from doing something and both are obligated to fulfill the promise.

bill of sale Written instrument that conveys title to personal property.

binding contract An agreement that can be enforced in a court of law if one of the parties to the agreement fails to fulfill any of its terms.

blind ad Ad in which the name of the person placing the ad is not mentioned.

blockbusting The practice on the part of unscrupulous speculators or real estate agents of inducing panic selling of homes at prices below-market value, especially by exploiting the prejudices of property owners in neighborhoods in which the racial makeup is changing or appears to be on the verge of changing.

bond An obligation; a real estate bond is a written obligation issued on security of a mortgage or trust deed.

book value The current value for accounting purposes of an asset expressed as original cost plus capital additions minus accumulated depreciation.

boot Cash received in an exchange of property in addition to the property.

bracing Use of one or more construction methods, such as plywood wall sheathing, to enable a structure to withstand the pressures caused by high winds and earth movement. Information on bracing systems can be found at the website of the Engineered Wood Association, www.wallbracing.org.

breach of contract The failure of a duty imposed by law or by contract, either by omission or commission.

broker-officer A licensed broker who is an officer of a brokerage that is set up as a corporation and who is designated as the broker responsible for supervision of licensed employees of the brokerage.

broker's price opinion (BPO) An estimate of property value that is not an appraisal but is developed by a real estate broker based on comparable sales in the area.

brownfield A site identified by the Environmental Protection Agency as containing hazardous substances, pollutants, or contaminants. Information on brownfields can be found at www.epa.gov/brownfields.

building code Standards for building, planning, and construction established by state law and local ordinance.

building permit Approval granted by the appropriate municipal, county, or other governing authority to begin construction of an improvement to real estate following review of the building plan submitted by the permit applicant and revision of the plan as required.

bulk transfer of goods Any transfer of a substantial part of the materials, supplies, merchandise, equipment, or other inventory of a business that is *not* in the ordinary course of the business's activities.

bundle of rights The legal rights of ownership of real property, including the rights of possession, use, disposition, and exclusion of others from the property.

Business and Professions Code California code that contains the Real Estate Law, which includes real estate licensing, transaction requirements, and the Subdivided Lands Law.

business opportunity The assets of an existing business enterprise, including its goodwill.

California Bureau of Real Estate (CalBRE) California agency that administers the Real Estate Law, including the licensing of real estate brokers and salespeople.

California Bureau of Real Estate Appraisers (BREA) California office that licenses and regulates real estate appraisers. Information can be found at www.brea.ca.gov.

California Department of Business Oversight (DBO) California agency that regulates licensees and industries formerly under the control of the Department of Corporations and Department of Financial Institutions. More information is available at www.dbo.ca.gov/Licensees/default.asp.

California Department of Insurance California agency that regulates insurers; found at www.insurance.ca.gov.

California Department of Public Health California agency that regulates construction activities affecting the water supply and other public health issues; formerly part of the California Department of Health Services. Information on the agency's mission and services can be found at www.cdph.ca.gov.

California finance lender Licensee under the California Finance Lenders Law who is in the business of making consumer loans or commercial loans in which personal property may be used as collateral. More information is available at www.dbo.ca.gov/Licensees/default.asp.

California Finance Lenders Law *See* California finance lender.

California Foreclosure Reduction Act Effective January 1, 2013, revised procedure for nonjudicial foreclosures; also known as the California Homeowner Bill of Rights.

California Franchise Tax Board California department that collects state personal income taxes and bank and corporation taxes.

California Homeowner Bill of Rights *See* California Foreclosure Reduction Act.

California Housing Finance Agency (CalHFA) Chartered in 1975 as a self-supported affordable housing bank to make low-interest loans funded by the sale of tax-exempt bonds. CalHFA bonds are repaid by mortgage loan revenue.

California Residential Mortgage Lending Act Part of the California Financial Code that regulates mortgage bankers. Information can be found at www.dbo.ca.gov/Licensees/default.asp.

California Solar Initiative State law effective January 1, 2008, that requires municipal utilities to offer a solar incentive program to customers.

CalVet loan Home or farm loan procured through the California Veterans Farm and Home Purchase Program.

capital assets Assets of a permanent nature used in the production of income, such as land, buildings, machinery, and equipment; usually distinguishable under income tax law from "inventory," assets held for sale to customers in the ordinary course of the taxpayer's trade or business.

capital gain The amount by which the net resale proceeds of a capital item exceed the adjusted cost basis of the item.

capitalization rate The rate of interest that is considered a reasonable return on an investment, used in the process of determining value based on net operating income; the yield necessary to attract investment.

capitalization recapture The return of an investment; an amortization rate based on the right of the investor to get back the purchase price at the end of the term of ownership or over the productive life of the improvements.

cash flow The net income generated by a property before depreciation and other noncash expenses.

caveat emptor Latin phrase meaning "Let the buyer beware."

CC&Rs Covenants, conditions, and restrictions; limitations on land use imposed by deed, usually when land is subdivided, as a means of regulating building construction, density, and use for the benefit of other property owners; may be referred to simply as *restrictions*.

certificate of discharge Document that is recorded by a mortgagee as evidence of the release of the mortgagee's lien rights.

certificate of eligibility Issued by the Department of Veterans Affairs (VA) to a veteran who qualifies for a loan guaranteed by the VA. Information on how to apply can be obtained at www.homeloans.va.gov.

certificate of occupancy (CO) Issued by the applicable building department of the municipal, county, or other jurisdiction in which the property is located when a structure has met all requirements and can be placed into service.

certificate of redemption Issued by the county tax collector when all past-due amounts have been paid.

certificate of sale Document received by the buyer at an execution or a judicial foreclosure sale; replaced by a sheriff's deed if the debtor fails to redeem the property during the statutory redemption period.

certificate of status Document issued by California secretary of state showing a corporation's place of domicile, date of incorporation, corporate number, name and address of agent for service of process, and other information.

certificate of title Statement of a property's owner of record as well as any existing encumbrances.

chain of title The history of the conveyances and encumbrances affecting the present owner's title to property, as far back as records are available.

change, principle of Effect on property value of constantly varying physical, economic, social, and political forces.

change in ownership statement Document indicating former and present owner of real estate that must be filed with the county recorder or assessor within 45 days of the date that the transfer is recorded.

chattel mortgage Use of personal property to secure or guarantee a promissory note.

chattel real An estate related to real estate, such as a lease of real property.

chattels Personal property; any property that is not real property.

city planning Land-use recommendations adopted by local jurisdiction, determined by use of demographic, geographic, economic, and other data.

civil law Legal system based on laws and regulations, without the influence of judicial decisions as in the common law system.

Civil Rights Act of 1866 Law that prohibits racial discrimination in every property transaction.

Civil Rights Housing Act of 2006 As of January 1, 2007, extends protected classifications of the Fair Employment and Housing Act (FEHA) to all California laws prohibiting discrimination in housing and housing-related areas, including real estate licensure and mortgage lending, and automatically includes any protected classes that are added to FEHA.

close of escrow Date on which all requirements of a real estate transaction have been fulfilled, documents are transmitted, and funds are transferred.

closing The completion of a real estate transaction, at which point required documents are transmitted and funds are transferred.

Closing Disclosure New form mandated by the TILA-RESPA rule that helps consumers to understand all the costs of the transaction. It must be provided to consumers three business days before closing.

cloud on the title Any claim, condition, or encumbrance that impairs title to real property.

coastal zone An area of about 1,800 square miles that runs the length of the state from the sea inland about 1,000 yards, with wider spots in coastal estuarine, habitat, and recreational areas; any development or improvement of land within the coastal zone must meet local requirements for coastal conservation and preservation of resources, as authorized by the California Coastal Act and subsequent legislation.

codes Bound volumes of laws and regulations.

codicil Written amendment to a will, made with the same legal formalities.

color of title A claim of possession to real property based on a document erroneously appearing to convey title to the claimant.

commercial acre That portion of an acre of newly subdivided land remaining after dedication for streets, sidewalks, parks, and so on.

commercial frustration Excuse for failure to perform contract obligation because of changed circumstances that make a purchase uneconomic; also called impracticability of performance.

commingling Placing funds in an inappropriate financial account, such as depositing a deposit check in a broker's business account instead of a trust account.

commission An agent's compensation for performing the duties of the agency; in real estate practice, typically a percentage of the selling price of property, rentals, or other property value.

common interest subdivision An area of land divided into separate parcels but with some of the land set aside for shared ownership by all of the owners of the separate parcels.

common law The body of law from England based on custom, usage, and court decisions.

common-law dedication Transfer of private land to public use or ownership, such as a roadway through a subdivision, by permitting such use or referencing the use in deeds to adjoining parcels.

community apartment project A form of subdivision in which the owner has an individual interest in the land and exclusive right of occupancy of an apartment on the land.

community property All property acquired by spouses during marriage except that qualifying as separate property.

community property with right of survivorship Method of property ownership by a married couple that specifically provides for transfer of the interest of the first to die to the spouse, instead of the interest being willed or passed by intestate succession.

community redevelopment agency (CRA) An agency authorized by state law but formed by a local governing body to rehabilitate existing structures, bringing new development, or both. All CRAs have been dissolved as of February 1, 2012.

comparative market analysis Informal estimate of market value performed by a real estate agent for either seller or buyer, utilizing the sales history of nearby properties; usually expressed as a range of values that includes the probable market value of the subject property.

compensation Money, goods, or other thing of value transferred in exchange for performance of a contract obligation.

competition, principle of Business profits encourage competition, which ultimately may reduce profits for any one business.

compound interest Interest paid on original principal and also on the accrued and unpaid interest that has accumulated as the debt matures.

comps Comparable properties that are used in an appraisal to determine the value of the property that is the subject of the appraisal.

concurrent ownership Ownership of property by more than one person, not necessarily in equal shares.

condemnation *See* eminent domain.

condition A qualification of an estate granted that can be imposed only in a conveyance; it can be a condition precedent or a condition subsequent. *See also* CC&Rs.

conditional delivery Transfer of documents and funds to escrow agent or settlement officer to be held until the transaction is closed, at which time they are transferred to the designated party.

conditional use permit Authorization for a land use that would otherwise not be permitted by zoning ordinances.

condition subsequent A stipulation in a contract or transfer of property that already has taken effect that will extinguish the contract or defeat the property transfer.

condominium A subdivision providing an exclusive ownership (fee) interest in the airspace of a particular portion of real property, as well as an interest in common in a portion of that property.

confidentiality Obligation to safeguard the principal's confidence and secrets (any information that might weaken the principal's bargaining position if it were revealed).

conflict of interest Anything that benefits an agent's self-interest or that of someone related to the agent, which would interfere with the objective fulfillment of an agent's obligations to a principal.

conforming loan A loan that meets the requirements established for purchase by Fannie Mae.

conformity, principle of Holds that property values are maximized when buildings are similar in design, construction, and age, particularly in residential neighborhoods.

consideration Anything of value given or promised by a party to induce another to enter into a contract; may be a benefit conferred on one party or a detriment suffered by the other.

construction loan *See* interim loan.

constructive eviction Interference by the landlord in a tenant's legitimate use of leased property, such as by making unwarranted alterations to the property.

constructive fraud Any representation made without a deliberate intent to deceive.

Consumer Financial Protection Bureau Federal agency created by the Dodd-Frank Wall Street Reform and Consumer Protection Act of 2010 to create and coordinate regulations intended to correct the mortgage lending practices that led to the housing crisis of 2007–2010.

contract A written or an oral agreement to do or not to do certain things. There may be an *express* agreement of the parties or a contract may be *implied* by their conduct. A *unilateral* contract imposes an obligation on only one of the parties, whereas both parties to a *bilateral* contract have an obligation to perform. A contract is *executory* when a contract obligation is to be performed in the future, and *executed* when all obligations have been performed and the contract transaction has been completed. A real estate contract must be a signed writing made by competent parties, for valuable consideration, with an offer by one party that is accepted by the other.

Contractor's State License Board State agency that licenses and regulates building contractors. Can be found at www.cslb.ca.gov.

contract rent The rent agreed to by lessor and lessee.

contractual obligation The agreed-on performance by one of the parties to a contract.

contribution, principle of A component part of a property is valued in proportion to its contribution to the value of the entire property, regardless of its separate actual cost.

conventional loan A loan secured by a mortgage or trust deed that is made without governmental underwriting (FHA-insured or VA-guaranteed).

cooperating broker The broker who finds a buyer for property listed for sale by another broker.

cooperating split Sharing of the compensation (usually, a commission) received by the listing broker with the broker who brings the buyer to the transaction.

cooperative apartment *See* stock cooperative.

corporation A legal entity that acts through its board of directors and officers, generally without liability on the part of the person or persons owning it. A domestic corporation is one chartered in California—any other corporation is a foreign corporation in California.

correction lines Guide meridians running every 24 miles east and west of a meridian, and standard parallels running every 24 miles north and south of a base line, used to correct inaccuracies in the rectangular survey system of land description caused by the earth's curvature.

correlative use Doctrine that states that property owners may use a reasonable amount of water from an underground source, but not to the detriment of adjoining property owners. Information about California water rights can be found at the website of the Bureau of Land Management, www.blm.gov/nstc /WaterLaws/california.html.

Costa-Hawkins Rental Housing Act California law that preempts rent control for new construction, single-family residences, and multiunit buildings in jurisdictions with vacancy control ordinances.

cost approach Appraisal method in which site value is added to the present reproduction or replacement cost of all property improvements, less depreciation, to determine market value.

counteroffer Any change to the terms of an offer, made in response to it.

county assessor Official responsible for determining property values for ad valorem taxation purposes.

covenant An agreement or a promise to do or not to do a particular act, usually imposed by deed. *See also* CC&Rs.

covenant of quiet enjoyment Promise of a landlord, implied by law, not to interfere in the possession or use of leased property by the tenant.

covenant to repair Express or legally implied obligation of the landlord to make necessary repairs to leased premises.

crawl space Area beneath lowest level of structure, usually unpaved, that is less than the height requirement to qualify as a basement.

creative financing Alternative (noninstitutional) financing that makes use of a seller carryback or other loan; useful when interest rates on institutional loans are relatively high or when borrower cannot qualify for a loan from a depository institution based on income or credit rating.

credit-bid Bid by lender at a foreclosure sale represented by the amount of the outstanding indebtedness owed to the lender by the defaulting borrower.

decedent Person who has died.

declaration of default Notice, accompanied by original note and trust deed, provided by lender (beneficiary) to trustee on default of trustor (borrower), stating the reason for the default.

declaration of homestead *See* homestead.

decline Period in which property loses value due to lack of maintenance.

dedication The giving of land by its owner for a public use, and the acceptance of the land for such use by the appropriate government officials.

deductions Amounts on which income tax need not be paid; the home mortgage interest deduction from taxable income benefits homeowners.

deed Written instrument that, when properly executed and delivered, conveys title to real property from a grantor to a grantee.

deed in lieu of foreclosure A deed to real property accepted by a lender from a defaulting borrower to avoid the necessity of foreclosure proceedings by the lender.

deed of reconveyance Deed from trustee to trustor, at the request of beneficiary of trust (lender), that returns title to the trustor on payment of the indebtedness secured by the deed of trust.

deed of trust *See* trust deed.

deed restriction Provision placed in a deed by the grantor that limits the property's use or requires the grantee to fulfill requirements of subdivision covenants, conditions, and restrictions (CC&Rs).

default Failure by one of the parties to a contract to fulfill one or more of the obligations imposed by the contract.

defendant A person against whom legal action is initiated for the purpose of obtaining criminal sanctions (in a case involving violation of a penal statute) or damages or other appropriate judicial relief (in a civil case).

deficiency judgment A judgment given by a court when the value of security pledged for a loan is insufficient to pay off the debt of the defaulting borrower.

demand for payoff Lender's statement of remaining indebtedness that will be paid at closing on transfer of the property securing the debt.

Department of Fair Employment and Housing California agency that enforces antidiscrimination laws; found at www.dfeh.ca.gov.

Department of Housing and Community Development State agency that carries out California's State Housing Law by adopting building standards and administrative regulations that ensure safe and durable housing while safeguarding affordability; found at www.hcd.ca.gov.

Department of Housing and Urban Development (HUD) Federal agency that carries out the purposes of the National Housing Act by, among other things, enforcing fair housing laws and supervising the activities of the Federal Housing Administration (FHA), which insures home mortgage loans; found at www.hud.gov.

depreciation Decrease in value of an asset that is allowed in computing property value for tax purposes; in appraising, a loss in the value of a property improvement from any cause; depreciation is *curable* when it can be remedied by a repair or an addition to the property, and it is *incurable* when there is no easy or economic way to cure the loss. *See also* physical deterioration, functional obsolescence, and external obsolescence.

devise Transfer of title to property by will. *See also* bequest.

devisee Person receiving title to property by will. *See also* legatee.

devisor One who wills property to another.

Direct Endorsement Plan Program that allows lenders to qualify to make FHA-insured loans without prior HUD review, except for construction projects.

discharged contract An agreement that has been terminated, whether by *performance* of its terms; *rescission* of the parties; *release* by one party at the request of the other party; formation of a new contract, called a *novation*; change in the terms of the agreement, called a *reformation*; *assignment* of the contract to a new party; or *breach* by one of the parties by failure to fulfill the terms of the agreement.

discount points *See* points.

discount rate Interest rate charged member banks by Federal Reserve Banks.

documentary transfer tax A tax applied on all transfers of real property located in a county that the county is authorized by the state to collect; notice of payment is entered on the face of the deed or on a separate paper filed with the deed.

dominant tenement *See* easement.

donee One who receives a gift.

donor One who makes a gift.

downspout Part of the rainwater drainage system that conducts water from a gutter that runs along a roof eave to ground level.

drywall Plasterboard, also called wallboard, used for interior wall finishing.

dual agency An agency relationship in which the agent represents two principals in their dealings with each other.

due diligence Acting with the appropriate degree of skill and care in fulfilling one's responsibilities under an agency or other contractual relationship.

due-on-sale clause An acceleration clause in a real estate financing instrument granting the lender the right to demand full payment of the remaining indebtedness on a sale of the property.

duty of care The obligation of principal to agent that the principal will not interfere with the agent's prospective economic advantage—the agent's business activities.

earthquake fault zone As defined by the state geologist, the area in such close proximity to an earthquake fault that movement of the fault presents a property hazard; location within an earthquake fault zone must be disclosed to a prospective purchaser by the seller (or seller's agent, if there is one).

easement The right to a specific use of or the right to travel over the land of another. The land being used or traveled over is the *servient tenement;* the land that is benefited by the use is the *dominant tenement.* An *easement appurtenant* is a property interest that belongs to the owner of the dominant tenement and is transferred with the land; an *easement in gross* is a personal right that usually is not transferable by its owner.

easement appurtenant An easement right that is transferred along with title to the land that benefits from the easement.

easement by condemnation Taking of an easement right by a public entity.

easement by implication of law An easement that will be created by law to provide access to a parcel of land that is otherwise landlocked.

easement by necessity An easement right over the land of the grantor of adjacent property that would otherwise be landlocked.

easement by prescription Acquiring a specific use of or the right to travel over the land of another by statutory requirements similar to those for adverse possession.

easement in gross An easement right with no accompanying property ownership right.

eave Portion of roof that extends over the exterior wall.

economic life The time over which an improved property will yield a return on investment over and above the return attributable solely to the land.

economic obsolescence *See* external obsolescence.

economic rent The reasonable rental expectancy if the property were available for renting at the time of its valuation.

effective gross income Property income from all sources, less allowance for vacancy and collection losses.

Electronic Signatures in Global and National Commerce Act Enacted by Congress in 2000 to facilitate the use of electronic records and signatures in interstate and foreign commerce by ensuring the validity and legal effect of contracts entered into electronically.

emancipated minor A person under the age of 18 who is married, in the military service, or determined by a court to be legally able to enter into a contract as an adult.

emblements Crops produced annually by labor and industry as distinguished from crops that grow naturally on the land.

eminent domain The right of the government to acquire title to property for public use by condemnation; the property owner receives compensation—generally fair market value. *See also* inverse condemnation.

employee Person who is hired by someone else to perform work; for purposes of the Real Estate Law, a real estate salesperson is always considered an employee under the supervision of the employing broker; for tax purposes, a real estate salesperson working for a real estate broker can be hired as an employee or as an independent contractor, if the requirements of the Internal Revenue Service are met.

employer Person who hires someone else to perform work. *See also* employee.

encroachment The unlawful intrusion of a property improvement onto adjacent property.

encumbrance Anything that affects or limits the fee simple title to or affects the condition or use of real estate.

energy-efficiency ratio (EER) Measure of an electrical appliance's energy consumption found by dividing its capacity measured in British thermal units (Btu) by the number of watts of electricity needed to run it. Information on the EER in a variety of applications can be found at www.energysavers.gov.

environmental impact report (EIR) Evaluation of effects on the environment of a proposed development; may be required by local government.

environmental obsolescence *See* external obsolescence.

Equal Credit Opportunity Act Federal law intended to ensure that all consumers are given an equal chance to obtain credit. Information is available at www.consumer.ftc.gov.

equal dignities rule Requires a writing if an agreement (such as a listing agreement) involves a transaction (such as the sale of real estate) that requires a writing.

equilibrium Period of stability in the life cycle of a building or neighborhood in which little change is evident.

equitable estoppel Common-law doctrine that requires transfer of title to property if seller acquires title only after a purported sale of the property to someone else; intended to prevent unjust enrichment.

equity Difference between current market value and the remaining indebtedness on a property; free-and-clear property value.

equity of redemption The right to redeem property during the foreclosure period, or during a statutorily prescribed time following a foreclosure sale.

erosion Process of wearing away of the surface of the land by the action of the elements, most conspicuously at a time of heavy rainfall.

escalator clause Provision in a lease agreement for an increase in payments based on an increase in an index such as the consumer price index.

escheat The reverting of property to the state when there are no heirs capable of inheriting.

escrow The deposit of instruments, funds (with instructions), or both with a neutral third party to carry out the provisions of an agreement or a contract.

escrow agent *See* escrow holder.

escrow holder Escrow agent or escrow officer; neutral third party who holds in trust the funds and documents necessary to complete a transaction until all of the terms of the underlying agreement have been fulfilled, at which time the funds are disbursed and documents transferred as required.

escrow instructions Written instructions to the escrow holder specifying the terms under which the escrow is to be conducted, including the contract or other requirements that are to be fulfilled as part of the escrow proceeding; change in the escrow instructions requires agreement of both parties to the underlying contract.

escrow officer *See* escrow holder.

estate The interest held by the owner of property.

estate at sufferance The occupancy of a tenant after the lease term expires.

estate at will A tenancy in which the tenant's time of possession is indefinite.

estate for years A tenancy for a fixed term.

estate from period to period Periodic tenancy; a tenancy for a fixed term, automatically renewed for the same term unless owner or tenant gives the other written notice of intention to terminate the tenancy.

estates of tenancy *See* leasehold estate.

estate tax Federal or state tax on the value of property owned by a decedent at the time of death.

estoppel A bar against future conduct. By acting as if an agency relationship exists, a principal is prevented by estoppel from denying it in future.

eviction Dispossession by process of law.

exchange A means of trading equities in two or more real properties, treated as a single transaction through a single escrow.

exclusive agency listing A listing agreement employing a broker as sole agent for a seller of real property under the terms of which the broker is entitled to compensation if the property is sold through any other broker, but not if a sale is negotiated by the owner without the services of an agent.

exclusive authorization and right-to-sell listing A listing agreement employing a broker as agent for a seller of real property under the terms of which the broker is entitled to compensation if the listed property is sold during the duration of the listing, whether by the listing agent, another agent, or the owner acting without the services of an agent.

executed contract Written agreement that has been signed by all parties; agreement that has been completed according to its terms.

executor Personal representative of the estate of a decedent, named in the decedent's will. *See also* administrator.

executory contract Agreement with terms that have not yet been completed.

express agent Agent identified in written or oral agency agreement.

express agreement An agreement established by written or oral communication of the parties that both parties acknowledge as their intention.

express contract *See* express agreement.

express reservation Property interest identified in deed as retained by grantor.

extended-coverage policy Policy of title insurance, primarily intended for the benefit of lenders, that includes coverage of items that would ordinarily be discovered by a property inspection, such as rights of parties in possession of the property.

external obsolescence Economic or environmental obsolescence; loss in value due to outside causes, such as changes in nearby land use.

Fair and Accurate Credit Transactions Act of 2003 (FACTA) Federal law that amended the Fair Credit Reporting Act (FCRA) to create procedures to assist consumers who are victims of identity theft.

Fair Credit Reporting Act (FCRA) Federal law detailing consumer rights in loan transactions involving credit reports.

Fair Employment and Housing Act (FEHA) California law that provides protection from harassment or discrimination in employment or housing on the basis of age (40 and over), ancestry, color, religious creed, denial of family and medical care leave, disability (mental and physical) including HIV and AIDS, marital status, medical condition (cancer and genetic characteristics), national origin, race, religion, sex, and sexual orientation. Information about enforcement procedures can be found at www.dfeh.ca.gov.

Fair Housing Act Federal law that prohibits discrimination in provision of housing on the basis of race, color, religion, sex, national origin, ancestry, disability, or familial status; Title VIII of the Civil Rights Act of 1968. Full text of the Fair Housing Act can be found at www.justice.gov/crt/about/hce.

Fair Housing Amendments Act of 1988 Expanded federal protections against discrimination in provision of housing to include families with children and persons with disabilities.

Fannie Mae Formerly the Federal National Mortgage Association; created in 1938 to provide a secondary mortgage market for federally related mortgage loans; now also purchases conventional mortgage loans. Information can be found at www.fanniemae.com and www.efanniemae.com.

Farmer Mac Provides financing of agricultural real estate and rural housing loans and liquidity to agricultural and rural housing lenders; found at www.farmermac.com.

Federal Depository Insurance Corporation (FDIC) Insures savings, checking, and other deposit accounts in insured institutions, up to $250,000 per depositor, per insured bank, for each ownership category; found at www.fdic .gov.

federal funds rate The interest rate at which depository institutions lend balances at the Federal Reserve to other depository institutions overnight. Discussion and historical rates can be found at www.federalreserve.gov /monetarypolicy/fomc.htm.

Federal Housing Administration (FHA) Created in 1934 to provide mortgage insurance on loans made by FHA-approved lenders throughout the United States; part of the Department of Housing and Urban Development; found at www.fha.com.

Federal Housing Finance Agency Federal agency created following the merger of the Federal Housing Finance Board (FHFB) and the Office of Federal Housing Enterprise Oversight (OFHEO).

federally related transaction Transaction that involves a federally chartered or insured lender.

Federal Reserve System (the Fed) Central banking system of the United States that regulates the flow of money and cost of credit; found at www.federalreserve.gov.

fee simple absolute A fee simple estate with no restrictions on its use.

fee simple defeasible An interest in land, such as a fee simple conditional or fee simple with special limitation, that may result in the estate of ownership being defeated.

fee simple estate The greatest interest in real property one can own, including the right to use the property at present and for an indeterminate period in the future.

fee simple qualified A fee simple estate with some restrictions on the right of possession.

FICO score Consumer credit score developed by the Fair Isaac Corporation; found at www.myfico.com.

fictitious business name statement Document indicating the name under which a business is operating; filed with the county where the business is located. Information is available at www.sos.ca.gov/business/corp/corp_irc. htm.

fiduciary A person in a position of trust and confidence who owes a certain loyalty to another, such as an agent to a principal.

final subdivision map *See* tentative subdivision map.

Financial Institutions Reform, Recovery, and Enforcement Act of 1989 (FIRREA) Federal legislation passed in response to the savings and loan crisis of the 1980s; established requirement for state appraiser licensing.

fire stops Wood blocks placed at intervals between wall studs to slow spread of fire.

fiscal year A business or an accounting year as distinguished from a calendar year.

fixed-rate mortgage Loan secured by mortgage or deed of trust on real estate that carries an interest rate that does not change over the life of the loan.

fixture Anything permanently attached to land or improvements so as to become real property.

flashing Metal strips intended to prevent water entry at openings in a roof for chimneys, vents, dormers, and changes in roof line.

foreclosure Sale of real property by mortgagee, trustee, or other lienholder on default by the borrower. *See also* judicial foreclosure.

forfeiture Breach of a condition subsequent in a deed; entitles grantor or grantor's successor to reacquire title to the property.

form appraisal report A short report, typically two pages plus addenda, using a preprinted form to summarize the data contributing to an appraiser's conclusion of value.

form-based planning Type of land use planning permitted in California that provides for a mix of land uses while taking into account the relationship of buildings and public areas. Information can be found at www.lgc.org/freepub /docs/community_design/fact_sheets/form_based_codes.pdf.

foundation Base of building, typically of poured concrete consisting of walls or footings.

frame Support posts, beams, and roof members, typically wood in residential construction; steel-frame construction is common for commercial structures and is also used for homes.

franchise A contract or agreement between the franchisor (grantor) and the franchisee (grantee).

franchise tax California tax on corporations.

fraud The intentional and successful use of any cunning, deception, collusion, or artifice to circumvent, cheat, or deceive another person, so that the other person acts on it to the loss of property and legal injury; *actual fraud* is a deliberate misrepresentation or a representation made in reckless disregard of its truth or falsity, the suppression of truth, a promise made without the intention to perform it, or any other act intended to deceive; *constructive fraud* is any misrepresentation made without fraudulent intent (the deliberate intent to deceive). Fraud is *affirmative* when it is a deliberate statement of a material fact that the speaker knows to be false and on which the speaker intends another person to rely, to her detriment. Fraud is *negative* when it is a deliberate concealment of something that should be revealed.

fraudulent misrepresentation Deliberate intent to deceive; fraudulent misrepresentation of a material fact in a real estate transaction is grounds for a legal action that may result in damages or rescission.

Freddie Mac Formerly the Federal Home Loan Mortgage Association; private corporation under federal supervision created by Congress in 1970 to provide a secondary market for conventional residential mortgage loans; found at www.freddiemac.com.

freehold estate An estate in land in which ownership is for an indeterminate length of time, as in a fee simple or life estate.

front foot Property measured by the front linear foot on its street line, each front foot extending the depth of the lot.

fructus industriales Plant growth that is the result of cultivation.

fructus naturales Plant growth that does not require cultivation, such as natural trees, grasses, and shrubbery.

full disclosure of material facts Obligation of real estate licensee to make known to the licensee's client as well as prospective purchasers all facts concerning the property and likely to affect its value that are known to the licensee and that the licensee is not otherwise prohibited by law from disclosing.

functional obsolescence Loss in value due to adverse factors within a structure that affect its marketability, such as its design, layout, or utility.

general agent *See* agent.

general indexes Lists of property owners and documents affecting property title maintained by title companies.

general lien Lien on all property of the debtor.

general partnership An association of two or more persons, called the partners, to carry on a business as co-owners for profit.

general plan Master plan; includes a statement of policy of the development and land uses within a city or county and a program to implement that policy.

general power of attorney Authority to act on behalf of someone else for financial purposes. *See also* power of attorney.

gentrification Renovation of run-down properties in neighborhoods that are in decline.

gift Voluntary transfer by an individual of any type of property for less than full consideration.

gift deed A deed for which the only consideration is "love and affection."

gift tax Federal tax owed by donor on gift in excess of allowable annual amount per individual; for 2008, gifts of no more than $12,000 per individual are not taxed.

Ginnie Mae Formerly the Government National Mortgage Association; created from the Federal National Mortgage Association (now known as Fannie Mae) in 1968 to provide a secondary market for federally backed residential mortgage loans; found at www.ginniemae.gov.

girders Beams that span foundation walls and footings to provide support for floor of structure.

good faith and honesty Obligation of real estate agent to act in the client's best interests while acting fairly to all parties in the transaction.

goodwill An intangible but a salable asset of a business derived from the expectation of continued public patronage.

graduated payment adjustable-rate mortgage Financing instrument that carries an interest rate that is subject to change based on a specified index, with loan payments limited to increases permitted at specified intervals.

graduated payment mortgage Financing instrument in which payments are increased during the first five years of the loan term and then remain fixed for the remainder of the term.

grant A conveyance of real estate.

grant deed A limited warranty deed using a granting clause—the word *grant* or words to that effect—assuring the grantee that the estate being conveyed is free from encumbrances placed on the property by the present owner (the grantor), and that the grantor has not previously conveyed the property to anyone else.

grantee A person to whom property is transferred by grant.

granting clause Portion of a deed that contains the words of conveyance.

grantor A person conveying property to another by grant.

gross income Total property income from all sources before any expenses are deducted.

gross income multiplier Gross rent multiplier; a number derived by dividing the sales price of a comparable property by the income it produces, which then is multiplied by the gross income produced by the subject property to derive an estimate of value.

gross lease Provides for the tenant to pay a fixed rental over the lease term, with the landlord paying all expenses of ownership, such as taxes, assessments, and insurance.

ground lease An agreement for the use of land only, sometimes secured by improvements placed on the land by the user.

ground rent Earnings of improved property credited to earnings of the ground itself after allowance is made for earnings of improvements.

growing equity mortgage Financing instrument in which payments of principal are increased based on the movement of a stated index, thereby decreasing the loan term.

growth Period of life cycle of a neighborhood in which property development is ongoing.

guarantee of title Guarantee of title as determined from examination of the public records and described in the guarantee document.

guide meridians *See* correction lines.

gutter Trough along roof line of structure that collects rainfall, which is diverted to a drainage pipe that carries it to the ground and away from the structure.

highest and best use In appraising real estate, the most profitable, physically possible, and legally permissible use for the property under consideration.

holder in due course Someone who takes a negotiable instrument for value, in good faith, and without notice of any defense against its enforcement that might be made by any person.

holdover tenancy Possession of property by a tenant who remains in possession after the expiration or termination of the lease term.

holographic will A will written entirely by hand, signed, and dated by the testator.

home energy rating program Program of the California Energy Commission that certifies home energy rating services and is intended to provide reliable information to differentiate the energy efficiency levels among California homes and to guide investment in cost-effective home energy efficiency measures; found at www.energy.ca.gov/HERS.

home equity sales contract Agreement to sell a homeowner's equity in the home; regulated by the California Civil Code, which requires specific notice, including right of cancellation, to homeowner.

Home Affordable Refinance Program (HARP) Legislation that allows borrowers with little or no equity in their home to refinance their mortgage with no new or additional mortgage insurance.

Home Loan Toolkit A guide published by the Consumer Finance Protection Bureau for consumers who apply for a consumer credit transaction secured by real property.

Homeowner Assistance Program California program for senior citizens and blind or disabled citizens of any age, providing property tax rebate for low-income taxpayers.

Homeowner's Bill of Rights of 2004 Law enacted after 2003 Southern California wildfires to clarify rights of homeowners under homeowner insurance policies.

homeowner's exemption Amount of property value of owner-occupied residence excluded from property taxation.

Homeowners Protection Act of 1998 (HPA) Federal law requiring that lenders or servicers provide certain disclosures and notifications concerning private mortgage insurance (PMI) on residential mortgage transactions completed on or after July 29, 1999.

homestead exemption A statutory exemption of real property used as a home from the claims of certain creditors and judgments up to a specified amount.

Housing Financial Discrimination Act (The Holden Act) California law effective January 1, 1978, that prohibits all financial institutions from discriminating in real estate loan decisions based on location or other property characteristic unless decision can be shown to have been based on sound business practice.

hypothecation Use of real property as collateral for a debt.

implied agency Action of a principal that causes a third party to rely on the representation of an agency relationship.

implied contract Agreement that can be established from the conduct of the parties rather than an express agreement.

implied warranties Warranties by grantor to grantee that will be implied by law, even if not mentioned in the deed; the grantor warrants that he has not already conveyed the property, and that there are no encumbrances on the property brought about by the grantor or any person who might claim title from the grantor.

impossibility of performance Event, such as destruction of property, that makes it impossible to perform a contract on its terms.

impound account A trust account established by a lender for accumulation of borrower funds to pay taxes and other recurring costs.

impracticability of performance *See* commercial frustration.

income capitalization approach Appraisal method in which the actual or likely net operating income of property is divided by its expected rate of return (capitalization rate) to arrive at an estimate of market value. *See also* capitalization rate.

independent contractor A person employed by another who has almost complete freedom to accomplish the purposes of the employment.

index method Way of estimating building reproduction cost by multiplying the original cost of the subject building by a factor that represents the percentage change in construction costs generally from the time of construction to the time of valuation.

inherent authority The authority of an agent to perform activities that are not specifically mentioned in the agency agreement but are necessary or customary to carry out an authorized act.

inheritance tax Tax on property received on the death of the previous owner; California no longer has an inheritance tax.

injunction A writ or an order issued by a court to restrain one or more parties to a suit or proceeding from doing an act deemed to be inequitable or unjust in regard to the rights of some other party or parties in the suit or proceeding.

installment note Promissory note that provides regular payments over the loan term, usually including both principal and interest.

installment sale Sale involving extension of credit by property seller, who receives regular payments from buyer on terms specified.

installment sales contract *See* sales contract.

institutional lenders A financial intermediary or depository, such as a savings and loan association, commercial bank, or life insurance company, that pools the money of its depositors and then invests funds in various ways, including trust deeds and mortgage loans.

insulation Use of wrapping and filling materials to reduce heat conductivity and improve energy efficiency of buildings and building components; measured in R-value.

interest A portion, share, or right in something; partial ownership; the charge in dollars for the use of money for a period.

interest rate The percentage of a sum of money borrowed that is charged for its use.

interest rate reduction refinancing loan (IRRRL) Type of VA-guaranteed loan that can be used for a loan refinancing.

interim loan A short-term temporary loan used until permanent financing is available, typically during building construction.

interim use The use to which a site or improved property may be put until ready for the more productive highest and best use.

internet Worldwide network of computers, originally created for military and university communications, making use of telephone lines or microwave links.

interpleader A court proceeding that may be brought by someone, such as an escrow agent, who holds property for another, for the purpose of deciding who among the claimants is legally entitled to the property.

inter vivos trust *See* living trust.

intestate Dying without leaving a valid will.

intestate succession Statutory method of distribution of property that belonged to someone who died intestate (without having made a valid will).

inverse condemnation A legal action brought by the owner of land when government puts nearby land to a use that diminishes the value of the owner's property.

involuntary lien Lien on property that can be imposed without the express permission of the property owner; tax liens are involuntary liens.

joint and several liability Obligation of all cosigners of a promissory note to repay the entire note, even if one defaults.

joint tenancy Ownership of property by two or more co-owners, each of whom has an equal share and the right of survivorship.

joint venture Two or more individuals or firms joining together on a single project as partners, typically with a lender contributing the necessary funds and the other partner(s) contributing his expertise.

joists Beams used to support flooring.

Jones v. Mayer The 1968 decision of the U.S. Supreme Court that upheld the Civil Rights Act of 1866; 392 U.S. 409. Text of the case is at http://law2.umkc.edu/faculty/projects/ftrials/conlaw/mayer.html.

judgment The final determination of a court of competent jurisdiction of a matter presented to it; may include an award of money damages.

judicial foreclosure Proceeding in which a mortgagee, a trustee, or another lienholder on property requests a court-supervised sale of the property to cover the unpaid balance of a delinquent debt.

junior lienor Lienholder whose rights are subordinate to those of another lienholder.

kickback An illegal fee paid by a nonlicensee to a salesperson or bank.

land The earth's surface, including substances beneath the surface extending downward to the center of the earth and the airspace above the surface for an indefinite distance upward.

land contract *See* sales contract.

landlord Lessor; one who leases her property to another.

lateral support The support that the soil of an adjoining owner gives to a neighbor's land.

lath and plaster Method of interior wall finishing used in older homes in which wet plaster is applied to a framework of wood slats, called laths, and wire.

lawful object Contract performance that does not violate any laws; requirement for a valid contract.

lead-based paint Paint, no longer allowed for use in buildings or products, that contains lead. Information on lead found in paint, dust, and soil is available at www.epa.gov/lead.

lease A contract between a property owner, called *lessor* or *landlord*, and another, called *lessee* or *tenant*, conveying and setting forth the conditions of occupancy and use of the property by the tenant.

lease assignment Transfer of leasehold interest by tenant to another party, with first tenant secondarily liable for lease obligations unless landlord agrees to a release of first tenant from those responsibilities.

leaseback *See* sale-leaseback.

leasehold Interest in land or an estate which gives right of use for a certain length of time.

leasehold estate Estate of tenancy; a tenant's right to occupy real estate during the term of the lease; a personal property interest.

lease option A lease accompanied by the right to purchase the leased property within a specified period for a specified or determinable price.

legacy Property, usually personal property, transferred by will.

legal capacity Person who is an adult or emancipated minor and mentally competent to enter into a contract.

legal description A land description used to define a parcel of land to the exclusion of all others that is acceptable by a court of law.

legatee Person who receives property, called a legacy, by bequest. *See also* devisee.

lessee One who leases property owned by someone else.

lessor Property owner; landlord.

letter of opinion A letter from appraiser to client presenting only the appraiser's conclusion of value, with no supporting data.

leverage Use of debt financing to purchase an investment, thus maximizing the return per dollar of equity invested; enables a purchaser to obtain possession for little or no initial cash outlay and relatively small periodic payments on the debt incurred.

license Permission to enter onto the land of another for a specific purpose, length of time, or both.

lien An encumbrance that makes property security for the payment of a debt or discharge of an obligation; a *voluntary lien* is one agreed to by the property owner, such as a deed of trust; an *involuntary lien* exists by operation of law to create a burden on property for certain unpaid debts, such as a tax lien.

lien release Filed by holder of mechanic's lien to voluntarily remove the encumbrance from the property owner's title.

lien release bond Filed with the county recorder by property owner who disputes the correctness or validity of a mechanic's lien to stop foreclosure of the property; must be in an amount equal to 150% of either the entire claim against the property or the portion of the claim allocated to the parcel(s) sought to be released; can also be filed by anyone having an interest in the property or by any other lienholder affected by the claim.

life estate An interest in real property conveying the right to possession and use for a term measured by the life or lives of one or more persons, most often the holder of the life estate.

life tenant Holder of a life estate.

limited equity housing cooperative A stock cooperative financed by the California Housing Finance Agency.

limited liability company (LLC) Form of business ownership in California that offers owners the limited liability of a corporation while still having the ability to take part in running the company.

limited partnership Partnership of one or more general partners, who run the business and are liable as partners, and limited partners, investors who do not run the business and are liable only up to the amount invested.

liquidated damages An amount agreed on by the parties to be full damages if a certain event occurs.

listing agreement Authorization by the owner of property, acting as principal, for a real estate broker to act as the agent of the principal in finding a person to buy, lease, or rent property; may be used to employ a real estate broker to act as agent for a person seeking property to buy, lease, or rent.

littoral rights Right to use of water from a lake or other body of still water by adjoining property owners.

living trust Inter vivos trust; established during lifetime of trustor/beneficiary to hold title to real property, other assets, or both and, on death of trustor, to pass title to contingent beneficiary without need for probate.

loan commitment Lender's agreement to make specified loan on indicated terms.

Loan Estimate New form mandated by the TILA-RESPA rule that helps consumers to understand the key features, costs, and risks of a mortgage loan. It must be provided to consumers no later than three business days after they submit a loan application.

loan-to-value ratio Amount of loan divided by purchase or market value of property.

lock-in clause Provision in a promissory note or land contract that prohibits the promissor from paying off the debt before the date set forth in the contract.

lot and block system Subdivision system; method of legal description of land using parcel maps identified by tract, block, and lot numbers.

lot books Catalogs maintained by title and abstract companies listing properties by location and showing deeds and other documents affecting title.

loyalty Obligation of agent to place interests of principal above those of the agent or any other party with whom the agent does business on behalf of the principal.

manufactured home A structure built on or after June 15, 1976, transportable in one or more sections, designed and equipped to contain no more than two dwelling units and to comply with HUD building specifications.

marker Natural or artificial object used to identify locations in a metes and bounds description. Also called monuments.

marketable title Title that a reasonably prudent purchaser, acting with full knowledge of the facts and their legal significance, would be willing and ought to accept.

market comparison approach *See* sales comparison approach.

market data approach *See* sales comparison approach.

market rent The rent that could be charged for property at the present time, based on demand and the number of available properties.

market value The most probable price property would bring in an arm's-length transaction under normal conditions on the open market. *See also* arm's-length transaction.

masonry Brick and stone products used for exterior building finishing, fireplaces, and other applications.

master plan The general plan; the comprehensive, long-term land-use plan for a jurisdiction.

material fact A fact that would be likely to affect the judgment of a person to whom it is known, such as information concerning the poor physical condition of a building that is for sale.

measuring life The person, usually the holder of a life estate, against whose life the duration of the life estate is determined.

mechanic's lien A statutory lien against real property in favor of persons who have performed work or furnished materials for the improvement of the property.

Mello-Roos Community Facilities Act California law that requires property owners benefiting from public improvements financed by bond issues to repay the bonds; requires notification to a prospective purchaser of lien assessments on the property.

meridians Imaginary lines that run north to south and intersect base lines that run east to west to form the starting point for land measurement using the rectangular survey system of land description.

metes and bounds Method of legal description of land using distances (called *metes*) measured from a point of beginning and using natural or artificial boundaries (called *bounds*) as well as single objects (called *monuments* or *markers*) as points of reference.

mineral rights Right of the owner of real estate to explore for and remove solid, liquid, and gaseous substances from the property; can be transferred independently of the right to occupy the property's surface.

minimum property requirements (MPRs) Minimally acceptable property condition for FHA-insured or VA-guaranteed loans; usually determined by compliance with loan building codes.

minor A person younger than 18 years of age.

mobilehome A factory-built home built before June 15, 1976, not to HUD standards. In California, a structure transportable in one or more sections, designed and equipped to contain no more than two dwelling units to be used with or without a foundation system.

mobilehome dealer Agent who displays or offers for sale two or more registered mobilehomes at the agent's place of business; requires licensure by the California Department of Housing and Community Development.

mobilehome park Any area or tract of land where two or more mobilehome lots are rented or leased or held out for rent or lease.

Mobilehome Residency Law (MRL) Portion of California Civil Code that regulates manufactured (mobile) home rental agreements, charges, grounds for eviction, and eviction procedures. The text of the law is available at www.hcd.ca.gov/codes/mp/2013MRL.pdf.

mold Naturally occurring organism, transmitted in the form of microscopic spores, that thrive in damp or humid conditions and can cause an allergic reaction in some individuals; certain types of mold are considered poisonous. For more information see www.epa.gov/mold/moldguide.html.

monument Natural or artificial object used to identify locations in a metes and bounds description. Also called markers.

Morgan Property Taxpayers' Bill of Rights California law effective January 1, 1994, to ensure that taxpayers are provided fair and understandable explanations of their rights and duties with respect to property taxation, prompt resolution of legitimate questions and appeals regarding their property taxes, and prompt corrections when errors have occurred in property tax assessments. Information can be found at www.boe.ca.gov/info/tra.htm.

mortgage A legal instrument by which property is pledged by a borrower, the *mortgagor,* as security for the payment of a debt or an obligation owed to a lender, the *mortgagee*.

mortgage-backed securities Debt instruments that consist of blocks or pools of mortgages on real estate.

mortgage bankers Those who make mortgage loans and may also serve as mortgage brokers; in California, mortgage bankers are licensed by the California Department of Business Oversight and subject to the California Residential Mortgage Lending Act (CRMLA), found in the California Financial Code.

mortgagee Lender to whom a property owner (mortgagor) gives a security interest in the property.

mortgage insurance Private mortgage insurance, required by lenders when mortgage indebtedness exceeds 80% of property value; also refers to a term life insurance policy that may be purchased by a borrower in an amount equal to the remaining mortgage indebtedness.

mortgage insurance premium Fee paid by borrower in exchange for lender's protection in the event of borrower's default in payment of mortgage debt.

mortgage loan brokerage Individual or company that brings borrowers and lenders together; in California, a real estate broker's license also includes authority to act as a mortgage broker. In California, a real estate licensee who conducts mortgage loan origination (MLO) activities for residential property of one to four units must obtain an MLO license endorsement that is attached to the real estate license and renewed annually.

mortgage loan disclosure statement The statement on a form approved by the Real Estate Commissioner that is required by law to be furnished by a mortgage loan broker to the prospective borrower of a loan of a statutorily prescribed amount before the borrower becomes obligated to complete the loan.

mortgage loan originator (MLO) Real estate licensee who conducts mortgage loan origination activities and must register annually on the Nationwide Mortgage Licensing System & Registry (NMLS), found at www.mortgage .nationwidelicensingsystem.org.

mortgage revenue bonds Method of financing community redevelopment projects through issuance of bonds that are repaid by property assessments.

mortgagor Property owner who gives security interest in the property to a lender (mortgagee) in exchange for a loan.

multiple listing clause Clause in a listing agreement, usually part of an exclusive authorization and right-to-sell listing, taken by a member of a multiple listing service (MLS), providing that the property will be made available through the MLS, in accordance with the MLS rules.

multiple listing service (MLS) An organization of real estate agents providing for a pooling of listings and the sharing of commissions on transactions involving more than one agent.

mutual consent Agreement of all parties to the specified terms; requirement for a valid contract.

mutuality of contract Agreement that imposes obligations on both parties.

narrative appraisal report The longest and most thorough appraisal report, containing a summary of all factual materials, techniques, and appraisal methods used in setting forth the appraiser's conclusion of value.

Natural Hazard Disclosure Statement Document indicating property location in a hazardous area that must be provided by seller to buyer in California residential transactions of one to four dwelling units, with certain exceptions. Information is available at http://ceres.ca.gov/planning/nhd.

negative amortization Increase in principal balance that occurs when monthly loan payment does not cover entire interest owed for the payment period.

negative declaration Statement that a proposed property use is not expected to have a significant impact on the environment and therefore does not require preparation of an environmental impact report.

negative fraud Deliberate concealment of something that should be revealed.

negligent misrepresentation A representation made carelessly that turns out to be false.

negotiable instrument An instrument, such as a promissory note, that is capable of being assigned or transferred in the ordinary course of business.

net listing A listing agreement providing that the agent may retain as compensation for her services all sums received over and above a net price to the owner.

net, net lease *See* triple-net lease.

net operating income Profit; the money remaining after expenses are deducted from income.

nominal rate The stated interest rate of a loan before taking into account loan fees, points, and other costs that make up the annual percentage rate (APR).

nonamortized A loan that includes payment of interest and may include payment of principal, but not enough principal to bring the outstanding balance of the loan to zero at the end of the loan term.

nonconforming use A property use that is not allowed by the current zoning ordinance.

nonexclusive listing *See* open listing.

notice Knowledge of a fact; *actual notice* is express or implied knowledge of a fact; *constructive notice* is knowledge of a fact that is imputed to a person by law because of the person's actual notice of circumstances and the inquiry that a prudent person would have been expected to make; *legal notice* is information required to be given by law.

notice of cessation Notice that can be filed by a property owner after work on a construction project has been stopped for 30 continuous days.

notice of completion Notice that can be filed by a property owner within 10 days following completion of a construction project.

notice of default Notice by trustee of the trustor's default in payment of the debt underlying the deed of trust and stating intention of the trustee to sell the property being held by the trustee as security for the debt.

notice of nonresponsibility Notice that must be filed by a property owner and posted in a conspicuous place on the property within 10 days of learning of construction, repair, or other work being performed on the property that the owner has not authorized.

notice of trustee's sale Notice of a sale of property under the terms of a deed of trust securing a debt on which the borrower has defaulted.

notice to pay or quit Notice by a landlord to a tenant who has defaulted in payment of rent that the amount owed must be paid within three days of the notice or the tenant must vacate and surrender possession of the premises.

novation The substitution or exchange of a new obligation or contract for an old one by mutual agreement of the parties.

null and void Of no legal validity or effect.

obedience Duty owed by agent to principal to follow all lawful instructions of the principal regarding the transaction.

observed condition method Breakdown method; depreciation computed by estimating the loss in value caused by every item of depreciation, whether curable or incurable.

offer and acceptance Required for a valid contract; an offer by one party that is accepted by the other.

offeree The party to whom an offer is made.

offeror The party who makes an offer.

open-ended mortgage A mortgage that permits additional amounts to be borrowed according to the note terms.

open listing Nonexclusive listing; the nonexclusive right to secure a purchaser, given by a property owner to a real estate agent; more than one agent may be given such authorization, and only the first to procure a ready, willing, and able buyer—or an offer acceptable to the seller—will be entitled to compensation.

opinion of title An attorney's written evaluation of the condition of the title to a parcel of land after examination of the abstract of title.

option A right given for a consideration to purchase or lease property on specified terms within a specified time, with no obligation on the part of the person receiving the right to exercise it.

option listing A listing agreement that gives the listing broker the right to purchase the listed property; because of the potential for the appearance of impropriety, if the option is exercised the principal should be informed of the broker's profit in the transaction and agree to it in writing.

oral contract A contract that is not in writing; because the statute of frauds requires a written agreement in certain cases, such as an agreement for the sale of real estate, an oral contract may not be enforceable.

ordinance Law established by the governing body of a municipal or county jurisdiction.

ordinary income Income that does not qualify for capital gains treatment.

orientation Placement of a structure on a site, ideally to take maximum advantage of street frontage, view, and access to light and air.

ostensible agency Holding out an agency relationship on which another relies.

overriding trust deed *See* wraparound mortgage or trust deed.

ownership in severalty Separate ownership; ownership of property by one person only.

parcel map Map that shows all property boundaries within a subdivision.

partition action Court proceeding by which co-owners may force a division of the property or its sale, with co-owners reimbursed for their individual shares.

partners *See* general partnership.

partnership *See* general partnership.

payment bond Bond that may be required of a building contractor to compensate the property owner if the contractor defaults in performance of contract obligations, such as payment of subcontractors, workers, and suppliers.

percentage lease Provides for rent as a percentage of the tenant's gross income, usually with a minimum base amount; the percentage may decrease as the tenant's income increases.

perc test Test to determine drainage capability of soil.

performance Obligation to be performed under the terms of a contract.

periodic tenancy *See* estate from period to period.

personal property All property that is not real property.

physical deterioration Loss in value brought about by wear and tear, disintegration, use, and action of the elements.

plaintiff The person who sues in a court action.

planned development *See* planned unit development.

planned unit development (PUD) A land-use design that provides intensive utilization of the land through a combination of private and common areas with prearranged sharing of responsibilities for the common areas; individual lots are owned in fee with joint ownership of open areas; primarily residential but may include commercial uses, industrial uses, or both.

planning commission An agency of local government charged with planning the development, redevelopment, or preservation of an area.

plasterboard Drywall; interior wall finishing material.

platform frame Construction technique in which each floor of a building provides support for the floor above it.

plat map Subdivision map showing division of property into tracts, blocks, and lots.

pledged Use of property as security for a debt by allowing lender to take possession of it until debt is repaid.

plottage Assemblage; an appraisal term for the increased value of two or more adjoining lots when they are placed under single ownership and available for use as a larger single lot.

pocket listing Property listing that the listing agent markets privately before entering it in the multiple listing service (MLS); usually a violation of MLS rules.

point of beginning The place at which a legal description using metes and bounds starts.

points One point represents one percentage point of a loan amount; may be charged by lenders at the time of loan funding to increase the loan's effective interest rate.

police power The right of government to enact laws and enforce them to benefit the public health, safety, and general welfare.

post-and-beam frame Construction technique in which interior posts support ceiling boards, allowing for more open space within a structure than is possible with other forms of construction.

potential gross income The maximum income that property is capable of producing.

power of attorney A written instrument authorizing an agent to act in the capacity of the principal; a *general power of attorney* provides authority to carry out all of the business dealings of the principal; a *special power of attorney* provides authority to carry out a specific act or acts.

power of eminent domain The government's right to take property for a public purpose on payment of just compensation to the property owner.

power of sale The power that may be given by a promissory note to a trustee, a mortgagee, or another lienholder to sell secured property without judicial proceedings if the borrower defaults.

power-of-sale clause A provision in a financing instrument that allows the property used as security for a debt to be sold in the event of the borrower's default without a judicial proceeding.

power of termination Right of the grantor of real estate to retake possession on violation of a limitation or condition on the deed to the grantee.

preliminary notice Notice of the right of a contractor, subcontractor, or material supplier to file a mechanic's lien; should be made within 20 days of the date on which the work begins or the material is provided.

preliminary report Title company's initial review of the status of a property's title; that is, the existence of liens or other encumbrances that could affect its marketability.

Prepaid Rental Listing Service (PRLS) Business that supplies prospective tenants with property listings on payment of a fee; may be performed by a licensed real estate broker or under the authority of a PRLS license.

primary mortgage market Composed of lenders that deal directly with borrowers. *See also* secondary mortgage market.

prime rate Interest rate banks charge their most favorably rated commercial borrowers.

principal The employer of an agent; one of the parties to a transaction; the amount of money borrowed.

priority of claims Order in which creditors will be paid when there are claims against a homestead that result in a judgment against the homeowner.

private mortgage insurance (PMI) Mortgage guaranty insurance available to conventional lenders on the high-risk portion of a loan, with payment included in the borrower's loan installments.

probate Court proceeding by which the property of a decedent is distributed according to the decedent's will or, if the decedent died intestate (without a will), according to the state law of intestate succession.

Probate Code The portion of California law that covers the court proceedings for disposition of property on the death of the property owner.

procuring cause The cause originating a series of events that lead directly to the intended objective; in a real estate transaction the procuring cause is the real estate agent who first procures a ready, willing, and able buyer.

progression, principle of The worth of a less valuable building tends to be enhanced by proximity to buildings of greater value.

promissory note A written promise to repay a loan under stipulated terms; establishes personal liability for payment by the person making the note.

property management A branch of the real estate business involving the marketing, operation, maintenance, and other day-to-day requirements of rental properties by an individual or a firm acting as agent of the owner.

property tax year Fiscal year for California property tax purposes runs from July 1 to June 30. Taxes charged for that period become a lien on the property on the preceding January 1.

Proposition 13 Passed by California voters in 1978; limits property tax rate and property value on which taxes may be based. Overview of property tax prepared by California State Board of Equalization can be found at www.boe.ca.gov/proptaxes/pdf/pub29.pdf.

proration Adjustment of interest, taxes, insurance, and other costs of property ownership on a pro rata basis as of the closing or agreed-on date; usually apportions those costs based on seller's and buyer's respective periods of ownership.

prospective economic advantage Legal term for one's expectations in doing business.

public report Real Estate Commissioner's report on a subdivision, including plans for improvements.

puffing Exaggerated comments or opinions that paint an overly optimistic picture of property attributes; may lead to a claim of misrepresentation.

purchase-money mortgage or trust deed A trust deed or mortgage given as part or all of the purchase consideration for real property.

quantity survey method Way of estimating building reproduction cost by making a thorough itemization of all construction costs, both direct (material and labor) and indirect (permits, overhead, profit), then totaling those costs.

quasi-community property Any California real estate acquired by an out-of-state married person that would be considered community property if acquired by a resident of California; any California real estate acquired in exchange for real or personal property located anywhere, when the California real estate would have been considered community property if it had been acquired by a California resident.

quiet title *See* action to quiet title.

quitclaim deed A deed that conveys any interest the grantor may have in the property at the time of the execution of the deed, without any warranty of title or interest.

radon Cancer-causing colorless, odorless radioactive gas caused by the breakdown of natural elements in soil; remediation includes external venting of basements and crawlspaces. Information can be found at www.epa.gov/radon.

rafters Beams that extend from ridge line of roof to eave.

ranges In the rectangular survey system of land description, townships running east and west of a meridian.

rate Interest rate is percentage of loan amount that must be paid as fee for loan.

ratification The adoption or approval of an act by the person on whose behalf it was performed, as when a principal ratifies conduct of an agent that was not previously authorized.

ready, willing, and able buyer A buyer who wants and is prepared to purchase property, including being able to finance the purchase, at the agreed-on price and terms.

real estate Real property; land; includes the surface of the earth, the substances beneath the surface, the airspace above the surface, fixtures, and anything incidental or appurtenant to the land.

Real Estate Advisory Commission Ten-member group appointed by the Real Estate Commissioner that makes recommendations to the Commissioner on matters involving the California Bureau of Real Estate.

real estate board A local organization whose members consist primarily of real estate brokers and salespeople.

real estate broker A person employed for a fee by another to carry on any of the activities listed in the Real Estate Law definition of a broker.

real estate brokerage Business licensed to conduct activities under authority of real estate broker's license.

Real Estate Education and Research Fund California fund financed by a fixed portion of real estate license fees, designed to encourage research in land use and real estate development.

Real Estate Fraud Prosecution Trust Fund Authorized by state law for any county that wishes to establish such a fund to help district attorneys and law enforcement agencies deter, investigate, and prosecute real property fraud crimes; up to $2 may be added to the county's recording fees for such a fund.

Real Estate Investment Trust (REIT) Way for investors to pool funds for investments in real estate and mortgages, with profits taxed to individual investors, rather than the corporation.

Real Estate Law Portion of the California Business and Professions Code regarding licensing of real estate brokers and salespeople and activities of the California Bureau of Real Estate; also includes Subdivided Lands Law.

real estate purchase contract and receipt for deposit Form of real estate sales contract commonly used in California.

real estate salesperson A person licensed under the provisions of the Real Estate Law to act under the control and supervision of a real estate broker in carrying on any of the activities listed in the license law.

Real Estate Settlement Procedures Act (RESPA) Federal law requiring certain disclosures by lenders in federally related mortgage loans involving the sale or transfer of residences of one to four dwelling units. Information on RESPA can be found at www.hud.gov/offices/hsg/rmra/res/respa_hm.cfm.

real estate syndicate An organization of real estate investors, typically in the form of a limited partnership.

Real Estate Transfer Disclosure Statement Information on property mechanical and structural conditions that must be disclosed by seller of California residential property of one to four units to a prospective buyer.

real property *See* real estate.

Real Property Loan Law Part of the California Real Estate Law that covers loans solicited or negotiated by a real estate broker.

reasonable care and skill Real estate agent's obligation to principal to conduct with appropriate expertise and consideration.

reassessment event Sale or other transaction, such as addition of improvements, that triggers a revaluation of property for tax purposes.

reconciliation In appraising, the final step, in which the estimates of value reached by each of the three appraisal approaches (sales comparison, cost, and income capitalization) are weighed in light of the type of property being appraised, the purpose of the appraisal, and other factors, to arrive at a final conclusion of value.

reconveyance deed Instrument by which the trustee returns title to the trustor after the debt underlying a deed of trust is paid.

recording Submitting a document to the county recorder for inclusion in the public records of the county on payment of the applicable recording fee.

Recovery Account State fund financed by real estate license fees and intended to help compensate victims of real estate licensee fraud, misrepresentation, deceit, or conversion of trust funds, when a court-ordered judgment cannot be collected.

recovery property Property that can be depreciated for income tax purposes, with the cost of the property deducted from income over a stated period.

rectangular survey system Section and township system; U.S. government survey system; method of legal description of land using areas called *townships* measured from meridians and base lines.

redemption Period following a court-ordered sale of mortgaged property in which the judgment debtor or the judgment debtor's successor in interest can buy back the property.

redlining An illegal lending policy of denying real estate loans on properties in certain areas because of alleged higher lending risks, without due consideration of the individual loan applicant.

reformation An action to correct a mistake in a contract, deed, or another document.

registered domestic partner One of two persons sharing a residence who have filed a Declaration of Domestic Partnership with the secretary of state.

regression, principle of A building's value will decline if the buildings around it have a lower value.

Regulations of the Real Estate Commissioner Rules that clarify and interpret the Real Estate Law and that are binding on real estate licensees.

Regulation Z Federal Reserve Board requirements, now subject to the Consumer Financial Protection Bureau, that implement the Truth in Lending Act.

reinstatement Revival of defaulted mortgage by payment of all delinquencies, including court costs and fees, before foreclosure sale.

rejection Refusal to accept an offer.

release Removal of part of a contract obligation, for consideration, by the party to whom the obligation is owed; removal of part of a property from a lien on payment of part of the debt owed.

reliction The increase of a landowner's property by the receding of an adjacent body of water.

remainder The right of future possession and use that will go to someone other than the grantor on termination of a life estate.

renegotiable-rate mortgage (RRM) A financing instrument in which the interest rate is adjusted after an agreed-to period following origination, such as three or five years.

rent The consideration paid for possession and use of leased property.

rent control A regulation imposed by a local governing body as a means of protecting tenants from relatively high rent increases over the occupancy period of a lease.

repair and deduct Tenant's remedy when landlord is on notice of and fails to make necessary repairs to leased premises.

replacement cost The cost of a new building using modern construction techniques, design, and materials but having the same utility as the subject property.

reproduction cost The cost of a new building of exactly the same design and materials as the subject property.

request for reconveyance Beneficiary's notice to trustee on payment of underlying debt that title to property is to be returned to the trustor.

rescission The cancellation of a contract and restoration of the parties to the same position they held before the contract was formed.

resident apartment manager Apartment manager who resides in one of the units; required of every California apartment building having at least 16 units.

restraint on alienation An illegal condition that would prohibit a property owner from transferring title to real estate.

restricted license Real estate license on which one or more conditions are imposed by the Real Estate Commissioner as the result of a disciplinary action.

restricted use report Property appraisal that will be limited in either the method of valuation used or the property interests valued.

restriction A limitation on the use of real property; public restrictions imposed by government include zoning ordinances; private restrictions imposed by deed may require the grantee to do or refrain from doing something. *See also* CC&Rs.

reverse annuity mortgage (RAM) Finance instrument that creates an increasing amount of debt secured by the borrower's residence, based on the amount paid out to the borrower, typically monthly.

reversion The right of future possession and use retained by the grantor of a life estate.

revitalization Period of property renovation and rebuilding in which neighborhood begins a new life cycle.

revocable transfer on death (TOD) deed Deed that transfers real property on the death of its owner without a probate proceeding, provided it is lawfully created.

revocation Cancellation of an offer before acceptance.

rezoning Change in the land use designation of an area.

ridge board Beam that runs along top of roof.

right of appropriation Right of government to take, impound, or divert water flowing on the public domain from its natural course for some beneficial purpose.

right of entry Right of the landlord to enter leased premises in certain circumstances.

right of redemption *See* redemption.

right of survivorship The right of surviving cotenants to share equally in the interest of a deceased cotenant; the last surviving cotenant is sole owner of the property.

right to rescind Consumer's three-day right to cancel a credit transaction involving a security interest in the consumer's principal dwelling, as provided by Regulation Z.

riparian rights The right of a landowner whose property borders a lake, river, or stream to the use and enjoyment of the water adjacent to or flowing over the property, provided the use does not injure other riparian landowners.

R-value Cumulative rating of the effectiveness of various types of insulation.

safety clause Provision that protects a listing broker's commission in the event that property is sold within a stated period to someone who was first brought to the property during the term of the listing.

sale-leaseback A transaction in which at the time of sale the seller retains occupancy by concurrently agreeing to lease the property from the purchaser.

sales associate *See* associate licensee.

sales comparison approach Market comparison approach; market data approach; appraisal method in which the sales prices of properties that are comparable in construction and location to the subject property are analyzed and adjusted to reflect differences between the comparables and the subject.

sales contract Land contract; installment sales contract; a contract used in a sale of real property whereby the seller retains title to the property until all or a prescribed part of the purchase price has been paid, but no earlier than one year from the date of possession.

sales tax Owed to the state by retailers of tangible personal property, whether or not paid by a customer; exception is made for some items, such as food, which incurs no sales tax.

salvage value In computing depreciation for tax purposes under all but the declining balance method, the reasonably anticipated fair market value of the property at the end of its useful life.

sandwich lease A leasehold interest between the primary lease and the operating lease.

satisfaction Discharge of an obligation before the end of its term by payment of the total debt owed.

scarcity Relative lack of supply of a product; one of the four basic elements of value that also include demand, utility, and transferability.

S corporation Business owned by no more than 35 shareholders and incorporated following requirements of Subchapter S of the Internal Revenue Code, which then allows income to flow directly to shareholders, avoiding double taxation.

secondary financing A loan secured by a second (or subsequent) mortgage or trust deed on real property.

secondary mortgage market Investment opportunities involving real property securities, other than direct loans from lender to borrower; loans may be bought, sold, or pooled to form the basis for mortgage-backed securities.

secret profit Compensation in any form received by a real estate licensee without the knowledge of the licensee's client.

section A standard land area of one mile square, containing 640 acres, used in the rectangular survey system of land description.

section and township system *See* rectangular survey system.

Secure and Fair Enforcement for Mortgage Licensing Act (SAFE Act) Law that law requires all real estate brokers (and salespersons acting under the supervision of a broker) who make, arrange, or service loans secured by real property to report that fact to the California Bureau of Real Estate by January 31, 2010 (or within 30 days of commencing the activity, whichever is later).

security deposit An amount paid at the start of a lease term and retained by the landlord until the tenant vacates the premises, all or part of which may be kept by the landlord at that time to cover costs of any default in rent payments or reasonable costs of repairs or cleaning necessitated by the tenant's use of the premises.

security instrument A written document executed by a debtor by which the described property is made security for the underlying debt.

seismic hazards zone Area specified by the California Department of Conservation as being at high risk of severe earth movement.

self-contained report Narrative report; most comprehensive type of appraisal report, including a thorough statement of the background data supporting the opinion of value.

separate property Property owned by a married person other than community property, including property owned before marriage, property acquired by gift or inheritance, income from separate property, and property acquired with the proceeds of separate property.

servient tenement *See* easement.

set-back ordinance An ordinance requiring improvements built on property to be a specified distance from the property line, street, or curb.

settlement statement Document provided to buyer and seller at closing that indicates all of the income and expenses of the transaction.

severalty, ownership in *See* ownership in severalty.

shared appreciation mortgage (SAM) Security instrument in which borrower receives below-market rate of interest and resulting lower payments in exchange for giving the lender an agreed-on portion of future property appreciation, if any.

shared equity mortgage A financing instrument that provides for the lender to share in the property's appreciation.

sheathing Insulating and bracing material, such as plywood, applied to exterior walls of wood-frame structure, to which exterior finishing material, such as siding or masonry, is applied.

sheriff's deed Deed given to the purchaser at a court-ordered sale to satisfy a judgment, without warranties.

short rate Increased premium charged by insurance company on early cancellation of policy to compensate insurer for the fact that the original rate was calculated on the full term of the policy.

siding Exterior wall finishing, applied in horizontal boards that can be wood, aluminum, vinyl, or a composite material.

sill Wood member placed directly on foundation; in California, state law requires anchor bolts to fasten sill to foundation for earthquake safety.

simple interest Interest computed on the principal amount of a loan only. *See also* compound interest.

single agency Representation of only one party to a transaction; for example, a seller's agent or buyer's agent.

sinking fund Fund set aside from the income from property that, with accrued interest, eventually will pay for replacement of the improvements.

site value Determination of land value exclusive of improvements.

six-month rule Time period in which a homeowner can sell one home and move into another, less costly one, to pay debts that would otherwise threaten a sale of the homestead.

soffit Encloses opening between outside wall of structure and end of room overhang.

solar heating System that uses warmth of sun; passive when sunlight is allowed to warm tiles or other materials; active when water is passed through solar collector, then recirculated.

sole proprietorship Business owned by only one owner.

special agent *See* agent.

special assessment Appropriation in the form of a tax on property that is enhanced by the addition or renovation of improvements, such as a light-rail line.

special limitation A limiting condition specified in a transfer of fee simple ownership that, if not complied with, will immediately and automatically extinguish the estate and return title to the grantor.

special power of attorney Authorization to act for someone else for a specific purpose, such as a real estate transaction.

special studies zone One of the areas, typically within a quarter-mile or more of an active earthquake fault, requiring a geologic report for any new project involving improvements or structures initiated after May 4, 1975; the report may be waived by city or county if the state geologist approves.

special warranty deed A deed in which the grantor warrants or guarantees the title only against defects arising during the grantor's ownership of the property and not against defects existing before the time of the grantor's ownership.

specific lien Creditor's right in identified property of the debtor.

specific performance An action to compel a breaching party to adhere to a contract obligation, such as an action to compel the sale of land as an alternative to money damages.

specific plan Formulated after adoption of a general plan by a city or county to give further details of community development, including projected population density and building construction requirements.

square-foot method Way of finding reproduction cost by multiplying the current cost per square foot of a comparable building by the number of square feet in the subject building.

standard parallels *See* correction lines.

standard policy Policy of title insurance that protects against fraud or other challenges to the owner's title that would not be discovered by an examination of the property or title records.

standard subdivision Area of land divided into parcels intended for separate ownership, with no common (shared) ownership by all of the owners of any of the land.

standby commitment Mortgage banker's promise, for which builder pays a standby fee, to make loans available to prospective purchasers on stated terms.

standby fee Fee paid by builder to mortgage banker in exchange for agreement to make mortgage loans available at a stated price at a future time.

starting time Date on which a construction project begins (work starts or materials are provided).

statute of frauds A state law requiring certain contracts to be in writing and signed before they will be enforceable, such as a contract for the sale of real estate.

statute of limitations Law that stipulates the specific time period during which a legal action must be brought following the act that gives rise to it.

statutory dedication Dedication of an easement for public use under the provisions of the California Subdivision Map Act.

statutory warranty deed A short-term warranty deed that warrants by inference that the seller is the undisputed owner, has the right to convey the property, and will defend the title if necessary; if the seller does not do so, the new owner can defend against said claims and sue the former owner.

steering The illegal act of directing prospective homebuyers to or from a particular residential area on the basis of the homebuyer's race or national origin.

stock cooperative A form of subdivision, typically of an apartment building, in which each owner in the stock cooperative is a shareholder in a corporation that holds title to the property, each shareholder being entitled to use, rent, or sell a specific apartment unit. *See also* limited equity housing cooperative.

straight-line method Depreciation computed at a constant rate over the estimated useful life of the improvement.

straight note A note in which a borrower repays the principal in a lump sum at maturity, with interest due in installments or at maturity.

stucco Type of plaster used for exterior finishing of walls.

studs Vertical wall supports; wood studs are used in a wood-frame structure and steel studs are used in a steel-frame structure.

subagent Person who works through agent on client's behalf.

Subdivided Lands Law Part of the California Real Estate Law found in the Business and Professions Code that regulates the formation, marketing, and financing of subdivisions under the authority of the Real Estate Commissioner. Information on zoning and planning laws can be found at http://www.ca.gov/

subdivision The division of real property into separate parcels or lots for the purpose of sale, lease, or financing.

subdivision map Document showing division of land into two or more parcels, required before subdivision approval.

Subdivision Map Act Part of the Government Code that sets out the procedure for filing a subdivision plan when property is divided into two or more parcels. Information on subdivisions can be found at http://www.ca.gov/

subdivision public report Issued by the Real Estate Commissioner after a subdivision developer has met the requirements of the Subdivided Lands Law; provides details of the project and financing, and a copy must be given to all prospective purchasers.

subdivision system *See* lot and block system.

subject to When a grantee takes title to real property "subject to" a mortgage or trust deed, the grantee is not responsible to the holder of the promissory note for the payment of the amount due, and the original maker of the note retains primary responsibility for the underlying debt.

sublease A lease given by a lessee (tenant).

subordination agreement An agreement by the holder of an encumbrance against real property to permit that claim to take an inferior position to other encumbrances against the property.

substitution Principle of Market value tends to be set by the present or recent cost of acquiring an equally desirable and valuable property, comparable in construction, utility, or both.

successor trustee Person who takes control of property held in trust on death or incapacitation of original trustee.

summary report Appraisal report using a standardized form, such as the Uniform Residential Appraisal Report (URAR) developed by Fannie Mae and Freddie Mac. A copy of the form can be downloaded from www.fanniemae.com/content/guide_form/1004.pdf.

supplemental assessment Additional "catch-up" property tax assessment following a sale or other reassessment event.

supply and demand, principle of Takes into account the effect on market value of the relationship between the number of properties on the market at a given time and the number of potential buyers.

survey The process by which a parcel of land is measured and its area determined.

syndicate, real estate *See* real estate syndicate.

tack Adding together successive periods of adverse possession.

take-out loan The loan arranged by the owner or builder/developer for a buyer; the permanent financing that pays off and replaces the interim loan used during construction.

taxable gross income Income from all sources, less certain payments, such as contributions to a qualified retirement plan.

taxable income Income that remains after allowed deductions from adjusted gross income.

tax bracket Tax rate applicable to a taxpayer's taxable income.

tax credit Reduction in tax owed.

tax deed Deed issued by the county tax collector when property is sold at public auction because of nonpayment of taxes.

tax-deferred exchange Transfer of property held for productive use in a trade or business or for investment in exchange for like-kind property in a transaction that meets the requirements of Section 1031 of the Internal Revenue Code.

tax increment funding Payments on bonds through collection of increased taxes on improvements financed by the bonds.

tax lien An involuntary lien that arises from a taxpayer's obligation to pay real property taxes, state income and estate taxes, or federal income, gift, and estate taxes.

Taxpayer Advocate's Office State office that assists taxpayers in explaining and resolving tax issues. Information on the program is available at www.ftb .ca.gov/aboutftb/taxpayer_advocate/index.shtml.

tax rate Percentage of income, proceeds, or consideration paid that is charged for a specific tax; the documentary transfer tax rate is 55 cents per $500 or fraction of $500 of the consideration paid for property.

tenancy in common Co-ownership of property in equal or unequal shares by two or more persons, each holding an undivided interest without right of survivorship.

tenancy in partnership Ownership by two or more persons, acting as partners, of property held for partnership purposes.

tenant Lessee under a lease; one who has the legal right to possession and use of property belonging to another.

tender An offer to perform a contracted obligation.

tentative subdivision map The initial or tentative map required of subdividers by the Subdivision Map Act, submitted to the local planning commission, which notes its approval or disapproval; a final map embodying any changes requested by the planning commission also must be submitted.

testamentary trust A trust established by will and funded with proceeds from the estate of the decedent.

testate Having a will upon death.

testator A person who makes a will.

tiers In the rectangular survey system of land description, townships running north and south of a base line.

TILA-RESPA Integrated Disclosure Rule (TRID) Federal rule that provides for Loan Estimate and Closing Disclosure forms in residential loan transactions.

time-share estate A right of occupancy in a time-share project (subdivision) coupled with an estate in the real property.

time-share project A form of subdivision of real property into rights to the recurrent, exclusive use or occupancy of a lot or unit of the property on an annual or other periodic basis, for a specified period.

time-share use A license or contractual or membership right of occupancy in a time-share project that is not coupled with an estate in the real property.

title insurance Insurance to protect a real property owner or lender up to a specified amount against certain types of loss affecting title or marketability.

title insurance company Business licensed by the state to insure buyers and lenders against losses due to defects in title to real estate.

title insurance fund Specified amount of premiums collected by a licensed California title insurance company that must be set aside each year.

title plant Database of a title insurance company that includes records of real estate transfers.

tort Any wrongful act, other than a breach of contract, for which a civil action may be brought by the person wronged.

township A standard land area of six miles square, divided into 36 sections of one mile square each, used in the rectangular survey system of land description.

trade fixtures Articles of personal property that are attached by a business tenant to real property that are necessary to the carrying on of a trade and are removable by the tenant.

transferability One of the four elements that must be present for a market to be created: demand, utility, scarcity, and transferability.

triple-net lease Guarantees a specified net income to the landlord, with the tenant paying that amount plus all operating and other property expenses, such as taxes, assessments, and insurance.

trust Method of property ownership in title is transferred by a trustor to a trustee to be held for the benefit of a beneficiary.

trust account An account separate from a broker's own funds (business and personal) in which the broker is required by law to deposit all funds collected for clients before disbursement.

trust deed A deed issued by a borrower of funds (the trustor) conveying title to a trustee on behalf of a lender, the beneficiary of the trust; the trust deed authorizes the trustee to sell the property to pay the remaining indebtedness to the beneficiary if the trustor defaults on the underlying obligation.

trustee One who holds property conveyed by a trustor on behalf of (in trust for) the beneficiary, to secure the performance of an obligation.

trustee in bankruptcy *See* bankruptcy.

trustee's deed Deed given to the purchaser at a foreclosure sale by the trustee acting under a deed of trust.

trustee's sale Sale of property held as security for payment of a loan on default of the trustor.

trustor One who conveys property to a trustee to hold on behalf of (in trust for) a beneficiary to secure the performance of an obligation; borrower under a deed of trust.

Truth in Lending Act (TILA) Federal law that requires certain disclosures in consumer credit transactions; implemented by Regulation Z that is now subject to the Consumer Financial Protection Bureau.

underground water rights Right to remove water from aquifers and other sources below the surface of the land.

undivided interest subdivision An area of land divided into parcels where each owner is a tenant in common with all other owners; for example, a campground with shared facilities.

undue influence Use of a fiduciary or confidential relationship to obtain a fraudulent or an unfair advantage over another's weakness of mind, distress, or necessity.

unenforceable contract Contract which, if enforced, would violate law.

uniform codes Building codes that are developed by national or international groups and adopted by states and local jurisdictions; the International Building Code is now the standard throughout the country, with additional requirements developed and adopted by states and local jurisdictions as warranted.

Uniform Commercial Code Establishes a unified and comprehensive method for regulation of security transactions in personal property.

Uniform Residential Appraisal Report (URAR) Summary form of appraisal report developed and required by Fannie Mae and Freddie Mac; available at www.fanniemae.com/content/guide_form/1004.pdf.

Uniform Residential Loan Application Standard form developed and required by Fannie Mae and Freddie Mac; available at www.fanniemae.com/content/guide_form/1003rev.pdf.

unilateral contract A contract that contains a promise of performance by only one party that is accepted by performance of the other party.

unit-in-place method Way of estimating building reproduction cost by adding the construction cost per unit of measure of each of the component parts of the subject property; each unit cost includes material, labor, overhead, and builder's profit.

unity of possession The essential element of a cotenancy or other form of co-ownership that gives all co-owners the right to possession of the entire property.

unlawful detainer Legal action that may be brought to evict a tenant who is in unlawful possession of leased premises.

Unruh Civil Rights Act California law that prohibits discrimination against persons in one of the identified groups in accommodations and business establishments.

untenantable dwelling Property lacking one or more necessary utilities, such as water, or in such poor condition that it falls below minimum property standards; uninhabitable.

urea-formaldehyde Chemical used in manufacturing process of many home building components and household goods that can emit toxic fumes.

URL Uniform resource locator, the address of a site on the internet, such as www.bre.ca.gov.

useful life The period of years in which a property improvement may be used for its originally intended purpose.

use tax California tax charged to the purchaser for storage, use, or other consumption of certain purchased or leased tangible personal property. Information can be found at www.boe.ca.gov/taxprograms/usetax/.

U.S. government survey system *See* rectangular survey system.

usury The charging of a rate of interest on a loan that is greater than the rate permitted by law.

utility One of the four elements necessary to create a market: demand, utility, scarcity, and transferability.

vacancy decontrol *See* rent control.

vacancy factor The percentage of a building's space that is unrented over a given period.

valid contract Contract which meets all of these required legal elements: legal capacity, offer and acceptance, lawful object, consideration, and in writing.

value in exchange The value of property expressed as the kind and amount of other property that would be acceptable in a transfer of ownership.

value in use The subjective value of property to its present owner, as opposed to market value, which should be objective.

vesting of title Time at which title to real estate is transferred to new owner.

veteran's entitlement Amount of loan guarantee available to eligible veteran.

veteran's exemption Amount by which value of eligible veteran's property is reduced for purposes of real property taxation.

void To have no force or effect; that which is unenforceable.

voidable That which can be adjudged void but is not void unless action is taken to make it so.

void contract Contract that has no legal effect from its inception.

voidable contract Contract that may be disavowed by one or both parties based on circumstances.

voluntary lien Encumbrance on property imposed on action or with consent of property owner; a mortgage or deed of trust is a voluntary lien on the property identified in the security instrument.

waiver The giving up of a right or privilege voluntarily.

wallboard Interior wall finishing material.

warranties Implied *See* implied warranties.

warranty deed A deed that expressly warrants that the grantor has good title; the grantor thus agrees to defend the premises against the lawful claims of third persons.

warranty of habitability Legally implied obligation of a landlord to meet minimal housing and building standards.

water rights Right to use of water found at surface of land and underground.

will A written, legal declaration of a person called a *testator*, expressing the testator's desires for the disposition of his property after death.

wraparound mortgage or trust deed Overriding or all-inclusive trust deed; a financing device in which a lender assumes payments on an existing debt and takes from the borrower a junior lien with a face value in an amount equal to the amount outstanding on the old instrument and the additional amount of money borrowed.

writ of execution A court order directing the sheriff or another officer to satisfy a money judgment out of the debtor's property, including real estate not exempt from execution.

writ of possession Order issued by the court directing the sheriff or marshal to take all legal steps necessary to remove the occupant(s) from the specified premises.

yield Profit; return; the interest earned by an investor on an investment or by a bank on the money it has loaned.

zones Defined land areas with designated land uses and building specifications.

zoning An act of city or county government specifying the possible uses of property in a particular area.

zoning ordinances Local laws, regulations, and codes requiring compliance with designated land uses.

zoning variance An exception to a requirement of a zoning ordinance to permit a use of the land that is reasonable in light of neighboring land uses.

ANSWER KEY

UNIT 1
Exercise 1-1, Page 7

No. The broker cannot delegate primary responsibility for all brokerage activities, which must be lawfully authorized.

Exercise 1-2, Page 28

Salesperson Sally has, arguably, engaged in a dishonest business practice that could result in suspension or revocation of her real estate license. Broker Bob should have reviewed the newsletter before allowing Sally to print and distribute it, particularly because she is a new, inexperienced salesperson. Bob thus shares in Sally's conduct.

Review Questions, Pages 33–35

1. b	8. c	15. d
2. b	9. d	16. d
3. a	10. d	17. d
4. d	11. d	18. c
5. a	12. d	19. d
6. c	13. b	20. a
7. b	14. c	

UNIT 2
Exercise 2-1, Page 48

A house is a fixture because it is permanently attached to land.

A room air conditioner is personal property if it is not installed in such a way that there is an alteration to the building.

A motor home is personal property because it is intended to be readily moved and is not attached to land.

A space heater that is a freestanding appliance is personal property. A wall-mounted space heater is a fixture.

A brick patio is a fixture because it is permanently attached.

A fireplace is a fixture.

Patio furnishings are personal property because they are not attached to the land.

Wall-to-wall carpeting is a fixture because it is attached to a building in such a way that it cannot be readily removed.

A wood deck on piers sunk into the ground is a fixture.

A room-size rug is personal property because it is not attached.

A hot tub may or may not be a fixture, depending on its installation. A hot tub built into the ground or a deck is a fixture, but a portable hot tub requiring no physical alteration of land or building to be installed is personal property.

A chandelier is a fixture, for it is a permanent attachment.

Review Questions, Pages 59–60

1.	c	8.	b	15.	d
2.	c	9.	b	16.	a
3.	d	10.	b	17.	d
4.	a	11.	d	18.	c
5.	c	12.	a	19.	c
6.	d	13.	a	20.	b
7.	a	14.	c		

UNIT 3
Exercise 3-1, Page 65

1. Life estate

2. Fee simple estate subject to a condition subsequent

3. Fee simple estate subject to a condition subsequent

4. Estate of tenancy

5. Simon has a life estate. Yvonne has a remainder while the life estate is in existence. If Simon dies before Annette, his heirs acquire the life estate until Annette's death. On Annette's death, Yvonne has a fee simple estate.

Exercise 3-2, Page 71

1. Joint tenancy

2. Community property

3. Tenancy in common

4. Tenancy in partnership

5. Separate property held in sole ownership

Exercise 3-3, Page 75

1. Corporation

2. Sole proprietorship

3. Syndicate held as a limited partnership

4. Trust

Review Questions, Pages 77–78

1.	a	8.	b	15.	b
2.	c	9.	d	16.	d
3.	c	10.	a	17.	a
4.	d	11.	d	18.	a
5.	d	12.	c	19.	c
6.	a	13.	b	20.	c
7.	c	14.	d		

UNIT 4
Exercise 4-1, Pages 90–91

1. Helen owns the condominium as separate property.

2. George and Helen own the house as community property.

3. Yes, by the power of eminent domain.

4. Perhaps not. George and Helen are entitled to the fair market value of their home, which may have appreciated from its initial purchase price. On the other hand, if property values have decreased since they purchased their home, George and Helen would probably be smart to accept the offer.

5. Yes. Community property may be willed by its owner.

6. No, because the "squatters" have perfected title to the "back 40" after five years of adverse possession.

7. Tim can bring a foreclosure action to force the sale of the property.

8. Henry died intestate. The law of intestate succession will be enforced through the legal process known as probate.

9. The other 70 feet of the property were lost in the flood by a process called avulsion.

Exercise 4-2, Page 93

1. No. No valid transaction can take place unless and until the grantor signs the deed.

2. Aunt Nellie still owns the condo, for she was incapable of making a valid deed.

3. There has been no conveyance. A deed must be in writing.

4. Diego may have a problem. The property description may be adequate, but only if there is no ambiguity as to the referenced parcel.

5. Perhaps, but title to the estate will pass through Uncle Anthony's will, if he has one, or by the laws of intestate succession, and not by the deed he prepared. The deed is invalid because it never was delivered to the grantee.

Exercise 4-3, Page 99

1. Grant deed

2. Quitclaim deed

3. Trust deed

4. Gift deed or grant deed

5. Reconveyance deed

6. Sheriff's deed

Review Questions, Pages 101–102

1. b	8. a	15. b
2. a	9. c	16. c
3. b	10. d	17. a
4. d	11. c	18. b
5. a	12. b	19. b
6. c	13. a	20. c
7. d	14. d	

UNIT 5
Exercise 5-1, Page 108

C. L. Drake has 90 days to file a mechanic's lien claim and 90 days after that to begin a foreclosure action, if necessary. These deadlines are in effect because work was stopped 60 days ago and neither a notice of completion nor a notice of cessation was filed.

Exercise 5-2, Page 115

The power company could put up its line if it already owned an easement over Harvey's property, or if that part of Harvey's property was condemned for that purpose. Of course, Harvey would have to be sent a notice of any condemnation proceeding, but it is up to Harvey to make sure that his mail is forwarded so that he receives any such notice.

The owner of the little house may have acquired an easement by prescription across Harvey's land, if he has used the new road continuously for five years and fulfilled all of the other requirements for such an easement.

Exercise 5-3, Page 119

1. Herb could make the upkeep of the property a condition of the deed he gives his grantee (the buyer). He also could impose a covenant or restriction to that effect, but the condition, covenant, or restriction would terminate when the grantee conveyed the property. Practically speaking, Herb might have a difficult time finding a buyer willing to accept such an encumbrance.

2. Aria cannot impose such a condition on her nephew's ownership of the property because it is a restraint on his free alienation of the property—that is, his right to sell it.

Exercise 5-4, Page 122

1. So long as the houseboat is their principal dwelling and place of residence, it can qualify as Harold's and Cynthia's homestead.

2. Because the equity the Potters have in their houseboat does not exceed the total amount of their mortgage balance and the $75,000 homestead exemption, creditors probably will not succeed in forcing a sale of their home.

Review Questions, Pages 124–125

1. d	8. d	15. d
2. a	9. a	16. c
3. c	10. b	17. b
4. d	11. b	18. a
5. a	12. b	19. c
6. b	13. a	20. d
7. c	14. c	

UNIT 6
Exercise 6-1, Page 137

1. There is no listing to take. Glenda has no control over the ranch, since title is held in trust for her. Even if Glenda did have title, because she is mentally incompetent she does not have the legal capacity to enter into a contract for the sale of real estate.

2. The salespeople of ABC Real Estate are independent contractors.

3. Certainly, Sam can sign a listing agreement on behalf of his broker for any property that he feels his firm is qualified to handle. If Sam does list the Nelson property, by showing the property to the Patels he would be acting in a dual agency capacity. Sam's broker then would be an agent for both the Patels and Jim Nelson. Sam should undertake such a representation only after fully informing Jim Nelson of the existence of his agreement with the Patels, informing the Patels of his agreement with Jim Nelson, and discussing the matter with his broker.

Exercise 6-2, Page 140

1. No. There is no written agreement between the Simpsons and broker Bonita.

2. No. There is no written agreement between the Simpsons and broker Bonita.

3. Yes. Now there is a written document, signed by both the Simpsons and broker Bonita, designating Bonita as sales agent. Because a selling price and commission rate had been discussed earlier, unless a different arrangement was specified in the contract, the earlier terms will apply. The Simpsons have ratified Bonita's conduct in bringing a prospective buyer to them.

Exercise 6-3, Page 143

1. No. Although Frank can delegate some of the responsibility of the listing agreement, he cannot turn over complete authority to someone else without the express consent of his principal. Frank's personal efforts and supervision of others in carrying out the terms of the listing agreement are what the seller bargained for, and Frank cannot transfer those responsibilities to someone else.

2. Because the offer is to be presented the next day, Frank should hold on to the check. If the offer is not accepted, he can simply return the check to the buyer. If the offer is accepted, he then can deposit the check in an escrow account. He should take precautions to safeguard the check while it is in his possession, as he could be liable for its loss.

3. No. Broker Rice has commingled his customer's funds with his own. Rice is subject to sanctions by the Real Estate Commissioner. Depending on when he noticed the error, Rice should have returned the check to the buyer or placed it in his trust account or an escrow depository if one already was stipulated.

Exercise 6-4, Page 167

Broker Carroll, in agreeing to act in the future for a buyer, has breached her fiduciary duty to Meyer. At the very least she owes Meyer the duty of full disclosure of her dealings with the buyer. She should have informed Meyer of both her relationship with the buyer and the intent of the buyer in making an offer. By actively working against Meyer's best interest in persuading her to accept the investor's offer, Carroll may be liable for fraud.

Review Questions, Pages 170–171

1.	a	8.	b	15.	c
2.	d	9.	d	16.	c
3.	b	10.	d	17.	c
4.	a	11.	b	18.	d
5.	b	12.	c	19.	c
6.	b	13.	d	20.	d
7.	a	14.	a		

UNIT 7
Exercise 7-1, Page 184

1. After Sally's first phone call to Clive, they do not have an agreement because they have no writing. If Clive accepts an offer that does not mention a commission for Sally, she still has no written agreement, and Clive is not obligated to pay her a commission. If the purchase offer accepted by Clive had stipulated a commission for Sally, she could have used that as the basis for her claim for a commission from Clive.

2. No, because no purchase price was specified.

3. No, because the identity of the house's designer, which would have a significant impact on the purchase price in this case, was misrepresented to him.

4. The oral lease for a term expiring more than one year from the date of agreement is unenforceable.

Exercise 7-2, Page 188

1. The Turners can ask Ted Markham to agree to rescind the contract. If he refuses, they can ask him to release them from their contract obligation on payment of some consideration, perhaps the earnest money deposit. The Turners also could refuse to go ahead with the sale, claiming impracticability of performance; if they succeed, they may be liable for damages.

2. The Wilsons can agree to rescind the contract if their deposit is returned. The Wilsons could sue for specific performance. Alternatively, they could sue for any damages they may have incurred as a result of the sale being canceled.

3. The condition of the living room ceiling indicates that the Davidsons may have concealed earlier water damage. The Harleys have up to three years from the discovery of the possibly fraudulent conduct to sue the Davidsons to recover the cost of repairs to the ceiling.

Exercise 7-3, Page 209

See the completed Residential Purchase Agreement and Joint Escrow Instructions on pages 558–567.

Review Questions, Pages 212–213

1.	b	8.	c	15.	c
2.	a	9.	c	16.	c
3.	a	10.	b	17.	d
4.	d	11.	b	18.	d
5.	b	12.	b	19.	b
6.	a	13.	c	20.	b
7.	b	14.	c		

UNIT 8
Exercise 8-1, Page 242

1. Mortgage

2. Mortgage with power of sale

3. Trust deed

4. Trust deed

Exercise 8-2, Page 256

You generally will find that interest rates on fixed-rate loans are higher than those initially set on adjustable-rate loans and that a longer loan term will have a higher interest rate than a shorter loan term.

Review Questions, Pages 269–270

1.	b	8.	b	15.	a
2.	b	9.	d	16.	b
3.	b	10.	a	17.	b
4.	d	11.	c	18.	c
5.	c	12.	a	19.	b
6.	a	13.	b	20.	c
7.	c	14.	c		

UNIT 9
Exercise 9-1, Pages 285–286

1. Yes, if the individual was a qualified California veteran.

2. Maximum loan amount would be $521,250.

3. The borrower's initial expenditure can be lowest with a VA-guaranteed loan, which need not involve a down payment, generally does not include discount points, and has a limit on closing costs.

EXERCISE 7-3

CALIFORNIA
ASSOCIATION
OF REALTORS®

**CALIFORNIA
RESIDENTIAL PURCHASE AGREEMENT
AND JOINT ESCROW INSTRUCTIONS**
(C.A.R. Form RPA-CA, Revised 12/15)

Date Prepared: _1/11/XX_

1. **OFFER:**
   A. **THIS IS AN OFFER FROM** Kenneth A. Plummer and Peggy M. Plummer ("Buyer").
   B. **THE REAL PROPERTY** to be acquired is 3840 Monroe Street , situated in Concord (City) Contra Costa County), California, (Zip Code), Assessor's Parcel No. ("Property").
   C. **THE PURCHASE PRICE** offered is three-hundred seventeen thousand dollars Dollars $ 317,000 .
   D. **CLOSE OF ESCROW** shall occur on _____ (date)(or 60 **Days** After Acceptance).
   E. Buyer and Seller are referred to herein as the "Parties." Brokers are not Parties to this Agreement.

2. **AGENCY:**
   A. **DISCLOSURE:** The Parties each acknowledge receipt of a ☑ "Disclosure Regarding Real Estate Agency Relationships" (C.A.R. Form AD).
   B. **CONFIRMATION:** The following agency relationships are hereby confirmed for this transaction:
      Listing Agent _____ (Print Firm Name) is the agent of (check one):
      ☐ the Seller exclusively; or ☐ both the Buyer and Seller.
      Selling Agent _____ (Print Firm Name) (if not the same as the Listing Agent) is the agent of (check one): ☐ the Buyer exclusively; or ☐ the Seller exclusively; or ☐ both the Buyer and Seller.
   C. **POTENTIALLY COMPETING BUYERS AND SELLERS:** The Parties each acknowledge receipt of a ☑ "Possible Representation of More than One Buyer or Seller - Disclosure and Consent" (C.A.R. Form PRBS).

3. **FINANCE TERMS:** Buyer represents that funds will be good when deposited with Escrow Holder.
   A. **INITIAL DEPOSIT**: Deposit shall be in the amount of .... $ 2,000
      (1) Buyer Direct Deposit: Buyer shall deliver deposit directly to Escrow Holder by electronic funds transfer, ☐ cashier's check, ☐ personal check, ☐ other _____ within 3 business days after Acceptance (or _____);
      OR **(2)X** ☐ **Buyer Deposit with Agent:** Buyer has given the deposit by personal check (or _____) to the agent submitting the offer (or to _____), made payable to _____ . The deposit shall be held uncashed until Acceptance and then deposited with Escrow Holder within **3** business days after Acceptance (or _____).
      Deposit checks given to agent shall be an original signed check and not a copy.
      (Note: Initial and increased deposits checks received by agent shall be recorded in Broker's trust fund log.)
   B. **INCREASED DEPOSIT:** Buyer shall deposit with Escrow Holder an increased deposit in the amount of .... $ _____
      within ____ **Days** After Acceptance (or _____).
      If the Parties agree to liquidated damages in this Agreement, they also agree to incorporate the increased deposit into the liquidated damages amount in a separate liquidated damages clause (C.A.R. Form RID) at the time the increased deposit is delivered to Escrow Holder.
   C. ☐ **ALL CASH OFFER:** No loan is needed to purchase the Property. This offer is NOT contingent on Buyer obtaining a loan. Written verification of sufficient funds to close this transaction IS ATTACHED to this offer or ☐ Buyer shall, within **3 (or _____) Days** After Acceptance, Deliver to Seller such verification.
   D. **LOAN(S):**
      (1) FIRST LOAN: in the amount of .... $ 253,600
      This loan will be conventional financing or ☐ FHA, ☐ VA, ☐ Seller financing (C.A.R. Form SFA), ☐ assumed financing (C.A.R. Form AFA), ☐ Other _____ . This loan shall be at a fixed rate not to exceed 6 ____% or, ☐ an adjustable rate loan with initial rate not to exceed _____%.
      Regardless of the type of loan, Buyer shall pay points not to exceed 2 ____% of the loan amount.
      (2) ☐ **SECOND LOAN** in the amount of .... $ _____
      This loan will be conventional financing or ☐ Seller financing (C.A.R. Form SFA), ☐ assumed financing (C.A.R. Form AFA), ☐ Other _____ . This loan shall be at a fixed rate not to exceed _____% or, ☐ an adjustable rate loan with initial rate not to exceed _____%. Regardless of the type of loan, Buyer shall pay points not to exceed _____% of the loan amount.
      (3) FHA/VA: For any FHA or VA loan specified in 3D(1), Buyer has **17 (or ___) Days** After Acceptance to Deliver to Seller written notice (C.A.R. Form FVA) of any lender-required repairs or costs that Buyer requests Seller to pay for or otherwise correct. Seller has no obligation to pay or satisfy lender requirements unless agreed in writing. A FHA/VA amendatory clause (C.A.R. Form FVAC) shall be a part of this Agreement.
   E. **ADDITIONAL FINANCING TERMS:** _____
      _____
   F. **BALANCE OF DOWN PAYMENT OR PURCHASE PRICE** in the amount of... $ 61,400
      to be deposited with Escrow Holder pursuant to Escrow Holder instructions.
   G. **PURCHASE PRICE (TOTAL):** .... $ 317,000

Buyer's Initials (_KAP_)(_KAP_)   Seller's Initials (_____)(_____)

RPA-CA REVISED 12/15 (PAGE 1 OF 10) Print Date

EQUAL HOUSING
OPPORTUNITY

CALIFORNIA RESIDENTIAL PURCHASE AGREEMENT (RPA-CA PAGE 1 OF 10)

EXERCISE 7-3 (continued)

Property Address: <u>3840 Monroe Street, Concord, California</u>   Date: <u>1/11/XX</u>

H. VERIFICATION OF DOWN PAYMENT AND CLOSING COSTS: Buyer (or Buyer's lender or loan broker pursuant to paragraph 3J(1)) shall, within **3 (or ___) Days** After Acceptance, Deliver to Seller written verification of Buyer's down payment and closing costs. (☐ Verification attached.)

I. APPRAISAL CONTINGENCY AND REMOVAL: This Agreement is (**or** ☐ **is NOT**) contingent upon a written appraisal of the Property by a licensed or certified appraiser at no less than the purchase price. Buyer shall, as specified in paragraph 14B(3), in writing, remove the appraisal contingency or cancel this Agreement within **17 (or ___) Days** After Acceptance.

J. LOAN TERMS:

(1) LOAN APPLICATIONS: Within **3 (or ___) Days** After Acceptance, Buyer shall Deliver to Seller a letter from Buyer's lender or loan broker stating that, based on a review of Buyer's written application and credit report, Buyer is prequalified or preapproved for any NEW loan specified in paragraph 3D. If any loan specified in paragraph 3D is an adjustable rate loan, the prequalification or preapproval letter shall be based on the qualifying rate, not the initial loan rate. (☐ Letter attached.)

(2) LOAN CONTINGENCY: Buyer shall act diligently and in good faith to obtain the designated loan(s). Buyer's qualification for the loan(s) specified above **is a contingency** of this Agreement unless otherwise agreed in writing. If there is no appraisal contingency or the appraisal contingency has been waived or removed, then failure of the Property to appraise at the purchase price does not entitle Buyer to exercise the cancellation right pursuant to the loan contingency if Buyer is otherwise qualified for the specified loan. Buyer's contractual obligations regarding deposit, balance of down payment and closing costs **are not contingencies** of this Agreement.

(3) LOAN CONTINGENCY REMOVAL:
Within **21 (or** <u>10</u> **) Days** After Acceptance, Buyer shall, as specified in paragraph 14, in writing, remove the loan contingency or cancel this Agreement. If there is an appraisal contingency, removal of the loan contingency shall not be deemed removal of the appraisal contingency.

(4) ☐ **NO LOAN CONTINGENCY:** Obtaining any loan specified above is NOT a contingency of this Agreement. If Buyer does not obtain the loan and as a result does not purchase the Property, Seller may be entitled to Buyer's deposit or other legal remedies.

(5) LENDER LIMITS ON BUYER CREDITS: Any credit to Buyer, from any source, for closing or other costs that is agreed to by the Parties ("Contractual Credit") shall be disclosed to Buyer's lender. If the total credit allowed by Buyer's lender ("Lender Allowable Credit") is less than the Contractual Credit, then (i) the Contractual Credit shall be reduced to the Lender Allowable Credit, and (ii) in the absence of a separate written agreement between the Parties, there shall be no automatic adjustment to the purchase price to make up for the difference between the Contractual Credit and the Lender Allowable Credit.

K. BUYER STATED FINANCING: Seller is relying on Buyer's representation of the type of financing specified (including but not limited to, as applicable, all cash, amount of down payment, or contingent or non-contingent loan). Seller has agreed to a specific closing date, purchase price and to sell to Buyer in reliance on Buyer's covenant concerning financing. Buyer shall pursue the financing specified in this Agreement. Seller has no obligation to cooperate with Buyer's efforts to obtain any financing other than that specified in the Agreement and the availability of any such alternate financing does not excuse Buyer from the obligation to purchase the Property and close escrow as specified in this Agreement.

4. SALE OF BUYER'S PROPERTY:

A. This Agreement and Buyer's ability to obtain financing are NOT contingent upon the sale of any property owned by Buyer.

OR B. ☐ This Agreement and Buyer's ability to obtain financing are contingent upon the sale of property owned by Buyer as specified in the attached addendum (C.A.R. Form COP).

5. ADDENDA AND ADVISORIES:

A. ADDENDA: ☐ Addendum # _____ (C.A.R. Form ADM)
☐ Back Up Offer Addendum (C.A.R. Form BUO)   ☐ Court Confirmation Addendum (C.A.R. Form CCA)
☐ Septic, Well and Property Monument Addendum (C.A.R. Form SWPI)
☐ Short Sale Addendum (C.A.R. Form SSA)   ☐ Other _____

B. BUYER AND SELLER ADVISORIES: ☑ Buyer's Inspection Advisory (C.A.R. Form BIA)
☐ Probate Advisory (C.A.R. Form PA)   ☐ Statewide Buyer and Seller Advisory (C.A.R. Form SBSA)
☐ Trust Advisory (C.A.R. Form TA)   ☐ REO Advisory (C.A.R. Form REO)
☐ Short Sale Information and Advisory (C.A.R. Form SSIA)   ☐ Other _____

6. OTHER TERMS: _____
_____
_____
_____

7. ALLOCATION OF COSTS

A. INSPECTIONS, REPORTS AND CERTIFICATES: Unless otherwise agreed in writing, this paragraph only determines who is to pay for the inspection, test, certificate or service ("Report") mentioned; it **does not determine who is to pay for any work recommended or identified in the Report.**

(1) ☐ Buyer ☒ Seller shall pay for a natural hazard zone disclosure report, including tax ☐ environmental ☐ Other: _____
_____ prepared by <u>Pet Away, Inc.</u>

(2) ☐ Buyer ☐ Seller shall pay for the following Report _____
prepared by_____

(3) ☐ Buyer ☐ Seller shall pay for the following Report _____
prepared by _____

B. GOVERNMENT REQUIREMENTS AND RETROFIT:

(1) ☐ Buyer ☐ Seller shall pay for smoke alarm and carbon monoxide device installation and water heater bracing, if required by Law. Prior to Close Of Escrow ("COE"), Seller shall provide Buyer written statement(s) of compliance in accordance with state and local Law, unless Seller is exempt.

Buyer's Initials (*KAP*)(*KAP*)   Seller's Initials (_____)(_____)

EXERCISE 7-3 (continued)

Property Address: 3840 Monroe Street, Concord, California   Date: 1/11/XX

(2) (i) ☐ Buyer ☐ Seller shall pay the cost of compliance with any other minimum mandatory government inspections and reports if required as a condition of closing escrow under any Law.

(ii) ☐ Buyer ☐ Seller shall pay the cost of compliance with any other minimum mandatory government retrofit standards required as a condition of closing escrow under any Law, whether the work is required to be completed before or after COE.

(iii) Buyer shall be provided, within the time specified in paragraph 14A, a copy of any required government conducted or point-of-sale inspection report prepared pursuant to this Agreement or in anticipation of this sale of the Property.

C. ESCROW AND TITLE:

(1) (a) ☒ Buyer ☐ Seller shall pay escrow fee _____.

(b) Escrow Holder shall be _____.

(c) The Parties shall, within **5 (or ___) Days** After receipt, sign and return Escrow Holder's general provisions.

(2) (a) ☐ Buyer ☒ Seller shall pay for **owner's** title insurance policy specified in paragraph 13E _____.

(b) Owner's title policy to be issued by _____

(Buyer shall pay for any title insurance policy insuring Buyer's **lender**, unless otherwise agreed in writing.)

D. OTHER COSTS:

(1) ☐ Buyer ☐ Seller shall pay County transfer tax or fee _____.

(2) ☐ Buyer ☐ Seller shall pay City transfer tax or fee _____.

(3) ☐ Buyer ☐ Seller shall pay Homeowners' Association ("HOA") transfer fee _____.

(4) Seller shall pay HOA fees for preparing documents required to be delivered by Civil Code §4525.

(5) ☐ Buyer ☐ Seller shall pay HOA fees for preparing all documents other than those required by Civil Code §4525.

(6) Buyer to pay for any HOA certification fee.

(7) ☐ Buyer ☐ Seller shall pay for any private transfer fee _____.

(8) ☐ Buyer ☐ Seller shall pay for _____.

(9) ☐ Buyer ☐ Seller shall pay for _____.

(10) ☐ Buyer ☒ Seller shall pay for the cost, not to exceed $ 350.00 _____, of a standard (or ☐ upgraded) one-year home warranty plan, issued by Home Plan, Inc. _____, with the following optional coverages: ☐ Air Conditioner ☐ Pool/Spa ☐ Other: _____

Buyer is informed that home warranty plans have many optional coverages in addition to those listed above. Buyer is advised to investigate these coverages to determine those that may be suitable for Buyer.

OR ☐ Buyer waives the purchase of a home warranty plan. Nothing in this paragraph precludes Buyer's purchasing a home warranty plan during the term of this Agreement.

8. ITEMS INCLUDED IN AND EXCLUDED FROM SALE:

A. NOTE TO BUYER AND SELLER: Items listed as included or excluded in the MLS, flyers or marketing materials are **not** included in the purchase price or excluded from the sale unless specified in paragraph 8 B or C.

B. ITEMS INCLUDED IN SALE: Except as otherwise specified or disclosed,

(1) All EXISTING fixtures and fittings that are attached to the Property;

(2) EXISTING electrical, mechanical, lighting, plumbing and heating fixtures, ceiling fans, fireplace inserts, gas logs and grates, solar power systems, built-in appliances, window and door screens, awnings, shutters, window coverings, attached floor coverings, television antennas, satellite dishes, air coolers/conditioners, pool/spa equipment, garage door openers/remote controls, mailbox, in-ground landscaping, trees/shrubs, water features and fountains, water softeners, water purifiers, security systems/alarms and the following if checked: ☐ all stove(s), except _____; ☐ all refrigerator(s) except _____; ☐ all washer(s) and dryer(s), except _____;

(3) The following additional items: _____

(4) Existing integrated phone and home automation systems, including necessary components such as intranet and Internet-connected hardware or devices, control units (other than non-dedicated mobile devices, electronics and computers) and applicable software, permissions, passwords, codes and access information, are (☐ are NOT) included in the sale.

(5) **LEASED OR LIENED ITEMS AND SYSTEMS:** Seller shall, within the time specified in paragraph 14A, (i) disclose to Buyer if any item or system specified in paragraph 8B or otherwise included in the sale is leased, or not owned by Seller, or specifically subject to a lien or other encumbrance, and (ii) Deliver to Buyer all written materials (such as lease, warranty, etc.) concerning any such item. Buyer's ability to assume any such lease, or willingness to accept the Property subject to any such lien or encumbrance, is a contingency in favor of Buyer and Seller as specified in paragraph 14B and C.

(6) Seller represents that all items included in the purchase price, unless otherwise specified, (i) are owned by Seller and shall be transferred free and clear of liens and encumbrances, except the items and systems identified pursuant to 8B(5) and _____, and (ii) are transferred without Seller warranty regardless of value.

C. ITEMS EXCLUDED FROM SALE: Unless otherwise specified, the following items are excluded from sale: (i) audio and video components (such as flat screen TVs, speakers and other items) if any such item is not itself attached to the Property, even if a bracket or other mechanism attached to the component or item is attached to the Property; (ii) furniture and other items secured to the Property for earthquake purposes; and (iii) _____

_____. **Brackets attached to walls, floors or ceilings for any such component, furniture or item shall remain with the Property (or ☐ will be removed and holes or other damage shall be repaired, but not painted).**

9. CLOSING AND POSSESSION:

A. Buyer intends (or ☐ does not intend) to occupy the Property as Buyer's primary residence.

B. **Seller-occupied or vacant property:** Possession shall be delivered to Buyer: (i) at 6 PM or (_____ ☐ AM/☒ PM) on the date of Close Of Escrow; (ii) ☐ no later than 2 calendar days after Close Of Escrow; or (iii) ☐ at _____ ☐ AM/☐ PM on _____.

Buyer's Initials (*KAP*)(*KAP*)   Seller's Initials (_____)(_____)

RPA-CA REVISED 12/15 (PAGE 3 OF 10) Print Date

CALIFORNIA RESIDENTIAL PURCHASE AGREEMENT (RPA-CA PAGE 3 OF 10)

EXERCISE 7-3 (continued)

Property Address: 3840 Monroe Street, Concord, California   Date: 1/11/XX

    C. **Seller remaining in possession After Close Of Escrow:** If Seller has the right to remain in possession after Close Of Escrow, (i) the Parties are advised to sign a separate occupancy agreement such as ☐ C.A.R. Form SIP, for Seller continued occupancy of less than 30 days, ☐ C.A.R. Form RLAS for Seller continued occupancy of 30 days or more; and (ii) the Parties are advised to consult with their insurance and legal advisors for information about liability and damage or injury to persons and personal and real property; and (iii) Buyer is advised to consult with Buyer's lender about the impact of Seller's occupancy on Buyer's loan.

    D. **Tenant-occupied property: Property shall be vacant** at least **5 (or ___) Days** Prior to Close Of Escrow, unless otherwise agreed in writing. **Note to Seller: If you are unable to deliver Property vacant in accordance with rent control and other applicable Law, you may be in breach of this Agreement.**

    OR ☐ **Tenant to remain in possession** (C.A.R. Form TIP).

    E. At Close Of Escrow, Seller assigns to Buyer any assignable warranty rights for items included in the sale; and Seller shall Deliver to Buyer available Copies of any such warranties. Brokers cannot and will not determine the assignability of any warranties.

    F. At Close Of Escrow, unless otherwise agreed in writing, Seller shall provide keys, passwords, codes and/or means to operate all locks, mailboxes, security systems, alarms, home automation systems and intranet and Internet-connected devices included in the purchase price, and garage door openers. If the Property is a condominium or located in a common interest subdivision, Buyer may be required to pay a deposit to the Homeowners' Association ("HOA") to obtain keys to accessible HOA facilities.

10. **STATUTORY AND OTHER DISCLOSURES (INCLUDING LEAD-BASED PAINT HAZARD DISCLOSURES) AND CANCELLATION RIGHTS:**

    A. **(1)** Seller shall, within the time specified in paragraph 14A, Deliver to Buyer: (i) if required by Law, a fully completed: Federal Lead-Based Paint Disclosures (C.A.R. Form FLD) and pamphlet ("Lead Disclosures"); and **(ii)** unless exempt, fully completed disclosures or notices required by sections 1102 et. seq. and 1103 et. seq. of the Civil Code ("Statutory Disclosures"). Statutory Disclosures include, but are not limited to, a Real Estate Transfer Disclosure Statement ("TDS"), Natural Hazard Disclosure Statement ("NHD"), notice or actual knowledge of release of illegal controlled substance, notice of special tax and/or assessments (or, if allowed, substantially equivalent notice regarding the Mello-Roos Community Facilities Act of 1982 and Improvement Bond Act of 1915) and, if Seller has actual knowledge, of industrial use and military ordnance location (C.A.R. Form SPQ or ESD).

        (2) Any Statutory Disclosure required by this paragraph is considered fully completed if Seller has answered all questions and completed and signed the Seller section(s) and the Listing Agent, if any, has completed and signed the Listing Broker section(s), or, if applicable, an Agent Visual Inspection Disclosure (C.A.R. Form AVID). Nothing stated herein relieves a Buyer's Broker, if any, from the obligation to (i) conduct a reasonably competent and diligent visual inspection of the accessible areas of the Property and disclose, on Section IV of the TDS, or an AVID, material facts affecting the value or desirability of the Property that were or should have been revealed by such an inspection or (ii) complete any sections on all disclosures required to be completed by Buyer's Broker.

        (3) **Note to Buyer and Seller:** Waiver of Statutory and Lead Disclosures is prohibited by Law.

        (4) Within the time specified in paragraph 14A, (i) Seller, unless exempt from the obligation to provide a TDS, shall, complete and provide Buyer with a Seller Property Questionnaire (C.A.R. Form SPQ); (ii) if Seller is not required to provide a TDS, Seller shall complete and provide Buyer with an Exempt Seller Disclosure (C.A.R. Form ESD).

        (5) Buyer shall, within the time specified in paragraph 14B(1), return Signed Copies of the Statutory, Lead and other disclosures to Seller.

        (6) In the event Seller or Listing Broker, prior to Close Of Escrow, becomes aware of adverse conditions materially affecting the Property, or any material inaccuracy in disclosures, information or representations previously provided to Buyer, Seller shall promptly provide a subsequent or amended disclosure or notice, in writing, covering those items. **However, a subsequent or amended disclosure shall not be required for conditions and material inaccuracies** of which Buyer is otherwise aware, or which are **disclosed in reports provided to or obtained by Buyer or ordered and paid for by Buyer.**

        (7) If any disclosure or notice specified in paragraph 10A(1), or subsequent or amended disclosure or notice is Delivered to Buyer after the offer is Signed, Buyer shall have the right to cancel this Agreement within **3 Days** After Delivery in person, or **5 Days** After Delivery by deposit in the mail, by giving written notice of cancellation to Seller or Seller's agent.

    B. **NATURAL AND ENVIRONMENTAL HAZARD DISCLOSURES AND OTHER BOOKLETS:** Within the time specified in paragraph 14A, Seller shall, if required by Law: **(i)** Deliver to Buyer earthquake guide(s) (and questionnaire), environmental hazards booklet, and home energy rating pamphlet; **(ii)** disclose if the Property is located in a Special Flood Hazard Area; Potential Flooding (Inundation) Area; Very High Fire Hazard Zone; State Fire Responsibility Area; Earthquake Fault Zone; and Seismic Hazard Zone; and **(iii)** disclose any other zone as required by Law and provide any other information required for those zones.

    C. **WITHHOLDING TAXES:** Within the time specified in paragraph 14A, to avoid required withholding, Seller shall Deliver to Buyer or qualified substitute, an affidavit sufficient to comply with federal (FIRPTA) and California withholding Law (C.A.R. Form AS or QS).

    D. **MEGAN'S LAW DATABASE DISCLOSURE:** Notice: Pursuant to Section 290.46 of the Penal Code, information about specified registered sex offenders is made available to the public via an Internet Web site maintained by the Department of Justice at **www.meganslaw.ca.gov**. Depending on an offender's criminal history, this information will include either the address at which the offender resides or the community of residence and ZIP Code in which he or she resides. (Neither Seller nor Brokers are required to check this website. If Buyer wants further information, Broker recommends that Buyer obtain information from this website during Buyer's inspection contingency period. Brokers do not have expertise in this area.)

    E. **NOTICE REGARDING GAS AND HAZARDOUS LIQUID TRANSMISSION PIPELINES:** This notice is being provided simply to inform you that information about the general location of gas and hazardous liquid transmission pipelines is available to the public via the National Pipeline Mapping System (NPMS) Internet Web site maintained by the United States Department of Transportation at **http://www.npms.phmsa.dot.gov/**. To seek further information about possible transmission pipelines near the Property, you may contact your local gas utility or other pipeline operators in the area. Contact information for pipeline operators is searchable by ZIP Code and county on the NPMS Internet Web site.

    F. **CONDOMINIUM/PLANNED DEVELOPMENT DISCLOSURES:**

        (1) **SELLER HAS: 7 (or ___) Days** After Acceptance to disclose to Buyer if the Property is a condominium, or is located in a planned development or other common interest subdivision (C.A.R. Form SPQ or ESD).

Buyer's Initials (*KAP*)(*KAP*)   Seller's Initials (_____)(_____)

RPA-CA REVISED 12/15 (PAGE 4 OF 10) Print Date

CALIFORNIA RESIDENTIAL PURCHASE AGREEMENT (RPA-CA PAGE 4 OF 10)

EQUAL HOUSING OPPORTUNITY

EXERCISE 7-3 (continued)

Property Address: _____3840 Monroe Street, Concord, California_____ Date: __1/11/XX__

(2) If the Property is a condominium or is located in a planned development or other common interest subdivision, Seller has **3 (or ___) Days** After Acceptance to request from the HOA (C.A.R. Form HOA1): **(i)** Copies of any documents required by Law; **(ii)** disclosure of any pending or anticipated claim or litigation by or against the HOA; **(iii)** a statement containing the location and number of designated parking and storage spaces; **(iv)** Copies of the most recent 12 months of HOA minutes for regular and special meetings; **(v)** the names and contact information of all HOAs governing the Property (collectively, "CI Disclosures"); **(vi)** private transfer fees; **(vii)** Pet fee restrictions; and **(viii)** smoking restrictions. Seller shall itemize and Deliver to Buyer all CI Disclosures received from the HOA and any CI Disclosures in Seller's possession. Buyer's approval of CI Disclosures is a contingency of this Agreement as specified in paragraph 14B(3). The Party specified in paragraph 7, as directed by escrow, shall deposit funds into escrow or direct to HOA or management company to pay for any of the above.

11. **CONDITION OF PROPERTY:** Unless otherwise agreed in writing: **(i)** the Property is sold (a) "AS-IS" in its PRESENT physical condition as of the date of Acceptance and (b) subject to Buyer's Investigation rights; **(ii)** the Property, including pool, spa, landscaping and grounds, is to be maintained in substantially the same condition as on the date of Acceptance; and **(iii)** all debris and personal property not included in the sale shall be removed by Close Of Escrow.
    A. Seller shall, within the time specified in paragraph 14A, DISCLOSE KNOWN MATERIAL FACTS AND DEFECTS affecting the Property, including known insurance claims within the past five years, and make any and all other disclosures required by law.
    B. Buyer has the right to conduct Buyer Investigations of the Property and, as specified in paragraph 14B, based upon information discovered in those investigations: (i) cancel this Agreement; or (ii) request that Seller make Repairs or take other action.
    C. **Buyer is strongly advised to conduct investigations of the entire Property in order to determine its present condition. Seller may not be aware of all defects affecting the Property or other factors that Buyer considers important. Property improvements may not be built according to code, in compliance with current Law, or have had permits issued.**
12. **BUYER'S INVESTIGATION OF PROPERTY AND MATTERS AFFECTING PROPERTY:**
    A. Buyer's acceptance of the condition of, and any other matter affecting the Property, is a contingency of this Agreement as specified in this paragraph and paragraph 14B. Within the time specified in paragraph 14B(1), Buyer shall have the right, at Buyer's expense unless otherwise agreed, to conduct inspections, investigations, tests, surveys and other studies ("Buyer Investigations"), including, but not limited to: **(i)** a general physical inspection; **(ii)** an inspection specifically for wood destroying pests and organisms. Any inspection for wood destroying pests and organisms shall be prepared by a registered Structural Pest Control company; shall cover the main building and attached structures; may cover detached structures; shall NOT include water tests of shower pans on upper level units unless the owners of property below the shower consent; shall NOT include roof coverings; and, if the Property is a unit in a condominium or other common interest subdivision, the inspection shall include only the separate interest and any exclusive-use areas being transferred, and shall NOT include common areas; and shall include a report ("Pest Control Report") showing the findings of the company which shall be separated into sections for evident infestation or infections (Section 1) and for conditions likely to lead to infestation or infection (Section 2); **(iii)** inspect for lead-based paint and other lead-based paint hazards; **(iv)** satisfy Buyer as to any matter specified in the attached Buyer's Inspection Advisory (C.A.R. Form BIA); **(v)** review the registered sex offender database; **(vi)** confirm the insurability of Buyer and the Property including the availability and cost of flood and fire insurance; and **(vii)** review and seek approval of leases that may need to be assumed by Buyer. Without Seller's prior written consent, Buyer shall neither make nor cause to be made: invasive or destructive Buyer Investigations, except for minimally invasive testing required to prepare a Pest Control Report; or inspections by any governmental building or zoning inspector or government employee, unless required by Law.
    B. Seller shall make the Property available for all Buyer Investigations. Buyer shall **(i)** as specified in paragraph 14B, complete Buyer Investigations and either remove the contingency or cancel this Agreement, and **(ii)** give Seller, at no cost, complete Copies of all such Investigation reports obtained by Buyer, which obligation shall survive the termination of this Agreement.
    C. Seller shall have water, gas, electricity and all operable pilot lights on for Buyer's Investigations and through the date possession is made available to Buyer.
    D. **Buyer indemnity and seller protection for entry upon property:** Buyer shall: **(i)** keep the Property free and clear of liens; **(ii)** repair all damage arising from Buyer Investigations; and **(iii)** indemnify and hold Seller harmless from all resulting liability, claims, demands, damages and costs. Buyer shall carry, or Buyer shall require anyone acting on Buyer's behalf to carry, policies of liability, workers' compensation and other applicable insurance, defending and protecting Seller from liability for any injuries to persons or property occurring during any Buyer Investigations or work done on the Property at Buyer's direction prior to Close Of Escrow. Seller is advised that certain protections may be afforded Seller by recording a "Notice of Non-Responsibility" (C.A.R. Form NNR) for Buyer Investigations and work done on the Property at Buyer's direction. Buyer's obligations under this paragraph shall survive the termination of this Agreement.
13. **TITLE AND VESTING:**
    A. Within the time specified in paragraph 14, Buyer shall be provided a current preliminary title report ("Preliminary Report"). The Preliminary Report is only an offer by the title insurer to issue a policy of title insurance and may not contain every item affecting title. Buyer's review of the Preliminary Report and any other matters which may affect title are a contingency of this Agreement as specified in paragraph 14B. The company providing the Preliminary Report shall, prior to issuing a Preliminary Report, conduct a search of the General Index for all Sellers except banks or other institutional lenders selling properties they acquired through foreclosure (REOs), corporations, and government entities. Seller shall within 7 Days After Acceptance, give Escrow Holder a completed Statement of Information.
    B. Title is taken in its present condition subject to all encumbrances, easements, covenants, conditions, restrictions, rights and other matters, whether of record or not, as of the date of Acceptance except for: **(i)** monetary liens of record (which Seller is obligated to pay off) unless Buyer is assuming those obligations or taking the Property subject to those obligations; and **(ii)** those matters which Seller has agreed to remove in writing.
    C. Within the time specified in paragraph 14A, Seller has a duty to disclose to Buyer all matters known to Seller affecting title, whether of record or not.
    D. At Close Of Escrow, Buyer shall receive a grant deed conveying title (or, for stock cooperative or long-term lease, an assignment of stock certificate or of Seller's leasehold interest), including oil, mineral and water rights if currently owned by Seller. Title shall vest as designated in Buyer's supplemental escrow instructions. THE MANNER OF TAKING TITLE MAY HAVE SIGNIFICANT LEGAL AND TAX CONSEQUENCES. CONSULT AN APPROPRIATE PROFESSIONAL.
    E. Buyer shall receive a CLTA/ALTA "Homeowner's Policy of Title Insurance", if applicable to the type of property and buyer. If not, Escrow Holder shall notify Buyer. A title company can provide information about the availability, coverage, and cost of other title policies and endorsements. If the Homeowner's Policy is not available, Buyer shall choose another policy, instruct Escrow Holder in writing and shall pay any increase in cost.

Buyer's Initials (_KAP_)(_KAP_)

Seller's Initials (_____)(_____)

RPA-CA REVISED 12/15 (PAGE 5 OF 10) Print Date

CALIFORNIA RESIDENTIAL PURCHASE AGREEMENT (RPA-CA PAGE 5 OF 10)

EQUAL HOUSING OPPORTUNITY

EXERCISE 7-3 (continued)

Property Address: ___3840 Monroe Street, Concord, California___   Date: __1/11/XX__

14. TIME PERIODS; REMOVAL OF CONTINGENCIES; CANCELLATION RIGHTS: The following time periods may only be extended, altered, modified or changed by mutual written agreement. Any removal of contingencies or cancellation under this paragraph by either Buyer or Seller must be exercised in good faith and in writing (C.A.R. Form CR or CC).

A. SELLER HAS: 7 (or ___) Days After Acceptance to Deliver to Buyer all Reports, disclosures and information for which Seller is responsible under paragraphs 5, 6, 7, 8B(5), 10A, B, C, and F, ~~11A~~ and 13A. If, by the time specified, Seller has not Delivered any such item, Buyer after first Delivering to Seller a Notice to Seller to Perform (C.A.R. Form NSP) may cancel this Agreement.   *KAP KAP*

B. (1) BUYER HAS: 17 (or 20) Days After Acceptance, unless otherwise agreed in writing, to: **(i)** complete all Buyer Investigations; review all disclosures, reports, lease documents to be assumed by Buyer pursuant to paragraph 8B(5), and other applicable information, which Buyer receives from Seller; and approve all matters affecting the Property; and **(ii)** Deliver to Seller Signed Copies of Statutory and Lead Disclosures and other disclosures Delivered by Seller in accordance with paragraph 10A.

(2) Within the time specified in paragraph 14B(1), Buyer may request that Seller make repairs or take any other action regarding the Property (C.A.R. Form RR). Seller has no obligation to agree to or respond to (C.A.R. Form RRRR) Buyer's requests.

(3) By the end of the time specified in paragraph 14B(1) (or as otherwise specified in this Agreement), Buyer shall Deliver to Seller a removal of the applicable contingency or cancellation (C.A.R. Form CR or CC) of this Agreement. However, if any report, disclosure or information for which Seller is responsible is not Delivered within the time specified in paragraph 14A, then Buyer has **5 (or ___) Days** After Delivery of any such items, or the time specified in paragraph 14B(1), whichever is later, to Deliver to Seller a removal of the applicable contingency or cancellation of this Agreement.

(4) Continuation of Contingency: Even after the end of the time specified in paragraph 14B(1) and before Seller cancels, if at all, pursuant to paragraph 14D, Buyer retains the right, in writing, to either (i) remove remaining contingencies, or (ii) cancel this Agreement based on a remaining contingency. Once Buyer's written removal of all contingencies is Delivered to Seller, Seller may not cancel this Agreement pursuant to paragraph 14D(1).

(5) Access to Property: Buyer shall have access to the Property to conduct inspections and investigations for **17 (or ___) Days** After Acceptance, whether or not any part of the Buyer's Investigation Contingency has been waived or removed.

C. ☐ **REMOVAL OF CONTINGENCIES WITH OFFER: Buyer removes the contingencies specified in the attached Contingency Removal form (C.A.R. Form CR). If Buyer removes any contingency without an adequate understanding of the Property's condition or Buyer's ability to purchase, Buyer is acting against the advice of Broker.**

D. SELLER RIGHT TO CANCEL:

(1) Seller right to Cancel; Buyer Contingencies: If, by the time specified in this Agreement, Buyer does not Deliver to Seller a removal of the applicable contingency or cancellation of this Agreement, then Seller, after first Delivering to Buyer a Notice to Buyer to Perform (C.A.R. Form NBP), may cancel this Agreement. In such event, Seller shall authorize the return of Buyer's deposit, except for fees incurred by Buyer.

(2) Seller right to Cancel; Buyer Contract Obligations: Seller, after first delivering to Buyer a NBP, may cancel this Agreement if, by the time specified in this Agreement, Buyer does not take the following action(s): **(i)** Deposit funds as required by paragraph 3A, or 3B or if the funds deposited pursuant to paragraph 3A or 3B are not good when deposited; **(ii)** Deliver a notice of FHA or VA costs or terms as required by paragraph 3D(3) (C.A.R. Form FVA); **(iii)** Deliver a letter as required by paragraph 3J(1); **(iv)** Deliver verification, or a satisfactory verification if Seller reasonably disapproves of the verification already provided, as required by paragraph 3C or 3H; **(v)** In writing assume or accept leases or liens specified in 8B5; **(vi)** Return Statutory and Lead Disclosures as required by paragraph 10A(5); or **(vii)** Sign or initial a separate liquidated damages form for an increased deposit as required by paragraphs 3B and 21B; or **(viii)** Provide evidence of authority to sign in a representative capacity as specified in paragraph 19. In such event, Seller shall authorize the return of Buyer's deposit, except for fees incurred by Buyer.

E. NOTICE TO BUYER OR SELLER TO PERFORM: The NBP or NSP shall: **(i)** be in writing; **(ii)** be signed by the applicable Buyer or Seller; and **(iii)** give the other Party at least **2 (or ___) Days** After Delivery (or until the time specified in the applicable paragraph, whichever occurs last) to take the applicable action. A NBP or NSP may not be Delivered any earlier than **2 Days** Prior to the expiration of the applicable time for the other Party to remove a contingency or cancel this Agreement or meet an obligation specified in paragraph 14.

F. EFFECT OF BUYER'S REMOVAL OF CONTINGENCIES: If Buyer removes, in writing, any contingency or cancellation rights, unless otherwise specified in writing, Buyer shall conclusively be deemed to have: **(i)** completed all Buyer Investigations, and review of reports and other applicable information and disclosures pertaining to that contingency or cancellation right; **(ii)** elected to proceed with the transaction; and **(iii)** assumed all liability, responsibility and expense for Repairs or corrections pertaining to that contingency or cancellation right, or for the inability to obtain financing.

G. CLOSE OF ESCROW: Before Buyer or Seller may cancel this Agreement for failure of the other Party to close escrow pursuant to this Agreement, Buyer or Seller must first Deliver to the other Party a demand to close escrow (C.A.R. Form DCE). The DCE shall: **(i)** be signed by the applicable Buyer or Seller; and **(ii)** give the other Party at least **3 (or ___) Days** After Delivery to close escrow. A DCE may not be Delivered any earlier than **3 Days** Prior to the scheduled close of escrow.

H. EFFECT OF CANCELLATION ON DEPOSITS: If Buyer or Seller gives written notice of cancellation pursuant to rights duly exercised under the terms of this Agreement, the Parties agree to Sign mutual instructions to cancel the sale and escrow and release deposits, if any, to the party entitled to the funds, less fees and costs incurred by that party. Fees and costs may be payable to service providers and vendors for services and products provided during escrow. Except as specified below, **release of funds will require mutual Signed release instructions from the Parties, judicial decision or arbitration award.** If either Party fails to execute mutual instructions to cancel escrow, one Party may make a written demand to Escrow Holder for the deposit (C.A.R. Form BDRD or SDRD). Escrow Holder, upon receipt, shall promptly deliver notice of the demand to the other Party. If, within 10 Days After Escrow Holder's notice, the other Party does not object to the demand, Escrow Holder shall disburse the deposit to the Party making the demand. If Escrow Holder complies with the preceding process, each Party shall be deemed to have released Escrow Holder from any and all claims or liability related to the disbursal of the deposit. Escrow Holder, at its discretion, may nonetheless require mutual cancellation instructions. **A Party may be subject to a civil penalty of up to $1,000 for refusal to sign cancellation instructions if no good faith dispute exists as to who is entitled to the deposited funds (Civil Code §1057.3).**

Buyer's Initials (*KAP*)(*KAP*)   Seller's Initials (_____)(_____)

RPA-CA REVISED 12/15 (PAGE 6 OF 10) Print Date

CALIFORNIA RESIDENTIAL PURCHASE AGREEMENT (RPA-CA PAGE 6 OF 10)

EQUAL HOUSING OPPORTUNITY

EXERCISE 7-3 (continued)

Property Address: 3840 Monroe Street, Concord, California   Date: 1/11/XX

15. FINAL VERIFICATION OF CONDITION: Buyer shall have the right to make a final verification of the Property within **5 (or ☒ 2) Days** Prior to Close Of Escrow, NOT AS A CONTINGENCY OF THE SALE, but solely to confirm: **(i)** the Property is maintained pursuant to paragraph 11; **(ii)** Repairs have been completed as agreed; and **(iii)** Seller has complied with Seller's other obligations under this Agreement (C.A.R. Form VP).

16. REPAIRS: Repairs shall be completed prior to final verification of condition unless otherwise agreed in writing. Repairs to be performed at Seller's expense may be performed by Seller or through others, provided that the work complies with applicable Law, including governmental permit, inspection and approval requirements. Repairs shall be performed in a good, skillful manner with materials of quality and appearance comparable to existing materials. It is understood that exact restoration of appearance or cosmetic items following all Repairs may not be possible. Seller shall: **(i)** obtain invoices and paid receipts for Repairs performed by others; **(ii)** prepare a written statement indicating the Repairs performed by Seller and the date of such Repairs; and **(iii)** provide Copies of invoices and paid receipts and statements to Buyer prior to final verification of condition.

17. PRORATIONS OF PROPERTY TAXES AND OTHER ITEMS: Unless otherwise agreed in writing, the following items shall be PAID CURRENT and prorated between Buyer and Seller as of Close Of Escrow: real property taxes and assessments, interest, rents, HOA regular, special, and emergency dues and assessments imposed prior to Close Of Escrow, premiums on insurance assumed by Buyer, payments on bonds and assessments assumed by Buyer, and payments on Mello-Roos and other Special Assessment District bonds and assessments that are now a lien. The following items shall be assumed by Buyer WITHOUT CREDIT toward the purchase price: prorated payments on Mello-Roos and other Special Assessment District bonds and assessments and HOA special assessments that are now a lien but not yet due. Property will be reassessed upon change of ownership. Any supplemental tax bills shall be paid as follows: **(i)** for periods after Close Of Escrow, by Buyer; and **(ii)** for periods prior to Close Of Escrow, by Seller (see C.A.R. Form SPT or SBSA for further information). TAX BILLS ISSUED AFTER CLOSE OF ESCROW SHALL BE HANDLED DIRECTLY BETWEEN BUYER AND SELLER. Prorations shall be made based on a 30-day month.

18. BROKERS:
    A. COMPENSATION: Seller or Buyer, or both, as applicable, agree to pay compensation to Broker as specified in a separate written agreement between Broker and that Seller or Buyer. Compensation is payable upon Close Of Escrow, or if escrow does not close, as otherwise specified in the agreement between Broker and that Seller or Buyer.
    B. SCOPE OF DUTY: Buyer and Seller acknowledge and agree that Broker: **(i)** Does not decide what price Buyer should pay or Seller should accept; **(ii)** Does not guarantee the condition of the Property; **(iii)** Does not guarantee the performance, adequacy or completeness of inspections, services, products or repairs provided or made by Seller or others; **(iv)** Does not have an obligation to conduct an inspection of common areas or areas off the site of the Property; **(v)** Shall not be responsible for identifying defects on the Property, in common areas, or offsite unless such defects are visually observable by an inspection of reasonably accessible areas of the Property or are known to Broker; **(vi)** Shall not be responsible for inspecting public records or permits concerning the title or use of Property; **(vii)** Shall not be responsible for identifying the location of boundary lines or other items affecting title; **(viii)** Shall not be responsible for verifying square footage, representations of others or information contained in Investigation reports, Multiple Listing Service, advertisements, flyers or other promotional material; **(ix)** Shall not be responsible for determining the fair market value of the Property or any personal property included in the sale; **(x)** Shall not be responsible for providing legal or tax advice regarding any aspect of a transaction entered into by Buyer or Seller; and **(xi)** Shall not be responsible for providing other advice or information that exceeds the knowledge, education and experience required to perform real estate licensed activity. Buyer and Seller agree to seek legal, tax, insurance, title and other desired assistance from appropriate professionals.

19. REPRESENTATIVE CAPACITY: If one or more Parties is signing this Agreement in a representative capacity and not for him/ herself as an individual then that Party shall so indicate in paragraph 31 or 32 and attach a Representative Capacity Signature Disclosure (C.A.R. Form RCSD). Wherever the signature or initials of the representative identified in the RCSD appear on this Agreement or any related documents, it shall be deemed to be in a representative capacity for the entity described and not in an individual capacity, unless otherwise indicated. The Party acting in a representative capacity (i) represents that the entity for which that party is acting already exists and (ii) shall Deliver to the other Party and Escrow Holder, within **3 Days** After Acceptance, evidence of authority to act in that capacity (such as but not limited to: applicable portion of the trust or Certification Of Trust (Probate Code §18100.5), letters testamentary, court order, power of attorney, corporate resolution, or formation documents of the business entity).

20. JOINT ESCROW INSTRUCTIONS TO ESCROW HOLDER:
    A. The following paragraphs, or applicable portions thereof, of this Agreement constitute the joint escrow instructions of Buyer and Seller to Escrow Holder, which Escrow Holder is to use along with any related counter offers and addenda, and any additional mutual instructions to close the escrow: paragraphs 1, 3, 4B, 5A, 6, 7, 10C, 13, 14G, 17, 18A, 19, 20, 26, 29, 30, 31, 32 and paragraph D of the section titled Real Estate Brokers on page 10. If a Copy of the separate compensation agreement(s) provided for in paragraph 18A, or paragraph D of the section titled Real Estate Brokers on page 10 is deposited with Escrow Holder by Broker, Escrow Holder shall accept such agreement(s) and pay out from Buyer's or Seller's funds, or both, as applicable, the Broker's compensation provided for in such agreement(s). The terms and conditions of this Agreement not set forth in the specified paragraphs are additional matters for the information of Escrow Holder, but about which Escrow Holder need not be concerned. Buyer and Seller will receive Escrow Holder's general provisions, if any, directly from Escrow Holder and will execute such provisions within the time specified in paragraph 7C(1)(c). To the extent the general provisions are inconsistent or conflict with this Agreement, the general provisions will control as to the duties and obligations of Escrow Holder only. Buyer and Seller will execute additional instructions, documents and forms provided by Escrow Holder that are reasonably necessary to close the escrow and, as directed by Escrow Holder, within **3 (or ___) Days**, shall pay to Escrow Holder or HOA or HOA management company or others any fee required by paragraphs 7, 10 or elsewhere in this Agreement.
    B. A Copy of this Agreement including any counter offer(s) and addenda shall be delivered to Escrow Holder within **3 Days** After Acceptance (or 5 calendar days ___). Buyer and Seller authorize Escrow Holder to accept and rely on Copies and Signatures as defined in this Agreement as originals, to open escrow and for other purposes of escrow. The validity of this Agreement as between Buyer and Seller is not affected by whether or when Escrow Holder Signs this Agreement. Escrow Holder shall provide Seller's Statement of Information to Title company when received from Seller. If Seller delivers an affidavit to Escrow Holder to satisfy Seller's FIRPTA obligation under paragraph 10C, Escrow Holder shall deliver to Buyer a Qualified Substitute statement that complies with federal Law.

Buyer's Initials (*KAP*)(*KAP*)   Seller's Initials (_____)(_____)

RPA-CA REVISED 12/15 (PAGE 7 OF 10) Print Date

CALIFORNIA RESIDENTIAL PURCHASE AGREEMENT (RPA-CA PAGE 7 OF 10)

EXERCISE 7-3 (continued)

Property Address: __3840 Monroe Street, Concord, California__   Date: __1/11/XX__

C. Brokers are a party to the escrow for the sole purpose of compensation pursuant to paragraph 18A and paragraph D of the section titled Real Estate Brokers on page 10. Buyer and Seller irrevocably assign to Brokers compensation specified in paragraph 18A, and irrevocably instruct Escrow Holder to disburse those funds to Brokers at Close Of Escrow or pursuant to any other mutually executed cancellation agreement. Compensation instructions can be amended or revoked only with the written consent of Brokers. Buyer and Seller shall release and hold harmless Escrow Holder from any liability resulting from Escrow Holder's payment to Broker(s) of compensation pursuant to this Agreement.

D. Upon receipt, Escrow Holder shall provide Seller and Seller's Broker verification of Buyer's deposit of funds pursuant to paragraph 3A and 3B. Once Escrow Holder becomes aware of any of the following, Escrow Holder shall immediately notify all Brokers: **(i)** if Buyer's initial or any additional deposit or down payment is not made pursuant to this Agreement, or is not good at time of deposit with Escrow Holder; or **(ii)** if Buyer and Seller instruct Escrow Holder to cancel escrow.

E. A Copy of any amendment that affects any paragraph of this Agreement for which Escrow Holder is responsible shall be delivered to Escrow Holder within **3 Days** after mutual execution of the amendment.

21. REMEDIES FOR BUYER'S BREACH OF CONTRACT:

A. **Any clause added by the Parties specifying a remedy (such as release or forfeiture of deposit or making a deposit non-refundable) for failure of Buyer to complete the purchase in violation of this Agreement shall be deemed invalid unless the clause independently satisfies the statutory liquidated damages requirements set forth in the Civil Code.**

B. **LIQUIDATED DAMAGES: If Buyer fails to complete this purchase because of Buyer's default, Seller shall retain, as liquidated damages, the deposit actually paid. If the Property is a dwelling with no more than four units, one of which Buyer intends to occupy, then the amount retained shall be no more than 3% of the purchase price. Any excess shall be returned to Buyer. Except as provided in paragraph 14G, release of funds will require mutual, Signed release instructions from both Buyer and Seller, judicial decision or arbitration award. AT THE TIME OF ANY INCREASED DEPOSIT BUYER AND SELLER SHALL SIGN A SEPARATE LIQUIDATED DAMAGES PROVISION INCORPORATING THE INCREASED DEPOSIT AS LIQUIDATED DAMAGES (C.A.R. FORM RID).**

Buyer's Initials _KAP_ / _KAP_   Seller's Initials _____ / _____

22. DISPUTE RESOLUTION:

A. **MEDIATION:** The Parties agree to mediate any dispute or claim arising between them out of this Agreement, or any resulting transaction, before resorting to arbitration or court action through the C.A.R. Real Estate Mediation Center for Consumers (**www.consumermediation.org**) or through any other mediation provider or service mutually agreed to by the Parties. The Parties **also agree to mediate any disputes or claims with Broker(s), who, in writing, agree to such mediation prior to, or within a reasonable time after, the dispute or claim is presented to the Broker.** Mediation fees, if any, shall be divided equally among the Parties involved. If, for any dispute or claim to which this paragraph applies, any Party (i) commences an action without first attempting to resolve the matter through mediation, or (ii) before commencement of an action, refuses to mediate after a request has been made, then that Party shall not be entitled to recover attorney fees, even if they would otherwise be available to that Party in any such action. THIS MEDIATION PROVISION APPLIES WHETHER OR NOT THE ARBITRATION PROVISION IS INITIALED. **Exclusions from this mediation agreement are specified in paragraph 22C.**

B. **ARBITRATION OF DISPUTES:**
The Parties agree that any dispute or claim in Law or equity arising between them out of this Agreement or any resulting transaction, which is not settled through mediation, shall be decided by neutral, binding arbitration. The Parties also agree to arbitrate any disputes or claims with Broker(s), who, in writing, agree to such arbitration prior to, or within a reasonable time after, the dispute or claim is presented to the Broker. The arbitrator shall be a retired judge or justice, or an attorney with at least 5 years of residential real estate Law experience, unless the parties mutually agree to a different arbitrator. The Parties shall have the right to discovery in accordance with Code of Civil Procedure §1283.05. In all other respects, the arbitration shall be conducted in accordance with Title 9 of Part 3 of the Code of Civil Procedure. Judgment upon the award of the arbitrator(s) may be entered into any court having jurisdiction. Enforcement of this agreement to arbitrate shall be governed by the Federal Arbitration Act. Exclusions from this arbitration agreement are specified in paragraph 22C.
      "NOTICE: BY INITIALING IN THE SPACE BELOW YOU ARE AGREEING TO HAVE ANY DISPUTE ARISING OUT OF THE MATTERS INCLUDED IN THE 'ARBITRATION OF DISPUTES' PROVISION DECIDED BY NEUTRAL ARBITRATION AS PROVIDED BY CALIFORNIA LAW AND YOU ARE GIVING UP ANY RIGHTS YOU MIGHT POSSESS TO HAVE THE DISPUTE LITIGATED IN A COURT OR JURY TRIAL. BY INITIALING IN THE SPACE BELOW YOU ARE GIVING UP YOUR JUDICIAL RIGHTS TO DISCOVERY AND APPEAL, UNLESS THOSE RIGHTS ARE SPECIFICALLY INCLUDED IN THE 'ARBITRATION OF DISPUTES' PROVISION. IF YOU REFUSE TO SUBMIT TO ARBITRATION AFTER AGREEING TO THIS PROVISION, YOU MAY BE COMPELLED TO ARBITRATE UNDER THE AUTHORITY OF THE CALIFORNIA CODE OF CIVIL PROCEDURE. YOUR AGREEMENT TO THIS ARBITRATION PROVISION IS VOLUNTARY."
      "WE HAVE READ AND UNDERSTAND THE FOREGOING AND AGREE TO SUBMIT DISPUTES ARISING OUT OF THE MATTERS INCLUDED IN THE 'ARBITRATION OF DISPUTES' PROVISION TO NEUTRAL ARBITRATION."

Buyer's Initials _KAP_ / _KAP_   Seller's Initials _____ / _____

C. **ADDITIONAL MEDIATION AND ARBITRATION TERMS:**
   (1) EXCLUSIONS: The following matters are excluded from mediation and arbitration: (i) a judicial or non-judicial foreclosure or other action or proceeding to enforce a deed of trust, mortgage or installment land sale contract as defined in Civil Code §2985; (ii) an unlawful detainer action; and (iii) any matter that is within the jurisdiction of a probate, small claims or bankruptcy court.

Buyer's Initials (_KAP_)(_____)   Seller's Initials (_____)(_____)

RPA-CA REVISED 12/15 (PAGE 8 of 10)   Print Date
CALIFORNIA RESIDENTIAL PURCHASE AGREEMENT (RPA-CA PAGE 8 OF 10)

EXERCISE 7-3 (continued)

Property Address: 3840 Monroe Street, Concord, California   Date: 1/11/XX

    (2) PRESERVATION OF ACTIONS: The following shall not constitute a waiver nor violation of the mediation and arbitration provisions: (i) the filing of a court action to preserve a statute of limitations; (ii) the filing of a court action to enable the recording of a notice of pending action, for order of attachment, receivership, injunction, or other provisional remedies; or (iii) the filing of a mechanic's lien.

    (3) BROKERS: Brokers shall not be obligated nor compelled to mediate or arbitrate unless they agree to do so in writing. Any Broker(s) participating in mediation or arbitration shall not be deemed a party to this Agreement.

23. SELECTION OF SERVICE PROVIDERS: Brokers do not guarantee the performance of any vendors, service or product providers ("Providers"), whether referred by Broker or selected by Buyer, Seller or other person. Buyer and Seller may select ANY Providers of their own choosing.

24. MULTIPLE LISTING SERVICE ("MLS"): Brokers are authorized to report to the MLS a pending sale and, upon Close Of Escrow, the sales price and other terms of this transaction shall be provided to the MLS to be published and disseminated to persons and entities authorized to use the information on terms approved by the MLS.

25. ATTORNEY FEES: In any action, proceeding, or arbitration between Buyer and Seller arising out of this Agreement, the prevailing Buyer or Seller shall be entitled to reasonable attorney fees and costs from the non-prevailing Buyer or Seller, except as provided in paragraph 22A.

26. ASSIGNMENT: Buyer shall not assign all or any part of Buyer's interest in this Agreement without first having obtained the separate written consent of Seller to a specified assignee. Such consent shall not be unreasonably withheld. Any total or partial assignment shall not relieve Buyer of Buyer's obligations pursuant to this Agreement unless otherwise agreed in writing by Seller (C.A.R. Form AOAA).

27. EQUAL HOUSING OPPORTUNITY: The Property is sold in compliance with federal, state and local anti-discrimination Laws.

28. TERMS AND CONDITIONS OF OFFER:
    This is an offer to purchase the Property on the above terms and conditions. The liquidated damages paragraph or the arbitration of disputes paragraph is incorporated in this Agreement if initialed by all Parties or if incorporated by mutual agreement in a counter offer or addendum. If at least one but not all Parties initial, a counter offer is required until agreement is reached. Seller has the right to continue to offer the Property for sale and to accept any other offer at any time prior to notification of Acceptance. The Parties have read and acknowledge receipt of a Copy of the offer and agree to the confirmation of agency relationships. If this offer is accepted and Buyer subsequently defaults, Buyer may be responsible for payment of Brokers' compensation. This Agreement and any supplement, addendum or modification, including any Copy, may be Signed in two or more counterparts, all of which shall constitute one and the same writing.

29. TIME OF ESSENCE; ENTIRE CONTRACT; CHANGES: Time is of the essence. All understandings between the Parties are incorporated in this Agreement. Its terms are intended by the Parties as a final, complete and exclusive expression of their Agreement with respect to its subject matter, and may not be contradicted by evidence of any prior agreement or contemporaneous oral agreement. If any provision of this Agreement is held to be ineffective or invalid, the remaining provisions will nevertheless be given full force and effect. Except as otherwise specified, this Agreement shall be interpreted and disputes shall be resolved in accordance with the Laws of the State of California. **Neither this Agreement nor any provision in it may be extended, amended, modified, altered or changed, except in writing Signed by Buyer and Seller.**

30. DEFINITIONS: As used in this Agreement:
    A. **"Acceptance"** means the time the offer or final counter offer is accepted in writing by a Party and is delivered to and personally received by the other Party or that Party's authorized agent in accordance with the terms of this offer or a final counter offer.
    B. **"Agreement"** means this document and any counter offers and any incorporated addenda, collectively forming the binding agreement between the Parties. Addenda are incorporated only when Signed by all Parties.
    C. **"C.A.R. Form"** means the most current version of the specific form referenced or another comparable form agreed to by the parties.
    D. **"Close Of Escrow"**, including **"COE"**, means the date the grant deed, or other evidence of transfer of title, is recorded.
    E. **"Copy"** means copy by any means including photocopy, NCR, facsimile and electronic.
    F. **"Days"** means calendar days. However, after Acceptance, the last **Day** for performance of any act required by this Agreement (including Close Of Escrow) shall not include any Saturday, Sunday, or legal holiday and shall instead be the next Day.
    G. **"Days After"** means the specified number of calendar days after the occurrence of the event specified, not counting the calendar date on which the specified event occurs, and ending at 11:59 PM on the final day.
    H. **"Days Prior"** means the specified number of calendar days before the occurrence of the event specified, not counting the calendar date on which the specified event is scheduled to occur.
    I. **"Deliver"**, **"Delivered"** or **"Delivery"**, unless otherwise specified in writing, means and shall be effective upon: personal receipt by Buyer or Seller or the individual Real Estate Licensee for that principal as specified in the section titled Real Estate Brokers on page 10, regardless of the method used (i.e., messenger, mail, email, fax, other).
    J. **"Electronic Copy"** or **"Electronic Signature"** means, as applicable, an electronic copy or signature complying with California Law. Buyer and Seller agree that electronic means will not be used by either Party to modify or alter the content or integrity of this Agreement without the knowledge and consent of the other Party.
    K. **"Law"** means any law, code, ordinance, regulation, rule or order, which is adopted by a controlling city, county, state or federal legislative, judicial or executive body or agency.
    L. **"Repairs"** means any repairs (including pest control), alterations, replacements, modifications or retrofitting of the Property provided for under this Agreement.
    M. **"Signed"** means either a handwritten or electronic signature on an original document, Copy or any counterpart.

31. EXPIRATION OF OFFER: This offer shall be deemed revoked and the deposit, if any, shall be returned to Buyer unless the offer is Signed by Seller and a Copy of the Signed offer is personally received by Buyer, or by _____,
who is authorized to receive it, by 5:00 PM on the third Day after this offer is signed by Buyer (or by ☐ _____ ☐AM/☐PM,
on _____ (date)).
☐ One or more Buyers is signing this Agreement in a representative capacity and not for him/herself as an individual. See attached Representative Capacity Signature Disclosure (C.A.R. Form RCSD-B) for additional terms.

Date _____ BUYER *Kenneth A. Plummer*
(Print name) Kenneth A. Plummer _____

Date _____ BUYER *Peggy M. Plummer*
(Print name) Peggy M. Plummer _____

☐ Additional Signature Addendum attached (C.A.R. Form ASA).

RPA-CA REVISED 12/15 (PAGE 9 of 10) Print Date   Seller's Initials (_____)(_____)

CALIFORNIA RESIDENTIAL PURCHASE AGREEMENT (RPA-CA PAGE 9 OF 10)

EXERCISE 7-3 (continued)

Property Address: 3840 Monroe Street, Concord, California   Date: 1/11/XX

32. ACCEPTANCE OF OFFER: Seller warrants that Seller is the owner of the Property, or has the authority to execute this Agreement. Seller accepts the above offer and agrees to sell the Property on the above terms and conditions. Seller has read and acknowledges receipt of a Copy of this Agreement, and authorizes Broker to Deliver a Signed Copy to Buyer.

☐ (If checked) SELLER'S ACCEPTANCE IS **SUBJECT TO ATTACHED COUNTER OFFER (C.A.R. Form SCO or SMCO) DATED:**
_____

☐ One or more Sellers is signing this Agreement in a representative capacity and not for him/herself as an individual. See attached Representative Capacity Signature Disclosure (C.A.R. Form RCSD-S) for additional terms.

Date _____ SELLER _____

(Print name) _____

Date _____ SELLER _____

(Print name) _____

☐ Additional Signature Addendum attached (C.A.R. Form ASA).

(____/____) **(Do not initial if making a counter offer.)** CONFIRMATION OF ACCEPTANCE: A Copy of Signed Acceptance was
(Initials) personally received by Buyer or Buyer's authorized agent on (date) _____ at _____
☐AM/☐PM. **A binding Agreement is created when a Copy of Signed Acceptance is personally received by Buyer or Buyer's authorized agent whether or not confirmed in this document. Completion of this confirmation is not legally required in order to create a binding Agreement; it is solely intended to evidence the date that Confirmation of Acceptance has occurred.**

REAL ESTATE BROKERS:
A. **Real Estate Brokers are not parties to the Agreement between Buyer and Seller.**
B. **Agency relationships are confirmed as stated in paragraph 2.**
C. If specified in paragraph 3A(2), Agent who submitted the offer for Buyer acknowledges receipt of deposit.
D. **COOPERATING BROKER COMPENSATION:** Listing Broker agrees to pay Cooperating Broker **(Selling Firm)** and Cooperating Broker agrees to accept, out of Listing Broker's proceeds in escrow, the amount specified in the MLS, provided Cooperating Broker is a Participant of the MLS in which the Property is offered for sale or a reciprocal MLS. If Listing Broker and Cooperating Broker are not both Participants of the MLS, or a reciprocal MLS, in which the Property is offered for sale, then compensation must be specified in a separate written agreement (C.A.R. Form CBC). Declaration of License and Tax (C.A.R. Form DLT) may be used to document that tax reporting will be required or that an exemption exists.

Real Estate Broker (Selling Firm) _____ CalBRE Lic. #_____
By _____ CalBRE Lic. #_____ Date _____
By _____ CalBRE Lic. #_____ Date _____
Address _____ City _____ State _____ Zip _____
Telephone _____ Fax _____ E-mail _____
Real Estate Broker (Listing Firm) _____ CalBRE Lic. #_____
By _____ CalBRE Lic. #_____ Date _____
By _____ CalBRE Lic. #_____ Date _____
Address _____ City _____ State _____ Zip _____
Telephone _____ Fax _____ E-mail _____

ESCROW HOLDER ACKNOWLEDGMENT:
Escrow Holder acknowledges receipt of a Copy of this Agreement, (if checked, ☐ a deposit in the amount of $ _____),
counter offer numbers _____ ☐ Seller's Statement of Information and _____
_____, and agrees to act as Escrow Holder subject to paragraph 20 of this Agreement, any supplemental escrow instructions and the terms of Escrow Holder's general provisions.

Escrow Holder is advised that the date of Confirmation of Acceptance of the Agreement as between Buyer and Seller is _____

Escrow Holder _____ Escrow # _____
By _____ Date_____
Address _____
Phone/Fax/E-mail _____
Escrow Holder has the following license number # _____
☐ Department of Business Oversight, ☐ Department of Insurance, ☐ Bureau of Real Estate.

PRESENTATION OF OFFER: (_____) Listing Broker presented this offer to Seller on _____(date).
Broker or Designee Initials

REJECTION OF OFFER: (_____)(_____) No counter offer is being made. This offer was rejected by Seller on_____(date).
Seller's Initials

Buyer Acknowledges that page 10 is part of this Agreement (_____)(_____)
Buyer's Initials

Reviewed by _____
Broker or Designee _____

RPA-CA REVISED 12/15 (PAGE 10 of 10)   **Print Date**
CALIFORNIA RESIDENTIAL PURCHASE AGREEMENT (RPA-CA PAGE 10 OF 10)

Exercise 9-2, Page 288

1. Sale-leaseback
2. Sales contract
3. Purchase-money mortgage
4. CalVet loan

Exercise 9-3, Page 292

The secondary market for real estate mortgage loans benefits borrowers by providing lenders with a source of funds from which to make additional loans.

Review Questions, Pages 294–295

1. a	8. a	15. b
2. b	9. b	16. c
3. a	10. c	17. c
4. c	11. c	18. c
5. b	12. c	19. d
6. c	13. c	20. d
7. d	14. d	

UNIT 10
Exercise 10-1, Page 303

1. No, unless both parties agree in writing to any changes in escrow instructions. The escrow agent is bound by the latest written instructions only.
2. Tom should immediately inform both seller and buyer of what he has learned, as the mud slide damage could have a serious impact on any potential use of the land.

Exercise 10-2, Page 313

See the completed Closing Disclosure form on pages 569–573.

Exercise 10-3, Page 331

1. Certificate of title
2. Guarantee of title
3. CLTA standard policy of title insurance
4. ALTA extended-coverage policy of title insurance
5. Abstract of title
6. CLTA standard policy of title insurance

Review Questions, Pages 333–334

1. a	8. b	15. a
2. c	9. a	16. b
3. d	10. b	17. c
4. b	11. a	18. b
5. c	12. b	19. a
6. c	13. a	20. a
7. c	14. c	

UNIT 11
Exercise 11-1, Page 341

Assessor's appraised value	$695,000
Less homeowner's exemption	7,000
Taxable amount	$688,000
Tax rate	0.01
Tax	$6,880
Installment	$3,440
Delinquent payment	$3,784

Exercise 11-2, Page 356

1. The Clocks' present rental expenses are $2,061 per month ($1,875 rent plus $186 utilities). In the fifth year they will be paying a total of $2,465.08, assuming a 5% increase per year and no increase in utility payments, and will start the sixth year at $2,579.03 per month. They will receive no tax break on the rental expenses.

EXERCISE 10-2

Closing Disclosure

This form is a statement of final loan terms and closing costs. Compare this document with your Loan Estimate.

Closing Information

Date Issued	4/15/2013
Closing Date	4/15/2013
Disbursement Date	4/15/2013
Settlement Agent	Epsilon Title Co.
File #	12-3456
Property	456 Somewhere Ave
	Anytown, ST 12345
Sale Price	$180,000

Transaction Information

Borrower	Michael Jones and Mary Stone
	123 Anywhere Street
	Anytown, ST 12345
Seller	Steve Cole and Amy Doe
	321 Somewhere Drive
	Anytown, ST 12345
Lender	Ficus Bank

Loan Information

Loan Term	30 years
Purpose	Purchase
Product	Fixed Rate
Loan Type	☒ Conventional ☐ FHA ☐ VA ☐ _____
Loan ID #	123456789
MIC #	000654321

Loan Terms

		Can this amount increase after closing?
Loan Amount	$162,000	**NO**
Interest Rate	3.875%	**NO**
Monthly Principal & Interest *See Projected Payments below for your Estimated Total Monthly Payment*	$761.78	**NO**
		Does the loan have these features?
Prepayment Penalty	**YES**	• **As high as $3,240** if you pay off the loan during the first 2 years
Balloon Payment		**NO**

Projected Payments

Payment Calculation	Years 1-7		Years 8-30	
Principal & Interest		$761.78		$761.78
Mortgage Insurance	+	82.35	+	—
Estimated Escrow *Amount can increase over time*	+	206.13	+	206.13
Estimated Total Monthly Payment		**$1,050.26**		**$967.91**

Estimated Taxes, Insurance & Assessments *Amount can increase over time* *See page 4 for details*	$356.13 a month	**This estimate includes** ☒ Property Taxes ☒ Homeowner's Insurance ☒ Other: Homeowner's Association Dues *See Escrow Account on page 4 for details. You must pay for other property costs separately.*	**In escrow?** YES YES NO

Costs at Closing

Closing Costs	$9,712.10	Includes $4,694.05 in Loan Costs + $5,018.05 in Other Costs – $0 in Lender Credits. *See page 2 for details.*
Cash to Close	$14,147.26	Includes Closing Costs. *See Calculating Cash to Close on page 3 for details.*

EXERCISE 10-2 (continued)

Closing Cost Details

Loan Costs		Borrower-Paid		Seller-Paid		Paid by Others
		At Closing	Before Closing	At Closing	Before Closing	
A. Origination Charges		**$1,802.00**				
01 0.25 % of Loan Amount (Points)		$405.00				
02 Application Fee		$300.00				
03 Underwriting Fee		$1,097.00				
04						
05						
06						
07						
08						
B. Services Borrower Did Not Shop For		**$236.55**				
01 Appraisal Fee	to John Smith Appraisers Inc.					$405.00
02 Credit Report Fee	to Information Inc.		$29.80			
03 Flood Determination Fee	to Info Co.	$20.00				
04 Flood Monitoring Fee	to Info Co.	$31.75				
05 Tax Monitoring Fee	to Info Co.	$75.00				
06 Tax Status Research Fee	to Info Co.	$80.00				
07						
08						
09						
10						
C. Services Borrower Did Shop For		**$2,655.50**				
01 Pest Inspection Fee	to Pests Co.	$120.50				
02 Survey Fee	to Surveys Co.	$85.00				
03 Title – Insurance Binder	to Epsilon Title Co.	$650.00				
04 Title – Lender's Title Insurance	to Epsilon Title Co.	$500.00				
05 Title – Settlement Agent Fee	to Epsilon Title Co.	$500.00				
06 Title – Title Search	to Epsilon Title Co.	$800.00				
07						
08						
D. TOTAL LOAN COSTS (Borrower-Paid)		**$4,694.05**				
Loan Costs Subtotals (A + B + C)		$4,664.25	$29.80			

Other Costs		Borrower-Paid		Seller-Paid		Paid by Others
E. Taxes and Other Government Fees		**$85.00**				
01 Recording Fees	Deed: $40.00 Mortgage: $45.00	$85.00				
02 Transfer Tax	to Any State			$950.00		
F. Prepaids		**$2,120.80**				
01 Homeowner's Insurance Premium (12 mo.) to Insurance Co.		$1,209.96				
02 Mortgage Insurance Premium (mo.)						
03 Prepaid Interest ($17.44 per day from 4/15/13 to 5/1/13)		$279.04				
04 Property Taxes (6 mo.) to Any County USA		$631.80				
05						
G. Initial Escrow Payment at Closing		**$412.25**				
01 Homeowner's Insurance $100.83 per month for 2 mo.		$201.66				
02 Mortgage Insurance per month for mo.						
03 Property Taxes $105.30 per month for 2 mo.		$210.60				
04						
05						
06						
07						
08 Aggregate Adjustment		– 0.01				
H. Other		**$2,400.00**				
01 HOA Capital Contribution	to HOA Acre Inc.	$500.00				
02 HOA Processing Fee	to HOA Acre Inc.	$150.00				
03 Home Inspection Fee	to Engineers Inc.	$750.00			$750.00	
04 Home Warranty Fee	to XYZ Warranty Inc.			$450.00		
05 Real Estate Commission	to Alpha Real Estate Broker			$5,700.00		
06 Real Estate Commission	to Omega Real Estate Broker			$5,700.00		
07 Title – Owner's Title Insurance (optional) to Epsilon Title Co.		$1,000.00				
08						
I. TOTAL OTHER COSTS (Borrower-Paid)		**$5,018.05**				
Other Costs Subtotals (E + F + G + H)		$5,018.05				

	Borrower-Paid		Seller-Paid		Paid by Others
J. TOTAL CLOSING COSTS (Borrower-Paid)	**$9,712.10**				
Closing Costs Subtotals (D + I)	$9,682.30	$29.80	$12,800.00	$750.00	$405.00
Lender Credits					

EXERCISE 10-2 (continued)

Calculating Cash to Close

Use this table to see what has changed from your Loan Estimate.

	Loan Estimate	Final	Did this change?
Total Closing Costs (J)	$8,054.00	$9,712.10	**YES** • See **Total Loan Costs (D)** and **Total Other Costs (I)**
Closing Costs Paid Before Closing	$0	– $29.80	**YES** • You paid these Closing Costs **before closing**
Closing Costs Financed (Paid from your Loan Amount)	$0	$0	**NO**
Down Payment/Funds from Borrower	$18,000.00	$18,000.00	**NO**
Deposit	– $10,000.00	– $10,000.00	**NO**
Funds for Borrower	$0	$0	**NO**
Seller Credits	$0	– $2,500.00	**YES** • See Seller Credits in **Section L**
Adjustments and Other Credits	$0	– $1,035.04	**YES** • See details in **Sections K and L**
Cash to Close	$16,054.00	$14,147.26	

Summaries of Transactions

Use this table to see a summary of your transaction.

BORROWER'S TRANSACTION

K. Due from Borrower at Closing	$189,762.30
01 Sale Price of Property	$180,000.00
02 Sale Price of Any Personal Property Included in Sale	
03 Closing Costs Paid at Closing (J)	$9,682.30
04	
Adjustments	
05	
06	
07	
Adjustments for Items Paid by Seller in Advance	
08 City/Town Taxes to	
09 County Taxes to	
10 Assessments to	
11 HOA Dues 4/15/13 to 4/30/13	$80.00
12	
13	
14	
15	

L. Paid Already by or on Behalf of Borrower at Closing	$175,615.04
01 Deposit	$10,000.00
02 Loan Amount	$162,000.00
03 Existing Loan(s) Assumed or Taken Subject to	
04	
05 Seller Credit	$2,500.00
Other Credits	
06 Rebate from Epsilon Title Co.	$750.00
07	
Adjustments	
08	
09	
10	
11	
Adjustments for Items Unpaid by Seller	
12 City/Town Taxes 1/1/13 to 4/14/13	$365.04
13 County Taxes to	
14 Assessments to	
15	
16	
17	

SELLER'S TRANSACTION

M. Due to Seller at Closing	$180,080.00
01 Sale Price of Property	$180,000.00
02 Sale Price of Any Personal Property Included in Sale	
03	
04	
05	
06	
07	
08	
Adjustments for Items Paid by Seller in Advance	
09 City/Town Taxes to	
10 County Taxes to	
11 Assessments to	
12 HOA Dues 4/15/13 to 4/30/13	$80.00
13	
14	
15	
16	

N. Due from Seller at Closing	$115,665.04
01 Excess Deposit	
02 Closing Costs Paid at Closing (J)	$12,800.00
03 Existing Loan(s) Assumed or Taken Subject to	
04 Payoff of First Mortgage Loan	$100,000.00
05 Payoff of Second Mortgage Loan	
06	
07	
08 Seller Credit	$2,500.00
09	
10	
11	
12	
13	
Adjustments for Items Unpaid by Seller	
14 City/Town Taxes 1/1/13 to 4/14/13	$365.04
15 County Taxes to	
16 Assessments to	
17	
18	
19	

CALCULATION

Total Due from Borrower at Closing (K)	$189,762.30
Total Paid Already by or on Behalf of Borrower at Closing (L)	– $175,615.04
Cash to Close ☒ From ☐ To Borrower	**$14,147.26**

CALCULATION

Total Due to Seller at Closing (M)	$180,080.00
Total Due from Seller at Closing (N)	– $115,665.04
Cash ☐ From ☒ To Seller	**$64,414.96**

EXERCISE 10-2 (continued)

Additional Information About This Loan

Loan Disclosures

Assumption

If you sell or transfer this property to another person, your lender

☐ will allow, under certain conditions, this person to assume this loan on the original terms.

☒ will not allow assumption of this loan on the original terms.

Demand Feature

Your loan

☐ has a demand feature, which permits your lender to require early repayment of the loan. You should review your note for details.

☒ does not have a demand feature.

Late Payment

If your payment is more than *15* days late, your lender will charge a late fee of *5% of the monthly principal and interest payment.*

Negative Amortization (Increase in Loan Amount)

Under your loan terms, you

☐ are scheduled to make monthly payments that do not pay all of the interest due that month. As a result, your loan amount will increase (negatively amortize), and your loan amount will likely become larger than your original loan amount. Increases in your loan amount lower the equity you have in this property.

☐ may have monthly payments that do not pay all of the interest due that month. If you do, your loan amount will increase (negatively amortize), and, as a result, your loan amount may become larger than your original loan amount. Increases in your loan amount lower the equity you have in this property.

☒ do not have a negative amortization feature.

Partial Payments

Your lender

☒ may accept payments that are less than the full amount due (partial payments) and apply them to your loan.

☐ may hold them in a separate account until you pay the rest of the payment, and then apply the full payment to your loan.

☐ does not accept any partial payments.

If this loan is sold, your new lender may have a different policy.

Security Interest

You are granting a security interest in

456 Somewhere Ave., Anytown, ST 12345

You may lose this property if you do not make your payments or satisfy other obligations for this loan.

Escrow Account

For now, your loan

☒ will have an escrow account (also called an "impound" or "trust" account) to pay the property costs listed below. Without an escrow account, you would pay them directly, possibly in one or two large payments a year. Your lender may be liable for penalties and interest for failing to make a payment.

Escrow		
Escrowed Property Costs over Year 1	$2,473.56	Estimated total amount over year 1 for your escrowed property costs: *Homeowner's Insurance Property Taxes*
Non-Escrowed Property Costs over Year 1	$1,800.00	Estimated total amount over year 1 for your non-escrowed property costs: *Homeowner's Association Dues* You may have other property costs.
Initial Escrow Payment	$412.25	A cushion for the escrow account you pay at closing. See Section G on page 2.
Monthly Escrow Payment	$206.13	The amount included in your total monthly payment.

☐ will not have an escrow account because ☐ you declined it ☐ your lender does not offer one. You must directly pay your property costs, such as taxes and homeowner's insurance. Contact your lender to ask if your loan can have an escrow account.

No Escrow		
Estimated Property Costs over Year 1		Estimated total amount over year 1. You must pay these costs directly, possibly in one or two large payments a year.
Escrow Waiver Fee		

In the future,

Your property costs may change and, as a result, your escrow payment may change. You may be able to cancel your escrow account, but if you do, you must pay your property costs directly. If you fail to pay your property taxes, your state or local government may (1) impose fines and penalties or (2) place a tax lien on this property. If you fail to pay any of your property costs, your lender may (1) add the amounts to your loan balance, (2) add an escrow account to your loan, or (3) require you to pay for property insurance that the lender buys on your behalf, which likely would cost more and provide fewer benefits than what you could buy on your own.

EXERCISE 10-2 (continued)

Loan Calculations

Total of Payments. Total you will have paid after you make all payments of principal, interest, mortgage insurance, and loan costs, as scheduled.	$285,803.36
Finance Charge. The dollar amount the loan will cost you.	$118,830.27
Amount Financed. The loan amount available after paying your upfront finance charge.	$162,000.00
Annual Percentage Rate (APR). Your costs over the loan term expressed as a rate. This is not your interest rate.	4.174%
Total Interest Percentage (TIP). The total amount of interest that you will pay over the loan term as a percentage of your loan amount.	69.46%

 Questions? If you have questions about the loan terms or costs on this form, use the contact information below. To get more information or make a complaint, contact the Consumer Financial Protection Bureau at **www.consumerfinance.gov/mortgage-closing**

Other Disclosures

Appraisal
If the property was appraised for your loan, your lender is required to give you a copy at no additional cost at least 3 days before closing. If you have not yet received it, please contact your lender at the information listed below.

Contract Details
See your note and security instrument for information about
- what happens if you fail to make your payments,
- what is a default on the loan,
- situations in which your lender can require early repayment of the loan, and
- the rules for making payments before they are due.

Liability after Foreclosure
If your lender forecloses on this property and the foreclosure does not cover the amount of unpaid balance on this loan,
[X] state law may protect you from liability for the unpaid balance. If you refinance or take on any additional debt on this property, you may lose this protection and have to pay any debt remaining even after foreclosure. You may want to consult a lawyer for more information.
[ ] state law does not protect you from liability for the unpaid balance.

Refinance
Refinancing this loan will depend on your future financial situation, the property value, and market conditions. You may not be able to refinance this loan.

Tax Deductions
If you borrow more than this property is worth, the interest on the loan amount above this property's fair market value is not deductible from your federal income taxes. You should consult a tax advisor for more information.

Contact Information

	Lender	Mortgage Broker	Real Estate Broker (B)	Real Estate Broker (S)	Settlement Agent
Name	Ficus Bank		Omega Real Estate Broker Inc.	Alpha Real Estate Broker Co.	Epsilon Title Co.
Address	4321 Random Blvd. Somecity, ST 12340		789 Local Lane Sometown, ST 12345	987 Suburb Ct. Someplace, ST 12340	123 Commerce Pl. Somecity, ST 12344
NMLS ID					
ST License ID			Z765416	Z61456	Z61616
Contact	Joe Smith		Samuel Green	Joseph Cain	Sarah Arnold
Contact NMLS ID	12345				
Contact ST License ID			P16415	P51461	PT1234
Email	joesmith@ficusbank.com		sam@omegare.biz	joe@alphare.biz	sarah@epsilontitle.com
Phone	123-456-7890		123-555-1717	321-555-7171	987-555-4321

Confirm Receipt

By signing, you are only confirming that you have received this form. You do not have to accept this loan because you have signed or received this form.

Applicant Signature	Date	Co-Applicant Signature	Date

2. As homeowners, the Clocks will have monthly expenses of $3,588.35 ($2,757.93 mortgage payment plus $488.75 as one month's share of the property tax plus $116.67 as one month's share of fire insurance plus $225 for utilities) before taxes. After taxes, taking into account that they will be paying $27,446.34 in interest and $5,865 in property tax the first year, their payment is effectively $2,811.09 ($27,446.34 interest + $5,865 property tax = $33,311.34 tax deductions; $33,311.34 × 28% tax rate = $9,327.18 by which the Clocks' taxes will be reduced; $9,327.18 ÷ 12 = $777.26 monthly tax benefit; $3,588.35 – $777.26 = $2,811.09 effective monthly housing expense).

In five years, when a greater share of the Clocks' mortgage payment is principal, they will have monthly expenses of $3,588.35 before taxes, and $2,846.74 after taxes. The after-tax amount is calculated as follows: $25,918.38 interest + $5,865 property tax = $31,783.38 tax deductions; $31,783.38 × 28% tax rate = $8,899.35 by which the Clocks' taxes will be reduced; $8,899.35 ÷ 12 = $741.61 monthly tax benefit; $3,588.35 – $741.61 = $2,846.74 effective monthly housing expense.

3. The Clocks also should take into account any reduction in their state income tax resulting from mortgage interest and property tax deductions, the possibility that they will move into a higher tax bracket and have a greater benefit from the allowable deductions, the condition of the house (Will it need major repairs in the near future?), the loss of income from the $115,000 used as a down payment, the equity buildup in the house over the loan term, the appreciation (or depreciation) of real estate, the fact that they may not qualify for the loan they want, the fact that as homeowners they will have to cut back on other expenses in the first years of ownership to cover their housing bills, the size of their family and their needs in the future, and the housing amenities that they have come to expect or would prefer to have.

Review Questions, Pages 358–359

1.	a	8.	b	15.	d
2.	b	9.	d	16.	a
3.	c	10.	c	17.	a
4.	c	11.	c	18.	a
5.	c	12.	c	19.	d
6.	d	13.	b	20.	d
7.	b	14.	b		

UNIT 12
Exercise 12-1, Pages 375–376

1. Estate for years

2. Estate at sufferance

3. A lease agreement must be written when the lease term will end more than one year from the date of the agreement.

4. No. The lease contract did not have a lawful object.

5. Yes. The landlord can demand a security deposit of no more than two months' rent for an unfurnished apartment—in this case, $1,300.

6. Sue will have a sublease.

7. No. The landlord has the right to enter the premises in an emergency.

Exercise 12-2, Page 379

1.	Landlord	6.	Tenant
2.	Tenant	7.	Landlord
3.	Tenant	8.	Landlord
4.	Landlord	9.	Tenant
5.	Landlord	10.	Tenant

Exercise 12-3, Page 388

1. 30 days

2. 15 days after personal service or 18 days after mailed notice of landlord's belief of abandonment

3. 3 days

4. 5 days

5. 15 days after personal notice, or 18 days after mailed notice

6. 3 days

7. 60 days

Exercise 12-4, Page 396

A percentage lease would be useful in this situation. It would allow for a base rent affordable for a new business and also provide for rent increases as the business grows.

Review Questions, Pages 398–399

1.	c	8.	a	15.	c
2.	c	9.	d	16.	b
3.	d	10.	a	17.	a
4.	b	11.	d	18.	d
5.	b	12.	d	19.	b
6.	c	13.	b	20.	b
7.	a	14.	a		

UNIT 13
Exercise 13-1, Pages 408–409

1. Contribution

2. Supply and demand, change, growth, anticipation

3. Growth, equilibrium, decline, change, supply and demand, competition, gentrification

4. Supply and demand, conformity, regression

Exercise 13-2, Pages 412–413

	Comparables		
	A	**B**	**C**
Sales price	$551,000	$538,000	$499,000
Adjustment variables			
Extra half-bath	–8,000		
No fireplace		+6,200	
No swimming pool			+25,000
Total adjustments	–8,000	+6,200	+25,000
Adjusted value	$543,000	$544,200	$524,000

Exercise 13-3, Page 419

Living area = 1,500 square feet
@ $125 per square foot = $187,500

Garage area = 625 square feet
@ $75 per square foot = $46,875

Total reproduction cost = $234,375

Yearly depreciation = $5,859

Total depreciation = $23,436

Reproduction cost – Total depreciation + Land value = $266,939

Estimate of value of house X by the cost approach is $266,939.

Exercise 13-4, Page 422

Subject's gross income multiplier = 207

Subject's market value = $2,800 × 207 = $579,600

Review Questions, Pages 429–430

1.	b	8.	c	15.	b
2.	d	9.	b	16.	c
3.	b	10.	c	17.	a
4.	c	11.	c	18.	c
5.	d	12.	b	19.	b
6.	c	13.	d	20.	a
7.	d	14.	b		

UNIT 14
Exercise 14-1, Page 436

Broker Bob may be charged with contracting without a license. Such extensive repairs surely cost more than $500; Bob does not qualify for any exception from the Contractors' License Law.

Exercise 14-2, Page 442

The photograph shows a one-story, ranch-style house with an attached two-car garage. The house has wood siding, brick trim, a brick chimney, stucco end wall, and wood shake roof.

Exercise 14-3, Page 445

Exercise 14-4, Page 461

(Clockwise, from top center) sheathing, ridge board, rafter, joist, firestop, stud, header, plate, foundation, footing, anchor bolt, crawl space, joist, sheathing, eave, flashing, building paper.

Review Questions, Pages 464–465

1. d	8. a	15. b
2. d	9. a	16. c
3. c	10. d	17. d
4. d	11. b	18. b
5. b	12. a	19. c
6. d	13. c	20. b
7. c	14. c	

UNIT 15
Exercise 15-1, Page 475

A city of two million would influence the expected population, commercial development, and property uses of a nearby suburban community. Increasing housing demand in the city would make surrounding property more desirable, just as the expense of commercial development in the city would bring business to outlying communities. The result would be greater demand for city and consumer services in the affected communities.

A county plan encouraging commercial development would increase the predictability of the above conditions.

If a community limits development, greater demand for both residential and commercial uses may be placed on nearby communities.

Development always will be limited by geologic features that prevent safe construction or require the imposition of strict controls.

Exercise 15-2, Page 483

1. Yes, because inclusion of more property restrictions is a material change in the subdivision offering.

2. See the completed chart below.

	Subdivision Map Act	Subdivided Lands Law
Number of subdivision units or parcels	Two or more	Five or more
Inclusion of undivided interests	No	Yes
Inclusion of time-shares	No	Yes
Inclusion of stock cooperatives	Only if five or more units are converted	Yes
Opportunity for notice and hearing	Only if significant deprivation of other landowner's property rights is involved	No

Exercise 15-3, Page 487

The Smiths are prohibited from all forms of unlawful discrimination in the sale of their house.

Review Questions, Pages 490–491

1. a	8. a	15. b
2. d	9. b	16. b
3. d	10. a	17. c
4. c	11. c	18. c
5. b	12. d	19. a
6. d	13. c	20. c
7. b	14. d	

APPENDIX A
Math Review Questions, Page 503

1. $756,000 × 2.5% = $18,900 buyer broker's commission

   $18,900 × 70% = $13,230 sales associate's commission

2. $175,000 × 6.625% = $11,593.75 annual interest

   $11,593.75 ÷ 12 = $966.15 first month's interest

   $1,120.54 − $966.15 = $154.39 first month's principal

3. $260,000 ÷ 1,000 = 260

   $8.99 × 260 = $2,337.40 monthly payment for 15 years

   $6.66 × 260 = $1,731.60 monthly payment for 30 years

4. 1,150 ft. × 2,400 ft. = 2,760,000 sq. ft.

   2,760,000 ÷ 43,560 = 63.36 acres

5. 7,200 sq. ft. × $265 = $1,908,000 construction cost

6. $780,000 × 80% = $624,000 loan amount

   624 × 6.33 = $3,949.92 monthly payment on 30-year loan at 6.5%

   624 × 8.17 = $5,098.08 monthly payment on 15-year loan at 5.5%

7. $230,000 × 112% = $257,600 appreciated value at end of year 1

   $257,600 × 112% = $288,512 appreciated value at end of year 2

   $288,512 × 112% = $323,133 appreciated value at end of year 3

   $323,133 × 112% = $361,909 appreciated value at end of year 4

8. $230,000 × 90% = $207,000 original loan amount

   $207,000 − $8,000 = $199,000 remaining loan amount

   $361,909 − $199,000 = $162,909 equity in the home

9. ½ × ¼ × ¼ × 640 = $\frac{1}{32}$ × 640 = 20 acres, so the descriptions match

   $26,600 × 20 = $532,000

10. $116,250

    $2,325,000 Rate

    $116,250 ÷ $2,325,000 = 0.05 = 5%

INDEX

Notes

Notes

Notes

Notes

Notes

Notes